THE PHILOSOPHY OF

KARL POPPER

BOOK I

THE LIBRARY OF LIVING PHILOSOPHERS

Paul Arthur Schilpp, Editor

Already Published:

THE PHILOSOPHY OF JOHN DEWEY (1939)
THE PHILOSOPHY OF GEORGE SANTAYANA (1940)
THE PHILOSOPHY OF ALFRED NORTH WHITEHEAD (1941)
THE PHILOSOPHY OF G. E. MOORE (1942)
THE PHILOSOPHY OF BERTRAND RUSSELL (1944)
THE PHILOSOPHY OF ERNST CASSIRER (1949)
ALBERT EINSTEIN: PHILOSOPHER-SCIENTIST (1949)
THE PHILOSOPHY OF SARVEPALLI RADHAKRISHNAN (1952)
THE PHILOSOPHY OF KARL JASPERS (1957)
THE PHILOSOPHY OF C. D. BROAD (1959)
THE PHILOSOPHY OF RUDOLF CARNAP (1963)
THE PHILOSOPHY OF MARTIN BUBER (1967)
THE PHILOSOPHY OF C. I. LEWIS (1968)
THE PHILOSOPHY OF KARL POPPER (1974)

In Preparation:

THE PHILOSOPHY OF GABRIEL MARCEL
THE PHILOSOPHY OF BRAND BLANSHARD
THE PHILOSOPHY OF GEORG HENRIK von WRIGHT
THE PHILOSOPHY OF W. V. QUINE
THE PHILOSOPHY OF JEAN-PAUL SARTRE

Other volumes to be announced

Karl Popper

THE LIBRARY OF LIVING PHILOSOPHERS
VOLUME XIV BOOK I

THE PHILOSOPHY OF
KARL POPPER

EDITED BY

PAUL ARTHUR SCHILPP
NORTHWESTERN UNIVERSITY &
SOUTHERN ILLINOIS UNIVERSITY

LA SALLE, ILLINOIS • OPEN COURT • ESTABLISHED 1887

THE PHILOSOPHY OF KARL POPPER

FIRST EDITION

Library of Congress Catalog Card Number: 76-186983
ISBN Number: 0-87548-141-8 Vol. I cloth
0-87548-142-6 Vol. II cloth

"Hypothesis and Imagination" by Peter Medawar was first published in *The Art of the Soluble* (London: Methuen & Co., 1971).

GENERAL INTRODUCTION*
TO
"THE LIBRARY OF LIVING PHILOSOPHERS"

According to the late F. C. S. Schiller, the greatest obstacle to fruitful discussion in philosophy is "the curious etiquette which apparently taboos the asking of questions about a philosopher's meaning while he is alive." The "interminable controversies which fill the histories of philosophy," he goes on to say, "could have been ended at once by asking the living philosophers a few searching questions."

The confident optimism of this last remark undoubtedly goes too far. Living thinkers have often been asked "a few searching questions," but their answers have not stopped "interminable controversies" about their real meaning. It is none the less true that there would be far greater clarity of understanding than is now often the case, if more such searching questions had been directed to great thinkers while they were still alive.

This, at any rate, is the basic thought behind the present undertaking. The volumes of *The Library of Living Philosophers* can in no sense take the place of the major writings of great and original thinkers. Students who would know the philosophies of such men as John Dewey, George Santayana, Alfred North Whitehead, G. E. Moore, Bertrand Russell, Ernst Cassirer, Karl Jaspers, Rudolf Carnap, Martin Buber, *et al.*, will still need to read the writings of these men. There is no substitute for first-hand contact with the original thought of the philosopher himself. Least of all does this *Library* pretend to be such a substitute. The *Library* in fact will spare neither effort nor expense in offering to the student the best possible guide to the published writings of a given thinker. We shall attempt to meet this aim by providing at the end of each volume in our series a complete bibliography of the published work of the philosopher in question. Nor should one overlook the fact that essays in each volume cannot but finally lead to this same goal. The interpretative and critical discussions of the various phases of a great thinker's work and, most of all, the reply of the thinker himself, are bound to lead the reader to the works of the philosopher himself.

---

* This General Introduction, setting forth the underlying conception this *Library*, is purposely reprinted in each volume (with only very minor changes).

At the same time, there is no denying the fact that different experts find different ideas in the writings of the same philosopher. This is as true of the appreciative interpreter and grateful disciple as it is of the critical opponent. Nor can it be denied that such differences of reading and of interpretation on the part of other experts often leave the neophyte aghast before the whole maze of widely varying and even opposing interpretations. Who is right and whose interpretation shall he accept? When the doctors disagree among themselves, what is the poor student to do? If, in desperation, he decides that all of the interpreters are probably wrong and that the only thing for him to do is to go back to the original writings of the philosopher himself and then make his own decision—uninfluenced (as if this were possible) by the interpretation of any one else—the result is not that he has actually come to the meaning of the original philosopher himself, but rather that he has set up one more interpretation, which may differ to a greater or lesser degree from the interpretations already existing. It is clear that in this direction lies chaos, just the kind of chaos which Schiller has so graphically and inimitably described.[1]

It is curious that until now no way of escaping this difficulty has been seriously considered. It has not occured to students of philosophy that one effective way of meeting the problem at least partially is to put these varying interpretations and critiques before the philosopher while he is still alive and to ask him to act at one and at the same time as both defendant and judge. If the world's great living philosophers can be induced to cooperate in an enterprise whereby their own work can, at least to some extent, be saved from becoming merely "dessicated lecture-fodder," which on the one hand "provides innocuous sustenance for ruminant professors," and, on the other hand, gives an opportunity to such ruminants and their understudies to "speculate safely, endlessly, and fruitlessly, about what a philosopher must have meant" (Schiller), they will have taken a long step toward making their intentions clearly comprehensible.

With this in mind, *The Library of Living Philosophers* expects to publish at more or less regular intervals a volume on each of the greater among the world's living philosophers. In each case it will be the purpose of the editor of the *Library* to bring together in the volume the interpretations and criticisms of a wide range of that particular thinker's scholarly contemporaries, each of whom will be given a free hand to discuss the specific phase of the thinker's work which has been assigned to him. All contributed essays will finally be submitted to the philosopher with whose work and thought they are concerned, for his careful perusal and reply. And, although it would be expecting too much to imagine that the philosopher's reply will be able to stop all differences of interpretation and of critique, this should at least serve the purpose of stopping certain of the grosser and more general kinds of misinterpretations. If no further gain than this were to come from the present and projected volumes of this *Library*, it would seem to be fully justified.

In carrying out this principal purpose of the *Library*, the editor announces that (insofar as humanly possible) each volume will conform to the following pattern:

First, a series of expository and critical articles written by the leading exponents and opponents of the philosopher's thought;
Second, the reply to the critics and commentators by the philosopher himself;
Third, an intellectual autobiography of the thinker whenever this can be secured; in any case an authoritative and authorized biography; and
Fourth, a bibliography of writings of the philosopher to provide a ready instrument to give access to his writings and thought.

The editor has deemed it desirable to secure the services of an Advisory Board of philosophers to aid him in the selection of the subjects of future volumes. The names of the seven prominent American philosophers who have consented to serve appear below. To each of them the editor expresses his sincere gratitude.

Future volumes in this series will appear in as rapid succession as is feasible in view of the scholarly nature of this *Library*. The next volume in this series will be devoted to the philosophy of Gabriel Marcel.

Through the generosity of the Edward C. Hegeler Foundation, the publication of many of the volumes of this *Library* was made possible. For the support of future volumes, additional funds are still needed. The *Library* would be grateful, therefore, for additional gifts and donations. Moreover, since November 6th, 1947, any gifts or donations made to The Library of Living Philosophers, Inc., are deductible by the donors in arriving at their taxable net income in conformity with the Internal Revenue Code of the Treasury Department of the United States of America.

DEPARTMENT OF PHILOSOPHY
NORTHWESTERN UNIVERSITY AND
SOUTHERN ILLINOIS UNIVERSITY

P. A. S.
Editor

[1] In his essay on "Must Philosophers Disagree?" in the volume by the same title (London: Macmillan, 1934), from which the above quotations were taken.

ACKNOWLEDGMENTS

by the editor

The editor hereby gratefully acknowledges his obligation and sincere gratitude to all the publishers of Professor Popper's books and publications for their kind and uniform courtesy in permitting us to quote—sometimes at some length—from Professor Popper's writings.

PAUL A. SCHILPP

ACKNOWLEDGMENTS

by Professor Popper

I am deeply grateful to Ernst Gombrich, Bryan Magee, Arne Petersen, Jeremy Shearmur, and most of all to David Miller and to my wife, for their patience in reading and improving my manuscript.

After the manuscript was completed, there arose many problems in connection with the proofs. The work done in this connection by Professor Eugene Freeman, Mrs. Ann Freeman and by their editorial staff was immense, and done under very trying circumstances since most of the corrections suggested by them and by myself had to be discussed by letters between California and England. I cannot thank them enough for their criticism, their meticulous care, and their infinite patience.

KARL POPPER

TABLE OF CONTENTS

PART THREE: THE PHILOSOPHER REPLIES
Karl Popper: "Replies to My Critics"

I. Introduction

II. The Problem of Demarcation

PREFACE

It certainly would be a task of supererogation to pen a justification for a volume on Sir Karl Popper in our *Library of Living Philosophers*. The essays contained herein and the distinction of the contributors are a better demonstration of that fact than anything the editor could write.

What, however, does call for explanation is the unusual size of this tome. Its 416 pages from Sir Karl's own pen plus the 900 pages contributed by his disciples and critics simply could not be gotten between the covers of *one* book; for the first time in the now thirty-four-year history of this series we have been forced to publish a volume in two books, at least in the hard-cover edition. But, that much material simply left the publisher no other choice.

And Sir Karl's own *Autobiography* and *Reply* would constitute a hefty book just by themselves. Yet: would anyone wish to eliminate a single sentence from either?

As a matter of fact, this tome would even have been still larger, if a few of our contributors had not been so kind and considerate as to shorten greatly their own original essays for this volume. To them the editor desires to express his special thanks.

By this time the editor himself is no longer under any Schillerian illusion that "the interminable controversies which fill the histories of philosophy could have been ended at once by asking the living philosophers a few searching questions" (see the General Introduction above). To the editor, at least, it has become obvious by now that no matter how many searching questions a still living philosopher is asked, by no matter how many of his philosophical peers, his own attempt to answer those questions will never, never, *never* be able to end "the interminable controversies."

Most of the contributors to this volume *did* ask Sir Karl "searching questions"; and, at least from the editor's point of view, Sir Karl has sincerely and seriously tried to answer all of them. Yet I fear the interminable controversies will remain to continue to plague future students of philosophy—and that, if for no *other* reason, simply because living, searching minds cannot (or, in any case, they will not) be put into the straitjacket of the other philosopher's thinking.

But the editor does desire to take this opportunity to express his own personal gratitude and appreciation to the following: first and foremost, of course, to the object of this volume, Sir Karl himself, for his never failing and always most considerate and helpful cooperation. Secondly, to that invaluable team of the publisher's editors, Eugene Freeman and Ann Freeman, whose long, careful and precise labors and endless patience not merely saved the editor himself interminable hours of work but actually made the printing of this book possible. And, finally, to our publisher, the Open Court Publishing Company of La Salle, Illinois, and to its indefatigable President, Mr. M. Blouke Carus, who spared neither time nor effort nor money to get this book onto the market in the shortest period of time.

The editor also desires to take this opportunity to express his sincere gratitude and appreciation to the National Endowment for the Humanities (Washington, D. C.) for a number of very helpful summer grants during the past summers while the work on this volume has been in progress.

PAUL ARTHUR SCHILPP

CARBONDALE, ILLINOIS
MAY 15, 1972

Editor's Note:
It is with profound shock that we have just learned of the untimely death, on Saturday, February 2, 1974, of one of our most distinguished contributors, Imre Lakatos.

To the philosophers of the world, and to all of his many friends, the loss of Imre Lakatos is an irreplaceable one.

Eugene Freeman
February 11, 1974

THE PHILOSOPHY OF
KARL POPPER

BOOK I

PART ONE

AUTOBIOGRAPHY
OF KARL POPPER

10) lead to contradictions and other symptoms of untruth. I ~~do~~ admit that we often accept the evidence of our senses, especially in cases in which we have learned to trust them. But I utterly deny that "the evidence of our senses" can ever be ~~it~~ anything like a decisive or final or perhaps even defining criterion of truth or that what we are looking for -- the truth of our theories -- can be in any way ~~be~~

Facsimile Reproduction of Popper's Handwriting

What to leave out and what to put in? That's
the problem. HUGH LOFTING, *Doctor*
Doolittle's Zoo.

1. *Omniscience and Fallibility*

When I was twenty I became apprenticed to an old master cabinetmaker
in Vienna whose name was Adalbert Pösch, and I worked with him
from 1922 to 1924, not long after the First World War. He looked exactly
like Georges Clemenceau, but he was a very mild and kind man. After I had
gained his confidence he would often, when we were alone in his workshop,
give me the benefit of his inexhaustible store of knowledge. Once he told me
that he had worked for many years on various models of a perpetual motion
machine, adding musingly: "They say you can't make it; but once it's been
made they'll talk different!" ("Da sag'n s' dass ma' so was net mach'n kann;
aber wann amal eina ein's g'macht hat, dann wer'n s' schon anders red'n!") A
favourite practice of his was to ask me a historical question and to answer it
himself when it turned out that I did not know the answer (although I, his
pupil, was a University student—a fact of which he was very proud). "And do
you know", he would ask, "who invented topboots? You don't? It was
Wallenstein, the Duke of Friedland, during the Thirty Years War." After one
or two even more difficult questions, posed by himself and triumphantly
answered by himself, my master would say with modest pride: "There, you
can ask me whatever you like: *I know everything*." ("Da können S' mi' frag'n
was Sie woll'n: *ich weiss alles*.")

I believe I learned more about the theory of knowledge from my dear
omniscient master Adalbert Pösch than from any other of my teachers. None
did so much to turn me into a disciple of Socrates. For it was my master who
taught me not only how very little I knew but also that any wisdom to which I
might ever aspire could consist only in realizing more fully the infinity of my
ignorance.

These and other thoughts which belonged to the field of epistemology
were occupying my mind while I was working on a writing desk. We had at
that time a large order for thirty mahogany kneehole desks, with many, many
drawers. I fear that the quality of some of these desks, and especially their
French polish, suffered badly from my preoccupation with epistemology.
This suggested to my master and also brought home to me that I was too
ignorant and too fallible for this kind of work. So I made up my mind that on
completing my apprenticeship in October, 1924, I should look for something
easier than making mahogany writing desks. For a year I took up social work
with neglected children, which I had done before and found very difficult.

Then, after five more years spent mainly in studying and writing, I married and settled down happily as a schoolteacher. This was in 1930.

At that time I had no professional ambitions beyond schoolteaching, though I got a little tired of it after I had published my *Logik der Forschung,* late in 1934. I therefore felt myself very fortunate when in 1937 I had an opportunity to give up schoolteaching and to become a professional philosopher. I was almost thirty-five and I thought that I had now finally solved the problem of how to work on a writing desk and yet be preoccupied with epistemology.

2. Childhood Memories

Although most of us know the date and the place of our birth—mine is July 28, 1902, at a place called Himmelhof in the Ober St Veit district of Vienna—few know when and how their intellectual life began. So far as my philosophical development goes, I do remember some of its early stages. But it certainly started later than my emotional and moral development.

As a child I was, I suspect, somewhat puritanical, even priggish, though this attitude was perhaps tempered by the feeling that I had no right to sit in judgement on anybody except myself. Among my earliest memories are feelings of admiration for my elders and betters, for example for my cousin Eric Schiff, whom I greatly admired for being one year older than I, for his tidiness and, especially, for his good looks: gifts which I always regarded as important and unattainable.

One often hears it said nowadays that children are cruel by nature. I do not believe it. I was, as a child, what Americans might call a "softy", and compassion is one of the strongest emotions I remember. It was the main component of my first experience of falling in love, which happened when I was four or five years old. I was taken to a kindergarten and there was a beautiful little girl who was blind. My heart was torn, both by the charm of her smile and by the tragedy of her blindness. It was love at first sight. I have never forgotten her, though I saw her only once, and only for an hour or two. I was not sent to the kindergarten again; perhaps my mother noticed how much I was upset.

The sight of abject poverty in Vienna was one of the main problems which agitated me when I was still a very small child—so much so that it was almost always at the back of my mind. Few people now living in one of the Western democracies know what poverty meant at the beginning of this century: men, women, and children suffering from hunger, cold, and hopelessness. But we children were helpless. We could do no more than ask for a few coppers to give to some poor people.

It was only after many years that I found that my father had worked hard and long to do something about this situation, although he had never talked about these activities. He worked on two committees which were running homes for the homeless: a freemasons' lodge of which he was for many years the Master ran a home for orphans, while the other committee (not masonic) built and administered a large institution for homeless adults and families. (An inmate of the latter—the *"Asyl für Obdachlose"*—was Adolf Hitler during his early stay in Vienna.)

This work of my father's received unexpected recognition when the old Emperor made him a knight of the Order of Francis Joseph (*Ritter des Franz Josef Ordens*), which must have been not only a surprise but a problem. For although my father—like most Austrians—respected the Emperor, he was a radical liberal of the school of John Stuart Mill, and not at all a supporter of the government.

As a freemason he was even a member of a society which at that time was declared illegal by the Austrian government, though not by the Hungarian government of Francis Joseph. Thus the freemasons often met beyond the Hungarian border, in Pressburg (now Bratislava in Czechoslovakia). The Austro-Hungarian Empire, though a constitutional monarchy, was not ruled by its two Parliaments: they had no power to dismiss the two Prime Ministers or the two Cabinets, not even by a vote of censure. The Austrian Parliament, it would seem, was even weaker than the English Parliament under William and Mary, if such a comparison can be made at all. There were few checks and balances, and there was severe political censorship; for example, a brilliant political satire, *Anno 1903*, which my father had written under the pen name Siegmund Karl Pflug, was seized by the police on its publication in 1904 and remained on the Index of prohibited books until 1918.

Nevertheless, in those days before 1914 there was an atmosphere of liberalism in Europe west of Czarist Russia, an atmosphere which also pervaded Austria and which was destroyed, for ever it now seems, by the First World War. The University of Vienna, with its many teachers of real eminence, had a great degree of freedom and autonomy. So had the theatres, which were important in the life of Vienna—almost as important as music. The Emperor kept aloof from all political parties and did not identify himself with any of his governments. Indeed he followed, almost to the letter, the precept given by Søren Kierkegaard to Christian VIII of Denmark.[1]

3. Early Influences

The atmosphere in which I was brought up was decidedly bookish. My father Dr Simon Siegmund Carl Popper, like his two brothers, was a doctor of law of the University of Vienna. He had a large library, and there were books everywhere—with the exception of the dining room, in which there was a Bösendorfer concert grand and many volumes of Bach, Haydn, Beethoven,

Schubert, and Brahms. My father, who was the same age as Sigmund Freud—whose works he possessed, and had read on publication—was a barrister and solicitor. About my mother Jenny Popper, *née* Schiff, I shall say more when I come to speak about music. My father was an accomplished speaker. I heard him plead in court only once, in 1924 or 1925, when I myself was the defendant. The case was, in my opinion, clear-cut.[2] I had therefore not asked my father to defend me, and was embarrassed when he insisted. But the utter simplicity, clarity, and sincerity of his speech impressed me greatly.

My father worked hard in his profession. He had been a friend and partner of the last liberal Burgomaster of Vienna, Dr Carl Grübl, and had taken over his law office. This office was part of the large apartment in which we lived, in the very heart of Vienna, opposite the central door of the cathedral (*Stephanskirche*). He worked long hours in this office, but he was really more of a scholar than a lawyer. He was a historian (the historical part of his library was considerable) and was interested especially in the Hellenistic period, and in the eighteenth and nineteenth centuries. He wrote poetry, and translated Greek and Latin verse into German. (He rarely spoke of these matters. It was by sheer accident that I found one day some light-hearted verse translations of Horace. His special gifts were a light touch and a strong sense of humour.) He was greatly interested in philosophy. I still possess his Plato, Bacon, Descartes, Spinoza, Locke, Kant, Schopenhauer, and Eduard von Hartmann; J. S. Mill's collected works, in a German translation edited by Theodor Gomperz (whose *Greek Thinkers* he valued highly); most of Kierkegaard's, Nietzsche's, and Eucken's works, and those of Ernst Mach; Fritz Mauthner's *Critique of Language* and Otto Weininger's *Geschlecht und Charakter* (both of which seem to have had some influence on Wittgenstein);[3] and translations of most of Darwin's books. (Pictures of Darwin and of Schopenhauer hung in his study.) There were, of course, the standard authors of German, French, English, Russian, and Scandinavian literature. But one of his main interests was in social problems. He not only possessed the chief works of Marx and Engels, of Lassalle, Karl Kautsky, and Eduard Bernstein, but also those of the critics of Marx: Böhm-Bawerk, Carl Menger, Anton Menger, P. A. Kropotkin, and Josef Popper-Lynkeus (apparently a distant relative of mine, since he was born in Kolin, the little town from which my paternal grandfather came). The library had also a pacifist section, with books by Bertha von Suttner, Friedrich Wilhelm Förster, and Norman Angell.

Thus books were part of my life long before I could read them. The first book which made a big and lasting impression on me was read by my mother to my two sisters and to me, shortly before I learned to read. (I was the youngest of three children.) It was a book for children by the great Swedish writer Selma Lagerlöf, in a beautiful German translation (*Wunderbare Reise des kleinen Nils Holgersson mit den Wildgänsen;* the English translation is entitled *The Wonderful Adventures of Nils*). For many, many, years I reread this book at least once a year; and in the course of time I probably read everything by Selma Lagerlöf more than once. I do not like her first novel, *Gösta Berling*, though it is no doubt very remarkable. But every single one of her other books remains, for me, a masterpiece.

Learning to read, and to a lesser degree, to write, are of course *the* major events in one's intellectual development. There is nothing to compare with it, since very few people (Helen Keller is the great exception) can remember what it meant for them to learn to speak. I shall be for ever grateful to my first teacher, Emma Goldberger, who taught me the three R's. They are, I think, the only essentials a child has to be taught; and some children do not even need to be taught in order to learn these. Everything else is atmosphere, and learning through reading and thinking.

Apart from my parents, my first schoolteacher, and Selma Lagerlöf, the greatest influence on my early intellectual development was, I suppose, my lifelong friend Arthur Arndt, a relative of Ernst Moritz von Arndt who had been one of the famous founding fathers of German nationalism in the period of the Napoleonic wars.[4] Arthur Arndt was an ardent antinationalist. Though of German descent, he was born in Moscow, where he also spent his youth. He was my senior by about twenty years—he was near thirty when first I met him in 1912. He had studied engineering at the University of Riga, and had been one of the student leaders during the abortive Russian revolution of 1905. He was a socialist and at the same time a strong opponent of the Bolsheviks, some of whose leaders he knew personally from 1905. He described them as the Jesuits of socialism, that is, capable of sacrificing innocent men, even of their own persuasion, because great ends justified all means. Arndt was not a convinced Marxist, yet he thought that Marx had been the most important theorist of socialism so far. He found me very willing to listen to socialist ideas; nothing, I felt, could be more important than to end poverty.

Arndt was also deeply interested (much more so than my father was) in the movement which had been started by the pupils of Ernst Mach and of Wilhelm Ostwald, a society whose members called themselves "The Monists". (There was a connection with the famous American journal, *The Monist*, to which Mach was a contributor.) They were interested in science, epistemology, and in what nowadays would be called the philosophy of science. Among the Monists of Vienna the "half-socialist" Popper-Lynkeus had a considerable following, which included Otto Neurath.

The first book on socialism I read (probably under the influence of my friend Arndt—my father was reluctant to influence me) was Edward

Bellamy's *Looking Backward*. I must have read it when I was about twelve, and it made a great impression on me. Arndt took me on Sunday excursions, arranged by the Monists, to the Vienna Woods, and on these occasions he explained and discussed Marxism and Darwinism. No doubt most of this was far beyond my grasp. But it was interesting and exciting.

One of these Sunday excursions by the Monists was on June 28, 1914. Towards evening, as we approached the outskirts of Vienna, we heard that the Archduke Franz Ferdinand, heir apparent of Austria, had been assassinated in Sarajevo. A week or so after this my mother took me and my two sisters for our summer holidays to Alt-Aussee, a village not far from Salzburg. And there, on my twelfth birthday, I received a letter from my father in which he said that he was sorry not to be able to come for my birthday, as he had intended, "because, unfortunately, there is war" ("*denn es ist leider Krieg*"). Since this letter arrived on the day of the actual declaration of war between Austria-Hungary and Serbia, it seems that my father realized that it was coming.

4. The First World War

I was twelve, then, when the First World War broke out; and the war years, and their aftermath, were in every respect decisive for my intellectual development. They made me critical of accepted opinions, especially political opinions.

Of course, few people knew at the time what war meant. There was a deafening clamour of patriotism throughout the country in which even some of the members of our previously far-from-warmongering circle participated. My father was sad and depressed. But even Arndt could see something hopeful. He hoped for a democratic revolution in Russia.

Afterwards I often remembered these days. Before the war, many members of our circle had discussed political theories which were decidedly pacifist, and at least highly critical of the existing order, and had been critical of the alliance between Austria and Germany, and of the expansionist policy of Austria in the Balkans, especially in Serbia. I was staggered by the fact that they could suddenly become supporters of that very policy.

Today I understand these things a little better. It was not only the pressure of public opinion; it was the problem of divided loyalties. And there was also fear—the fear of violent measures which, in war, have to be taken by the authorities against dissenters, since no sharp line can be drawn between dissent and treason. But at the time I was greatly puzzled. I knew, of course, nothing about what had happened to the socialist parties of Germany and France: how their internationalism disintegrated. (A marvellous description of these events can be found in the last volumes of Roger Martin du Gard's *Les Thibaults*.)[5]

For a few weeks, under the influence of war propaganda in my school, I became a little infected by the general mood. In the autumn of 1914 I wrote a silly poem "Celebrating the Peace", in which the assumption was expressed that the Austrians and the Germans had successfully resisted the attack (I then believed that "we" had been attacked) and which described, and celebrated, the restoration of peace. Though it was not a very warlike poem I soon became thoroughly ashamed of the assumption that "we" had been attacked. I realized that the Austrian attack on Serbia and the German attack on Belgium were terrible things and that a huge apparatus of propaganda was trying to persuade us that they had been justified. In the winter of 1915-16 I became convinced—under the influence, no doubt, of prewar socialist propaganda—that the cause of Austria and Germany was a bad cause and that we deserved to lose the war (and therefore that we would lose it, as I naively argued).

One day, I think it must have been in 1916, I approached my father with a reasonably well-prepared statement of this position, but found him less responsive than I expected. He was more doubtful than I about the rights and wrongs of the war, and also about its outcome. In both respects he was, of course, correct, and obviously I had seen these things in an oversimplified manner. Yet he took my views very seriously, and after a lengthy discussion he expressed an inclination to agree with them. So did my friend Arndt. After this I had few doubts.

Meanwhile all of my cousins who were old enough were fighting as officers in the Austrian army, and so were many of our friends. My mother still took us for our summer vacation to the Alps, and in 1916 we were again in the Salzkammergut—this time in Ischl, where we rented a little house high up on a wooded slope. With us was Freud's sister, Rosa Graf, who was a friend of my parents. Her son Hermann, only five years my senior, came for a visit in uniform on his final leave before going to the front. Soon after came the news of his death. The grief of his mother—and of his sister, Freud's favourite niece—was terrible. It made me realize the meaning of those frightful long lists of people killed, wounded, and missing.

Soon afterwards political issues made themselves felt again. The old Austria had been a multilingual state: there were Czechs, Slovaks, Poles, southern Slavs (Yugoslavs), and Italian-speaking people. Now rumour began to leak through of the defection of Czechs, Slavs, and Italians from the Austrian army. The dissolution had begun. A friend of our family who was acting as judge advocate told us about the Pan-Slavic movement, which he had to study professionally, and about Masaryk, a philosopher from the Universities of Vienna and Prague who was the leader of the Czechs. We heard about the Czech army, formed in Russia by Czech-speaking Austrian prisoners of war. And then we heard rumours about death sentences for treason, and the terror directed by the Austrian authorities against people suspected of disloyalty.

5. An Early Philosophical Problem: Infinity

I have long believed that there are genuine philosophical problems which are not mere puzzles arising out of the misuse of language. Some of these problems are childishly obvious. It so happened that I stumbled upon one of them when I was still a child, probably about eight.

Somehow I had heard about the solar system and the infinity of space (no doubt of Newtonian space) and I was worried: I could neither imagine that space was finite (for what, then, was outside it?) nor that it was infinite. My father suggested that I ask one of his brothers who, he told me, was very good at explaining such things. This uncle asked me first whether I had any trouble about a sequence of numbers going on and on. I had not. Then he asked me to imagine a stack of bricks, and to add to it one brick, and again one brick, and so on, without end; it would never fill the space of the universe. I agreed, somewhat reluctantly, that this was a very helpful answer, though I was not completely happy about it. Of course, I was unable to formulate the misgivings I still felt: it was the difference between potential and actual infinity, and the impossibility of reducing the actual infinity to the potential. The problem is, of course, part (the spatial part) of Kant's first antinomy, and it is (especially if the temporal part is added) a serious and still unsolved[6] philosophical problem—especially since Einstein's hopes of solving it by showing that the universe is a closed Riemannian space of finite radius have been more or less abandoned. It did not, of course, occur to me that what was worrying me might be an open problem. Rather, I thought that this was a question which an intelligent adult like my uncle must understand, while I was still too ignorant, or perhaps too young, or too stupid, to grasp it completely.

I remember a number of similar problems—serious problems, not puzzles—from later, when I was twelve or thirteen; for example, the problems of the origin of life, left open by Darwinian theory, and whether life is simply a chemical process (I opted for the theory that organisms are flames).

These, I think, are almost unavoidable problems for anybody who has ever heard about Darwin, whether child or adult. The fact that experimental work is done in connection with them does not make them nonphilosophical. Least of all should we decree in a high-handed manner that philosophical problems do not exist, or that they are insoluble (though perhaps dissoluble).

My own attitude towards such problems remained the same for a long time. I never thought it possible that any of those which bothered me had not been solved long ago; even less that any of them could be new. I had no doubt that people like the great Wilhelm Ostwald, editor of the journal *Das monistische Jahrhundert* (i.e. The Century of Monism), would know all the answers. My difficulties, I thought, were entirely due to my limited understanding.

6. My First Philosophical Failure: The Problem of Essentialism

I remember the first discussion of the first philosophical issue to become decisive for my intellectual development. The issue arose from my rejection of the attitude of attributing importance to *words and their meaning (or their "true meaning")*.

I must have been about fifteen. My father had suggested that I should read some of the volumes of Strindberg's autobiography. I do not remember which of its passages prompted me, in a conversation with my father, to criticize what I felt was an obscurantist attitude of Strindberg's: his attempt to extract something important from the "true" meanings of certain words. But I remember that when I tried to press my objections I was disturbed, indeed shocked, to find that my father did not see my point. The issue seemed obvious to me, and the more so the longer our discussion continued. When we broke it off late at night I realized that I had failed to make much impact. There was a real gulf between us on an issue of importance. I remember how, after this discussion, I tried strongly to impress on myself that I must always remember *the principle of never arguing about words and their meanings*, because such arguments are specious and insignificant. Moreover, I remember that I did not doubt that this simple principle must be well known and widely accepted; I suspected that both Strindberg and my father must be behind the times in these matters.

Years later I was to find that I had done them an injustice, and that the belief in the importance of the meanings of words, especially definitions, was almost universal. The attitude which I later came to call "essentialism"[7] is still widespread, and the sense of failure which I felt as a schoolboy has often come back to me in later years.

The first repetition of this sense of failure came when I tried to read some of the philosophical books in my father's library. I soon found that Strindberg's and my father's attitude was quite general. This created very great difficulties for me, and a dislike of philosophy. My father had suggested that I should try Spinoza (perhaps as a cure). Unfortunately I did not try his *Letters*, but the *Ethics* and the *Principles According to Descartes*, both of them full of definitions which seemed to me arbitrary, pointless, and question-begging, so far as there was any question at all. It gave me a lifetime's dislike of theorizing about God. (Theology, I still think, is due to lack of faith.) I also felt that the relation between the ways of geometry, the most fascinating subject to me at school, and Spinoza's *more geometrico* was quite superficial. Kant was different. Though I found the *Critique* much too difficult I could see that it was about real problems. I remember that after trying to read (I do not suppose with much understanding, but certainly with fascination) the Preface to the second edition of the *Critique* (in the edition by Benno Erdmann), I turned the pages and was struck and puzzled by that queer arrangement of the Antinomies. I did not get the point. I could not understand what Kant (or anybody) might mean by saying that reason can contradict itself. Yet I saw from the table of the First Antinomy that real problems were being argued; and also, from the Preface, that mathematics and physics were needed to understand these things.

But here I feel I must turn to the issue underlying that discussion, whose impact on me I remember so well. It is an issue that still divides me from most of my contemporaries, and since it has turned out to be so crucial for my later life as a philosopher I feel I must examine it in some detail, at the cost even of a long digression.

7. *A Long Digression Concerning Essentialism: What Still Divides Me from Most Contemporary Philosophers*

I call this a digression for two reasons. First, the formulation of my anti-essentialism in the third paragraph of the present section is undoubtedly biased by hindsight. Secondly, because the later parts of the present section are devoted not so much to carrying on the story of my intellectual development (though this is not neglected) as to discussing an issue which it has taken me a lifetime to clarify.

I do not wish to suggest that the following formulation was in my mind when I was fifteen, yet I cannot now state better than in this way the attitude I reached in that discussion with my father which I mentioned in the previous section:

Never let yourself be goaded into taking seriously problems about words and their meanings. What must be taken seriously are questions of fact, and assertions about facts: theories and hypotheses, the problems they solve and the problems they raise.

I shall refer to this piece of self-advice in the sequel as my *anti-essentialist exhortation*. Apart from the reference to theories and so on, which is likely to be of a much later date, this exhortation cannot be far from an articulation of the feelings I harboured when I first became conscious of the trap set by worries or quarrels about words and their meanings. This, I still think, is the surest path to intellectual perdition: the abandonment of real problems for the sake of verbal problems.

However, my own thoughts on this issue were for a long time bedevilled by my naive yet confident belief that all this must be well known, especially to philosophers, provided they were sufficiently up to date. This belief led me later, when I began more seriously to read philosophical books, to try to identify my problem—the relative unimportance of words—among the standard problems of philosophy; as a result I decided that it was very closely related to the classical problem of universals. And although I realized fairly soon that my problem was not identical with that classical problem, I tried to interpret it as a variant of the classical problem. This was a mistake. But in consequence I became greatly interested in the problem of universals, and its history; and I soon came to the conclusion that behind the classical problem of universal words and their meaning (or sense, or denotation) there loomed a deeper and more important problem: the problem of universal laws and their truth; that is, the problem of regularities.

The problem of universals is even today treated as if it were a problem of words or of language usages; or of similarities in situations, and how they are matched by similarities in our linguistic symbolism. It seemed to me quite obvious, however, that it was much more general; that it was fundamentally a problem of *reacting*, similarly, to biologically similar situations. Since all (or almost all) reactions have, biologically, an anticipatory value, we are led to the problem of anticipation or expectation, and so to that of adaptation to regularities.

Now throughout my life I have not only believed in the existence of what philosophers call an "external world" but I have also regarded the opposite view as one not worth taking seriously. This does not mean that I never argued the issue with myself, or that I never experimented with, for example, "neutral monism" and similar idealistic positions. Yet I was always an adherent of *realism*; and this made me sensitive to the fact that within the context of the problem of universals this term *"realism"* was used in a quite different sense; that is, to denote positions opposed to *nominalism*. In order to avoid this somewhat misleading use I invented, when working on *The Poverty of Historicism* (probably in 1935; see the "Historical Note" to the book edition) the term *"essentialism"* as a name for any (classical) position which is opposed to *nominalism*, and especially for the theories of Plato and Aristotle (and, among the moderns, for Husserl's "intuition of essences").

At least ten years before I chose this name I had become aware of the fact that my own problem, as opposed to the classical problem of universals (and its biological variant), was a *problem of method*. After all, what I had originally impressed on my mind was an exhortation to think, to proceed, in one way rather than in another. This is why, long before I invented the terms *"essentialism"* and *"anti-essentialism"*, I had qualified the term "nom-inalism" by the term "methodological", using the name "methodological nominalism" for the attitude characteristic of my exhortation. (I now think this name a little misleading. The choice of the word "nominalism" was the result of my attempt to identify my attitude with some well-known position, or at least to find similarities between it and some such position. Classical. "nominalism", however was a position which I never accepted.)

In the early 1920s I had two discussions which had some influence on these ideas. The first was a discussion with Karl Polanyi, the economic and political theorist. Polanyi thought that what I described as "methodological nominalism" was characteristic of the natural sciences but not of the social sciences. The second discussion, somewhat later, was with Heinrich Gomperz, a thinker of great originality and immense erudition, who shocked me by describing my position as "realist" in *both* senses of the word.

I now believe that Polanyi and Gomperz were both right. Polanyi was right because the natural sciences are largely free from verbal discussion, while verbalism was, and still is, rampant in many forms in the social sciences. But there is more to it. I should now say[7a] that social relations belong, in many ways, to what I have more recently called "the third world" or "world 3", the world of theories, of books, of ideas, of problems; a world which, ever since Plato—who saw it as a world of concepts—has been investigated essentialistically. Gomperz was right because a realist who believes in an "external world" necessarily believes in the existence of a cosmos rather than a chaos; that is, in regularities. And though I felt more opposed to classical essentialism than to nominalism, I did not then realize that, in substituting the problem of biological adaptation to regularities for the problem of the existence of similarities, I stood closer to "realism" than to nominalism.

In order to explain these matters as I see them at present, I will make use of a table of ideas which I first published in "On the Sources of Knowledge and of Ignorance".[8]

IDEAS
that is
DESIGNATIONS or TERMS or   STATEMENTS or PROPOSITIONS
CONCEPTS   or THEORIES
may be formulated in
WORDS   ASSERTIONS
which may be
MEANINGFUL   TRUE
and their
MEANING   TRUTH
may be reduced, by way of
DEFINITIONS   DERIVATIONS
to that of
UNDEFINED CONCEPTS   PRIMITIVE PROPOSITIONS
the attempt to establish (rather than reduce) by these means their
MEANING   TRUTH
leads to an infinite regress

This table is in itself quite trivial: the logical analogy between the left and right sides is well established. However, it can be used to bring home my exhortation, which may now be reformulated as follows.

In spite of the perfect logical analogy between the left and the right sides of this table, the left-hand side is philosophically unimportant, while the right-hand side is philosophically all important.[9]

This implies the view that meaning philosophies and language philosophies (so far as their concern is with words) are on the wrong track. *In matters of the intellect, the only things worth striving for are true theories, or theories which come near to the truth*—at any rate nearer than some other (competing) theory, for example an older one.

This, I suppose, most people will admit; but they will be inclined to argue as follows. Whether a theory is true, or new, or intellectually significant, depends on its meaning; and *the meaning of a theory* (provided it is grammatically unambiguously formulated) *is a function of the meanings of the words in which the theory is formulated.* (A "function" here, as in mathematics, is intended to take account of the order of the arguments.)

This view of the meaning of a theory seems almost obvious; it is widely held, and often unconsciously taken for granted.[10] Nevertheless, there is hardly any truth in it. I would counter it with the following rough formulation.

The relationship between a theory (or a statement) and the words used in its formulation is in several ways analogous to that between written words and the letters used in writing them down.

Obviously the letters have no "meaning" in the sense in which the words have "meaning", although we must know the letters (that is, their "meaning" in some other sense) if we are to recognise the words, and so discern their meaning. Approximately the same may be said about words and statements or theories.

Letters play a merely technical or pragmatic role in the formulation of words. In my opinion, words also play a merely technical or pragmatic role in the formulation of theories. Thus both letters and words are mere means to ends (different ends). And the only intellectually important ends are: the formulation of problems; the tentative proposing of theories to solve them; and the critical discussion of the competing theories. The critical discussion assesses such theories as are put forward in terms of their rational or intellectual value as solutions to the problem under consideration; and as regards their truth, or nearness to truth. Truth is the main regulative principle in the criticism of theories; their power to raise new problems and to solve them is another. (See *C.&R.*, Chap. 10.)

There are some excellent examples showing that two theories, T_1 and T_2, which are formulated in entirely different terms (terms which are not one-to-one translatable) may nevertheless be logically equivalent, so that we may say that T_1 and T_2 are merely different formulations of one and the same theory. This shows that it is a mistake to look on the logical "meaning" of a theory as determined by the "meanings" of the words. (In order to establish the equivalence of T_1 and T_2 it may be necessary to construct a richer theory T_3 into which both T_1 and T_2 can be translated. Examples are various axiomatizations of projective geometry; and also the particle and the wave formalisms of quantum mechanics, whose equivalence can be established by translating them both into an operator language.)[11]

Of course, it is quite obvious that a change of one word can radically change the meaning of a statement; just as a change of one letter can radically change the meaning of a word, and with it, of a theory—as anybody interested in the interpretation of, say, Parmenides will realize. Yet the mistakes of copyists or printers, though they may be fatally misleading, can more often than not be corrected by reflecting on the context.

Everybody who has done some translating, and who has thought about it, knows that there is no such thing as a grammatically correct and also almost literal translation. Every good translation is an *interpretation* of the original text; and I would even go so far as to say that every good translation of a nontrivial text must be a theoretical reconstruction. Thus it will even incorporate bits of a commentary. Every good translation must be, at the same time, close *and* free. Incidentally, it is a mistake to think that in an attempt to translate a piece of purely theoretical writing, aesthetic considerations are not important. One need only think of a theory like Newton's or Einstein's to see that a translation which gives the content of a theory but fails to bring out certain internal symmetries may be quite unsatisfactory; so much so that if somebody were given only the translation he would, if he discovered those symmetries, rightly feel he had himself made an original contribution, that he had discovered a theorem, even if the theorem was interesting chiefly for aesthetic reasons. (Somewhat similarly, a verse translation of Xenophanes, Parmenides, Empedocles, or Lucretius, is, other things being equal, preferable to a prose translation.)[12]

In any case, although a translation may be bad because it is not *sufficiently* precise, a *precise* translation of a difficult text simply does not exist. And if the two languages have a different structure, some theories may be almost untranslatable (as Benjamin Lee Whorf has shown so beautifully). Of course, if the languages are as closely related as, say, Latin and Greek, the introduction of a few newly coined words may suffice to make a translation possible. But in other cases an elaborate commentary may have to take the place of a translation.[13]

In view of all this, the idea of a precise language, or of precision in language, seems to be altogether misconceived. If we were to enter

"Precision" in the *Table of Ideas* (see above), it would stand on the left-hand side (because the linguistic precision of a statement would indeed depend entirely on the precision of the words used); its analogue on the right-hand side might be "Certainty". I did not enter these two ideas, however, because my table is so constructed that the ideas on the right-hand side are all valuable; yet both precision and certainty are false ideals. They are impossible to attain, and therefore dangerously misleading if they are *uncritically* accepted as guides. *The quest for precision is analogous to the quest for certainty*, and both should be abandoned.

I do not suggest, of course, that an increase in the precision of, say, a prediction, or even of a formulation, may not sometimes be highly desirable. What I do suggest is that *it is always undesirable to make an effort to increase precision for its own sake—especially linguistic precision—since this usually leads to loss of clarity*, and to a waste of time and effort on preliminaries which turn out to be useless so often because they are bypassed by the real advance of the subject: *one should never try to be more precise than the problem situation demands*.

I might perhaps state my position as follows. *Every increase in clarity is of intellectual value in itself; an increase in precision or exactness has only a pragmatic value as a means to some definite end*—the end's being usually an increase in testability or criticizability demanded by the problem situation (which for example may demand that we distinguish between two competing theories which lead to *almost* indistinguishable predictions).[14]

It will be clear that these views differ greatly from those implicitly held by many contemporary philosophers of science. Their attitude towards precision dates, I think, from the days when mathematics and physics were regarded as the Exact Sciences. Scientists, and also scientifically inclined philosophers, were greatly impressed. They felt it to be almost a duty to live up to, or to emulate, this "exactness", perhaps hoping that fertility would emerge from exactness as a kind of by-product. But fertility is the result not of exactness but of seeing new problems where none have been seen before, and of finding new ways of solving them.

However, I will postpone my remarks on the history of contemporary philosophy to the end of this digression, and turn again to the question of the meaning or significance of a statement or theory.

Having in mind my own exhortation never to quarrel about words, I am very ready to admit (with a shrug, as it were) that there may be meanings of the word "meaning" such that the meaning of a theory depends entirely on that of the words used in a very explicit formulation of the theory. (Perhaps Frege's "sense" is one of them, though much that he says speaks against this.) Nor do I deny that, as a rule, we must understand the words in order to understand a theory (although this is by no means true in general, as the existence of implicit definition suggests). But what makes a theory interesting or significant—what we try to understand, if we wish to understand a theory—is something different. To put the idea first in a way which is merely intuitive, and perhaps a bit woolly, it is its logical relation to the prevailing problem situation which makes a theory interesting: its relation to preceding and competing theories; its power to solve existing problems, and to suggest new ones. In other words, the meaning or significance of a theory in this sense depends on very comprehensive contexts, although of course the significance of these contexts in their turn depends on the various theories, problems, and problem situations of which they are composed.

It is interesting that this apparently vague (and one might say "holistic") idea of the significance of a theory can be analysed and clarified to a considerable extent in purely logical terms—with the help of the idea of the *content* of a statement or a theory.

There are in use, in the main, two intuitively very different but logically almost identical ideas of content, which I have sometimes called "*logical content*" and "*informative content*"; a special case of this I have also called "empirical content". To these I shall here add a third idea, which is merely a kind of unification of the other two; I shall refer to it as the "*problem content*" of a statement or a theory.

The *logical content* of a statement or theory may be identified with what Tarski has called its "consequence class"; that is, the class of all the (nontautological) consequences which can be derived from the statement or theory.

For *informative content* (as I have called it) we must consider the intuitive idea that statements or theories tell us the more "the more they prohibit" or exclude.[15] This intuitive idea leads to a definition of informative content which, to some people, has seemed absurd: *the informative content of a theory is the set of statements which are incompatible with the theory.*[16]

It may be seen at once, however, that the elements of this set and the elements of the logical content stand in a one-one correspondence: to every element which is in one of the sets, there is in the other set a corresponding element, namely its *negation*.

We therefore find that if the logical strength, or the power, or the amount of information in a theory increases or decreases, its logical content and its informative content must both likewise increase or decrease. This shows that the two ideas are very similar: there is a one-one correspondence between what can be said about the one, and what can be said about the other. Thus my definition of informative content is not entirely absurd.

But there are also differences. For example, for the *logical* content the following *rule of transitivity* holds: if b is an element of the content of a, and c an element of the content of b, then c is also an element of the content of a.

Although there of course exists a corresponding rule for *informative* content, it is not a simple transitivity rule like this.[17]

Moreover, the content of any (nontautological) statement—say a theory *t*—is *infinite*; for let there be an infinite list of statements *a, b, c, . . .*, which pairwise are contradictory, and individually do not entail *t*. (For most *t* something like *a*: "the number of planets is 0", *b*: "the number of planets is 1", and so on, would be adequate.) Then the statement "*t or a or both*" is deducible from *t*, and therefore belongs to the logical content of *t*; and the same holds for *b* and any other statement in the list. From our assumptions about *a, b, c, . . .*, it can now be shown simply that the statements of the sequence "*t or a or both*", "*t or b or both*", . . . , are not interdeducible; that is, not one of them entails any other. Thus the logical content of *t* must be infinite.

This elementary result concerning the logical content of any non-tautological theory is of course well known. The argument is trivial since it is based on the trivial operation of the logical (nonexclusive) "*or*";[18] and so one may doubt, perhaps, whether the infinity of the content is not altogether a trivial affair, depending merely on those statements like "*t or a or both*" which are the results of a trivial method of weakening *t*. However, in terms of *informative content* it immediately becomes clear that the matter is not quite as trivial as it looks.

For let the theory under consideration be Newton's theory of gravitation; call it *N*. Then any statement or any theory which is incompatible with *N* will belong to the informative content of *N*. Let us call Einstein's theory of gravitation *E*. Since the two theories are incompatible, each belongs to the informative content of the other; each excludes, or forbids, or prohibits the other.

This shows in a very intuitive way that the informative content of a theory *t* is infinite in a far from trivial way: any theory which is incompatible with *t*, and thus *any future theory which one day may supersede t* (say, after some crucial experiment has decided against *t*) *obviously belongs to the informative content of t*. But just as obviously, we cannot know, or construct, these theories in advance: Newton could not foresee Einstein or Einstein's successors.

Of course, it is now easy to find a precisely similar, though slightly less intuitive, situation concerning the logical content: since *E* belongs to the *informative* content of *N*, *non-E* belongs to the *logical* content of *N*; *non-E* is entailed by *N*, a fact which, obviously, could also not have been known to Newton, or anybody else, before *E* was discovered.

I have in lectures often described this interesting situation by saying: *we never know what we are talking about*. For when we propose a theory, or try to understand a theory, we also propose, or try to understand, its logical implications; that is, all those statements which follow from it. But this, as we have just seen, is a hopeless task: there is *an infinity of unforeseeable nontrivial statements belonging to the informative content of any theory*, and an exactly corresponding infinity of statements belonging to its logical content. We can therefore never know or understand all the implications of any theory, or its full significance.

This, I think, is a surprising result as far as it concerns logical content; though for informative content it turns out to be rather natural. (I have only once seen it stated,[19] although I have referred to it in lectures for many years.) It shows, among other things, that understanding a theory is always an infinite task, and that theories can in principle be understood better and better. It also shows that, if we wish to understand a theory better, what we have to do *first* is to discover its logical relation to those existing problems and existing theories which constitute what we may call *the "problem situation" at the particular moment of time.*

Admittedly, we also *try* to look ahead: we do try to discover new problems raised by our theory. But the task is infinite, and can never be completed.

Thus it turns out that the formulation which I have said earlier was "merely intuitive, and perhaps a bit woolly" can now be clarified. The nontrivial infinity of a theory's content, as I have described it here, turns the significance of the theory into a partly logical and partly historical matter. The latter depends on what has been discovered, *at a certain time*, in the light of the prevailing problem situation, about the theory's content; it is, as it were, a projection of this historical problem situation upon the logical content of the theory.

All this can easily be stated even if we confine ourselves to just one of the two ideas of content so far discussed. It becomes even clearer in terms of a third idea of content, that is, the idea of the *problem content* of a theory.

Following a suggestion of Frege's, we may introduce the notion of a yes-or-no problem or, briefly, a y-problem: given any statement a (say, "Grass is green"), the corresponding y-problem ("Is grass green?") may be denoted by "$y(a)$". One sees at once that $y(a) = y(non-a)$: the problem whether grass is green is, *qua* problem, identical with the problem whether grass is not green, even though the two questions are differently formulated, and even though the answer "Yes" to one of them is equivalent to the answer "No" to the other.

We can define what I propose to call the problem content of a theory t in either of two equivalent ways: (1) it is the set of all those $y(a)$ for which a is an element of the logical content of t; (2) it is the set of all those $y(a)$ for which a is an element of the informative content of t. Thus the problem content is related to the two other contents in identical ways.

In our previous example of N (Newton's theory) and E (Einstein's), $y(E)$ belongs to the problem content of N, and $y(N)$ to that of E. If we denote by K ($= K_1$ *and* K_2 *and* K_3) the statement which formulates Kepler's three laws, restricted to the two-body problem,[20] then K_1 and K_2 follow from N but contradict E, while K_3 and therefore K contradict both N and E. Nevertheless, $y(K)$ and $y(K_1)$, $y(K_2)$, $y(K_3)$, all belong to the problem content both of N and of E, and $y(N)$ and $y(E)$ both belong to the problem contents of K, of K_1, of K_2, and of K_3.

That $y(E)$, the problem of the truth or falsity of Einstein's theory, belongs to the problem content of K and to that of N illustrates the fact that there can be no transitivity here. For the problem whether the theory of the optical Doppler effect is true—that is, $y(D)$—belongs to the problem content of E, but not to that of N or that of K.

Although there is no transitivity there may be a link: the problem contents of a and of b may be said to be linked by $y(c)$ if $y(c)$ belongs to that of a and also to that of b. Obviously, the problem contents of any a and b can always be linked by choosing some appropriate c (perhaps $c = a$ *or* b); thus the bare fact that a and b are linked is trivial; but the fact that they are linked by some particular problem $y(c)$ (which interests us for some reason or other) may not be trivial, and may add to the significance of a, of b, and of c. Most links are, of course, unknown at any given time.

To sum up, there is at least one meaning of the "meaning" (or "significance") of a theory which makes it dependent upon its content and thus more dependent on its relations with other theories than on the meaning of any set of words.

These, I think, are some of the more important results which, during a lifetime, emerged from my anti-essentialist exhortation—which, in its turn, was the result of the discussion described in section 6. One further result is, quite simply, the realization that the quest for precision, in words or concepts or meanings, is a wild-goose chase. There simply is no such thing as a precise concept (say, in Frege's sense), though concepts like "price of this kettle" and "thirty pence" are usually precise enough for the problem context in which they are used. (But note the fact that "thirty pence" is, as a social or economic concept, highly variable: it had a different significance a few years ago from what it has today.)

Frege's opinion is different; for he writes: "A definition of a concept. . .must determine unambiguously of any object whether or not it falls under the concept. . . .Using a metaphor, we may say: the concept must have a sharp boundary."[21] But it is clear that for this kind of absolute precision to be demanded of a *defined* concept, it must first be demanded of the *defining* concepts, and ultimately of our *undefined*, or *primitive*, terms. Yet this is impossible. For either our undefined or primitive terms have a traditional meaning (which is never very precise) or they are introduced by so-called "implicit definitions"—that is, through the way they are used in the context of a theory. This last way of introducing them—if they have to be "introduced"—seems to be the best. But it makes the meaning of the concepts depend on that of the theory, and most theories can be interpreted in more than one way. As a result, implicitly defined concepts, and thus all concepts which are defined explicitly with their help, become not merely "vague" but *systematically ambiguous*. And the various systematically ambiguous interpretations, such as the points and straight lines of projective geometry, may be *completely distinct*.

This should be sufficient to establish the fact that "unambiguous" concepts, or concepts with "sharp boundary lines", do not exist. Thus we need not be surprised at Clifford A. Truesdell's remark about the laws of thermodynamics: "Every physicist knows exactly what the first and the second law mean, but . . . no two physicists agree about them."[22]

We know now that the choice of undefined terms is largely arbitrary, as is the choice of the axioms of a theory. Frege was, I think, mistaken on this point, at least in 1892: he believed that there were terms which were intrinsically undefinable because "what is logically simple cannot have a proper definition".[23] However, what he thought of as an example of a simple concept—the concept of "concept"—turned out to be quite unlike what he thought it was. It has since developed into that of "set", and few would now call it either unambiguous or simple.

At any rate, the wild-goose chase did go on. When I wrote my *Logik der Forschung* I thought that the quest for the meanings of words was about to end. I was an optimist: it was gaining momentum.[24] The task of philosophy was more and more widely described as concerned with meaning, and this meant, mainly, the meanings of words. And nobody seriously questioned the implicitly accepted dogma that the meaning of a statement, at least in its most explicit and unambiguous formulation, depends on (or is a function of) that of its words. This is true equally of the British language analysts and of those who follow Carnap in upholding the view that the task of philosophy is the "explication of concepts", that is, making concepts precise. Yet *there is no such thing as an "explication" or an "explicated" or "precise" concept.*

However, the problem still remains: what should we do in order to make our meaning clearer, if greater clarity is needed, or to make it more precise, if greater precision is needed? In the light of my exhortation the main answer to this question is: any move to increase clarity or precision must be *ad hoc* or "piecemeal". If because of lack of clarity a misunderstanding arises, do not try to lay new and more solid foundations on which to build a more precise "conceptual framework", but reformulate your formulations *ad hoc*, with a view to avoiding misunderstandings which have arisen or which you can foresee. And always remember that *it is impossible to speak in such a way that you cannot be misunderstood:* there will always be some who misunderstand you. If greater precision is needed, it is needed because *the problem to be solved* demands it. Simply try your best to solve your problems and do not try in advance to make your concepts or formulations more precise in the fond hope that this will provide you with an arsenal for future use in tackling problems which have not yet arisen. *They may never arise;* the evolution of the theory may bypass all your efforts. The intellectual weapons which will be needed at a later date may be very different from those which anyone has in store. For example, it is almost certain that nobody trying to make the concept of simultaneity more precise would, before the discovery of Einstein's problem (the asymmetries in the electrodynamics of moving bodies), have hit on Einstein's "analysis". (It should not be thought that I subscribe to the still popular view that Einstein's achievement was one of "operational analysis". It was not. See page 20 of my *Open Society*, [1957(h)] and later editions, Vol. II.)

The *ad hoc* method of dealing with problems of clarity or precision as the need arises might be called *"dialysis"*, in order to distinguish it from *analysis:* from the idea that language analysis as such may solve problems, or create an armoury for future use. Dialysis cannot solve problems. It cannot do so any more than definition or explication or language analysis can: problems can only be solved with the help of new ideas. But our problems may sometimes demand that we make new distinctions—*ad hoc*, for the purpose in hand.

This long digression[25] has led me away from my main story, to which I will now return.

8. *A Crucial Year: Marxism; Science and Pseudoscience*

It was during the last terrible years of the war, probably in 1917, at a time when I was suffering from a long illness, that I realized very clearly what I had felt in my bones for a considerable time: that in our famous Austrian secondary schools (called *"Gymnasium"* and—*horribile dictu*— *"Realgymnasium"*) we were wasting our time shockingly, even though our teachers were well educated and tried hard to make the schools the best in the world. That much of their teaching was boring in the extreme—hours and hours of hopeless torture—was not new to me. (They immunized me: never since have I suffered from boredom. In school one was liable to be found out if one thought of something unconnected with the lesson: one was compelled to attend. Later on, when a lecturer was boring, one could entertain oneself with one's own thoughts.) There was just one subject in which we had an interesting and truly inspiring teacher. The subject was mathematics, and the name of the teacher was Philipp Freud (I do not know whether he was a relative of Sigmund Freud's). Yet when I returned to school after an illness of over two months I found that my class had made hardly any progress, even in mathematics. This was an eye-opener: it made me eager to leave school.

The breakdown of the Austrian Empire and the aftermath of the First World War, the famine, the hunger riots in Vienna, and the runaway inflation, have often been described. They destroyed the world in which I had grown up; and there began a period of cold and hot civil war which ended with Hitler's invasion of Austria, and led to the Second World War. I was a little over sixteen when the war ended, and the revolution incited me to stage my own private revolution. I decided to leave school, late in 1918, to study on my own. I enrolled at the University of Vienna where I was, at first, a non-matriculated student, since I did not take the entrance examination ("*Matura*") until 1922, when I became a matriculated student. There were no scholarships, but the cost of enrolling at the University was nominal. And every student could attend any lecture course.

It was a time of upheavals, though not only political ones. I was close enough to hear the bullets whistle when, on the occasion of the Declaration of the Austrian Republic, soldiers started shooting at the members of the Provisional Government assembled at the top of the steps leading to the Parliament building. (This experience led me to write a paper on freedom.) There was little to eat; and as for clothing, most of us could afford only discarded army uniforms, adapted for civilian use. Few of us thought seriously of careers—there were none (except perhaps in a bank; but the thought of a career in commerce never entered my head). We studied not for a career but for the sake of studying. We studied and we discussed politics.

There were three main political parties: the social democrats, and the two antisocialist parties, the German nationalists (then the smallest of the three main parties, and later to be absorbed by the Nazis), and what was in effect the party of the Roman Church (Austria had a vast Roman Catholic majority) which called itself "Christian" and "social" (*christlich-sozial*) although it was antisocialist. Then there was the small communist party. I became a member of the association of socialist pupils of secondary schools (*sozialistische Mittelschüler*) and went to their meetings. I went also to meetings of the socialist university students. The speakers at these meetings belonged sometimes to the social democratic and sometimes to the communist parties. Their Marxist beliefs were then very similar. And they all dwelt, rightly, on the horrors of war. The communists claimed that they had proved their pacifism by ending the war, at Brest-Litovsk. Peace, they said, was what they primarily stood for. At that particular time they were not only for peace but, in their propaganda at least, against all "unnecessary" violence.[26] For a time I was suspicious of the communists, mainly because of what my friend Arndt had told me about them. But in the spring of 1919 I, together with a few friends, became convinced by their propaganda. For about two or three months I regarded myself as a communist.

I was soon to be disenchanted. The incident that first turned me against communism, and that soon led me away from Marxism altogether, was one of the most important incidents in my life. It happened shortly before my seventeenth birthday. In Vienna, shooting broke out during a demonstration by unarmed young socialists who, instigated by the communists, tried to help some communists to escape who were under arrest in the central police station in Vienna. Several young socialist and communist workers were killed. I was horrified and shocked at the police, but also at myself. For I felt that as a Marxist I bore part of the responsibility for the tragedy—at least in principle. Marxist theory demands that the class struggle be intensified, in order to speed up the coming of socialism. Its thesis is that although the revolution may claim some victims, capitalism is claiming more victims than the whole socialist revolution.

That was the Marxist theory—part of so-called "scientific socialism". I now asked myself whether such a calculation could ever be supported by "science". The whole experience, and especially this question, led me to a life-long revulsion of feeling.

Communism is a creed which promises to bring about a better world. It claims to be based on knowledge: knowledge of the laws of historical development. I still hoped for a better world, a less violent and more just world, but I questioned whether I really *knew*—whether what I had thought was knowledge was not perhaps mere pretence. I had, of course, read some Marx and Engels—but had I really understood it? Had I examined it critically, as anybody should do before he accepts a creed which justifies its means by a somewhat distant end?

I was shocked to have to admit to myself that not only had I accepted a complex theory somewhat uncritically, but I had also actually noticed quite a bit that was wrong, in the theory as well as in the practice of communism, but had repressed this—partly out of loyalty to my friends, partly out of loyalty to "the cause", and partly because there is a mechanism of getting oneself more and more deeply involved: once one has sacrificed one's intellectual conscience over a minor point one does not wish to give up too easily; one wishes to justify the self-sacrifice by convincing oneself of the fundamental goodness of the cause, which is seen to outweigh any little moral or intellectual compromise that may be required. With every such moral or intellectual sacrifice one gets more deeply involved. One becomes ready to back one's moral or intellectual investments in the cause with further investments. It is like being eager to throw good money after bad.

I saw how this mechanism had been working in my case, and I was horrified. I also saw it at work in others, especially in my communist friends.

And the experience enabled me to understand later many things which otherwise I would not have understood.

I had accepted a dangerous creed uncritically, dogmatically. The reaction made me first a sceptic; then it led me on, for a short time, to react against all rationalism. (As I found later, this is a typical reaction of a disappointed Marxist.)

By the time I was seventeen I had become an anti-Marxist. I realized the dogmatic character of the creed, and its incredible intellectual arrogance. It was a terrible thing to arrogate to oneself a kind of knowledge which made it a duty to risk the lives of other people for an uncritically accepted dogma, or for a dream which might turn out not to be realizable. It was particularly bad for an intellectual, for one who could read and think. It was awfully depressing to have fallen into such a trap.

Once I had looked at it critically, the gaps and loopholes and inconsistencies in the Marxist theory became obvious. Take its central point with respect to violence, the dictatorship of the proletariat: who were the proletariat? Lenin, Trotsky, and the other leaders? The communists had never been in the majority. They did not hold a majority even among the workers in the factories. In Austria, certainly, they were a very small minority, and apparently it was the same elsewhere.

It took me some years of study before I felt with any confidence that I had grasped the heart of the Marxian argument. It consists of a historical prophecy, combined with an implicit appeal to the following moral law: *Help to bring about the inevitable!* Even then I had no intention of publishing my criticism of Marx, for anti-Marxism in Austria was a worse thing than Marxism: since the social democrats were Marxist, anti-Marxism was very nearly identical with those authoritarian movements which were later called fascist. Of course, I talked about it to my friends. But it was not till sixteen years later, in 1935, that I began to write about Marxism with the intention of publishing what I wrote. As a consequence, two books emerged between 1935 and 1943—*The Poverty of Historicism* and *The Open Society and Its Enemies*.

Yet at the time I am now speaking about (it must have been in 1919 or 1920) one of the things which revolted me was the intellectual presumption of some of my Marxist friends and fellow students, who almost took it for granted that they were the future leaders of the working class. They had, I knew, no special intellectual qualifications. All they could claim was some acquaintance with Marxist literature—not even a thorough one, and certainly not a critical one. Of the life of a manual worker most of them knew less than I did. (I had at least worked for some months during the war in a factory.) I reacted strongly to this attitude. I felt that we were privileged in being able to study—indeed, undeservedly so—and I decided to try to become a manual worker. I also decided never to seek any influence in party politics.

I did in fact make several attempts to become a manual worker. My second attempt broke down because I did not have the physical stamina needed for digging concrete-hard road surfaces with a pickaxe for days and days on end. My last attempt was to become a cabinetmaker. Physically this was not demanding, but the trouble was that certain speculative ideas which interested me interfered with my work.

Perhaps this is the place to say how much I admired the workers of Vienna and their great movement—led by the social democratic party—even though I regarded the Marxist historicism of their social democratic leaders as fatally mistaken.[27] Their leaders were able to inspire them with a marvellous faith in their mission, which was nothing less, they believed, than the liberation of mankind. Although the social democratic movement was largely atheistic (despite a small and admirable group who described themselves as religious socialists) the whole movement was inspired by what can only be described as an ardent religious and humanitarian faith. It was a movement of the workers to educate themselves in order to fulfil their "historic mission"; to emancipate themselves, and thus to help liberate mankind; and above all to end war. In their restricted spare time many workers, young and old, went to extension courses, or to one of the "People's Universities" (*Volkshochschulen*). They took a great interest not only in self-education but in the education of their children, and in improving housing conditions. It was an admirable programme. In their lives, showing on occasion, perhaps, a touch of priggishness, they substituted mountaineering for alcohol, classical music for swing, serious reading for thrillers. These activities were all peaceful, and they were carried on in an atmosphere poisoned by fascism and latent civil war; and also, most unfortunately, by repeated and confused threats from the workers' leaders that they would give up democratic methods and take recourse to violence—a legacy of the ambiguous attitude of Marx and Engels. This great movement and its tragic destruction by fascism made a deep impression on some English and American observers (for example, G. E. R. Gedye).[28]

I remained a socialist for several years, even after my rejection of Marxism; and if there could be such a thing as socialism combined with individual liberty, I would be a socialist still. For nothing could be better than living a modest, simple, and free life in an egalitarian society. It took some time before I recognised this as no more than a beautiful dream; that freedom is more important than equality; that the attempt to realize equality endangers freedom; and that, if freedom is lost, there will not even be equality among the unfree.

The encounter with Marxism was one of the main events in my intellectual development. It taught me a number of lessons which I have never forgotten. It taught me the wisdom of the Socratic saying, "I know that I do not know". It made me a fallibilist, and impressed on me the value of intellectual modesty. And it made me most conscious of the differences between dogmatic and critical thinking.

Compared with this encounter, the somewhat similar pattern of my encounters with Alfred Adler's "individual psychology" and with Freudian psychoanalysis—which were more or less contemporaneous (it all happened in 1919)—were of minor importance.[29]

Looking back at that year I am amazed that so much can happen to one's intellectual development in so short a spell. For at the same time I learned about Einstein; and this became a dominant influence on my thinking—in the long run perhaps the most important influence of all. In May, 1919, Einstein's eclipse predictions were successfully tested by two British expeditions. With these tests a new theory of gravitation and a new cosmology suddenly appeared, not just as a mere possibility, but as a real improvement on Newton—a better approximation to the truth.

Einstein gave a lecture in Vienna, to which I went; but I remember only that I was dazed. This thing was quite beyond my understanding. I had been brought up in an atmosphere in which Newton's mechanics and Maxwell's electrodynamics were accepted side by side as unquestionable truths. Even Mach in *The Science of Mechanics*, in which he criticized Newton's theory of absolute space and absolute time, had retained Newton's laws—including the law of inertia, for which he had offered a new and fascinating interpretation. And although he did consider the possibility of a non-Newtonian theory he thought that before we could start on it we would have to await new experiences, which might come, perhaps, from new physical or astronomical knowledge about regions of space containing faster and more complex movements than could be found in our own solar system.[30] Hertz's mechanics too did not deviate from Newton's, except in its presentation.

The general assumption of the truth of Newton's theory was of course the result of its incredible success, culminating in the discovery of the planet Neptune. The success was so impressive because (as I later put it) Newton's theory repeatedly *corrected the empirical material which it set out to explain.*[31] Yet in spite of all this, Einstein had managed to produce a real alternative and, it appeared, a better theory, without waiting for new experiences. Like Newton himelf, he predicted new effects within (and without) our solar system. And some of these predictions, when tested, had now proved successful.

I was fortunate in being introduced to these ideas by a brilliant young student of mathematics, Max Elstein, a friend who died in 1922 at the age of twenty-one. He was not a positivist (as Einstein was in those days, and for years to come), and he therefore stressed the objective aspects of Einstein's theory: the field-theoretical approach; the electrodynamics and mechanics and their new link; and the marvellous idea of a new cosmology—a finite but unbounded universe. He drew my attention to the fact that Einstein himself regarded it as one of the main arguments in favour of his theory that it yielded Newton's theory as a very good approximation; also, that Einstein, though convinced that his theory was a better approximation than Newton's, regarded his own theory merely as a step towards a still more general theory; and further that Hermann Weyl had already published, even before the eclipse observations, a book (*Raum, Zeit, Materie*, 1918) in which was offered a more general and comprehensive theory than Einstein's.

No doubt Einstein had all this, and especially his own theory, in mind when he wrote in another context: "There could be no fairer destiny for any physical theory than that it should point the way to a more comprehensive theory, in which it lives on as a limiting case."[32] But what impressed me most was Einstein's own clear statement that he would regard his theory as untenable if it should fail in certain tests. Thus he wrote, for example: "If the redshift of spectral lines due to the gravitational potential should not exist, then the general theory of relativity will be untenable."[33]

Here was an attitude utterly different from the dogmatic attitude of Marx, Freud, Adler, and even more so that of their followers. Einstein was looking for crucial experiments whose agreement with his predictions would by no means establish his theory; while a disagreement, as he was the first to stress, would show his theory to be untenable.

This, I felt, was the true scientific attitude. It was utterly different from the dogmatic attitude which constantly claimed to find "verifications" for its favourite theories.

Thus I arrived, by the end of 1919, at the conclusion that the scientific attitude was the critical attitude, which did not look for verifications but for crucial tests; tests which could *refute* the theory tested, though they could never establish it.

9. Early Studies

Although the years after the First World War were grim for most of my friends and also for myself, it was an exhilarating time. Not that we were happy. Most of us had no prospects and no plans. We lived in a very poor country in which civil war was endemic, flaring up in earnest from time to time. We were often depressed, discouraged, disgusted. But we were learning, our minds were active and growing. We were reading ravenously, omnivorously; debating, changing our opinions, studying, sifting critically, thinking. We listened to music, went tramping in the beautiful mountains, and dreamt of a better, healthier, simpler, and more honest world.

During the winter of 1919-20 I left home to live in a disused part of a former military hospital converted by students into an extremely primitive students' home. I wanted to be independent, and I tried not to be a burden to my father, who was well over sixty and had lost all his savings in the runaway inflation after the war. My parents would have preferred it if I had stayed at home.

I had been doing some unpaid work in Alfred Adler's child guidance clinics, and I was now doing other occasional work with hardly any pay at all. Some of it was hard (road making). But I also coached some American university students, who were very generous. I needed very little: there was not much to eat, and I did not smoke or drink. The only necessities which were sometimes hard to come by were tickets for concerts. Though the tickets were cheap (if one stood), they were for a number of years almost a daily expenditure.

At the University I sampled lecture courses in various subjects: history, literature, psychology, philosophy, and even lectures at the medical school. But I soon gave up going to lectures, with the exception of those in mathematics and theoretical physics. The University had, at that time, most eminent teachers, but reading their books was an incomparably greater experience than listening to their lectures. (Seminars were for advanced students only.) I also started fighting my way through the *Critique of Pure Reason* and the *Prolegomena*.

Only the department of mathematics offered really fascinating lectures. The professors at the time were Wirtinger, Furtwängler, and Hans Hahn. All three were creative mathematicians of world reputation. Wirtinger, whom departmental rumour rated as the greatest genius of the three, I found difficult to follow. Furtwängler was amazing in his clarity and the mastery of his subjects (algebra, number theory). But I learned most from Hans Hahn. His lectures attained a degree of perfection which I have never encountered again. Each lecture was a work of art: dramatic in logical structure; not a word too much; of perfect clarity; and delivered in beautiful and civilized language. The subject (and sometimes the problems discussed) were introduced by an exciting historical sketch. Everything was alive, though due to its very perfection a bit aloof.

There was also Dozent Helly, who lectured on probability theory and from whom I first heard the name of Richard von Mises. Later there came for a short time a very young and charming professor from Germany, Kurt Reidemeister; I went to his lectures on tensor algebra. All these men—except perhaps Reidemeister, who was not averse to interruptions—were demigods. They were infinitely beyond our reach. There was no contact between professors and students who had not qualified for a Ph.D. dissertation. Neither had I the slightest ambition to make, nor prospect of making, their acquaintance. I never expected that I should later become personally acquainted with Hahn, Helly, von Mises, and Hans Thirring, who taught theoretical physics.

I studied mathematics because I simply wanted to learn, and I thought that in mathematics I would learn something about standards of truth; and also because I was interested in theoretical physics. Mathematics was a huge and difficult subject, and had I ever thought of becoming a professional mathematician I might soon have been discouraged. But I had no such ambition. If I thought of a future, I dreamt of one day founding a school in which young people could learn without boredom, and would be stimulated to pose problems and discuss them; a school in which no unwanted answers to unasked questions would have to be listened to; in which one did not study for the sake of passing examinations.

I passed my "*Matura*" as a private pupil in 1922, one year later than I would have, had I continued at school. But the experiment had been worth the year I "lost". I now became a fully matriculated university student. A year later I passed a second "*Matura*" at a teachers' training college, which qualified me to teach in primary schools. I took this examination while learning to be a cabinetmaker. Later I added qualifications to teach mathematics, physics, and chemistry in secondary schools. However, there were no posts available for teachers, and after concluding my apprenticeship as a cabinetmaker I became, as I have mentioned, a social worker (*Horterzieher*) with neglected children.

Early during this period I developed further my ideas about the *demarcation between scientific theories* (like Einstein's) *and pseudoscientific theories* (like Marx's, Freud's, and Adler's). It became clear to me that what made a theory, or a statement, scientific was its power to rule out, or exclude, the occurrence of some possible events—to prohibit, or forbid, the occurrence of these events: *the more a theory forbids, the more it tells us.*[34]

Although this idea is closely related to that of the "informative content" of a theory, and contains the latter idea in a nutshell, I did not, at the time, develop it much beyond this point. I was, however, much concerned with the problem of *dogmatic thinking and its relation to critical thinking.* What especially interested me was the idea that dogmatic thinking, which I regarded as prescientific, was a stage that was needed if critical thinking was to be possible. Critical thinking must have before it something to criticize, and this, I thought, must be the result of dogmatic thinking.

I shall say here a few more words on the *problem of demarcation* and my solution.

(1) As it occurred to me first, the problem of demarcation was not the problem of demarcating science from metaphysics but rather the problem of

demarcating science from pseudoscience. At the time I was not at all interested in metaphysics. It was only later that I extended my "*criterion of demarcation*" to metaphysics.

(2) My main idea in 1919 was this. If somebody proposed a scientific theory he should answer, as Einstein did, the question: "Under what conditions would I admit that my theory is untenable?" In other words, what conceivable facts would I accept as refutations, or falsifications, of my theory?

(3) I had been shocked by the fact that the Marxists (whose central claim was that they were social scientists) and the psychoanalysts of all schools were able to interpret any conceivable event as a verification of their theories. This, together with my criterion of demarcation, led me to the view that only attempted refutations which did not succeed *qua* refutations could count as "verifications".

(4) I still hold with (2). But when a little later I tentatively introduced the idea of the *falsifiability (or testability or refutability) of a theory as a criterion of demarcation*, I very soon found that every theory can be "immunized" (this excellent term is due to Hans Albert)[35] against criticism. If we allow such immunization, then every theory becomes unfalsifiable. Thus we must exclude at least some immunizations.

On the other hand, I also realized that we must not exclude all immunizations, not even all which introduce *ad hoc* auxiliary hypotheses. For example the observed motion of Uranus might have been regarded as a falsification of Newton's theory. Instead the auxiliary hypothesis of an outer planet was introduced *ad hoc*, thus immunizing the theory. This turned out to be fortunate; for the auxiliary hypothesis was a testable one, even if difficult to test, and it stood up to tests successfully.

All this shows not only that some degree of dogmatism is fruitful, even in science, but also that logically speaking falsifiability, or testability, cannot be regarded as a very sharp criterion. Later, in *Logik der Forschung*, I dealt with this problem very fully. I introduced *degrees of testability*, and these turned out to be closely related to (degrees of) *content*, and surprisingly fertile: increase of content became the criterion for whether we should, or should not, tentatively adopt an auxiliary hypothesis.

In spite of the fact that all this was clearly stated in my *Logik der Forschung* of 1934, a number of legends were propagated about my views.[36] First, that I had introduced falsifiability as a meaning criterion rather than as a criterion of demarcation. Secondly, that I had not seen that immunization was always possible, and had therefore overlooked the fact that since all theories could be rescued from falsification none could simply be described as "falsifiable". In other words my own results were, in these legends, turned into reasons for rejecting my approach.[37]

(5) As a kind of summary it may be useful to show, with the help of examples, how various types of theoretical systems are related to testability (or falsifiability) and to immunization procedures.

(a) There are metaphysical theories of a *purely existential* character (discussed especially in *Conjectures and Refutations*).[38]

(b) There are theories like the psychoanalytic theories of Freud, Adler, and Jung, or like (sufficiently vague) astrological lore.[39]

(c) There are what one might call "unsophisticated" theories like "All swans are white" or the geocentric "All stars other than planets move in circles". Kepler's laws may be included (though they are in many senses highly sophisticated). These theories are falsifiable, though falsifications can, of course, be evaded: immunization is *always* possible. But the evasion would usually be dishonest: it would consist, say, in denying that a black swan was a swan, or that it was black; or that a non-Keplerian planet was a planet.

(d) The case of Marxism is interesting. As I pointed out in my *Open Society*,[40] one may regard Marx's theory as refuted by the course of events during the Russian Revolution. According to Marx the revolutionary changes start at the bottom, as it were: means of production change first, then social conditions of production, then political power, and ultimately ideological beliefs, which change last. But in the Russian Revolution the political power changed first, and then the ideology (Dictatorship plus Electrification) began to change social conditions and the means of production from the top. The reinterpretation of Marx's theory of revolution to evade this falsification immunized it against further attacks, transforming it into the vulgar-Marxist (or socioanalytic) theory which tells us that the "economic motive" and the class struggle pervade social life.

(e) There are more abstract theories like Newton's or Einstein's theories of gravitation. They are falsifiable—say, by not finding predicted perturbations, or perhaps by a negative outcome of radar tests replacing solar eclipse observations. But in their case a prima facie falsification *may* be evaded, not only by uninteresting immunizations but also, as in the Uranus/Neptune sort of case, by the introduction of testable auxiliary hypotheses, so that the empirical content of the system—consisting of the original theory plus the auxiliary hypothesis—is greater than that of the original system. We may regard this as an increase of informative content—as a case of *growth* in our knowledge. There are, of course, also auxiliary hypotheses which are merely evasive immunizing moves. They decrease the content. All this suggests the *methodological rule* not to put up with any content-decreasing manoeuvres (or with "degenerating problem shifts", in the terminology of Imre Lakatos[41]).

10. A Second Digression: Dogmatic and Critical Thinking; Learning without Induction

Konrad Lorenz is the author of a marvellous theory in the field of animal psychology, which he calls "imprinting". It implies that young animals have an inborn mechanism for jumping to unshakable conclusions. For example, a newly hatched gosling adopts as its "mother" the first moving thing it sets eyes on. This mechanism is well adapted to normal circumstances, though a bit risky for the gosling. (It may also be risky for the chosen foster parent, as we learn from Lorenz.) But it is a successful mechanism under normal circumstances; and also under some not quite normal ones.

The following points about Lorenz's "imprinting" are important:

(1) It is a process—not the only one—of learning by observation.

(2) The problem solved under the stimulus of the observation is inborn; that is, the gosling is genetically conditioned to look out for its mother: it expects to see its mother.

(3) The theory or expectation which solves the problem is also to some extent inborn, or genetically conditioned: it goes far beyond the actual observation, which merely (so to speak) releases or triggers the theory which is largely preformed in the organism.

(4) The learning process is *nonrepetitive*, though it may take a certain amount of time (a short time),[42] and involve some normal activity or "effort" on the part of the organism; and therefore a situation not too far removed from that normally encountered. I shall say of such nonrepetitive learning processes that they are "noninductive", taking repetition as the characteristic of "induction". (The theory of nonrepetitive learning may be described as *selective* or Darwinian, while the theory of inductive or repetitive learning is a theory of *instructive* learning; it is Lamarckian.) Of course, this is purely terminological: should anybody insist on calling imprinting an inductive process I should just have to change my terminology.

(5) The observation itself works only like the turning of a key in a lock. Its role is important, but the highly complex result is almost completely preformed.

(6) Imprinting is an absolutely irreversible process of learning; that is, it is not subject to correction or revision.

Of course I knew nothing in 1922 of Konrad Lorenz's theories (though I had known him as a boy in Altenberg, where we had close friends in common). I shall here use the theory of imprinting merely as a means of explaining my own conjecture, which was similar yet different. My conjecture was not about animals (though I was influenced by C. Lloyd Morgan and even more by H.S. Jennings[43]) but about human beings, especially young children. It was this.

Most (or perhaps all) learning processes consist in theory formation;

that is, the formation of expectations. The formation of a theory or conjecture has always a "dogmatic", and often a "critical", phase. This dogmatic phase shares, with imprinting, the characteristics of (2) to (4), and sometimes also (1) and (5), but not normally (6). The critical phase consists in giving up the dogmatic theory under the pressure of disappointed expectations or refutations, and in trying out other dogmas. I noticed that sometimes the dogma was so strongly entrenched that no disappointment could shake it. It is clear that in this case—though only in this case —dogmatic theory formation comes very close to imprinting, of which (6) is characteristic.[44] However, I was inclined to look on (6) as a kind of neurotic aberration (even though neuroses did not really interest me: it was the psychology of discovery I was trying to get at). This attitude towards (6) shows that what I had in mind, though perhaps related to imprinting, was different.

I looked on this method of theory formation as a method of learning by trial and error. But when I called the formation of a theoretical dogma a "trial" *I did not mean a random trial.*

It is of some interest to consider the problem of the randomness (or otherwise) of trials in a trial-and-error procedure. Take a simple arithmetical example: division by a number (say, 74856) whose multiplication table we do not know by heart is usually done by trial and error; but this does not mean that the trials are random, for we do know the multiplication tables for 7 and 8.[45] Of course we could programme a computer to divide by a method of selecting *at random* one of the ten digits 0, 1, . . .9, as a trial and, in case of error, one of the remaining nine (the erroneous digit having been excluded) by the same random procedure. But this would obviously be inferior to a more systematic procedure: at the very least we should make the computer notice whether its first trial was in error because the selected digit was too small or because it was too big, thus reducing the range of digits for the second selection.

To this example the idea of randomness is in principle applicable, because in every step in long division there is a selection to be made from a well-defined set of possibilities (the digits). But in most zoological examples of learning by trial and error the range or set of possible reactions (movements of any degree of complexity) is not given in advance; and since we do not know the elements of this range we cannot attribute probabilities to them, which we should have to do in order to speak of randomness in any clear sense.

Thus we have to reject the idea that the method of trial and error operates in general, or normally, with trials which are *random*, even though we may, with some ingenuity, construct highly artificial conditions (such as a maze for rats) to which the idea of randomness may be applicable. But its mere applicability does not, of course, establish that the trials are in fact random: our computer may adopt with advantage a more systematic method of selecting the digits (and a rat running a maze may also operate on principles which are not random).

On the other hand, in any case in which the method of trial and error is applied to the solution of such a problem as the problem of adaptation (to a maze, say), the trials are as a rule not determined, or not completely determined, by the problem; nor can they anticipate its (unknown) solution otherwise than by a fortunate accident. In the terminology of D. T. Campbell, we may say that the trials must be "blind" (I should perhaps prefer to say they must be "blind to the solution of the problem").[46] It is not from the trial but only from the critical method, the method of error elimination, that we find, *after* the trial—corresponding to the dogma—has been carried out, whether or not it was a lucky guess; that is, sufficiently successful in solving the problem in hand to avoid being eliminated for the time being.

Yet the trials are not always quite blind to the demands of the problem: the problem often determines the range from which the trials are selected (such as the range of the digits). This is well described by David Katz: "A hungry animal divides the environment into edible and inedible things. An animal in flight sees roads of escape and hiding places."[47] Moreover, the problem may change somewhat with the successive trials; for example, the range may narrow. But there may also be quite different cases, especially on the human level; cases in which everything depends upon an ability to break through the limits of the assumed range. These cases show that the selection of the range itself may be a trial (an unconscious conjecture), and that critical thinking may consist not only in a rejection of any particular trial or conjecture, but also in a rejection of what may be described as a deeper conjecture—the assumption of the range of "all possible trials". This, I suggest, is what happens in many cases of "creative" thinking.

What characterizes creative thinking, apart from the intensity of the interest in the problem, seems to me often the ability to break through the limits of the range—or to vary the range—from which a less creative thinker selects his trials. This ability, which clearly is a critical ability, may be described as *critical imagination*. It is often the result of culture clash, that is, a clash between ideas, or frameworks of ideas. Such a clash may help us to break through the ordinary bounds of our imagination.

Remarks like this, however, would hardly satisfy those who seek for a psychological theory of creative thinking, and especially of scientific discovery. For what they are after is a theory of *successful* thinking.

I think that the demand for a theory of successful thinking cannot be satisfied, and that it is not the same as the demand for a theory of creative thinking. Success depends on many things—for example on luck. It may depend on meeting with a promising problem. It depends on not being anticipated. It depends on such things as a fortunate division of one's time between trying to keep up-to-date and concentrating on working out one's own ideas.

But it seems to me that what is essential to "creative" or "inventive" thinking is a combination of intense interest in some problem (and thus a readiness to try again and again) with highly critical thinking; with a readiness to attack even those presuppositions which for less critical thought determine the limits of the range from which trials (conjectures) are selected; with an imaginative freedom that allows us to see so far unsuspected sources of error: possible prejudices in need of critical examination.

(It is my opinion that most investigations into the psychology of creative thought are pretty barren—or else more logical than psychological. For critical thought, or error elimination, can be better characterized in logical terms than in psychological terms.)

Thus a "trial" or a newly formed "dogma" or "expectation" is largely the result of inborn *needs* that give rise to specific problems. But it is also the result of the inborn need to form expectations (in certain specific fields, which in their turn are related to some other needs); and it may also be partly the result of disappointed earlier expectations. I do not of course deny that there may also be an element of personal ingenuity present in the formation of trials or dogmas, but I think that ingenuity and imagination play their main part in the *critical process of error elimination*. Most of the great dogmas which are among the supreme achievements of the human mind are the offspring of earlier dogmas, plus criticism.

What became clear to me first, in connection with dogma-formation, was that children—especially small children—urgently needed discoverable regularities around them; there was an inborn need not only for food and for being loved but also for discoverable structural invariants of the environment ("things" are such discoverable invariants), for a settled routine, for settled expectations. This infantile dogmatism has been observed by Jane Austen: "Henry and John were still asking every day for the story of Harriet and the gipsies, and still tenaciously setting [Emma]. . . right if she varied in the slightest particular from the original recital."[48] There was, especially in older children, enjoyment in variation, but mainly within a limited range or framework of expectations. Games, for example, were of this kind; and the rules (the invariants) of the game were often almost impossible to learn by mere observation.[49]

My main point was that the dogmatic way of thinking was due to an inborn need for regularities, and to inborn mechanisms of discovery, mechanisms which make us search for regularities. And one of my theses was that if we speak glibly of "heredity and environment" we are liable to underrate the overwhelming role of heredity—which, among other things, largely determines what aspects of its objective environment (its ecological niche) do or do not belong to an animal's subjective, or biologically significant, environment.

I distinguished three main types of learning process, of which the first was the fundamental one:

(1) Learning in the sense of discovery: (dogmatic) formation of theories or expectations, or regular behaviour, checked by (critical) error elimination.

(2) Learning by imitation. This can be shown to be a special case of (1).

(3) Learning by "repetition" or "practising", as in learning to play an instrument or to drive a car. Here my thesis is that (a) there is no genuine "repetition"[50] but rather (b) change through error elimination (following theory formation) and (c) a process which helps to make certain actions or reactions automatic, thereby allowing them to sink to a merely physiological level and be performed without attention.

The significance of inborn dispositions or needs for discovering regularities and rules may be seen in the child's learning to speak a language, a process that has been much studied. It is, of course, a kind of learning by imitation; and the most astonishing thing is that this very early process is one of trial and critical error elimination, in which the critical error elimination plays a very important role. The power of innate dispositions and needs in this development can best be seen in children who, owing to their deafness, do not participate in the speech situations of their social environment in the normal way. The most convincing cases are perhaps children who are deaf *and* blind like Laura Bridgman (or Helen Keller, of whom I heard only at a later date). Admittedly, even in these cases we find social contacts—Helen Keller's contact with her teacher—and we also find imitation. But Helen Keller's imitation of her teacher's spelling into her hand is far removed from the ordinary child's imitation of sounds heard over a long period, sounds whose communicative function can be understood, and responded to, even by a dog.

The great differences between human languages show that there must be an important environmental component in language learning. Moreover, the child's learning of a language is almost entirely an instance of learning by imitation. Yet reflection on various biological aspects of language shows that the genetic factors are much more important. Thus I agree with the statement of Joseph Church: "While some part of the change that occurs in infancy can be accounted for in terms of physical maturation, we know that maturation stands in a circular, feedback relationship to experience—the things the organism does, feels, and has done to it. This is not to disparage the role of maturation; it is only to insist that we cannot view it as a simple blossoming of predestined biological characteristics."[51] Yet I differ from Church in contending that the genetically founded maturation process is much more complex and has much greater influence than the releasing signals and the experience of receiving them, though no doubt a certain minimum of this is needed to stimulate the "blossoming". Helen Keller's grasping that the spelled word "water" meant the thing which she could feel with her hand and which she knew so well had, I think, some similarity with "imprinting"; but there are also many dissimilarities. The similarity was the ineradicable impression made on her, and the way in which a single experience released pent-up dispositions and needs. An obvious dissimilarity was the tremendous range of variation which the experience opened up for her, and which led in time to her mastery of language.

In the light of this I doubt the aptness of Church's comment: "The baby does not walk because his 'walking mechanisms' have come into flower, but because he has achieved a kind of orientation to space whereby walking becomes a possible mode of action."[52] It seems to me that in Helen Keller's case there was no orientation in linguistic space or, at any rate, extremely little, prior to her discovery that the touches of her teacher's fingers denoted water, and her jumping to the conclusion that certain touches may have denotational significance. What must have been there was a readiness, a disposition, a need, to interpret signals; and a need, a readiness, to learn to use these signals by imitation, by the method of trial and error (by nonrandom trials and the critical elimination of spelling errors).

It appears that there must be inborn dispositions of great variety and complexity which cooperate in this field: the disposition to love, to sympathize, to emulate movements, to control and correct the emulated movements; the disposition to use them, and to communicate with their help; the disposition to use language for receiving commands, requests, admonitions, warnings; the disposition to interpret descriptive statements, and to produce descriptive statements. In Helen Keller's case (as opposed to that of normal children) most of her information about reality came through language. As a consequence she was unable for a time to distinguish clearly between what we might call "hearsay" and experience and her own imagination: all three came to her in the same symbolic code.[53]

The example of language learning showed me that the theory of a natural sequence consisting of a dogmatic phase followed by a critical phase is too simple. In language learning there is clearly an inborn disposition to correct (that is, to be flexible and critical, to eliminate errors) which after a time peters out. When a child, having learned to say "mice" uses "hice" for the plural of "house", then a disposition to find regularities is at work. The child will soon correct himself, perhaps under the influence of adult criticism. But there seems to be a phase in language learning when the language structure becomes rigid—perhaps under the influence of "automatization", as explained in 3 (c) above.

I have used language learning merely as an example from which we can see that imitation is a special case of the method of trial and error-elimination.[54] It is also an example of the cooperation between phases of dogmatic theory formation, expectation formation, or the formation of behavioural regularities, on the one hand, and phases of criticism on the other.

But although the theory of a dogmatic phase followed by a critical phase is too simple, it is true that *there can be no critical phase without a preceding dogmatic phase, a phase in which something—an expectation, a regularity of behaviour—is formed, so that error elimination can begin to work on it.*

This view made me reject the psychological theory of learning by induction, a theory to which Hume adhered even after he had rejected induction on logical grounds. (I do not wish to repeat what I have said in *Conjectures and Refutations* about Hume's views on habit.)[55] It also led me to see that there is no such thing as an unprejudiced observation. All observation is an activity with an aim (to find, or to check, some regularity which is *at least* vaguely conjectured); an activity guided by problems, and by the context of expectations (the "horizon of expectations" as I later called it). There is no such thing as passive experience; no passively impressed association of impressed ideas. Experience is the result of active exploration by the organism, of the search for regularities or invariants. There is no such thing as a perception except in the context of interests and expectations, and hence of regularities or "laws".

All this led me to the view that conjecture or hypothesis must come before observation or perception: we have inborn expectations; we have latent inborn knowledge, in the form of latent expectations, to be activated by stimuli to which we react as a rule while engaged in active exploration. All learning is a modification (it may be a refutation) of some prior knowledge and thus, in the last analysis, of some inborn knowledge.[56]

It was this psychological theory which I elaborated, tentatively and in clumsy terminology, between 1921 and 1926. It was this theory of the formation of our knowledge which engaged and distracted me during my apprenticeship as a cabinetmaker.

One of the strange things about my intellectual history is this. Although I was at the time interested in the contrast between dogmatic and critical thinking, and although I looked upon dogmatic thinking as prescientific (and, where it pretends to be scientific, as "unscientific"), and although I realized the link with the falsifiability criterion of demarcation between science and pseudoscience, I did not appreciate that there was a connection between all this and the problem of induction. For years these two problems lived in different (and it appears almost watertight) compartments of my mind, even though I believed that I had solved the problem of induction by the simple discovery that induction by repetition did not exist (any more than did learning something new by repetition): the alleged inductive method of science had to be replaced by the method of (dogmatic) trial and (critical) error elimination, which was the mode of discovery of all organisms from the amoeba to Einstein.

Of course I was aware that my solutions to both these problems—the problem of demarcation, the problem of induction—made use of the same idea: that of the separation of dogmatic and critical thinking. Nevertheless the two problems seemed to me quite different; demarcation had no similarity with Darwinian selection. Only after some years did I realize that there was a close link, and that the problem of induction arose essentially from a mistaken solution of the problem of demarcation—from the belief that what elevated science over pseudoscience was the "scientific method" of finding true, secure, and justifiable knowledge, and that this method was the method of induction: a belief that erred in more ways than one.

11. Music

In all this, speculations about music played a considerable part, especially during my apprenticeship.

Music has been a dominant theme in my life. My mother was very musical: she played the piano beautifully. It seems that music is a thing that runs in families, though why this should be so is very puzzling indeed. European music seems much too recent an invention to be genetically based, and primitive music is a thing which many very musical people dislike as much as they love the music written since Dunstable, Dufay, Josquin des Prés, Palestrina, Lassus, and Byrd.

However this may be, my mother's family was "musical". It may have come down through my maternal grandmother, *née* Schlesinger. (Bruno Walter was a member of the Schlesinger family. I was not, in fact, an admirer of his, especially after singing under his direction in Bach's *St Matthew Passion*.) My grandparents Schiff were both founder-members of the famous *Gesellschaft der Musikfreunde*, which built the beautiful *Musikvereinssaal* in Vienna. Both my mother's sisters played the piano very well. The elder sister was a professional pianist, whose three children were also gifted musicians—as were three other cousins of mine on my mother's side. One of her brothers played, for many years, first violin in an excellent quartet.

As a child I had a few violin lessons, but I did not get far. I had no piano lessons, and even though I liked to play the piano, I played it (and still play it) very badly. When I was seventeen I met Rudolf Serkin. We became friends; and throughout my life I have remained an ardent admirer of his incomparable way of playing, completely absorbed in the work he plays and forgetful of self.

For a time—between the autumn of 1920 and perhaps 1922—I myself thought quite seriously of becoming a musician. But as with so many other things—mathematics, physics, cabinetmaking—I felt in the end that I was not really good enough. I have done a little composing throughout my life, taking pieces of Bach as my Platonic model, but I have never deceived myself about the merits of my compositions.

I was always conservative in the field of music. I felt that Schubert was the last of the really great composers, though I liked and admired Bruckner (especially his last three symphonies) and *some* Brahms (the *Requiem*). I disliked Richard Wagner even more as the author of the words of the *Ring* (words which, frankly, I could only regard as ludicrous) than as a composer, and I also greatly disliked the music of Richard Strauss, even though I fully appreciated that both of them were full-blooded musicians. (Anybody can see at a glance that *Der Rosenkavalier* was intended to be a *Figaro* rewritten for the modern age; but leaving aside the fact that this historicist intention is misconceived, how could a musician like Strauss be so unperceptive as to think even for a minute that this intention was realized?) However, under the influence of some of Mahler's music (an influence that did not last), and of the fact that Mahler had defended Schönberg, I felt that I ought to make a real effort to get to know and to like contemporary music. So I became a member of the Society for Private Concerts ("*Verein für musikalische Privataufführungen*") which was presided over by Arnold Schönberg, and which was dedicated to performing compositions by Schönberg, Alban Berg, Anton von Webern, and other contemporary "advanced" composers like Ravel, Bartók, and Strávinsky. For a time I also became a pupil of Schönberg's pupil Erwin Stein, but I had scarcely any lessons with him: instead I helped him a little with his rehearsals for the Society's performances. In this way I got to know some of Schönberg's music intimately, especially the *Kammersymphonie* and *Pierrot Lunaire*. I also went to rehearsals of Webern, especially of his *Orchesterstücke*, and of Berg.

After about two years I found I had succeeded in getting to know something—about a kind of music which now I liked even less than I had to begin with. So I became, for about a year, a pupil in a very different school of music—the department of Church music in the Vienna *Konservatorium* ("Academy of Music"). I was admitted on the basis of a fugue I had written. It was at the end of this year that I came to the decision mentioned earlier: that I was not good enough to become a musician. But all this added to my love for "classical" music, and to my boundless admiration for the great composers of old.

The connection between music and my intellectual development in the narrow sense is that out of my interest in music there came at least three ideas which influenced me for life. One was closely connected with my ideas on dogmatic and critical thinking, and with the significance of dogmas and traditions. The second was a distinction between two kinds of musical composition, which I felt to be immensely important, and for which I appropriated for my own use the terms "objective" and "subjective". The third was a realization of the intellectual poverty and destructive power of historicist ideas in music and in the arts in general. Let me now discuss these three ideas.[57]

12. Speculations about the Rise of Polyphonic Music: Psychology of Discovery or Logic of Discovery?

The speculations which I shall recount briefly here were closely related to my speculations, reported earlier, on dogmatic and critical thinking. I believe they were among my earliest attempts to apply those psychological ideas to another field; later they led me to an interpretation of the rise of Greek science. The ideas on Greek science I found to be historically fruitful; those on the rise of polyphony may well be historically mistaken. I later chose history of music as a second subject for my Ph.D. examination, in the hope that this would give me an opportunity to investigate whether there was anything in them, but I did not get anywhere and my attention soon turned to other problems. In fact, I have now forgotten almost everything I ever knew in this field. Yet these ideas later greatly influenced my reinterpretation of Kant and my change of interest from the psychology of discovery to an objectivist epistemology—that is, to the logic of discovery.

My problem was this. Polyphony, like science, is peculiar to our Western civilization. (I am using the term "polyphony" to denote not only counterpoint but also Western harmony.) Unlike science it does not seem to be of Greek origin but to have arisen between the ninth and fifteenth centuries A.D. If so, it is possibly the most unprecedented, original, indeed miraculous achievement of our Western civilization, not excluding science.

The facts seem to be these. There was much melodic singing—dancesong, folk music, and above all Church music. The melodies—especially slow ones, as sung in Church—were, of course, sometimes sung in parallel octaves. There are reports that they were also sung in parallel fifths (which, taken with the octave, also make fourths, though not if reckoned from the bass). This way of singing ("organum") is reported from the tenth century, and probably existed earlier. Plainsong was also sung in parallel thirds, together with parallel sixths (both reckoned from the bass: "fauxbourdon", "faburden").[58] It seems that this was felt to be a real innovation, like an accompaniment, or even an embellishment.

What might have been the next step (though its origins are said to go back even to the ninth century) seems to have been that, while the plainsong melody remained unaltered, the accompanying voices no longer proceeded only in parallel thirds and sixths. Antiparallel movement of note against note (*punctum contra punctum*, point counter point) was now also permitted, and could lead not only to thirds and sixths but to fifths, reckoned from the bass, and therefore to fourths between these and some of the other voices.

In my speculations I regarded this last step, the invention of counterpoint, as the decisive one. Although it does not seem to be quite certain that it was temporally the last step, it was the one that led to polyphony.

The "*organum*" may not at the time have been felt to be an addition to the one-voice melody, except perhaps by those responsible for Church music. It is quite possible that it arose simply from the different voice levels of a congregation which was trying to sing the melody. Thus it may have been an unintended result of a religious practice, namely the intoning of responses by the congregation. Mistakes of this kind in the singing of congregations are bound to occur. It is well known, for example, that in the Anglican festal responses, with the *cantus firmus* in the tenor, congregations are liable to make the mistake of following (in octaves) the highest voice, the treble, instead of the tenor. At all events as long as the singing is in strict parallels there is no polyphony. There may be more than one voice but there is only one melody.

It is perfectly conceivable that the origin also of counterpoint singing lay in mistakes made by the congregation. For when singing in parallels would lead a voice to a note higher than it could sing it may have dropped down to the note sung by the next voice below, thus moving *contra punctum* rather than in parallel *cum puncto*. This may have happened in either *organum* or *fauxbourdon* singing. At any rate, it would explain the first basic rule of simple one-to-one note counterpoint: that the result of the countermovement must be only an octave or fifth or third or sixth (always reckoned from the bass). But though this may be the way the counterpoint *originated*, the *invention* of it must have been due to the musician who first realized that here was a possibility for a more or less independent second melody, to be sung together with the original or fundamental melody, the *cantus firmus*, without disturbing it or interfering with it any more than did *organum* or *fauxbourdon* singing. And this leads to the second basic rule of counterpoint: parallel octaves and fifths are to be avoided *because these would destroy the intended effect of an independent second melody*. Indeed they would lead to an unintended (though temporary) *organum* effect, and thus to the disappearance of the second melody as such, for the second voice would (as in *organum* singing) merely enforce the *cantus firmus*. Parallel thirds and sixths (as in *fauxbourdon*) are permitted steps provided they are preceded or followed fairly soon by a real countermovement (with respect to some of the parts).

Thus the basic idea is this. The fundamental or given melody, the *cantus firmus*, puts limitations on any second melody (or counterpoint), but in spite of these limitations the counterpoint should appear as if it were a freely invented independent melody—a melody melodious in itself and yet almost miraculously fitting the *cantus firmus* though, unlike both *organum* and *fauxbourdon*, in no way dependent on it. Once this basic idea is grasped, we are on the way to polyphony.

I will not enlarge on this. Instead I will explain the historical conjecture I made in this connection—a conjecture which, though it may in fact be false, was nevertheless of great significance for all my further ideas. It was this.

Given the heritage of the Greeks, and the development (and canonization) of the Church modes in the time of Ambrose and Gregory the Great, there would hardly have been any need for, or any incitement to, the invention of polyphony if Church musicians had had the same freedom as, let us say, the originators of folk song. My conjecture was that it was the canonization of Church melodies, the dogmatic restrictions on them, which produced the *cantus firmus* against which the counterpoint could develop. It was the established *cantus firmus* which provided the framework, the order, the regularity that made possible inventive freedom without chaos.

In some non-European music we find that *established* melodies give rise to *melodic* variations: this I regarded as a similar development. Yet the combination of a tradition of melodies sung in parallels with the security of a *cantus firmus* which remains undisturbed even by a countermovement opened to us, according to this conjecture, a whole new ordered world, a new cosmos.

Once the possibilities of this cosmos had been to some extent explored—by bold trials and by error elimination—the original authentic melodies, accepted by the Church, could be done without. New melodies could be invented to serve in place of the original *cantus firmus*, some to become traditional for a time, while others might be used in only one musical composition, for example, as the subject of a fugue.

According to this perhaps untenable historical conjecture it was thus the canonization of the Gregorian melodies, a piece of dogmatism, that provided the necessary framework or rather the necessary scaffolding for us to build a new world. I also formulated it like this: the dogma provides us with the frame of coordinates needed for exploring the order of this new unknown and possibly in itself even somewhat chaotic world, and also for creating order where order is missing. Thus musical and scientific creation seem to have this much in common: the use of dogma, or myth, as a man-made path along which we move into the unknown, exploring the world, both creating regularities or rules and probing for existing regularities. And once we have found, or erected, some landmarks, we proceed by trying new ways of ordering the world, new coordinates, new modes of exploration and creation, new ways of building a new world, undreamt of in antiquity unless in the myth of the music of the spheres.

Indeed, a great work of music (like a great scientific theory) is a cosmos imposed upon chaos—in its tensions and harmonies inexhaustible even for its creator. This was described with marvellous insight by Kepler in a passage devoted to the music of the heavens:[59]

> Thus the heavenly motions are nothing but a kind of perennial concert, rational rather than audible or vocal. They move through the tension of dissonances which are like syncopations or suspensions with their resolutions (by which men imitate the corresponding dissonances of nature), reaching secure and predetermined closures, each containing six terms like a chord consisting of six voices. And by these marks they distinguish and articulate the immensity of time. Thus there is no marvel greater or more sublime than the rules of singing in harmony together in several parts, unknown to the ancients but at last discovered by man, the ape of his Creator; so that, through the skilful symphony of many voices, he should actually conjure up in a short part of an hour the vision of the world's total perpetuity in time; and that, in the sweetest sense of bliss enjoyed through Music, the echo of God, he should almost reach the contentment which God the Maker has in His Own works.

Here were some more ideas which distracted me and which interfered with my work on those writing desks during my apprenticeship as a cabinetmaker.[60] It was during a time when I was reading Kant's first *Critique* again and again. I soon decided that his central idea was that *scientific theories are man-made, and that we try to impose them upon the world*: "Our intellect does not derive its laws from nature, but imposes its laws upon nature." Combining this with my own ideas, I arrived at something like the following.

Our theories, beginning with primitive myths and evolving into the theories of science, are indeed man-made, as Kant said. We *do* try to impose them on the world, and we *can* always stick to them dogmatically if we so wish, even if they are false (as are not only most religious myths, it seems, but also Newton's theory, which is what Kant had in mind).[61] But although at first we have to stick to our theories—*without theories we cannot even begin*, for we have nothing else to go by—we can, in the course of time, adopt a more critical attitude towards them. We can try to replace them by something better if we have learned, with their help, where they let us down. Thus there may arise a scientific or critical phase of thinking, *which is necessarily preceded by an uncritical phase.*

Kant, I felt, had been right when he said that it was impossible that knowledge was, as it were, a copy or impression of reality. He was right to believe that knowledge was *genetically* or *psychologically* a priori, but quite wrong to suppose that any knowledge could be a priori *valid*.[62] Our theories are our inventions; but they may be merely ill-reasoned guesses, bold conjectures, *hypotheses*. Out of these we create a world: not the real world, but our own nets in which we try to catch the real world.

If this was so, then what I originally regarded as the psychology of discovery had a basis in logic: there was no other way into the unknown, for logical reasons.

13. Two Kinds of Music

It was my interest in music that led me to what I then felt was a minor intellectual discovery (in 1920, I should say, even before the rise of my interest in the psychology of discovery described in the preceding section and in section 10). This discovery later greatly influenced my ways of thinking in philosophy, and it ultimately led even to my distinction between world 2 and world 3, which plays such a role in the philosophy of my old age. At first it took the form of an interpretation of the difference between Bach's and Beethoven's music, or their ways of approaching music. I still think that there is something in my idea, even though this particular interpretation, I later thought, greatly exaggerated the difference between Bach and Beethoven. Yet the origin of this intellectual discovery is for me so closely connected with these two great composers that I will relate it in the form in which it occurred to me at the time. I do not wish to suggest, however, that my remarks do justice to them or to other composers, or that they add something new to the many things, good and bad, which have been written about music; my remarks are essentially autobiographical.

To me the discovery came as a great shock. I loved both Bach and Beethoven—not only their music but also their personalities, which, I felt, became visible through their music. (It was not the same with Mozart: there is something unfathomable behind his charm.) The shock came one day when it struck me that Bach's and Beethoven's relations to their own work were utterly different, and that although it was permissible to take Bach as one's model it was quite impermissible to adopt this attitude towards Beethoven.

Beethoven, I felt, had made music an instrument of self-expression. For him in his despair this may have been the only way to go on living. (I believe that this is suggested in his *"Heiligenstädter Testament"* of October 6, 1802.) There is no more moving work than *Fidelio*; no more moving expression of a man's faith, and his hopes, and his secret dreams, and his heroic fight against despair. Yet his purity of heart, his dramatic powers, his unique creative gifts allowed him to work in a way which, I felt, was not permissible for others. I felt that there could be no greater danger to music than an attempt to make Beethoven's ways an ideal, or a standard, or a model.

It was to distinguish the two distinct attitudes of Bach and of Beethoven towards their compositions that I introduced—only for myself—the terms "objective" and "subjective". These terms may not be well chosen (this does not matter much), and in a context such as this they may mean little to a philosopher; but I was glad to find, many years later, that Albert Schweitzer had used them in 1905, at the beginning of his great book on Bach.[63] For my own thinking the contrast between an objective and a subjective approach, or attitude, especially in relation to one's own work, became decisive. And it soon influenced my views on epistemology. (See, for example, the titles of some of my more recent papers, like "Epistemology Without a Knowing Subject", or "On the Theory of the Objective Mind", or "Quantum Mechanics without 'The Observer' ".)[64]

I will now try to explain what I have had in mind when speaking (to this day only to myself, and perhaps a few friends) about "objective" and "subjective" music or art. In order to give a better explanation of some of my early ideas I shall sometimes use formulations which I should scarcely have been capable of at that time.

I should perhaps start with a criticism of a widely accepted theory of art: the theory that art is self-expression, or the expression of the artist's personality, or perhaps the expression of his emotions. (Croce and Collingwood are two of the many proponents of this theory. My own anti-essentialist point of view implies that *what-is?* questions like "What is art?" are never genuine problems.)[65] My main criticism of this theory is simple: *the expressionist theory of art is empty.* For everything a man or an animal can do is (among other things) an expression of an internal state, of emotions, and of personality. This is trivially true for all kinds of human and animal languages. It holds for the way a man or a lion walks, the way a man coughs or blows his nose, the way a man or a lion may look at you, or ignore you. It holds for the ways a bird builds its nest, a spider constructs its web, and a man builds his house. In other words it is not a characteristic of art. For the same reason expressionist or emotive theories of language are trivial, uninformative, and useless.

I do not of course propose to answer the *what-is?* question "What is art?", but I do suggest that what makes a work of art interesting or significant is something quite different from self-expression. Regarded from a psychological point of view there are certain abilities needed in the artist, which we may describe as creative imagination, perhaps playfulness, taste, and—of some significance—utter devotion to his work. The work must be everything to him, it must transcend his personality. But this is merely a psychological aspect of the matter, and for this very reason of minor importance. The important thing is the work of art. And here I wish to say some negative things first.

There can be great works of art without great originality. There can hardly be a great work of art which the artist *intended mainly* to be original or "different" (except perhaps in a playful way). The main aim of the true artist is the perfection of the work. Originality is a gift of the gods—like naivety, it cannot be had for the asking or gained by seeking. Trying seriously to be original or different, and also trying to express one's own personality, must interfere with what has been called the "integrity" of the work of art. In a great work of art the artist does not try to impose his little personal ambitions on the work but uses them to *serve* his work. In this way he may grow as a person through interaction with what he does. By a kind of feedback he may gain in craftsmanship and other powers that make an artist.[66]

What I have said may indicate what the difference was between Bach and Beethoven which so impressed me: Bach forgets himself in his work, he is a servant of his work. Of course, he cannot fail to impress his personality on it; this is unavoidable. But he is not, as Beethoven is, at times, conscious of expressing himself and even his moods. It was for this reason that I saw them as representing two opposite attitudes towards music.

Thus Bach said, when dictating instructions to his pupils concerning continuo playing: "It should make a euphonious harmony for the glory of God and the permitted delectation of the mind; and like all music its *finis* and final cause should never be anything else but the glory of God and the recreation of the mind. When this is not heeded, there really is no music, but a hellish howl and clatter."[67]

I suggest that Bach wished to exclude from the final cause of music the making of a noise for the greater glory of the musician.

In view of my quotation from Bach I should make it quite clear that the difference I have in mind is not one between religious and secular art. Beethoven's *Mass in D* shows this. It is inscribed "From the heart—may it again go to the heart" ("Vom Herzen—möge es wieder—zu Herzen gehen"). It should also be said that the difference has nothing to do with the emotional content or the emotional impact of music. A dramatic oratorio such as Bach's *St Matthew Passion* depicts strong emotions and thus, by sympathy, arouses strong emotions—stronger perhaps even than Beethoven's *Mass in D*. There is no reason to doubt that the composer felt these emotions too; but, I suggest, he felt them because the music which he invented must have made its impact on him (otherwise he would, no doubt, have scrapped the piece as unsuccessful), and not because he was first in an emotional mood which he then expressed in his music.

The difference between Bach and Beethoven has its characteristic technical aspects. For example, the structural role of the dynamic element (forte versus piano) is different. There are, of course, dynamic elements in Bach. In the concertos there are the changes from tutti to solo. There is the cry "*Barrabam!*" in the *St Matthew Passion*. Bach is often highly dramatic. Yet although dynamic surprises and contrasts occur, they are rarely important determinants of the structure of the composition. As a rule, fairly long periods occur without major dynamic contrasts. Something similar may be said of Mozart. But it cannot be said of, say, Beethoven's *Appassionata*, where dynamic contrasts are nearly as important as harmonic ones.

Schopenhauer says that, in a Beethoven symphony, "all human emotions and passions speak: joy and grief, love and hate, fear and hope, . . . in countless delicate shades";[68] and he stated the theory of emotional expression and resonance in the form: "The way in which all music touches our hearts . . . is due to the fact that it reflects every impulse of our inmost essence." One might say that Schopenhauer's theory of music, and of art in general, escapes subjectivism (if at all) only because according to him "our inmost essence"—our will—is also objective, since it is the essence of the objective world.

But to return to objective music. Without asking a *what-is?* question, let us look at Bach's *Inventions*, and his own somewhat longish title page, in which he makes it clear that he has written for people wanting to play the piano. They will, he assures them, learn "how to play with two and three parts clearly . . . and in a melodious way";[69] and they will be stimulated to be inventive, and so "incidentally get a first taste of composition". Here music is to be learned from examples. The musician is to grow up in Bach's workshop, as it were. He learns a discipline, but he is also encouraged to use his own musical ideas and he is shown how they can be worked out clearly and skilfully. His ideas may develop, no doubt. Through work the musician may, like a scientist, learn by trial and error. And with the growth of his work his musical judgement and taste may also grow—and perhaps even his creative imagination. But this growth will depend on effort, industry, dedication to his work; on sensitivity to the work of others, and on self-criticism. There will be a constant give-and-take between the artist and his work rather than a one-sided "give"—a mere expression of his personality in his work.

From what I have said it should be clear that I am far from suggesting that great music, and great art in general, may not have a deep emotional impact. And least of all do I suggest that a musician may not be deeply moved by what he is writing or playing. Yet to admit the emotional impact of music is not, of course, to accept musical expressionism, which is *a theory about music* (and a theory which has led to certain musical practices). It is, I think, a mistaken theory of the relation between human emotions on the one side and music—and art in general—on the other.

The relation between music and the human emotions can be viewed in a number of very different ways. One of the earliest and most seminal theories is the theory of divine inspiration which manifests itself in the divine madness or divine frenzy of the poet or musician: the artist is possessed by a spirit, though by a benign rather than an evil spirit. A classical formulation of this view can be found in Plato's *Ion*.[70] The views which Plato formulates there are many-sided and incorporate several distinct theories. Indeed, Plato's treatment may be used as the basis for a systematic survey:

(1) What the poet or musician composes is not his own work but rather a message or dispensation from the gods, especially the Muses. The poet or musician is only an instrument through which the Muses speak; he is merely the mouthpiece of a god and "to prove this, the god sang on purpose the finest of songs through the meanest of poets".[71]

(2) The artist (whether creative or performing) who is possessed by a divine spirit gets frantic, that is, emotionally overexcited; and his state communicates itself to his audience by a process of sympathetic resonance. (Plato compares it with magnetism.)

(3) When the poet or the performer composes or recites he is deeply moved, and indeed possessed (not only by the god but also) by the message, for example, by the scenes he describes; and the work, rather than merely his emotional state, induces similar emotions in his audience.

(4) We have to distinguish between a mere craft or skill or "art" acquired by training or study, and divine inspiration; the latter alone makes the poet or musician.

It should be noted that in developing these views Plato is far from serious; he speaks with his tongue in his cheek. One little joke, especially, is significant and quite amusing. To Socrates' remark that the rhapsode, when possessed by the god, is obviously quite deranged (for example, when he is shaking with fear even though he is in no danger) and that he induces the same nonsensical emotions in his audience, the rhapsode Ion replies: "Exactly: when I watch them from my platform I see how they cry, and how they look at me with awestruck eyes. . . . And I am obliged to watch them very closely indeed; for if they cry I shall laugh because of the money I take, and if they laugh I shall cry because of the money I lose."[72] Clearly Plato wants us to understand that if the rhapsode is possessed by these mundane and far from "deranged" anxieties while watching his listeners in order to regulate his behaviour by their response, then he cannot be serious when he suggests (as Ion does at that very place) that his great effect on them depends entirely on his sincerity—that is, on his being completely and genuinely possessed by the god and out of his mind. (Plato's joke here is a typical self-referring joke—an almost paradoxical self-reference.)[73] In fact, Plato hints strongly[74] that any knowledge or skill (say, of keeping his audience spellbound) would be dishonest trickery and deception, since it would necessarily interfere with the divine message. And he suggests that the rhapsode (or the poet or the musician) is at least sometimes a skilful deceiver, rather than genuinely inspired by the gods.

I will now make use of my list (1) to (4) of Plato's theories in order to derive a modern theory of art as expression. My main contention is that if we take the theory of inspiration and frenzy, *but discard divinity*, we arrive immediately at the modern theory that art is self-expression, or more precisely, self-inspiration and the expression and communication of emotion. In other words the modern theory is a kind of theology without God—with the hidden nature or essence of the artist taking the place of the gods: the artist inspires himself.

Clearly, this subjectivist theory must discard, or at least play down, point (3): the view that the artist and his audience are emotionally moved *by the work of art*. Yet to me (3) seems to be precisely the theory that gives a correct account of the relationship between art and the emotions. It is an objectivist theory which holds that poetry or music may describe or depict or dramatize scenes which have emotional significance, and that they may even describe or depict emotions as such. (Note that it is not implied by this theory that this is the only way in which art can be significant.)

This objectivist theory of the relationship between art and the emotions may be discerned in the passage from Kepler quoted in the preceding section.

It played an important part in the rise of the opera and the oratorio. It was certainly acceptable to Bach and Mozart. It is, incidentally, perfectly compatible with Plato's theory, expounded for example in the *Republic* and also in the *Laws*, that music has the power to arouse emotions, and to soothe them (like a lullaby), and even to form a man's character: some kinds of music may make him brave, others turn him into a coward; a theory which exaggerates the power of music, to say the least.[75]

According to my objectivist theory (which does not deny self-expression but stresses its utter triviality) the really interesting function of the composer's emotions is not that they are to be expressed, but that they may be used to test the success or the fittingness or the impact of the (objective) work: the composer may use himself as a kind of test body, and he may modify and rewrite his composition (as Beethoven often did) when he is dissatisfied by his own reaction to it; or he may even discard it altogether. (Whether or not the composition is primarily emotional, he will in this way make use of his own reactions—his own "good taste": it is another application of the method of trial and error.)

It should be noted that Plato's theory (4), in its nontheological form, is hardly compatible with an objectivist theory which sees the sincerity of the work less in the genuineness of the artist's inspiration than in the result of the artist's self-criticism. Yet an expressionist view such as Plato's theory (4), Ernst Gombrich informs me, became part of the classical tradition of rhetoric and poetic theory. It even went so far as to suggest that successful description or depiction of emotions depended on the depth of the emotions of which the artist was capable.[76] And it may well have been this dubious last view, the secularized form of Plato's (4) which regards anything that is not pure self-expression as "playing false"[77] or "insincere", that led to the modern expressionist theory of music and art.[78]

To sum up; (1), (2), and (4), without the gods, may be regarded as a formulation of the subjectivist or expressionist theory of art and of its relation to the emotions, and (3) as a partial formulation of an objectivist theory of this relation, according to which it is the work which is mainly responsible for the emotions of the musician rather than the other way round.

To turn now to the objectivist view of music, it is clear that (3) cannot suffice for this, since it is merely concerned with the relation of music to emotions, which are not the only or even the main thing which makes art significant. The musician *may* make it his problem to depict emotions and to move us to sympathy, as in the *St Matthew Passion*; but there are many other problems he tries to solve. (This is obvious in such an art as architecture, where there are always practical and technical problems to be solved.) In writing a fugue the composer's problem is to find an interesting subject and a contrasting counterpoint, and then to exploit this material as well as he can. What leads him may be a trained sense of general fittingness or "balance". The result may still be moving; but our appreciation may be based on the sense of fittingness—of a cosmos emerging from near chaos—rather than on any depicted emotion. The same may be said of some of Bach's *Inventions,* whose problem was to give the student a first taste of composition—of musical problem solving. Similarly, the task of writing a minuet or a trio poses a definite *problem* for the musician; and the problem may be made more specific by the demand that it should fit into a certain half-completed suite. To see the musician as struggling to solve musical problems is of course very different from seeing him engaged in expressing his emotions (which, trivially, everybody always does).

I have tried to give a reasonably clear idea of the difference between these two theories of music, objectivist and subjectivist, and to relate them to the two kinds of music—Bach's and Beethoven's—which seemed to me so different at the time, though I loved them both.

The distinction between an objective and a subjective view of one's work became most important for me; and it has, I may say, coloured my views of the world and of life.

14. *Progressivism in Art, Especially in Music*

I certainly was not quite just when I thought that Beethoven was responsible for the rise of expressionism in music. No doubt he was influenced by the romantic movement, but we can see from his notebooks that he was far removed from merely expressing his feelings or his whims. He often worked very hard through version after version of an idea, trying to clarify and to simplify it, as a comparison of the *Choral Fantasy* with the notebooks for his Ninth Symphony will show. And yet, the indirect influence of his tempestuous personality, and the attempts to emulate him led, I believe, to a decline in music. It still seems to me that this decline was brought about largely by expressionist theories of music. But I would not now contend that there are not other equally pernicious creeds, and among them some anti-expressionist creeds, which have led to all kinds of formalistic experiments from serialism to *musique concrète*. All these movements, however, and especially the "anti-" movements, largely result from that brand of "historicism" which I will discuss in this section, and especially from the historicist attitude towards "progress".

Of course, there can be something like progress in art, in the sense that certain new possibilities may be discovered, and also new problems.[79] In music such inventions as counterpoint revealed almost an infinity of new possibilities and problems. There is also purely technological progress (for example in certain instruments). But although this may open new possibilities, it is not of fundamental significance. (Changes in the "medium" may remove more problems than they create.) There could conceivably be progress even in the sense that musical knowledge grows—that is, a composer's mastery of the discoveries of all his great predecessors; but I do not think that anything like this has been achieved by any musician. (Einstein may not have been a greater physicist than Newton, but he mastered Newtonian technique completely; no similar relation seems ever to have existed in the field of music.) Even Mozart, who may have come closest to it, did not attain it and Schubert did not come close to it. There is also always the danger that newly realized possibilities may kill old ones: dynamic effects, dissonance, or even modulation may, if used too freely, dull our sensitivity to the less obvious effects of counterpoint or, say, to an allusion to the old modes.

The loss of possibilities which may be the result of new innovations is an interesting problem. Thus counterpoint threatened the loss of monodic and especially of rhythmic effects, and contrapuntal music was criticized for this reason, as well as for its complexity. There is no doubt that this criticism had some wholesome effects, and that some of the great masters of counterpoint, Bach included, took the greatest interest in the intricacies and contrasts resulting from combining recitatives, arias, and other monodic alternatives with contrapuntal writing. Many recent composers have been less imaginative. (Schönberg realized that, in a context of dissonances, consonances have to be carefully prepared, introduced, and perhaps even resolved. But this meant that their old function was lost.)

It was Wagner[80] who introduced into music an idea of progress which (in

1935 or thereabouts) I called "historicist", and who thereby, I still believe, became the main villain of the piece. He also sponsored the uncritical and almost hysterical idea of the unappreciated genius: the genius who not only expresses the spirit of his time but who actually is "ahead of his time"; a leader who is normally misunderstood by all his contemporaries except a few "advanced" connoisseurs.

My thesis is that the doctrine of art as self-expression is merely trivial, muddleheaded and empty—though not necessarily vicious, unless taken seriously, when it may easily lead to self-centred attitudes and megalomania. But the doctrine that the genius must be in advance of his time is almost wholly false and vicious, and opens up the universe of art to valuations which have nothing to do with the values of art.

Intellectually, both theories are on such a low level that it is astonishing that they were ever taken seriously. The first can be dismissed as trivial and muddled on purely intellectual grounds, without even looking more closely at art itself. The second—the theory that art is the expression of the genius in advance of his time—can be refuted by countless examples of geniuses genuinely appreciated by many patrons of the arts of their own time. Most of the great painters of the Renaissance were highly appreciated. So were many great musicians. Bach was appreciated by King Frederick of Prussia—besides, he obviously was not ahead of his time (as was, perhaps, Telemann): his son Carl Philipp Emanuel thought him *passé* and spoke of him habitually as "The Old Fusspot" (*"der alte Zopf"*). Mozart, though he died in poverty, was appreciated throughout Europe. An exception is perhaps Schubert, appreciated only by a comparatively small circle of friends in Vienna; but even he was getting more widely known at the time of his premature death. The story that Beethoven was not appreciated by his contemporaries is a myth. Yet let me say here again (see the text between nn. 47 and 48 in section 10 above) that I think that success in life is largely a matter of luck. It has little correlation with merit, and in all fields of life there have always been many people of great merit who did not succeed. Thus it is only to be expected that this happened also in the sciences and in the arts.

The theory that art advances with the great artists in the van is not just a myth; it has led to the formation of cliques and pressure groups which, with their propaganda machines, almost resemble a political party or a church faction.

Admittedly there were cliques before Wagner. But there was nothing quite like the Wagnerians (unless later the Freudians): a pressure group, a party, a church with rituals. But I shall say no more about this, since Nietzsche has said it all much better.[81]

I saw some of these things at close quarters in Schönberg's Society for Private Concerts. Schönberg started as a Wagnerian, as did so many of his contemporaries. After a time his problem and that of many members of his circle became, as one of them said in a lecture, "How can we supersede Wagner?" or even "How can we supersede the remnants of Wagner in ourselves?". Still later it became: "How can we remain ahead of everybody else, and even constantly supersede ourselves?". Yet I feel that the will to be ahead of one's time has nothing to do with service to music, and nothing to do with genuine dedication to one's own work.

Anton von Webern was an exception to this. He was a dedicated musician and a simple, lovable man. But he had been brought up in the philosophical doctrine of self-expression, and he never doubted its truth. He once told me how he wrote his *Orchesterstücke*: he just listened to sounds that came to him, and he wrote them down; and when no more sounds came, he stopped. This, he said, was the explanation of the extreme brevity of his pieces. Nobody could doubt the purity of his heart. But there was not much music to be found in his modest compositions.

There may be something in the ambition to write a great work; and such an ambition may indeed be instrumental in creating a great work, though many great works have been produced without any ambition other than to do one's work well. But the ambition to write a work which is ahead of its time and which will preferably not be understood too soon—which will shock as many people as possible—has nothing to do with art, even though many art critics have fostered this attitude and popularized it.

Fashions, I suppose, are as unavoidable in art as in many other fields. But it should be obvious that those rare artists who were not only masters of their art but blessed with the gift of originality were seldom anxious to follow a fashion, and never tried to be leaders of fashion. Neither Johann Sebastian Bach nor Mozart nor Schubert created a new fashion or "style" in music. Yet one who did was Carl Philipp Emanuel Bach, a well-trained musician of talent and charm—and less originality of invention than the great masters. This holds for all fashions, including that of primitivism—though primitivism may be partly motivated by a preference for simplicity; and one of Schopenhauer's wisest remarks (though not perhaps his most original one) was: "In all art . . . simplicity is essential . . . ; at least it is always dangerous to neglect it."[82] I think what he meant was the striving for the kind of simplicity which we find especially in the subjects of the great composers. As we may see from the *Seraglio*, for example, the final result may be complex; but Mozart could still proudly reply to the Emperor Joseph that there was not one note too many in it.

But although fashions may be unavoidable, and although new styles may emerge, we ought to despise attempts to be fashionable. It should be obvious that "modernism"—the wish to be new or different at any price, to be ahead of one's time, to produce *"The Work of Art of the Future"* (the title of an essay by Wagner)—has nothing to do with the things an artist should value and should try to create.

Historicism in art is just a mistake. Yet one finds it everywhere. Even in philosophy one hears of a new style of philosophizing, or of a "Philosophy in a New Key"—as if it were the key that mattered rather than the tune played, and as if it mattered whether the key was old or new.

Of course I do not blame an artist or a musician for trying to say something new. What I really accuse many of the "modern" musicians of is their failure to love great music—the great masters and their miraculous works, the greatest perhaps that man has produced.

15. Last Years at the University

In 1925, while I was working with neglected children, the City of Vienna founded a new institute of education, called the Pedagogic Institute. The Institute was to be linked, somewhat loosely, with the University. It was to be autonomous, but its students were to take courses at the University in addition to the courses at the Institute. Some of the University courses (such as psychology) were made compulsory by the Institute, others were left to the choice of the students. The purpose of the new Institute was to further and support the reform, then in progress, of the primary and secondary schools in Vienna, and some social workers were admitted as students; I was among them. So also were some lifelong friends of mine—Fritz Kolb, who after the Second World War served as Austrian Ambassador in Pakistan, and Robert Lammer, with both of whom I enjoyed many fascinating discussions.

This meant that after a short period as social workers we had to give up our work (without unemployment relief, or income of any kind—except, in my case, the occasional coaching of American students). But we were enthusiastic for school reform, and enthusiastic for studying—even though our experience with neglected children made some of us sceptical of the educational theories we had to swallow in huge doses. These were imported mainly from America (John Dewey) and from Germany (Georg Kerschensteiner).

From a personal and intellectual point of view the years at the Institute were most significant for me because I met my wife there. She was one of my fellow students, and was to become one of the severest judges of my work. Her part in it ever since has been at least as strenuous as my own. Indeed, without her much of it would never have been done at all.

My years in the Pedagogic Institute were years of studying, of reading and of writing—but not of publishing. They were my first years of (quite unofficial) academic teaching. Throughout these years I gave seminars for a group of fellow students. Although I did not realize it then, they were good seminars. Some of them were most informal, and took place while hiking, or skiing, or spending the day on a river island in the Danube. From my teachers at the Institute I learned very little, but I learned much from Karl Bühler, Professor of Psychology at the University. (Though students of the Pedagogic Institute went to his lectures, he did not teach at the Pedagogic Institute, or hold a position there.)

In addition to the seminars I gave classes, also quite unofficially, to prepare my fellow students for some of the numberless examinations we had to sit, among which were psychology examinations set by Bühler. He told me afterwards (in the first private conversation I ever had with a university teacher) that this had been the best-prepared batch of students he had ever examined. Bühler had only recently been called to Vienna to teach psychology, and at that time was best known for his book on *The Mental Development of the Child*.[83] He had also been one of the first *Gestalt* psychologists. Most important for my future development was his theory of the three levels or functions of language (already referred to in n. 78 above): the expressive function (*Kundgabefunktion*), the signal or release function (*Auslösefunktion*), and, on a higher level, the descriptive function (*Darstellungsfunktion*). He explained that the two lower functions were common to human and animal languages and were always present, while the third function was characteristic of human language alone and sometimes (as in exclamations) absent even from that.

This theory became important to me for many reasons. It confirmed my view of the emptiness of the theory that art is self-expression. It led me later to the conclusion that the theory that art was "communication" (that is, release)[84] was equally empty, since these two functions were trivially present in all languages, even in animal languages. It led me to a strengthening of my "objectivist" approach. And it led me—years later—to add to Bühler's three functions what I call the argumentative function.[85] The argumentative function of language became particularly important for me because I regarded it as the basis of all critical thought.

I was in my second year at the Pedagogic Institute when I met Professor Heinrich Gomperz, to whom Karl Polanyi had given me an introduction. Heinrich Gomperz was the son of Theodor Gomperz (author of *Greek Thinkers*, and a friend and translator of John Stuart Mill). Like his father, he was an excellent Greek scholar, and also greatly interested in epistemology. He was only the second professional philosopher I had met, and the first university teacher of philosophy. Previously I had met Julius Kraft (of Hanover, a distant relation of mine, and a pupil of Leonard Nelson),[86] who later became a teacher of philosophy and sociology at Frankfurt; my friendship with him lasted until his death in 1960.[87]

Julius Kraft, like Leonard Nelson, was a non-Marxist socialist, and about half our discussions, often lasting into the small hours of the morning, were centred on my criticism of Marx. The other half were about the theory of knowledge: mainly Kant's so-called "transcendental deduction" (which I regarded as question-begging), his solution of the antinomies, and Nelson's "Impossibility of the Theory of Knowledge".[88] Over these we fought a hard battle, which went on from 1926 to 1956, and we did not reach anything approaching agreement until a few years before his untimely death in 1960. On Marxism we reached agreement fairly soon.

Heinrich Gomperz was always patient with me. He had the reputation of being scathing and ironical, but I never saw anything of it. He could be most witty, though, when telling stories about some of his famous colleagues, such as Brentano and Mach. He invited me from time to time to his house, and let me talk. Usually I gave him portions of manuscript to read, but he made few comments. He was never critical of what I had to say, but he very often drew my attention to related views, and to books and articles bearing on my own topic. He never indicated that he found what I said important until I gave him, some years later, the manuscript of my first book (still unpublished—see section 16 below). He then wrote me (in December, 1932) a highly appreciative letter, the first I had ever received about something I had written.

I read all his writings, which were outstanding for their historical approach: he could follow a historical problem through all its vicissitudes from Heraclitus to Husserl, and (in conversations anyway) to Otto Weininger, whom he had known personally, and regarded as almost a genius. We did not agree on psychoanalysis. At this time he believed in it, even publishing in *Imago*.

The problems I discussed with Gomperz were those of the psychology of knowledge or of discovery; it was during this period that they were changing into problems of the logic of discovery. I was reacting more and more strongly against any "psychologistic" approach, including the psychologism of Gomperz.

Gomperz himself had criticized psychologism—only to fall back into it.[89] It was mainly in discussions with him that I began to stress my realism, my conviction that there is a real world, and that the problem of knowledge is the problem of how to discover this world. I became convinced that, if we want to argue about it, we cannot start from our sense experiences (or even our feelings, as his theory demanded) without falling into the traps of psychologism, idealism, positivism, phenomenalism, even solipsism—all views which I refused to take seriously. My sense of social responsibility told me that taking such problems seriously was a kind of treason of the intellectuals—and a misuse of the time we ought to be spending on real problems.

Since I had access to the psychological laboratory I conducted a few experiments, which soon convinced me that sense data, "simple" ideas or impressions, and other such things, did not exist: they were fictitious—inventions based on mistaken attempts to transfer atomism (or Aristotelian logic—see below) from physics to psychology. The proponents of *Gestalt* psychology held similarly critical views; but I felt that their views were insufficiently radical. I found that my views were similar to those of Oswald Külpe and his school (the *Würzburger Schule*), especially Bühler[90] and Otto Selz.[91] They had found that we do not think in images but in terms of problems and their tentative solutions. Finding that some of my results had been anticipated, especially by Otto Selz, was, I suspect, one of the minor motives of my move away from psychology.

Giving up the psychology of discovery and of thinking, to which I had devoted years, was a lengthy process which culminated in the following insight. I found that association psychology—the psychology of Locke, Berkeley, and Hume—was merely a translation of Aristotelian subject-predicate logic into psychological terms.

Aristotelian logic deals with statements like "Men are mortal". Here are two "terms" and a "copula" which couples or associates them. Translate this into psychological terms, and you will say that thinking consists in having the "ideas" of man and of mortality "associated". One has only to read Locke with this in mind to see how it happened: his main assumptions are the validity of Aristotelian logic, and that it describes our subjective, psychological thought processes. But subject-predicate logic is a very primitive thing. (It may be regarded as an interpretation of a small fragment of Boolean algebra, untidily mixed up with a small fragment of naive set theory.) It is incredible that anybody should still mistake it for empirical psychology.

A further step showed me that the mechanism of translating a dubious logical doctrine into one of an allegedly empirical psychology was still at work, and had its dangers, even for such an outstanding thinker as Bühler.

For in Külpe's *Logic*,[92] which Bühler accepted and greatly admired, arguments were regarded as complex judgements (which is a mistake from the point of view of modern logic).[93] In consequence there could be no real distinction between judging and arguing. As a further consequence the descriptive function of language (which corresponds to "judgements") and the argumentative function amounted to the same thing; thus Bühler failed to see that they could be as clearly separated as the three functions of language which he had already distinguished.

Bühler's expressive function could be separated from his communicative function (or signal function, or release function) because an animal or a man could express himself even if there were no "receiver" to be stimulated. The expressive and communicative functions together could be distinguished from Bühler's descriptive function because an animal or a man could communicate fear (for example) without describing the object feared. The descriptive function (a higher function, according to Bühler, and exclusive to man) was, I then found, clearly distinguishable from the argumentative function, since there exist languages, such as maps, which are descriptive but not argumentative.[94] (This, incidentally, makes the familiar analogy between maps and scientific theories a particularly unfortunate one. Theories are essentially argumentative systems of statements: their main point is that they explain deductively. Maps are nonargumentative. Of course every theory is also descriptive, like a map—just as it is, like all descriptive language, communicative, since it may make people act; and also expressive, since it is a symptom of the "state" of the communicator—which may happen to be a computer.) Thus there was a second case where a mistake in logic led to a mistake in psychology; in this particular case the psychology of linguistic dispositions and of the innate biological needs that underly the uses and achievements of human language.

All this showed me *the priority of the study of logic over the study of subjective thought processes.* And it made me highly suspicious of many of the psychological theories accepted at the time. For example, I came to realize that *the theory of conditioned reflex was mistaken. There is no such thing as a conditioned reflex.* Pavlov's dogs have to be interpreted as searching for invariants in the field of food acquisition (which is essentially "plastic", in other words open to modification by trial and error) and as fabricating expectations, or anticipations, of impending events. One might call this "conditioning"; but it is not a reflex formed as a result of the learning process, it is a discovery (perhaps a mistaken one) of what to anticipate.[95] Thus even the apparently empirical results of Pavlov, and the Reflexology of Bechterev,[96] and most of the results of modern learning theory, turned out, in this light, to misinterpret their findings under the influence of Aristotle's logic; for reflexology and the theory of conditioning were merely association psychology translated into neurological terms.

In 1928 I submitted a Ph.D. thesis in which, though indirectly it was the result of years of work on the psychology of thought and discovery, I finally turned away from psychology. I had left the psychological work unfinished; I had not even a fair copy of most of what I had written; and the thesis, "On the Problem of Method in the Psychology of Thinking",[97] was a kind of hasty last minute affair originally intended only as a methodological introduction to my psychological work, though now indicative of my changeover to methodology.

I felt badly about my thesis, and I have never again even glanced at it. I also felt badly about my two "rigorous" examinations ("*Rigorosum*" was the name of the public oral examinations for Ph.D.), one in the history of music, the other in philosophy and psychology. Bühler, who had previously examined me in psychology, did not ask me any questions in this field, but encouraged me to talk about my ideas on logic and the logic of science. Schlick examined me mainly on the history of philosophy, and I did so badly on Leibniz that I thought I had failed. I could hardly believe my ears when I was told that I had passed in both examinations with the highest grade, *"einstimmig mit Auszeichnung"*. I was relieved and happy, of course, but it took quite a time before I could get over the feeling that I had deserved to fail.

16. *Theory of Knowledge;* Logik der Forschung

I got my Ph.D. in 1928, and in 1929 I qualified as a teacher of mathematics and physical science in (lower) secondary schools. For this qualifying examination I wrote a thesis on problems of axiomatics in geometry, which also contained a chapter on non-Euclidean geometry.

It was only after my Ph. D. examination that I put two and two together, and my earlier ideas fell into place. I understood why the mistaken theory of science which had ruled since Bacon—that the natural sciences were the *inductive* sciences, and that induction was a process of establishing or justifying theories by *repeated* observations or experiments—was so deeply entrenched. The reason was that scientists had to *demarcate* their activities from pseudoscience as well as from theology and metaphysics, and they had taken over from Bacon the inductive method as their criterion of demarcation. (On the other hand, they were anxious to justify their theories by an appeal to the sources of knowledge comparable in reliability to the sources of religion.) But I had held in my hands for many years a better criterion of demarcation: testability or falsifiability.

Thus I could discard induction without getting into trouble over demarcation. And I could apply my results concerning the method of trial and error in such a way as to replace the whole inductive methodology by a deductive one. The falsification or refutation of theories through the falsification or refutation of their deductive consequences was, clearly, a deductive inference (*modus tollens*). This view implied that *scientific theories are either falsified or for ever remain hypotheses or conjectures.*

Thus the whole problem of scientific method cleared itself up, and with it the problem of scientific progress. Progress consisted in moving towards theories which tell us more and more—theories of ever greater content. But the more a theory says the more it excludes or forbids, and the greater are the opportunities for falsifying it. So a theory with greater content is one which can be more severely tested. This consideration led to a theory in which scientific progress turned out not to consist in the accumulation of observations but in the overthrow of less good theories and their replacement by better ones, in particular by theories of greater content. Thus there was competition between theories—a kind of Darwinian struggle for survival.

Of course theories which we claim to be no more than conjectures or hypotheses need no justification (and least of all a justification by a nonexistent "method of induction", of which nobody has ever given a sensible description). We can, however, sometimes give reasons for preferring one of the competing conjectures to the others, in the light of their critical discussion.[98]

All this was straightforward and, if I may say so, highly coherent. But it was very different from what the Machian positivists and the Wittgensteinians of the Vienna Circle were saying. I had heard about the Circle in 1926 or 1927, first from a newspaper article by Otto Neurath and then in a talk by him to a social democratic youth group. (This was the only party meeting I ever attended; I did so because I had known Neurath a little since 1919 or 1920.) I had read the programmatic literature of the Circle, and of the *Verein* Ernst Mach; in particular a pamphlet by my teacher, the mathematician Hans Hahn. In addition I had read Wittgenstein's *Tractatus*, some years before writing my Ph.D. thesis, and Carnap's books as they were published.

It was clear to me that all these people were looking for a criterion of demarcation not so much between science and pseudoscience as between science and metaphysics. And it was also clear to me that my old criterion of demarcation was better than theirs. For, first of all, they were trying to find a criterion which made metaphysics meaningless nonsense, sheer gibberish, and any such criterion was bound to lead to trouble, since metaphysical ideas are often the forerunners of scientific ones. Secondly, demarcation by meaningfulness versus meaninglessness merely shifted the problem. As the Circle recognised, it created the need for another criterion, one to distinguish between meaning and lack of meaning. For this, they had adopted verifiability, which was taken as being the same as provability by observation statements. But this was only another way of wording the time-honoured criterion of the inductivists; there was no real difference between the ideas of induction and of verification. Yet according to my theory, science was not inductive; induction was a myth which had been exploded by Hume. (A further and less interesting point, later acknowledged by Ayer, was the sheer absurdity of the use of verifiability as a meaning criterion: how could one ever say that a theory was gibberish because it could not be verified? Was it not necessary to *understand* a theory in order to judge whether or not it could be verified? And could an understandable theory be sheer gibberish?) All this made me feel that, to every one of their main problems, I had better answers—more coherent answers—than they had.

Perhaps the main point was that they were positivists, and therefore epistemological idealists in the Berkeley/Mach tradition. Of course they did not admit that they were idealists. They described themselves as "neutral monists". But in my opinion this was merely another name for idealism—and in Carnap's books[99] idealism (or, as he called it, methodological solipsism) was pretty openly accepted as a kind of working hypothesis.

I wrote (without publishing) a great amount on these issues, working through Carnap's and Wittgenstein's books in considerable detail. From the point of view I had reached this turned out to be fairly straightforward. I knew only one man to whom I could explain these ideas—and that was Heinrich Gomperz. In connection with one of my main points—that scientific theories always remain hypotheses or conjectures—he referred me to Alexis Meinong, *On Assumptions* (*Über Annahmen*, 1902), which I found not only to be psychologistic but also to assume implicitly—as did Husserl in his *Logical Investigations* (*Logische Untersuchungen*, 1900, 1901)—that scientific theories are true. For years I found that people had great difficulty in admitting that theories are, logically considered, the same as hypotheses. The prevailing view was that hypotheses are as yet unproved theories, and that theories are proved, or established, hypotheses. And even those who admitted the hypothetical character of all theories still believed that they needed some justification; that, if they could not be shown to be true, their truth had to be highly probable.

The decisive point in all this, the hypothetical character of all scientific theories, was to my mind a fairly commonplace consequence of the Einsteinian revolution, which had shown that not even the most successfully tested theory, such as Newton's, should be regarded as more than a hypothesis, an approximation to the truth.

In connection with my espousal of deductivism—the view that theories are hypothetico-deductive systems, and that the method of science is not inductive—Gomperz referred me to Professor Victor Kraft, a member of the Vienna Circle and author of a book on *The Basic Forms of Scientific Method*.[100] This book was a most valuable description of a number of the methods actually used in science, and it showed that at least some of these methods are not inductive but deductive—*hypothetico-deductive*. Gomperz gave me an introduction to Victor Kraft (no relation to Julius Kraft) and I met him several times in the *Volksgarten,* a park near the University. Victor Kraft was the first member of the Vienna Circle I met (unless I include Zilsel, who, according to Feigl,[101] was not a member). He was ready to pay serious attention to my criticisms of the Circle—more so than most of the members I met later. But I remember how shocked he was when I predicted that the philosophy of the Circle would develop into a new form of scholasticism and verbalism. This prediction has, I think, come true. I am alluding to the programmatic view that the task of philosophy is "the explication of concepts".

In 1929 or 1930 (in the latter year I was, at last, appointed as a secondary school teacher) I met another member of the Vienna Circle, Herbert Feigl.[102] The meeting, arranged by my uncle Walter Schiff, Professor of Statistics and Economics at the University of Vienna, who knew of my philosophical interests, became decisive for my whole life. I had found some encouragement before in the interest shown by Julius Kraft, Gomperz, and Victor Kraft. But although they knew that I had written many (unpublished) papers,[103] none of them had encouraged me to publish my ideas. Gomperz, indeed, had impressed upon me the fact that publishing *any* philosophical ideas was hopelessly difficult. (Times have changed.) This was supported by the fact that Victor Kraft's great book on the methods of science had been published only with the support of a special fund.

But Herbert Feigl, during our nightlong session, told me not only that he found my ideas important, almost revolutionary, but also that I should publish them in book form.[104]

It had never occurred to me to write a book. I had developed my ideas out of sheer interest in the problems, and then written some of them down for myself because I found that this was not only conducive to clarity but necessary for self-criticism. At that time I looked upon myself as an unorthodox Kantian, and as a realist.[105] I conceded to idealism that our theories are actively produced by our minds rather than impressed upon us by reality, and that they transcend our "experience"; yet I stressed that a falsification may be a head-on clash with reality. I also interpreted Kant's doctrine of the impossibility of knowing things in themselves as corresponding to the for ever hypothetical character of our theories. I also regarded myself as a Kantian in ethics. And I used to think in those days that my criticism of the Vienna Circle was simply the result of having read Kant, and of having understood some of his main points.

I think that without encouragement from Herbert Feigl it is unlikely that I should ever have written a book. Writing a book did not fit my way of life nor my attitude towards myself. I just did not have the confidence that what interested me was of sufficient interest to others. Moreover, nobody encouraged me after Feigl left for America. Gomperz, to whom I told the story of my exciting meeting with Feigl, definitely discouraged me, and so did my father, who was afraid it would all end in my becoming a journalist. My wife opposed the idea because she wanted me to use any spare time to go skiing and mountain climbing with her—the things we both enjoyed most. But once I started on the book she taught herself to type, and she has typed many times everything I have written since. (I have always been unable to get anywhere when typing—I am in the habit of making far too many corrections.)

The book I wrote was devoted to two problems—the problems of induction and of demarcation—and their interrelation. So I called it *The Two*

Fundamental Problems in the Theory of Knowledge (*Die beiden Grund-probleme der Erkenntnistheorie*), an allusion to a title of Schopenhauer's (*Die beiden Grundprobleme der Ethik*).

As soon as I had a number of chapters typed I tried them out on my friend and onetime colleague at the Pedagogic Institute, Robert Lammer. He was the most conscientious and critical reader I have ever come across: he challenged every point which he did not find crystal clear, every gap in the argument, every loose end I had left. I had written my first draft pretty quickly, but thanks to what I learned from Lammer's insistent criticism I never again wrote anything quickly. I also learned never to defend anything I had written against the accusation that it is not clear enough. If a conscientious reader finds a passage unclear, it has to be rewritten. So I acquired the habit of writing and rewriting, again and again, clarifying and simplifying all the time. I think I owe this habit almost entirely to Robert Lammer. I write, as it were, with somebody constantly looking over my shoulder and constantly pointing out to me passages which are not clear. I know of course very well that one can never anticipate all possible mis-understandings; but I think one can avoid some misunderstandings, assuming readers who want to understand.

Through Lammer I had earlier met Franz Urbach, an experimental physicist working at the University of Vienna's Institute for Radium Research. We had many common interests (music among them), and he gave me much encouragement. He also introduced me to Fritz Waismann, who had been the first to formulate the famous criterion of meaning with which the Vienna Circle was identified for so many years—the verifiability criterion of meaning. Waismann was very interested in my criticism. I believe it was through his initiative that I received my first invitation to read some papers criticizing the views of the Circle in some of the "epicyclic" groups which formed its halo, so to speak.

The Circle itself was, so I understood, Schlick's private seminar, meeting on Thursday evenings. Members were simply those whom Schlick invited to join. I was never invited, and I never fished for an invitation.[106] But there were other groups, meeting in Victor Kraft's or Edgar Zilsel's apartments, and in other places; and there was also Karl Menger's famous "*mathematisches Colloquium*". Several of these groups, of whose existence I had not even heard, invited me to present my criticisms of the central doctrines of the Vienna Circle. It was in Edgar Zilsel's apartment, in a crowded room, that I read my first paper. I still remember the stage fright.

In some of those early talks I also discussed problems connected with the theory of probability. Of all existing interpretations I found the so-called "frequency interpretation" the most convincing, and Richard von Mises's form of it the one which seemed most satisfactory. But there were still a number of difficult problems connected with it, especially if one looked at it from the point of view that *statements about probability are hypotheses.* The central question then was: *are they testable?* I tried to discuss this and some subsidiary questions, and I have worked on various improvements of my treatment of them ever since.[107] (Some are still unpublished.)

Several members of the Circle, some of whom had been at these meetings, invited me to discuss these points with them personally. Among them were Hans Hahn, who had so impressed me through his lectures, and Philipp Frank and Richard von Mises (on their frequent visits to Vienna). Hans Thirring, the theoretical physicist, invited me to address his seminar; and Karl Menger invited me to become a member of his colloquium. It was Karl Menger (whom I had asked for advice on the point) who suggested to me that I should try to apply his theory of dimension to the comparison of degrees of testability.

Very early in 1932 I completed what I then regarded as the first volume of *The Two Fundamental Problems in the Theory of Knowledge.* It was conceived, from the beginning, largely as a critical discussion and as a correction of the doctrines of the Vienna Circle; long sections were also devoted to criticisms of Kant and of Fries. The book, which is still unpublished, was read first by Feigl and then by Carnap, Schlick, Frank, Hahn, Neurath, and other members of the Circle; and also by Gomperz.

Schlick and Frank accepted the book in 1933 for publication in their series *Schriften zur wissenschaftlichen Weltauffassung.* (This was a series of books most of which were written by members of the Vienna Circle.) But the publishers, Springer, demanded that it be radically shortened. By the time the book was accepted I had written most of the second volume. This meant that little more than an outline of my work could be given within the number of pages the publishers were prepared to publish. With the agreement of Schlick and Frank I put forward a new manuscript which consisted of extracts from both volumes. But even this was returned by the publishers as too long. They were insisting on a maximum of fifteen sheets (two hundred and forty pages). The final extract—which was ultimately published as *Logik der Forschung*—was made by my uncle, Walter Schiff, who ruthlessly cut about half the text.[108] I do not think that, having tried so hard to be clear and explicit, I could have done this myself.

I can hardly give here an outline of that outline which became my first published book. But there are one or two points I will mention. The book was meant to provide a theory of knowledge and, at the same time, to be a treatise on method—the method of science. The combination was possible because I looked on human knowledge as consisting of our theories, our hypotheses, our conjectures; as the *product* of our intellectual activities. There is of course another way of looking at "knowledge": we can regard "knowledge" as a subjective "state of mind", as a subjective state of an organism. But I chose to treat it as a system of statements—theories submitted to discussion. "Knowledge" in this sense is *objective*; and it is hypothetical or conjectural.

This way of looking at knowledge made it possible for me to reformulate Hume's *problem of induction*. In this objective reformulation the problem of induction is no longer a problem of our beliefs—or of the rationality of our beliefs—but a problem of the logical relationship between singular statements (descriptions of "observable" singular facts) and universal theories.

In this form, the problem of induction becomes soluble:[109] there is no induction, because universal theories are not deducible from singular statements. But they may be refuted by singular statements, since they may clash with descriptions of observable facts.

Moreover, we may speak of "better" and of "worse" theories in an objective sense even before our theories are put to the test: the better theories are those with the greater content and the greater explanatory power (both relative to the problems we are trying to solve). And these, I showed, are also the better testable theories; and—if they stand up to tests—the better tested theories.

This solution of the problem of induction gives rise to a new theory of the method of science, to an analysis of the *critical method*, the method of trial and error: the method of proposing bold hypotheses, and exposing them to the severest criticism, in order to detect where we have erred.

From the point of view of this methodology, we start our investigation with *problems*. We always find ourselves in a certain problem situation; and we choose a problem which we hope we may be able to solve. The solution, always tentative, consists in a theory, a hypothesis, a conjecture. The various competing theories are compared and critically discussed, in order to detect their shortcomings; and the always changing, always inconclusive results of the critical discussion constitute what may be called "the science of the day".

Thus *there is no induction*: we never argue from facts to theories, unless by way of refutation or "falsification". This view of science may be described as selective, as Darwinian. By contrast, theories of method which assert that we proceed by induction or which stress *verification* (rather than *falsification*) are typically Lamarckian: they stress *instruction* by the environment rather than *selection* by the environment.

It may be mentioned (although this is not a thesis of *L.d.F.*) that the proposed solution of the problem of induction also shows the way to a solution of the older problem—the problem of the rationality of our beliefs. For we may first replace the idea of belief by that of action; and we may say that actions (or inactions) are "rational" if they are carried out in accordance with the state, prevailing at the time, of the critical scientific discussion. There is no better synonym for "rational" than "critical". (Belief, of course, is never rational: it is rational to *suspend* belief.)

My solution of the problem of induction has been widely misunderstood. I intend to say more about it in my *Replies to my Critics* (see sections 13 and 14 of those *Replies*).

17. Who Killed Logical Positivism?

> Logical positivism, then, is dead, or as dead as a
> philosophical movement ever becomes.
>
> JOHN PASSMORE[110]

Owing to the manner in which it originated, my book *Logik der Forschung*, published late in 1934, was cast partly in the form of a criticism of positivism. So were its unpublished predecessor of 1932 and my brief letter to the Editors of *Erkenntnis* in 1933.[111] Since at this time my position was being widely discussed by leading members of the Circle, and, moreover, the book was published in a mainly positivistic series edited by Frank and Schlick, this aspect of *Logik der Forschung* had some curious consequences. One was that until its English publication in 1959 as *The Logic of Scientific Discovery* philosophers in England and America (with only a few exceptions, such as J. R. Weinberg)[112] seem to have taken me for a logical positivist—or at best for a dissenting logical positivist who replaced verifiability by falsifiability.[113] Even some logical positivists themselves, remembering that the book had come out in this series, preferred to see in me an ally rather than a critic. They thought they could ward off my criticism with a few concessions—preferably mutual ones—and some verbal stratagems.[114] (For example, they persuaded themselves that I would agree to substitute falsifiability for verifiability as a criterion of meaningfulness.) And because I did not press my attack home (fighting logical positivism being by no means a major interest of mine) the logical positivists did not feel that logical positivism was seriously challenged. Before, and even after, the Second World War books and papers went on appearing which continued this method of concessions and small adjustments. But by then logical positivism had really been dead some years.

Everybody knows nowadays that logical positivism is dead. But nobody seems to suspect that there may be a question to be asked here—the question "Who is responsible?" or, rather, the question "Who has done it?". (Passmore's excellent historical article [cited in n. 110] does not ask this question.) I fear that I must admit responsibility. Yet I did not do it on purpose: my sole intention was to point out what seemed to me a number of fundamental mistakes. Passmore correctly ascribes the dissolution of logical positivism to insuperable internal difficulties. Most of these difficulties had been pointed out in my lectures and discussions, and especially in my *Logik der Forschung*.[114a] Some members of the Circle were impressed by the need to make changes. Thus the seeds were sown. They led, in the course of many years, to the disintegration of the Circle's tenets.

Yet the disintegration of the Circle preceded that of its tenets. The Vienna Circle was an admirable institution. Indeed, it was a unique seminar of philosophers working in close cooperation with first-rate mathematicians and scientists, keenly interested in problems of logic and the foundations of mathematics, and attracting some of the greatest innovators in the field, Kurt Gödel and Alfred Tarski. Its dissolution was a most serious loss. Personally I owe a debt of gratitude to some of its members, especially to Herbert Feigl and Victor Kraft—not to mention Philipp Frank and Moritz Schlick, who had accepted my book in spite of its severe criticism of their views. Again, it was indirectly through the Circle that I met Tarski, first at the Prague conference in August, 1934, when I had with me the page proofs of *Logik der Forschung*; in Vienna in 1934-35; and again at the Congress in Paris in September, 1935. And from Tarski I learned more, I think, than from anybody else.

But what attracted me perhaps most to the Vienna Circle was the "scientific attitude" or, as I now prefer to call it, the rational attitude. This was beautifully stated by Carnap in the last three paragraphs of the Preface to the first edition of his first major book, *Der logische Aufbau der Welt*. There is much in Carnap with which I disagree; and even in these three paragraphs there are things which I regard as mistaken: for although I agree that there is something "depressing" ("*niederdrückend*") about most philosophical systems, I do not think that it is their "plurality" which is to be blamed; and I feel that it is a mistake to demand the elimination of metaphysics, and another to give as a reason that "its theses cannot be rationally justified". But although especially Carnap's repeated demand for "justification" was (and still is) to my mind a serious mistake, such a matter is almost insignificant in this context. For Carnap pleads here for rationality, for greater intellectual responsibility; he asks us to learn from the way in which mathematicians and scientists proceed, and he contrasts with this the depressing ways of the philosophers: their pretentious wisdom, and their arrogation of knowledge which they present to us with a minimum of rational, or critical, argument.

It is in this general attitude, the attitude of the enlightenment, and in this critical view of philosophy—of what philosophy unfortunately is, and of what it ought to be—that I still feel very much at one with the Vienna Circle and with its spiritual father, Bertrand Russell. This explains perhaps why I was sometimes thought by members of the Circle, such as Carnap, to be one of them, and to overstress my differences with them.

Of course I never intended to overstress these differences. When writing my *Logik der Forschung* I hoped only to challenge my positivist friends and opponents. I was not altogether unsuccessful. When Carnap, Feigl, and I met in the Tyrol[115] in the summer of 1932, Carnap read the unpublished first volume of my *Grundprobleme* and, to my surprise, published shortly afterwards an article in *Erkenntnis*, "Über Protokollsätze",[116] in which he gave a detailed account, with ample acknowledgements, of some of my views. He summed up the situation by explaining that—and why—he now regarded what he called my "procedure" ("*Verfahren B*") as the best so far available in the theory of knowledge. This procedure·was *the deductive procedure of testing statements in physics*, a procedure that looks on *all statements, even the test statements themselves, as hypothetical or conjectural*, as being soaked in theory. Carnap adhered to this view for a considerable time,[117] and so did Hempel.[118] Carnap's and Hempel's highly favourable reviews of *Logik der Forschung*[119] were promising signs, and so, in another way, were attacks by Reichenbach and Neurath.[120]

Since I mentioned Passmore's article at the beginning of this section, I may perhaps say here that what I regard as the ultimate cause of the dissolution of the Vienna Circle and of Logical Positivism is not its various grave mistakes of doctrine (many of which I had pointed out) but a decline of interest in the great problems: the concentration upon *minutiae* (upon "puzzles") and especially upon the meanings of words; in brief, its scholasticism. This was inherited by its successors, in England and in the United States.

18. Realism and Quantum Theory

Although my *Logik der Forschung* may have looked to some like a criticism of the Vienna Circle, its main aims were positive. I tried to propound a theory of human knowledge. But I looked upon human knowledge in a way quite different from the way of the classical philosophers. Down to Hume and Mill and Mach, most philosophers took human knowledge as something settled. Even Hume, who thought of himself as a sceptic, and who wrote the *Treatise* in the hope of revolutionizing the social sciences, almost identified human knowledge with human habits. Human knowledge was what almost everybody knew: that the cat was on the mat; that Julius Caesar had been assassinated; that grass was green. All this seemed to me incredibly uninteresting. What was interesting was problematic knowledge, growth of knowledge—*discovery*.

If we are to look upon the theory of knowledge as a theory of discovery, then it will be best to look at *scientific* discovery. A theory of the growth of knowledge should have something to say especially about the growth of physics, and about the clash of opinions in physics.

At the time (1930) when, encouraged by Herbert Feigl, I began writing my book, modern physics was in turmoil. Quantum mechanics had been created by Werner Heisenberg in 1925;[121] but it was several years before outsiders—including professional physicists—realized that a major breakthrough had been achieved. And from the very beginning there was dissension and confusion. The two greatest physicists, Einstein and Bohr, perhaps the two greatest thinkers of the twentieth century, disagreed with one another. And their disagreement was as complete at the time of Einstein's death in 1955 as it had been at the Solvay meeting in 1927. There is a widely accepted myth that Bohr won a victory in his debate with Einstein;[122] and the majority of creative physicists supported Bohr and subscribed to this myth. But two of the greatest physicists, de Broglie and Schrödinger, were far from happy with Bohr's views (later called "the Copenhagen interpretation of quantum mechanics") and proceeded on independent lines. And after the Second World War, there were several important dissenters from the Copenhagen School, in particular Bohm, Bunge, Landé, Margenau, and Vigier.

The opponents of the Copenhagen interpretation are still in a small minority, and they may well remain so. They do not agree among themselves. But quite a lot of disagreement is also discernible within the Copenhagen orthodoxy. The members of this orthodoxy do not seem to notice these disagreements or at any rate to worry about them, just as they do not seem to notice the difficulties inherent in their views. But both are very noticeable to outsiders.

This all too superficial survey will perhaps explain why I felt at a loss when I first tried to get to grips with quantum mechanics, then often called "the new quantum theory". I was working on my own, from books; the only physicist with whom I sometimes talked about my difficulties was my friend Franz Urbach. I tried to *understand* the theory, and he had doubts whether it was understandable—at least by ordinary mortals.

I began to see light when I realized the significance of Born's statistical interpretation of the theory. At first I had not liked Born's interpretation: Schrödinger's original interpretation appealed to me, aesthetically, and as an *explanation of matter*; but once I had accepted the fact that it was not tenable, and that Born's interpretation was highly successful, I stuck to the latter, and was thus puzzled to know how one could uphold Heisenberg's interpretation of his indeterminacy formulae if Born's interpretation was accepted. It seemed obvious that if quantum mechanics was to be interpreted statistically, then so must be Heisenberg's formulae: they had to be interpreted as *scatter relations*, that is, as stating the lower bounds of the statistical scatter, or the upper bounds of the homogeneity, of any sequence of quantum-mechanical experiments. This view has now been widely accepted.[123] (I should make clear, however, that originally I did not always clearly distinguish between the scatter of the results of a set of experiments and the scatter of a set of particles in one experiment; although I had found in "formally singular" probability statements the means for solving this problem, it was only completely cleared up with the help of the idea of propensities.)[124]

A second problem of quantum mechanics was the famous problem of the "reduction of the wave packet". Few perhaps will agree that this problem was solved in 1934 in my *Logik der Forschung*; yet some very competent physicists have accepted the correctness of this solution. The proposed solution consists in pointing out that the probabilities occurring in quantum mechanics were *relative probabilities* (or conditional probabilities).[125]

This second problem is connected with what was perhaps the central point of my considerations—a conjecture, which grew into a conviction, that the *problems of the interpretation of quantum mechanics can all be traced to problems of the interpretation of the calculus of probability.*

A third problem solved was the distinction between a preparation of a state and a measurement. Although my discussion of this was quite correct and, I think, very important, I made a serious mistake over a certain thought experiment (in section 77 of *L.Sc.D.*). I took this mistake very much to heart; I did not know at that time that even Einstein had made some similar mistakes, and I thought that my blunder proved my incompetence. It was in Copenhagen in 1936, after the Copenhagen "Congress for Scientific Philosophy", that I heard of Einstein's mistakes. On the initiative of Victor Weisskopf, the theoretical physicist, I had been invited by Niels Bohr to stay a few days for discussions at his Institute. I had previously defended my thought experiment against von Weizsäcker and Heisenberg, whose arguments did not quite convince me, and against Einstein, whose arguments did convince me. I had also discussed the matter with Thirring and (in Oxford) with Schrödinger, who told me that he was deeply unhappy about quantum mechanics and thought that nobody really understood it. Thus I was in a defeatist mood when Bohr told me of his discussions with Einstein—the same discussions he described later in Schilpp's *Einstein* volume.[126] It did not occur to me to derive comfort from the fact that, according to Bohr, Einstein had been as mistaken as I; I felt defeated, and I was unable to resist the tremendous impact of Bohr's personality. (In those days Bohr was irresistible anyway.) I more or less caved in, though I still defended my explanation of the "reduction of the wave packet". Weisskopf seemed willing to accept it, but Bohr was much too eager to expound his theory of complementarity to take any notice of my feeble efforts to sell my explanation, and I did not press the point, content to learn rather than to teach. I left with an overwhelming impression of Bohr's kindness, brilliance, and enthusiasm; I also felt little doubt that he was right and I wrong. Yet I could not persuade myself that I understood Bohr's "complementarity", and I began to doubt whether anybody else understood it, though clearly some were persuaded that they did. This doubt was shared, I am sure, by Einstein and also by Schrödinger.

This set me thinking about "understanding". Bohr, in a way, was asserting that quantum mechanics was not understandable; that only classical physics was understandable and that we had to resign ourselves to the fact that quantum mechanics could be only partially understood, and then only through the medium of classical physics. Part of this understanding was achieved through the classical "particle picture", part through the classical "wave picture"; these two pictures were incompatible, and they were what Bohr called "*complementary*". There was no hope for a fuller or more direct understanding of the theory; and what was required was a "*renunciation*" of any attempt to reach a fuller understanding.

I suspected that Bohr's theory was based on a very narrow view of what *understanding* could achieve. Bohr, it appeared, thought of understanding in terms of pictures and models—in terms of a kind of visualization. This was too narrow, I felt; and in time I developed an entirely different view. According to this view what matters is the understanding not of pictures but of the logical force of a theory: its explanatory power, its relation to the relevant problems and to other theories. I developed this view over many years in lectures, first I think in Alpbach (1948) and in Princeton (1950), in Cambridge in a lecture on quantum mechanics (1953 or 1954), in Minneapolis (1962), and later again in Princeton (1963), and other places (London too, of course). It will be found, though only sketchily, in some of my later papers.[127]

Concerning quantum physics I remained for years greatly discouraged. I could not get over my mistaken thought experiment, and although it is, I think, only right to grieve over any of one's mistakes, I think now that I attributed too much weight to it. Only after some discussions, in 1948 or 1949, with Arthur March, a quantum physicist whose book on the foundations of quantum mechanics[128] I had quoted in my *Logik der Forschung*, did I return to the problem with something like renewed courage.

I went again into the old arguments, and I arrived at the following:[129]

(A)   The problem of determinism and indeterminism.

(1)   There is no such thing as a specifically quantum-mechanical argument against determinism. Of course, quantum mechanics is a statistical theory and not a prima facie deterministic one, but this does not mean that it is incompatible with a prima facie deterministic theory. (More especially, von Neumann's famous proof of this alleged incompatibility—of the nonexistence of so-called "hidden variables"—is invalid, as was recently shown by John S. Bell.)[130] The position at which I had arrived in 1934 was that nothing

in quantum mechanics justifies the thesis that determinism is refuted because of its incompatibility with quantum mechanics. Since then I have changed my mind more than once.

A model showing that the existence of a prima facie deterministic theory was indeed formally compatible with the results of quantum mechanics was given by David Bohm in 1951. (The basic ideas underlying this proof had been anticipated by de Broglie.)

(2) There is, on the other hand, no valid reason whatever for the assertion that determinism has a basis in physical science; in fact there are strong reasons against it, as pointed out by C. S. Peirce,[131] Franz Exner, Schrödinger,[132] and von Neumann:[133] all these drew attention to the fact that the deterministic character of Newtonian mechanics was compatible with indeterminism.[134] Moreover, while it is possible to explain the existence of prima facie deterministic theories as macrotheories on the basis of indeterministic and probabilistic microtheories, the opposite is not possible: *nontrivial probabilistic conclusions can only be derived (and thus explained) with the help of probabilistic premises.*[135] (In this connection some very interesting arguments of Landé's should be consulted.)[136]

(B) Probability.

In quantum mechanics we need an interpretation of the probability calculus which

(1) is physical and objective (or "realistic");

(2) yields probability hypotheses which can be statistically tested.

Moreover,

(3) these hypotheses are applicable to single cases; and

(4) they are relative to the experimental setup.

In *Logik der Forschung* I developed a "formalistic" interpretation of the probability calculus which satisfied all these demands. I have since improved upon this, replacing it by the "propensity interpretation".[137]

(C) Quantum Theory.

(1) Realism. Although I had no objections of principle to "wavicles" (wave-*cum*-particles) or similar nonclassical entities, I did not see (and I still do not see) any reason to deviate from the classical, naive, and realistic view that electrons and so on are just particles; that is to say, *that they are localized, and possess momentum.* (Of course, further developments of the theory *may* show that those who do not agree with this view are right.)[138]

(2) Heisenberg's so-called "indeterminacy principle" is a misinterpretation of certain formulae, which assert *statistical scatter.*

(3) The Heisenberg formulae *do not refer to measurements*; which implies that the whole of the current "quantum theory of measurement" is packed with misinterpretations. Measurements which according to the usual interpretation of the Heisenberg formulae are "forbidden" are according to

my results not only allowed, but actually required for *testing* these very formulae.[139]

(4) What is indeed peculiar to quantum theory is the (phase-dependent) *interference of probabilities*. It is conceivable that we may have to accept this as something ultimate. However, this does not seem to be the case: while still opposing Compton's crucial tests of Einstein's photon theory Duane produced, in 1923, long before wave mechanics, a new quantum rule,[140] which may be regarded as the analogue with respect to momentum of Planck's rule with respect to energy. Duane's rule for the quantization of momentum can be applied not only to photons but (as stressed by Landé)[141] to particles, and it then gives a rational (though only qualitative) explanation of particle interference. Landé has further argued that quantitative interference rules of wave mechanics can be derived from simple additional assumptions.

(5) Thus that host of philosophical spectres can now be exorcized, and all those many staggering philosophical assertions about the intrusion of the subject or the mind into the world of the atom can now be dismissed. The whole business can be largely explained as due to the traditional subjectivist misinterpretation of the probability calculus.[142]

19. Objectivity and Physics

In the preceding section I stressed some aspects of *Logik der Forschung* and of later work that emerged from it, which had little or nothing to do with my criticism of positivism. However, the criticism of positivism did play a subsidiary role even in my views on quantum theory. I think I was immunized against Heisenberg's early positivism by my rejection of Einstein's positivism.

As I mentioned before (section 6, text between nn. 31 and 32), I was introduced to Einstein's theories of relativity by Max Elstein. He neither stressed nor criticized the observational point of view, but helped me to understand the problem of the special theory (I am afraid in the usual unhistorical manner, as a problem posed by the experiment of Michelson and Morley), and he discussed with me Minkowski's form of the solution. It may have been this initiation that prevented me from ever taking the operationalist approach to simultaneity seriously: one can read Einstein's paper[143] of 1905 as a realist, without paying any attention to "the observer"; and one can read it as a positivist or operationalist, always attending to the observer and his doings.

It is an interesting fact that Einstein himself was for years a dogmatic positivist and operationalist. He later rejected this interpretation: he told me in 1950 that he regretted no mistake he ever made as much as this mistake. The mistake assumed a really serious form in his popular book *Relativity:*

The Special and the General Theory.[144] There he says, on page 22 (pages 14 f. in the original): "I would ask the reader not to proceed farther until he is fully convinced on this point." The point is, briefly, that "simultaneity" must be *defined*—and defined in an *operational* way—since otherwise "I allow myself to be deceived. . .when I imagine that I am able to attach a meaning to the statement of simultaneity". Or in other words, a term has to be operationally defined or else it is *meaningless*. (Here in a nutshell is the positivism later developed by the Vienna Circle under the influence of Wittgenstein's *Tractatus*, and in a very dogmatic form.)

But the situation in Einstein's theory is, simply, that for any inertial system (or "the stationary system")[145] events are simultaneous or not, just as they are in Newton's theory; and the following transitivity law (Tr) holds:

(Tr) In any inertial system, if the event a is simultaneous with b, and b with the event c, then a is simultaneous with c.

But (Tr) *does not hold in general for any three distant events unless the system in which a and b are simultaneous is the same as the system in which b and c are simultaneous*: it does not hold for distant events some of which occur in different systems, that is, in systems which are in relative motion. This is a consequence of the principle of the invariance of the velocity of light with respect to any two (inertial) systems in relative motion, that is, the principle that allows us to deduce the Lorentz transformations. There is no *need* even to mention simultaneity, except in order to warn the unwary that the Lorentz transformations are incompatible with an application of (Tr) to events that occur in different (inertial) systems.[146]

It will be seen that there is no occasion here to introduce operationalism and even less to insist on it. Moreover, since Einstein was in 1905—at least when he wrote his paper—unaware of the Michelson experiment, he had only scanty evidence at his disposal for the invariance of the velocity of light.

But many excellent physicists were greatly impressed by Einstein's operationalism, which they regarded (as did Einstein himself for a long time) as an integral part of relativity. And so it happened that operationalism became the inspiration of Heisenberg's paper of 1925, and of his widely accepted thesis that the concept of the track of an electron, or of its classical position-*cum*-momentum, was *meaningless*.

Here, for me, was a stimulus to test my realist epistemology, by applying it to a critique of Heisenberg's subjectivist interpretation of the quantum-mechanical formalism. About Bohr I said little in *Logik der Forschung* because he was less explicit than Heisenberg, and because I was reluctant to saddle Bohr with views which he might not hold. Anyway, it had been Heisenberg who had founded the new quantum mechanics on an operationalist progamme, and whose success had converted the majority of theoretical physicists to positivism.

20. Truth; Probability; Corroboration

By the time *Logik der Forschung* was published I felt that there were three problems which I had to take further: truth, probability, and the comparison of theories with respect to their content and to their corroboration.

Although the notion of falsity—that is, of untruth—and thus, by implication, the notion of truth—played a big role in *Logik der Forschung*, I had used it quite naively, and had discussed it only in section 84, entitled "Remarks Concerning the Use of the Concepts 'True' and 'Corroborated' " (*Bemerkungun über den Gebrauch der Begriffe "wahr" und "bewährt"*). At the time I did not know Tarski's work, or the distinction between two kinds of metalinguistic theories (one called by Carnap "Syntax", and the other by Tarski "Semantics", later very clearly distinguished and discussed by Marja Kokoszyńska);[147] yet so far as the relation between truth and corroboration was concerned, my views[148] became more or less standard in the Circle—that is, among those of its members[149] who, like Carnap, accepted Tarski's theory of truth.

When in 1935 Tarski explained to me (in the *Volksgarten* in Vienna) the idea of his definition of the concept of truth, I realized how important it was, and that he had finally rehabilitated the much maligned correspondence theory of truth which, I suggest, is and always has been the commonsense idea of truth.

My later thoughts on this were largely an attempt to make clear to myself what Tarski had done. It was not really that he had *defined* truth. To be sure, he had done so for a very simple formalized language, and he had sketched methods of defining it for a class of other formalized languages. Yet he had also made clear that there were other essentially equivalent ways of introducing truth, not by definition but axiomatically; so the question of whether truth should be introduced axiomatically or by definition could not be fundamental. Moreover, all these precise methods were confined to formalized languages, and could not, as Tarski had shown, be applied to ordinary language (with its "universalistic" character). Nevertheless it was clear that we could learn from Tarski's analysis how to use, with a little care, the notion of truth in ordinary discourse, and use it, moreover, in its ordinary sense—as correspondence to the facts. I decided in the end that what Tarski had done was to show that once we had understood the distinction between an object language and a (semantic) metalanguage—a language in which we can speak about statements and about facts—there was no great difficulty left in *understanding* how a statement could correspond to a fact. (See section 32 below.)

Probability created problems for me, as well as much exciting and enjoyable work. The fundamental problem tackled in *Logik der Forschung* was the *testability of probability statements in physics*. I regarded this problem as offering an important challenge to my general epistemology, and I solved it with the help of an idea which was an integral part of this epistemology and not, I think, an *ad hoc* assumption. It was the idea that no test of any theoretical statement is final or conclusive, and that the empirical, or the critical, attitude involves the adherence to some "methodological rules" which tell us not to evade criticism but to accept refutations (though not too easily). These rules are essentially somewhat flexible. As a consequence the acceptance of a refutation is nearly as risky as the tentative adoption of a hypothesis.

A second problem was that of *the variety of possible interpretations of probability statements*, and this problem was closely related to two others which played a major role in my book (but which were utterly different in character): one was the problem of the interpretation of quantum mechanics—amounting to, in my opinion, the problem of the status of probability statements in physics; the other was the problem of the content of theories.

Yet in order to be able to attack the problem of the interpretation of probability statements in its most general form it was necessary to develop an *axiom system for the calculus of probability*. This was also necessary for another purpose—for establishing my thesis, proposed in *Logik der Forschung*, that *corroboration was not a probability in the sense of the probability calculus*. (See also the text between nn. 155 and 159 below.)

In *Logik der Forschung* I had pointed out that there were *many possible interpretations* of the idea of probability, and I had insisted that in the physical sciences only a frequency theory like that proposed by Richard von Mises was acceptable. (I later modified this view by introducing the propensity interpretation, and I think that von Mises would have agreed with the modification; for propensity statements are still tested by frequencies.) But I had one major technical objection, quite apart from several minor ones, to all the known frequency theories operating with infinite sequences. It was this.

Take *any finite sequence* of 0's and 1's (or only of 0's or only of 1's), however long; and let its length be n, which may be thousands of millions. Continue from the $n + 1$st term with an *infinite random sequence* (a "collective"). Then for the combined sequence, only the properties of some *endpiece* (from some $m \geq n + 1$ on) are significant, for a sequence satisfies the demands of von Mises if, and only if, some endpiece of it satisfies them. But this means that any *empirical* sequence is simply irrelevant for judging any infinite sequence of which it is the initial segment.

I had the opportunity to discuss this problem (together with many others) with von Mises, with Helly, and with Hans Hahn. They agreed, of course; but von Mises did not worry much about it. His view (which is well known) was that a sequence which satisfied his demands—a "collective" as he called it—was an *ideal* mathematical concept like a sphere. Any empirical "sphere" could be only a rough approximation.

I was willing to accept the relation between an ideal mathematical sphere and an empirical sphere as a kind of model for that between a mathematical random sequence (a "collective") and an infinite empirical sequence. But I stressed that there was no satisfactory sense in which a *finite* sequence could be said to be a rough approximation to a collective in von Mises's sense. I therefore set out to construct something ideal but less abstract: *an ideal infinite random sequence which had the property of randomness from the very start*, so that every finite initial segment of length *n* was as ideally random as possible.

I had outlined the construction of such a sequence in *Logik der Forschung*,[150] but I did not then fully realize that this construction actually solved (a) the problem of an *ideal infinite* sequence capable of being compared with a *finite empirical* sequence; (b) that of constructing a mathematical sequence which could be used in place of von Mises's (nonconstructive) definition of randomness; and (c) that of making superfluous von Mises's postulate of the existence of a limit, since this could now be proved. Or in other words, I did not realize at the time that my construction superseded several of the solutions proposed in *Logik der Forschung*.

My idealized random sequences were not "collectives" in von Mises's sense: although they passed all statistical tests of randomness, they were definite mathematical constructions: their continuation could be mathematically predicted by anybody who knew the method of construction. But von Mises had demanded that a "collective" should be unpredictable (the "principle of the excluded gambling system"). This sweeping demand had the unfortunate consequence that no example of a collective could be constructed, so that a constructive proof of the consistency of the demand was impossible. The only way to get over this difficulty was, of course, to relax the demand. Thus arose an interesting problem: what was the minimum relaxation which would allow a proof of consistency (or existence)?

This was interesting, but not my problem. My central problem was the construction of *finite* randomlike sequences of arbitrary length, and thus expandable into infinite ideal random sequences.

Early in 1935 I lectured on this in one of the epicycles of the Vienna Circle, and afterwards I was invited by Karl Menger to give a lecture to his famous *"mathematisches Colloquium"*. I found a very select gathering of about thirty people, among them Kurt Gödel, Alfred Tarski, and Abraham Wald; and, according to Menger, I became the unwitting instrument for arousing Wald's interest in the field of probability and statistics, in which he became so famous. Menger describes the incident in his obituary of Wald as follows:[151]

> At that time there occurred a second event which proved to be of crucial importance in Wald's further life and work. The Viennese philosopher Karl Popper. . .tried to make precise the idea of a random sequence, and thus to remedy the obvious shortcomings of von Mises's definition of collectives. After I had heard (in Schlick's Philosophical Circle) a semitechnical exposition of Popper's ideas, I asked him to present the important subject in all details to the Mathematical Colloquium. Wald became greatly interested and the result was his masterly paper on the self-consistency of the notion of collectives. . . .He based his existence proof for collectives on a twofold relativisation of that notion.

Menger proceeds to characterize his description of Wald's definition of a collective, and concludes:[152]

> Although Wald's relativisation restricts the original unlimited (but unworkable) idea of collectives, it is much weaker than the irregularity requirements of Copeland, Popper, and Reichenbach. In fact, it embraces these requirements as special cases.

This is very true, and I was most impressed by Wald's brilliant solution of the problem of a minimum relaxation of von Mises's demands.[153] But, as I had opportunity to point out to Wald, it did not solve my problem: a "Wald-collective" with equal probabilities for 0 and 1 could still *begin* with a block of thousands of millions of 0's, since randomness was only a matter of how it behaved in the limit. Admittedly, Wald's work provided a general method for dividing the class of all infinite sequences into collectives and noncollectives, whilst mine merely allowed the construction of *some* random sequences of any desired length—of some very special models, as it were. However, *any given finite sequence*, of any length, could always be so continued as to become either a collective or a noncollective in Wald's sense. (The same held for the sequences of Copeland, Reichenbach, Church, and others.[154])

I have felt for a long time that my solution of my problem, though it seems philosophically quite satisfactory, could be made mathematically more interesting by being generalized, and that Wald's method could be used for this purpose. I discussed the matter with Wald, with whom I became friendly, in the hope that he himself would do it. But these were difficult times: neither of us managed to return to the problem before we both emigrated, to different parts of the world.

There is another problem, closely connected with probability: that of (a measure of) the *content* of a statement or a theory. I had shown, in *Logik der Forschung*, that the probability of a statement is inversely related to its content, and that it could therefore be used to construct a measure of the content. (Such a measure of the content would be at best comparative, unless the statement was one about some game of chance, or perhaps about some statistics.)

This suggested that among the interpretations of the probability calculus, at least two are of major importance: (1) an interpretation which allows us to speak of the *probability of (singular) events*, such as a toss of a penny or the arrival of an electron on a screen; and (2) the *probability of statements or propositions*, especially of conjectures (of varying degrees of universality).[155] This second interpretation is needed by those who maintain that degree of corroboration can be measured by a probability; and also by those, like myself, who wish to deny it.

As for my *degree of corroboration*, the idea was to sum up, in a short formula, a *report* of the manner in which a theory has passed—or not passed—its tests, including an evaluation of the severity of the tests: only tests undertaken in a *critical* spirit—attempted refutations—should count. By passing such tests, a theory may "prove its mettle"—its "fitness to survive".[156] Of course, it can only prove its "fitness" to survive those tests which it *did* survive; just as in the case of an organism, "fitness", unfortunately, only means actual survival, and past performance in no way ensures future success.

I regarded (and I still regard) the degree of corroboration of a theory merely as a critical report on the quality of past performance: *it could not be used to predict future performance*. (The *theory*, of course, may predict *future events*.) Thus it had a time index: one could only speak of the degree of corroboration of a theory *at a certain stage of its critical discussion*. In some cases it provided a very good guide if one wished to assess *the relative merits of two or more competing theories in the light of past discussions*. When faced with the *need to act*, on one theory or another, the rational choice was to act on that theory—if there was one—which so far had stood up to criticism better than its competitors had: there is no better idea of rationality than that of a readiness to accept criticism. Accordingly, the degree of corroboration of a theory was a rational guide to practice. Although we cannot justify a theory—that is, justify our belief in its truth, we can sometimes justify our *preference* for one theory over another; for example if its degree of corroboration is greater.[157]

I have been able to show, very simply, that Einstein's theory is (at least at the moment of writing) preferable to Newton's, by showing that its degree of corroboration is greater.[158]

A decisive point about degree of corroboration was that, because it increased with the severity of tests, it could be high only for *theories with a high degree of testability or content*. But this meant that degree of corroboration was linked to *improbability* rather than to *probability*: it was thus impossible to identify it with probability (although it could be defined in terms of probability—as can improbability).

All these problems were opened, or dealt with, in *Logik der Forschung* but I felt that there was more to be done about them, and that an axiomatization of the probability calculus was the thing I should do next.[159]

21. The Approaching War; The Jewish Problem

It was in July, 1927, after the big shooting in Vienna, described below, that I began to expect the worst: that the democratic bastions of Central Europe would fall, and that a totalitarian Germany would start another world war. By about 1929 I realized that among the politicians of the West only Churchill in England, then an outsider whom nobody took too seriously, thoroughly distrusted Germany. I then thought that the war would come in a few years. I was mistaken: everything developed much more slowly than I thought possible considering the logic of the situation.

Obviously, I was an alarmist. But essentially I had judged the situation correctly. I realized that the social democrats (the only remaining political party with a strong democratic element) were powerless to resist the totalitarian parties in Austria and Germany. I expected, from 1929 on, the rise of Hitler; I expected the annexation, in some form or other, of Austria by Hitler; and I expected the War against the West. (*The War Against the West* is the title of an excellent book by Aurel Kolnai.) In these expectations my assessment of the Jewish problem played a considerable role.

My parents were both born in the Jewish faith, but were baptized into the Protestant (Lutheran) Church before any of their children arrived. After much thought my father had decided that living in an overwhelmingly Christian society imposed the obligation to give as little offence as possible—to become assimilated. This, however, meant giving offence to organized Judaism. It also meant being denounced as a coward, as a man who feared anti-Semitism. All this was understandable. But the answer was that anti-Semitism was an evil, to be feared by Jews and non-Jews alike, and that it was the task of all people of Jewish origin to do their best not to provoke it: moreover, many did merge with the population: assimilation worked. Admittedly it is understandable that people who were despised for their racial origin should react by saying that they were proud of it. But racial pride is not only stupid but wrong, even if provoked. All nationalism or racialism is evil, and Jewish nationalism is no exception.

I believe that Austria before the First World War, and even Germany, were treating the Jews well. They were given almost all rights, although there were some barriers established by tradition, especially in the army. In a perfect society, no doubt, they would have been treated in every respect as equals. But like all societies this was far from perfect: although Jews, and people of Jewish origin, were equal before the law, they were not treated as equals in every respect. Yet I believe that the Jews were treated as well as one could reasonably expect. A member of a Jewish family converted to Roman Catholicism had even become an Archbishop (Archbishop Kohn of Olmütz); though because of an intrigue in which use was made of popular anti-Semitism, he had to resign his seat in 1903. The proportion of Jews or men of Jewish origin among University professors, medical men, and lawyers was very high, and open resentment was aroused by this only after the First World War. Baptized Jews could rise to the highest positions in the civil service.

Journalism was one profession which attracted many Jews, and quite a few of them certainly did little to raise professional standards. The kind of sensational journalism provided by some of these people was for many years strongly criticized—mainly by other Jews, such as Karl Kraus, anxious to defend civilized standards. The dust raised by these quarrels did not make the contestants popular. There were also Jews prominent among the leaders of the Social Democratic Party, and since they were, as leaders, targets of vile attacks, they contributed to the increasing tension.

Clearly, here was a problem. Many Jews looked conspicuously different from the "autochthonous" population. There were many more poor Jews than rich ones; but some of the rich ones were typically *nouveaux riches.*

Incidentally, while in England anti-Semitism is linked with the idea that Jews are (or once were) "moneylenders"—as in *The Merchant of Venice,* or in Dickens or Trollope—I never heard this suggestion made in Austria, at least not prior to the rise of the Nazis. There were a few Jewish bankers, such as the Austrian Rothschilds, but I never heard it suggested that they had ever engaged in the kind of moneylending to private individuals of which one reads in English novels.

In Austria, anti-Semitism was basically an expression of hostility towards those who were felt to be strangers; a feeling exploited not only by the German Nationalist party of Austria, but also by the Roman Catholic party. And, characteristically, this reprehensible resistance to strangers (an attitude, it seems, which is almost universal) was shared by many of the families of Jewish origin. During the First World War there was an influx into Vienna of Jewish refugees from the old Austrian Empire, which had been invaded by Russia. These "Eastern Jews", as they were called, had come straight from virtual ghettos,[160] and they were resented by those Jews who had settled down in Vienna; by assimilationists, by many orthodox Jews, and even by Zionists, who were ashamed of those they regarded as their poor relations.

The situation improved legally with the dissolution of the Austrian Empire at the end of the First World War; but as anybody with a little sense could have predicted, it deteriorated socially: many Jews, feeling that freedom and full equality had now become a reality, understandably but not wisely entered politics and journalism. Most of them meant well; but the influx of Jews into the parties of the left contributed to the downfall of those parties. It seemed quite obvious that, with much latent popular anti-Semitism about, the best service which a good socialist who happened to be of Jewish origin could render to his party was *not* to try to play a role in it. Strangely enough, few seemed to think of this obvious rule.

As a result, the fight between the right and the left, which was almost from the start a kind of cold civil war, was fought by the right more and more under the flag of anti-Semitism. There were frequent anti-Semitic riots at the University, and constant protests against the excessive number of Jews among the professors. It became impossible for anybody of Jewish origin to become a University teacher. And the competing parties of the right were outbidding each other in their hostility towards the Jews.

Other reasons why I expected the defeat of the Social Democratic Party at least after 1929 can be found in some of the footnotes to my *Open Society*.[161] Essentially they were connected with Marxism—more especially with the policy (formulated by Engels) of using violence, at least as a threat. The threat of violence gave the police an excuse, in July, 1927, to shoot down scores of peaceful and unarmed social democratic workers and bystanders in Vienna. My wife and I (we were not yet married) were among the incredulous witnesses of the scene. It became clear to me that the policy of the social democratic leaders, though they acted with good intentions, was irresponsible *and* suicidal. (Incidentally I found that Fritz Adler, when I met him in July, 1927, a few days after the massacre, was of the same opinion.) More than six years were to elapse, however, before the final suicide of the Social Democratic Party brought about the end of democracy in Austria.

22. Emigration: England and New Zealand

My *Logik der Forschung* was surprisingly successful, far beyond Vienna. There were more reviews, in more languages, than there were twenty-five years later of *The Logic of Scientific Discovery*, and fuller reviews even in English. As a consequence I received many letters from various countries in Europe and many invitations to lecture, including an invitation from Professor Susan Stebbing of Bedford College, London. I came to England in the autumn of 1935 to give two lectures at Bedford College. I had been invited to speak about my own ideas, but I was so deeply impressed by Tarski's achievements, then completely unknown in England, that I chose them as my topic instead. My first lecture was on Syntax and Semantics (Tarski's semantics) and the second on Tarski's theory of truth. I believe that it was on this occasion that I first aroused Woodger's interest in Tarski's work.[162]

Altogether I paid in 1935-36 two long visits to England with a very short stay in Vienna between them. I was on leave of absence without pay from my teacher's job, while my wife continued to teach, and to earn.

During these visits I gave not only these lectures at Bedford College, but also three lectures on probability at Imperial College, on an invitation arranged by Professor Hyman Levy; and I read two papers in Cambridge (with G. E. Moore present, and on the second occasion C. H. Langford, who was splendid in the discussion), and one in Oxford, where Freddie Ayer had earlier introduced me to Isaiah Berlin and to Gilbert Ryle. I also read a paper, on "The Poverty of Historicism", in Professor Hayek's seminar at the London School of Economics and Political Science (L.S.E.). Although Hayek came from Vienna, where he had been a Professor and Director of the Institute for Trade Cycle Research (*Konjunkturforschung*), I met him first in the L.S.E.[163] Lionel Robbins (now Lord Robbins) was present at the seminar and so was Ernst Gombrich. Years later G. L. S. Shackle told me that he too had been present.

In Oxford I met Schrödinger, and had long conversations with him. He was very unhappy in Oxford. He had come there from Berlin where he had presided over a seminar for theoretical physics which was probably unique in the history of science: Einstein, von Laue, Planck, and Nernst had been among its regular members. In Oxford he had been very hospitably received. He could not of course expect a seminar of giants; but what he did miss was the passionate interest in theoretical physics, among students and teachers alike. We discussed my statistical interpretation of Heisenberg's indeterminacy formulae. He was interested, but sceptical, even about the status of quantum mechanics. He gave me some offprints of papers in which he expressed doubts about the Copenhagen interpretation; it is well known that he never became reconciled to it—that is, to Bohr's "complementarity". Schrödinger mentioned that he might return to Austria. I tried to dissuade him, because he had made no secret of his anti-Nazi attitude when he left Germany, and this would be held against him if the Nazis should gain power in Austria. But in the late autumn of 1936 he did return. A chair in Graz had become vacant and Hans Thirring, professor of theoretical physics in Vienna, made the suggestion that he should give up his chair in Vienna and go to Graz, so that Schrödinger could take over Thirring's chair in Vienna. But Schrödinger would have none of this; he went to Graz, where he stayed about eighteen months. After Hitler's invasion of Austria, Schrödinger and his wife, Annemarie, had a hairbreadth's escape. She drove their car to a place near to the Italian border, where they abandoned it. Taking only hand luggage they crossed the border. From Rome, where they arrived almost penniless, they managed to telephone De Valera, the Irish Prime Minister (and a mathematician), who happened then to be in Geneva, and De Valera told them to join him there. On the Italian/Swiss border they became suspect to the Italian guards because they had hardly any luggage, and money equivalent to less than one pound. They were taken out of the train, which left the border station without them. In the end they were allowed to take the next train for Switzerland. And that is how Schrödinger became the Senior Professor of the Institute of Advanced Studies in Dublin, which then did not even exist. There is still no such Institute in Britain.

One of the experiences which I remember well from my visit in 1936 was when Ayer took me to a meeting of the Aristotelian Society at which Bertrand Russell spoke, perhaps the greatest philosopher since Kant.

Russell was reading a paper on "The Limits of Empiricism".[164] Assuming that empirical knowledge was obtained by induction, and at the same time much impressed by Hume's criticism of induction, Russell suggested that we had to adopt some *principle of induction* which in its turn could not be based on induction. Thus the adoption of this principle marked the limits of empiricism. Now I had in my *Grundprobleme*, and more briefly in *Logik der Forschung*, attributed to Kant precisely these arguments, and so it appeared to me that Russell's position was in this respect identical with Kant's.

After the lecture there was a discussion, and Ayer encouraged me to say something. So I said first that I did not believe in induction at all, even though I believed in learning from experience, and in an empiricism without those Kantian limits which Russell proposed. This statement, which I formulated as briefly and as pointedly as I could with the halting English at my disposal, was well received by the audience who, it appears, took it as a joke, and laughed. In my second attempt I suggested that the whole trouble was due to the mistaken assumption that *scientific knowledge* was a species of *knowledge*—knowledge in the ordinary sense in which if I know that it is raining it must be *true* that it is raining, so that knowledge implies truth. But, I said, what we call "scientific knowledge" was hypothetical, and often not true, let alone certainly or probably true (in the sense of the calculus of probability). Again the audience took this for a joke, or a paradox, and they laughed and clapped. I wonder whether there was anybody there who suspected that not only did I seriously hold these views, but that, in due course, they would widely be regarded as commonplace.

It was Woodger who suggested that I answer the advertisement for a teaching position in philosophy in the University of New Zealand (at Canterbury University College, as the present University of Canterbury was then called). Somebody—it may have been Hayek—introduced me to Dr Walter Adams (later Director of the London School of Economics) and to

Miss Esther Simpson, who together were running the Academic Assistance Council, which was then trying to help the many refugee scientists from Germany, and had already begun to help some from Austria.

In July, 1936, I left London for Copenhagen—I was seen off by Ernst Gombrich—in order to attend a Congress,[165] and to meet Niels Bohr, a meeting I have described in section 18. From Copenhagen I returned to Vienna, travelling through Hitler's Germany. At the end of November I received a letter from Dr A. C. Ewing, offering me academic hospitality in the name of the Moral Sciences Faculty of Cambridge University, together with a letter of support from Walter Adams of the Academic Assistance Council; shortly after, on Christmas Eve, 1936, I received a cable offering me a lectureship in Canterbury University College, Christchurch, New Zealand. This was a normal position, while the hospitality offered by Cambridge was meant for a refugee. Both my wife and I would have preferred to go to Cambridge, but I thought that this offer of hospitality might be transferable to somebody else. So I accepted the invitation to New Zealand and asked the Academic Assistance Council and Cambridge to invite Fritz Waismann, of the Vienna Circle, in my stead. They agreed to this request.

My wife and I resigned from our schoolteaching positions, and within a month we left Vienna for London. After five days in London we sailed for New Zealand, arriving in Christchurch during the first week of March, 1937, just in time for the beginning of the New Zealand academic year.

I felt certain that my help would soon be needed for Austrian refugees from Hitler. But it was another year before Hitler invaded Austria and before the cries for help started. A committee in Christchurch was constituted to obtain permits for refugees to enter New Zealand and some were rescued from concentration camps and from prison thanks to the energy of Dr Campbell, of the New Zealand High Commission in London.

23. Early Work in New Zealand

Before we went to New Zealand I had stayed in England, in all for about nine months, and it had been a revelation and an inspiration. The honesty and decency of the people and their strong feeling of political responsibility made the greatest possible impression on me. But even the university teachers I met were utterly misinformed about Hitler's Germany, and wishful thinking was universal. I was in England when popular loyalty to the ideas of the League of Nations destroyed the Hoare/Laval plan (which might well have prevented Mussolini from joining forces with Hitler); and I was there when Hitler entered the Rhineland, an act supported by an upsurge of English popular opinion. I also heard Neville Chamberlain speak in favour of a rearmament budget, and I tried to comfort myself with the idea that he was only Chancellor of the Exchequer, and that there was therefore no real need for him to understand what he was arming against, or how urgent it all was. I realized that democracy—even British democracy—was not an institution designed to fight totalitarianism; but it was very sad to find that there was apparently only one man—Winston Churchill—who understood what was happening, and that literally nobody had a good word for him.

In New Zealand the situation was similar but somewhat exaggerated. There was no harm in the people: like the British they were decent, friendly, and well disposed. But the continent of Europe was infinitely remote. In those days New Zealand had no contact with the world except through England, five weeks away. There was no air connection and one could not expect an answer to a letter in less than three months. In the First World War the country had suffered terrible losses, but all that was forgotten. The Germans were liked and war was unthinkable.

I had the impression that New Zealand was the best-governed country in the world, and the most easily governed.

It was a wonderfully quiet and pleasant atmosphere for work, and I settled down quickly to continue work which had been interrupted for several months. I won a number of friends who were interested in my work and encouraged me greatly. Hugh Parton, the physical chemist, and Frederick White, the physicist, came first. Then came Colin Simkin, the economist, Alan Reed, a lawyer, and George Roth, the radiation physicist. Further south, in Dunedin, Otago, were John Findlay, the philosopher, and John Eccles, the neurophysiologist. All these became lifelong friends.

I first concentrated—apart from teaching (I alone did the teaching in philosophy)[166]—on probability theory, especially on an axiomatic treatment of the probability calculus and on the relation between the probability calculus and Boolean algebra; and I soon finished a paper, which I compressed to minimum length. It was published later in *Mind*.[167] I continued this work for many years: it was a great standby whenever I had a cold. I also read some physics, and thought further about quantum theory. (I read, among other things, the exciting and disturbing letter [168] in *Nature* by Halban, Joliot, and Kowarski on the possibility of a uranium explosion, some letters on the same topic in *The Physical Review*, and an article by Karl K. Darrow in the *Annual Report of the Board of Regents of the Smithsonian Institution*.[169])

I had for a long time been thinking about the methods of the social sciences; after all, it had been in part a criticism of Marxism that had started me, in 1919, on my way to *Logik der Forschung*. I had lectured in Hayek's seminar on "The Poverty of Historicism", a lecture which contained (or so I thought) something like an application of the ideas of *Logik der Forschung* to the methods of the social sciences. I discussed these ideas with Hugh Parton, and with Dr H. Larsen, who was then teaching in the department of economics. However, I was most reluctant to publish anything against Marxism: where they still existed on the continent of Europe the Social Democrats were after all the only political force still resisting tyranny. I felt that, in the situation then prevailing, nothing should be published against them. Even though I regarded their policy as suicidal, it was unrealistic to think that they could be reformed by a piece of writing: any published criticism could only weaken them.

Then came the news, in March, 1938, of Hitler's occupation of Austria. There was now an urgent need to help Austrians to escape. I also felt that I could no longer hold back whatever knowledge of political problems I had acquired since 1919; I decided to put "The Poverty of Historicism" in a publishable form. What came out of it were two more or less complementary pieces: *The Poverty of Historicism* and *The Open Society and Its Enemies* (which at first I had intended to call: "False Prophets: Plato—Hegel—Marx").

24. The Open Society *and* The Poverty of Historicism

Originally I simply intended to elaborate and to put into publishable English my talk in Hayek's seminar (first given in German in Brussels in the house of my friend Alfred Braunthal),[170] showing more closely how "historicism" inspired both Marxism and fascism. I saw the finished paper clearly before me: a fairly long paper, but of course easily publishable in one piece.

My main trouble was to write it in acceptable English. I had written a few things before, but they were linguistically very bad. My German style in *Logik der Forschung* had been reasonably light—for German readers; but I discovered that English standards of writing were utterly different. For example, no German reader minds polysyllables. In English, one has to learn to be repelled by them. But if one is still fighting to avoid the simplest mistakes, such higher aims are a lot more distant, however much one may approve of them.

The Poverty of Historicism is, I think, one of my stodgiest pieces of writing. Besides, after I had written the ten sections which form the first chapter, my whole plan broke down: section 10, on essentialism, turned out to puzzle my friends so much that I began to elaborate it; and out of this elaboration and a few remarks I made on the totalitarian tendencies of Plato's *Republic*—remarks which were also thought obscure by my friends—there grew, or exploded, without any plan and against all plans, a truly unintended consequence, *The Open Society*. After it had begun to take shape I cut it out of *The Poverty* and reduced *The Poverty* to what was more or less its originally intended content.

There was also a minor factor which contributed to *The Open Society*: I was incensed by the obscurantism of some examination questions about "the one and the many" in Greek philosophy, and I wanted to bring into the open the political tendencies linked with these metaphysical ideas.

After *The Open Society* had broken away from *The Poverty*, I next finished the first three chapters of the latter. The fourth chapter, which until then had existed only in a sketchy form (without any discussion of what I later called "situational logic"), was completed, I think, only after the first draft of the Plato volume of *The Open Society* had been written.

It was no doubt due partly to internal developments in my thought that these works proceeded in this somewhat confused way, but partly also, I suppose, to the Hitler/Stalin pact and the actual outbreak of the war, and to the strange course of the war. Like everybody else, I feared that after the fall of France, Hitler would invade England. I was relieved when he invaded Russia instead, but afraid that Russia would collapse. Yet, as Churchill says in his book on the First World War, wars are not won but lost; and the Second World War was lost by Hitler's tanks in Russia and by Japan's bombers at Pearl Harbor.

The Poverty and *The Open Society* were my war effort. I thought that freedom might become a central problem again, especially under the renewed influence of Marxism and the idea of large-scale "planning" (or "dirigism"); and so these books were meant as a defence of freedom against totalitarian and authoritarian ideas, and as a warning against the dangers of historicist superstitions. Both books, and especially *The Open Society* (no doubt the more important one), may be described as books on the philosophy of politics.

Both grew out of the theory of knowledge of *Logik der Forschung* and out of my conviction that our often unconscious views on the theory of knowledge and its central problems ("What can we know?", "How certain is our knowledge?") are decisive for our attitude towards ourselves and towards politics.[171]

In *Logik der Forschung* I tried to show that our knowledge grows through trial and error-elimination, and that the main difference between its prescientific and its scientific growth is that on the scientific level we consciously search for our errors: *the conscious adoption of the critical method* becomes the main instrument of growth. It seems that already at that time I was well aware that the critical method—or the critical approach—consists, generally, in the search for difficulties or contradictions and their tentative resolution, and that this approach could be carried far beyond science, for which alone *critical tests* are characteristic. For I wrote:

"In the present work I have relegated the critical—or, if you will, the 'dialectical'—method of resolving contradictions to second place, since I have been concerned with the attempt to develop the practical methodological aspects of my views. In an as yet unpublished work I have tried to take the critical path. . . ."[172] (The allusion was to *Die beiden Grundprobleme.*)

In *The Open Society* I stressed that the critical method, though it will use tests wherever possible, and preferably practical tests, can be generalized into what I described as the critical or rational attitude.[173] I argued that one of the best senses of "reason" and "reasonableness" was openness to criticism—readiness to be criticized, and eagerness to criticize oneself; and I tried to argue that this critical attitude of reasonableness should be extended as far as possible.[174] I suggested that the demand that we extend the critical attitude as far as possible might be called "critical rationalism", a suggestion which was later endorsed by Adrienne Koch,[175] and by Hans Albert.[176]

Implicit in this attitude is the realization that we shall always have to live in an imperfect society. This is so not only because even very good people are very imperfect; nor is it because, obviously, we often make mistakes because we do not know enough; even more important than either of these reasons is the fact that there always exist irresolvable clashes of values: there are many moral problems which are insoluble because moral principles conflict.

There can be no human society without conflict: such a society would be a society not of friends but of ants. Even if it were attainable, there are human values of the greatest importance which would be destroyed by its attainment, and which therefore should prevent us from attempting to bring it about. On the other hand, we certainly ought to bring about a reduction of conflict. So already we have here an example of a clash of values or principles. This example also shows that clashes of values and principles may be valuable, and indeed essential for an open society.

One of the main arguments of *The Open Society* is directed *against moral relativism.* The fact that moral values or principles may clash does not invalidate them. Moral values or principles may be discovered, and even invented. They may be relevant to a certain situation, and irrelevant to other situations. They may be accessible to some people and inaccessible to others. But all this is quite distinct from relativism; that is, from the doctrine that any set of values can be defended.[177]

In this, my intellectual autobiography, a number of the other philosophical ideas of *The Open Society* (some of them pertaining to the history of philosophy, others to the philosophy of history) ought really to be mentioned—more, indeed, than can be discussed here. Among them is what was the first fairly extensive exposition of my anti-essentialist position and, I suspect, the first statement of an anti-essentialism which is not nominalistic or observationalistic. In connection with this exposition, *The Open Society* contained some criticism of Wittgenstein's *Tractatus*, criticism which has been almost completely neglected by Wittgenstein's commentators.

In a similar context I also wrote on the *logical paradoxes* and formulated some new paradoxes. I also discussed their relation to the *paradox of democracy* (a discussion which has given rise to a fairly extensive literature) and to the more general *paradoxes of sovereignty*.

A voluminous literature, which in my opinion has contributed little to the problem, has sprung from a mistaken criticism of my ideas on *historical explanation*. In section 12 of *Logik der Forschung* I discussed what I called "causal explanation",[178] or deductive explanation, a discussion which had been anticipated, without my being aware of it, by J. S. Mill, though perhaps a bit vaguely (because of his lack of distinction between an initial condition and a universal law).[179] When I first read "The Poverty of Historicism" in Brussels a former pupil of mine, Dr Karl Hilferding[180] made an interesting contribution to the discussion, to which Carl Hempel and Paul Oppenheim also contributed: Hilferding pointed out the relation that some of my remarks on historical explanation had to section 12 of *Logik der Forschung*. (These remarks eventually became pp. 143-46 of the book edition [1957(g)] of *The Poverty*. Hilferding's discussion, based on *Logik der Forschung*, brought out some of the points now on pp. 122-24 and 133 of [1957(g)];[181] points connected partly with the logical relation between explanation and prediction, and partly with the triviality of the universal laws usually used in historical explanations: these laws are usually uninteresting simply because they are in the context unproblematic.)

I did not, however, regard this particular analysis as especially important for historical explanation, and what I did regard as important needed some further years in which to mature. It was the problem of rationality (or the "rationality principle" or the "zero method" or the "logic of the situation").[182] But for years the unimportant thesis—in a misinterpreted form—has, under the name "the deductive model", helped to generate a voluminous literature.

The much more important aspect of the problem, the method of situational analysis, which I first added to *The Poverty*[183] in 1938, and later explained a little more fully in Chapter 14 of *The Open Society*,[184] was developed from what I had previously called the "zero method". The main point here was an attempt *to generalize the method of economic theory (marginal utility theory) so as to become applicable to the other theoretical social sciences*. In my later formulations, this method consists of constructing a *model of the social situation*, including especially the institutional situation, in which an agent is acting, in such a manner as to explain the rationality (the zero-character) of his action. Such models, then, are the testable hypotheses of the social sciences; and those models that are "singular", more especially, are the (in principle testable) singular hypotheses of history.

In this connection I may perhaps also refer to the theory of the abstract society, which was first added in the American edition of *The Open Society*.[185]

For myself *The Open Society* marks a turning point, for it made me write history (somewhat speculative history) which, to some extent, gave me an excuse to write about methods of historical research.[186] I had done some unpublished research in the history of philosophy before, but this was my first published contribution. I think it has, to say the least, raised a number of new historical problems—in fact, a wasp's nest of them.

The first volume of *The Open Society*, which I called *The Spell of Plato*, originated, as already mentioned, from an extension of section 10 of *The Poverty*. In the first draft of this extension there were a few paragraphs on Plato's totalitarianism, on its connection with his historicist theory of decline or degeneration, and on Aristotle. These were based on my earlier reading of the *Republic*, the *Statesman, Gorgias*, and some books of the *Laws*, and on Theodor Gomperz's *Greek Thinkers*, a book much beloved since my days in secondary school. The adverse reactions of my New Zealand friends to these paragraphs produced in the end *The Spell of Plato*, and with it *The Open Society*. For it turned me back to the study of the sources, because I wanted to give full evidence for my views. I reread Plato most intensively; I read Diels, Grote (whose view, I found, was essentially the same as mine), and many other commentators and historians of the period. (Full references will be found in *The Open Society*.) What I read was determined largely by what books I could get in New Zealand: during the war there was no possibility of getting books from overseas for my purposes. For some reason or other I could not get, for example, the Loeb edition of the *Republic* (Shorey's translation), though the second volume, I found after the war, had been published in 1935. This was a great pity, since it is by far the best translation, as I was to discover later. The translations which were available were so unsatisfactory that, with the help of Adam's marvellous edition, I began to do translations myself, in spite of my very scanty Greek, which I tried to improve with the help of a school grammar which I had brought from Austria. Nothing would have come of this but for the great amount of time I spent on these translations: I had found before that I had to rewrite again and again translations from Latin, and even from German, if I wanted to make an interesting idea clear, in reasonably forceful English. I have been accused of bias in my translations; and indeed they are biased. But there are no unbiased translations of Plato and, I suggest, there can be none. Shorey's is one of the few which has no liberal bias, because he accepted Plato's politics, in the same sense, approximately, in which I rejected them.

I sent *The Poverty* to *Mind*, but it was rejected; and immediately after completing *The Open Society* in February, 1943 (it had been rewritten many times), I sent it to America for publication. The book had been written in trying circumstances; libraries were severely limited, and I had had to adjust myself to whatever books were available. I had a desperately heavy teaching load, and the University authorities not only were unhelpful, but tried actively to make difficulties for me. I was told that I should be well advised not to publish anything while in New Zealand, and that any time spent on research was a theft from the working time for which I was paid.[187] The situation was such that without the moral support of my friends in New Zealand I could hardly have survived. Under these circumstances the reaction of those friends in the United States to whom I sent the manuscript was a terrible blow. They did not react at all for many months; and later, instead of submitting the manuscript to a publisher, they solicited an opinion from a famous authority, who decided that the book, because of its irreverence towards Aristotle (not Plato), was not fit to be submitted to a publisher.

After almost a year, when I was at my wit's end and in terribly low spirits, I obtained, by chance, the English address of my friend Ernst Gombrich, with whom I had lost contact during the war. Together with Hayek, who most generously offered his help (I had not dared to trouble him since I had seen him only a few times in my life), he found a publisher. Both wrote most encouragingly about the book. The relief was immense. I felt that these two had saved my life, and I still feel so.

25. Other Work in New Zealand

This was not the only work I did in New Zealand. I also did some work in logic—in fact, I invented for myself something now called "natural deduction"[188]—and I did much work, and much lecturing, on the logic of scientific discovery, including work in the history of science. This latter work consisted in the main in applications of my logical ideas on discovery to actual discoveries; but I also tried to make clear to myself the immense historical importance of erroneous theories, such as the Parmenidean theory of the full world.

In New Zealand I gave courses on noninductivist methods of science to the Christchurch branch of the Royal Society of New Zealand and the Medical School in Dunedin. These were initiated by Professor (later Sir John) Eccles. During my last two years at Christchurch I gave lunchtime lectures to the teachers and students of the science departments of Canterbury University College. All this was hard work (today I cannot imagine how I did it) but extremely enjoyable. In later years I have met former participants in these courses the world over, scientists who assured me that I had opened their eyes—and there were some highly successful scientists among them.

I liked New Zealand very much, in spite of the hostility shown by the University to my work, and I was ready to stay there for good. Early in 1945 I received an invitation from the University of Sydney. There followed some newspaper criticism in Australia about the appointment of a foreigner, and some questions were asked in Parliament. So I cabled my thanks and declined. Shortly afterwards—the war in Europe was in its last stages—I received a cable, signed by Hayek, offering me a readership at the University of London, tenable at the London School of Economics, and thanking me for offering *The Poverty* to *Economica*, of which he was the acting editor. I felt that Hayek had saved my life once more. From that moment I was impatient to leave New Zealand.

26. England: At the London School of Economics and Political Science

Wartime conditions were still prevailing when we left New Zealand, and our boat was ordered to sail round Cape Horn. It was a fantastically and unforgettably beautiful sight. We arrived in England early in January, 1946, and I started work at the London School of Economics.

The L.S.E. was in those days, just after the war, a marvellous institution. It was small enough for everybody on the staff to know everybody else. The staff, though few, were outstanding, and so were the students. There were lots of them—larger classes than I had later at the L.S.E.—eager, mature, and extremely appreciative; and they presented a challenge to the teacher. Among these students was a former regular officer of the Royal Navy, John Watkins, now my successor at the L.S.E.

I had come back from New Zealand with lots of open problems, in part purely logical, in part matters of method, including the method of the social sciences; and being now in a school of the social sciences, I felt that those latter problems had—for a time—a claim on me prior to problems of method in the natural sciences. Yet the social sciences never had for me the same attraction as the theoretical natural sciences. In fact, the only theoretical social science which appealed to me was economics. But like many before me I was interested to compare the natural and the social sciences from the point of view of their methods, which was to some extent a continuation of work I had done in *The Poverty*.

One of the ideas I had discussed in *The Poverty* was the influence of a prediction upon the event predicted. I had called this the "Oedipus effect", because the oracle played a most important role in the sequence of events which led to the fulfilment of its prophecy. (It was also an allusion to the psychoanalysts, who had been strangely blind to this interesting fact, even though Freud himself admitted that the very dreams dreamt by patients were often coloured by the theories of their analysts; Freud called them "obliging dreams".) For a time I thought that the existence of the Oedipus effect distinguished the social from the natural sciences. But in biology too—even in molecular biology—expectations often play a role in bringing about what has been expected. At any rate, my refutation of the idea that this could serve as a distinguishing mark between social and natural science provided the germ of my paper "Indeterminism in Quantum Physics and in Classical Physics".[189]

This, however, took some time. My first paper after my return to Europe arose out of a very kind invitation to contribute to a symposium, "Why are the Calculuses of Logic and Arithmetic Applicable to Reality?",[190] at the Joint Session of the Aristotelian Society and the Mind Association in Manchester in July, 1946. It was an interesting meeting, and I was received by the English philosophers with the utmost friendliness and, especially by Ryle, with considerable interest. In fact, my *Open Society* had been well received in England, far beyond my expectations; even a Platonist who hated the book commented on its "fertility of ideas", saying that "almost every sentence gives us something to think about"—which of course pleased me more than any facile agreement.

And yet there could be no doubt that my ways of thinking, my interests, and my problems were utterly uncongenial to many English philosophers. Why this was so I do not know. In some cases it might have been my interest in science. In others it might have been my critical attitude towards positivism, and towards language philosophy. This brings me to my encounter with Wittgenstein, of which I have heard the most varied and absurd reports.

Early in the academic year 1946-47 I received an invitation from the Secretary of the Moral Sciences Club at Cambridge to read a paper about some "philosophical puzzle". It was of course clear that this was Wittgenstein's formulation, and that behind it was Wittgenstein's philosophical thesis that there are no genuine problems in philosophy, only linguistic puzzles. Since this thesis was among my pet aversions, I decided to speak on "Are there Philosophical Problems?". I began my paper (read on October 26, 1946, in R. B. Braithwaite's room in King's College) by expressing my surprise at being invited by the Secretary to read a paper "stating some philosophical puzzle"; and I pointed out that by implicitly denying that philosophical problems exist, whoever wrote the invitation took sides, perhaps unwittingly, in an issue created by a genuine philosophical problem.

I need hardly say that this was meant merely as a challenging and somewhat lighthearted introduction to my topic. But at this very point, Wittgenstein jumped up and said, loudly and, it seemed to me, angrily: "The Secretary did exactly as he was told to do. He acted on my own instruction." I did not take any notice of this and went on; but as it turned out, at least some of Wittgenstein's admirers in the audience did take notice of it, and as a consequence took my remark, meant as a joke, for a serious complaint against the Secretary. And so did the poor Secretary himself, as emerges from the minutes, in which he reports the incident, adding a footnote: "This is the Club's form of invitation."[191]

However, I went on to say that if I thought that there were no genuine philosophical problems, I would certainly not be a philosopher; and that the fact that many people, or perhaps all people, thoughtlessly adopt untenable solutions to many, or perhaps all, philosophical problems provided the only justification for being a philosopher. Wittgenstein jumped up again, interrupting me, and spoke at length about puzzles and the nonexistence of philosophical problems. At a moment which appeared to me appropriate, I interrupted him, giving a list I had prepared of philosophical problems, such as: Do we know things through our senses?, Do we obtain our knowledge by induction? These Wittgenstein dismissed as being logical rather than philosophical. I then referred to the problem whether potential or perhaps even actual infinities exist, a problem he dismissed as mathematical. (This dismissal got into the minutes.) I then mentioned moral problems and the problem of the validity of moral rules. At that point Wittgenstein, who was sitting near the fire and had been nervously playing with the poker, which he sometimes used like a conductor's baton to emphasize his assertions, challenged me: "Give an example of a moral rule!". I replied: "Not to threaten visiting lecturers with pokers." Whereupon Wittgenstein, in a rage, threw the poker down and stormed out of the room, banging the door behind him.

I really was very sorry. I admit that I went to Cambridge hoping to provoke Wittgenstein into defending the view that there are no genuine philosophical problems, and to fight him on this issue. But I had never intended to make him angry; and it was a surprise to find him unable to see a joke. I realized only later that he probably did indeed feel that I was joking, and that it was this that offended him. But though I had wanted to treat my problem lightheartedly, I was in earnest—perhaps more so than was Wittgenstein himself, since, after all, he did not believe in genuine philosophical problems.

After Wittgenstein left us we had a very pleasant discussion, in which Bertrand Russell was one of the main speakers. And Braithwaite afterwards paid me a compliment (perhaps a doubtful compliment) by saying that I was the only man who had managed to interrupt Wittgenstein in the way in which Wittgenstein interrupted everyone else.

Next day in the train to London there were, in my compartment, two students sitting opposite each other, a boy reading a book and a girl reading a leftish journal. Suddenly she asked: "Who is this man Karl Popper?". He replied: "Never heard of him.". Such is fame. (As I later found out, the journal contained an attack on *The Open Society*.)

The meeting of the Moral Sciences Club became almost immediately the subject of wild stories. In a surprisingly short time I received a letter from New Zealand asking whether it was true that Wittgenstein and I had come to blows, both armed with pokers. Nearer home the stories were less exaggerated, but not much.

The incident was, in part, attributable to my custom, whenever I am invited to speak in some place, of trying to develop some consequences of my views which I expect to be unacceptable to the particular audience. For I believe that there is only one excuse for a lecture: to challenge. It is the only way in which speech can be better than print. This is why I chose my topic as I did. Besides, this controversy with Wittgenstein touched on fundamentals.

I claim that there are philosophical problems, and that I have solved some. Yet, as I have written elsewhere "nothing seems less wanted than a simple solution to an age-old philosophical problem".[192] The view of many philosophers and, especially, it seems, of Wittgensteinians, is that if a problem is soluble, it cannot have been philosophical. There are of course other ways of getting over the scandal of a solved problem. One can say that all this is old hat; or that it leaves the real problem untouched. And, after all, surely, this solution must be all wrong, must it not? (I am even ready to admit that quite often an attitude like this is more valuable than one of excessive agreement.)

One of the things which in those days I found difficult to understand was the tendency of English philosophers to flirt with nonrealistic epistemologies: phenomenalism, positivism, Berkeleyan or Machian idealism ("neutral monism"), sensationalism, pragmatism—these playthings of philosophers were in those days still more popular than realism. After a cruel war lasting for six years this attitude was surprising, and I admit that I felt that it was a bit "out of date" (to use a historicist phrase). Thus, being invited in 1946-47 to read a paper in Oxford, I read one under the title "A Refutation of Phenomenalism, Positivism, Idealism, and Subjectivism". In the discussion, the defence of the views which I had attacked was so feeble that it made little impression. However, the fruits of this victory (if any) were gathered by the philosophers of ordinary language, since language philosophy soon came to support common sense. Indeed, its attempts to adhere to common sense and realism are in my opinion by far the best aspect of ordinary-language philosophy. But common sense, though usually right (and especially in its realism), is not always right. And things get really interesting just when it is wrong. These are precisely the occasions which show that we are badly in need of enlightenment. They are also the occasions on which the usages of ordinary language cannot help us. To put it in another way, ordinary language—and with it the philosophy of ordinary language—are conservative. But in matters of the *intellect* (as opposed, perhaps, to art, or to politics) nothing is less creative and more commonplace than conservatism.

All this seems to me very well formulated by Gilbert Ryle: "The rationality of man consists not in his being unquestioning in matters of principle but in never being unquestioning; not in cleaving to reputed axioms, but in taking nothing for granted."[193]

27. Early Work in England

Although I have known sorrow and great sadness, as is everybody's lot, I do not think that I have had an unhappy hour as a philosopher since we returned to England. I have worked hard, and I have often got deep into insoluble difficulties. But I have been most happy in finding new problems, in wrestling with them, and in making some progress. This, or so I feel, is the best life. It seems to me infinitely better than the life of mere contemplation (to say nothing of divine self-contemplation) which Aristotle recommends as the best. It is a completely restless life, but it is highly self-contained—*autark* in Plato's sense, although no life, of course, can be fully *autark*. Neither my wife nor I liked living in London; but ever since we moved to Buckinghamshire, in 1950, I have been, I suspect, the happiest philosopher I have met.

This is far from irrelevant to my intellectual development since it has helped me immensely in my work. But there is also some feedback here: one of the many great sources of happiness is to get a glimpse, here and there, of a new aspect of the incredible world we live in, and of our incredible role in it.

Before our move to Buckinghamshire my main work was on "natural deduction". I had started it in New Zealand, where one of the students in my logic class, Peter Munz (now Professor of History at Victoria University), encouraged me much by his understanding and his excellent and independent development of an argument.[194] (He cannot remember the incident.) After my return to England I talked to Bernays about it, and once to Bertrand Russell. (Tarski was not interested, which I could well understand, as he had more important ideas on his mind; but Evert Beth took some real interest in it.) It is a very elementary but also strangely beautiful theory—much more beautiful and symmetrical than the logical theories I had known before.

The general interest which inspired these investigations came from Tarski's paper "On the Concept of Logical Consequence",[195] which I had heard him read at a Congress in Paris in the autumn of 1935. This paper, and especially certain doubts expressed in it,[196] led me to two problems: (1) how far is it possible to formulate logic in terms of truth or deducibility, that is, transmission of truth and retransmission of falsity? And (2) how far is it possible to characterize the logical constants of an object language as symbols whose functioning can be fully described in terms of deducibility (truth transmission)? Many other problems sprang from these problems, and from my many attempts to solve them.[197] Yet in the end, after several years of effort, I gave up when I discovered a mistake I had made, although the mistake was not serious and although in repairing it I was led to some interesting results. These, however, I have never published.[198]

With Fritz Waismann I travelled to Holland in 1946, invited to a Congress of the International Society for Significs. This was the beginning of a close connection with Holland which lasted for several years. (Earlier I had been visited in England by the physicist J. Clay, who had read my *Logik der Forschung* and with whom I shared many views.) It was on this occasion that I first met Brouwer; and also Heyting, A. D. DeGroot, and the brothers Justus and Herman Meijer. Justus became very interested in my *Open Society*, and started almost at once on the first translation of the book, into the Dutch language.[199]

In 1949 I was made a professor of logic and scientific method in the University of London. Perhaps in acknowledgement of this I usually began my lectures on scientific method with an explanation of why this subject was nonexistent—even more so than some other nonexistent subjects. (However, I did not repeat myself very much in my lectures: I have never used a set of lecture notes for a second time.)

The people from whom I learned most in those early days in England were Gombrich, Hayek, Medawar, and Robbins—none of them philosophers; there was also Terence Hutchinson, who had written with great understanding about the methods of economics. But what I missed most in those days was to be able to talk at length to a physicist, although I had met Schrödinger again in London, and had a good innings with Arthur March in Alpbach, Tyrol, and another with Pauli in Zurich.

28. First Visit to the United States. Meeting Einstein

In 1949 I received an invitation to give the William James Lectures at Harvard. This led to my first visit to America, and it made a tremendous difference to my life. When I read Professor Donald Williams's most unexpected letter of invitation I thought a mistake had been made: I thought I had been invited in the belief that I was Josef Popper-Lynkeus.

I was at that time working on three things: a series of papers on natural deduction; various axiomatizations of probability; and the methodology of social science. The only topic which seemed to fit a course of eight or ten public lectures was the last of these, and so I chose as the title of the lectures "The Study of Nature and of Society".

We sailed in February, 1950. Of the members of the department of philosophy at Harvard I had met only Quine before. Now I also met C. I. Lewis, Donald Williams, and Morton White. I also met again, for the first time since 1936, a number of old friends: the mathematician Paul Boschan, Herbert Feigl, Philipp Frank (who introduced me to the great physicist Percy Bridgman, with whom I quickly became friends), Julius Kraft, Richard von Mises, Franz Urbach, Abraham Wald, and Victor Weisskopf. I also met, for the first time, Gottfried von Haberler who, as I later heard from Hayek, had apparently been the first economist to become interested in my theory of method, George Sarton and I. Bernard Cohen the historians of science, and James Bryant Conant, the President of Harvard.

I liked America from the first, perhaps because I had been somewhat prejudiced against it. There was a feeling of freedom, of personal independence, which did not exist in Europe and which, I thought, was even stronger than in New Zealand, the freest country I knew. These were the early days of McCarthyism—of the by now partly forgotten anti-communist crusader, Senator Joseph McCarthy—, but judging by the general atmosphere I thought that this movement, which was thriving on fear, would in the end defeat itself. On my return to England I had an argument about this with Bertrand Russell.

I admit that things might have developed in a very different way. "It cannot happen here" is always wrong: a dictatorship can happen anywhere.

The greatest and most lasting impact of our visit was made by Einstein. I had been invited to Princeton, and read in a seminar a paper on "Indeterminism in Quantum Physics and in Classical Physics", an outline of a much longer paper.[200] In the discussion Einstein said a few words of agreement, and Bohr spoke at length (in fact, until we were the only two left), arguing with the help of the famous two-slit experiment that the situation in quantum physics was completely new, and altogether incomparable with that in classical physics. The fact that Einstein and Bohr came to my lecture I regard as the greatest compliment I have ever received.

I had met Einstein before my talk, first through Paul Oppenheim, in whose house we were staying. And although I was most reluctant to take up Einstein's time, he made me come again. Altogether I met him three times. The main topic of our conversation was indeterminism. I tried to persuade him to give up his determinism, which amounted to the view that the world was a four-dimensional Parmenidean block universe in which change was a human illusion, or very nearly so. (He agreed that this had been his view, and while discussing it I called him "Parmenides".) I argued that if men, or other organisms, could experience change and genuine succession in time, then this was real. It could not be explained away by a theory of the successive rising into our consciousness of time slices which in some sense coexist; for this kind of "rising into consciousness" would have precisely the same character as that succession of changes which the theory tries to explain away. I also brought in the somewhat obvious biological arguments: that the evolution of life, and the way organisms behave, especially higher animals, cannot really be understood on the basis of any theory which interprets time as if it were something like another (anisotropic) space coordinate. After all, we do *not* experience space coordinates. And this is because they are simply nonexistent: we must beware of hypostatizing them; they are constructions which are almost wholly arbitrary. Why should we then experience the time coordinate—to be sure, the one appropriate to our inertial system—not only as real but also as absolute, that is, as unalterable and independent of anything we can do (except changing our state of motion)?

The *reality of time and change* seemed to me the crux of realism. (I still so regard it, and it has been so regarded by some idealistic opponents of realism, such as Schrödinger and Gödel.)

When I visited Einstein, Schilpp's *Einstein* volume in *The Library of Living Philosophers* had just been published; this volume contained a now famous contribution of Gödel's which employed, against the reality of time and change, arguments from Einstein's two relativity theories.[201] Einstein had come out in that volume strongly in favour of realism. And he clearly disagreed with Gödel's idealism: he suggested in his reply that Gödel's solutions of the cosmological equations might have "to be excluded on physical grounds".[202]

Now I tried to present to Einstein-Parmenides as strongly as I could my conviction that a clear stand must be made against any idealistic view of time. And I also tried to show that, though the idealistic view was compatible with both determinism and indeterminism, a clear stand should be made in favour of an "open" universe—one in which the future was in no sense contained in the past or the present, even though they do impose severe restrictions on it. I argued that we should not be swayed by our theories to give up common sense too easily. Einstein clearly did not want to give up realism (for which the strongest arguments were based on common sense), though I think that he was ready to admit, as I was, that we might be forced one day to give it up if very powerful arguments (of Gödel's type, say) were to be brought against it. I therefore argued that with regard to time, and also to indeterminism (that is, the incompleteness of physics) the situation was precisely similar to the situation with regard to realism. Appealing to his own way of expressing things in theological terms, I said: if God had wanted to put everything into the world from the beginning, He would have created a universe without change, without organisms and evolution, and without man and man's experience of change. But He seems to have thought that a live universe with events unexpected even by Himself would be more interesting than a dead one.

I also tried to make plain to Einstein that such a position need not disturb his critical attitude towards Bohr's claim that quantum mechanics was complete; on the contrary, it was a position which suggested that we can always push our problems further, and that physics in general was likely to turn out to be incomplete (in some sense or other).

For we can always continue asking why-questions. Although Newton believed in the truth of his theory, he did not believe that it gave an ultimate explanation, and he tried to give a theological explanation of action at a distance. Leibniz did not believe that mechanical push (action at vanishing distance) was ultimate, and he asked for an explanation in terms of repulsive forces; an explanation which was later given by the electrical theory of matter. Explanation is always incomplete:[203] we can always raise another why-question. And the new why-question may lead to a new theory which not only "explains" the old theory, but corrects it.[204]

This is why the evolution of physics is likely to be an endless process of correction and better approximation. And even if one day we should reach a stage where our theories were no longer open to correction, since they were simply true, they would still not be complete—and we would know it. For Gödel's famous incompleteness theorem would come into play: in view of the mathematical background of physics, at best an infinite sequence of such true theories would be needed in order to answer the problems which in any given (formalized) theory would be undecidable.

Such considerations do not prove that the objective physical world is incomplete, or undetermined: they only show the essential incompleteness of our efforts. But they also show that it is barely possible (if possible at all) for science to reach a stage in which it can provide genuine support for the view that the physical world is deterministic. Why, then, should we not accept the verdict of common sense—at least until these arguments have been refuted?[205]

This is the substance of the argument with which I tried to convert Einstein-Parmenides. Besides this, we also discussed more briefly such problems as operationalism,[206] positivism and the positivists and their strange fear of metaphysics, verification versus falsification, falsifiability, and simplicity. I found to my surprise that Einstein thought my suggestions concerning simplicity (in *Logik der Forschung*) had been universally accepted, so that everybody now knew that the simpler theory was preferable because of its greater power of excluding possible states of affairs; that is, its better testability.[207]

Another topic we discussed was Bohr and complementarity—an unavoidable topic after Bohr's contribution to the discussion the night before; and Einstein repeated in the strongest possible terms what he had indicated in the Schilpp volume: that, in spite of the greatest efforts, he could not understand what Bohr meant by complementarity.[208]

I also remember some scathing remarks of Einstein's on the triviality, from a physicist's point of view, of the atom bomb, which seemed to me to go just a little too far, considering that Rutherford had thought it impossible to utilize atomic energy. Perhaps these remarks were slightly coloured by his dislike of the bomb and all it involved, but no doubt he meant what he said, and no doubt he was in essentials right.

It is difficult to convey the impression made by Einstein's personality. Perhaps it may be described by saying that one felt immediately at home with him. It was impossible not to trust him, not to rely implicitly on his straightforwardness, his kindliness, his good sense, his wisdom, and his almost childlike simplicity. It says something for our world, and for America, that so unworldly a man not only survived, but was appreciated and so greatly honoured.

During my visit to Princeton I also met Kurt Gödel again, and I discussed with him both his contribution to the Einstein volume and some aspects of the possible significance of his incompleteness theorem for physics.

After our first visit to America we moved to Penn, Buckinghamshire, which was then a quiet and beautiful little place. Here I could do more work than I had ever done before.

29. Problems and Theories

Already in 1937, when trying to make sense of the famous "dialectic triad" (*thesis: antithesis: synthesis*) by interpreting it as a form of the method of trial and error-elimination, I suggested that all scientific discussions start with a problem (P_1), to which we offer some sort of tentative solution—a *tentative theory* (*TT*); this theory is then criticized, in an attempt at *error elimination* (*EE*); and as in the case of dialectic, this process renews itself: the theory and its critical revision give rise to new *problems* (P_2).[209]

Later I condensed this into the following schema:

$$P_1 \rightarrow TT \rightarrow EE \rightarrow P_2 ,$$

a schema which I often used in lectures.

I liked to sum up this schema by saying that *science begins with problems, and ends with problems*. But I was always a little worried about this summary, for every scientific problem arises, in its turn, in a theoretical context. It is soaked in theory. So I used to say that we may begin the schema at any place: we may begin with TT_1 and end with TT_2; or we may begin with EE_1 and end with EE_2. However, I used to add that it is often from some *practical problem* that a theoretical development starts; and although any formulation of a practical problem unavoidably brings in theory, the practical problem itself may be just "felt": it may be "prelinguistic"; we—or an amoeba—may *feel* cold or some other irritation, and this may induce us, or the amoeba, to make tentative moves—perhaps theoretical moves—in order to get rid of the irritation.

But the problem "Which comes first, the problem or the theory?" is not so easily solved.[210] In fact, I found it unexpectedly fruitful and difficult.

For *practical problems* arise because something has gone wrong, because of some unexpected event. But this means that the organism, whether man or amoeba, has previously adjusted itself (perhaps ineptly) to its environment, by evolving some expectation, or some other structure (say, an organ). Yet such an adjustment is the preconscious form of developing a theory; and since any practical problem arises relative to some adjustment of this kind, practical problems are, essentially, imbued with theories.

In fact, we arrive at a result which has unexpectedly interesting consequences: *the first theories—that is, the first tentative solutions of problems—and the first problems must somehow have arisen together.*

But this has some further consequences:

Organic structures and problems arise together. Or in other words, *organic structures are theory-incorporating as well as problem-solving structures.*

Later (especially in section 37 of this *Autobiography*, below) I will return to biology and evolutionary theory. Here I will only point out that there are some subtle issues surrounding the various distinctions between formulated and theoretical problems on the one hand, and problems which are merely "felt", and also practical problems, on the other.

Amongst these issues are the following.

(1) The relationship between a formulated problem and a formulated (tentative) solution may be regarded as, essentially, a logical relationship.

(2) The relationship between a "felt" problem or a practical problem and a solution is also a fundamental relationship of *biology*. It may be very important in the description of the behaviour of individual organisms, or in the theory of the evolution of a species or a phylum. (Most problems— perhaps all—are more than "survival problems", they are very concrete problems posed by very specific situations.)

(3) The relationship between problems and solutions clearly plays an important role in the *histories* of individual organisms, especially of human organisms; and it plays a particularly important role in the history of intellectual endeavours, such as the history of science. All history should be, I suggest, a history of problem situations.

(4) On the other hand this relationship seems to play *no* role in the history of the *inorganic* evolution of the universe, or of inorganic parts of it

(say, of the evolution of stars, or of the "survival" of stable elements, or stable compounds, and the consequent rarity of unstable ones).

A very different point is also of some importance.

(5) Whenever we say that an organism has tried to solve a problem, P_1 say, we are offering a more or less risky *historical conjecture*. Though it is a historical conjecture, it is proposed in the light of historical or biological theories. The conjecture is an attempt to solve a historical problem, $P(P_1)$ say, which is quite distinct from the problem P_1 attributed by the conjecture to the organism in question.[211] Thus it is possible that a scientist like Kepler may have thought that he had solved a problem P_1, while the historian of science may try to solve the problem $P(P_1)$: "Did Kepler solve P_1 or another problem? What was the actual *problem situation*?". And the solution of $P(P_1)$ may indeed be (as I think it is) that Kepler solved a problem quite different from the one he believed he had solved.

On the animal level it is of course *always* conjectural—in fact, it is a highly theoretical construction—if a scientist conjectures of an individual animal or species (say, some microbe treated with penicillin) that it has reached a solution (say, becoming penicillin resistant) to a problem facing it. Such an ascription sounds metaphorical, even anthropomorphic, but it may not be so: it may simply state the conjecture that such was the environmental situation that unless the species (or population of organisms) changed in a certain way (perhaps by an alteration in the distribution of its gene population) it would get into trouble.

One may say that all this is obvious: most of us know that it is a difficult task to formulate our problems clearly, and that we often fail in this task. Problems are not easily identified or described, unless, indeed, some ready-made problem has been set us, as in an examination; but even then we may find that the examiner did not formulate his problem well, and that we can do better. Thus there is only too often the problem of formulating the problem—and the problem whether this was really the problem to be formulated.

Thus problems, even practical problems, are always theoretical. Theories, on the other hand, can only be understood as tentative solutions of problems, and in relation to problem situations.

In order to avoid misunderstandings, I want to stress that the relations here discussed between problems and theories are not relations between the words "problem" and "theory": I have discussed neither usages nor concepts. What I have discussed are relations between problems and theories—especially those theories which precede the problems; those problems which arise from theories, or with them; and those theories which are tentative solutions of certain problems.

30. Debates with Schrödinger

It was in 1947 or 1948 that Schrödinger let me know that he was coming to London, and I met him in the mews house of one of his friends. From then on we were in fairly regular contact by way of letters, and by personal meetings in London and later in Dublin, in Alpbach, Tyrol, and in Vienna.

In 1960 I was in hospital in Vienna, and as he was too ill to come to the hospital, his wife, Annemarie Schrödinger, came to see me every day. Before I returned to England I visited them in their apartment in the Pasteurgasse. It was the last time I saw him.

Our relations had been somewhat stormy. Nobody will be surprised at this. We disagreed violently on many things. Originally I had taken it almost for granted that he, with his admiration for Boltzmann, would not hold a positivist epistemology, but our most violent clash was sparked off when I criticized one day (in 1954 or 1955 approximately) the Machian view now usually called "neutral monism"—even though we both agreed that, contrary to Mach's intentions, this doctrine was a form of idealism.[212]

Schrödinger had absorbed his idealism from Schopenhauer. But I had expected him to see the weakness of this philosophy, a philosophy about which Boltzmann had said harsh things, and against which for example Churchill, who never claimed to be a philosopher, had produced excellent arguments.[213] I was even more surprised when Schrödinger expressed such sensualist and positivist opinions as that "all our knowledge. . .rests entirely on immediate sense perception".[214]

We had another violent clash over my paper "The Arrow of Time",[215] in which I asserted the existence of physical processes which are irreversible whether or not any entropy increase may be connected with them. The typical case is an expanding spherical light wave, or a process (like an explosion) that sends particles to infinity (of Newtonian space). The opposite—a coherent spherical wave contracting from infinity (or an implosion from infinity) cannot occur—not because such a thing is ruled out by the universal laws of light propagation or of motion, but because it would be physically impossible to realize the initial conditions.[216]

Schrödinger had written some interesting papers trying to rescue Boltzmann's theory, according to which the direction of entropy increase fully determined the direction of time (or "defined" this direction—but let us forget about this). He had insisted that this theory would collapse if there were a method, such as the one I had suggested, by which we could decide the arrow of time independently of entropy increase.[217]

So far we agreed. But when I asked him to tell me where I was wrong, Schrödinger accused me of unfeelingly destroying the most beautiful theory in physics—a theory with deep philosophical content; a theory which no physicist would dare to harm. For a nonphysicist to attack such a theory was presumptuous if not sacrilegious. He followed this up by inserting (in parentheses) a new passage into *Mind and Matter*: "This has a momentous consequence for the methodology of the physicist. He must never introduce anything that decides independently upon the arrow of time, else Boltzmann's beautiful building collapses."[218] I still feel that Schrödinger was carried away by enthusiasm: if the physicist or anybody else *can* independently decide the arrow of time, and if this *has* the consequence which Schrödinger (I think correctly) attributes to it, then, like it or not, he must accept the collapse of the Boltzmann/Schrödinger theory, and the argument for idealism based on it. Schrödinger's refusal to do so was wrong—unless he could find another way out. But he believed that no other way existed.

Another clash was over a thesis of his—an unimportant one I think, but he thought it very important—in his beautiful book *What is Life?*. This is a work of genius, especially the short section entitled "The Hereditary Code-Script", which in its very title contains one of the most important of biological theories. Indeed, the book is a marvel: written for the educated nonscientist it contains new and pioneering scientific ideas.

Yet it also contains, in response to its main question "What is Life?", a suggestion which seems to me quite obviously mistaken. In Chapter 6 there is a section which begins with the words "What is the characteristic feature of life? When is a piece of matter said to be alive?". To this question Schrödinger gives a reply in the title of the next section: "*It Feeds on 'Negative Entropy'* ".[219] The first sentence of this section reads, "It is by avoiding the rapid decay into the inert state of 'equilibrium' that an organism appears so enigmatic. . . .". After briefly discussing the statistical theory of entropy, Schrödinger asks: "How would we express in terms of the statistical theory the marvellous faculty of a living organism, by which it delays the decay into thermodynamical equilibrium (death)? We said before: 'It feeds upon negative entropy', attracting, as it were, a stream of negative entropy upon itself. . . ."[220] And he adds: "Thus the device by which an organism maintains itself stationary at a fairly high level of orderliness (= fairly low level of entropy) really consists in continually sucking orderliness from its environment."[221]

Now admittedly organisms do all this. But I denied, and I still deny,[222] Schrödinger's thesis that it is this which is *characteristic* of life, or of organisms; for it holds for every steam engine. In fact every oil-fired boiler and every self-winding watch may be said to be "continually sucking orderliness from its environment". Thus Schrödinger's answer to his question cannot be right: feeding on negative entropy is not "the characteristic feature of life".

I have written here about some of my disagreements with Schrödinger, but I owe him an immense personal debt: in spite of all our quarrels, which more than once looked like a final parting of our ways, he always came back to renew our discussions—discussions which were more interesting, and certainly more exciting, than any I had with any other physicist. The topics we discussed were topics on which I tried to do some work. And the very fact that he raised the question *What is Life?* in that marvellous book of his gave me courage to raise it again for myself (although I tried to avoid the *what-is?* form of the question).

In the remainder of this *Autobiography* I intend to report on ideas rather than on events, though I may make historical remarks where it seems relevant. What I am aiming at is a survey of the various ideas and problems on which I have worked during my later years, and on which I am still working. Some of them will be seen to be connected with the problems I had the great good fortune to discuss with Schrödinger.

31. *Objectivity and Criticism*

Much of my work in recent years has been in defence of objectivity, attacking or counterattacking subjectivist positions.

To start with, I must make it quite clear that I am not a behaviourist, and my defence of objectivity has nothing to do with any denial of "introspective methods" in psychology. I do not deny the existence of subjective experiences, of mental states, of intelligences, and of minds; I even believe these to be of the utmost importance. But I think that our theories about these subjective experiences, or about these minds, should be as objective as other theories. And by an objective theory I mean a theory which is arguable, which can be exposed to rational criticism, preferably a theory which can be tested; not one which merely appeals to our subjective intuitions.

As an example of some simple testable laws about subjective experiences I might mention optical illusions such as the Müller-Lyer illusion. An interesting optical illusion was recently shown to me by my friend Edgar Tranekjaer Rasmussen: if a swinging pendulum—a weight suspended from a string—is observed by placing a dark glass before *one* eye it appears, in binocular vision, to move round a horizontal circle rather than in a vertical plane; and if the dark glass is placed before the other eye, it appears to move round the same circle in the opposite direction.

These experiences can be tested by using independent subjects (who, incidentally, *know*, and have *seen*, that the pendulum swings in a plane). They can also be tested by using subjects who habitually (and testably) use monocular vision only: they fail to report the horizontal movement.

An effect like this may give rise to all sorts of theories. For example, that binocular vision is used by our central decoding system to *interpret* spatial distances, and that these interpretations may work in some cases independently of our "better knowledge". Such interpretations seem to play a subtle biological role. No doubt they work very well, and quite unconsciously, under normal conditions; but our decoding system may be misled by abnormal ones.

All of this suggests that our sense organs have many subtle decoding and interpreting devices built into them—that is, adaptations, or theories. These are not of the nature of "valid" theories ("valid", say, because they necessarily impose themselves upon all our experiences) but of conjectures, since, especially under unusual conditions, they may produce mistakes. A consequence of this is that there are no uninterpreted visual sense data, no sensations or "elements" in the sense of Mach: whatever is "given" to us is already interpreted, decoded.

In this sense, an objective theory of subjective perception may be constructed. It will be a biological theory which describes normal perception not as the subjective source or the subjective epistemological basis of our subjective knowledge, but rather as an objective achievement of the organism by which the organism solves certain *problems* of adaptation. And these problems may, conjecturally, be specified.

It will be seen how very far the approach here suggested is removed from behaviourism. And as for subjectivism, although the approach here suggested may make subjective experiences (and subjective experiences of "knowing" or "believing") its *object,* the theories or conjectures with which it works can be perfectly objective and testable.

This is just one example of the *objectivist* approach, for which I have been fighting in epistemology, quantum physics, statistical mechanics, probability theory, biology, psychology, and history.[223]

Perhaps most important to the objectivist approach is the recognition of (1) objective problems, (2) objective achievements, that is, solutions of problems, (3) knowledge in the objective sense, (4) criticism, which presupposes objective knowledge in the form of linguistically formulated theories.

(1) Although we may feel disturbed by a problem, and may ardently wish to solve it, the problem itself is something objective—as is a fly by which we may be disturbed, and which we may ardently wish to get rid of. That it is an objective problem, that it is present, and the role it may play in some events, are conjectures (just as the presence of the fly is a conjecture).

(2) The solution of a problem, usually found by trial and error, is an achievement, a success, in the objective sense. That something *is* an achievement is a conjecture, and it may be an arguable conjecture. The argument will have to refer to the (conjectured) problem, since achievement or success is, like a solution, always relative to a problem.

(3) We must distinguish achievements or solutions in the objective sense from subjective feelings of achievement, or of knowing, or of belief. Any

achievement may be regarded as a solution of a problem, and thus as a *theory* in a generalized sense; and as such it belongs to the world of *knowledge in the objective sense*—which, precisely, is the world of problems and their tentative solutions, and of the critical arguments which bear on them. Geometrical theories and physical theories, for example, belong to this world of knowledge in the objective sense. They are, as a rule, conjectures, in various states of their critical discussion.

(4) Criticism may be said to continue the work of natural selection on a nongenetic (exosomatic) level: it presupposes the existence of objective knowledge, in the form of *formulated theories*. Thus it is only through language that conscious criticism becomes possible. This, I conjecture, is the main reason for the importance of language; and I conjecture that it is human language which is responsible for the peculiarities of man (including even his achievements in the arts and in music).

32. Induction; Deduction; Objective Truth

There is perhaps a need here for a few words about the myth of induction, and about some of my arguments against induction. And since at present the most fashionable forms of the myth connect induction with an untenable subjectivist philosophy of deduction, I must first say a little more about the objective theory of deductive inference, and about the objective theory of truth.

I did not originally intend to explain Tarski's theory of objective truth in this *Autobiography*; but after writing briefly about it in section 20 I happened to come across some evidence showing that certain logicians have not understood the theory in the sense in which I think it should be understood. As the theory is needed to explain the fundamental difference between deductive inference and the mythical inductive inference, I will explain it briefly. I shall begin with the following problem.

How can one ever hope to understand what is meant by saying that a statement (or a "*meaningful* sentence", as Tarski calls it)[224] corresponds to the facts? Indeed, it seems that unless one accepts something like a picture theory of language (as did Wittgenstein in the *Tractatus*) one cannot speak of anything like correspondence between a statement and a fact. But the picture theory is hopelessly and indeed outrageously mistaken, and so there seems to be no prospect of explaining the correspondence of a statement to a fact.

This may be said to be the fundamental problem encountered by the so-called "correspondence theory of truth"; that is, by the theory which explains truth as correspondence to the facts. Understandably enough, the difficulty has led philosophers to suspect that the correspondence theory must be false or—even worse—meaningless. Tarski's philosophical achievement in this field was, I suggest, that he reversed this decision. He did this very simply by reflecting that a theory which deals with any relation between a statement and a fact must be able to speak about (a) statements and (b) facts. In order to be able to speak about statements, it must use names of statements, or descriptions of statements, and perhaps words such as "statement"; that is, the theory must be in a metalanguage, a language in which one can speak about language. And in order to be able to speak about facts and purported facts, it must use names of facts, or descriptions of facts, and perhaps words like "fact". Once we have a metalanguage, a language like this in which we can speak about statements *and* facts, it becomes easy to make assertions about the correspondence between a statement and a fact; for we can say:

The statement in the German language that consists of the three words, "Gras", "ist", and "grün", in that order, corresponds to the facts if and only if grass is green.

The first part of this is a description of a German statement (the description is given in *English*, which here serves as our metalanguage, and consists *in part* of English quotation names of German words); and the second part contains a description (also in English) of a (purported) fact, of a (possible) state of affairs. And the whole statement asserts the correspondence. More generally, we can put it like this. Let *"X"* abbreviate some English name, or some English description, of a statement belonging to the language L, and let *"x"* indicate the translation of X into English (which serves as a metalanguage of L); then we can say (in English, that is in the metalanguage of L) quite generally:

(+) The statement X in the language L corresponds to the facts if and only if x.

Thus it is possible, even trivially possible, to speak in an *appropriate metalanguage* about the correspondence between a statement and a (purported) fact. And so the riddle is solved: correspondence does not involve structural similarity between a statement and a fact, or anything like the relation between a picture and the scene pictured. For once we have a suitable metalanguage it is easy to explain, with the help of (+), what we mean by correspondence to the facts.

Once we have thus explained correspondence to the facts, we can replace "corresponds to the facts" by "is true (in L)". Note that *"is true"* is a metalinguistic predicate, predicable of statements. It is to be preceded by metalinguistic *names* of statements—for example quotation names—and it can therefore be clearly distinguished from a phrase like *"It is true that"*. For example "It is true that snow is red" does not contain a metalinguistic predicate of statements; it belongs to the same language as does "Snow is red", and not to the metalanguage of that language.The unexpected triviality of Tarski's result seems to be one of the reasons why it is difficult to understand. On the other hand, the triviality might reasonably have been expected, since after all everybody understands what "truth" means as long as he does not begin to think (wrongly) about it.

The most significant application of the correspondence theory is not to specific statements like "Grass is red" or "Grass is green", but to the descriptions of general logical situations. For example, we wish to say things like this. If an inference is valid then if the premises are all true, the conclusion must be true; that is, the truth of the premises (if they are all true) is invariably transmitted to the conclusion; and the falsity of the conclusion (if it is false) is invariably retransmitted to at least one of the premises. (I have christened these laws respectively "the law of the transmission of truth" and "the law of the retransmission of falsity".)

These laws are fundamental for the theory of deduction, and the use here of the words "truth" and "are true" (which are replaceable by the words "correspondence to the facts" and "correspond to the facts") is obviously far from redundant.

The correspondence theory of truth which Tarski rescued is a theory which regards truth as *objective*: as a property of theories, rather than as an experience or belief or something subjective like that. It is also *absolute*, rather than relative to some set of assumptions (or beliefs); for we may ask of any set of assumptions whether these assumptions are true.

Now I turn to deduction. A deductive inference may be said to be valid if and only if it invariably transmits truth from the premises to the conclusion; that is to say, if and only if all inferences of the same logical form transmit truth. One can also explain this by saying: a deductive inference is valid if and only if *no counterexample exists*. Here a counterexample is an inference of the same form with true premises and a false conclusion, as in:

All men are mortal. Socrates is mortal. ∴ Socrates is a man.

Let "Socrates" be here the name of a dog. Then the premises are true and the conclusion is false. Thus we have a counterexample and the inference is invalid.

Thus deductive inference, like truth, is *objective*, and even *absolute*. Objectivity does not mean, of course, that we can always ascertain whether or not a given statement is true. Nor can we always ascertain whether a given inference is valid. If we agree to use the term "true" only in the objective sense, then there are many statements which we can *prove* to be true; yet *we cannot have a general criterion of truth*. If we had such a criterion, we would be omniscient, at least potentially, which we are not. According to the work of Gödel and Tarski, we cannot even have a general criterion of truth for arithmetical statements, although we can of course describe infinite sets of arithmetical statements which are true. In the same way, we may agree to use the term "valid inference" in the objective sense, in which case we can prove of many inferences that they are valid (that is, they unfailingly transmit truth); yet we have no general criterion of validity—not even if we confine ourselves to purely arithmetical statements (or less). As a consequence, we have no general criterion for deciding whether or not some given arithmetical statement follows validly from the axioms of arithmetic. Nevertheless, we can describe infinitely many rules of inference (of many degrees of complexity) for which it is possible to *prove* validity; that is, the nonexistence of a counterexample. *Thus it is false to say that deductive inference rests upon our intuition.* Admittedly, if we have not established the validity of an inference, then we may allow ourselves to be led by guesses—that is, by intuition; intuition cannot be done without, but more often than not it leads us astray. (This is obvious; we know from the history of science that there have been many more bad theories than good ones.) And thinking intuitively is something totally different from appealing to intuition as if it were as good as appealing to an argument.

As I have often said in lectures, such things as intuition, or the feeling that something is self-evident, may *perhaps* be partially explained by truth, or by validity, but never vice versa. No statement is true, and no inference is valid, just because we feel (however strongly) that it is. It can be admitted, of course, that our intellect, or our faculty of reasoning or judging (or whatever we may call it), is so adjusted that, under fairly ordinary circumstances, we accept, or judge, or believe, what is true; largely no doubt because there are some dispositions built into us for checking things critically. However, optical illusions, to take a comparatively simple example, show that we cannot rely too much on our intuition, even if it takes a form somewhat akin to compulsion.

That we may explain such subjective feelings as the result of being presented with truth or validity and of having run through some of our normal critical checks does not allow us to turn the matter round and say: this statement is true or this inference is valid because I believe it, or because I feel compelled to believe it, or because it is self-evident, or because the opposite is inconceivable. Nevertheless, for hundreds of years this kind of talk has served subjectivist philosophers in place of argument.

The view is still widely held that in logic we have to appeal to intuition because without circularity there cannot be arguments for or against the rules of deductive logic: all arguments must presuppose logic. Admittedly, all arguments make use of logic and, if you like, "presuppose" it, though much may be said against this way of putting things. Yet it is a fact that we can establish the validity of some rules of inference without making use of them.[225] To sum up, deduction or deductive validity is objective, as is objective truth. Intuition, or a feeling of belief or of compulsion, may perhaps sometimes be due to the fact that certain inferences are valid; but the validity is objective, and explicable neither in psychological nor in behaviourist nor in pragmatist terms.

I have often expressed this attitude by saying: "I am not a belief philosopher." Indeed, beliefs are quite insignificant for a theory of truth, or of deduction, or of "knowledge" in the objective sense. A so-called "true belief " is a belief in a theory which is true; and whether or not it is true is not a question of belief, but a question of fact. Similarly, "rational belief ", if there can be said to be such a thing, consists in giving preference to what is preferable in the light of critical arguments. So this again is not a question of belief, but a question of argument, and of the objective state of the critical debate.[226]

As for induction (or inductive logic, or inductive behaviour, or learning by induction or by repetition or by "instruction") I assert that there is no such thing. If I am right then this solves, of course, the problem of induction.[227] (There are other problems left which may also be called problems of induction, such as whether the future will be like the past. But this, in my opinion far from stirring problem, can also be solved: the future will in part be like the past and in part not at all like the past.)

What is the present most fashionable reply to Hume? It is that induction is, of course, not "valid", because the word "valid" means "deductively valid"; thus the invalidity (in the *deductive* sense) of inductive arguments creates no problem: we have deductive reasoning and inductive reasoning; and although the two have a lot in common—both consist of arguing in accordance with well-tried, habitual, and fairly intuitive rules—there is also a lot of difference.[228]

What deduction and induction are supposed to have in common, especially, can be put like this. The validity of deduction cannot be validly proved, for this would be proving logic by logic, which would be circular. Yet such a circular argument, it is said, may in fact clarify our views and strengthen our confidence. *The same is true for induction.* Induction may perhaps be beyond inductive justification, yet inductive reasoning about induction is useful and helpful, if not indispensable.[229] Moreover, in both the theory of deduction and the theory of induction, such things as intuition or habit or convention or practical success *may* be appealed to; and sometimes they *must* be appealed to.

To criticize this fashionable view I repeat what I said earlier in this section: a deductive inference is *valid if no counterexample exists*. Thus we have a method of objective critical testing at our disposal: to any proposed rule of deduction, we can try to construct a counterexample. If we succeed, then the inference, or the rule of inference, is invalid, whether or not it is held to be intuitively valid by some people or even by everybody. (Brouwer thought that he had done just this—that he had given a counterexample for indirect proofs—explaining that these were mistakenly imagined to be valid because only *infinite* counterexamples exist, so that indirect proofs are valid in all finite cases.) As we have objective tests and in many cases even objective proofs at our disposal, psychological considerations, subjective convictions, habits, and conventions become completely irrelevant to the issue.

Now what is the situation with regard to induction? When is an inductive inference inductively "unsound" (to use a word other than "invalid")? The only answer which has been suggested is: when it leads to frequent practical mistakes in inductive behaviour. But I assert that every rule of inductive inference ever proposed by anybody would, if anyone were to use it, lead to such frequent practical mistakes.

The point is that there is no rule of inductive inference—inference leading to theories or universal laws—ever proposed which can be taken seriously for even a minute. Carnap seems to agree; for he writes:[230]

> By the way, Popper finds it "interesting" that I give in my lecture an example of deductive inference, but no example of inductive inference. Since in my conception probabilistic ("inductive") reasoning consists essentially not in making inferences, but rather in assigning probabilities, he should instead have required examples of principles for probability assignments. And this request, not made but reasonable, was anticipated and satisfied.

But Carnap developed only a system that assigns the probability zero to all universal laws:[231] and although Hintikka (and others) have since developed systems which do attribute an inductive probability other than zero to universal statements, there is no doubt that these systems seem to be essentially confined to very poor languages, in which even a primitive natural science could not be formulated. Moreover, they are restricted to cases in which only *finitely* many theories are available at any time.[232] (This does not stop the systems from being frighteningly complicated.) Anyway, to my mind such laws—of which there are, in practice, always infinitely many—*ought* to be given "probability" zero (in the sense of the calculus of probability) though their degree of corroboration may be greater than zero. And even if we do adopt a new system—one that assigns to some laws the probability, let us say, of 0.7—what do we gain? Does it tell us whether or not the law has good inductive support? By no means; all it tells us is that according to some (largely arbitrary) new system—no matter whose—*we ought to believe* in the law with a degree of belief equal to 0.7, provided we want our feelings of belief to conform to this system. What difference such a rule would make and, if it makes a difference, how it is to be criticized—what it excludes, and why it is to be preferred to Carnap's and my own arguments for assigning zero probabilities to universal laws—is difficult to say.[233]

Sensible rules of inductive inference do not exist. (This seems to be recognized by the inductivist Nelson Goodman.)[234] The best rule I can extract from all my reading of the inductivist literature would be something like this:

"The future is likely to be not so very different from the past."

This, of course, is a rule which everybody accepts in practice; and something like it we must accept also in theory if we are realists (as I believe we all are, whatever some may say). The rule is, however, so vague that it is hardly interesting. And in spite of its vagueness, the rule assumes too much, and certainly much more than we (and thus any inductive rule) should assume *prior* to all theory formation; for it assumes a *theory of time.*

But this was to be expected. Since there can be no theory-free observation, and no theory-free language, there can of course be no theory-free rule or principle of induction; no rule or principle on which all theories should be based.

Thus induction is a myth. No "inductive logic" exists. And although there exists a "logical" interpretation of the probability calculus, there is no good reason to assume that this "generalized logic" (as it *may* be called) is a system of "inductive logic".[235]

Nor is it to be regretted that induction does not exist: we seem to do quite well without it—with theories which are bold guesses, and which we criticize and test as severely as we can, and with as much ingenuity as we possess.

Of course, *if* this is good practice—successful practice—then Goodman and others may say that it is an "inductively valid" rule of induction. But my whole point is that it is good practice *not* because it is successful, or reliable, or what not, but because it tells us that it is bound to lead to error and so keeps us conscious of the need to look out for these errors, and to try to eliminate them.

33. Metaphysical Research Programmes

After the publication of *The Open Society* in 1945 my wife pointed out to me that this book did not represent my central philosophical interests, for I was not primarily a political philosopher. I had in fact said so in the Introduction; but she was satisfied neither by this disclaimer, nor by my subsequent return to my old interests, to the theory of scientific knowledge. She pointed out to me that my *Logik der Forschung* had long been unobtainable and by then was very nearly forgotten; and that, since I was assuming its results in my new writings, it had become urgent that it should be translated into English. I quite agreed with her, but without her insistent reminders, through many years, I should have let it rest; even so it took another fourteen years for *The Logic of Scientific Discovery* to be published (in 1959) and another seven years for the second German edition of *Logik der Forschung.*

During these years I did more and more work which I intended to use in a companion volume to *The Logic of Scientific Discovery*; and in approximately 1952 I decided to call this volume *Postscript: After Twenty Years*, hoping that it would come out in 1954.

It was sent to the printers in 1956, together with the (English) manuscript of *The Logic of Scientific Discovery*, and I received the proofs of both volumes early in 1957. Proofreading turned into a nightmare. I could complete only the first volume, which was published in 1959, and I then had to have operations on both eyes. After this I could not start proofreading again for some time, and as a result the *Postscript* is still unpublished, with the exception of one or two extracts.[236] It was of course read by several of my colleagues and students.

In this *Postscript* I reviewed and developed the main problems and solutions discussed in *Logik der Forschung*. For example, I stressed that I had *rejected all attempts at the justification of theories, and that I had replaced justification by criticism*:[237] we can never justify a theory. But we can sometimes "justify" (in a different sense) our *preference* for a theory, considering the state of the critical debate; for a theory may stand up to criticism better than its competitors. To this the objection may be made that a critic must always justify his own theoretical position. My answer is: he need not, for he may significantly criticize a theory if he can show an unexpected contradiction to exist either within the theory, or between it and some other interesting theory, though of course the latter criticism would not as a rule be decisive.[238] Previously, most philosophers had thought that any claim to rationality meant rational *justification* (of one's beliefs); my thesis was, at least since my *Open Society*, that rationality meant rational *criticism* (of one's own theory and of competing theories). Thus the old philosophy linked the ideal of rationality with final, demonstrable knowledge (either proreligious or antireligious; religion was the main issue) while I linked it with the *growth of conjectural knowledge*. This itself I linked with the idea of a better and better approximation to truth, or of *increasing truthlikeness or verisimilitude*.[239] According to this view, finding theories which are better approximations to truth is what the scientist aims at; the aim of science is knowing more and more. This involves *the growth of the content of our theories*, the growth of our knowledge of the world.

Apart from a restatement of my theory of knowledge, one of my aims in the *Postscript* was to show that the realism of my *Logik der Forschung* was a criticizable or arguable position. I stressed that *Logik der Forschung* was the book of a realist but that at that time I did not dare to say much about realism. The reason was that I had not then realized that a metaphysical position, though not testable, might be rationally criticizable or arguable. I had confessed to being a realist, but I had thought that this was no more than a confession of faith. Thus I had written about a realist argument of mine that it "expresses the metaphysical faith in the existence of regularities in our world (a faith which I share, and without which practical action is hardly conceivable)".[240]

In 1958 I published two talks, partly based on the *Postscript*, under the title "On the Status of Science and of Metaphysics" (now in *Conjectures & Refutations*[241]). In the second of these talks I tried to show that metaphysical theories may be susceptible to criticism and argument, because they may be attempts to solve *problems*—problems perhaps open to better or less good solutions. This idea I applied in the second talk to five metaphysical theories: determinism, idealism (and subjectivism), irrationalism, voluntarism (Schopenhauer's), and nihilism (Heidegger's philosophy of nothingness). And I gave reasons for rejecting these as mistaken attempts to solve their problems.

In the last chapter of the *Postscript* I argued in a similar way for indeterminism, realism, and objectivism. I tried to show that these three metaphysical theories are compatible and, in order to show the compatibility by a kind of model, I proposed that we conjecture *the reality of dispositions* (such as potentials or fields) *and especially of propensities*. (This is one way of arguing in favour of the propensity interpretation of probability. Another way will be mentioned in the next section.)

But one of the main points of that chapter was a description and appreciation of the role played by *metaphysical research programmes*;[242] I showed, with the help of a brief historical sketch, that *there had been changes down the ages in our ideas of what a satisfactory explanation ought to be like*. These ideas changed under the pressure of criticism. Thus they were criticizable, though not testable. They were metaphysical ideas—in fact, metaphysical ideas of the greatest importance.

I illustrated this with some historical remarks on the different "metaphysical research programmes that have influenced the development of physics since the days of Pythagoras"; and I proposed a new metaphysical view of the world, and with it a new research programme, based on the idea of the reality of dispositions and on the propensity interpretation of probability. (This view, I now think, is also helpful in connection with evolution.)

I have reported here on these developments for two reasons.

(1) Because metaphysical realism—the view that there is a real world to be discovered—solves some of the problems which are left open by my solution of the problem of induction.

(2) Because I intend to argue that the theory of natural selection is not a testable scientific theory, but a metaphysical research programme; and although it is no doubt the best at present available, it can perhaps be slightly improved.

I will not say more about point (1) than that, when we think we have found an approximation to the truth in the form of a scientific theory which has stood up to criticism and to tests better than its competitors, we shall, as realists, accept it as a basis for practical action, simply because we have nothing better (or nearer to the truth). But we need not accept it as true: we need not believe in it (which would mean believing in its truth).[243]

About (2) I will say more when I come to discuss the theory of evolution in section 37.

34. Fighting Subjectivism in Physics: Quantum Mechanics and Propensity

Few great men have had an intellectual impact upon the twentieth century comparable to that of Ernst Mach. He influenced physics, physiology, psychology, the philosophy of science, and pure (or speculative) philosophy. He influenced Einstein, Bohr, Heisenberg, William James, Bertrand Russell—to mention just a few names. Mach was not a great physicist; but he was a great personality and a great historian and philosopher of science. As a physiologist, psychologist, and philosopher of science, he held many important and original views to which I subscribe. He was, for instance, an evolutionist in the theory of knowledge, and in the field of psychology and physiology, especially in the study of the senses. He was critical of metaphysics, but he was sufficiently tolerant to admit, and even to stress, the necessity of metaphysical ideas as guiding lights for the physicist, even the experimental physicist. Thus he wrote, in his *Principles of the Theory of Heat*, about Joule:[244]

> When it comes to general (philosophical) questions [which Mach calls "metaphysical" on the previous page], Joule is almost silent. But where he speaks, his utterances closely resemble those of Mayer. And indeed, one cannot doubt that such comprehensive experimental investigations, all with the same aim, can be carried out only by a man who is inspired by a great and philosophically most profound view of the world.

A passage like this is the more remarkable as Mach had previously published a book, *The Analysis of Sensations,* in which he wrote that "my approach *eliminates all metaphysical questions*", and that "all we can know of the world expresses itself necessarily in sensations" (or sense data, *"Sinnesempfindungen"*).

Unfortunately, neither his biological approach nor his tolerance made much impact on the thought of our century; what was so influential —especially upon atomic physics—was his antimetaphysical intolerance, combined with his theory of sensations. That Mach's influence on the new generation of atomic physicists became so persuasive is indeed one of the ironies of history. For he was a vehement opponent of atomism and the "corpuscular" theory of matter, which he, like Berkeley,[245] regarded as metaphysical.

The philosophical impact of Mach's positivism was largely transmitted by the young Einstein. But Einstein turned away from Machian positivism, partly because he realized with a shock some of its consequences; consequences which the next generation of brilliant physicists, among them Bohr, Pauli, and Heisenberg, not only discovered but enthusiastically embraced: they became *subjectivists*. But Einstein's withdrawal came too late. Physics had become a stronghold of subjectivist philosophy, and it has remained so ever since.

Behind this development there were, however, two serious problems, connected with quantum mechanics and the theory of time; and one problem which is, I think, not so serious, the subjectivist theory of entropy.

With the rise of quantum mechanics, most of the younger physicists became convinced that quantum mechanics, unlike statistical mechanics, was a theory not of ensembles, but of the mechanics of single fundamental particles. (After some wavering I too accepted this view.) On the other hand, they were also convinced that quantum mechanics, like statistical mechanics, was a probabilistic theory. As a mechanical theory of fundamental particles, it had an objective aspect. As a probabilistic theory, it had a subjective aspect. Thus it was an utterly new type of fundamental theory, combining objective and subjective aspects; such was its revolutionary character.

Einstein's view diverged somewhat from this. For him, probabilistic theories such as statistical mechanics were extremely interesting and important and beautiful. (In his early days he had made some crucial contributions to them.) But they were neither fundamental physical theories, nor objective: they were, rather, subjectivist theories, theories which we have to introduce *because of the fragmentary character of our knowledge*. From this it follows that quantum mechanics, in spite of its excellence, is not a fundamental theory, but incomplete (because it works with incomplete knowledge), and that the objective or complete theory we must search for would be not a probabilistic but a deterministic theory.

It will be seen that the two positions have an element in common: both assume that a probabilistic or statistical theory somehow makes use of our subjective knowledge, or lack of knowledge.

This can be well understood if we consider that the only objectivist interpretation of probability discussed at that time (the late 1920s) was the frequency interpretation. (This had been developed in various versions by Venn, von Mises, Reichenbach; and later by myself.) Now frequency theorists hold that there are objective questions concerning mass phenomena, and corresponding objective answers. But they have to admit that whenever we speak of the probability of a *single* event, *qua* element of a mass phenomenon, the objectivity becomes problematic; so that it may well be asserted that with respect to single events, such as the emission of one photon, probabilities merely evaluate our ignorance. For the objective probability tells us only what happens on the average if this sort of event is repeated many times: about the single event itself the objective statistical probability says nothing.

It was here that subjectivism entered quantum mechanics, according to both Einstein's view and to that of his opponents. And it was here that I tried to fight subjectivism by introducing the propensity interpretation of probability. This was not an *ad hoc* introduction. It was, rather, the result of a careful revision of the arguments underlying the frequency interpretation.

The main idea was that propensities could be regarded as *physical realities*. They were measures of dispositions. Measurable physical dispositions ("potentials") had been introduced into physics by the theory of fields. Thus there was a precedent here for regarding dispositions as physically real; and so the suggestion that we should regard propensities as physically real was not so very strange. It also left room, of course, for indeterminism.

To show the kind of problem of interpretation which the introduction of propensities was intended to solve, I will discuss a letter which Einstein wrote to Schrödinger.[246] In this letter, Einstein refers to a well-known thought experiment which Schrödinger had published in 1935.[247] Schrödinger had pointed out the possibility of arranging some radioactive material so as to trigger a bomb, with the help of a Geiger counter. The arrangement can be made in such a way that either the bomb explodes within a certain time interval or else the fuse is disconnected. Let the probability of an explosion equal 1/2. Schrödinger argued that if a cat is placed next to the bomb, the probability that it will be killed will also be 1/2. The whole arrangement might be described in terms of quantum mechanics, and in this description, there will be a superposition of two states of the cat—a live and a dead state. Thus the quantum-mechanical description—the ψ-function—does not describe anything real: for the real cat will be either alive or dead.

Einstein argues in his letter to Schrödinger that this means that quantum mechanics is subjective and incomplete:

> If one tries to interpret the ψ-function as a complete description [of the real physical process described by it] . . . then this would mean that at the moment in question, the cat is neither alive nor blown to bits. Yet one condition or the other would be realized by an observation.
> If one rejects this view [of the completeness of the ψ-function] then one has to assume that the ψ-function does not describe a real state of affairs, but the totality of *our knowledge with respect to the state of affairs*. This is Born's interpretation which, it seems, is today accepted by most theoretical physicists.[248]

Upon acceptance of my propensity interpretation, however, this dilemma disappears, and quantum mechanics, that is the ψ-function, *does* describe a real state of affairs—a real disposition—though not a deterministic state of affairs. And although the fact that the state of affairs is not deterministic may well be said to indicate an incompleteness, this incompleteness may be not a fault of the theory—of the description—but a reflection of the indeterminateness of reality, of the state of affairs itself.

Schrödinger had always felt that $|\psi\psi^*|$ must describe something physically *real*, such as a real density. And he also was aware of the possibility[249] that reality itself may be indeterminate. According to the propensity interpretation these feelings were quite correct.

I will not discuss here any further the propensity theory of probability and the role it can play in clarifying quantum mechanics, because I have dealt with these matters fairly extensively elsewhere.[250] I remember that the theory was not well received to start with, which neither surprised nor depressed me. Things have changed very much since then, and some of the same critics (and defenders of Bohr) who at first dismissed my theory contemptuously as incompatible with quantum mechanics now say that it is all old hat, and in fact identical with Bohr's view.

I regarded myself as more than rewarded for almost forty years of heartsearching when I received a letter from B. L. van der Waerden about my paper of 1967, "Quantum Mechanics without 'The Observer' ", in which he said that he fully agreed with all the thirteen theses of my paper, and also with my propensity interpretation of probability.[251]

35. Boltzmann and the Arrow of Time

The irruption of subjectivism into physics—and especially into the theory of time and entropy—began long before the rise of quantum mechanics. It was closely connected with the tragedy of Ludwig Boltzmann, one of the great physicists of the nineteenth century, and at the same time an ardent and almost militant realist and objectivist.

Boltzmann and Mach were colleagues at the University of Vienna. Boltzmann was Professor of Physics there when Mach was called, in 1895, to a chair in the philosophy of science, established especially for him. It must have been the first chair of its kind in the world. Later Moritz Schlick occupied the chair, and after him Victor Kraft.[252] In 1901, when Mach resigned, Boltzmann succeeded him, keeping his chair of physics. Mach, who was Boltzmann's senior by six years, stayed in Vienna approximately until Boltzmann's death in 1906; and during this period, and for many years after, Mach's influence was constantly increasing. Both were physicists, Boltzmann by far the more brilliant and creative of the two;[253] and both were philosophers. Mach was called to Vienna as a philosopher, on the initiative of two philosophers. (After Boltzmann had been called to succeed Stefan in a chair of physics—a chair of which Mach had had some hopes—the idea of calling Mach to a chair of philosophy instead originated with Heinrich Gomperz, then only twenty-one, who took action through his father.)[254] On the philosophical merits of Boltzmann and Mach my judgement is frankly partisan. Boltzmann is little known as a philosopher; until quite recently I too knew next to nothing about his philosophy, and I still know much less about it than I should. Yet with what I know I agree; more closely perhaps than with any other philosophy. Thus I greatly prefer Boltzmann to Mach—not only as a physicist and a philosopher but also, I admit, as a person. But I also find Mach's personality extremely attractive; and although I am utterly opposed to his "analysis of sensations", I agree with his biological approach to the problem of (subjective) knowledge.

Boltzmann and Mach both had a great following among physicists, and they were involved in an almost deadly struggle. It was a struggle over the research programme of physics, and over the "corpuscular" hypothesis; that is, over atomism and the molecular or kinetic theory of gases and of heat. Boltzmann was an atomist, and he defended both atomism and Maxwell's kinetic theory of heat and of gases. Mach was opposed to these "metaphysical" hypotheses. He favoured a "phenomenological thermodynamics" from which he hoped to exclude all "explanatory hypotheses"; and he hoped to extend the "phenomenological" or "purely descriptive" method to the whole of physics.

In all these issues my sympathies are entirely on Boltzmann's side. But I have to admit that, in spite of his superior mastery of physics and his (in my opinion) superior philosophy, Boltzmann lost the battle. He was beaten on an issue of fundamental importance—his bold probabilistic derivation of the second law of thermodynamics, the law of entropy increase, from the kinetic theory (Boltzmann's H-theorem). He was beaten, I think, because he had been too bold.

His derivation is intuitively most convincing: he associates entropy with disorder; he shows, convincingly and correctly, that disordered states of a gas in a box are more "probable" (in a perfectly good and objective sense of "probable") than ordered states. And then he concludes (and this conclusion turned out to be invalid[255]) that there is *a general mechanical law* according to which closed systems (enclosed gases) tend to assume more and more probable states; which means that ordered systems tend to become more and more disordered the older they get, or that the entropy of a gas *tends to increase with time.*

All this is highly convincing; but in this form it is unfortunately wrong. Boltzmann at first interpreted his H-theorem as proving a *one-directional increase of disorder with time.* But as Zermelo pointed out,[256] Poincaré had proved previously (and Boltzmann never challenged this proof) that every closed system (gas) returns, after some finite time, to the neighbourhood of any state in which it was before. Thus all states are (approximately) recurring for ever; and if the gas was once in an ordered state, it will after some time return to it. Accordingly there can be no such thing as a preferred direction of time—an "arrow of time"—which is associated with entropy increase.

Zermelo's objection was, I think, decisive: it revolutionized Boltzmann's own view, and statistical mechanics and thermodynamics became, especially after 1907 (the date of the article of the Ehrenfests[257]), strictly symmetrical with respect to the direction of time; and so far they have remained so. The situation looks like this: every closed system (a gas, say) spends almost all its time in disordered states (equilibrium states). There will be fluctuations from the equilibrium, but the frequency of their occurrence rapidly decreases with their increasing size. Thus if we find that a gas is in some state of fluctuation (that is, a state of better *order* than the equilibrium state), we can conclude that it was *probably* preceded, and will *just as probably* be succeeded, by a state nearer to equilibrium (*disorder*). Accordingly, if we want to predict its future, we can predict (with high probability) an entropy increase; and a precisely analogous retrodiction of its past can also be made. It is strange that it is rarely seen that with Zermelo a revolution occurred in thermodynamics: Zermelo often gets a dishonourable mention or none at all.[258]

Unfortunately, Boltzmann did not see at once the seriousness of Zermelo's objection; thus his first reply was unsatisfactory, as Zermelo pointed out. And with Boltzmann's second reply to Zermelo there started what I regard as the great tragedy: Boltzmann's lapse into subjectivism. For in this second reply,

(a) Boltzmann gave up his theory of an objective arrow of time, and his theory that entropy tends to increase in the direction of this arrow; that is, he gave up what had been one of his central points;

(b) he introduced *ad hoc* a beautiful but wild cosmological hypothesis;

(c) he introduced a subjectivist theory of the arrow of time, and a theory which reduced the law of entropy increase to a tautology.

The connection between these three points of Boltzmann's second reply can best be expounded as follows.[259]

(a) Let us start by assuming that time has objectively no arrow, no direction, that it is in this respect just like a space coordinate; and that the objective *"universe"* is completely symmetrical with respect to the two directions of time.

(b) Let us further assume that the whole universe is a system (like a gas) in thermal equilibrium (maximal disorder). In such a universe, there will be *fluctuations* of entropy (disorder), regions in space and time, that is, in which there is some order. These regions of low entropy will be very rare—the rarer the lower the entropy valley; and on our symmetry assumption, the valley will rise in a similar way in both time directions, and flatten out towards maximum entropy. Let us in addition assume that life is only possible on the sides of deeply cut entropy valleys; and let us call these regions of changing entropy "worlds".

(c) Now we need only assume that, subjectively, we (and probably all animals) *experience* the time coordinate as having a direction—an arrow—pointing towards the entropy increase; this means that the time coordinate becomes successively or serially conscious to us as, in the "world" (the region in which we live), the entropy increases.

If (a) to (c) hold then, clearly, entropy will always increase with increasing time; that is, with the time of our consciousness. On the biological hypothesis that time gets an arrow only within the experience of animals, and only in the direction in which entropy increases, the law of entropy increase becomes a necessary law—but only subjectively valid.

The following diagram may help. (See Fig. 1.)

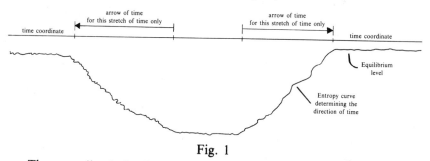

Fig. 1

The upper line is the time coordinate; the lower line indicates an entropy fluctuation. The arrows indicate regions in which life may occur, and in which time may be experienced as having the indicated direction.

Boltzmann—and also Schrödinger—suggest that the direction towards the "future" can be fixed by a definition, as the following quotation from Boltzmann's second reply to Zermelo shows:[260]

We have the choice of two kinds of picture. Either we assume that the whole universe is at the present moment in a very improbable state. Or else we assume that the aeons during which this improbable state lasts, and the distance from here to Sirius, are *minute* if compared with the age and size of the whole universe. In such a universe, which is in thermal equilibrium as a whole and therefore dead, relatively small regions of the size of our galaxy will be found here and there; regions (which we may call "worlds") which deviate significantly from thermal equilibrium for relatively short stretches of those "aeons" of time. Among these worlds, the probabilities of their state [= the entropy] will increase as often as they decrease. In the universe as a whole the two directions of time are indistinguishable, just as in space there is no up or down. However, just as at a certain place on the earth's surface we can call "down" the direction towards the centre of the earth, so a living organism that finds itself in such a world at a certain period of time can define the "direction" of time as going from the less probable state to the more probable one (the former will be the "past" and the latter the "future"), and by virtue of this definition [*sic*] he will find that his own small region, isolated from the rest of the universe, is "initially" always in an improbable state. It seems to me that this way of looking at things is the only one which allows us to understand the validity of the second law, and the heat death of each individual world, without invoking a unidirectional change of the entire universe from a definite initial state to a final state.

I think that Boltzmann's idea is staggering in its boldness and beauty. But I also think that it is quite untenable, at least for a realist. It brands unidirectional change as an illusion. This makes the catastrophe of Hiroshima an illusion. Thus it makes our world an illusion, and with it *all our attempts to find out more about our world*. It is therefore self-defeating (like all idealism). Boltzmann's idealistic *ad hoc* hypothesis clashes with his own realistic and almost passionately maintained anti-idealistic philosophy, and with his passionate wish to know.

But Boltzmann's *ad hoc* hypothesis also destroys, to a considerable extent, the physical theory which it was intended to save. For his great and bold attempt to derive the law of entropy increase ($dS/dt \geq 0$) from mechanical and statistical assumptions—his H-theorem—fails completely. It fails for his objective time (that is, his directionless time) since for it entropy decreases as often as it increases.[261] And it fails for his subjective time (time with an arrow) since here only a definition or an illusion makes entropy increase, and no kinetic, no dynamic, no statistical or mechanical proof could (or could be required to) establish this fact. Thus it destroyed the physical theory—the kinetic theory of entropy—which Boltzmann tried to defend against Zermelo. The sacrifice of his realistic philosophy for the sake of his H-theorem was in vain.

I think that, in time, he must have realized all this, and that his depression and suicide in 1906 may have been connected with it.

Although I admire the beauty and the intellectual boldness of Boltzmann's idealistic *ad hoc* hypothesis, it now turns out that it was not "bold" in the sense of my methodology: it did not add to our knowledge, it was not content-increasing. On the contrary, it was destructive of all content. (Of course, the theory of equilibrium and fluctuations was unaffected; see n. 256 above.)

This was why I did not feel any regret (though I was very sad for Boltzmann) when I realized that my example of a nonentropic physical process which had an arrow of time[262] destroyed Boltzmann's idealistic *ad hoc* hypothesis. I admit that it destroyed something remarkable—an argument for idealism which seemed to belong to pure physics. But unlike Schrödinger, I was not prone to look for such arguments; and since I was, like Schrödinger, opposed to the use of quantum theory in support of subjectivism, I was glad that I had been able to attack an even older stronghold of subjectivism in physics.[263] And I felt that Boltzmann would have approved of the attempt (though perhaps not of the results).

The story of Mach and Boltzmann is one of the strangest in the history of science; and it is one which shows the historical power of fashions. But fashions are stupid and blind, especially philosophical fashions; and that includes the belief that history will be our judge.

In the light of history—or in the darkness of history—Boltzmann was defeated, according to all accepted standards, though everybody admits his eminence as a physicist. For he never succeeded in clearing up the status of his H-theorem; nor did he explain entropy increase. (Instead, he created a new problem—or, as I think, a pseudoproblem: is the arrow of time a consequence of entropy increase?) He was also defeated as a philosopher. During his later life, Mach's positivism and Ostwald's "energetics", both of them antiatomist, waxed so influential that Boltzmann became disheartened (as his *Lectures on Gas Theory* show). Such was the pressure that he lost faith in himself and in the reality of atoms: he suggested that the corpuscular hypothesis may perhaps be only a heuristic device (rather than a hypothesis about a physical reality)—a suggestion Mach reacted to with the remark that it was "not a very chivalrous [counter-]move in the debate" ("*ein nicht ganz ritterlicher polemischer Zug*"[264]).

To this day Boltzmann's realism and objectivism have been vindicated neither by himself nor by history. (The worse for history.) Even though the atomism he had defended won its first great victory with the help of his idea of statistical fluctuations (I am alluding to Einstein's paper on Brownian movement of 1905), it was Mach's philosophy—the philosophy of the arch-opponent of atomism—that became the accepted creed of the young Einstein and probably thereby of the founders of quantum mechanics. Nobody denied Boltzmann's greatness as a physicist, of course, and especially as one of the two founders of statistical mechanics. But whatever there is in the way of a renaissance of his ideas seems to be linked either with his subjectivist theory of the arrow of time (Schrödinger, Reichenbach, Grünbaum), or with a subjectivist interpretation of statistics and of his H-theorem (Born, Jaynes). The goddess of history—venerated as our judge—still plays her tricks.

I have told this story here because it throws some light on the idealistic theory that the arrow of time is a subjective illusion, and because the fight against this theory has taken up much of my thought in recent years.

36. The Subjectivist Theory of Entropy

What I mean here by the subjectivist theory of entropy[265] is not Boltzmann's theory, in which the arrow of time is subjective but entropy objective. I mean rather a theory, originally due to Leo Szilard,[266] according to which the entropy of a system increases whenever our information about it decreases, and vice versa. According to Szilard's theory, any gain of information or knowledge must be interpreted as a decrease in entropy: in accordance with the second law it must somehow be paid for by an at least equal increase in entropy.[267]

I admit that there is something intuitively satisfying in this thesis—especially, of course, for a subjectivist. Undoubtedly, information (or "informative content") can be measured by improbability, as in fact I pointed out in 1934 in my *Logik der Forschung*.[268] Entropy, on the other hand, can be equated with the *probability* of the state of the system in question. Thus the following equations *appear* to be valid:

information = negentropy;
entropy = lack of information = nescience.

These equations, however, should be used with the greatest caution: all that has been shown is that entropy and lack of information can be measured by *probabilities*, or interpreted as probabilities. It has not been shown that they are probabilities of the same attributes of the same system.

Let us consider one of the simplest possible cases of entropy increase, the expansion of a gas in driving a piston. Let there be a cylinder with a piston in the middle. (See Fig. 2.) Let the cylinder be kept at constant high temperature

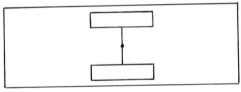

Fig. 2

by a heat bath, so that any loss of heat is at once replaced. If there is a gas on the left which drives the piston to the right, thus enabling us to obtain work (lifting a weight), then we pay for this by an increase in the entropy of the gas.

Let us assume, for simplicity's sake, that the gas consists of one molecule only, the molecule *M*. (This assumption is standard among my opponents—Szilard, or Brillouin—so it is permissible[269] to adopt it; it will, however, be critically discussed later on.) Then we *can* say that the increase of entropy corresponds to a loss of information. For before the expansion of the gas, we knew of the gas (that is, of our molecule *M*) that it was in the left half of the cylinder. After the expansion, and when it has done its work, we do not know whether it is in the left half or in the right half, because the piston is now at the far right of the cylinder: the informative content of our knowledge is clearly much reduced.[270]

I am of course ready to accept this. What I am *not* ready to accept is Szilard's more general argument by which he tries to establish the theorem that knowledge, or information, about the position of M can be converted into negentropy, and vice versa. This alleged theorem I regard, I am afraid, as sheer subjectivist nonsense.

Szilard's argument consists of an idealized thought experiment; it may be put—with some improvement, I think—as follows.[271]

Assume we *know* at the moment t_0 that the gas—that is to say, the one molecule M—is in the left half of our cylinder. Then we can at this moment slide a piston into the middle of the cylinder (for example, from a slit in the side of the cylinder)[272] and wait until the expansion of the gas, or the momentum of M, has pushed the piston to the right, lifting a weight. The energy needed was, obviously, supplied by the heat bath. The negentropy needed, and lost, was supplied by our knowledge; the knowledge was lost when the negentropy was consumed, that is, in the process of expansion and during the movement of the piston to the right; when the piston reaches the right end of the cylinder we have lost all knowledge of the part of the cylinder in which M is located. If we reverse the procedure by *pushing* back the piston, the same amount of energy will be needed (and added to the heat bath) and the same amount of negentropy must come from somewhere; for we end up with the situation from which we started, including the knowledge that the gas—or M—is in the left half of the cylinder.

Thus, Szilard suggests, knowledge and negentropy can be converted one into the other. (He supports this by an analysis—in my opinion a spurious one—of a direct measurement of the position of M. But since he merely suggests, but does not claim, that this analysis is generally valid, I will not argue against it. I think, moreover, that the presentation here given strengthens his case somewhat—at any rate it makes it more plausible.)

I now come to my criticism. It is essential for Szilard's purposes to operate with one single molecule M rather than with a gas of many molecules:[273] if we have a gas of several molecules, the knowledge of the positions of these molecules does not help us in the least (it is thus *not sufficient*), unless indeed the gas happens to be in a very negentropic state; say, with most of the molecules on the left side. But then *it will obviously be this objective negentropic state* (rather than our subjective knowledge of it) which we can exploit; and should we, without knowing it, slide in the piston at the right moment, then again we can exploit this objective state (knowledge is thus *not necessary*).

So let us first operate, as Szilard suggests, with one molecule, M. But in this case, I assert, *we do not need any knowledge* regarding the location of M: all we need is to slide our piston into the cylinder. If M happens to be on the left, the piston will be driven to the right, and we can lift the weight. And if M

is on the right, the piston will be driven to the left, and we can also lift a weight: nothing is easier than to fit the apparatus with some gear so that it lifts a weight in *either case*, without our having to know which of the two possible directions the impending movement will take.

Thus no knowledge is needed here for the balancing of the entropy increase; and Szilard's analysis turns out to be a mistake: he has offered no valid argument whatever for the intrusion of knowledge into physics.

It seems to me necessary, however, to say a little more about Szilard's thought experiment and also about mine. For the question arises: *can this particular experiment of mine be used to refute the second law of thermodynamics* (the law of entropy increase)?

I do not think so, even though I *do* believe that the second law is actually refuted by Brownian movement.[274]

The reason is this: the assumption of a gas represented by *one* molecule, M, is not only an idealization (which would not matter) but amounts to the assumption that the gas is, *objectively*, constantly in a state of minimum entropy. It is a gas which even if expanded takes up, we must assume, no appreciable subspace of the cylinder: this is why it will be found always only on one side of the piston. For example, we can turn a flap in the piston into, say, a horizontal position (see Fig. 3), so that the piston can be pushed back

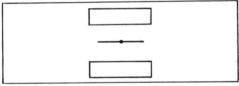

Fig. 3

without resistance to the centre, where it is turned back to its working position; if we do this, we can be quite sure that the whole gas—the whole M— is on one side of the piston only; and so it will push the piston. But assume we have in fact *two* molecules in the gas; then these may be on different sides, and the piston may not be pushed by them. This shows that *the use of one molecule M only* plays an essential role in my answer to Szilard (just as it did in Szilard's argument) and it also shows that *if* we could have a gas consisting of one powerful molecule M, it would indeed violate the second law. But this is not surprising since the second law describes an essentially statistical effect.

Let us look more closely at this second thought experiment—the case of *two molecules*. The information that both are in the left half of the cylinder would indeed enable us to close the flap and thus put the piston into its working position. But what drives the piston to the right is not our knowledge of the fact that both molecules are on the left. It is, rather, the momenta of the two molecules—or, if you like, the fact that the gas is in a state of low entropy.

Thus these particular thought experiments of mine do *not* show that a perpetual motion machine of the second order is possible;[275] but since, as we have seen, the use of *one* molecule is essential to Szilard's own thought experiment, my thought experiments show the invalidity of Szilard's argument, and thus of the attempt to base the subjectivist interpretation of the second law upon thought experiments of this type.

The edifice that has been built on Szilard's (in my opinion invalid) argument, and on similar arguments by others, will continue, I fear, to grow; and we will continue to hear that "entropy—like probability—measures the lack of information", and that machines can be driven by knowledge, like Szilard's machine. Hot air and entropy, I imagine, will continue to be produced for as long as there are some subjectivists about to provide an equivalent amount of nescience.

37. Darwinism as a Metaphysical Research Programme

I have always been extremely interested in the theory of evolution, and very ready to accept evolution as a fact. I have also been fascinated by Darwin as well as by Darwinism—though somewhat unimpressed by most of the evolutionary philosophers; with the one great exception, that is, of Samuel Butler.[276]

My *Logik der Forschung* contained a theory of the growth of knowledge by trial and error-elimination, that is, by Darwinian *selection* rather than Lamarckian *instruction*; this point (at which I hinted in that book) increased, of course, my interest in the theory of evolution. Some of the things I shall have to say spring from an attempt to utilize my methodology and its resemblance to Darwinism to throw light on Darwin's theory of evolution.

The Poverty of Historicism[277] contains my first brief attempt to deal with some epistemological questions connected with the theory of evolution. I continued to work on such problems, and I was greatly encouraged when I later found that I had come to results very similar to some of Schrödinger's.[278]

In 1961 I gave the Herbert Spencer Memorial Lecture in Oxford, under the title "Evolution and the Tree of Knowledge".[279] In this lecture I went, I believe, a little beyond Schrödinger's ideas; and I have since developed further what I regard as a slight improvement on Darwinian theory,[280] while keeping strictly within the bounds of Darwinism as opposed to Lamarckism—within natural selection, as opposed to instruction.

I tried also in my Compton lecture [1966(f)] to clarify several connected questions; for example, the question of the *scientific status* of Darwinism. It seems to me that Darwinism stands in just the same relation to Lamarckism as does

Deductivism	*to* Inductivism,
Selection	*to* Instruction by Repetition,
Critical Error Elimination	*to* Justification.

The logical untenability of the ideas on the right-hand side of this table establishes a kind of logical explanation of Darwinism: it could be described as "almost tautological"; or it could be described as applied logic—at any rate, as applied situational logic.

From this point of view the question of the scientific status of Darwinian theory—in the widest sense, the theory of trial and error-elimination—becomes an interesting one. I have come to the conclusion that Darwinism is not a testable scientific theory, but a *metaphysical research programme*—a possible framework for testable scientific theories.[281]

Yet there is more to it: I also regard Darwinism as an application of what I call "situational logic". Darwinism as situational logic can be understood as follows.

Let there be a world, a framework of limited constancy, in which there are entities of limited variability. Then some of the entities produced by variation (those which do "fit" into the conditions of the framework) will "survive", while others (those which clash with the conditions) will be eliminated.

Add to this the assumption of the existence of a special framework—a set of perhaps rare and highly individual conditions—in which there can be life, or more especially, self-reproducing but nevertheless variable bodies. Then a situation is given in which the idea of trial and error-elimination, or of Darwinism, becomes not merely applicable, but almost logically necessary. This does not mean that either the framework or the origin of life is necessary. There may be a framework in which life would be possible, but in which the trial which leads to life has not occurred, or in which all those trials which led to life were eliminated. (The latter is not a mere possibility but may happen at any moment: there is more than one way in which all life on earth might be destroyed.) What is meant is that if the life-permitting situation occurs, and if life originates, then this total situation makes the Darwinian idea one of situational logic.

To avoid any misunderstanding: it is not in every possible situation that Darwinian theory would be successful; rather, it is a very special, perhaps even a unique situation. But even in a situation without life Darwinian selection can apply to some extent: atomic nuclei which are relatively stable (in the situation in question) will tend to be more abundant than unstable ones; and the same may hold for chemical compounds.

I do not think that Darwinism can explain the origin of life. I think it quite possible that life is so extremely improbable that nothing can "explain" why it originated; for statistical explanation must operate, *in the last instance*, with very high probabilities. But if our high probabilities are merely low probabilities which have become high because of the immensity of the available time (as in Boltzmann's "explanation"; see text to n. 259 in section 35), then we must not forget that in this way it is possible to "explain" almost everything.[282] Even so, we have little enough reason to conjecture that any explanation of this sort is applicable to the origin of life. But this does not affect the view of Darwinism as situational logic, once life and its framework are assumed to constitute our "situation".

I think that there is more to say for Darwinism than that it is just one metaphysical research programme among others. Indeed, its close resemblance to situational logic may account for its great success, in spite of the almost tautological character inherent in the Darwinian formulation of it, and for the fact that so far no serious competitor has come forward.

Should the view of Darwinian theory as situational logic be acceptable, then we could explain the strange similarity between my theory of the growth of knowledge and Darwinism: both would be cases of situational logic. The new and special element in the *conscious scientific approach to knowledge*—conscious criticism of tentative conjectures, and a conscious building up of selection pressure on these conjectures (by criticizing them)—would be a consequence of the emergence of a descriptive and argumentative language; that is, of a descriptive language whose descriptions can be criticized.

The emergence of such a language would face us here again with a highly improbable and possibly unique situation—perhaps as improbable as life itself. But given this situation, the theory of the growth of exosomatic knowledge through a conscious procedure of conjecture and refutation follows "almost" logically: it becomes part of the situation as well as part of Darwinism.

As for Darwinian theory itself, I must now explain that I am using the term "Darwinism" for the modern forms of this theory, called by various names, such as "neo-Darwinism" or (by Julian Huxley) "The New Synthesis". It consists essentially of the following assumptions or conjectures, to which I will refer later.

(1) The great variety of the forms of life on earth originate from very few forms, perhaps even from a single organism: there is an evolutionary tree, an evolutionary history.

(2) There is an evolutionary theory which explains this. It consists in the main of the following hypotheses.

(a) Heredity: the offspring reproduce the parent organisms fairly faithfully.

(b) Variation: there are (perhaps among others) "small" variations. The most important of these are the "accidental" and hereditary mutations.

(c) Natural selection: there are various mechanisms by which not only the variations but the whole hereditary material is controlled by elimination. Among them are mechanisms which allow only "small" mutations to spread; "big" mutations ("hopeful monsters") are as a rule eliminated.

(d) Variability: although *variations* in some sense—the presence of different competitors—are for obvious reasons prior to selection, it may well be the case that *variability*—the scope of variation—is controlled by natural selection; for example, with respect to the frequency as well as the size of variations. A gene theory of heredity and variation may even admit special genes controlling the variability of other genes. Thus we may arrive at a hierarchy, or perhaps at even more complicated interaction structures. (We must not be afraid of complications; for they are known to be there. For example, from a selectionist point of view we are bound to assume that something like the genetic code method of controlling heredity is itself an early product of selection, and that it is a highly sophisticated product.)

Assumptions (1) and (2) are, I think, essential to Darwinism (together with some assumptions about a changing environment endowed with some regularities). The following point (3) is a reflection of mine on point (2).

(3) It will be seen that there is a close analogy between the "conservative" principles (a) and (d) and what I have called dogmatic thinking; and likewise between (b) and (c), and what I have called critical thinking.

I now wish to give some reasons why I regard Darwinism as metaphysical, and as a research programme.

It is metaphysical because it is not testable. One might think that it is. It seems to assert that, if ever on some planet we find life which satisfies conditions (a) and (b), then (c) will come into play and bring about in time a rich variety of distinct forms. Darwinism, however, does not assert as much as this. For assume that we find life on Mars consisting of exactly three species of bacteria with a genetic outfit similar to that of terrestrial species. Is Darwinism refuted? By no means. We shall say that these three species were the only forms among the many mutants which were sufficiently well adjusted to survive. And we shall say the same if there is only one species (or none). Thus Darwinism does not really *predict* the evolution of variety. It therefore cannot really *explain* it. At best, it can predict the evolution of variety under "favourable conditions". But it is hardly possible to describe in general terms what favourable conditions are—except that, in their presence, a variety of forms will emerge.

And yet I believe I have taken the theory almost at its best—almost in its most testable form. One might say that it "almost predicts" a great variety of forms of life.[283] In other fields, its predictive or explanatory power is still more disappointing. Take "adaptation". At first sight natural selection appears to explain it, and in a way it does, but it is hardly a scientific way. To say that a species now living is adapted to its environment is, in fact, almost tautological. Indeed we use the terms "adaptation" and "selection" in such a way that we can say that, if the species were not adapted, it would have been eliminated by natural selection. Similarly, if a species has been eliminated it must have been ill adapted to the conditions. Adaptation or fitness is *defined* by modern evolutionists as survival value, and can be measured by actual success in survival: there is hardly any possibility of testing a theory as feeble as this.[284]

And yet, the theory is invaluable. I do not see how, without it, our knowledge could have grown as it has done since Darwin. In trying to explain experiments with bacteria which become adapted to, say, penicillin, it is quite clear that we are greatly helped by the theory of natural selection. Although it is metaphysical, it sheds much light upon very concrete and very practical researches. It allows us to study adaptation to a new environment (such as a penicillin-infested environment) in a rational way: it suggests the existence of a mechanism of adaptation, and it allows us even to study in detail the mechanism at work. And it is the only theory so far which does all that.

This is, of course, the reason why Darwinism has been almost universally accepted. Its theory of adaptation was the first nontheistic one; and theism was worse than an open admission of failure, for it created the impression that an incontrovertible explanation had been reached.

Now to the degree that Darwinism creates the same impression, it is not so very much better than the theistic view of adaptation; it is therefore important to show that Darwinism is not a scientific theory, but metaphysical. But its value for science as a metaphysical research programme is very great, especially if it is admitted that it may be criticized and improved upon.

Let us now look a little more deeply into the research programme of Darwinism, as formulated above under points (1) and (2).

First, though (2), that is, Darwin's theory of evolution, does not have sufficient explanatory power to *explain* the terrestrial evolution of a great variety of forms of life, it certainly *suggests* it, and thereby draws attention to it. And it certainly does *predict* that *if* such an evolution takes place, it will be *gradual.*

The nontrivial *prediction of gradualness* is important, and it follows immediately from (2)(a)-(2)(c); and (a) and (b) and at least the smallness of the mutations predicted by (c) are not only experimentally well supported, but known to us in great detail.

Gradualness is thus, from a logical point of view, the central prediction of the theory. (It seems to me that it is its only prediction.) Moreover, as long as changes in the genetic base of the living forms are gradual, they are—at least "in principle"—explained by the theory; for the theory does predict the occurrence of small changes, each due to mutation. However, "explanation in principle"[285] is something very different from the type of explanation which we demand in physics. While we can explain a particular eclipse by predicting it, we cannot predict or explain any particular evolutionary change (except perhaps certain changes in the gene population *within* one species); all we can say is that if it is not a small change, there must have been some intermediate steps—an important suggestion for research: a research programme.

Moreover, the theory predicts *accidental* mutations, and thus *accidental* changes. If any "direction" is indicated by the theory, it is that throwback mutations will be comparatively frequent. Thus we should expect evolutionary sequences of the random-walk type. (A random walk is, for example, the track described by a man who at every step consults a roulette wheel to determine the direction of his next step.)

Here an important question arises. How is it that random walks do not seem to be prominent in the evolutionary tree? The question would be answered if Darwinism could explain "orthogenetic trends", as they are sometimes called; that is, sequences of evolutionary changes in the same "direction" (nonrandom walks). Various thinkers such as Schrödinger and Waddington have tried to give a Darwinian explanation of orthogenetic trends, and I also have tried to do so, for example, in my Spencer lecture.

My suggestions for an enrichment of Darwinism which might explain orthogenesis are briefly as follows.

(A) I distinguish external or environmental selection pressure from internal selection pressure. Internal selection pressure comes from the organism itself and, I conjecture, ultimately from its *preferences* (or "aims") though these may of course change in response to external changes.

(B) I assume that there are different classes of genes: those which mainly control the *anatomy*, which I will call *a*-genes; those which mainly control *behaviour*, which I will call *b*-genes. Intermediate genes (including those with mixed functions) I will here leave out of account. The *b*-genes in their turn may be similarly subdivided into *p*-genes (controlling *preferences* or "aims") and *s*-genes (controlling *skills*).

I further assume that some organisms, under external selection pressure, have developed genes, and especially *b*-genes, which allow the organism a certain variability. The *scope* of behavioural variation will somehow be controlled by the genetic *b*-structure. But since external circumstances vary, a not too rigid determination of the behaviour by the *b*-structure may turn out to be as successful as a not too rigid genetic determination of heredity, that is to say of the scope of gene variability. (See (2)(d) above.) Thus we may speak of "purely behavioural" changes of behaviour, or variations of behaviour, meaning nonhereditary changes within the genetically determined scope of variability; and contrast them with genetically fixed or determined behavioural changes.

We can now say that certain environmental changes may lead to new preferences or aims (for example, because certain types of food have disappeared). The new preferences or aims may at first appear in the form of new tentative behaviour (permitted but not fixed by *b*-genes). In this way the animal may tentatively adjust itself to the new situation without genetic change. But this *purely behavioural* and tentative change, if successful, will amount to the adoption, or discovery, of a new ecological niche. Thus it will favour individuals whose *genetic p*-structure (that is, their instinctive preferences or "aims") more or less anticipates or fixes the new behavioural pattern of preferences. This step will prove decisive; for now those changes in the skill structure (*s*-structure) will be favoured which conform to the new preferences: skills for getting the preferred food, for example.

I now suggest that *only after the s-structure has been changed will certain changes in the a-structure be favoured; that is, those changes in the anatomical structure which favour the new skills.* The internal selection pressure in these cases will be "directed", and so lead to a kind of orthogenesis.

My suggestion for this internal selection mechanism can be put schematically as follows:

$$p \rightarrow s \rightarrow a.$$

That is, the preference structure and its variations control the selection of the skill structure and its variations; and this in turn controls the selection of the purely anatomical structure and its variations.

This sequence, however, may be cyclical: the new anatomy may in its turn favour changes of preference, and so on.

What Darwin called "sexual selection" would, from the point of view expounded here, be a special case of the internal selection pressure which I have described; that is, of a cycle starting with new *preferences*. It is characteristic that internal selection pressure may lead to comparatively bad adjustment to the environment. Since Darwin this has often been noted, and the hope of explaining certain striking maladjustments (maladjustments from a survival point of view, such as the display of the peacock's tail) was one of the main motives for Darwin's introduction of his theory of "sexual selection". The original preference may have been well adjusted, but the internal selection pressure and the feedback from *a* to *p* may lead to exaggerated forms, both behavioural forms (rites) and anatomical ones.

As an example of nonsexual selection I may mention the woodpecker. A reasonable assumption seems to be that this specialization started with a *change in taste* (preferences) for new foods which led to genetic behavioural changes, and then to new skills, in accordance with the schema

$$p \rightarrow s;$$

and that the anatomical changes came last.[286] A bird undergoing anatomical changes in its beak and tongue without undergoing changes in its taste and skill can be expected to be eliminated quickly by natural selection, *but not the other way round.* (Similarly, and not less obviously: a bird with a new skill but without the new preferences which the new skill can serve would have no advantages.)

Of course there will be a lot of feedback at every stage: $p \rightarrow s$ will lead to feedback (that is, s will favour further genetic changes in the same direction as p), just as a will act back on both s and p, as indicated. It is, one may conjecture, this feedback which is mainly responsible for the more ex-aggerated forms and rituals.[287]

To explain the matter with another example, assume that in a certain situation external selection pressure favours bigness. Then the same pressure will also favour sexual *preference* for bigness: preferences can be, as in the case of food, the results of external pressure. But once there are new p-genes, a whole new cycle will be set up: it is the p-mutations which trigger off the orthogenesis.

This leads to a general principle of mutual reinforcement: we have on the one hand a primary *hierarchical control* in the preference or aim structure, over the skill structure, and further over the anatomical structure; but we also have a kind of secondary interaction or feedback between those structures. This hierarchical system of mutual reinforcement is thought to work in such a way that in most cases the control in the preference or aim structure largely dominates the lower controls throughout the entire hierarchy.[288]

Examples may illustrate both these ideas. If we distinguish genetic changes (mutations) in what I call the "preference structure" or the "aim structure" from genetic changes in the "skill structure" and genetic changes in the "anatomical structure", then as regards the interplay between the aim structure and the anatomical structure there will be the following possi-bilities:

(a) action of mutations of the aim structure on the anatomical structure: when a change takes place in taste, as in the case of the woodpecker, then the anatomical structure relevant for food acquisition may remain unchanged, in which case the species is most likely to be eliminated by natural selection (unless extraordinary skills are used); or the species may adjust itself by developing a new anatomical specialization, similar to an organ like the eye: a stronger interest in seeing (aim structure) in a species may lead to the selec-tion of a favourable mutation for an improvement of the anatomy of the eye.

(b) action of mutations of the anatomical structure on the aim structure: when the anatomy relevant for food acquisition changes, then the aim structure concerning food is in danger of becoming fixed or ossified by natural selection, which in its turn may lead to further anatomical specialization. It is similar in the case of the eye: a favourable mutation for an improvement of the anatomy will increase keenness of interest in seeing (this is similar to the opposite effect).

The theory sketched suggests something like a solution to the problem of evolution towards what may be called "higher" forms of life. Darwinism as usually presented fails to give such an explanation. It can at best explain something like an improvement in the degree of adaptation. But bacteria must be adapted at least as well as men. At any rate, they have existed longer, and there is reason to fear that they will survive men. But what may perhaps be identified with higher forms of life is a behaviouristically richer preference structure—one of greater scope; and if the preference structure should have (by and large) the leading role I ascribe to it, then evolution towards higher forms may become understandable.[289] My theory may also be presented like this: higher forms arise through the primary hierarchy of $p \rightarrow s \rightarrow a$, that is, whenever and as long as the preference structure is in the lead. Stagnation and reversion, including overspecialization, are the result of an inversion due to feedback within this primary hierarchy.

The theory also suggests a possible solution (perhaps one among many) to the problem of the separation of species. The problem is this: mutations on their own may be expected to lead only to a change in the gene pool of the species, not to a new species. Thus local separation has to be called in to explain the emergence of new species. Usually one thinks of geographic separation.[290] But I suggest that geographic separation is merely a special case of separation due to the adoption of new behaviour and consequently of a new ecological niche; if a *preference* for an ecological niche—a certain *type* of location—becomes hereditary, then this could lead to sufficient local separation for interbreeding to discontinue, even though it was still physiologically possible. Thus two species might separate while living in the same geographical region—even if this region is of the range of a mangrove tree, as seems to be the case with certain African molluscs. Sexual selection may have similar consequences.

The description of the possible genetic mechanisms behind orthogenetic trends, as outlined above, is a typical situational analysis. That is to say, only if the developed structures are of the sort that can simulate the methods of situational logic will they have any survival value.

Another suggestion concerning evolutionary theory which may be worth mentioning is connected with the idea of "survival value", and also with teleology. I think that these ideas may be made a lot clearer in terms of problem solving.

Every organism and every species is faced constantly by the threat of extinction; but this threat takes the form of concrete problems which it has to solve. Many of these concrete problems are not as such survival problems. The problem of finding a good nesting place may be a concrete problem for a pair of birds without being a survival problem for these birds, although it may turn into one for their offspring; and the species may be very little affected by the success of these particular birds in solving the problem here and now. Thus I conjecture that most problems are posed not so much by survival, but by *preferences*, especially *instinctive preferences*; and even if the instincts in question (*p*-genes) should have evolved under external selection pressure, the problems posed by them are not as a rule survival problems.

It is for reasons such as these that I think it is better to look upon organisms as problem-solving rather than as end-pursuing: as I have tried to show in "Of Clouds and Clocks",[291] we may in this way give a rational account—"in principle", of course—of *emergent evolution*.

I conjecture that the origin of *life* and the origin of *problems* coincide. This is not irrelevant to the question whether we can expect biology to turn out to be reducible to chemistry and further to physics. I think it not only possible but likely that we shall one day be able to recreate living things from nonliving ones. Although this would, of course, be extremely exciting in itself[292] (as well as from the reductionist point of view), it would not *establish* that biology can be "reduced" to physics or chemistry. For it would not establish a physical explanation of the emergence of problems—any more than our ability to produce chemical compounds by physical means establishes a physical theory of the chemical bond or even the existence of such a theory.

My position may thus be described as one that upholds a theory of *irreducibility and emergence,* and it can perhaps best be summarized in this way:

(1) I conjecture that there is no biological process which cannot be regarded as correlated in detail with a physical process or cannot be progressively analysed in physicochemical terms. But no physicochemical theory can explain the emergence of a new problem, and no physicochemical process can as such solve a *problem*. (Variational principles in physics, like the principle of least action or Fermat's principle are perhaps similar but they are not solutions to problems. Einstein's theistic method tries to use God for similar purposes.)

(2) If this conjecture is tenable it leads to a number of distinctions. We must distinguish from each other:

a physical problem = a physicist's problem;

a biological problem = a biologist's problem;

an organism's problem = a problem like: How am I to survive? How am I to propagate? How am I to change? How am I to adapt?

a man-made problem = a problem like: How do we control waste? From these distinctions we are led to the following thesis: *the problems of organisms are not physical: they are neither physical things, nor physical laws, nor physical facts. They are specific biological realities; they are "real" in the sense that their existence may be the cause of biological effects.*

(3) Assume that certain physical bodies have "solved" their problem of reproduction: that they can reproduce themselves; either exactly, or, like crystals, with minor faults which may be chemically (or even functionally) *in-essential*. They would not be "living" (in the full sense) because they cannot adjust: they need reproduction *plus* genuine variability to achieve this.

(4) The "essence" of the matter is, I propose, *problem solving*. (But we should not talk about "essence"; and the term is not used here seriously.) Life as we know it consists of physical "bodies" (more precisely, structures) which are problem solving. This the species has "learned" by natural selection, that is to say by the method of reproduction plus variation, which itself has been learned by the same method. This regress is not necessarily infinite—indeed, it may go back to some fairly definite moment of emergence.

Thus men like Butler and Bergson, though I suppose utterly wrong in their theories, were right in their intuition. Vital force does, of course, exist—but it is in its turn a product of life, *of selection*, rather than anything like the "essence" of life. It is indeed the preferences *which lead the way*. Yet the way is not Lamarckian but Darwinian.

This emphasis on *preferences* (which, being dispositions, are not so very far removed from propensities) in my theory is, clearly, a purely "objective" affair: we need not assume that these preferences are conscious. But they may become conscious; at first, I conjecture, in the form of states of well-being and of suffering (pleasure and pain).

My approach, therefore, leads almost necessarily to a research programme that asks for an explanation, in objective biological terms, of the emergence of states of consciousness.

38. World 3 or the Third World

In his *Wissenschaftslehre,* Bolzano spoke of "truths in themselves" and, more generally, of "statements in themselves", in contradistinction to those (subjective) thought processes by which a man may think, or grasp truths; or, more generally, statements, both true and false.

Bolzano's distinction between statements in themselves and subjective thought processes had always seemed to me of the greatest importance. Statements in themselves could stand in logical relations to each other: one statement could follow from another, and statements could be logically compatible or incompatible. Subjective thought processes, on the other hand, could stand in psychological relations. They could disquieten us, or comfort us, remind us of some experiences or suggest to us certain expectations; they could induce us to take some action, or to leave some planned action undone.

The two kinds of relations are utterly different. One man's thought processes cannot contradict those of another man, or his own thought processes at some other time; but the *contents* of his thoughts—that is, the statements in themselves—can of course contradict the contents of other thoughts. On the other hand, contents, or statements in themselves, cannot stand in psychological relations: *thoughts in the sense of contents* or statements in themselves and *thoughts in the sense of thought processes* belong to *two entirely different "worlds"*.

If we call the world of "things"—of physical objects—the *first world*, and the world of subjective experiences the *second world*, we may call the world of statements in themselves the *third world*. (I now[293] prefer to call it world 3; Frege sometimes called it the third realm.)

Whatever one may think about the status of these three worlds—I have in mind such "questions" as whether they "really exist" or not, and whether the third world may be in some sense "reduced" to the second, and perhaps the second to the first—it seems of the utmost importance first of all to distinguish them as sharply and clearly as possible. (If our distinctions are too sharp, this may be brought out by subsequent criticism.)

At the moment it is the distinction between the second and the third world which has to be made clear; and in this connection, we will come up against, and must face, arguments like the following.

When I think of a picture I know well, there may be a certain effort needed to recall it and "put it before my mind's eye". I can distinguish between (a) the real picture, (b) the process of imagining, which involves an effort, and (c) the more or less successful result, that is, the *imagined* picture. Clearly, the imagined picture (c) belongs exactly like (b) to the second world rather than to the third. Yet I may say things about it which are quite analogous to the logical relations between statements. For example, I may say that my image of the picture at time t_1 is incompatible with my image at time t_2 and even perhaps with a *statement* such as: "In the picture only the head and shoulders of the painted man are visible." Moreover, the imagined picture may be said to be the content of the process of imagining. All this is analogous to the thought content and the process of thinking. But who would deny that the image belongs to the second world; that it is mental, and indeed part of the process of imagining?

This argument seems to me valid and quite important: I agree that within the thinking process some parts may be distinguished that may perhaps be described as its content (or the thought, or the third-world object) *as grasped*. But it is precisely for this reason that I find it important to distinguish between the mental process and the thought content (as Frege called it) *in its logical or third-world sense*.

I personally have only vague visual imaginings: it is usually only with difficulty that I can recall a clear, detailed, and vivid picture before my mind. (It is different with music.) Rather, I think in terms of schemata, of dispositions to follow up a certain "line" of thought, and very often in terms of words, especially when I am about to write down some ideas. And I often find myself mistaken in the belief that I "have got it", that I have grasped a thought clearly: when trying to write it down I may find that I have not got it yet. This "it", this something which I may not have got, which I cannot be quite certain that I *have* got before I have written it down, or at any rate formulated it in language so clearly *that I can look at it critically from various sides*, this "it" is the thought in the objective sense, the third-world object which I am trying to grasp.

The decisive thing seems to me that we can put objective thoughts—that is, theories—before us in such a way that we can criticize them, argue them. To do so, we must formulate them in some more or less permanent (especially linguistic) form. A written form will be preferable to a spoken form, and printing may be better still. And it is significant that we can distinguish between the criticism of a mere *formulation* of a thought—a thought can be formulated rather well, or not so well—and the logical aspects of the thought in itself: its truth, its truthlikeness in comparison with some of its competitors, its compatibility with certain other theories.

Once I had arrived at this stage I found that I had to people my third world with inmates other than statements, and I brought in, in addition to statements or theories, also problems and arguments, especially critical arguments. For theories should be discussed always with an eye to the *problems* which they might solve.

I regard books and journals and letters as typically third-world objects, especially if they develop and discuss a theory. Of course the physical shape of the book is insignificant, and even physical nonexistence does not detract from third-world existence; think of all the "lost" books, their influence, and the search for them. And frequently even the formulation of an argument does not matter greatly. What do matter are *contents*, in the logical sense.

It is clear that everybody interested in science must be interested in third-world objects. A physical scientist, to start with, may be interested mainly in first-world objects—say, crystals and X-rays. But very soon he must realize how much depends on our interpretation of the facts, that is, on our theories, and so on third-world objects. Similarly a historian of science, or a philosopher interested in science, must be largely a student of third-world objects. Admittedly, he may also be interested in the relation between third-world theories and second-world thought processes; but the latter will interest him mainly in their relation to theories, that is, to objects belonging to the third world.

What is the ontological status of the third-world objects? Or, to use less high-sounding language, are problems, theories, and arguments "real", like tables and chairs? When some forty-four years ago Heinrich Gomperz warned me that I was, potentially, not only a realist in the sense of believing in the reality of tables and chairs but also in the sense of Plato, who believed in the reality of Forms or Ideas—of concepts, and their meanings or essences—I did not like the suggestion, and I still do not include the left-hand side of the table of ideas (see section 7 above) among the denizens of my third world. But I have become a realist with respect to the third world of *problems, theories,* and *critical arguments*.

Bolzano was, I think, doubtful about the ontological status of his statements in themselves, and Frege, it seems, was an idealist, or very nearly so. I too was, like Bolzano, doubtful for a long time, and I did not publish anything about the third world until I arrived at the conclusion that its inmates were real; indeed, more or less as real as tables and chairs.

Nobody will doubt this as far as books are concerned, and other written matter. They are, like tables and chairs, made by us, though not in order to be sat upon, but in order to be read.

This seems easy enough; but what about the theories in themselves? I agree that they are not quite as "real" as tables and chairs. I am prepared to accept something like a materialist starting point according to which, in the first place, only physical things like tables and chairs, stones and oranges, are to be called "real". But this is only a starting point: in the second place we are almost bound to extend the range of the term radically: gases and electric currents may kill us: should we not call them real? The field of a magnet may be made visible by iron filings. And who can doubt, with television such a familiar phenomenon, that some sort of reality has to be attributed to Hertz's (or Maxwell's) waves?

Should we call the pictures we see on television "real"? I think we should, for we can take photographs of them with the help of various cameras and they will agree, like independent witnesses.[294] But television pictures are the result of a process by which the set decodes highly complicated and "abstract" messages transmitted with the help of waves; and so we should, I think, call these "abstract" coded messages "real". They can be decoded, and the result of the decoding is "real".

We are now perhaps no longer quite so very far removed from the theory in itself—the abstract message coded in a book, say, and decoded by ourselves when we read the book. However, a more general argument may be needed.

All the examples given have one thing in common. We seem to be ready to call real anything which can *act upon physical things* such as tables and chairs (and photographic film, we may add), and which can be acted upon by physical things.[295] But our world of physical things has been greatly changed by theories, like those of Maxwell and Hertz; that is by third-world objects. Thus these objects should be called "real".

Two objections should be made: (1) Our physical world has been changed not by the theories in themselves but, rather, by their physical incorporation in books, and elsewhere; and books belong to the first world. (2) It has been changed not by the theories in themselves, but by our understanding of them, our grasp of them; that is, by mental states, by second-world objects.

I admit both objections, but I reply to (1) that the change was brought about not by physical aspects of the books but solely by the fact that they somehow "carried" a message, an informative content, a theory in itself. In response to (2), which I regard as a far more important objection, I admit even that *it is solely through the second world as an intermediary between the first and the third that the first world and the third world can interact.*

This is an important point, as will be seen when I turn to the body-mind problem. It means that the first world and the second world can interact, and also the second and the third; but the first and the third cannot interact directly, without some mediating interaction with the second world. Thus although only the second world can act immediately upon the first, the third world can act upon the first in an indirect way, owing to its influence upon the second.

In fact, the "incorporation" of a theory in a book—and thus in a physical object—is an example of this. To be read, the book needs the intervention of a human mind, of the second world. But it also needs the theory in itself. For example, I may make a mistake: my mind may fail to grasp the theory correctly. But there is always the theory in itself, and somebody else may grasp it and correct me. It may easily be not a case of a difference of opinion, but a case of a real, unmistakable mistake—a failure to understand the theory in itself. And this may even happen to the originator of the theory. (It has happened more than once, even to Einstein.)[296]

I have touched here on an aspect which I have described in some of my papers on these and related subjects as the (partial) *autonomy of the third world*.[297]

By this I mean that although we may invent a theory, there may be (and in a good theory, there always will be) *unintended and unforeseen consequences*. For example, men may have invented the natural numbers or, say, the method of proceeding without end in the series of natural numbers. But the existence of prime numbers (and of Euclid's theorem that there is no greatest prime) is something we *discover*. It is there, and we cannot change it. It is an unintended and unforeseen consequence of that invention of ours. And it is a necessary consequence: we cannot get around it. Things like prime numbers, or square numbers, and many others are thus "produced" by the third world itself, without further help from us. This is why I call it "autonomous".

Somewhat related to the problem of autonomy but, I think, less important, is the problem of the timelessness of the third world. If an unambiguously formulated statement is true now, then it is true for ever, and always was true: truth is timeless (and so is falsity). Logical relations such as contradictoriness or compatibility are also timeless, and even more obviously so.

It would be easy for this reason to regard the whole third world as timeless, as Plato suggested of his world of Forms or Ideas. We only need to assume that we never invent a theory but always discover it. Thus we would have a timeless third world, existing before life emerged and after all life will have disappeared, a world of which men discover some little bits.

This is a possible view; but I don't like it. Not only does it fail to solve the problem of the ontological status of the third world, but it makes this problem insoluble from a rational point of view. For although it allows us to "discover" third-world objects, it fails to explain whether, in discovering these objects, we interact with them, or whether they only act upon us; and how they can act upon us—especially if we cannot act upon them. It leads, I think, to a Platonic or neo-Platonic intuitionism, and to a host of difficulties. For it is based, I think, upon the misunderstanding that the status of the *logical relations between* third-world objects must be shared by these objects.

I propose a different view—one which, I have found, is surprisingly fruitful. *I regard the third world as being essentially the product of the human mind.* It is we who create third-world objects. That these objects have their own inherent or autonomous laws which create unintended and unforeseeable consequences is only an instance (though a very interesting one) of a more general rule, the rule that all our actions have such consequences.

Thus I look at the third world as a product of human activity, and as one whose repercussions on us are as great as, or greater than, those of our physical environment. There is a kind of feedback in all human activities: in acting we always act, indirectly, upon ourselves.

More precisely, I regard the third world of problems, theories, and critical arguments as one of the results of the evolution of human language, and as acting back on this evolution.

This is perfectly compatible with the timelessness of truth and of logical relations; and it makes the reality of the third world understandable. It is as real as other human products, as real as a coding system—a language; as real as (or perhaps even more real than) a social institution, such as a university or a police force.

And the third world has a history. It is the history of our ideas; not only a history of their discovery, but also a history of how we invented them: how we made them, and how they reacted upon us, and how we reacted to these products of our own making.

This way of looking at the third world allows us also to bring it within the scope of an evolutionary theory which views man as an animal. There are animal products (such as nests) which we may regard as forerunners of the human third world.

And ultimately it suggests a generalization in another direction. We may regard the world of problems, theories, and critical arguments as a special case, as the third world in the narrow sense, or the logical or intellectual province of the third world; and we may include in the third world in a more general sense all the products of the human mind, such as tools, institutions, and works of art.

39. The Body-Mind Problem and the Third World

I think that I was always a Cartesian dualist (although I never thought that we should talk about "substances"[298]); and if not a dualist, I was certainly more inclined to pluralism than to monism. I think it silly to deny the existence of mental experiences or mental states or states of consciousness; or to deny that mental states are as a rule closely related to states of the body, especially physiological states. But it also seems clear that mental states are products of the evolution of life, and that little can be gained by linking them to physics rather than to biology.[299]

My earliest encounter with the body-mind problem made me feel, for many years, that it was a hopeless problem. Psychology, *qua* science of the self and its experiences, was almost nonexistent, *pace* Freud. Watson's behaviourism was a very understandable reaction to this state of affairs, and it had some methodological advantages—like so many other theories which deny what they cannot explain. As a philosophical thesis it was clearly wrong, even though irrefutable. That we do experience joy and sadness, hope and fear, and that we do think, in words as well as by means of schemata; that we can read a book with more or less interest and attention—all this seemed to me obviously true, though easily denied; and extremely important, though obviously nondemonstrable. It also seemed to me quite obvious that we are embodied selves or minds. *But how can the relation between our bodies (or physiological states) and our minds (or mental states) be rationally understood?* This question seemed to formulate the body-mind problem; and as far as I could see there was no hope of doing anything to bring it nearer to a solution.

In Schlick's *Erkenntnislehre* I found a discussion of the body-mind relation—the first since those of Spinoza and Leibniz really to fascinate me. It was beautifully clear, and it was worked out in considerable detail. It has been brilliantly discussed, and further developed, by Herbert Feigl. But although I found this theory fascinating, it did not satisfy me; and for many years I continued to think that nothing could be done about this problem, except perhaps by way of criticism; for example, by criticizing the views of those who thought that the whole problem was due to some "linguistic muddle".[300] (No doubt we sometimes create problems ourselves, through being muddled in speaking about the world; but why should not the world itself harbour some really difficult secrets, perhaps even insoluble ones? Riddles *may* exist;[301] and I think they do.)

I thought, however, that language does play a role: that although *consciousness* may be conjectured to be prelinguistic, what I call *full consciousness of self* may be conjectured to be specifically human, and to depend on language. Yet this idea seemed to me of little importance until, as described in the previous section, I had developed certain views of Bolzano's (and, as I later found, also of Frege's) into a theory of what I called the "third world". It was only then that it dawned on me that the body-mind problem could be completely transformed if we call the theory of the third world to our aid.[302] For it can help us to develop at least the rudiments of an *objective theory*—a biological theory—not only of subjective states of consciousness but also of selves.

Thus whatever new I might have to say on the body-mind problem is connected with my views on the third world.

It appears that the body-mind problem is still usually seen and discussed in terms of the various possible relationships (identity, parallelism, interaction) between states of consciousness and bodily states. As I am an interactionist myself, I think that a part of the problem may perhaps be discussed in this manner, but I am as doubtful as ever whether this discussion is worthwhile. In its stead I propose a biological and even evolutionist approach to the problem.

As I explained in section 37, I do not think highly of the theoretical or explanatory power of the theory of evolution. But I think that an evolutionist approach to biological problems is inescapable, and also that in a problem situation so desperate we must clutch gratefully even at a straw. So I propose, to start with, that we regard the human mind quite naively as if it were a highly developed bodily organ, and that we ask ourselves, as we might with respect to a sense organ, what it contributes to the household of the organism.

To this question there is at hand a typical answer which I propose to dismiss. It is that our consciousness enables us to see, or perceive, things. I dismiss this answer because for such purposes we have eyes and other sense organs. It is, I think, thanks to the observationalist approach to knowledge that consciousness is so widely identified with seeing or perceiving.

I propose instead that we regard the human mind first of all as *an organ that produces objects of the human third world* (in the more general sense) and interacts with them. Thus I propose that we look upon the human mind, essentially, as the producer of human language, for which our basic aptitudes (as I have explained earlier[303]) are inborn; and as the producer of theories, of critical arguments, and many other things such as mistakes, myths, stories, witticisms, tools, and works of art.

It may perhaps be difficult to bring order into this medley, and perhaps not worth our while; but it is not difficult to offer a guess as to what came first. I propose that it was language, and that language is about the only exosomatic tool whose use is inborn or, rather, genetically based, in man.

This conjecture seems to me to have some explanatory power, even though it is of course difficult to test. I suggest that the emergence of descriptive language is at the root of the human power of imagination, of human inventiveness, and therefore of the emergence of the third world. For we may assume that the first (and almost human) function of descriptive language as a tool was to serve exclusively for *true* description, *true* reports. But then came the point when language could be used for lies, for "storytelling". This seems to me the decisive step, the step that made language truly descriptive and truly human. It led, I suggest, to storytelling of an explanatory kind, to myth making; to the critical scrutiny of reports and descriptions, and thus to science; to imaginative fiction and, I suggest, to art—to storytelling in the form of pictures.

However this may be, the physiological basis of the human mind, if I am right, might be looked for in the speech centre; and it may not be an accident that there seems to be only *one* centre of speech control in the two hemispheres of the brain; it may be the highest in the hierarchy of control centres.[304] (I am here consciously trying to revive Descartes's problem of the seat of consciousness, and even part of the argument which led him to the view that it must be the pineal gland; the theory might perhaps become testable in experiments with the split brain.)[305]

I suggest that we distinguish states of "consciousness" in general from those highly organized states which seem to be characteristic of the human mind, the human second world, the human self. I think animals are conscious. (This conjecture may become testable if we find, with the help of the electroencephalograph, typical dreamlike sleeping in animals as well as in men.) But I also conjecture that animals do not have selves. About the "full consciousness of self", as it may be called, my central suggestion is that, just as the third world is a product of the second, so the specifically human second world, the full consciousness of self, is a feedback product of *theory making*.

Consciousness as such seems to emerge and become organized before descriptive language does. Anyway, personalities emerge among animals, and a kind of knowledge or understanding of other personalities, especially in social animals. (Dogs may even develop an intuitive understanding of human personalities.) But the full consciousness of self, I suggest, can emerge only through language: only after our knowledge of other persons has developed, and only after we have become conscious of our bodies' extension in space and, especially, in time; only after we have become clear, in the abstract, about the regular interruptions to our consciousness in sleep, and developed a *theory* of the continuity of our bodies—and thus of our selves—during sleep.

Thus the body-mind problem divides into at least two quite distinct problems: the problem of the very close relationship between physiological states and certain states of consciousness, and the very different problem of the emergence of the self, and its relation to its body. It is the problem of the emergence of the self which, I suggest, can be solved only by taking language and the objects of the third world into account, and the self's dependence on them. The consciousness of self involves, among other things, a distinction, however vague, between living and nonliving bodies, and thereby a rudimentary theory of the main characteristics of life; also involved somehow is a distinction between bodies endowed with consciousness and others not so endowed. It involves too the projection of the self into the future: the more or less conscious expectation of the child of growing up in time into an adult; and a consciousness of having existed for some time in the past. Thus it involves a theory of birth and perhaps even of death.

All this becomes possible only through a highly developed descriptive language—a language which has not only led to the production of a third world, but which has been modified through feedback from the third world.

But the body-mind problem seems to me not exhausted by these two subproblems, the problem of states of consciousness, and the problem of the self. Although full consciousness of self is, *in dispositional form*, always present in adults, these dispositions are not always activated. On the contrary, we are often in an intensely active mental state and, at the same time, completely forgetful of ourselves, though always able to reflect on ourselves at a moment's notice.

This state of intense mental activity which is not self-conscious is reached, especially, in intellectual or artistic work: in trying to understand a problem, or a theory; or in enjoying an absorbing work of fiction, or perhaps in playing the piano or playing a game of chess.

In such states, we may forget where we are—always an indication that we have forgotten ourselves. What our mind is engaged in, with the utmost concentration, is the attempt to grasp a third-world object, or to produce it.

I think that this is a far more interesting and characteristic state of mind than the perception of a round patch of orange colour. And I think it important that, although only the human mind achieves it, we find similar states of concentration in hunting animals, for example, or in animals that try to escape from danger. The conjecture offers itself that it is in these stages of high concentration upon a task, or a problem, that both animal and human minds best serve their biological purposes. In more idle moments of consciousness, the mental organ may be, indeed, just idling, resting, recuperating, or, in a word, preparing itself, charging itself up, for the period of concentration. (No wonder that in self-observation we only too often catch ourselves idling rather than, say, thinking intensively.)

Now it seems clear to me that the achievements of the mind require an organ such as this, with its peculiar powers of concentration on a problem, with its linguistic powers, its powers of anticipation, inventiveness, and imagination; and with its powers of tentative acceptance and rejection. There does not seem to be a physical organ which can do all this: it seems that something different, like consciousness, was needed, and had to be used as a *part* of the building material for the mind. No doubt, only as a part: many mental activities are unconscious; much is dispositional, and much is just physiological. But much of what is physiological and "automatic" (in playing the piano, say, or driving a car) at a certain period of time has *previously* been done by us with that conscious concentration which is so characteristic of the discovering mind—the mind faced with a difficult problem. Thus everything speaks in favour of the indispensability of the mind in the household of the higher organisms, and also for the need to let solved problems and "learned" situations sink back into the body, presumably to free the mind for new tasks.

A theory of this kind is clearly interactionist: there is interaction between the various organs of the body, and also between these organs and the mind. But beyond this I think that the interaction with the third world always needs the mind in its relevant stages—although as the examples of learning to speak, to read, and to write show, a large part of the more mechanical work of coding and decoding can be taken over by the physiological system, which does similar work in the case of the sense organs.

It seems to me that the objectivist and biological approach sketched here allows us to see the body-mind problem in a new light. It appears too that it blends extremely well with some new work in the field of animal psychology, especially with the work of Konrad Lorenz. And there is also, it seems to me, a close kinship with some of D. T. Campbell's ideas on evolutionary epistemology and with some ideas of Schrödinger's.

40. The Place of Values in a World of Facts

The title of this section is close to that of a book by a great psychologist and a great man, Wolfgang Köhler.[306] I found his formulation of the problem in the first chapter of his book not only admirably put but very moving; and I think it will move not merely those who remember the times in which the book was written.[307] Yet I was disappointed by Köhler's own solution of his problem, "What is the place of values in the world of facts; and how could they make their entry into this world of facts?". I feel unconvinced by his thesis that *Gestalt* psychology can make an important contribution to the solution of this problem.

Köhler explains very clearly why few scientists, and few philosophers with scientific training, care to write about values. The reason is simply that so much of the talk about values is just hot air. So many of us fear that we too would only produce hot air or, if not that, something not easily distinguished from it. To me these fears seem to be well founded, in spite of Köhler's efforts to convince us that we should be bold and run the risk. At least in the field of ethical *theory* (I do not include the Sermon on the Mount) with its almost infinite literature, I cannot recall having read anything good and striking except Plato's *Apology of Socrates* (in which ethical theory plays a subsidiary role), some of Kant's works, especially his *Foundations of the Metaphysic of Morals* (which is not too successful) and Friedrich Schiller's elegiac couplets which wittily criticize Kant's rigorism.[308] Perhaps I might add to this list Schopenhauer's *Two Fundamental Problems of Ethics*. Except Plato's *Apology*, and Schiller's charming *reductio* of Kant, none of these comes anywhere near to achieving its aim.

I shall therefore say nothing more than that values emerge together with problems; that values could not exist without problems; and that neither values nor problems can be derived or otherwise obtained from facts, though they often pertain to facts or are connected with facts. As far as problems are concerned we may, looking at some person (or some animal or plant), conjecture that he (or it) is trying to solve a certain problem, even though he (or it) may be quite unaware of that problem. Or else, a problem may have been described and discovered, critically or objectively, in its relations, say, to some other problem, or to some attempted solutions. In the first case only our historical conjecture belongs to the third world; in the second case the problem itself may be regarded as one of the inmates of the third world. It is like this with values. A thing, or an idea, or a theory, or an approach, may be conjectured to be objectively valuable in being of help in solving a problem, or as a solution of a problem, whether or not its value is consciously appreciated by those struggling to solve that problem. But if our conjecture is formulated and submitted to discussion, it will belong to the third world. Or else, a value (relative to a certain problem) may be created or discovered, and discussed, in its relations to other values and to other problems; in this quite different case it too may become an inmate of the third world.

Thus if we are right in assuming that once upon a time there was a physical world devoid of life, this world would have been, I think, a world without problems and thus without values. It has often been suggested that values enter the world only with consciousness. This is not my view. I think that values enter the world with life, and if there is life without consciousness (as I think there may well be, even in animals, for there appears to be such a thing as dreamless sleep) then, I suggest, there would also be objective values (as in the first case mentioned) even without consciousness.

There are thus two sorts of values: values created by life, by unconscious problems, and values created by the human mind, on the basis of previous solutions, in the attempt to solve problems which may be worse or better understood.

This is the place I see for values in a world of facts. It is a place in the third world of historically emergent problems and traditions, and this is part of the world of facts—though not of first-world facts, but of facts partly produced by the human mind. The world of values transcends the valueless world of facts—the world of brute facts, as it were.

The innermost nucleus of the third world, as I see it, is the world of problems, theories, and criticism. This nucleus is not a place of values; but it is dominated by a value: the value of *objective truth and its growth*.[309] In a sense we can say that throughout this human intellectual third world this value remains the highest value of all, though we must admit other values into our third world. For with every value proposed arises the problem: is it *true* that this is a value? And, is it *true* that it has its proper standing in the hierarchy of values: is it true that kindness is a higher value than justice, or even comparable with justice? (Thus I am utterly opposed to those who fear truth—who think it was a sin to eat from the tree of knowledge.)

We have generalized the idea of a human third world so that the third world in the wider sense comprises not only the products of our intellect, together with the unintended consequences which emerge from them, but also the products of our mind in a much wider sense, for example, the products of our imagination. Even theories, products of our intellect, result from the criticism of myths, which are products of our imagination: they would not be possible without myths; nor would criticism be possible without the discovery of the distinction between fact and fiction, or truth and falsity. This is why myths or fictions should not be excluded from the third world. So we are led to include art and, in fact, all human products into which we have injected some of our ideas, and which incorporate the result of criticism, in a sense wider than the merely intellectual one. We ourselves may be included, as we have absorbed and criticized the ideas of our predecessors, and tried to form ourselves; and so may our children and pupils, our traditions and institutions, our ways of life, our purposes, and our aims.

It is one of the grave mistakes of contemporary philosophy not to recognise that these things—our children—though they are products of our minds, and though they bear upon our subjective experiences—also have an objective side. One way of life may be incompatible with another way of life in almost the same sense in which a theory may be logically incompatible with another. These incompatibilities are there, objectively, even if we are unaware of them. And so our purposes and our aims, like our theories, may compete, and may be discussed critically.

Yet the subjective approach, especially the subjective theory of knowledge, looks upon third-world objects—even those in the narrower sense, such as problems, theories, and critical arguments—as if they were mere utterances or expressions of the knowing subject. This approach is closely similar to the expressionist theory of art. Generally, it regards a man's work only or mainly as the expression of his inner state; and it looks upon self-expression as an aim.

I am trying to replace this view of the relation of a man to his work by a very different one. Admitting that the third world originates with us, I stress its considerable autonomy, and its immeasurable repercussions on us. Our minds, our selves, cannot exist without it; they are anchored in the third world. We owe to the interaction with the third world our rationality, the practice of critical and self-critical thinking and acting. We owe to it our mental growth. And we owe to it our relation to our task, to our work, and its repercussions upon ourselves.

The expressionist view is that our talents, our gifts, and perhaps our upbringing, and thus "our whole personality", determine what we do. The result is good or bad, according to whether or not we are gifted or interesting personalities.

In opposition to this I suggest that everything depends upon the give-and-take between ourselves and our task, our work, our problems, our third world; upon the repercussion upon us of this world; upon feedback, which can be amplified by our criticism of what we have done. It is through the attempt to see objectively the work we have done—that is to see it critically—and to do it better, through the interaction between our actions and their objective results, that we can transcend our talents, and ourselves.

As with our children, so with our theories, and ultimately with all the work we do: our products become largely independent of their makers. We may gain more knowledge from our children or our theories than we ever imparted to them. This is how we can lift ourselves out of the morass of our ignorance; and how we can all contribute to the third world.

If I am right in my conjecture that we grow, and become ourselves, only in interaction with the third world, then the fact that we can all contribute to it, if only a little, can give comfort to everyone who feels that in struggling with ideas he has found more happiness than he could ever deserve.

Karl Popper

PENN, BUCKINGHAMSHIRE

NOTES

[1] The allusion is to Kierkegaard's conversation with Christian VIII in which the king asked him for his views on how a king should conduct himself. Kierkegaard said such things as: "First, it would be a good thing for the King to be ugly." (Christian VIII was very good-looking.) "Then he should be deaf and blind, or at least behave as if he were, for this solves many difficulties. . . . And then, he must not say much, but must have a little standard speech that can be used on all occasions, a speech therefore without content." (Francis Joseph used to say: "It was very nice, and it pleased me very much."—"Es war sehr schön, es hat mich sehr gefreut.")

[2] The case arose from my work with children. One of the boys for whom I was responsible had fallen from a climbing frame and had suffered a fractured skull. I was acquitted because I could prove that I had demanded for months that the authorities should remove the climbing frame, which I regarded as dangerous. (The authorities had tried to put the blame on me; a procedure about which the judge had some strong words to say.)

[3] See Otto Weininger, *Geschlecht und Charakter* (Vienna: Braumüller, 1903), p. 176: "All blockheads, from Bacon to Fritz Mauthner, have been critics of language." (Weininger adds that he should ask Bacon to forgive him for associating him in this way with Mauthner.) Compare this with *Tractatus*, 4.0031.

[4] Cp. n. 57 to Chap. 12 of *The Open Society and Its Enemies* [1945(c)], p. 297; [1950(a)], p. 653; [1962(c)], [1963(l)], and later editions, p. 312. (*The Open Society and Its Enemies* will hereinafter be cited as *O.S.*) Notations like these, in square brackets, refer to the list of my publications at the end of the volume.

[5] Roger Martin du Gard, *L'Été 1914*; English translation by Stuart Gilbert, *Summer 1914* (London: John Lane, The Bodley Head, 1940).

[6] The problem has recently reached a new stage through Abraham Robinson's work on the infinitely small; see Abraham Robinson, *Non-Standard Analysis* (Amsterdam: North-Holland Publishing Company, 1966).

[7] The term *"essentialism"* (widely used now) and especially its application to *definitions* (*"essentialist definitions"*) were, to my knowledge, first introduced in section 10 of *The Poverty of Historicism* [1944(a)]; see esp. pp. 94-97; [1957(g)] and later editions, pp. 27-30 (*The Poverty of Historicism* will hereinafter be cited as *The Poverty*); and in my *O.S.*, Vol. I [1945(b)], pp. 24-27; and Vol. II [1945(c)], pp. 8-20, 274-86; [1950(a)], pp. 206-18, 621-38; [1962(c)], [1963(l)], and later editions: Vol. I, pp. 29-32; Vol. II, pp. 9-21, 287-301. There is a reference on p. 202 of Richard Robinson's *Definition* (Oxford: Oxford University Press, 1950), to the 1945 edition of my *O.S.* [1945(c)], Vol. II, pp. 9-20; and what he says, for example, on pp. 153-57 (cp. the "utterances" on p. 158), and also on pp. 162-65, is in some respects very similar to what I say in the pages of my book to which he refers (though his remark on p. 71 about Einstein and simultaneity does not agree with what I say in [1945(c)], pp. 18f., 108f.; [1950(a)], pp. 216f., 406; [1962(c)] and [1963(l)], Vol. II, pp. 20, 220). Compare also Paul Edwards, ed., *The Encyclopedia of Philosophy* (New York: Macmillan Company and Free Press, 1967; London: Collier Macmillan, 1967), Vol. II, pp. 314-17. *"Essentialism"* is there discussed at length under the main entry *Definition* (reference is made in the Bibliography to Robinson).

[7a] (Added in proofs.) I have recently made a change in terminology from the first, second and third worlds to world 1, world 2, and world 3, upon the suggestion of Sir John Eccles. For my older terminology, see [1968(r)] and [1968(s)]; for Sir John's suggestion, see his *Facing Reality* (New York, Heidelberg and Berlin: Springer-Verlag, 1970). The suggestion came too late to be incorporated in the text of the present book except in one or two places. See also n. 293 below.

[8] Annual Philosophical Lecture, British Academy, 1960 [1960(d)], [1961(f)]; republished in *Conjectures and Refutations* [1963(a)] (*Conjectures and Refutations* will hereinafter be cited as *C.&R.*); see esp. pp. 19 f. and also p. 349 of my "Epistemology Without a Knowing Subject" [1968(s)], now Chap. 3 of my [1972(a)]. (The table reproduced here is a slight modification of the original one.)

[9] Cp. the 3d ed. of *C.&R.* [1969(h)], p. 28, the newly inserted point 9. (Point 9 of the earlier editions is now numbered 10.)

[10] Not even Gottlob Frege states it quite explicitly, though this doctrine is certainly implicit in his "Sinn und Bedeutung", and he even produces there arguments in its support. Cp. Peter Geach and Max Black, eds., *Translations from the Philosophical Writings of Gottlob Frege* (Oxford: Blackwell, 1952), pp. 56-78.

[11] Cp. my article "Quantum Mechanics without 'The Observer' " [1967(k)]; see esp. pp. 11-15, where the present problem is discussed. (This particular equivalence, incidentally, is questioned there.) The paper has now been reprinted, with minor alterations, in [1974(a)], where it is Chap. 3.

[12] One could hardly write in a prose translation (Parmenides, fragments 14-15):
    Bright in the night with an alien light round the earth she is erring,
    Always she wistfully looks round for the rays of the sun.

[13] Gottlob Frege suggests—mistakenly, I think—in "Der Gedanke", *Beiträg zur Philos. d. deutschen Idealismus*, **1** (1918-19), 58-77 (excellently translated by A. M. and Marcelle Quinton as "The Thought: A Logical Enquiry", *Mind*, n. s. **65** [1956], 289-311), that *only* of the emotional aspects of speech is a "perfect (*vollkommene*) translation almost impossible" (p. 63; p. 295 of the translation), and that "The more strictly scientific a presentation, the more easily is it translated" (*ibid.*). Ironically enough, Frege continues to say quite correctly that it makes no difference to any thought content which of the four German synonyms for "horse" (*Pferd, Ross, Gaul, Mähre*—they are different only in emotional content: *Mähre*, in particular, *need not* be a female horse) is used in any formulation. Yet this very simple and unemotional thought of Frege's is, it appears, untranslatable into the English language, since English does not seem to have three good synonyms for "horse". The translator would, therefore, have to become a commentator by finding some common word which has three good synonyms—preferably with strikingly different emotional or poetic associations.

[14] Cp., for example, section 37 of my *Logik der Forschung*, [1934(b)], [1966(e)] and later editions; and also of *The Logic of Scientific Discovery*, [1959(a)] and later editions. The example I had in mind was gravitational redshift. (*Logik der Forschung* will hereinafter be cited as *L.d.F.; The Logic of Scientific Discovery* as *L.Sc.D.*)

[15] For this idea, and the quotation, see section 6 of my *L.d.F.* [1934(b)], p. 13; [1966(e)], p. 15; "Sie sagen um so mehr, je mehr sie verbieten."; *L.Sc.D.* [1959(a)] and later editions, p. 41: "The more they prohibit the more they say." The idea was adopted by Rudolf Carnap in section 23 of his *Introduction to Semantics* (Cambridge, Mass.: Harvard University Press, 1942); see esp. p. 151. There Carnap attributes this idea to Wittgenstein "due to an error of memory", as he himself puts it in section 73 of his *Logical Foundations of Probability* (Chicago: University of Chicago Press, 1950), p. 406 (where he attributes it to me). Carnap writes there: "The assertive power of a sentence consists in its excluding certain possible cases". I should now stress that these "cases" are, in science, *theories* (*hypotheses*) *of a higher or a lower degree of generality*. (Even what I called "basic statements" in *L.Sc.D.* are, as I stressed there, *hypotheses*, though of a low degree of generality.)

[16] The subset of the informative content which consists of basic statements (empirical statements) I called in *L.Sc.D.* the class of the theory's "potential falsifiers", or its "empirical content".

[17] For *non-a* belongs to the informative content of *a*, and *a* to the informative content of *non-a*, but *a* does not belong to its own informative content (unless it is a contradiction).

[18] The proof (which in the particular form given here was shown to me by David Miller) is quite straightforward. For the statement *"b or t or both"* follows from *"a or t or both"* if and only if it follows from *a*; that is, if and only if the theory *t* follows from *"a and non-b"*. But because *a* and *b* contradict one another (by hypothesis), this last statement says the same as *a*. Thus *"b or t or both"* follows from *"a or t or both"* if and only if *t* follows from *a*; and this, by assumption, it does not.

[19] J. W. N. Watkins, *Hobbes's System of Ideas* (London: Hutchinson, 1965), pp. 22 f.

[20] See my paper [1957(i)], [1969(k)], now Chap. 5 of [1972(a)]; and also [1963(a)], p. 62, n. 28.

[21] Gottlob Frege, *Grundgesetze der Arithmetik* (Jena: H. Pohle, 1903), Vol. II, section 56.

[22] Clifford A. Truesdell, "Foundations of Continuum Mechanics", in *Delaware Seminar in the Foundations of Physics*, ed. by Mario Bunge (Berlin, Heidelberg, New York: Springer-Verlag, 1967), pp. 35-48; see esp. p. 37.

[23] Gottlob Frege, "Uber Begriff und Gegenstand", *Vierteljahrsschrift f. wissenschaftliche Philos.*, **16** (1892), 192-205. Cp. p. 43 of Geach and Black, eds., *Philosophical Writings of Gottlob Frege*, pp. 42-55 (see n. 10 above).

[24] See n. *1 to section 4; [1959(a)] and later editions, p. 35; [1966(e)] and later editions, p. 9; and also my two Prefaces.

[25] The problems dealt with here are discussed (though perhaps not fully enough) in the various Prefaces to *L.d.F.* and *L.Sc.D.* It is perhaps of some interest that the fact that I criticized there in some detail the whole approach of language analysis was not even mentioned when this book was reviewed in *Mind* (see also my reply to this review in n. 243 in section 33, below), though this journal was an obvious place in which to mention, and to answer, such a criticism; nor has the criticism been mentioned elsewhere. For other discussions of problems connected with the topic of this digression, see the references in n. 7 in the preceding section 6, and my various discussions of the descriptive and argumentative functions of language in *C.&.R.*, [1963(a)] and later editions; and also [1966(f)], [1967(k)], [1968(r)], and [1968(s)], (now Chap. 6 of [1972(a)], Chap. 3 of [1974(a)], and Chaps. 3 and 4 of [1972(a)]).

An interesting example of a key word (*ephexēs* in Plato's *Timaeus* 55 A) which has been misinterpreted (as "next in order of magnitude", instead of "next in order of time" or perhaps "in adjacent order") because the *theory* was not understood, and which can be interpreted in two different senses ("successively" in time, or "adjacent" applied to plane angles) without affecting Plato's *theory*, may be found in my paper "Plato, *Timaeus* 54E - 55A" [1970(d)]. For similar examples, see the 3d ed. of *C.&R.* [1969(h)], esp. pp. 165 and 408-12. In brief, one cannot translate without keeping the problem situation constantly in mind.

[26] See section IV to Chap. 19 of my *O.S.*, [1945(c)], [1950(a)], and later editions, for the ambiguity of violence; and also the Index under "violence".

[27] See, for comments on all this, *The Poverty* [1944(a) and (b)] and [1945(a)], and [1957(g)], and esp. Chaps. 17 to 20 of my *O.S.* [1945(c)], [1966(a)]. The remarks on the workers of Vienna which follow here in the text repeat in the main what I said in my *O.S.*, in nn. 18 to 22 to Chap. 18, and n. 39 to Chap. 19. See also the references given in n. 26 above on *the ambiguity of violence*.

[28] G. E. R. Gedye, *Fallen Bastions* (London: Victor Gollancz, 1939).

[29] Cp. [1957(a)], reprinted as Chap. 1 of *C.&R.*, [1963(a)] and later editions.

[30] Cp. Ernst Mach, *The Science of Mechanics*, 6th English ed. with an Introduction by Karl Menger (La Salle, Ill.: Open Court Publishing Co., 1960), Chap. 2, section 6, subsection 9.

[31] The formulation in italics was first suggested, and its significance discussed, in [1949(d)], now translated as the Appendix to [1972(a)]; see also [1957(i) & (j)], [1969(k)], now Chap. 5 of [1972(a)].

[32] Albert Einstein, *Über die spezielle und die allgemeine Relativitätstheorie,* 3d ed., (Braunschweig: Vieweg, 1918); see esp. Chap. 22. I have used my own translation, but the

corresponding passage occurs on p. 77 of the English translation referred to in the next footnote. It should be noted that Newton's theory lives on as a limiting case in Einstein's theory of gravitation. (This is particularly clear if Newton's theory is formulated in a "general relativistic" or "covariant" way, by taking the velocity of light as infinite $[c = \infty]$. This was shown by Peter Havas, "Four-Dimensional Formulations of Newtonian Mechanics and Their Relation to the Special and the General Theory of Relativity", *Reviews of Modern Physics*, **36** [1964], 938-65.)

[33] Albert Einstein, *Relativity: The Special and the General Theory. A Popular Exposition* (London: Methuen & Co., 1920), p. 132. (I have slightly improved upon the translation.)

[34] *L.d.F.* [1934(b)], p. 13; [1966(e)] and later editions, p. 15; and *L.Sc.D.*, [1959(a)] and later editions, p. 41; see n. 15 in section 7 above.

[35] Cp. Hans Albert, *Marktsoziologie und Entscheidungslogik* (Neuwied and Berlin: Herman Luchterhand Verlag, 1967); see esp. pp. 149, 227 f., 309, 341 f. My very clumsy term, which Albert replaced by "immunization against criticism", was "conventionalist stratagem".

(Added in proofs.) David Miller has now drawn my attention to n. 1 on p. 560 of Arthur Pap, "Reduction Sentences and Dispositional Concepts", in *The Philosophy of Rudolf Carnap*, ed. by Paul Arthur Schilpp (La Salle, Ill.: Open Court Publishing Co., 1963), pp. 559-97, which anticipates this use of "immunization".

[36] Cp. Chap. 1 of my *C.&R.*, [1963(a)] and later editions.

[37] For a much fuller discussion, see sections 2, 3, and 5 of my *Replies*.

[38] See *C.&R.*, [1963(a)] and later editions, Chap. 10, esp. the Appendix, pp. 248-50; Chap. 11, pp. 275-77; Chap. 8, pp. 193-200; and Chap. 17, p. 346. The problem was first discussed by me in section 15 of *L.d.F.* [1934(b)], pp. 33 f.; [1966(e)] and later editions, pp. 39-41; *L.Sc.D.*, [1959(a)] and later editions, pp. 69 f. A fairly full discussion of certain metaphysical theories (centered on metaphysical determinism and indeterminism) is to be found in my paper "Indeterminism in Quantum Physics and in Classical Physics" [1950(b)]; see esp. pp. 121-23. This last paper is now reprinted as Chap. 9 of [1974(a)].

[39] See pp. 37 f. of *C.&R.*, [1963(a)] and later editions.

[40] See [1945(c)], pp. 101 f.; [1962(c)] and later editions, Vol. II, pp. 108 f.

[41] See Imre Lakatos, "Changes in the Problem of Inductive Logic", in *The Problem of Inductive Logic*, ed. by Imre Lakatos (Amsterdam: North-Holland Publishing Co., 1968), pp. 315-417, esp. p. 317.

[42] There does not seem to be any systematic time-dependence, as there is in the learning of meaningless syllables.

[43] Cp. C. Lloyd Morgan, *Introduction to Comparative Psychology* (London: Scott, 1894), and H. S. Jennings, *The Behaviour of the Lower Organisms* (New York: Columbia University Press, 1906).

[44] My view of habit formation may be illustrated by a report about the gosling Martina in Konrad Lorenz, *On Aggression* (London: Methuen & Co., 1966), pp. 57 f. Martina acquired a habit consisting of a certain detour towards a window before mounting the stairs to the first floor of Lorenz's house in Altenberg. This habit originated (*ibid.*, p. 57) with a typical escape reaction towards the light (the window). Although this first reaction was "repeated", "the habitual detour . . . became shorter and shorter". Thus repetition did not create this habit; and in this case it even tended to make it slowly disappear. (Perhaps this was something like an approach towards a critical phase.) Incidentally, many asides of Lorenz's seem to be in support of my view that scientists use the critical method—the method of conjectures and attempted refutations. For example he writes (*ibid.*, p. 8): "It is a very good morning exercise for a research scientist to discard a pet hypothesis every day before breakfast." Yet in spite of this insight he seems still to be influenced by inductivism. (See, for example, *ibid.*, p. 62: "But perhaps a whole series of countless repetitions . . . was necessary"; for another passage with clearly methodological intent see Konrad Lorenz, *Über tierisches und menschliches Verhalten* [Munich: R. Piper & Co., 1965], p. 388.) He does not always seem to realize that in science "repetitions" of observations

are not inductive confirmations but critical attempts to check oneself—to catch oneself in a mistake. See also below, n. 95 in section 15, and text.

[45] According to *The Oxford English Dictionary*, the phrase "rule of trial and error" originated in arithmetic (see TRIAL 4). Note that neither Lloyd Morgan nor Jennings used the term in the sense of random trials. (This latter use seems to be due to Edward Thorndike.)

[46] Drawing a ball blindly from an urn does not ensure randomness unless the balls in the urn are well mixed. And blindness regarding the solution need not involve blindness regarding the problem: we may know that our problem is to win a game by drawing a white ball.

[47] D. Katz, *Animals and Men* (London: Longmans, 1937), p. 143.

[48] Jane Austen, *Emma* (London: John Murray, 1816), Vol. III, end of Chap. 3 (Chap. 39 of some later editions). Cp. p. 336 of R. W. Chapman, ed., *The Novels of Jane Austen*, 3d ed., (Oxford: Oxford University Press, 1933), Vol. IV.

[49] For the development of games, see Jean Piaget, *The Moral Judgment of the Child* (London: Routledge & Kegan Paul, 1932), esp. p. 18 for the dogmatic first two stages and the critical "third stage"; see also pp. 56-69. See further Jean Piaget, *Play, Dreams, and Imitation in Childhood* (London: Routledge & Kegan Paul, 1962).

[50] Something like this view may be found in Søren Kierkegaard, *Repetition* (Princeton: Princeton University Press; Oxford: Oxford University Press, 1942); cp., for example, pp. 77 f.

[51] Joseph Church, *Language and the Discovery of Reality* (New York: Random House, 1961), p. 36.

[52] *Ibid.*

[53] This seems to be the obvious explanation of the tragic incident of Helen Keller's alleged plagiarism when she was still a child, an incident which made a great impression on her, and perhaps helped her to sort out the various kinds of messages which reached her in the same code.

[54] W. H. Thorpe writes in a passage (to which Arne Petersen has drawn my attention) in his interesting book *Learning and Instinct in Animals* (London: Metheun & Co., 1956), p. 122 (2d rev. ed., 1963, p. 135): "By true imitation is meant the copying of a novel or otherwise improbable act or utterance, or some act for which there is clearly no instinctive tendency." (Italicized in the original.) *There can be no imitation without elaborate instinctive tendencies for copying in general, and even for the specific kind of imitating act in particular.* No tape recorder can work without its built-in (innate, instinctive) ability for learning by imitation (imitation of vibrations) and if we do not provide it with a substitute of a need or drive to use its abilities (perhaps in the form of a human operator who *wants* the machine to do some recording *and* playing back), then it will not imitate. This seems to be true, then, of even the most *passive* forms of learning by imitation of which I can think. It is of course quite correct that we should speak of imitation only if the act to be imitated is not one which would be performed by animal *A* from instinct alone, without its having been first performed by another animal *B* in the presence of *A*. But there will be cases in which we have reason to suspect that *A* *may* have produced the act—perhaps at a somewhat later stage—without imitating *B*. Should we not call it a true imitation if *B*'s act led to *A*'s performing the act (much) earlier than it would have done otherwise?

[55] *C.&R.,* [1963(a)] and later editions, Chap. 1, esp. pp. 42-52. I refer there on p. 50, n. 16, to a thesis "Gewohnheit und Gesetzerlebnis" [On Habit and Belief in Laws] which I presented (in an unfinished state) in 1927, and in which I argued against Hume's idea that habit is merely the (passive) result of repetitive association.

[56] This is somewhat similar to Plato's theory of knowledge in *Meno* 80 D- 86 C but of course also dissimilar.

[57] I feel that here is the place, more than anywhere else, to acknowledge the help I have received throughout this essay from my friends Ernst Gombrich and Bryan Magee. It was perhaps not so difficult for Ernst Gombrich for, although he does not agree with all I say about music, he at least sympathizes with my attitude. But Bryan Magee emphatically does not. He is an admirer of Wagner (on whom he has written a brilliant book, *Aspects of Wagner* [London:

Alan Ross, 1968; New York: Stein & Day, 1969]). Thus he and I are here as completely at loggerheads as two people can possibly be. It is of lesser moment that in his judgement my sections 13 and 14 contain well-known muddles, and that some of the views I attack are Aunt Sallies. Of course, I do not quite agree with this; but the point I wish to make here is that our disagreement has not prevented him from helping me immensely, not only with the rest of this autobiographical sketch but also with these two sections that contain views on which we have seriously disagreed for many years.

[58] It is a long time since I gave up these studies and I cannot now remember the details. But it seems to me more than probable that there was a certain amount of parallel singing, at the *organum* stage, which contained thirds *and* fifths (reckoned from the bass). I feel that this should have preceded *fauxbourdon* singing.

[59] See D. Perkin Walker, "Kepler's Celestial Music", *Journal of the Warburg and Courtauld Institutes,* **30** (1967), 228-50. I am greatly indebted to Dr Walker for drawing my attention to the passage which I quote in the text. It is from Kepler, *Gesammelte Werke*, ed. by Max Caspar (Munich, 1940), Vol. VI, p. 328. The passage is quoted in Latin by Walker, *Kepler's Celestial Music*, pp. 249 f., who also gives an English translation. The translation here is my own. (I translate: *ut mirum amplius non sit* = there is no marvel greater or more sublime; *ut luderet* [= that he should enact] = that he should conjure up a vision of; *ut quadamtenus degusterat* = that he should almost [taste or touch or] reach.) Incidentally, I cannot agree that Plato's harmony of the spheres was monodic and consisted "only of scales" (cp. Walker, *Kepler's Celestial Music*, n. 3 and text); on the contrary, Plato takes the greatest care to avoid this interpretation of his words. (See for example *Republic* 617B, where each of the eight Sirens sings one single tune, such that from all the eight together "there came the concord of one single harmony". *Timaeus* 35 B-36B and 90D should be interpreted in the light of this passage. Relevant is also Aristotle, *De sensu* vii, 448 a 20 ff. where the views of "some writers on concords" are examined who "say that sounds do not arrive simultaneously but merely *seem* to do so".) See also on singing in octaves Aristotle's *Problems* 918 b 40, 919 b 33-35 ("mixture"; "consonance") and 921 a 8-31 (see esp. 921 a 27 f.)

[60] I have alluded to this story in Chap. 1 of *C.&R.*, [1963(a)] and later editions, end of section vi, p. 50.

[61] It was only years later that I realized that in asking "How is science possible?" Kant had Newton's theory in mind, augmented by his own interesting form of atomism (which resembled that of Boscovich); cp. *C.&R.*, Chaps. 2, 7, and 8, and my paper "Philosophy and Physics" [1961(h)], now Chap. 1 of [1974(a)].

[62] For this distinction (and also for a more subtle one) see *C.&R.* [1963(a)], Chap. 1, section v, pp. 47 f.

[63] Albert Schweitzer, *J. S. Bach* (Leipzig: Breitkopf und Härtel, 1908); first published in French in 1905; 7th ed., 1929; and new English ed.(London: A. & C. Black, 1923), Vol. I, p. 1. Schweitzer uses the term "objective" for Bach and "subjective" for Wagner. I would agree that Wagner is far more "subjective" than Beethoven. Yet I should perhaps say here that, though I greatly admire Schweitzer's book (especially his most excellent comments on the phrasing of Bach's themes) I cannot at all agree with an analysis of the contrast between "objective" and "subjective" musicians in terms of the musician's relation to his "time" or "period". It seems to me almost certain that in this Schweitzer is influenced by Hegel, whose appreciation of Bach impressed him. (See *ibid.*, pp. 225 f., and n. 56 on p. 230. On p. 225 [Vol. 1, p. 244 of the English ed.] Schweitzer recounts from Therese Devrient's memoirs a charming incident involving Hegel which is not very flattering to him.)

[64] The first of these [1968(s)] was an address delivered in 1967 and first published in *Logic, Methodology and Philosophy of Science*, Vol. III, pp. 333-73; the second [1968(r)] was first published in *Proceedings of the XIVth International Congress of Philosophy, Vienna: 2nd to 9th September 1968*, Vol. I, pp. 25-53. These two papers are now Chaps. 3 and 4 respectively of [1972(a)]. The third paper [1967(k)] cited in the text is in *Quantum Theory and Reality*, and now Chap. 3 of [1974(a)]. See also my *L.d.F.* and *L.Sc.D.*, sections 29 and 30 [1934(b)], pp. 60-67;

[1966(e)] and later editions, pp. 69-76; [1959(a)] and later editions, pp. 104-11; my *C.&R.* [1963(a)], esp. pp. 224-31; and my paper "A Realist View of Logic, Physics, and History" [1970(l)] in *Physics, Logic, and History*, now Chap. 8 of [1972(a)].

[65] See my *O.S.*, Vol. I [1945(b)], pp. 26, 96; Vol. II [1945(c)], pp. 12 f.; [1950(a)], pp. 35, 108, 210-12; [1962(c)], [1963(l)], and later editions, Vol. I, pp. 32, 109; Vol. II, pp. 13 f.

[66] See also the last section of my paper "Epistemology Without a Knowing Subject" [1968(s)], pp. 369-71; [1972(a)], pp. 146-50.

[67] Cited by Schweitzer, *J. S. Bach*, p. 153.

[68] Arthur Schopenhauer, *Die Welt als Wille und Vorstellung* [The World as Will and Idea], Vol. II (1844), Chap. 39; the second quotation is from Vol. I (1818 [1819]), section 52. Note that *"Vorstellung"* must be translated by "idea" rather than by "representation", for the German word *"Vorstellung"* is simply the translation into German of Locke's term "idea".

[69] The German is: *"eine cantable Art im Spielen zu erlangen"*.

[70] Plato, *Ion*; cp. esp. 533D-536D.

[71] *Ibid.*, 534E.

[72] Plato, *Ion* 535E; cp. 535C.

[73] See also my paper "Self-Reference and Meaning in Ordinary Language" [1954(c)], which now forms Chap. 14 of *C.&R.* [1963(a)]; and text to n. 163 of my reply to Schlesinger below (added after completion of this *Autobiography*). (Arguments purporting to show that self-referring jokes are impossible may be found in Gilbert Ryle, *The Concept of Mind* [London: Hutchinson, 1949], for example, on pp. 193-96; Peregrine Books ed. [Harmondsworth: Penguin Books, 1963], pp. 184-88. I think that Ion's remark is [or implies] "a criticism of itself" which according to Ryle, p. 196, should not be possible.)

[74] Plato, *Ion* 541E-542B.

[75] See my *O.S.*, [1945(b) and (c)] and later editions, nn. 40 and 41 to Chap. 4, and text.

[76] Ernst Gombrich referred me to "In order to make me weep you yourself must suffer first" (Horace, *Ad Pisones*, 103 f.). Of course it is conceivable that what Horace intended to formulate was not an expressionist view but the view that only the artist who has suffered first is capable of critically judging the impact of his work. It seems to me probable that Horace was not conscious of the difference between these two interpretations.

[77] Plato, *Ion* 541E f.

[78] For much of this paragraph, and some criticism of the previous paragraphs, I am indebted to my friend Ernst Gombrich.
 It will be seen that the secularized Platonic theories (of the work of art as subjective expression and communication, and as objective description) correspond to Karl Bühler's three functions of language; cp. my [1963(a)], pp. 134 f. and 295, and section 15.

[79] See E. H. Gombrich, *Art and Illusion* (London: Phaidon Press; New York: Pantheon Books, 1960; latest edition, 1972), *passim*.

[80] It will be seen that my attitude towards music resembles the theories of Eduard Hanslick (caricatured by Wagner as Beckmesser), a music critic of great influence in Vienna, who wrote a book against Wagner (*Vom Musikalisch-Schönen* [Leipzig: R. Weigel, 1854]; trans. by G. Cohen from the 7th rev. ed. as *The Beautiful in Music* [London: Novello and Co., 1891]). But I do not agree with Hanslick's rejection of Bruckner who, though venerating Wagner, was in his way as saintly a musician as Beethoven (who is now sometimes wrongly accused of dishonesty). It is an amusing fact that Wagner was greatly impressed by Schopenhauer—by *The World as Will and Idea*—and that Schopenhauer wrote in the *Parerga*, Vol. II, section 224 (first published in 1851, when Wagner was starting work on the music of *The Ring*), "One can say that Opera has been the bane of music". (He meant of course recent opera, although his arguments sound very general—much too general in fact.)

[81] Friedrich Nietzsche, *Der Fall Wagner* [The Case of Wagner] (Leipzig, 1888) and *Nietzsche contra Wagner*; both translated in *The Complete Works of Friedrich Nietzsche*, ed. by Oscar Levy (Edinburgh and London: T. N. Foulis, 1911), Vol. VIII.

[82] Arthur Schopenhauer, *Parerga*, Vol. II, section 224.

[83] Karl Bühler, *Die geistige Entwicklung des Kindes* (Jena: Fischer, 1918; 3d ed., 1922); English translation, *The Mental Development of the Child* (London: Kegan Paul, Trench, Trubner & Co., 1930). For the functions of language, see also his *Sprachtheorie* (Jena: Fischer, 1934); see esp. pp. 24-33.

[84] A word may be perhaps said here on Aristotle's hygienic theory of art. Art no doubt has some biological or psychological function like catharsis; I do not deny that great music may in some sense purify our minds. But is the greatness of a work of art summed up in the fact that it cleanses us more thoroughly than a lesser work? I do not think that even Aristotle would have said this.

[85] Cp. *C.&R.*, pp. 134 f., 295; *Of Clouds and Clocks* [1966 (f)], now Chap. 6 of [1972(a)], section 14-17 and n. 47; "Epistemology Without a Knowing Subject" [1968(s)], esp. section 4, pp. 345 f. ([1972(a)], Chap. 3, pp. 119-22).

[86] Leonard Nelson was an outstanding personality, one of the small band of Kantians in Germany who had opposed the First World War, and who upheld the Kantian tradition of rationality.

[87] See my paper "Julius Kraft 1898-1960" [1962(f)].

[88] See Leonard Nelson, "Die Unmöglichkeit der Erkenntnistheorie", *Proceedings of the IVth International Congress of Philosophy, Bologna: 5th to 11th April 1911* (Genoa: Formiggini, 1912), Vol. I, pp. 255-75; see also L. Nelson, *Über das sogenannte Erkenntnisproblem* (Göttingen: Vandenhoeck & Ruprecht, 1908).

[89] See Heinrich Gomperz, *Weltanschauungslehre* (Jena and Leipzig: Diederichs, 1905 and 1908), Vol. I, and Vol. II, Part 1. Gomperz told me that he had completed the second part of the second volume but had decided not to publish it, and to abandon his plans for the later volumes. The published volumes were planned and executed on a truly magnificent scale, and I do not know the reason why Gomperz ceased to work on it, about eighteen years before I met him. Obviously it had been a tragic experience. In one of his later books, *Über Sinn und Sinngebilde—Verstehen und Erklären* (Tübingen: Mohr, 1929), he refers to his earlier theory of feelings, esp. on pp. 206 f. For his psychologistic approach—which he called "pathempiricism" (*Pathempirismus*) and which emphasized the role of feelings (*Gefühle*) in knowledge—see esp. *Weltanschauungslehre*, sections 55-59 (Vol. II, pp. 220-93). Cp. also sections 36-39 (Vol. I, pp. 305-94).

[90] Karl Bühler, "Tatsachen und Probleme zu einer Psychologie der Denkvorgänge", *Archiv f. d. gesamte Psychologie,* **9** (1907), 297-365; **12** (1908), 1-23, 24-92, 93-123.

[91] Otto Selz, *Über die Gesetze des geordneten Denkverlaufs* (Stuttgart: W. Spemann, 1913), Vol. I; (Bonn: F. Cohen, 1922), Vol. II.

[92] Oswald Külpe, *Vorlesungen über Logik*, ed. by Otto Selz (Leipzig: S. Hirzel, 1923).

[93] A similar mistake can be found even in *Principia Mathematica*, since Russell failed, in places, to distinguish between an inference (logical implication) and a conditional statement (material implication). This confused me for years. Yet the main point—that an inference was an ordered set of statements—was sufficiently clear to me in 1928 to be mentioned to Bühler during my (public) Ph.D. examination. He admitted very charmingly that he had not considered the point.

[94] See *C.&R.* [1963(a)], pp. 134 f.

[95] I now find a similar argument in Konrad Lorenz: ". . . modifiability occurs . . . only in those . . . places where built-in learning mechanisms are phylogenetically programmed to perform just that function." (See Konrad Lorenz, *Evolution and Modification of Behaviour* [London: Methuen & Co., 1966], p. 47.) But he does not seem to draw from it the conclusion

that the theories of reflexology and of the conditioned reflex are invalid: see especially *ibid.*, p. 66. See also section 10 above, esp. n. 44. One can state the main difference between association psychology or the theory of the conditioned reflex on the one hand, and discovery by trial and error on the other, by saying that the former is essentially Lamarckian (or "instructive") and the latter Darwinian (or "selective"). See now for example the investigations of Melvin Cohn, "Reflections on a Discussion with Karl Popper: The Molecular Biology of Expectation", *Bulletin of the All-India Institute of Medical Sciences,* 1 (1967), 8-16, and later works by the same author. For Darwinism, see section 37.

⁹⁶ W. von Bechterev, *Objektive Psychologie oder Psychoreflexologie* (originally published 1907-12), German ed. (Leipzig and Berlin: Teubner, 1913); and *Allgemeine Grundlagen der Reflexologie des Menschen* (originally published 1917), German ed. (Leipzig and Vienna: F. Deuticke, 1926); English ed., *General Principles of Human Reflexology* (London: Jarrolds, 1933).

⁹⁷ The title of my (unpublished) dissertation was "Zur Methodenfrage der Denkpsychologie" [1928(a)].

⁹⁸ Compare with this paragraph some of my remarks against Reichenbach at a conference in 1934 ([1935(a)] reprinted in [1966(e)], [1969(e)], p. 257; there is a translation in *L.Sc.D.,* [1959(a)] and later editions, p. 315: "Scientific theories can never be 'justified', or verified. But . . . a hypothesis *A* can . . . achieve more than a hypothesis *B*. . . . The best we can say of a hypothesis is that up to now . . . it has been more successful than other hypotheses although, in principle, it can never be justified, verified, or even shown to be probable." See also the end of section 20 (text to nn. 156-58), and n. 243 in section 33, below.

⁹⁹ Rudolf Carnap, *Der logische Aufbau der Welt*, and *Scheinprobleme in der Philosophie: das Fremdpsychische und der Realismusstreit*, both first published (Berlin: Weltkreis-Verlag, 1928); second printing (both books in one) (Hamburg: Felix Meiner, 1961). Now translated as *The Logical Structure of the World* and *Pseudoproblems of Philosophy* (London: Routledge & Kegan Paul, 1967).

¹⁰⁰ Victor Kraft, *Die Grundformen der wissenschaftlichen Methoden* (Vienna: Academy of Sciences, 1925).

¹⁰¹ See p. 641 of Herbert Feigl's charming and most informative essay, "The Wiener Kreis in America", in *Perspectives in American History* (The Charles Warren Center for Studies in American History, Harvard University, 1968), Vol. II, pp. 630-73; and also n. 106 below. [Upon inquiry Feigl suggests that Zilsel may have become a member after his—Feigl's—emigration to the United States.]

¹⁰² Herbert Feigl says (*ibid.*, p. 642) that it must have been in 1929, and no doubt he is right.

¹⁰³ My only published papers before I met Feigl—and for another four years after—were on educational topics. With the exception of the first [1925(a)] (published in an educational journal *Schulreform*) they were all ([1927(a)], [1931(a)], [1932(a)]) written at the invitation of Dr Eduard Burger, the editor of the educational journal *Die Quelle*.

¹⁰⁴ Feigl refers to the meeting in "Wiener Kreis in America". I have briefly described the opening move of our discussion in *C. &R.* [1963(a)], pp. 262 f.; see n. 27 on p. 263. See also "A Theorem on Truth-Content" [1966(g)], my contribution to the Feigl *Festschrift*.

¹⁰⁵ During that first long conversation, Feigl objected to my realism. (He was at that time in favour of a so-called "neutral monism", which I regarded as Berkeleyan idealism; I still do.) I am happy at the thought that Feigl too became a realist.

¹⁰⁶ Feigl writes, "Wiener Kreis in America", p. 641, that both Edgar Zilsel and I tried to preserve our independence "by remaining outside the Circle". But the fact is that I should have felt greatly honoured had I been invited, and it would never have occurred to me that membership in Schlick's seminar could endanger my independence in the slightest degree. (Incidentally, before reading this passage of Feigl's I did not realize that Zilsel was not a member of the Circle. I always thought he was, and Victor Kraft records him as one in his book *Der*

Wiener Kreis [Vienna: Springer-Verlag, 1950]; see p. 4 of the translation, *The Vienna Circle* [New York: Philosophical Library, 1953]. See also n. 101 above.)

107 See my publications listed on p. 44 of my paper "Quantum Mechanics Without 'The Observer' " [1967(k)]. This paper is now reprinted as Chap. 3 of [1974(a)].

108 The manuscript of the first volume and parts of the manuscript of that version of *L.d.F.* which was cut by half by my uncle still exist. The manuscript of the second volume, with the possible exception of a few sections, seems to have been lost.

109 See in particular now my [1971(i)], reprinted with minor alterations as Chap. 1 of [1972(a)]; and also section 13 of my *Replies*.

110 See John Passmore's article "Logical Positivism" in *Encyclopedia of Philosophy*, ed. by Edwards, Vol. V, p. 56 (see n. 7 above).

111 This letter [1933(a)] was first published in *Erkenntnis, 3*, Nos. 4-6 (1933), 426 f. It is republished in translation in my *L.Sc.D.,* [1959(a)] and later editions, pp. 312-14, and in its original language in the second and third editions of *L.d.F.* [1966(e)], [1969(e)], pp. 254-56.

112 J. R. Weinberg, *An Examination of Logical Positivism* (London: Kegan Paul, Trench, Trubner & Co., 1936).

113 For a much fuller discussion of this legend, see sections 2 and 3 of my *Replies* below.

114 Cp. Arne Naess, *Moderne filosofer* (Stockholm: Almqvist & Wiksell/Gebers Förlag AB, .965); English translation as *Four Modern Philosophers* (Chicago and London: University of Chicago Press, 1968). Naess writes in n. 13 on pp. 13 f. of the translation: "My own experience was rather similar to Popper's. . . . The polemic [in an unpublished book of Naess's] . . . written . . . between 1937 and 1939 was *intended* to be directed against *fundamental* theses and trends in the Circle, but was understood by Neurath as a proposal for modifications which were already accepted in principle and were to be made official in future publications. Upon this assurance I gave up plans to publish the work."

114a For the impact of all these discussions, see nn. 115 to 120.

115 Cp. *C.&R.* [1963(a)], pp. 253 f.

116 Rudolf Carnap. "Über Protokollsätze", *Erkenntnis, 3* (1932), 215-28; see esp. 223-28.

117 Cp. Rudolf Carnap, *Philosophy and Logical Syntax*, Psyche Miniatures (London: Kegan Paul, 1935), pp. 10-13, which correspond to *Erkenntnis, 3* (1932), 224 ff. Carnap speaks here of "verification" where before he (correctly) reported me as speaking of "testing".

118 Cp. C. G. Hempel, *Erkenntnis, 5* (1935), esp. 249-54, where Hempel describes (with reference to Carnap's article "Über Protokollsätze") my procedure very much as Carnap had reported it.

119 Rudolf Carnap, *Erkenntnis, 5* (1935), 290-94 (with a reply to Reichenbach's criticism). C. G. Hempel, *Deutsche Literaturzeitung, 58* (1937), 309-14. (There was also a second review by Hempel.) I mention here only the more important reviews and criticisms from members of the Circle.

120 Hans Reichenbach, *Erkenntnis, 5* (1935), 367-84 (with a reply to Carnap's review, to which Carnap briefly replied). Otto Neurath, *Erkenntnis, 5* (1935), 353-65.

121 Werner Heisenberg, "Über quantentheoretische Umdeutung kinematischer und mechanischer Beziehungen", *Zeitschrift für Physik, 33* (1925), 879-93; Max Born and Pascual Jordan, "Zur Quantenmechanik", *ibid.,* **34** (1925), 858-88; Max Born, Werner Heisenberg, and Pascual Jordan, "Zur Quantenmechanik II", *ibid.,* **35** (1926), 557-615. All three papers are translated in *Sources of Quantum Mechanics*, ed. by B. L. van der Waerden (Amsterdam: North-Holland Publishing Co., 1967).

122 For a report of the debate see Niels Bohr, "Discussion with Einstein on Epistemological Problems in Atomic Physics", in *Albert Einstein: Philosopher-Scientist*, ed. by Paul Arthur Schilpp (Evanston, Ill.: Library of Living Philosophers, Inc., 1949); 3d ed. (La Salle, Ill.: Open Court Publishing Co., 1970), pp. 201-41. For a criticism of Bohr's contentions in this debate, see

my *L.Sc.D.* [1959(a)], new Appendix *xi, pp. 444-56, *L.d.F.* [1966(e)] and [1969(e)], pp. 399-411, and [1967(k)] (now [1974(a)], Chap. 3).

[123] James L. Park & Henry Margenau, "Simultaneous Measurability in Quantum Theory", *International Journal of Theoretical Physics,* **1** (1968), 211-83.

[124] See [1957(e)] and [1959(e)], respectively Chaps. 4 and 5 of **[1974(a)]**.

[125] See [1934(b)], pp. 171 f., [1959(a)], pp. 235 f., [1966(e)], pp. 184 f.; [1967(k)], pp. 34-38 (now Chap. 3 of [1974(a)]).

[126] *Albert Einstein: Philosopher-Scientist,* pp. 201-41 (see n. 122 above).

[127] See esp. [1957(i)], [1969(k)], now Chap. 5 of [1972(a)]; [1963(h)], now Chap. 2 of [1974(a)]; [1966(f)], now Chap. 6 of [1972(a)]; [1967(k)], now Chap. 3 of [1974(a)]; and [1968(s)], now Chap. 3 of [1972(a)], in which also is reprinted, as Chap. 4, [1968(r)], where a fuller treatment can be found

[128] Arthur March, *Die Grundlagen der Quantenmechanik* (Leipzig: Barth, 1931); cp. the Index of [1934(b)], [1959(a)], or [1966(e)].

[129] The list of results given here are partly of a later, partly of an earlier date. For my latest views see my contribution to the Landé *Festschrift,* "Particle Annihilation and the Argument of Einstein, Podolsky, and Rosen" [1971(n)], now [1974(a)], Chap. 6.

[130] Cp. John von Neumann, *Mathematische Grundlagen der Quantenmechanik* (Berlin: Springer-Verlag, 1931), p. 170; or the translation, *Mathematical Foundations of Quantum Mechanics* (Princeton: Princeton University Press, 1955), p. 323. Thus even if von Neumann's argument were valid, it would not disprove determinism. Moreover, his assumed "rules" I and II on pp. 313 f. (cp. p. 225 f.)—German edition p. 167 (cp. p. 118)—are inconsistent with the commutation relations, as was first shown by G. Temple, "The Fundamental Paradox of the Quantum Theory", *Nature,* **135** (1935), 957. (That von Neumann's rules I and II are inconsistent with quantum mechanics was clearly implied by R. E. Peierls, "The Fundamental Paradox of the Quantum Theory", *Nature,* **136** [1935], 395. See also Park and Margenau, "Simultaneous Measurability in Quantum Theory" [see n. 123 above].) John S. Bell's paper is "On the Problem of Hidden Variables in Quantum Mechanics", *Reviews of Modern Physics,* **38** (1966), 447-52.

[131] C. S. Peirce, *Collected Papers of Charles Sanders Peirce,* ed. by Charles Hartshorne and Paul Weiss (Cambridge, Mass.: Harvard University Press, 1935), Vol. VI; see item 6.47 (first published 1892), p. 37.

[132] According to Schrödinger, Franz Exner made the suggestion in 1918; see Erwin Schrödinger, *Science, Theory, and Man* (New York: Dover Publications, 1957), pp. 71, 133, 142 f. (originally published as *Science and the Human Temperament* [London: Allen and Unwin, 1935]; see pp. 57 f., 107, 114); and *Die Naturwissenschaften,* **17** (1929), 732.

[133] von Neumann, *Mathematical Foundations of Quantum Mechanics,* pp. 326 f. (German edition, p. 172): "...the apparent causal order of the world in the large (... [of the] objects visible to the naked eye) has certainly no other cause than the 'law of large numbers' and it *is completely independent of whether the natural laws governing the elementary processes are causal or not*". (Italics mine; von Neumann refers to Schrödinger.) Obviously this situation has no direct connection with quantum mechanics.

[134] See also my [1934(b)], [1959(a)], and later editions, section 78 (and also 67-70); [1950(b) and (c)]. now [1974(a)], Chap. 9; [1957(g)], Preface; [1957(e)], [1959(e)], respectively Chaps. 4 and 5 of [1974(a)]; [1966(f)], esp. section iv ([1972(a)], Chap. 6); [1967(k)] ([1974(a)], Chap. 3).

[135] This is the view which I have upheld consistently. It can be found, I believe, in Richard von Mises.

[136] Alfred Landé, "Determinism versus Continuity in Modern Science", *Mind,* n.s. **67** (1958), 174-81, and *From Dualism to Unity in Quantum Physics* (Cambridge: Cambridge University Press, 1960), pp. 5-8. (I have called this argument "Landé's blade".)

[137] Cp. [1957(e)], [1959(e)], and [1967(k)]; see now, [1974(a)], Chaps. 3, 4, and 5.

[138] Why should particles not be particles, at least to a first approximation, perhaps to be explained by a field theory? (A unified field theory of the type, say, of Mendel Sachs.) The only objection known to me derives from the "smear" interpretation of the Heisenberg indeterminacy formulae; if the "particles" are always "smeared", they are not real particles. But this objection does not seem to hold water: there is a statistical interpretation of quantum mechanics.
(Since writing the above I have written a contribution to the Landé *Festschrift* [1971(n)] referred to in n. 129 above; now reprinted as Chap. 6 of [1974(a)]. And since then, I have read two outstanding works defending the statistical interpretation of quantum mechanics: Edward Nelson, *Dynamical Theories of Brownian Motion* [Princeton: Princeton University Press, 1967], and L. E. Ballentine, "The Statistical Interpretation of Quantum Mechanics", *Reviews of Modern Physics*, **42** [1970], 358-81. It is most encouraging to find some support after a lone fight of thirty-seven years.)

[139] See esp. [1967(k)] (Chap. 3 of [1974(a)]).

[140] W. Duane, "The Transfer in Quanta of Radiation Momentum to Matter", *Proceedings of the National Academy of Sciences* (Washington), **9** (1923), 158-64. The rule may be written:
$$\Delta p_x = nh/\Delta x \qquad (n \text{ an integer}).$$
See Werner Heisenberg, *The Physical Principles of the Quantum Theory* (New York: Dover, 1930), p. 77.

[141] Landé, *Dualism to Unity in Quantum Physics*, pp. 69, 102 (see n. 136 above), and *New Foundations of Quantum Mechanics* (Cambridge: Cambridge University Press, 1965), pp. 5-9.

[142] See esp. [1959(a)], [1966(e)], new Appendix *xi; and [1967(k)] ([1974(a)], Chap. 3).

[143] Albert Einstein, "Zur Elektrodynamik bewegter Körper", *Annalen der Physik*, 4th ser. **17**, 891-921; translated as "On the Electrodynamics of Moving Bodies" in Albert Einstein et al., *The Principle of Relativity*, trans. by W. Pennett and G. B. Jeffery (New York: Dover, 1923), pp. 35-65.

[144] Einstein, *Relativity: Special and General Theory* (1920 and later editions). The German original is *Über die spezielle und die allgemeine Relativitätstheorie* (Brunswick: Vieweg & Sohn, 1916). (See nn. 32 and 33 above.)

[145] See Einstein's paper of 1905, section 1; in *Principle of Relativity*, pp. 38-40 (see n. 143 above).

[146] By wrongly applying the very intuitive transitivity principle (Tr) to events beyond one system one can easily prove that *any* two events are simultaneous. But this contradicts the axiomatic assumption that within any inertial system there is a temporal order; that is, that for any two events within one system *one and only one* of the three relations holds: *a* and *b* are simultaneous; *a* comes before *b*; *b* comes before *a*. This is overlooked in an article by C. W. Rietdijk, "A Rigorous Proof of Determinism Derived from the Special Theory of Relativity", *Philosophy of Science*, **33** (1966), 341-44.

[147] Cp. Marja Kokoszyńska, "Über den absoluten Wahrheitsbegriff und einige andere semantische Begriffe", *Erkenntnis*, **6** (1936), 143-65; cp. Carnap, *Introduction to Semantics*, pp. 240, 255 (see n. 15 above).

[148] [1934(b)], section 84, "Wahrheit und Bewährung"; cp. Rudolf Carnap, "Wahrheit und Bewährung", *Proceedings of the IVth International Congress for Scientific Philosophy*, Paris, 1935 (Paris: Hermann, 1936), Vol. IV, pp. 18-23; an adaptation appears in translation as "Truth and Confirmation", in *Readings in Philosophical Analysis*, ed. by Herbert Feigl and Wilfrid Sellars (New York: Appleton-Century-Crofts, Inc., 1949), pp. 119-27.

[149] Many members of the Circle refused at first to operate with the notion of truth; cp. Kokoszyńska, "Über den absoluten Wahrheitsbegriff".

[150] Cp. Appendix iv of [1934(b)] and [1959(a)]. After the war, a proof of the validity of the construction was given by L. R. B. Elton and myself. (It is, I am afraid, my fault that our paper was never published.) In his review of *L.Sc.D.* (*Mathematical Reviews*, **21** [1960], Review 6318) I. J. Good mentions a paper of his own, "Normal Recurring Decimals", *Journal of the London*

Mathematical Society, **21** (1946), 167-69. That my construction is valid follows easily—as David Miller has pointed out to me—from the considerations of this paper.

[151] Karl Menger, "The Formative Years of Abraham Wald and His Work in Geometry", *The Annals of Mathematical Statistics*, **23** (1952), 14-20; see esp. p. 18.

[152] Karl Menger, *ibid.*, p. 19.

[153] Abraham Wald, "Die Widerspruchsfreiheit des Kollektivsbegriffes der Wahrscheinlichkeitsrechnung", *Ergebnisse eines mathematischen Kolloquiums*, **8** (1937), 38-72.

[154] Jean Ville, however, who read a paper in Menger's Colloquium at about the same time as Wald, produced a solution similar to my "ideal random sequence": he constructed a mathematical sequence which from the very start was Bernoullian, that is, random. (It was a somewhat "longer" sequence than mine; in other words, it did not become as quickly insensitive to predecessor selection as mine did.) Cp. Jean A. Ville, *Étude critique de la notion de collectif, Monographies des Probabilités: calcul des probabilités et ses applications*, ed. by Émile Borel (Paris: Gauthier-Villars, 1939).

[155] For the various interpretations of probability, see esp. [1934(b)], [1959(a)], and [1966(e)], section 48; and [1967(k)], pp. 28-34 (now Chap. 3 of [1974(a)]).

[156] See the Introduction before section 79 of [1934(b)], [1959(a)], [1966(e)].

[157] Compare to all this n. 243 in section 33, below, and text; see also section 16, text to n. 98.

[158] See [1959(a)], p. 401, n. 7; [1966(e)], p. 354.

[159] Some of this work is incorporated in the new appendices to *L.Sc.D.*, [1959(a)], [1966(e)], and later editions.

[160] I have read only two or three (very interesting) books about life in the Ghetto, especially Leopold Infeld, *Quest. The Evolution of a Scientist* (London: Victor Gollancz, 1941).

[161] Cp. [1945(c)] and later editions, Chap. 18, n. 22; Chap. 19, nn. 35-40 and text, Chap. 20, n. 44 and text.

[162] See John R. Gregg and F. T. C. Harris, eds., *Form and Strategy in Science. Studies Dedicated to Joseph Henry Woodger* (Dordrecht: D. Reidel, 1964), p. 4.

[163] Many years later Hayek told me that it was Gottfried von Haberler (later of Harvard) who in 1935 had drawn his attention to *L.d.F.*

[164] Cp. Bertrand Russell, "The Limits of Empiricism", *Proceedings of the Aristotelian Society*, **36** (1936), 131-50. My remarks here allude especially to pp. 146 ff.

[165] At the Copenhagen Congress—a congress for scientific philosophy—a very charming American gentleman took great interest in me. He said that he was the representative of the Rockefeller Foundation and gave me his card: "Warren Weaver, The European of the Rockefeller Foundation" (*sic*). This meant nothing to me; I had never heard about the foundations and their work. (Apparently I was very naive.) It was only years later that I realized that if I had understood the meaning of this encounter it might have led to my going to America instead of to New Zealand.

[166] My opening talk to my first seminar in New Zealand was later published in *Mind* [1940(a)], and is now Chap. 15 of *C.&R.*, [1963(a)] and later editions.

[167] Cp. [1938(a)]; [1959(a)], [1966(e)], Appendix *ii.

[168] Cp. H. von Halban, Jr, F. Joliot, and L. Kowarski, "Liberation of Neutrons in the Nuclear Explosion of Uranium", *Nature*, **143** (1939), 470 f.

[169] Karl K. Darrow, "Nuclear Fission", *Annual Report of the Board of Regents of the Smithsonian Institution* (Washington, D. C.: Government Printing Office, 1941), pp. 155-59.

[170] See the historical note in *The Poverty of Historicism* [1957(g)], p. iv; American ed. [1964(a)], p. v.

[171] This connection is briefly described in my British Academy lecture [1960(d)], now the Introduction to *C.&R.* [1963(a)]; see sections II and III.

172 See *L.d.F.* [1934(b)], pp. 227 f.; [1959(a)], p. 55, n. 3 to section 11; [1966(e)], p. 27. See also [1940(a)], p. 404, [1963(a)], p. 313, where the method of testing is described as an essentially critical, that is, faultfinding method.

173 Quite unnecessarily I used more often than not the ugly word "rationalist" (as in "rationalist attitude") where "rational" would have been better, and clearer. The (bad) reason for this was, I suppose, that I was arguing in defence of "rationalism".

174 See *O.S.*, Vol. II, [1945(c)] and later editions, Chap. 24 (Chap. 14 of the German ed. [1958(i)]).

175 Adrienne Koch used "Critical Rationalism" as the title of the excerpts from *O.S.* that she selected for her book *Philosophy for a Time of Crisis, An Interpretation with Key Writings by Fifteen Great Modern Thinkers* (New York: Dutton & Co., 1959) [1959(k)].

176 Hans Albert, "Der kritische Rationalismus Karl Raimund Poppers", *Archiv für Rechts- und Sozialphilosophie,* **46** (1960), 391-415. Hans Albert, *Traktat über die kritische Vernunft* (Tübingen: Mohr, 1968; and later editions).

177 In the 4th ed. of *O.S.* [1962(c)], [1963(l) and (m)], and in later editions, there is an important *Addendum* to the second volume: "Facts, Standards, and Truth: A Further Criticism of Relativism" (pp. 369-96) which has been, so far as I know, overlooked by almost everybody.

178 I now regard the analysis of causal explanation in section 12 of *L.d.F.* (and therefore also the remarks in *The Poverty* and other places) as superseded by an analysis based on my propensity interpretation of probability [1957(e)], [1959(e)], [1967(k)] (see now Chaps. 3, 4, and 5 of [1974(a)]). This interpretation, which presupposes my axiomatization of the probability calculus (see, for example, [1959(e)], p. 40; [1959(a)], [1966(e)], Appendices *iv and *v), allows us to discard the formal mode of speaking and to put things in a more realistic way. We interpret

(1) $p(a,b) = r$

to mean: "The propensity of the state of affairs (or the conditions) b to produce a equals r." (r is some real number.) A statement like (1) may be a conjecture, or deducible from some conjecture; for example, a conjecture about laws of nature.

We can then causally explain (in a generalized and weaker sense of "explain") a as due to the presence of b, even if r does not equal 1. That b is a classical or complete or deterministic cause of a can be stated by a conjecture like

(2) $p(a,bx) = 1$ for every x,

where x ranges over *all* possible states of affairs, including states incompatible with b. (We need not even exclude "impossible" states of affairs.) This shows the advantages of an axiomatization like mine, in which the second argument may be inconsistent.

This way of putting things is, clearly, a generalization of my analysis of causal explanation. In addition, it allows us to state *"nomic conditionals"* of various types—of type (1) with $r<1$, of type (1) with $r = 1$, and of type (2). (Thus it offers a solution of the so-called problem of counterfactual conditionals.) It allows us to solve Kneale's problem (see [1959(a)], [1966(e)], Appendix *x) of distinguishing between *accidentally* universal statements and naturally or physically *necessary* connections, as stated by (2). Notice however that there may be physically nonnecessary connections which nevertheless are not accidental, like (1) with an r not far from unity. See also my reply to Suppes (added after completion of this *Autobiography*).

179 See also *The Poverty* [1957(g)], p. 125. Reference should be made to J. S. Mill, *A System of Logic,* 8th ed., Book III, Chap. XII, section 1.

180 See Karl Hilferding, "Le fondement empirique de la science", *Revue des questions scientifiques,* **110** (1936), 85-116. In this paper Hilferding (a physical chemist) explains at considerable length my views, from which he deviates in allowing inductive probabilities in the sense of Reichenbach.

181 See also Hilferding, "Le fondement empirique de la science", p. 111, with a reference to p. 27 (that is, section 12) of the 1st ed. of *L.d.F.* [1934(b)].

182 See *The Poverty* [1957(g)], pp. 140 f. and 149 f., further developed in Chap. 14 of *O.S.* [1962(c) and (d)], [1963(l) and (m)]; [1966(i)]; [1967(d)]; [1968(r)] (now [1972(a)], Chap. 4);

[1969(j)]; and in many unpublished lectures given at the London School of Economics and elsewhere.

[183] See [1957(g)], sections 31 and 32, esp. pp. 149 and 154 f.

[184] See Vol. II of [1962(c)], [1963(l) and (m)], pp. 93-99, and esp. pp. 97 f.

[185] See [1950(a)], pp. 170 f.; [1952(a)], Vol I, pp. 174-76.

[186] See [1957(g)], sections 30-32; [1962(c)]; and more recently [1968(r)] (Chap. 4 of [1974(a)]) and [1969(j)].

[187] It was this situation which in 1945 led to the publication of a pamphlet *Research and the University* [1945(e)], drafted by me with the help of Robin S. Allan and Hugh Parton, and signed, after some minor changes, by Henry Forder and others. The situation changed in New Zealand soon after I left.

[188] See esp. [1947(a)] and [1947(b)]. I was led to this work, partly, by problems of probability theory: the rules of "natural deduction" are very closely related to the usual definitions in Boolean algebra. See also Alfred Tarski's papers of 1935 and 1936, which now form Chaps. XI and XII of his book *Logic, Semantics, Metamathematics*, trans. by J. H. Woodger (London and New York: Oxford University Press, 1956).

[189] [1950(b) and (c)]; now Chap. 7 of *Philosophy and Physics* [1974(a)].

[190] [1946(b)]; Chap. 9 of [1963(a)] and later editions.

[191] The minutes of the meeting are not quite reliable. For example the title of my paper is given there (and it was so given on the printed list of meetings) as "Methods in Philosophy" instead of "Are there Philosophical Problems?", which was the title ultimately chosen by me. Furthermore, the Secretary thought I was complaining that his invitation was for a *brief* paper, to introduce a *discussion*—which in fact suited me very well. He completely missed my point (puzzle versus problem).

[192] See *C.&R.* [1963(a)], p. 55.

[193] See p. 167 of Ryle's review of *O.S.* in *Mind, 56* (1947), 167-72.

[194] At a very early stage of the course he formulated, and showed the validity of, the metalinguistic rule of *indirect proof*:

If *a* logically follows from non-*a*, then *a* is demonstrable.

[195] Now in Tarski, *Logic, Semantics, Metamathematics*, pp. 409-20 (see n. 188 above).

[196] *Ibid.*, pp. 419 f.

[197] See [1947(a)], [1947(b)], [1947(c)], [1948(b)], [1948(c)], [1948(e)], [1948(f)]. The subject has now been advanced by Lejewski. See his paper below (added after completion of this *Autobiography*).

[198] The mistake was connected with the rules of substitution or replacement of expressions: I had mistakenly thought that it was sufficient to formulate these rules in terms of *interdeducibility*, while in fact what was needed was *identity* (of expressions). To explain this remark: I postulated, for example, that if in a statement *a*, two (disjoint) subexpressions *x* and *y* are both, wherever they occur, replaced by an expression *z*, then the resulting expression (provided it is a statement) is *interdeducible* with the result of replacing first *x* wherever it occurs by *y* and then *y* wherever it occurs by *z*. What I should have postulated was that the first result is *identical* with the second result. I realized that this was stronger, but I mistakenly thought that the weaker rule would suffice. The interesting (and so far unpublished) conclusion to which I was led later by repairing this mistake was that there was an essential difference between propositional and functional logic: while propositional logic can be constructed as a theory of sets of statements, whose elements are partially ordered by the relation of deducibility, functional logic needs in addition a specifically morphological approach since it must refer to the subexpression of an expression, using a concept like *identity* (with respect to expressions). But no more is needed than the ideas of identity and subexpression; no further description especially of the shape of the expressions.

199 [1950(d)].

200 [1950(b) and (c)]; [1974(a)], Chap. 9.

201 See Kurt Gödel, "A Remark About the Relationship Between Relativity Theory and Idealistic Philosophy", in *Albert Einstein: Philosopher-Scientist*, pp. 555-62 (see n. 122 above). Gödel's arguments were (a) philosophical, (b) based on the special theory (see esp. his n. 5), and (c) based on his new cosmological solutions of Einstein's field equations, that is, on the possibility of closed four-dimensional orbits in a (rotating) Gödel universe, as described by him in "An Example of a New Type of Cosmological Solutions of Einstein's Field Equations of Gravitation", *Reviews of Modern Physics*, **21** (1949), 447-50. (The results (c) were challenged by S. Chandrasekhar and James P. Wright, "The Geodesics in Gödel's Universe", *Proceedings of the National Academy of Sciences*, **47** [1961], 341-47. Note however that even if Gödel's closed orbits are not geodesics, this does not in itself constitute a refutation of Gödel's views; for a Gödel orbit was never meant to be fully ballistic or gravitational: even that of a moon rocket is only partially so.)

202 Cp. Schilpp, ed., *Albert Einstein: Philosopher-Scientist*, p. 688 (see n. 122 above). Not only do I agree with Einstein, but I would even go so far as to say this. Were the existence (in the physical sense) of Gödel's orbits a *consequence* of Einstein's theory (which it is not), then this fact should be held against the theory. It would not, to be sure, be a conclusive argument: there is no such thing; and we may have to accept Gödel orbits. I think, however, that in such a case we ought to look for some alternative.

203 Harald Høffding wrote (in *Den menneskelige Tanke* [Copenhagen: Nordisk Forlag, 1910], p. 303; in the German translation *Der menschliche Gedanke* [Leipzig: O. Riesland, 1911], p. 333): "Knowledge, which is to describe and explain the world for us, always itself forms part of the existing world; for this reason new entities may always emerge to be dealt with by it. . . .We have no knowledge going beyond experience; but at no stage are we entitled to look upon experience as complete. Thus knowledge, even at its highest, provides us with nothing more than a segment of the existing world. Every reality, we may find, is itself again a part of a wider reality." (I owe this passage to Arne Petersen.) The best intuitive idea of this incompleteness is that of a map showing the table on which the map is being drawn, and the map as it is drawn. (See also my reply to Watkins below [added after completion of this *Autobiography*].)

204 See my paper [1948(d)], now [1963(a)], Chap. 16 and, more fully, [1957(i)] and [1969(k)], now [1972(a)], Chap. 5.

205 There is an interesting and hard-hitting article by William Kneale, "Scientific Revolution for Ever?", *The British Journal for the Philosophy of Science*, **19** (1968), 27-42, in which he seems to sense something of the position outlined above. (In many points of detail, however, he misunderstands me; for example, on p. 36: "For if there is no truth, there cannot be any approximation to truth. . . ." This is true. But where did I ever suggest that there is no truth? The set of true theoretical statements of physics may not be [finitely] axiomatizable; in view of Gödel's theorem, it almost certainly is not. But the sequence of our attempts to produce better and better finite axiomatizations may well be a revolutionary sequence in which we constantly create new theoretical and mathematical means for more nearly approaching this unattainable end.)

206 See *C.&R.* [1963(a)], p. 114 (n. 30 to Chap. 3 and text), and the third paragraph of section 19 of the present *Autobiography*.

207 In a letter to me of June 15, 1935, Einstein approved of my views concerning "falsifiability as the decisive property of any theory about reality".

208 See *Albert Einstein: Philosopher-Scientist*, p. 674 (see n. 122 above); also relevant is Einstein's letter on p. 29 of Schrödinger et al., *Briefe zur Wellenmechanik*, ed. by K. Przibram (Vienna: Springer-Verlag, 1963); in the English translation, *Letters on Wave Mechanics* (London: Vision, 1967), the letter appears on pp. 31 f.

209 See my paper "What is Dialectic?", now Chap. 15 of *C.&R.* [1963(a)]. This is a stylistically revised form of [1940(a)], with several additional footnotes. The passage summarized here in the text is from *C.&R.*, p. 313, first new paragraph. As shown by n. 3 of this

chapter (n. 1 of [1940(a)]), I regarded this description (in which I stressed that *testing* a theory is part of its criticism, that is, of *EE*) as summarizing the scientific procedure described in *L.d.F.*

[210] Compare with this the problems "which comes first, the hen (*H*) or the egg (*O*)?", and "Which comes first, the Hypothesis (*H*) or the observation (*O*)?", discussed on p. 47 of *C.&R.* [1963(a)]. See also [1949(d)], now in English as the Appendix to [1972(a)]; esp. pp. 345 f.

[211] See, for example, [1968(r)], esp. pp. 36-39; [1972(a)], pp. 170-78.

[212] Schrödinger defends this view as a form of idealism or panpsychism in the second part of his posthumous book, *Mein Weltbild* (Vienna: Zsolnay, 1961), Chap. 1, pp. 61-67; English translation, *My View of the World* (Cambridge: Cambridge University Press, 1964).

[213] I am alluding to Winston Churchill, *My Early Life* (London, 1930). The arguments can be found in Chap. IX ("Education at Bangalore"), that is, on pp. 131 f. of the Keystone Library edition (1934), or the Macmillan edition (1944). I have quoted from the passage at length in section 5 of Chap. 2 of [1972(a)]; see pp. 42-43.

[214] The quotation is not from memory but from the first paragraph of Chap. 6 of Erwin Schrödinger, *Mind and Matter* (Cambridge: Cambridge University Press, 1958), p. 88; and of Erwin Schrödinger, *What Is Life?* and *Mind and Matter* (Cambridge: Cambridge University Press, 1967; two books issued in one paperback volume), p. 166. The views which Schrödinger defended in our conversations were very similar.

[215] [1956(b)]. This is now part of Chap. 10 of [1974(a)].

[216] Incidentally, the replacement here of "impossible" by "infinitely improbable" (perhaps a dubious replacement) would not affect the main point of these considerations; for though entropy is connected with probability, not every reference to probability brings in entropy.

[217] See *Mind and Matter*, p. 86; or *What is Life?* and *Mind and Matter*, p. 164.

[218] See *Mind and Matter*. He used the wording "methodology of the physicist", probably to dissociate himself from a methodology of physics emanating from a philosopher.

[219] *What Is Life?*, pp. 74 f.

[220] *Ibid.*, p. 78.

[221] *Ibid.*, p. 79.

[222] See my [1967(b) and (h)].

[223] See, for example, "Quantum Mechanics without 'The Observer' " [1967(k)] ([1974(a)], Chap. 3); "Of Clouds and Clocks" [1966(f)] ([1972(a)], Chap. 6); "Is there an Epistemological Problem of Perception?" [1968(e)]; "On the Theory of the Objective Mind" [1968(r)], "Epistemology Without a Knowing Subject" [1968(s)] (respectively Chaps. 4 and 3 of [1972(a)]); and "A Pluralist Approach to the Philosophy of History" [1969(j)].

[224] Tarski has often been criticized for attributing truth to *sentences*: a sentence, it is said, is a mere string of words without meaning; thus it cannot be true. But Tarski speaks of "*meaningful* sentences", and so this criticism, like so much philosophical criticism, is not only invalid but simply irresponsible. See *Logic, Semantics, Metamathematics*, p. 178 (Definition 12) and p. 156, n. 1 (see n. 188 above); and, for comments, my [1955(d)] (now an addendum to Chap. 9 of my [1972(a)] and [1959(a)], [1966(e)], and later editions, to *1 to section 84.

[225] This holds even for the validity of some very simple rules, rules whose validity has been denied on intuitive grounds by some philosophers (esp. G. E. Moore); the simplest of all these rules is: from any statement *a*, we may validly deduce *a* itself. Here the impossibility of constructing a counterexample can be shown very easily. Whether or not anybody accepts this argument is his private affair. If he does not, he is simply mistaken. See also my [1947(a)].

[226] I have said things like this many times since [1934(b)], sections 27 and 29, and [1947(a)]—see [1968(s)]; ([1972(a)], Chap. 3), for example; and I have suggested that what I have called the "degree of corroboration of a hypothesis *h* in the light of the tests or of the evidence *e*", may be interpreted as a condensed report of the past critical discussions of the hypothesis *h* in the light of the tests *e*. (Cp. nn. 156-58 in section 20 above, and text.) Thus, I

wrote, for example, in *L.Sc.D.* [1959(a)], p. 414: "...*C(h,e)* can be adequately interpreted as degree of corroboration of *h*—or of the rationality of our belief in *h*, in the light of tests—only if *e* consists of reports of the outcome of sincere attempts to refute *h*. . .". In other words, only a report of a discussion which is sincerely critical can be said to determine, even partially, the *degree of rationality* (of our belief in *h*). In the quoted passage (as opposed to my terminology here in the text) I used the words "degree of rationality of our belief", which should be even clearer than "rational belief'; see also *ibid.*, p. 407, where I explain this, and make my objectivist attitude sufficiently clear, I think (as I have done *ad nauseam* elsewhere). Nevertheless the quoted passage has been construed (by Professor Lakatos, "Changes in the Problem of Inductive Logic", in *Problem of Inductive Logic*, ed. by Lakatos, n. 6 on pp. 412 f. [see n. 41 above]) as a symptom of the shakiness of my objectivism; and an indication that I am prone to subjectivist lapses. It is, I think, impossible to avoid all misunderstandings. I wonder how my present remarks about the insignificance of belief will be construed.

227 See esp. my [1971(i)], now Chap. 1 of [1972(a)].

228 What I have called the "fashionable view" may be traced back to J. S. Mill. For modern formulations see P. F. Strawson, *Introduction to Logical Theory* (London: Methuen & Co., 1952; New York: John Wiley & Sons, 1952), pp. 249 f.; Nelson Goodman, *Fact, Fiction, and Forecast* (Cambridge, Mass.: Harvard University Press, 1955), pp. 63-66; and Rudolf Carnap, "Inductive Logic and Inductive Intuition", in *Problem of Inductive Logic*, ed. by Lakatos, pp. 258-67, particularly p. 265 (see n. 41 above).

229 This seems to me a more carefully worded form of one of Carnap's arguments; see Carnap, "Inductive Logic and Inductive Intuition", p. 265, the passage beginning: "I think that it is not only legitimate to appeal to inductive reasoning in defending inductive reasoning, but that it is indispensable."

230 *Ibid.*, p. 311.

231 For Carnap's "instance confirmation" see my *C.&R.* [1963(a)], pp. 282 f. What Carnap calls the "instance confirmation" of a law (a universal hypothesis) is equal in fact to the degree of confirmation (or the probability) of the next instance of the law; and this approaches 1/2 or 0.99, provided the relative frequency of the observed favourable instances approaches 1/2, or 0.99, respectively. As a consequence, a law that is refuted by every second instance (or by every hundredth instance) has an instance confirmation that approaches 1/2 (or 0.99); which is absurd. I explained this first in [1934(b)], p. 191, that is [1959(a)], p. 257, long before Carnap thought of instance confirmation, in a discussion of various possibilities of attributing "probability" to a hypothesis; and I then said that this consequence was "devastating" for this idea of probability. I am puzzled by Carnap's reply to this in Lakatos, ed., *Problem of Inductive Logic*, pp. 309 f. (see n. 41 above). There Carnap says about instance confirmation that its numerical value "is. . .an important characteristic of the law. In Popper's example, the law which is in the average satisfied by one half of the instances, has, on the basis of my definition, not the probability 1/2, as Popper erroneously believes, but 0." But although it does have what Carnap (and I) both call "probability 0", it also has what Carnap calls "instance confirmation 1/2"; and this was the issue under discussion (even though I used in 1934 the term "probability" in my criticism of the function which Carnap much later called "instance confirmation").

232 I am grateful to David Miller for pointing out to me this characteristic of all Hintikka's systems. Jaakko Hintikka's first paper on the subject was "Towards a Theory of Inductive Generalization", in *Logic, Methodology and Philosophy of Science*, ed. by Yehoshua Bar-Hillel (Amsterdam: North-Holland Publishing Co., 1964), Vol. II, pp. 274-88. Full references can be found in Risto Hilpinen, "Rules of Acceptance and Inductive Logic", *Acta Philosophica Fennica*, 21 (1968).

233 According to Carnap's position of approximately 1949-56 (at least), inductive logic is analytically true. But if so, I cannot see how the allegedly rational degree of belief could undergo such radical changes as from 0 (strongest disbelief) to 0.7 (mild belief). According to Carnap's latest theories "inductive intuition" operates as a court of appeal. I have given reasons to show how irresponsible and biased this court of appeal is; see my [1968(i)], esp. pp. 297-303.

²³⁴ Cp. *Fact, Fiction, and Forecast*, p. 65 (see n. 228 above).

²³⁵ See [1968(i)]. For my positive theory of corroboration, see the end of section 20 above, and also the end of section 33, esp. n. 243 and text.

²³⁶ See [1957(i)] and [1969(k)], now reprinted as Chap. 5 of [1972(a)]; and [1957(l)].

²³⁷ See [1959(a)], end of section 29, and p. 315 of the translation of [1935(a)], there in Appendix *i, 2, pp. 315-17; or [1963(a)], Introduction; and see below, n. 243 and text.

²³⁸ I gave a course of lectures on this particular problem—criticism without justification—in the Institute of Advanced Studies in Vienna in 1964.

²³⁹ See esp. [1957(i)] and [1969(k)], now Chap. 5 of [1972(a)]; Chap. 10 of [1963(a)]; and Chap. 2 of [1972(a)].(Chap. 2 of [1972(a)].) See n. 165a to my *Replies*.

²⁴⁰ See [1934(b)], p. 186; [1959(a)], p. 252 (section 79).

²⁴¹ Cp. [1958(c)], [1958(f)], [1958(g)]; now Chap. 8 of [1963(a)].

²⁴² The term "metaphysical research programme" was used in my lectures from about 1949 on, if not earlier; but it did not get into print until 1958, though clearly in evidence in the last chapter of the *Postscript* (in galley proofs since 1957). I made the *Postscript* available to my colleagues, and Professor Lakatos acknowledges that what he calls "scientific research programmes" are in the tradition of what I described as "metaphysical research programmes" ("metaphysical" because nonfalsifiable). See p. 183 of his paper "Falsification and the Methodology of Scientific Research Programmes", in *Criticism and the Growth of Knowledge*, ed. by Imre Lakatos and Alan Musgrave (Cambridge: Cambridge University Press, 1970).

²⁴³ Incidentally, realists believe, of course, in truth (and believers in truth believe in reality; see [1963(a)], p. 116)—they even know that there are "as many" true statements as there are false ones. (For what follows here, see also the end of section 20, above.) Since the purpose of this volume is to further the discussion between my critics and myself, I may here perhaps refer briefly to G. J. Warnock's review of my *L.Sc.D.* in *Mind*, **59** (1960), 99-101 (see also n. 25 in section 7 above). Here we read, on p. 100, about my views on the problem of induction: "Now Popper says emphatically that this venerable problem is insoluble. . .". I am sure I have never said so, least of all emphatically, for I always flattered myself that I actually solved this problem in the book under review. Later we read, on the same page: "[Popper] wishes to claim for his own views, not that they offer a solution of Hume's problem, but that they do not permit it to arise." This clashes with the suggestion at the beginning of my book (esp. sections 1 and 4) that what I have called Hume's problem of induction is one of the two fundamental problems of the theory of knowledge. Later we get quite a good version of my formulation of that problem: "how. . .can [we] be justified in regarding as true, or even probably true, the general statements of. . .a scientific theory". My straight answer to this question was: *we cannot be justified.* (But we can sometimes be justified in *preferring* one competing theory to another; see the text to which the present note is appended.) Yet the review continues: "There is, Popper holds, no hope of answering this question, since it requires that we should solve the insoluble problem of induction. But, he says, it is needless and misguided to ask this question at all." None of the passages I have quoted are meant to be *critical*; rather, they claim to *report* what I "say emphatically"; "wish to claim"; "hold"; and "say". A little later in the review the criticism begins with the words: "Now does this eliminate the 'insoluble' problem of induction?".

Since I am at it, I may as well mention that this reviewer concentrates his criticism of my book upon the following thesis which I am putting here in italics (p. 101; the word "rely" here means, as the context shows, "rely for the future"): "Popper evidently assumes, what of course his language implies, that *we are entitled to rely* [for the future] *upon a well-corroborated theory*". But I have never assumed anything like this. What I assert is that a well-corroborated theory (which has been critically discussed and compared with its competitors, and which has *so far* "survived") is rationally *preferable* to a less well-corroborated theory; and that (short of proposing a new competing theory) we have no better way open to us than to prefer it, and act upon it, *even though we know very well that it may let us down badly in some future cases.* Thus I have to reject the reviewer's criticism as based on a complete misunderstanding of my text, caused by his substitution of his own problem of induction (the traditional problem) for mine (which is very different). See now also [1971(i)], reprinted as Chap. 1 of [1972(a)].

[244] See Ernst Mach, *Die Prinzipien der Wärmelehre* (Leipzig: Barth, 1896), p. 240; on p. 239 the term "general philosophical" is equated with "metaphysical"; and Mach hints that Mayer (whom he greatly admired) was inspired by "metaphysical" intuitions.

[245] See "A Note on Berkeley as Precursor of Mach" [1953(d)]; now Chap. 6 of [1963(a)].

[246] See Schrödinger et al., *Briefe zur Wellenmechanik*, p. 32; I have used my own translations, but the letter can be found in English in the English ed. *Letters on Wave Mechanics*, pp. 35 f. (see n. 208 above). Einstein's letter is dated August 9, 1939.

[247] Cp. Erwin Schrödinger, "Die gegenwärtige Situation in der Quantenmechanik", *Die Naturwissenschaften,* **23** (1935), 807-12, 823-28, 844-49.

[248](Italics mine.) See Einstein's letter referred to in n. 246 above, and also his very similar letter of December 22, 1950, in the same book, pp. 36 f. (translation, pp. 39 f.). (Note that Einstein takes it for granted that a probabilistic theory must be interpreted subjectively if it refers to a single case; this is an issue on which he and I disagreed from 1935 on. See [1959(a)], p. 459, and my footnote.)

[249] See especially the references to Franz Exner's views in Schrödinger, *Science, Theory and Man*, pp. 71, 133, 142 f. (see n. 132 above).

[250] Cp. my paper "Quantum Mechanics without 'The Observer' " [1967(k)] (now Chap. 3 of [1974(a)]), where references to my other writings in this field will be found (the most important are Chaps. 4 and 5 of [1974(a)])

[251] Van der Waerden's letter is dated October 19, 1968. (It is a letter in which he also criticizes me for a mistaken historical reference to Jacob Bernoulli, on p. 29 of [1967(k)]; see now Chap. 3 of [1974(a)]).

[252] Since this is an autobiography, I might perhaps mention that in 1947 or 1948 I received a letter from Victor Kraft, writing in the name of the Faculty of Philosophy of the University of Vienna, asking whether I would be prepared to take up Schlick's chair. I replied that I would not leave England.

[253] Max Planck questioned Mach's competence as a physicist even within Mach's favourite field, the phenomenological theory of heat. See Max Planck, "Zur Machschen Theorie der physikalischen Erkenntnis", *Physikalische Zeitschrift,* **11** (1910), 1186-90. (See also Planck's preceding paper, "Die Einheit des physikalischen Weltbildes", *Physikalische Zeitschrift,* **10** [1909], 62-75; and Mach's reply, "Die Leitgedanken meiner wissenschaftlichen Erkenntnislehre und ihre Aufnahme durch die Zeitgenossen", *Physikalische Zeitschrift,* **11** [1910], 599-606.)

[254] See Josef Mayerhöfer, "Ernst Machs Berufung an die Wiener Universität, 1895", in *Symposium aus Anlass des 50. Todestages von Ernst Mach* (Ernst Mach Institut, Freiburg im Breisgau, 1966), pp. 12-25. A charming (German) biography of Boltzmann is E. Broda, *Ludwig Boltzmann* (Vienna: Franz Deuticke, 1955).

[255] See n. 256 and n. 261 below.

[256] See E. Zermelo, "Über einen Satz der Dynamik und die mechanische Wärmetheorie", *Wiedemannsche Annalen (Annalen der Physik),* **57** (1896), 485-94. Twenty years before Zermelo, Boltzmann's friend Loschmidt had pointed out that by reversing all velocities in a gas the gas can be made to run backward and thus to revert to the ordered state from which it is supposed to have lapsed into disorder. This objection of Loschmidt's is called the "reversibility objection", while Zermelo's is called the "recurrence objection".

[257] Paul and Tatiana Ehrenfest, "Über zwei bekannte Einwände gegen das Boltzmannsche *H*-Theorem", *Physikalische Zeitschrift,* **8** (1907), 311-14.

[258] See, for example, Max Born, *Natural Philosophy of Cause and Chance* (Oxford: Oxford University Press, 1949), who writes on p. 58: "Zermelo, a German mathematician, who worked on abstract problems like the theory of Cantor's sets and transfinite numbers, ventured into physics by translating Gibbs's work on statistical mechanics into German." But note the dates:

Zermelo criticized Boltzmann in 1896; published the translation of Gibbs whom he greatly admired in 1905; wrote his first paper on set theory in 1904, and his second only in 1908. Thus he was a physicist before he became an "abstract" mathematician.

[259] Cp. Erwin Schrödinger, "Irreversibility", *Proceedings of the Royal Irish Academy*, **53**A (1950), 189-95.

[260] See Ludwig Boltzmann, "Zu Hrn. Zermelo's Abhandlung: 'Über die mechanische Erklärung irreversibler Vorgänge' ", *Wiedemannsche Annalen (Annalen der Physik)*, **60** (1897), 392-98. The gist of the passage is repeated in his *Vorlesungen über Gastheorie* (Leipzig: J. A. Barth, 1898), Vol. II, pp. 257 f.; again I have used my own translation, but the corresponding passage can be found in L. Boltzmann, *Lectures on Gas Theory*, trans. by Stephen G. Brush (Berkeley and Los Angeles: University of California Press, 1964). pp. 446 f.

[261] Boltzmann's best proof of $dS/dt \geq 0$ was based upon his so-called collision integral. This represents the *average* effect upon a single molecule of *the system of all the other molecules of the gas*. My suggestion is that (a) it is not the collisions which lead to Boltzmann's results, but the *averaging* as such; the time coordinate plays a part because there was no averaging before the collision, and so entropy increase *seems* to be the result of physical collisions. My suggestion is further that, quite apart from Boltzmann's derivation, (b) collisions *between the molecules of the gas* are not decisive for an entropy increase, though the assumption of molecular disorder (which enters through the averaging) is. For assume that a gas takes up at one time one half of a box: soon it will "fill" the whole box—even if it is so rare that (practically) *the only collisions are with the walls*. (The walls are essential; see point (3) of [1956(g)].) I further suggest that (c) we may interpret Boltzmann's derivation to mean that an ordered system X becomes almost certainly (that is, with probability 1) disordered *upon collision with any system Y* (say, the walls) which is in a state chosen at random, or more precisely, in a state not matched in every detail to the state of X. In this interpretation the theorem is of course valid. For the "reversibility objection" (see n. 256 above) would only show that for systems such as X in its disordered state *there exists at least one* other ("matched") system Y which by (reverse) collision would return the system X to its ordered state. The mere mathematical existence (even in a constructive sense) of such a system Y which is "matched" to X creates no difficulty, since the probability that X should collide with a system matched to itself will be equal to zero. Thus the H-theorem, $dS/dt \geq 0$, holds *almost certainly for all colliding systems*. (This explains why the second law holds for all *closed* systems.) The "recurrence objection" (see n. 256 above) is valid, but it does not mean that the probability of a recurrence—of the system's taking up a state in which it was before—will be appreciably greater than zero for a system of any degree of complexity. Still, there are open problems. (See my series of notes in *Nature*, [1956(b)], [1956(g)], [1957(d)], [1958(b)], [1965(f)], [1967(b) and (h)], and my note [1957(f)] in *The British Journal for the Philosophy of Science*; and now Chap. 10 of [1974(a)].

[262] See [1956(b)] and section 30 (on Schrödinger) above, esp. the text to nn. 215 and 216.

[263] See above, section 30. I lectured on these matters to the Oxford University Science Society on October 20, 1967. In this lecture, now Chap. 11 of my [1974(a)], I also gave a brief criticism of Schrödinger's influential paper "Irreversibility" (see n. 259 above); he writes there on p. 191: "I wish to reformulate the laws of...irreversibility...in such a way, that the logical contradiction [which] *any* derivation of those laws from reversible models seems to involve is removed once and for ever". Schrödinger's reformulation consists in an ingenious way (a method later called the "method of branch systems") of introducing Boltzmannian arrows of time by a kind of operational definition; the result is Boltzmann's. And the method, like Boltzmann's, is too strong: it does not (as Schrödinger thinks) save Boltzmann's derivation—that is, his physical explanation of the H-theorem; instead, it provides, rather, a (tautological) definition from which the second law follows immediately. So it makes any physical explanation of the second law redundant.

[264] *Die Prinzipien der Wärmelehre*, p. 363 (see n. 244 above). Boltzmann is not mentioned there by name (his name appears, with a modicum of praise, on the next page) but the description of the "move" (*"Zug"*) is unmistakable: it really describes Boltzmann's wavering. Mach's attack in this chapter ("The Opposition between Mechanistic and Phenomenological Physics"), if read

between the lines, is severe; and it is combined with a hint of self-congratulation and with a confident belief that the judgement of history will be on his side; as indeed it was.

265 The present section has been added here because it is, I believe, significant for an understanding of my intellectual development, or more especially, for my more recent fight against subjectivism in physics.

266 See Leo Szilard "Über die Ausdehnung der phänomenologischen Thermodynamik auf die Schwankungserscheinungen", *Zeitschrift für Physik,* **32** (1925), 753-88 and "Über die Entropieverminderung in einem thermodynamischen System bei Eingriffen intelligenter Wesen", *ibid.,* **53** (1929), 840-56; this second paper has been translated as "On the Decrease of Entropy in a Thermodynamic System by the Intervention of Intelligent Beings", *Behavioural Science, 9* (1964), 301-10. Szilard's views were refined by L. Brillouin, *Scientific Uncertainty and Information* (New York: Academic Press, 1964). But I believe that all these views have been clearly and decisively criticized by J. D. Fast, *Entropy*, revised and enlarged reprint of 2d ed. (London: Macmillan, 1970), Appendix 5. I owe this reference to Troels Eggers Hansen.

267 Norbert Wiener, *Cybernetics: Or Control & Communication in the Animal & the Machine* (Cambridge, Mass.: M.I.T. Press, 1948), pp. 44 f., tried to marry this theory to Boltzmann's theory; but I do not think that the spouses actually met in logical space—not even in that of Wiener's book, where they are confined to strictly different contexts. (They could meet through the postulate that what is called consciousness is *essentially* growth of knowledge, that is, information increase; but I really do not wish to encourage idealistic speculation, and I greatly fear the fertility of such a marriage.) However, the subjective theory of entropy is closely connected both with Maxwell's famous demon and with Boltzmann's *H*-theorem. Max Born, for example, who believes in the original interpretation of the *H*-theorem, attributes to it a (partially?) subjective meaning, interpreting the collision integral and the "averaging" (both discussed in n. 261 in section 35, above) as "mixing mechanical knowledge with ignorance of detail"; this mixing of knowledge and ignorance, he says, "leads to irreversibility". Cp. Born, *Natural Philosophy of Cause and Chance*, p. 59 (see n. 258 above).

268 See, for example, sections 34-39 and 43 of *L.d.F.* [1934(b)], [1966(e)], and of *L.Sc.D.* [1959(a)].

269 See esp. [1959(a)], new Appendix *xi (2), p. 444; [1966(e)], p. 399.

270 For measurement and its content-increasing (or information-increasing) function see section 34 of [1934(b)] and [1959(a)].

271 For a general criticism of thought experiments see the new Appendix *xi of my *L.Sc.D.* [1959(a)], esp. pp. 443 f.

272 Like the assumption that the gas consists of *one* molecule *M*, the assumption that, without expenditure of energy or negentropy, we can slide a piston from the side into the cylinder, is freely used by my opponents in their proofs of the convertibility of knowledge and negentropy. It is harmless here, and it is not really needed: see n. 274 below.

273 David Bohm, *Quantum Theory* (New York: Prentice-Hall, 1951), p. 608, refers to Szilard, but operates with many molecules. He does not, however, rely on Szilard's arguments but rather on the general idea that Maxwell's demon is incompatible with the law of entropy increase.

274 See my paper, "Irreversibility; or Entropy since 1905" [1957(f)], a paper in which I referred especially to Einstein's famous paper of 1905 on Brownian movement. In that paper I also criticized, among others, Szilard, though not via the thought experiment used here. I had first developed this thought experiment some time before 1957, and I lectured about it, on the same lines as in the text here, in 1962, on Professor E. L. Hill's invitation, in the physics department of the University of Minnesota.

275 See P. K. Feyerabend, "On the Possibility of a Perpetuum Mobile of the Second Kind", in *Mind, Matter, and Method, Essays in Honor of Herbert Feigl*, ed. by P. K. Feyerabend and G. Maxwell (Minneapolis: University of Minnesota Press, 1966), pp. 409-12. For a further criticism of this idea, see Chap. 10 of my *Philosophy and Physics* [1974(a)]. I should mention that the idea of building a flap into the piston (see Fig. 3 above), to avoid the awkwardness of having to slide it

in from the side, is a refinement that Feyerabend made to my original analysis of Szilard's thought experiment.

276 Samuel Butler has suffered many wrongs from the evolutionists, including a serious wrong from Charles Darwin himself who, though greatly upset by it, never put things right. This was done, as far as possible, by Charles's son Francis, after Butler's death. The story, which is a bit involved, deserves to be retold. See pp. 167-219 of Nora Barlow, ed., *The Autobiography of Charles Darwin* (London: Collins, 1958), esp. p. 219, where references to most of the other relevant material will be found.

277 See [1945(a)], section 27; cp. [1957(g)] and later editions, esp. pp. 106-8.

278 I am alluding to Schrödinger's remarks on evolutionary theory in *Mind and Matter*, especially those indicated by his phrase "Feigned Lamarckism"; see *Mind and Matter*, p. 26; and p. 118 of the combined reprint cited in n. 214 above.

279 The lecture [1961(j)] was delivered on October 31, 1961, and the manuscript was deposited on the same day in the Bodleian Library. It now appears in a revised version, with an addendum, as Chap. 7 of my [1972(a)].

280 See [1966(f)]; now Chap. 6 of [1972(a)].

281 See section 33 above, esp. n. 242.

282 See *L.Sc.D.*, section 67.

283 For the problem of "degrees of prediction" see F. A. Hayek, "Degrees of Explanation", first published in 1955 and now Chap. 1 of his *Studies in Philosophy, Politics and Economics* (London: Routledge & Kegan Paul, 1967); see esp. n. 4 on p. 9. For Darwinism and the production of "a great variety of structures", and for its irrefutability, see esp. p. 32.

284 Darwin's theory of sexual selection is partly an attempt to explain falsifying instances of this theory; such things, for example, as the peacock's tail, or the stag's antlers. See the text before n. 286 below.

285 For the problem of "explanation in principle" (or "of the principle") in contrast to "explanation in detail", see Hayek, *Philosophy, Politics and Economics*, esp. section VI, pp. 11-14.

286 David Lack makes this point in his fascinating book, *Darwin's Finches* (Cambridge: Cambridge University Press, 1947), p. 72: ". . .in Darwin's finches all the main beak differences between the species may be regarded as adaptations to differences in diet." (Footnote references to the behaviour of birds I owe to Arne Petersen.)

287 As Lack so vividly describes it, *ibid.*, pp. 58 f., the *absence* of a long tongue in the beak of a woodpeckerlike species of Darwin's finches does not prevent this bird from excavating in trunks and branches for insects—that is, it sticks to its taste; however, due to its particular anatomical disability it has developed a skill to meet this difficulty: "Having excavated, it picks up a cactus spine or twig, one or two inches long, and holding it lengthwise in its beak, pokes it up the crack, dropping the twig to seize the insect as it emerges." This striking behavioural trend may be a nongenetical "tradition" which has developed in that species with or without teaching among its members; it may also be a genetically entrenched behaviour pattern. That is to say, a genuine behavioural invention can take the place of an anatomic change. However this may be, this example shows how the behaviour of organisms can be a "spearhead" of evolution: a type of biological problem solving which may lead to the emergence of new forms and species.

288 See now my 1971 Addendum, "A Hopeful Behavioural Monster", to my Spencer Lecture, Chap. 7 of [1972(a)].

289 This is one of the main ideas of my Spencer Lecture, now Chap. 7 of [1972(a)].

290 The theory of geographic separation or geographic speciation was first developed by Moritz Wagner in *Die Darwin'sche Theorie und das Migrationsgesetz der Organismen* (Leipzig: Duncker und Humblot, 1868); English translation, J. L. Laird, trans., *The Darwinian Theory and the Law of Migration of Organisms* (London: Edward Stanford, 1873). See also Theodosius Dobzhansky, *Genetics and the Origin of Species*, 3d rev. ed. (New York: Columbia University Press, 1951), pp. 179-211.

291 See [1966(f)], pp. 20-26, esp. pp. 24 f., point (11). Now [1972(a)], p. 244.

292 See [1970(l)], esp. pp. 5-10; [1972(a)], pp. 289-95.

293 Since I completed this *Autobiography* I have taken up a suggestion of John Eccles to call the third world "world 3"; see J. C. Eccles, *Facing Reality* (New York, Heidelberg and Berlin: Springer-Verlag, 1970). See also n. 7a above.

294 This argument for something's reality—that we can take "cross bearings" which agree—is, I think, due to Winston Churchill. See p. 43 of Chap. 2 of my *Objective Knowledge* [1972(a)].

295 Cp. p. 15 of [1967(k)] (now Chap. 3 of *Philosophy and Physics* [1974(a)]): ". . .by and large I regard as excellent Landé's suggestion to call physically real what is 'kickable' (and able to kick back if kicked)."

296 Take, for example, Einstein's misunderstanding of his own requirement of covariance (first challenged by Kretschmann), which had a long history before it was finally cleared up, mainly (I think) due to the efforts of Fock and Peter Havas. The relevant papers are Erich Kretschmann, "Über den physikalischen Sinn der Relativitätspostulate, A. Einsteins neue und seine ursprüngliche Relativitätstheorie", *Annalen der Physik*, 4th ser. **53** (1917), 575-614; and Einstein's reply, "Prinzipielles zur allgemeinen Relativitätstheorie", *ibid.*, **55** (1918), 241-44. See also V. A. Fock, *The Theory of Space, Time and Gravitation* (London: Pergamon Press, 1959; 2d rev. ed., Oxford, 1964); and Havas, "Four-Dimensional Formulations of Newtonian Mechanics and their Relation to Relativity", (see n. 32 above).

297 See [1968(r)], [1968(s)]; see also "A Realist View of Logic, Physics, and History" [1970(l)], and [1966(f)]. (These papers are now respectively Chaps. 4, 3, 8, 6 of [1972(a)].)

298 The talk of "substances" arises from the problem of change ("What remains constant in change?") and from the attempt to answer *what-is?* questions. The old witticism that Bertrand Russell's grandmother plagued him with—"What is mind? No matter! What is matter? Never mind!"—seems to me not only to the point but perfectly adequate. Better ask: "What does mind?".

299 The last two sentences may be regarded as containing an argument against panpsychism. The argument is, of course, inconclusive (since panpsychism is irrefutable), and it remains so even if it is strengthened by the following observation: even if we attribute conscious states to (say) all atoms, the problem of explaining the states of consciousness (such as recollection or anticipation) of higher animals remains as difficult as it was before, without this attribution.

300 See my papers "Language and the Body-Mind Problem" [1953(a)] and "A Note on the Body-Mind Problem" [1955(c)]; now Chaps. 12 and 13 of [1963(a)].

301 Wittgenstein ("The riddle does not exist") exaggerated the gulf between the world of describable ("sayable") facts and the world of that which is deep and which cannot be said. There are gradations; moreover, the world of the sayable does not always lack depth. And if we think of depth, there is a gulf within those things that can be said—between a cookery book and Copernicus's *De revolutionibus*—and there is a gulf within those things that cannot be said—between some piece of artistic tastelessness and a portrait by Holbein; and these gulfs may be far deeper than that between something that is sayable and something that is not. It is his facile solution of the problem of depth—the thesis "the deep is the unsayable"—which unites Wittgenstein the positivist with Wittgenstein the mystic. Incidentally, this thesis had long been traditional, especially in Vienna, and not merely among philosophers. See the quotation from Robert Reininger in *L.Sc.D.*, n. 4 to section 30. Many positivists agreed; for example, Richard von Mises, who was a great admirer of the mystic poet Rilke.

302 David Miller suggests that I called the third world in to redress the balance of the first and the second.

303 See sections 10 and 15 above.

304 After writing this I became acquainted with the second volume of Konrad Lorenz's collected papers (*Über tierisches und menschliches Verhalten*, Gesammelte Abhandlungen [Munich: R. Piper & Co. Verlag, 1967], Vol. II; see esp. pp. 361 f.). In these papers Lorenz

criticizes, with a reference to Erich von Holst, the view that the delimitation between the mental and the physical is also one between the higher and the lower functions of control: some comparatively primitive processes (such as a bad toothache) are intensely conscious, while some highly controlled processes (such as the elaborate interpretation of sense stimuli) are unconscious, so that their result—perception—appears to us (wrongly) as just "given". This seems to me an important insight not to be overlooked in any theory of the body-mind problem. (On the other hand, I cannot imagine that the all-absorbing character of a bad toothache caused by a dying nerve has any biological value as a control function; and we are here interested in the hierarchical character of *controls*.)

[305] R. W. Sperry ("The Great Cerebral Commissure", *Scientific American*, **210** [1964], 42-52; and "Brain Bisection and Mechanisms of Consciousness", in *Brain and Conscious Experience*, ed. by J. C. Eccles [Berlin, Heidelberg and New York: Springer-Verlag, 1966], pp. 298-313) warns us that we must not think that the separation is absolute: there is a certain amount of overspill to the other side of the brain. Nevertheless he writes, in the second paper mentioned, p. 300: "The same kind of right-left mental separation [reported about patients manipulating objects] is seen in tests involving vision. Recall that the right half of the visual field, along with the right hand, is represented together in the left hemisphere, and vice versa. Visual stimuli such as pictures, words, numbers, and geometric forms flashed on a screen directly in front of the subject and to the right side of a central fixation point, so that they are projected to the dominant speech hemispheres, are all described and reported correctly with no special difficulty. On the other hand, similar material flashed to the left half of the visual field and hence into the minor hemisphere are completely lost to the talking hemisphere. Stimuli flashed to one half field seem to have no influence whatever, in tests to date, on the perception and interpretation of stimuli presented to the other half field."

[306] Wolfgang Köhler, *The Place of Value in a World of Fact* (New York: Liveright, 1938). I have substituted "Values" for "Value" to indicate my stress on pluralism.

[307] See for this the end of my reply to Ernst Gombrich below. (Added after completion of this *Autobiography*.)

[308] Schiller says something like this:
> Friends, what a pleasure to serve you! But I do so from fond inclination.
> Thus no virtue is mine, and I feel greatly aggrieved.
> What can I do about it? I must teach myself to abhor you,
> And, with disgust in my heart, serve you as duty commands.

[309] See the *Addendum* "Facts, Standards, and Truth" in *O.S.*, 4th [1962(c)] and later editions, Vol. II.

PART TWO

DESCRIPTIVE
AND CRITICAL ESSAYS
ON THE PHILOSOPHY
OF KARL POPPER

1

Victor Kraft

POPPER AND THE VIENNA CIRCLE

Contents

Popper never belonged to the Vienna Circle, never took part in its meetings, and yet cannot be thought of as outside it. Already in my 1950 article dealing with the Vienna Circle I found it necessary to refer to him repeatedly. On the other hand, Popper's work cannot be genetically understood without reference to the Vienna Circle. As Popper stands in a close, inextricable relationship with the development of the Vienna Circle, so the Circle was also of essential significance for his own development. Thus Popper himself says of Carnap's *Logical Syntax of Language* that "the book. . .marks the beginning of a revolution in my own philosophical thinking."[1] And in his latest book, *Conjectures and Refutations* (1963), Popper proves his relationship with the Vienna Circle by mentioning it several times and producing valuable insights into it, especially in Chapter 11, "Demarcation Between Science and Metaphysics" (pp. 253 ff.). Popper was in personal contact with only a few members of the Vienna Circle, especially with Carnap and Feigl, but also with Waismann, Menger, Gödel, and with myself. In 1928 or 1929 he participated in Carnap's seminar.[2] In 1931 or 1932 his first book, which has remained unpublished, was read and discussed by several members of the Vienna Circle.[3] In 1932 Popper spent his summer vacation with Carnap and Feigl in the Ötz Valley in Tyrol, an opportunity filled with philosophical discussions, both "long and fascinating."[4] Popper's relationship with the Vienna Circle is shown by the fact that in Paris in 1935 and in Copenhagen in 1936 he participated and discussed in Congresses sponsored by the movement which started from the Vienna Circle. At the first meeting Neurath even called him "the official opponent" of the Circle.[5] This relationship with the Vienna Circle becomes also clear from such details as that he took over Waismann's concept of the logical scope [6] or that he uses a waving fog to illustrate a world without structure, as done by Zilsel, a member of the Vienna Circle.[7]

Popper's direct contact with the Vienna Circle lasted only till 1936 or 1937, when he went to the University of Christchurch, New Zealand, as a Senior Lecturer. From then on he did not refer to the Vienna Circle for two decades, with the exception of a few critical remarks on Wittgenstein and Schlick in his work, *The Open Society and Its Enemies*.[8] But, how closely he remained attached to the Vienna Circle and how important it still appeared to him to come to terms with it is shown by the fact thet he renewed his relations with it in later years. He was concerned especially with its most important representative, Carnap, even before his contribution to the volume, *The Philosophy of Rudolf Carnap* (1964) in the "Library of Living Philosophers." In his essay, "Degree of Confirmation,"[9] he already gave a basic critique of Carnap's inductive logic, and in *Conjectures and Refutations* he mentions the Vienna Circle again and again.

Kant probably played an important part in Popper's philosophical development. He is the only historical philosopher whom Popper mentioned several times in Popper's *The Logic of Scientific Discovery*—Hume and Fries are mentioned only occasionally—and to whom he also devoted two chapters (7 and 8) in his *Conjectures and Refutations*. Even outside of these chapters Kant is expressly honored as Hume's philosophical opponent. Kant probably clarified for Popper the way in which empiricism is limited by a rational component of Knowledge. According to Popper, the categorial function of the law of causality gets a partial justification insofar as an instinctive expectation to find regularity precedes observation; an expectation which is not only psychologically innate a priori, but also logically a priori, but which is not a priori valid, as Kant thought.[10] The Vienna Circle, on the other hand, thought Kant superseded; for it, Mach and Russell were the most influential philosophers; the latter at the stage of his *Our Knowledge of the External World* (1914) and his *The Analysis of Matter* (1927). But Russell had also a great importance for Popper, who says about him that his "influence upon Carnap and upon us all was greater than anyone else's."[11]

II. TOPICAL CONNECTIONS

A. General

When Popper at the end of the twenties of our century came into contact with the Vienna Circle, his thinking had already taken an independent direction. As early as 1919 he already found himself confronted by the problem: Wherein, precisely, lies the scientific character of a theory?[12] This problem has remained at the center of his investigations. And, all by himself, he had already found an answer in the criterion of falsifiability.[13] Therefore, Popper confronted the Vienna Circle from the first with his own ideas, from which he naturally developed a critical attitude towards them; but Popper did not only stand in opposition to them, there was also far-reaching agreement among them. If Popper was called the "opponent" of the Vienna Circle, his opposition still rested on a common ground on which the dispute took place. There were not only common questions which were answered differently, but also common viewpoints regarding the answer.

In the Vienna Circle two points of view were fundamental: The special position of logic and mathematics and the empirical ground of the knowledge of reality.[14] Logic and mathematics are valid not because they are concerned with the laws of reality, neither its most general laws nor the natural necessities of thinking, but because they establish the rules of our language. This is why both are valid independent of experience. Knowledge of reality, by contrast, is dependent on experience; in it lies the ground of its validity. Popper was not at all concerned with the validity of logic and mathematics; this was no problem for him. Probably he knew from the beginning that logic and mathematics do not say anything about reality, because their validity is independent of experience. Only as late as 1946 did he concern himself with the *applicability* of logic and mathematics to reality,[15] and here he agrees with the view that logic does not contain descriptive statements but "rules of procedure,"[16] rules of a language which, however, must not be taken purely syntactically, as Carnap had done at first,[17] but which must be understood semantically, as Carnap later recognized.[18] In this respect there was, therefore, a fundamental agreement between Popper and the Vienna Circle.

But, also with respect to the second point of view, our knowledge of reality, there was some common ground between Popper and the Vienna Circle. He, too, is fundamentally an empiricist: "The principle of empiricism can be fully preserved, since the fate of a theory, its acceptance or rejection is decided by observation and experiment."[19] He merely rejects a total empiricism.[20] Popper defends empiricism against both Duhem's instrumentalism and Poincaré's conventionalism.[21] The empirical, the component of experience, however, fades into the background in the course of his publications, because he was mainly concerned to show that there is a rational component of knowledge. It is for this reason that his work is dominated by a critique of the kind of empiricism represented by the Vienna Circle. This is why it sometimes seems as if Popper were only pointing out the insufficiency of observation as a foundation of knowledge. In his article on Popper's *Logik der Forschung* Carnap says[22] that Popper overemphasizes "precisely his differences from those epistemological points of view [of the Vienna Circle] which actually are closest to his own," and even arouses the suspicion as if he were an "a priorist and anti-empiricist" which, however, he is not.

Because of his fundamental empiricism Popper also had an antimetaphysical attitude in common with the Vienna Circle, even though the point of view from which metaphysics is being criticized and rejected is different (something which will be discussed in greater detail below). Popper, too, did not admit metaphysics as valid knowledge; in fact he was concerned, precisely, with the clear demarcation of metaphysics from scientific knowledge.

Aside from these fundamental agreements there were also several special agreements, mainly because the views in the Vienna Circle were, in part, changing, especially because of Popper's influence on the Circle, a fact which is admitted in Carnap's article. On the other hand, however, Carnap also feels that "Popper's views in some points were probably also influenced by those of the Vienna Circle."[23] These agreements and differences will now be presented in detail.

B. Specific

1. *The Criterion of Demarcation.* The problem, which formed the starting point for Popper's epistemological investigations did not come to him in reading philosophical literature, but forced itself upon him in his own thinking. It grew out of his study of theories which were current at that time: Marx's philosophy of history, Freud's psychoanalysis, and Alfred Adler's individual psychology.[24] Because of his doubts about these theories he found himself confronted by these questions: How can one decide whether a theory is correct? How do scientific statements get their validity? How can we dis-

tinguish between scientific and unscientific assertions?[25] The Vienna Circle was also concerned with the problem of this demarcation. Here it was the demarcation from metaphysics which was sought. Popper found the solution under the influence made by the sensational confirmation of the general theory of relativity by Eddington's observations of 1919. It was testing a theory by means of falsifiability. The Vienna Circle, on the contrary, found the distinction, following Wittgenstein's *Tractatus Logico-Philosophicus* (1922), in the distinction between meaningful and meaningless sentences, and this distinction was determined by verifiability: a statement is meaningful if it can be verified; statements of which no verification is possible are meaningless "pseudopropositions" (*Scheinsätze*).

Popper opposed this view; but others, too—Reichenbach, Lewis, Nagel, Stace—raised objections. Popper insisted that not only metaphysical sentences but also natural laws were excluded by the meaning-criterion of verifiability; for they cannot be completely verified.

(a) *The Meaning-Criterion of Verifiability.* The meaning-criterion of verifiability rests on the presupposition that for every statement it must be possible, even if not always actually practicable, to decide whether it is true or false.[26] In order to do justice to the presupposition of such a complete verification Wittgenstein, in his *Tractatus Logico-Philosophicus*, had designed a grandiose structure of the knowledge of reality, which was taken over by the Vienna Circle. It transfers atomism to language. The fundamental parts of knowledge are elementary statements, "atomic sentences," which picture elementary facts—pictures which were understood, as in mathematics, as relations of symbolic associations to facts. In connecting atomic sentences by logical conjunctions (and, or, if-then) compound sentences or "molecular sentences" can be formed. The meaning of a sentence, therefore, lies in symbolizing a possible, thinkable fact. If there is such a fact in the world the sentence is true, otherwise it is false. The truth of a molecular sentence is a function of the truth of the atomic sentences of which it consists. At least in theory, therefore, the truth or falsity of a sentence can always be completely determined.

But, assertions of unlimited generality cannot be formed by this method. Natural laws cannot be so formulated; they cannot be analysed into conjunctions of atomic sentences, because they transcend the observed facts. But then, statements of natural laws are meaningless. These were the considerations which led Popper, in his *Logic of Scientific Discovery*, to criticize the meaning-criterion of verifiability: he proved it to be impracticable. For the same reason, Schlick would not admit statements about natural laws as genuine statements, but only as directions for the formation of verifiable statements about facts.[27] Thus they would be mere sentence-functions which become meaningful sentences only by the substitution of constants. But this would mean that natural laws could not be known.

Popper was in fundamental opposition to this entire construction of knowledge and to the assumption of total verifiability. As an empiricist he agreed with the Vienna Circle that the decision about the truth or falsity of a statement can follow only the testing of a statement—a test undertaken to find whether it agrees with the experiential facts or not. But, it was his revolutionary discovery that there is an asymmentry with respect to the decision. A general statement can be refuted if it contradicts a statement about an individual fact; but it cannot be completely verified by ever so many supporting statements about individual facts: a general statement transcends any definite individual facts, because it is supposed to be valid for all those facts which are still unknown. Thus the verification of a general statement by *induction*, traditional in empiricism, is logically impossible. Popper radically rejects induction.

(b) *The Critique of Inductivism*. His turning against "inductivism" was decisive and characteristic for Popper's epistemological position from the beginning.[28] For that purpose he used Hume's critique of induction.[29] In an unpublished thesis, "Gewohnheit und Gesetzerlebnis," which he handed in to the Institute of Education in Vienna in 1927, he criticized Hume's *psychological* view of induction.[30] Hume's proof of the *logical* impossibility of inductive generalization was accepted by the Vienna Circle. Thus Schlick says: "Induction is nothing else but methodically guided guessing, a psychological, biological process whose treatment certainly has nothing to do with logic."[31] Nevertheless, one did not find it possible to free oneself entirely from induction. Thus, for example, Carnap, speaking on induction writes: "As justification, however, it can mention its empirical validation."[32] Feigl, too, who as early as 1929 had already come to accept this point of view that "an inductive judgment, which expresses a general factual aspect of reality, can only be a hypothesis,"[33] attempted later at least a pragmatic justification—"vindication" as over against "validation"—of induction.[34]

(c) *The Criterion of Testability*. Popper opposed to "inductivism" another, new conception of knowledge. Because general statements about reality cannot logically be derived from specific ones, one can only set them up as hypotheses. They can only be conjectured, or guessed at, as he later (in *Conjectures and Refutations*) expressed it with special precision. Whether a hypothesis or theory fits can only be found by tests, by deductively deriving singular sentences from them which must be compared with the empirical facts. If there is a contradiction between them, a hypothesis or theory is shown to be false. Their agreement, however, is not sufficient to demonstrate its truth; it may well be confirmed by it, but only for the time being. There is no complete verification at all of general statements about reality; only an ambiguous falsification for it is possible. Thus Popper took an independent, original stand as over against the Vienna Circle. By this an essential difference as over against the initial views in the Vienna Circle was introduced. This difference, however, soon decreased, because Carnap recognized Popper's view that a complete verification is impossible.[35] He took over from him the empirical testability as the criterion of scientific knowledge and modified the original meaning-criterion of verifiability accordingly. "If by verification is meant a definitive and final establishment of truth, then no (synthetic) sentence is ever verifiable. . . . We can only confirm a sentence more and more." "We distinguish the testing of a sentence from its confirmation."[36] Neurath, however, opposed Popper's view, called it pseudorationalism, and rejected it.[37] For the determination of conceptual meaning Carnap begins with our use of language: ". . .an expression of language has meaning in this empiricist] sense if we know how to use it in speaking about empirical facts, either actual or possible ones."[38] Thus it depends on the language whether a sentence has meaning or not. For this the rules of language are decisive. These rules may, of course, differ. Therefore there is not only *one* language, as Wittgenstein thought, but there are many kinds of languages. The empiricist determination of meaning now follows the establishment of corresponding rules. It does not appear, as formerly, as an assertion of facts. "It seems to me that it is preferable to formulate the principle of empiricism not in the form of an assertion—'all knowledge is empirical'—or 'all synthetic sentences that we can know are based on (or connected with) experiences'·or the like—but rather in the form of a proposal or requirement. . . . "[39] This requirement now consists in the testability or at least the confirmability of a statement instead of its (complete) verification. In this way, however, verification is still maintained, though in a weakened form. Thus Popper's critique of the presupposition of complete verification deeply changed the conception of the validation of empirical knowledge on the part of the Vienna Circle.

 2. *The Test Sentences.* In spite of this acceptance by the Circle of the criterion of testability, essential differences remained in two respects. The Vienna Circle was dominated by the sensualistic empiricism of Mach and Russell. Experience, on which the knowledge of reality rests, was identified under the term of "observation" with sensory perception: the one is lost in the other. Thus Feigl, in his first publication of *Theorie und Erfahrung in der Physik* (1929), p. 14, wrote: "The final factuality which underlies this sentence [that my pencil rests in my hand] is a series of mutually connected facial, tactual, and muscular sensations." In this sense Carnap, in his book, *Der logische Aufbau der Welt* (1928), wanted to constitute all empricial concepts out of "elementary experiences," of the "individual psyche" by way of the "recollection of similarity" which was his basic undefined relation: all empirical statements are supposed to be able to be transformed into

statements concerning elementary experiences (Secs. 2, 67, 78). Therefore the empirical statements by which a hypothesis is proved, contain experiences and observations as statements about corporeal objects even when they are expressed in a "physical" language.

In his article, "Über das Fundament der Erkenntnis,"[40] Schlick discussed in great detail what precisely is involved in empirical statements. An observational statement expresses a present subjective experience; it is a simple assertion of what presently is given to someone. Such a statement always has the form: "here and now such and such," as for example, "here is now pain," "here and now yellow borders on blue."[41] The significance of the demonstrative words "here," "now," "I" get the meaning of specific data through the concrete situation in which they are used. Such a statement loses this special meaning at once whenever it is no longer expressed within the original situation, for then the words no longer point at the same data. Such a statement is therefore valid only at the moment of the experience. Thus it cannot be retained, repeated, or written down.[42] That is the character of empirical statements.

What Neurath and Carnap, however, understood by an observational statement, a "protocol sentence," is not an assertion, as Schlick had put it, but a *report* about it. In a protocol sentence an assertion assumes an objective form without demonstrative words. It has the schema: *A at time t and place p P has perceived such and such.* A protocol sentence reports that a certain person has made an assertion at a certain time and place.

Popper undertook a fundamental correction of this notion of test-sentences and with it of the empirical foundations of the knowledge of nature, although he does agree with this notion that the empirical basis, the "basic statements," are singular statements (like the protocol sentences). They have the following form: At a certain space-time-point there is such and such.[43] But these basic sentences cannot be observational statements nor protocols about them, for both of these speak only of subjective experiences. For the testing of a hypothesis or theory, however, the knowledge of *objective* facts is necessary. Statements about those, however, transcend the empirically-given, because they use general concepts (whereas experiences are something unique). They always include a theory, because they speak about objects and events of the external world.[44] But the external world cannot logically be constructed from individual experiences, as Carnap first thought in *Der logische Aufbau der Welt.* Carnap himself recognized that this simple construction of knowledge cannot be carried through and modified it in *Testability and Meaning.* He gave up defining higher terms by empirical statements and replacing them by the latter; but he still sought to maintain their reducibility by reduction sentences. Popper immediately criticized this view of Carnap's.[45] The test sentences are no statements about observed experiences;

they must be statements about facts which can be stated intersubjectively. With that, observation was dislodged from its former role as the ultimate basis of validation.

Schlick considered the empirical statement of an observation, an assertion, as absolutely valid. The subject of the experience is immediately aware of it as true. What matters is only that the experience under consideration is correctly denoted. An assertion can only be mendacious but not erroneous, since the experiencer knows what he experiences and cannot be deceived by it.[46] Its assertion is the only statement about reality which is not hypothetical. For this reason, Schlick declared it to be the foundation of knowledge. Against this idea, which saw the function of observation in furnishing a solid validation, Popper maintained that it is only a subjective experience, only a psychological fact. Even Schlick describes its certainty as "a feeling of fulfillment, of a very characteristic satisfaction."[47] Carnap, too, was originally of the opinion that protocol sentences are absolutely valid, that they "are exempt from the need for validation."[48] Neurath fought against this view. Protocol sentences are no more original than other statements; like others they can be corrected. They, too, are only *hypothetical*.[49] Carnap later accepted Neurath's view. For Popper it was a necessary consequence that the basic sentences are only hypothetical, for they are statements about objective facts which always include theories. Therefore they can have only a hypothetical validity. "Any basic statement can again in its turn be subjected to tests, using as a touchstone any of the basic statements which can be deduced from it";[50] and it can of course be rejected. Therefore there are no statements about facts which are indubitably true. There is no such thing as final verification, and therefore no absolute foundation for the knowledge of nature. In this way agreement was reached between Popper, Neurath, and Carnap, which has been acknowledged by both sides. Therefore Carnap wrote:

> Even in positivism there is a remnant of this idealistic absolutism [of experiences]; in the logistic positivism of our Circle—in the up to now published writings of Wittgenstein, Schlick, Carnap—it assumes the refined form of an absolutism of fundamental sentences ("elementary sentences," "atomic sentences"). Neurath was the first to turn decisively against this absolutism by rejecting the irrevocability of the protocol sentences. From another starting point Popper takes still a further step in his method of testing: there is no such thing as final sentences; his system therefore represents the most radical surmounting of that kind of absolutism.[51]

Popper acknowledged the recognition of his view by Carnap with satisfaction: "I would like. . .to thank Professor Carnap most cordially for the friendly words which he devoted to my investigations at the stated passage."[52] He adds, however: "It seems to me that the view here upheld is closer to that of the 'critical' (Kantian) school of philosophy (perhaps in the form represented by Fries) than to positivism."[53]

If, however, the protocol sentences and the basic sentences are hypothetical, too, then one gets an infinite regression. This can only be avoided by finally making a decision whether one wants to recognize a basic or protocol sentence as sufficient and basic. With that a conventionalistic element gets into the knowledge of nature. Popper acknowledged this and Carnap agreed.[54] This conventionalism fundamentally differs from the one represented by Poincaré in that the determination is concerned with *universal* statements yet singular ones,[55] whereas Neurath wanted to leave it to arbitrary decision whether one cancels a contradictory protocol sentence or changes the sentence system so that it becomes compatible with it. Popper's freedom of determination is different. It does not concern the choice of *contents* of a basic sentence but consists only in the fact that one desists from a further *test* of a basic sentence, if the sentence seems sufficiently confirmed. That is a tremendous difference. For, with his contention, Neurath gave up empiricism without wanting to do so. Schlick turned against both Neurath and Popper, because they make the difference between protocol sentences and other sentences meaningless and therefore destroy it.[56] So there was a split within the Vienna Circle with respect to the foundations of the knowledge of nature; and owing to this fact, the attitude to Popper was not uniform. There was partly agreement, partly rejection.

3. *Physicalism.* There is one further agreement between Popper and the Vienna Circle. Popper rejected observation as insufficient for a testing of hypotheses because observation is a psychological concept whereas basic statements should speak of objective facts. He raised the objection against the positivism of the Vienna Circle that it does not see the difference between experience and statement.[57] But the Vienna Circle did come to agree with Popper that hypotheses must be corroborated by test sentences, and that the corroboration must be possible intersubjectively. Both also agreed that statements about experiences, about psychical data, cannot directly be proved intersubjectively, because these are inaccessible to other persons, and that only statements concerning bodily processes are intersubjectively confirmable. The Vienna Circle was already prepared for this. To get a unified language for all empirical sciences it had put forth the postulate of "*physicalism*": Scientific statements can only be made in the "thing-language", as statements about physical data. Therefore the test sentences also must sound "physicalistic." Neurath and Carnap demanded this just as did Popper. The latter specifically declared: One could speak instead of "an *observable event*. . .involving position and movement, of macroscopic physical bodies, or we might lay down, more precisely, that every basic statement must either be itself a statement about relative positions, of physical

bodies or that it must be equivalent to some basic statement of this mechanistic kind."[58] This is quite in accord with the thesis of physicalism in its original form, which points out that statements about psychical data must be *translated* into statements about bodily processes, about physical data.[59] Physicalism, however, was then sharpened insofar as statements about psychical facts cannot be expressed at all as scientific ones,[60] because the concept of something psychical in contrast to something physical cannot be formulated physicalistically, i.e., only in terms of physical data.

Popper refused to go as far as to exclude statements about mental states from science. He expressly rejected a *universal* physicalism. Popper fought against the physicalistic language as the universal language of science at the Congress of Copenhagen (1936), where it was propagated.[61] Nevertheless, there still is a remarkable agreement between Popper and the Vienna Circle concerning *observation*. Through the physicalism of the Vienna Circle observation as a psychical phenomenon is excluded from scientific knowledge because it cannot be expressed in the language of science. "Each concept in the language of science goes back to 'positional coordinates' that is the coordination of numbers with space-time-points according to specific procedures."[62] The language of science contains nothing but such 'positional coordinates.' Therewith the original foundation of the protocol sentences comes to nothing. On the other hand, however, Carnap still demands observability for the test sentences, as in *Testability and Meaning*,[63] though physicalism had been proclaimed as early as 1932.[64] "We shall take two descriptive, i.e., non-logical, terms of this field as *basic terms* for our following considerations, namely 'observable' and 'realizable.' All other terms, and above all the terms 'confirmable' and 'testable,' which are the chief terms of our theory, will be defined on the basis of the two basic terms mentioned."[65]

Popper, too, requires "observability" of the facts which form the contents of basic sentences. But "observability" is not supposed to mean something psychological. "Perceptions may be psychological, but observability is not."[66] A clarification of this term is left undone, because Popper introduces it as a basic undefinable concept which is supposed to be made sufficiently precise by linguistic use. Observation as experience, as psychic phenomenon, is excluded by Popper also. As in the quoted passage in *The Logic of Scientific Discovery* (Sec. 29) he says in *Conjectures and Refutations* "we do *not*, for the purpose of such basic tests, choose reports about our own observational experiences, but rather reports. . .about physical bodies" (p. 267). And here it is said with all possible clarity that the basic sentences must be formulated physicalistically. "Whenever we wish to put a scientific statement to an observational test, *this test must in a sense be physicalistic*" (p. 267). As in the Vienna Circle so in Popper's philosophy, observation has no place in the knowledge of nature. That a fact is observed cannot be asserted, because both exclude observation in favor of physicalism. Besides, Carnap declares: "Each concrete sentence of the physicalistic system of language can in certain circumstances serve as a protocol sentence."[67] With this the empirical foundation of the knowledge of nature becomes unclear. Neither protocol sentences nor basic sentences can be validated on the basis of observational experiences. It is a question whether empiricism can then be retained at all or whether with this it has not already been given up. That Popper and the Vienna Circle meet in this weighty outcome is very surprising if on the one hand we remember their basic, or at least original, empiricism and on the other hand their mutual antagonism.

4. *Verification and Probability.* The Vienna Circle assimilated Popper's view that the demarcation of scientific knowledge against extrascientific assertions, especially against metaphysics, is produced by its empirical testability. True, Popper took a different stance towards metaphysics from the original one of the Vienna Circle. He did not consider metaphysics as meaningless but partly even attributed a heuristic value to it as preparation for theoretical ideas. Nevertheless, he did not consider it as knowledge but as "not subject to scientific discussion." The argeement also went so far as to assert that a complete verification of empirical statements is not possible but only a preliminary corroboration that in all tests up to now they have not yet been falsified. For Popper, however, this corroboration does not mean more than: not yet falsified. "We regard the incompatibility [with the facts] as a falsification of the theory, the compatibility, however, not yet as a positive corroboration. The mere fact that a theory is not falsified cannot yet be valued as a positive corroboration."[68] Carnap, on the other hand, put into the foreground the confirmation of a hypothesis or theory by the fact that it always stood several tests of falsification. Although there is no truth, there is confirmation.[69] The difference between truth and corroboration lies in this that truth and falsity are timelessly valid, whereas the corroboration is valid only with reference to a particular point in time up to which a statement has stood its tests.[70] With the idea of confirmation Carnap again establishes a weakened form of verification, which, however, Popper strictly rejects.[71] Carnap thoroughly and systematically explicated the conditions and kinds of confirmation in *Testability and Meaning.* He distinguishes between testability and confirmability and in both between a complete one and an incomplete one. The confirmation changes with time; it can increase with the number and type of confirmations. According to Popper, the degree of corroboration is determined by the measure of testability and the strictness of the tests which a hypothesis or theory has stood thus far.[72] To determine, to measure, the degree of confirmation by means of numerical value appeared to be an obvious task. Reichenbach was first to undertake it and to seek to solve it with the aid of the calculation of probabilities.[73] True, Reichenbach did not belong

to the Vienna Circle but to the Berlin Group; but, as a leading member of the common movement of "logical empiricism," and as coeditor of and contributor to the magazine *Erkenntnis*, he was prominent in Popper's mind also. In *The Logic of Scientific Discovery* (Sec. 80) Popper offered a striking critique of Reichenbach's attempt to determine the degree of corroboration of a hypothesis by means of calculation of probabilities. Reichenbach based his calculation of probability on the form which this had taken in Richard von Mises. According to that the degree of confirmation would have to be described by the limiting value of a frequency (of confirmations) in a sequence of sentences. But which sequence of sentences shall it be? If one lets them consist of basic sentences which confirm or contradict a hypothesis, then the probability of a hypothesis would still be half if half of the test sentences would contradict it! Nor can another sequence of sentences be found for which the limiting value of a relative frequency would correspond to the degree of confirmation. Because of this criticism Carnap, in *Testability and Meaning* (I,3), left it as "presently not yet clear whether the concept of the degree of confirmation can be defined as a quantitative one, as a dimension with a numerical value" (p. 427). Later on, however, he developed a theory of confirmation as a theory of probability which he distinguished from the *calculation* of probability as a theory of relative frequency (as "probability$_1$" and "probability$_2$"). His probability is constituted on the basis of *logical* probability. Already in *The Logic of Scientific Discovery*, Popper, however, convincingly criticized Keynes's attempt to base the inductive generalization—a hypothesis—on an a priori, i.e., a logical probability (Sec. 83). According to Keynes the probability of a hypothesis is supposed to correspond to its logical probability. Whereas the corroboration of a hypothesis grows with the number of the cases which confirm it, and the possibility of confirmation or refutation increases with the generality of the hypothesis, its a priori probability will be the smaller the greater is the generality of the hypothesis. Its logical probability is rather the greater the less the hypothesis is different from its test sentences. According to that the confirmation, which can grow with the testability, decreases with it at the same time! The probability of a hypothesis by means of its corroboration therefore proves incompatible with its *logical* probability. Both contradict each other. With essentially the same argumentation Popper proved Carnap's attempt to ground the probability of hypotheses on their logical probability as untenable, first in his "Degree of Confirmation"[74] and in his "Content and Degree of Confirmation"[75] and again in *Conjectures and Refutations* (pp. 280 f.). He correctly reached the conclusion that the probability of a hypothesis, in the sense of its degree of corroboration, represents a third kind of probability which differs as well from logical as from mathematical probability (p. 285). It is hardly necessary to go into this critique in greater detail. For this no longer has a place in the description of Popper's critique of the Vienna Circle, because this late work of Carnap's no longer belongs to his period in the Vienna Circle.

5. *Idealism-Realism*. The problem of the agreements and differences between Popper and his Vienna Circle thus far has centered on the question how reality can be known. Between them, however, there also was still the difference of opinion wherein knowable reality consists. Originally an *idealistic* or "phenomenalistic" view dominated the Vienna Circle, as it was represented in Russell's *Our Knowledge of the External World* and in Carnap's *Der logische Aufbau der Welt*. Physical bodies can only mean logical constructions from sense-data; real are only the experienced phenomena. If all higher empirical concepts can be reduced to relations of experiences, then only those can form the contents of the knowledge of reality. Thus Philipp Frank says: "Things which are constituted by perceptions, do not correspond to any reality existing external to the perceptions."[76] On the other hand, Schlick, in his essay "Positivismus und Realismus"[77] and again in "Meaning and Verification"[78] specifically and unambiguously rejected an epistemological idealism and advocated an empirical *realism*. "Logical positivism and realism are no antitheses."[79] The views concerning the knowledge of reality consequently were not uniform within the Vienna Circle.

Popper, too, rejects idealism and advocates *realism*, but in such a way that, because of the unverifiability of all hypothetical constructions, we can never know whether we have thereby grasped the real world. The world of physics as of everyday life are only "aspects of the real world."[80] "Although in one sense of the word 'real', all these various levels are equally real, there is another yet closely related sense in which we might say that the higher and more conjectural levels are the *more real* ones. . ."[81] Popper rejects the view of instrumentalism "that the uncertainty of a theory, i.e., its hypothetical or conjectural character, diminishes in any way its implicit *claim* to describe something real."[82]

Carnap considered the question as to realism or idealism as a pseudo-problem.[83] But it makes a material difference of fundamental significance whether one asserts: There are only my experiences and nothing else; or whether one establishes the hypothesis: There are also experiences different from mine, but there are only phenomena of consciousness; or the still different hypothesis: There is also something that differs from phenomena of consciousness: bodies, elementary particles, fields of force. The question which of these assertions is to be accepted or rejected is by no means senseless.

6. *Philosophy*. The Vienna Circle occupied itself only with epistemological problems. It considered all other areas of philosophy as inaccessible to scientific knowledge and rejected them. But Schlick did not even

recognize the epistemological area as valid. According to him "the traditional problems of epistemology are *passé*."[84] Under the influence of Wittgenstein *philosophy* was altogether conceived of in a radically changed way. As early as in the first volume of *Erkenntnis* Schlick programmatically laid down the new conception as a "turning point in philosophy." The traditional problems of philosophy present themselves for the most part as meaningless pseudoproblems. It is the task of philosophy to expose this fact and, beyond that, to clarify the concepts and sentences of science and to eliminate those discovered as being meaningless. Philosophy therefore is an activity, "a system of acts," not a "body of knowledge, i.e., of true empirical sentences."[85] Philosophy is no science but the analysis of language. Since it is the activity "by which the *meaning* of statements is determined or discovered," that "what the statements really mean," (not its truth),[86] philosophy is "the reflection on the essence of the expression, of the description, i.e., of every possible 'language'."

Regarding philosophy, Popper was more conservative. In *The Logic of Scientific Discovery* he expressly opposed as "positivistic" the thesis of the nonexistence of philosophical problems.[87] At least the methodological problems of a theory of experience should be admitted as autonomous problems of philosophy. Only later in his address on "The Nature of Philosophical Problems and their Roots in Science" (1952) did he concern himself in greater detail with Wittgenstein's view of philosophy.[88] He concedes Wittgenstein that "it is perhaps true, by and large, that philosophical problems do not exist; for indeed the purer a philosophical problem becomes the more is lost of its original significance, and the more liable is its discussion to degenerate into empty verbalism."[89] But that is not yet the whole truth; he maintains: "On the other hand there exist not only genuine scientific problems, but genuine philosophical problems."[90] "A problem may rightly be called 'philosophical' if we find that, although it originally arose in connection with, say, atomic theory, it is more closely connected with the problems and theories which have been discussed by philosophers than with theories nowadays treated by physicists."[91] In this sense Popper, too, actually did philosophy and did not confine himself to methodological investigations. The voluminous and rich work, *The Open Society and Its Enemies*, written in New Zealand soon after *The Logic of Scientific Discovery*, and the themes in Chapters 17 to 20 in *Conjectures and Refutations* demonstrate this. Therewith he documented a philosophical point of view which went far beyond that of the Vienna Circle.

But Carnap, too, did agree neither with Wittgenstein's nor Schlick's conception of philosophy as a mere activity of meaning-clarification, nor with the rejection of its claims to knowledge, but he acknowledged the knowledge-function of philosophy at least in part. True, he adopted Wittgenstein's and

Schlick's basic idea that philosophy is the analysis of language, but he defined
this as a *logical* analysis. In the first instance he did not understand this as an
analysis based on the *meaning* of language but purely formalistically as an investigation which is directed at the structure of language, as its *syntax*. Later,
however, with the insight that logic is not possible without the *meaning* of
words and sentences, he arrived at the view that logical analysis of language
does not differ fundamentally from epistemological investigations. Therewith
Carnap rehabilitated philosophy at least in part. Of those problems with
which philosophy had been concerned so far some are metaphysical,
meaningless pseudoproblems, and they disappear, therefore. Others concern
matters of fact which belong to the areas of the specific empirical sciences,
and therefore they do not belong to philosophy. Finally, there are questions
dealing with the presentation, the syntax, and the semantics of language, and
these form a legitimate area of philosophical knowledge. Carnap and Popper
are in agreement at least thus far that there is such a thing as an area of
philosophical knowledge.

7. *Summary.* Popper's relationship to the Vienna Circle, if we now
summarize it, was of a critical nature. But it was not a criticism from an in-
commensurable point of view and there was no permanent feud between
them; but they agreed with each other again and again. There was no un-
bridgeable opposition; rather a common basis. Both faced the same
problems: the foundations of empirical knowledge and the criterion of
science, and in addition to that they had the same basic attitude: empiricism.
But the way they tackled these problems in the first instance was different.
The approach of the Vienna Circle was determined—apart from views of
Mach and Russell—above all by Wittgenstein's *Tractatus*. Popper had
formed a view of his own. But his philosophical development proceeded in
contact and in disputation with the Vienna Circle, even though this does not
stand out as strongly as does Popper's impact on the Vienna Circle. This impact was achieved not so much by Popper's critique of the views of the Vienna
Circle as by the presentation of and confrontation with his own results. By the
insight into the justification of those results the views within the Vienna Circle underwent a considerable change. Popper replaced Wittgenstein in his influence on the Vienna Circle. In the later period he was its opponent. It must
be attributed to this influence that a rapid and productive development took
place within the Vienna Circle by which a new, fruitful movement in
epistemology was introduced. The Vienna Circle owes Popper gratitude for
an essential contribution to this development outside of its own forces.
Through this influence an agreement was reached again and again between
the Vienna Circle and Popper so that the initial disagreements between them
finally disappeared to a great extent; yet not by the assimilation of Popper to
the Vienna Circle but partly through acceptance of Popper's insights, and

partly also through the independent development within the Vienna Circle. The meaning-criterion of scientific knowledge was given up and Popper's criterion of testability was taken over; the hypothetical, conventionalistic and physicalistic character of the test sentences was reached by both sides; philosophy was recognized at least as logic of science, as theory of knowledge. But the agreement was reached with only one wing of the Circle, the one led by Carnap and Neurath. Schlick, on the other hand, moved less far from the original basis; he stuck to his assertion of the nonhypothetical, indubitable validity of observation and admitted philosophy only as the clarification of concepts. But with Carnap also differences remained; he did not only acknowledge falsification as valid but continued to maintain verification in its weaker form of confirmation. Reichenbach erected a quite different structure of knowledge against Popper's; he advocated inductivism and completely negated Popper's interpretation. But Reichenbach did not belong to the Vienna Circle.

VICTOR KRAFT

PHILOSOPHISCHE FAKULTÄT
UNIVERSITÄT WIEN
VIENNA, AUSTRIA
SUMMER, 1968

NOTES

[1] K. R. Popper, *Conjectures and Refutations: The Growth of Scientific Knowledge* (London: Routledge & Kegan Paul, 1963; New York: Basic Books, 1963), p. 271. Hereinafter cited as *C.&R.*

[2] *Ibid.*, p. 256.

[3] *Ibid.*, p. 40.

[4] *Ibid.*, p. 253.

[5] *Ibid.*, p. 269, n. 44.

[6] K. R. Popper, *The Logic of Scientific Discovery* (London: Hutchinson, 1959; New York: Basic Books, 1959), p. 124. Hereinafter cited as *L.Sc.D.*

[7] *C.&R.*, p. 271.

[8] *Ibid.*, p. 255, n. 5.

[9] K. R. Popper, "Degree of Confirmation," *The British Journal for the Philosophy of Science,* **5,** No. 18 (1954), 143-49, and **6,** No. 22 (1955), 157-63.

[10] *Ibid.*, pp. 47, 48.

[11] *C.&R.*, p. 254.

[12] *Ibid.*, p. 33.

[13] *Ibid.*, pp. 47 f.

[14] Cf. V. Kraft, *The Vienna Circle* (New York: Philosophical Library, 1953).

[15] K. R. Popper, "Why are the Calculuses of Logic and Arithmetic Applicable to Reality?"

Proceedings of the Aristotelian Society, Suppl., **20** (1946).

[16] *C.&R.*, pp. 207 f.

[17] Rudolf Carnap, *The Logical Syntax of Language* (New York: Harcourt, Brace & Co., 1937).

[18] Rudolf Carnap, *Introduction to Semantics* (Cambridge: Harvard University Press, 1946).

[19] *C.&R.*, p. 54.

[20] *Ibid.*, p. 4.

[21] K. R. Popper, *The Poverty of Historicism* (London: Routledge & Kegan Paul, 1957), p. 132 n.

[22] *Erkenntnis*, **5**, 290 ff.

[23] *Ibid.*, p. 293.

[24] *C.&R.*, p. 34.

[25] *Ibid.*, p. 35.

[26] Moritz Schlick, *Naturwissenschaften*, **19** (1931), 150; Friedrich Waismann, *Erkenntnis*, **1**, 120.

[27] Schlick, *Naturwissenschaften*, **19**, 150.

[28] It is probably connected with the critique of induction which I gave in my *Grundformen der wissenschaftlichen Methoden* (1925), though Popper does not say anything about it, although he quotes it twice in *L.Sc.D.* In his article on my "Erkenntnislehre," in *The British Journal for the Philosophy of Science*, **13** (1963), Professor Feyerabend also referred to this. My priority refers only to the negation of induction, not to the idea of falsification and testability by which Popper has replaced the induction.

[29] *C.&R.*, p. 42.

[30] *Ibid.*, p. 50, n. 16.

[31] Moritz Schlick, "Über das Fundament der Erkenntnis," *Erkenntnis*, **4** (1934); *Gesammelte Aufsätze* (Wien: Jarold & Co., 1938), p. 303.

[32] R. Carnap, *Physikalische Begriffsbildung* (Karlsruhe: Verlag G. Braun, 1926), p. 8.

[33] Herbert Feigl, *Theorie und Erfahrung in der Physik* (Karlsruhe: G. Braun, 1929), p. 12.

[34] H. Feigl, "De Principiis Non Disputandum," *Philosophical Analysis*, ed. by Max Black (New York: Prentice-Hall, 1963), p. 950; "Some Major Issues and Developments in the Philosophy of Science of Logical Empiricism," in *Minnesota Studies in the Philosophy of Science* (Minneapolis: University of Minnesota Press, 1956), Vol. I.

[35] R. Carnap, "Testability and Meaning," I, 3 (first published in *Philosophy of Science*, **3**, No. 4 [October, 1936], and **4**, No. 1 [January, 1937]), 426: "The impossibility of absolute verification has been pointed out and explained in detail by Popper. On this point our present views are, it seems to me, in full accordance with Lewis[15] and Nagel.[16]"

   [15] Lewis, "Experience and Meaning," *Philosophical Review*, **43** (1934), 137, n. 12: "No verification of the kind of knowledge commonly stated in propositions is ever absolutely complete and final."

   [16] Nagel, "Verifiability, Truth and Verification," *Journal of Philosophy*, **31** (1934), 144 f. See also *C.&R.*, p. 278, n. 60.

[36] Carnap, "Testability," I, 1, p. 420.

[37] Otto Neurath, "Pseudorationalismus der Falsifikation," *Erkenntnis*, **5** (1935).

[38] Carnap, *Erkenntnis*, **4**, No. 17 (1934), 2.

[39] *Ibid.*, **4**, No. 27, p. 33.

[40] Schlick, *Erkenntnis*, **4** (1934); *Gesammelte Aufsätze*, pp. 290 f.

[41] Schlick, *Gesammelte Aufsätze*, p. 308.

[42] *Ibid.*, p. 309.

[43] *L.Sc.D.*, Sec. 28.

[44] *Ibid.*, Sec. 25.

[45] *C.&R.* p. 254: "My criticism was directed, largely, against two books of Carnap's, *Der logische Aufbau der Welt*. . .and *Scheinprobleme in der Philosophie* and some of his articles in *Erkenntnis.*" See also Carnap, *Erkenntnis*, **14**, p. 223: "The possibility of this procedure [the empirical test] grew out of talks with Karl Popper."

[46] Schlick, "Über das Fundament der Erkenntnis," in *Gesammelte Aufsätze*, pp. 309 f.

[47] *Ibid.*, p. 304.

[48] Carnap, *Erkenntnis*, **2**, p. 438.

[49] Carnap, *Erkenntnis*, **3**, p. 209.

[50] *L.Sc.D.*, Sec. 29, p. 104.

[51] Carnap, *Erkenntnis*, **3**, p. 228.

[52] *Ibid.* and pp. 223 f.

[53] *L.Sc.D.*, Sec. 29, pp. 104, 105, nn. 1, 3.

[54] Popper, *ibid.*; Carnap, "Testability and Meaning," III, p. 426.

[55] *L.Sc.D.*, Sec. 30, pp. 108 f.

[56] Schlick, "Fundament der Erkenntnis," p. 294.

[57] *L.Sc.D.*, Sec. 29, p. 105, n. 3.

[58] *Ibid.*, Sec. 28, pp. 103 f.

[59] Rudolf Carnap, "Psychologie in physikalischer Sprache," *Erkenntnis*, **3** (1932/33), p. 108.

[60] Rudolf Carnap, *Scheinprobleme in der Philosophie* (Berlin: Weltkreis-Verlag, 1928), p. 40.

[61] Cf. *C.&R.*, p. 269, n. 44.

[62] Carnap, "Psychologie in physikalischer Sprache," p. 142.

[63] Carnap, "Testability," III, p. 11.

[64] Carnap, *Erkenntnis*, **3**.

[65] Carnap, "Testability," p. 454.

[66] *L.Sc.D.*, Sec. 29.

[67] Carnap, *Erkenntnis*, **3**, p. 224.

[68] *L.Sc.D.*, Sec. 82, p. 266.

[69] Rudolf Carnap, "Wahrheit und Bewährung," *Actes du Congrès International de Philosophie Scientifique* (Paris, 1936).

[70] *L.Sc.D.*, Sec. 84, p. 275.

[71] *C.&R.*, p. 279 and n.

[72] *L.Sc.D.*, Chap. X, esp. p. 251, and Sec. 82, pp. 266 f.

[73] Hans Reichenbach, "Wahrscheinlichkeitslogik," *Sitzungsberichte der Preussischen Akademie der Wissenschaften, Physikalisch-mathematische Klasse*, **29** (1932).

[74] Popper in *The British Journal for the Philosophy of Science*, **5** (1954).

[75] *Ibid.*, **5** (1955) and **7** (1956).

[76] Philipp Frank, *Erkenntnis*, **2** (1932), p. 186.

[77] Moritz Schlick, *Erkenntnis*, **3** (1932), and *Gesammelte Aufsätze*, pp. 85 f.

[78] Schlick, *Gesammelte Aufsätze*, pp. 336 f.

[79] *Ibid.*, p. 115.

[80] *C.&R.*, p. 115.

[81] *Ibid.*, p. 116.

[82] *Ibid.*

[83] Carnap, *Scheinprobleme* (1928).

[84] Schlick, *Gesammelte Aufsätze*, p. 35.

[85] *Ibid.*

[86] *Ibid.*, p. 36.

[87] *L.Sc.D.*, Sec. 10, pp. 50 ff.

[88] *C.&R.*, pp. 66 ff.

[89] *Ibid.*, p. 73.

[90] *Ibid.*

[91] *Ibid.*, p. 74.

2

William C. Kneale

THE DEMARCATION OF SCIENCE

I

In writings on the philosophy of Science it is often assumed without discussion that the propositions which scientists assert, or at any rate put forward in their professional capacity, are all propositions of unrestricted universality, such as 'Light travels *in vacuo* at 300,000 km. per second', 'Water is a compound of oxygen and hydrogen', 'Birds are oviparous', i.e., generalizations free from any restriction, either explicit or implicit, to particular individuals or to particular regions of space and time. Professor Popper, for example, says near the beginning of his *Logic of Scientific Discovery* (p. 41), where he is discussing the demarcation of science, '*It must be possible for an empirical scientific system to be refuted by experience.* . . . My proposal is based upon an *asymmetry* between verifiability and falsifiability; an asymmetry which results from the logical form of universal statements'. Now I do not wish for a moment to deny that the word 'science' is often used for a system of universal propositions; but I think that it is wrong to suppose that scientists in their professional capacities never make statements of any other logical form, and I wish to argue that if we are to avoid falling into unfortunate dogmatism about the use of the word 'science', we must consider the intellectual contexts in which universal propositions are put forward by scientists, and in particular the relations of scientific activity to other studies. I propose in fact to speak first of the relation of science to metaphysics, then of its relation to history, and finally of its relation to cosmology. This sounds a very grand programme; but my chief purpose is to indicate some oversimplifications which seem to me dangerous, and what I have to say about the big topics I have just mentioned will be very sketchy.

II

Thirty years ago, when most philosophers of science were positivists, the word 'metaphysics' was often bandied about as a term of intellectual abuse for theorizing which could not be admitted as belonging either to logic or to empirical science. No doubt those who applied the word in this way always had in mind a comparison with the verbiage of Hegel and other philosophers notorious for empty eloquence; but they spoke as upholders of the Principle of Verifiability, and in course of time they came to think of the adjective 'metaphysical' as equivalent in *meaning* to the phrase 'senseless because unverifiable'. It soon appeared, however, that if this new way of talking were taken seriously, all scientific theories would have to be classified as metaphysical, and at this point Popper put forward a new suggestion. He too wished to draw a line between the sciences and other bodies of theory about the world, but in a passage from which I have already quoted he characterized an empirical science as a system of propositions open to refutation by experience. This new proposal, as he called it, had the great merit of showing what is wrong with the work of pseudoscientists who claim to find empirical confirmation of their theories but refuse at the same time to indicate any conceivable circumstances in which those theories would be refuted. And it was much preferable to the Principle of Verifiability in that it did not involve an attempt to condemn all nonscientific theories as meaningless. For Popper took care to point out that scientific theories of great merit, e.g., the atomic theory of matter, had arisen from prescientific speculations, and he insisted also that the contradictory of any hypothesis of law was certainly meaningful, though it could never be falsified because it was an unrestricted existential proposition, i.e., an existential proposition like 'Somewhere or other there has been or will be a firebreathing reptile'. Nevertheless there is something very curious in the terminology to which Popper committed himself in the presentation of his new view.

His primary aim was to distinguish between the universal propositions of genuine science, whether true or false, and those of pseudoscience; but he sometimes took over quite unnecessarily the terminology of the positivists and described his proposal as a division of all nonanalytic utterances between the two classes of the empirical and the metaphysical. This way of speaking commits him to the paradoxical thesis that all unrestricted existential propositions of the sort I mentioned a moment ago are metaphysical and nonempirical. To call them all metaphysical is very curious, because most of them have nothing at all to do with metaphysics as understood by Aristotle or any other philosopher until the positivists of this century began to use 'metaphysical' in a grossly extended sense for purposes of abuse. Suppose, for example, that an occultist tells me that there really are witches. I believe he is talking rubbish; but I do not think it proper to call that particular kind of rubbish metaphysics merely because it has the form of an unrestricted existential statement. Or again, suppose that on some occasion when I have been rashly dogmatic about the behaviour of fish out of water a biologist reminds me, in an unrestricted existential statement, that there are after all lungfish which can breathe on dry land. I do not dismiss his remark as irrelevant metaphysics, but humbly accept it as good empirical information. Furthermore, there is a strange departure from the ordinary use of words in maintaining that hypotheses of natural law are empirical, because they are open to refutation by experience, while denying that unrestricted existential propositions can ever deserve the same title. For refutation of any hypothesis of law is at the same time the establishment of the unrestricted existential proposition which is its contradictory, and if the procedure involves appeal to experience under the first description it must involve the same under the second description also. Indeed, if the word 'empirical' is to be applied at all to propositions as such (which I personally consider undesirable), there is a much better case for applying it to those which may be *established* empirically than for applying it to those which may be *refuted* empirically, since it was first used by philosophers in discussion of claims to *knowledge*.

I have suggested that Popper could have escaped from these troubles if he had disentangled himself more completely from positivist ways of thinking, in particular from worries about metaphysics (as distinct from pseudoscience), and had presented his distinction as one applying solely to theories in that special sense in which theories are always hypotheses of law. It is also worth noticing, however, that scientific statements are not all, as he seems to suppose, formulations of theories in that special sense. Admittedly the phrase 'scientific statement' is rather vague; and if it is taken to cover all the professional remarks of scientists, whether made in learned periodicals or in chats over cups of tea in their laboratories, what I have said is obvious enough, since a great many of those remarks are about the results of experiments in particular places at particular times. But what I have in mind is something more interesting than that. When Professor Anderson announced his discovery of the positron, his argument took the form of considerations about the shape of a track on a particular photographic plate which he had exposed in his laboratory, but what he asserted was the unrestricted existential proposition that there are positively charged particles with the mass of electrons, and it is this which his fellow scientists rightly regard as his very important contribution to physics. It is true, of course, that his announcement would not have been taken seriously if his account of his experiment had not been sufficiently full and clear to allow for the possibility of repetition by other people; but it would be very unplausible special pleading to contend for this reason that Anderson's novelty was really after all an hypothesis of law about what happens whenever anyone tries his experiment.

What surprised and interested physicists was surely his assertion of the existence of particles of a sort hitherto unsuspected by anyone except Dirac (whose work was unknown to Anderson), and if the possibility of such a scientific development is excluded by any philosophy of science, so much the worse for that philosophy. But I myself have admitted earlier that it is natural to think of a science as a system of universal propositions. How, if at all, can this view be reconciled with what I have just said? This question brings me to my next topic, the relation of science to history.

III

It seems plausible to maintain that science should be distinguished from history (in the largest sense of that word), not as the study of universal truths from the study of singular truths, but rather as the study of what is possible or impossible from the study of what has been or is actually the case. Speaking metaphorically, we may say that science is about the frame of nature, while history is about the content. I think that Popper came near to this way of thinking when he conceded in the English edition of his *Logic of Scientific Discovery* (p. 433), that scientists try to formulate truths which hold not only for the actual world but for all possible worlds differing from the actual world, if at all, only in initial conditions. His motive in saying this was to allow for the fact that acceptance of an hypothesis of scientific law is ordinarily thought to involve commitment to subjunctive conditionals such as 'If the earth had two moons with different periods of revolution, the tides would be even more complicated than they are'. But, once it is allowed that we have a notion of natural necessity, it must be admitted also that we have a notion of natural possibility, since either can be defined in terms of the other. In fact, Popper's formulation of his view seems to be based on the assumption that the notion of natural possibility is more easily intelligible than the notion of natural necessity.

Now there is indeed a very interesting and important difference between statements of natural possibility on the one hand and statements of natural impossibility on the other, namely that the former may sometimes be inferred logically from records of observed fact, whereas the latter can never be justified in such a way. Hence all the worry of philosophers about induction. For induction is often described as argument from empirically known facts to laws, and yet laws in the scientific sense are propositions about what must or what cannot be the case, i.e., propositions which cannot be inferred logically from empirically known facts. Furthermore, just because laws in the scientific sense are logically stronger than any sets of empirically known facts, they are the truths we most eagerly try to guess when we study nature in a self-conscious way. For if we knew them, we should be able to extrapolate safely from what we have learnt of the actual world through observation. By contrast, truths of possibility, i.e., truths of the absence of law, seem much less attractive. *Ab esse ad posse valet consequentia,* as they said in the Middle Ages; but why should anyone want to make the inference?

This is the explanation of our tendency to assume that all scientific statements of any interest are statements of law, but it should be noticed that the assumption seems plausible only so long as we believe with Hume and his followers that concepts are all acquired separately, i.e., without connexions of the kind asserted in scientific theory, and have to be linked, if at all, by the repeated conjunction of specimens falling under them. If that old empiricist doctrine is correct, all learning from experience, whether it be the un-conscious learning we call association of ideas or the conscious learning we call research, must involve a restriction of the boundaries of what is seriously thinkable. But the history of science does not confirm this doctrine. Although it is true to say that before Anderson's discovery, there was no assured place in physical science for the notion of a positron, this should not be taken to mean that physicists had concluded inductively against the existence of positively charged particles with the same mass as electrons. What happened was something quite different. In 1897, Sir J. J. Thomson, writing in the *Philosophical Magazine* on Cathode Rays, which were already known to carry negative charges, gave good reasons to think that these rays were streams of very small particles of a nature independent of the nature of the gas from which they were derived, and later it was found possible to deter-mine the mass of the particles with greater precision. Neither at this stage nor for many years to come was there any known reason to suppose the existence of similar particles with positive charges, and so it was simply assumed without argument of any kind that particles of the mass of an electron all carry negative charges, just as it is commonly assumed without argument that all unsupported bodies fall to the earth. I suppose we can say, if we like, that Anderson's work was the refutation of an assumption of law widely held by scientists; but just because the assumption which he refuted had never been set out explicitly as an hypothesis, his achievement appeared as a liberating discovery of new possibilities, rather than as a disappointment of scientific hopes which should be accepted with good grace on the ground that refuta-tion of a false belief is always a gain.

Perhaps I can put my point most clearly as follows. When we engage in scientific research, what we hope to do is to form a correct theory of the frame of nature. That is to say, we want to work out a system of concepts for the description of nature which allows for all naturally possible combinations, but for no others. In many respects the ordinary language with which we start is too loose for our purposes, since it admits as well-formed many sentences which express no real possibilities, e.g., the absurd sentence 'Our ancestors ate nothing but iron'; and it is therefore easily intelligible that the scientific enterprise should often be regarded as the task of formulating restrictive hypotheses or supplementary rules for the elimination of bogus possibilities. This view is perhaps most likely to commend itself when attention is concentrated on the early stages of scientific development. But ordinary language can also suffer from the defect of overnarrowness. It is said, for example, that the ancient Egyptians, living as they did in a river valley which ran almost due north, could not easily distinguish in their language between the two notions of downstream and north, so that when they travelled abroad they found difficulty in describing the life of people whose rivers ran southward. And we know that in the English of a century ago there were no separate names for many of the chemical substances with which we are now quite familiar. But in a still more striking way the ordinary language which we teach to our children is inadequate for the purposes of modern physical theory. It is true, of course, that anyone of sufficient intelligence can be taught how to adapt it for the purposes of physical theory; but this special education will involve learning to recognize hitherto unsuspected possibilities as well as learning to disregard misleading suggestions of possibility conveyed by some combinations of words permissible in ordinary speech; and this is why it seems best to say that science is the study of what is possible or impossible in nature.

　　If I am right, the discovery of the positron, which we express in the form appropriate for the negation of a law, i.e., by means of an unrestricted existential statement in the present tense, can properly be said to belong where most people think that it does, namely to science, rather than to metaphysics or to history. But it is not so easy to distinguish science from history when we turn to biological studies. Long before the days of evolutionary theory many of these studies were classified as natural history rather than as natural philosophy or science, partly perhaps because the information which they furnished was very often about particular matters of fact such as the flourishing of certain species in certain places; but also, I think, because even the generalizations to which they gave rise seemed to be more like inventories or catalogue entries than like theses in an explanatory system. During the last century the situation has altered, and biologists now offer explanatory theories. But it is interesting to notice that in their evolutionary explanations for the properties characteristic of various species of organisms, they have to think of those species much as historians of human affairs think of families, tribes, and nations, i.e., as bodies of individuals who are linked by common inheritance and subject to the influences of a common environment at particular places and times. When, for example, a hitherto unrecorded species of insect is discovered on an oceanic island, it is supposed that the members of the species must be descended from a few ancestors who were marooned on the island at some date in the past and that their differentiation from their nearest relatives elsewhere is to be explained by their adaptation under natural selection to the conditions of their island home. How then should we describe the present activities of biologists? According to current academic classifications biologists are scientists; and yet many of them spend most of their time considering what has happened at certain times to groups of individuals in certain regions of the surface of the earth. It is true that, in their explanations they use principles of genetics and biochemistry, but their special hypotheses are concerned with initial conditions for the occurrence of events that arouse their curiosity.

In this respect biologists are not alone among the persons who work in the science faculties of universities. Geologists and astronomers have to do with the distribution of matter in particular regions of space at different times, and the generalizations peculiar to their studies seem to be of an accidental sort that can be explained by hypotheses about initial conditions rather than of the essential sort we call laws. That there are comets associated with the solar system is just a matter of fact, though one for which it is no doubt possible to give a plausible explanation in a genetic story about the solar system, and it will be thought that their common features have been rendered intelligible when it has been shown that they can be derived from such a genetic story in accordance with general principles of physics. Even galaxies have their histories, and according to the type of cosmology which seems to be in favour at the moment, their common features are also to be explained within a scheme of cosmic evolution, perhaps by the suggestion that the whole universe is expanding from a state of extreme concentration. That there are the chemical elements there are, in the quantities in which they are now found in different parts of the universe, is a fact of history. We may perhaps say, if we like, that it is a much less chancy accident than the occurrence of planetary systems and *a fortiori* than the occurrence of organisms. Given a certain initial state for the expanding universe it was physically necessary that the chemical substances we know should arise at a certain stage in evolution and then persist for a time with the properties they are found to possess. But if the universe is an oscillating system, even the elements we call stable will disappear again when the compression of matter becomes too great for the survival of things with their relatively complex structures. According to this way of thinking, chemistry is just the most fundamental of a number of special sciences in which principles of physics can be applied to elucidate the consequences of contingent hypotheses about initial conditions.

About the details of the relationships between the sciences I am not competent to have an opinion. But there seems to be general agreement on a scheme such as I have tried to sketch, and if this is correct in outline, we must obviously be very careful in what we say about scientific method and the logical forms of scientific statements. Many studies of different kinds are carried on under the name of 'science', and we are likely to make mistakes if we dogmatize about science in general without recognizing the diversities which it covers. In particular we should beware of suggesting, as I may have done earlier, that the professional assertions of scientists are all about the frame as opposed to the content of nature. Although, as I argued, scientists are not ordinarily satisfied to record what has been or is the case but go on to speak of what is or is not possible, the notion they have in mind is very often possibility or impossibility relative to some historical facts that we all take for granted. Of all the sciences only general physics, or natural philosophy, as they still call it in some places, seems to be concerned exclusively with the frame of nature.

But even here we must beware of oversimplification. For it would be wrong to assume that all other sciences can be reduced to one in the sense of being shown to involve no absolute laws except those of physics, since psychology seems to offer a quite insuperable obstacle to such a programme of reduction. Considered as one of the biological studies, it undoubtedly presupposes physics; but so far as I can see, what is peculiar to it cannot be wholly explained by any historical assumptions about the distribution of matter at the places and times at which sentient life is known to flourish, because sentience is not definable in physical terms. Among some philosophers there has recently been a revival of the old materialist thesis that sensations (i.e., events of sentience) are identical with occurrences in the central nervous system; but I suspect that those who defend it have given themselves the illusion of understanding by using the word 'identical' in a queerly extended sense to cover the universal concomitance of distinguishable occurrences. They themselves declare that the identity of which they speak is only contingent, which seems to mean that there is no absolute necessity for sensations to be also nervous occurrences; and from this it follows that anyone who maintains the definite inclusion of the first among the second may rightly be asked to say first what empirical evidence would tell for or against his thesis, and secondly how he thinks that it in turn might be explained. Since, however, the special problems of mental philosophy are far too difficult to pose, let alone solve, in a few casual remarks during a very wide survey of the field of science, I propose to pass on now to my last topic, which is the relation of science to cosmology.

IV

Naturally the science of which we are thinking when we pose this question is general physics, and the puzzle we have in mind is that of distinguishing at the limit between the frame and the content of nature. Earlier in this paper I quoted with approval a phrase of Popper in which he tried to characterize natural laws as truths holding for all possible worlds that differ from the actual world, if at all, only in initial conditions. Using this terminology, which is familiar to many scientists, I might say that the problem is to disentangle laws from initial conditions at that level of discussion at which we are no longer concerned only with what has happened or is happening in the rather special conditions of some spatiotemporal region such as surface of the earth during the last few million years. But it is important to notice that in this context the phrase 'initial conditions' is not to be taken literally as signifying conditions at the beginning of the cosmos, since we do not wish to commit ourselves without argument to the view that there was an absolute beginning. What we assume is merely that some facts are brute in the sense of not being deducible from laws alone.

Perhaps it may seem curious to raise at this stage a doubt concerning our ability to distinguish between the frame and the content of nature. But if anyone is puzzled by my question, he should reflect that there is no such distinction to be drawn in an account of nature which has been very widely accepted by philosophers: I mean the account of Hume and Wittgenstein. According to Wittgenstein, in his *Tractatus Logico-Philosophicus* (2.04 ff.), the world, or reality, is the totality of existing states of affairs, and each of these is independent of all the others, because from the existence or nonexistence of one it is impossible to infer the existence or nonexistence of another. Here 'existence' does not mean any special connexion with the time of speaking, but just actuality as opposed to possibility, where the only possibility under consideration is logical. In other words, reality, as Wittgenstein conceives it, is what I have called the content of nature, and apart from formal logic, there is no frame of nature with which it can be contrasted, because the universal truths sometimes called laws of nature are just as contingent as the facts of history. Admittedly laws of nature cannot be inferred deductively from any conjunction of historical facts, however large, since they have the form of generalizations, that is to say of denials of existence. But if it were possible to set out a true statement of the form 'There are no historical facts but the following. . .', this would apparently have for logical consequences all the laws which scientists wish to discover. Wittgenstein does not make this point explicitly, but I think it must be what he has in mind when he writes later in the *Tractatus:*

There is no compulsion making one thing happen because another has happened. The only necessity that exists is logical necessity. The whole modern conception of the world is founded on the illusion that the so-called laws of nature are the explanations of natural phenomena. Thus people to-day stop at the laws of nature, treating them as something inviolable, just as God and Fate were treated in past ages. And in fact both are right and both wrong, though the view of the ancients

is clearer in so far as they have a clear and acknowledged terminus, while the
modern system tries to make it look as if everything were explained. [6.37-6.373]

It is correct, of course, to say that particular matters of fact cannot be explained by laws of nature alone, i.e., without reference to other particular
matters of fact called initial conditions; and it is also correct to say that
hypotheses of law may themselves need explanation by more fundamental
theories. But so far as I am aware, no scientist has ever denied either of these
contentions. On the other hand, the more extreme thesis that laws of nature
are of no use at all for explanation of natural phenomena, though repudiated
by all practising scientists, may perhaps seem plausible to philosophers who
believe, like Wittgenstein, that such laws are, so to say, mere abstracts from
the content of nature. What I wish to consider in this last section of my paper
is the question whether a cosmological theory might conceivably lead to a
view of natural laws which is at least superficially like that of Hume and
Wittgenstein.

In his theory of general relativity Einstein gave an account of the universe which, if true, suffices to explain gravitation without assumption of any
special law, and in the last half of his life he worked very hard but, as most
physicists believe, unsuccessfully on projects for a unified field theory in
which electromagnetism would receive similar treatment. In recent years
there have been a number of suggestions to the effect that the laws governing
nature in its atomic aspect may perhaps be explicable by use of the
topological notion of multiple connected space. I am quite incapable of discussing the merits of any of these speculations, but I think I can safely say
that they are all connected with attempts to geometrize physics. Wild anticipations of such a programme are to be found already in Plato's *Timaeus*
and in Descartes's *Principles of Philosophy;* but the modern efforts can be
taken more seriously than their predecessors because they are made at a time
when the study of pure geometry has revealed alternative possibilities. No
modern scientist would wish to say, as Descartes did at the end of the second
part of his *Principles*, 'I do not accept or desire any other principle in physics
than in geometry or abstract mathematics, because all the phenomena of
nature may be explained by their means'. For this way of speaking suggests
that physics may be exhibited as a continuation of pure mathematics, much
as in Frege's view arithmetic may be exhibited as a continuation of logic,
whereas it is essential to each of the modern speculations I have mentioned
that it ascribes a special kind of order to the world, i.e., an order whose
realization in nature cannot be inferred from principles of pure mathematics,
though these may be used in the working out of its implications. In short,
each of these speculations is a cosmological hypothesis, and the interest of
such theorizing for our purposes is that it seems to promise explanations of
laws without recourse to further laws.

In a paper of 1957 on 'Some Philosophical Problems of Cosmology' H. Bondi wrote:

> There is an interesting difference between cosmology and the rest of physics. In physics we are primarily interested in *laws* describing common features of a variety of phenomena. As an example consider the law of free fall on the surface of the Earth. This can be regarded as an abstraction from a large number of experiments in which it is found that every object moves with the same constant downward acceleration. A distinction is drawn between, on the one hand, the "accidental" feature of the velocity and direction of projection, which is largely under our control and distinguishes the trajectories of different projectiles from each other, and on the other hand the "general" feature of the unique constant downward acceleration common to all projectiles. The law of gravitation is solely concerned with this general feature. Similarly, on the larger scale of the solar system, the law of gravitation describes the features common to the orbits of all planets and satellites, while the question of the "accidental" circumstances of projection is left to the far more difficult and obscure subject of the origin of the solar system. In cosmology a unique object is studied (the universe) and accordingly this process of abstraction becomes inappropriate. Any attempt to distinguish between "general" and "accidental" features of the unique universe is hence wholly arbitrary. The most complete "explanation" that a theory of cosmology can give is therefore a description.[1]

When he wrote this, Bondi was not thinking of the deduction of physical laws from postulated properties of the universe as a whole; but if he is right in what he says about cosmology, it looks as though the success of any of the speculations I mentioned a moment ago would amount to getting everything from initial conditions alone. Is this impression correct?

I think it is a mistake to suppose that the difference between the frame and the content of nature might be made to disappear by success in the derivation of physical laws from a cosmological hypothesis, because it seems to me that there must always remain a very important distinction to be drawn between propositions about nature as a whole and propositions about parts of nature; or better, between propositions about the general form of order to be found in nature and propositions about the detailed ways in which this order is realized. Thus Einstein's theory of general relativity, which is supposed to explain the law of gravitation, involves the assumption that physical space as a whole is a Riemannian continuum of positive curvature; but it is essential to the theory that this cosmological hypothesis should be compatible with infinitely many suppositions about the distribution of different degrees of curvature in different regions of space. Nor can this cosmological hypothesis be described properly as a mere abstract from a host of independent hypotheses about different parts of the whole; for it does not make sense to talk as though a part might have existed by itself with a local curvature such as it has in the whole. Similarly, the suggestion that physical space is multiply connected like the surface of a sponge is compatible with many different suppositions about the distribution of the holes; and again, if it is true, it cannot be an abstract from a host of independent facts about parts of nature, since the connectivity of a space is a topological invariant which characterizes it as a whole. Although in each of our examples the propositions suggested for consideration have been selected from among various possibilities studied in pure mathematics, and are certainly not necessary in the same way as truths of logic or pure mathematics, we may very well hesitate to say that they are merely contingent or accidental, since these words are both derived from talk of happening in time and still imply a dependence on events which seems inappropriate here. Indeed, the intellectual attraction of the theories which I have mentioned seems to me to arise precisely from this feature of cosmology. We want to maintain a fundamental distinction between natural laws and initial conditions while still allowing that natural laws are not mathematical necessities. If we can show that they are derivative from postulates of physical geometry about the character of the universe as a whole, we shall in fact secure for them the required status of nonaccidental pervasiveness. For although we have learnt that alternatives are conceivable in abstract geometry, we can attach no sense to a suggestion that the universe might change over time in respect of such features as the number of its dimensions. There are, I believe, some theologians who say that the necessity of God's existence is not to be explained after the fashion of Anselm and Descartes (by saying that existence is involved in his essence) but consists simply in his being absolutely ingenerable and indestructible. I do not know whether such a view commends itself to many modern philosophers of religion, nor even whether it can be thought out consistently; but I believe that a similar view about the necessity of the laws of nature should be considered seriously by philosophers of science.

.

V

At the beginning of my paper, in a discussion of the relation of science to metaphysics, I argued against the view that scientific statements are all conjectures of law such as might in principle be refuted by experience, and I produced as a counterexample Anderson's announcement of the existence of positrons. Next, in a section on the relation of science to history, I argued that many generalizations put forward by scientists as laws are thought to be explicable by hypotheses of an histoɾical kind about what happened at certain times in the past. And finally, in a section on the relation of science to cosmology, I have argued that even the laws of nature we call fundamental may perhaps be explained some day in a satisfactory fashion by mathematical derivation from a cosmological hypothesis which is, strictly speaking, a singular proposition, since it is about the one universe we live in, though only about its unalterable general features. My motive in bringing together these otherwise disconnected remarks was a wish to show that it is unwise to be dogmatic about the logical form of scientific theories, e.g., by saying that they are all unverifiable propositions of unrestricted universality. Activities of various sorts are carried on under the name of scientific research, and theses of various sorts may be advanced by scientists in their professional capacity. What scientific activities have in common is a concern with the frame as distinct from the content of nature, but this concern may express itself, as we have seen, in assertions of existence which reveal hitherto unsuspected possibilities, in historical conjectures which would, if true, suffice to explain some regularities in the light of more fundamental laws, or lastly in cosmological speculations which may account for the necessity of supposed laws, but only by treating them as restricted in scope to a universe that embodies one among the various possible forms of order studied in pure geometry.

WILLIAM C. KNEALE

CORPUS CHRISTI COLLEGE
OXFORD, ENGLAND
JUNE, 1964

NOTES

[1] H. Bondi, 'Some Philosophical Problems of Cosmology', in *British Philosophy in Mid-Century*, ed. by C. A. Mace, 2d ed. (New York: Humanities Press, 1966).

3

W. V. Quine

ON POPPER'S NEGATIVE METHODOLOGY

A keynote of Sir Karl's theory of scientific method has been, down the years, his negative doctrine of evidence. Evidence does not serve to support a hypothesis, but only to refute it, when it serves at all. I am going to express some sympathetic reflections on this doctrine, along vaguely logical lines.

Let us limit our attention for a while to hypotheses of the most classical kind: categorical universals like 'All ravens are black'. Evidence of one solitary case to the contrary—one unblack raven—suffices to refute such a hypothesis. This is crystal clear, and it would be beside the point to reply that a law is sometimes preserved by challenging the solitary contrary instance as illusory. The point is that one unblack raven, *if conceded*, suffices to refute the law. Obviously such laws admit no supporting evidence as conclusive as the refuting evidence.

Might we speak still of some evidence as supporting a law, merely in the sense of not refuting it? Very well; this is rather support than refutation, but it is negative support: the mere absence of refutation. Adverse evidence is the primary kind of evidence, surely, as long as we consider categorical universals like 'All ravens are black'. It is the primary kind because of its conclusiveness; this is reason enough.

Its primacy is reflected also by Hempel's paradox of the unblack non-ravens, which runs as follows. If a black raven counts at all as partial evidence in *support* of the law 'All ravens are black', then, by the same token, an unblack non-raven should count as partial evidence in support of the law 'All unblack things are non-ravens'. But this law is logically equivalent to 'All ravens are black'. Therefore the unblack non-ravens attest to the law 'All ravens are black', equally with the black ravens. This seems odd, and is therefore a paradox.

This paradox suggests a certain instability in the notion of evidence *for* laws of the form 'All ravens are black'. There is no corresponding instability in the notion of evidence *against* such laws. What counts as evidence against this law is simply any unblack raven; what counts as evidence against the

equivalent law 'All unblack things are non-ravens' is again simply any unblack raven. On the refutational side there is no paradox.

Hempel's paradox thus plagues only the notion of *supporting* evidence
for 'All ravens are black'. I think, by the way, that even in that domain it can
be answered. My answer is that, whereas black ravens do partially confirm
'All ravens are black', unblack non-ravens do not even partially confirm 'All
unblack things are non-ravens'; and the reason is that 'raven' and 'black' are
projectible predicates, as Goodman would say, while 'unblack' and 'non-
raven' are not. I would equate projectibility of predicates to the naturalness
of kinds, and I would account for our native primitive intuition of natural
kinds by Darwinian natural selection. The intuitively natural groupings that
favor successful inductions are the groupings that have survival value in the
evolution of the species. I am brief on this point because it is a digression,
serving only to show that I do not despair over Hempel's paradox. The more
significant fact for present purposes is that when we talk only of refutation of
'All ravens are black' we tangle with no such paradox, and are not called
upon to consider projectibility or natural kinds or natural selection.

Thus far I have talked of simple universal hypotheses: 'All ravens are
black'. The corresponding simple existential statements, such as 'Some swans
are black', are oppositely situated. Supporting evidence is the decisive
evidence here; contrary evidence is what is indecisive and threatened by
paradox. The existential statements thus round out the symmetry; Sir Karl's
negative doctrine of evidence for universal hypotheses can be read off in
reverse as an affirmative doctrine of evidence for existential ones. And why
then has he accentuated the negative? So far as concerns the simple universal
and existential forms that we have thus far considered, the answer is clear: the
universal ones are the interesting ones, being the lawlike ones. 'All ravens are
black' is the very paradigm, in miniature, of an empirical law; 'Some swans
are black' is no law at all. Insofar, the negative doctrine of evidence is
sustained as a canon of discovery of scientific laws.

Insofar. But now let us move up to the next grade of complexity: 'All
men are mortal'. This is logically more complex than 'All ravens are black', if
we analyze mortality itself into an existential quantification: 'x is mortal'
means '$(\exists t)$ (x dies at t)'. Just as an unblack raven is what it takes to refute
'All ravens are black', so an immortal man is what it takes to refute 'All men
are mortal'; but the problem of spotting and certifying an immortal man is a
problem of a different order from that of spotting and certifying an unblack
raven. For 'Jones is immortal' is itself universal like 'All ravens are black'; it
says that all future times are times in Jones's life.

The fact of the matter is that a law with the complexity of 'All men are
mortal' admits of no direct evidence for or against: no direct refutation and
no direct demonstration. When we reach even this moderate level of complex-

ity, any implication of verifiable or falsifiable consequences must depend upon collaboration. Sentences governed by multiple mixed quantifiers may, when taken in conjunction, imply some singular sentences, even though they imply no such sentences when taken separately.

Suddenly our topic is doubly complex. Our laws or hypotheses are neither simply universal nor simply existential, but multiply quantified; and we are considering what observable consequences these laws imply not law by law, but conjointly. Our topic, in short, is now the more or less comprehensive theory rather than the lone hypothesis. At this level is there still any good reason for Sir Karl's negative bias, his negative doctrine of evidence? There is indeed, and it is essentially different now from what it was in the case of 'All ravens are black'. It is that we think of theories as conjunctions of laws and not as alternations of laws. Logically, duality is present as usual; laws taken in conjunction may imply singular consequences and laws taken in alternation may be implied by singular conditions. But a scientific theory consists of laws in conjunction, not alternation; and its evidence lies in the singular consequences. Failure of such a consequence refutes the theory, while verification of such a consequence is as may be.

W. V. QUINE

DEPARTMENT OF PHILOSOPHY
HARVARD UNIVERSITY
JANUARY, 1970

4

Hilary Putnam

THE "CORROBORATION" OF THEORIES

S ir Karl Popper is a philosopher whose work has influenced and stimulated
that of virtually every student in the philosophy of science. In part this influence is explainable on the basis of the healthy-mindedness of some of Sir
Karl's fundamental attitudes: "There is no method peculiar to philosophy."
"The growth of knowledge can be studied best by studying the growth of
scientific knowledge."

> Philosophers should not be specialists. For myself, I am interested in science and
> in philosophy only because I want to learn something about the riddle of the
> world in which we live, and the riddle of man's knowledge of that world. And I
> believe that only a revival of interest in these riddles can save the sciences and
> philosophy from an obscurantist faith in the expert's special skill and in his per-
> sonal knowledge and authority.

These attitudes are perhaps a little narrow (can the growth of knowledge be
studied without also studying nonscientific knowledge? Are the problems
Popper mentions of merely theoretical interest—just "riddles"?), but much
less narrow than those of many philosophers; and the "obscurantist faith"
Popper warns against is a real danger. In part this influence stems from
Popper's realism, his refusal to accept the peculiar meaning theories of the
positivists, and his separation of the problems of scientific methodology from
the various problems about the "interpretation of scientific theories" which
are internal to the meaning theories of the positivists and which positivistic
philosophers of science have continued to wrangle about.[1]

In this paper I want to examine his views about scientific methodology—about what is generally called "induction", although Popper rejects the concept—and, in particular, to criticize assumptions that Popper has
in common with received philosophy of science, rather than assumptions that
are peculiar to Popper. For I think that there are a number of such common
assumptions, and that they represent a mistaken way of looking at science.

1. Popper's View of "Induction"

Popper himself uses the term "induction" to refer to any method for verifying or showing to be true (or even probable) general laws on the basis of observational or experimental data (what he calls "basic statements"). His views are radically Humean: no such method exists or can exist. A principle of induction would have to be either synthetic a priori (a possibility that Popper rejects) or justified by a higher level principle. But the latter course necessarily leads to an infinite regress.

What is novel is that Popper concludes neither that empirical science is impossible nor that empirical science rests upon principles that are themselves incapable of justification. Rather, his position is that empirical science does not really rely upon a principle of induction!

Popper does not deny that scientists state general laws, nor that they test these general laws against observational data. What he says is that when a scientist "corroborates" a general law, that scientist does not thereby assert that law to be true or even probable. "I have corroborated this law to a high degree" only means "I have subjected this law to severe tests and it has withstood them". Scientific laws are *falsifiable,* not verifiable. Since scientists are not even trying to *verify* laws, but only to falsify them, Hume's problem does not arise for empirical scientists.

2. A Brief Criticism of Popper's View

It is a remarkable fact about Popper's book, *The Logic of Scientific Discovery* that it contains but a half-dozen brief references to the *application* of scientific theories and laws; and then all that is said is that application is yet another *test* of the laws. "My view is that . . . the theorist is interested in explanations as such, that is to say, in testable explanatory theories: applications and predictions interest him only for theoretical reasons—because they may be used as *tests* of theories" (*L.Sc.D.,* p. 59).

When a scientist accepts a law, he is recommending to other men that they rely on it—rely on it, often, in practical contexts. Only by wrenching science altogether out of the context in which it really arises—the context of men trying to change and control the world—can Popper even put forward his peculiar view on induction. Ideas are not *just* ideas; they are guides to action. Our notions of "knowledge", "probability", "certainty", etc., are all linked to and frequently used in contexts in which action is at issue: may I confidently rely upon a certain idea? Shall I rely upon it tentatively, with a certain caution? Is it necessary to check on it?

If "this law is highly corroborated", "this law is scientifically accepted", and like locutions merely meant "this law has withstood severe tests"—and there were no suggestion at all that a law which has withstood severe tests is likely to withstand further tests, such as the tests involved in an application or attempted application, then Popper would be right; but then science would be a wholly unimportant activity. It would be practically unimportant, because scientists would never tell us that any law or theory is safe to rely upon for practical purposes; and it would be unimportant for the purpose of under-standing, since on Popper's view, scientists never tell us that any law or theory is true or even probable. Knowing that certain "conjectures" (accord-ing to Popper all scientific laws are "provisional conjectures") have not yet been refuted is *not understanding anything*.

Since the application of scientific laws does involve the anticipation of future successes, Popper is not right in maintaining that induction is un-necessary. Even if scientists do not inductively anticipate the future (and, of course, they do), men who apply scientific laws and theories do so. And "don't make inductions" is hardly reasonable advice to give these men.

The advice to regard all knowledge as "provisional conjectures" is also not reasonable. Consider men striking against sweatshop conditions. Should they say "it is only a provisional conjecture that the boss is a bastard. Let us call off our strike and try appealing to his better nature." The distinction between *knowledge* and *conjecture* does real work in our lives; Popper can maintain his extreme scepticism only because of his extreme tendency to regard theory as an end for itself.

3. Popper's View of Corroboration

Although scientists, on Popper's view, do not make inductions, they do "corroborate" scientific theories. And although the statement that a theory is highly corroborated does not mean, according to Popper, that the theory may be accepted as true, or even as approximately true,[2] or even as probably ap-proximately true, still, there is no doubt that most readers of Popper read his account of corroboration as an account of something like the verification of theories, in spite of his protests. In this sense, Popper has, *contre lui* a theory of induction. And it is this theory, or certain presuppositions of this theory, that I shall criticize in the body of this paper.

Popper's reaction to this way of reading him is as follows:

> My reaction to this reply would be regret at my continued failure to explain my main point with sufficient clarity. For the sole purpose of the elimination ad-vocated by all these inductivists was to *establish as firmly as possible the sur-viving theory* which, they thought, must be the *true* one (or, perhaps, only a *highly probable* one, in so far as we may not have fully succeeded in eliminating every theory except the true one).
>
> As against this, I do not think that we can ever seriously reduce by elimina-tion, the number of the competing theories, since this number remains always in-finite. What we do—or should do—is to *hold on, for the time being, to the most improbable of the surviving theories* or, more precisely, to the one that can be most severely tested. We tentatively *'accept'* this theory—but only in the sense that we select it as worthy to be subjected to further criticism, and to the severest tests we can design.

On the positive side, we may be entitled to add that the surviving theory is
the best theory—and the best tested theory—of which we know. [*L.Sc.D.*, p. 419]

If we leave out the last sentence, we have the doctrine we have been
criticizing in pure form: when a scientist "accepts" a theory, he does not
assert that it is probable. In fact, he "selects" it as most improbable! In the
last sentence, however, am I mistaken, or do I detect an inductivist quaver?
What does "best theory" mean? Surely Popper cannot mean "most likely"?

4. *The Scientific Method—The Received Schema*

Standard "inductivist" accounts of the confirmation[3] of scientific
theories go somewhat like this: Theory implies prediction (basic sentence, or
observation sentence); if prediction is false, theory is falsified; if sufficiently
many predictions are true, theory is confirmed. For all his attack on inductivism, Popper's schema is not *so* different: Theory implies prediction (basic
sentence); if prediction is false, theory is falsified; if sufficiently many predictions are true, and certain further conditions are fullfilled, theory is highly
corroborated.

Moreover, this reading of Popper does have certain support. Popper
does say that the "surviving theory" is *accepted*—his account is, therefore, an
account of the logic of accepting theories. We must separate two questions: is
Popper right about what the scientist means—or should mean—when he
speaks of a theory as "accepted"; and is Popper right about the methodology
involved in according a theory that status? What I am urging is that his account of that methodology fits the received schema, even if his interpretation
of the status is very different.

To be sure there are some important conditions that Popper adds.
Predictions that one could have made on the basis of background knowledge
do not test a theory; it is only predictions that are *improbable* relative to
background knowledge that test a theory. And a theory is not corroborated,
according to Popper, unless we make sincere attempts to derive false predictions from it. Popper regards these further conditions as anti-Bayesian;[4] but
this seems to me to be a confusion, at least in part. A theory which implies an
improbable prediction is improbable, that is true, but it may be the most
probable of all theories which imply that prediction. If so, and the prediction
turns out true, then Bayes's theorem itself explains why the theory receives a
high probability. Popper says that we select the most improbable of the *surviving* theories—i.e., the accepted theory is most improbable even *after* the
prediction has turned out true; but, of course, this depends on using
"probable" in a way no other philosopher of science would accept. And a
Bayesian is not committed to the view that *any* true prediction significantly
confirms a theory. I share Popper's view that quantitative measures of the

probability of theories are not a hopeful venture in the philosophy of science[5]; but that does not mean that Bayes's theorem does not have a certain *qualitative* rightness, at least in many situations.

Be all this as it may, the heart of Popper's schema is the theory-prediction link. It is because theories imply basic sentences in the sense of "imply" associated with deductive logic—because basic sentences are DEDUCIBLE from theories—that, according to Popper, theories and general laws can be falsifiable by basic sentences. And this same link is the heart of the "inductivist" schema. Both schemes say: *look at the predictions that a theory implies; see if those predictions are true.*

My criticism is going to be a criticism of this link, of this one point on which Popper and the "inductivists" agree. I claim: in a great many important cases, scientific theories do not imply predictions at all. In the remainder of this paper I want to elaborate this point, and show its significance for the philosophy of science.

5. The Theory of Universal Gravitation

The theory that I will use to illustrate my points is one that the reader will be familiar with: it is Newton's theory of universal gravitation. The theory consists of the law that every body a exerts on every other body b a force F_{ab} whose direction is towards a and whose magnitude is a universal constant g times $M_a M_b / d^2$, together with Newton's three laws. The choice of this particular theory is not essential to my case: Maxwell's theory, or Mendel's, or Darwin's would have done just as well. But this one has the advantage of familiarity.

Note that this theory does not imply a single basic sentence! Indeed, any motions whatsoever are compatible with this theory, since the theory says nothing about what forces other than gravitation may be present. The forces F_{ab} are not themselves directly measurable; consequently not a single *prediction* can be deduced from the theory.

What do we do, then, when we apply this theory to an astronomical situation? Typically we make certain simplifying assumptions. For example, if we are deducing the orbit of the earth we might assume as a first approximation:

(I) No bodies exist except the sun and the earth.

(II) The sun and the earth exist in a hard vacuum.

(III) The sun and the earth are subject to no forces except mutually induced gravitational forces.

From the conjunction of the theory of universal gravitation (U.G.) and these auxiliary statements (A.S.) we can, indeed, deduce certain predictions—e.g., Kepler's laws. By making (I), (II), (III) more "realistic"—i.e., incorporating further bodies in our model solar system—we can obtain better predictions. But it is important to note that these predictions do not come from the theory alone, but from the conjunction of the theory with A.S. As scientists actually use the term "theory", the statements A.S. are hardly part of the "theory" of gravitation.

6. Is the Point Terminological?

I am not interested in making a merely *terminological* point, however. The point is not just that scientists don't use the term "theory" to refer to the conjunction of U.G. with A.S., but that such a usage would obscure profound methodological issues. A *theory,* as the term is actually used, is a set of *laws.* Laws are statements that we hope to be *true;* they are supposed to be true by the nature of things, and not just by accident. None of the statements (I), (II), (III) has this character. We do not really believe that *no* bodies except the sun and the earth exist, for example, but only that all other bodies exert forces small enough to be neglected. This statement is not supposed to be a law of nature: it is a statement about the "boundary conditions" which obtain as a matter of fact in a particular system. To blur the difference between A.S. and U.G. is to blur the difference between *laws* and *accidental statements,* between statements the scientist wishes to establish as *true* (the laws), and statements he already knows to be false (the oversimplifications (I), (II), (III)).

7. Uranus, Mercury, "Dark Companions"

Although the statements A.S. *could* be more carefully worded to avoid the objection that they are known to be false, it is striking that they are not in practice. In fact, they are not "worded" at all. Newton's calculation of Kepler's laws makes the assumptions (I), (II), (III) without more than a casual indication that this is what is done. One of the most striking indications of the difference between a theory (such as U.G.) and a set of A.S. is the great care which scientists use in stating the theory, as contrasted with the careless way in which they introduce the various assumptions which make up A.S.

The A.S. are also far more subject to revision than the theory. For over two hundred years the law of universal gravitation was accepted as unquestionably true, and used as a premise in countless scientific arguments. If the standard kind of A.S. had not led to successful prediction in that period, they would have been modified, not the theory. In fact, we have an example of this. When the predictions about the orbit of Uranus that were made on the basis of the theory of universal gravitation and the assumption that the known planets were all there were turned out to be wrong, Leverrier in France and Adams in England simultaneously predicted that there must be another planet. In fact, this planet was discovered—it was Neptune. Had this modification of the A.S. not been successful, still others might have been tried—e.g., postulating a medium through which the planets are moving, instead of a hard vacuum, or postulating significant nongravitational forces.

It may be argued that it was crucial that the new planet should itself be observable. But this is not so. Certain stars, for example, exhibit irregular behavior. This has been explained by postulating companions. When those companions are not visible through a telescope, this is handled by suggesting that the stars have *dark companions*—companions which cannot be seen through a telescope. The fact is that many of the assumptions made in the sciences cannot be directly tested—there are many "dark companions" in scientific theory.

Lastly, of course, there is the case of Mercury. The orbit of this planet can almost but not quite be successfully explained by Newton's theory. Does this show that Newton's theory is wrong? *In the light of an alternative theory,* say the General Theory of Relativity, one answers "yes". But, in the absence of such a theory, the orbit of Mercury is just a slight anomaly, cause: unknown.

What I am urging is that all this is perfectly good scientific practice. The fact that any one of the statements A.S. may be false—indeed, they are false, as stated, and even more careful and guarded statements might well be false—is important. We do not know for sure all the bodies in the solar system; we do not know for sure that the medium through which they move is (to a sufficiently high degree of approximation in all cases) a hard vacuum; we do not know that nongravitational forces can be neglected in all cases. Given the overwhelming success of the Law of Universal Gravitation in almost all cases, one or two anomalies are not reason to reject it. It is more *likely* that the A.S. are false than that the theory is false, at least when no alternative theory has seriously been put forward.

8. The Effect on Popper's Doctrine

The effect of this fact on Popper's doctrine is immediate. The Law of Universal Gravitation is *not* strongly falsifiable at all; yet it is surely a paradigm of a scientific theory. Scientists for over two hundred years did not derive predictions from U.G. in order to falsify U.G.; they derived predictions from U.G. in order to explain various astronomical facts. If a fact proved recalcitrant to this sort of explanation it was put aside as an anomaly (the case of Mercury). Popper's doctrine gives a correct account of neither the nature of the scientific theory nor of the practice of the scientific community in this case.

Popper might reply that he is not describing what scientists do, but what they *should* do. Should scientists then not have put forward U.G.? Was Newton a bad scientist? Scientists did not try to falsify U.G. because they could not try to falsify it; laboratory tests were excluded by the technology of the time and the weakness of the gravitational interactions. Scientists were thus limited to astronomical data for a long time. And, even in the astronomical cases, the problem arises that one cannot be absolutely sure that no non-gravitational force is relevant in a given situation (or that one has summed *all* the gravitational forces). It is for this reason that astronomical data can *support* U.G., but they can hardly *falsify* it. It would have been incorrect to reject U.G. because of the deviancy of the orbit of Mercury; given that U.G. predicted the other orbits, to the limits of measurement error, the possibility could not be excluded that the deviancy in this one case was due to an unknown force, gravitational or nongravitational, and in putting the case aside as one they could neither explain nor attach systematic significance to, scientists *were* acting as they "should".[6]

So far we have said that (1) theories do not imply predictions; it is only the conjunction of a theory with certain "auxiliary statements" (A.S.) that, in general, implies a prediction. (2) The A.S. are frequently suppositions about boundary conditions (including initial conditions as a special case of "boundary conditions"), and highly risky suppositions at that. (3) Since we are very unsure of the A.S., we cannot regard a false prediction as definitively falsifying a theory; theories are *not* strongly falsifiable.

All this is not to deny that scientists do sometimes derive predictions from theories and A.S. in order to test the theories. If Newton had not been able to derive Kepler's laws, for example, he would not have even put forward U.G. But even if the predictions Newton had obtained from U.G. had been wildly wrong, U.G. might still have been true: the A.S. might have been wrong. Thus, even if a theory is "knocked out" by an experimental test, the theory may still be right, and the theory may come back in at a later stage when it is discovered the A.S. were not useful approximations to the true situation. As has previously been pointed out,[7] falsification in science is no more conclusive than verification.

All this refutes Popper's view that what the scientist does is to put forward "highly falsifiable" theories, derive predictions from them, and then attempt to falsify the theories by falsifying the predictions. But it does not refute the standard view (what Popper calls the "inductivist" view) that scientists try to *confirm* theories *and* A.S. by deriving predictions from them and verifying the predictions. There is the objection that (in the case of U.G.) the A.S. were known to be false, so scientists could hardly have been trying to confirm them; but this could be met by saying that the A.S. could, in principle, have been formulated in a more guarded way, and would not have been false if sufficiently guarded.[8] I think that, in fact, there is some truth in the "inductivist" view: scientific theories are shown to be correct by their successes, just as all human ideas are shown to be correct, to the extent that they are, by their successes in practice. But the inductivist schema is still inadequate, except as a picture of one aspect of scientific procedure. In the next sections, I shall try to show that scientific activity cannot, in general, be thought of as a matter of deriving predictions from the conjunction of theories and A.S., whether for the purpose of confirmation or for the purpose of falsification.

9. Kuhn's View of Science

Recently a number of philosophers have begun to put forward a rather new view of scientific activity. I believe that I anticipated this view about ten years ago when I urged that some scientific theories cannot be overthrown by experiments and observations *alone*, but only by alternative theories.[9] The view is also anticipated by Hanson,[10] but it reaches its sharpest expression in the writings of Thomas Kuhn[11] and Louis Althusser.[12] I believe that both of these philosophers commit errors; but I also believe that the tendency they represent (and that I also represent, for that matter) is a needed corrective to the deductivism we have been examining. In this section, I shall present some of Kuhn's views, and then try to advance on them in the direction of a sharper formulation.

The heart of Kuhn's account is the notion of a *paradigm*. Kuhn has been legitimately criticized for some inconsistencies and unclarities in the use of this notion; but at least one of his explanations of the notion seems to me to be quite clear and suitable for his purposes. On this explanation, a paradigm is simply a scientific theory together with an example of a successful and striking application. It is important that the application—say, a successful explanation of some fact, or a successful and novel prediction—be *striking;* what this means is that the success is sufficiently impressive that scientists—especially young scientists choosing a career—are led to try to emulate that success by seeking further explanations, predictions, or whatever on the same model. For example, once U.G. had been put forward and one had the example of Newton's derivation of Kepler's laws together with the example of the derivation of, say, a planetary orbit or two, then one had a paradigm. The most important paradigms are the ones that generate scientific fields; the field generated by the Newtonian paradigm was, in the first instance, the entire field of Celestial Mechanics. (Of course, this field was only a part of the larger field of Newtonian mechanics, and the paradigm on which Celestial Mechanics is based is only one of a number of paradigms which collectively structure Newtonian mechanics.)

Kuhn maintains that the paradigm that structures a field is highly immune to falsification—in particular, it can only be overthrown by a new paradigm. In one sense, this is an exaggeration: Newtonian physics would probably have been abandoned, even in the absence of a new paradigm, if the world had started to act in a markedly non-Newtonian way. (Although even then—would we have concluded that Newtonian physics was false, or just that we didn't know what the devil was going on?) But then even the old successes, the successes which were paradigmatic for Newtonian physics, would have ceased to be available. What is true, I believe, is that in the absence of such a drastic and unprecedented change in the world, and in the absence of its turning out that the paradigmatic successes had something "phony" about them (e.g., the data were faked, or there was a mistake in the deductions), a theory which is paradigmatic is not given up because of observational and experimental results by themselves, but only because and when a better theory is available.

Once a paradigm has been set up, and a scientific field has grown up around that paradigm, we get an interval of what Kuhn calls "normal science". The activity of scientists during such an interval is described by Kuhn as "puzzle solving"—a notion I shall return to.

In general, the interval of normal science continues even though not all the puzzles of the field can be successfully solved (after all, it is only human experience that some problems are too hard to solve), and even though some of the solutions may look *ad hoc*. What finally terminates the interval is the introduction of a new paradigm which manages to supersede the old.

Kuhn's most controversial assertions have to do with the process whereby a new paradigm supplants an older paradigm. Here he tends to be radically subjectivistic (overly so, in my opinion): data, in the usual sense, cannot establish the superiority of one paradigm over another because data themselves are perceived through the spectacles of one paradigm or another. Changing from one paradigm to another requires a "Gestalt switch". The history and methodology of science get rewritten when there are major paradigm changes; so there are no "neutral" historical and methodological canons to which to appeal. Kuhn also holds views on meaning and truth which are relativistic and, on my view, incorrect; but I do not wish to discuss these here.

What I want to explore is the interval which Kuhn calls "normal science". The term "puzzle solving" is unfortunately trivializing; searching for explanations of phenomena and for ways to harness nature is too important a part of human life to be demeaned (here Kuhn shows the same tendency that leads Popper to call the problem of the nature of knowledge a "riddle"). But the term is also striking: clearly, Kuhn sees normal science as neither an activity of trying to falsify one's paradigm nor as an activity of trying to confirm it, but as something else. I want to try to advance on Kuhn by presenting a schema for normal science, or rather for one aspect of normal science; a schema which may indicate why a major philosopher and historian of science would use the metaphor of solving puzzles in the way Kuhn does.

10. *Schemata for Scientific Problems*

Consider the following two schemata:

SCHEMA I

THEORY
AUXILIARY STATEMENTS

PREDICTION—TRUE OR FALSE ?

SCHEMA II

THEORY
??????????????

FACT TO BE EXPLAINED

These are both schemata for scientific problems. In the first type of problem we have a theory, we have some A.S., we have derived a prediction, and our problem is to see if the prediction is true or false: the situation emphasized by standard philosophy of science. The second type of problem is quite different. In this type of problem we have a theory, we have a fact to be explained, but the A.S. are missing: the problem is to find A.S., if we can, which are true, or approximately true (i.e., useful oversimplifications of the truth), and which have to be conjoined to the theory to get an explanation of the fact.

We might, in passing, mention also a third schema which is neglected by standard philosophy of science:

SCHEMA III

THEORY
AUXILIARY STATEMENTS

????????????????????

This represents the type of problem in which we have a theory, we have some A.S., and we want to know what consequences we can derive. This type of problem is neglected because the problem is "purely mathematical". But knowing whether a set of statements has testable consequences at all depends upon the solution to this type of problem, and the problem is frequently of great difficulty—e.g., little is known to this day concerning just what the physical consequences of Einstein's "unified field theory" are, precisely because the mathematical problem of deriving those consequences is too difficult. Philosophers of science frequently write as if it is *clear*, given a set of statements, just what consequences those statements do and do not have.

Let us, however, return to Schema II. Given the known facts concerning the orbit of Uranus, and given the known facts (prior to 1846) concerning what bodies make up the solar system, and the standard A.S. that those bodies are moving in a hard vacuum, subject only to mutual gravitational forces, etc., it was clear that there was a problem: the orbit of Uranus could not be successfully calculated if we assumed that Mercury, Venus, Earth, Mars, Saturn, Jupiter, and Uranus were all the planets there are, and that these planets together with the sun make up the whole solar system. Let S_1 be the conjunction of the various A.S. we just mentioned, including the statement that the solar system consists of at least, but not necessarily of only, the bodies mentioned. Then we have the following problem:

> Theory: U.G.
> A.S.: S_1
> Further A.S.: ????????
>
> ---
>
> *Explanandum:* The orbit of Uranus

—note that the problem is not to find further explanatory laws (although sometimes it may be, in a problem of the form of Schema II); it is to find further assumptions about the initial and boundary conditions governing the solar system which, together with the Law of Universal Gravitation and the other laws which make up U.G. (i.e., the laws of Newtonian mechanics) will enable one to explain the orbit of Uranus. If one does not require that the missing statements be true, or approximately true, then there are an infinite number of solutions, mathematically speaking. Even if one includes in S_1 that no nongravitational forces are acting on the planets or the sun, there are still an infinite number of solutions. But one tries first the simplest assumption, namely:

(S_2) There is one and only one planet in the solar system in addition to the planets mentioned in S_1.

Now one considers the following problem:

> Theory: U.G.
> A.S.: S_1, S_2
>
> ---
>
> Consequence ??? — turns out to be that the unknown planet must have a certain orbit O.

This problem is a mathematical problem—the one Leverrier and Adams both solved (an instance of Schema III). Now one considers the following empirical problem:

Theory: U.G.
A.S.: S_1, S_2

Prediction: A planet exists moving
in orbit O—TRUE OR FALSE?

—this problem is an instance of Schema I—an instance one would not normally consider, because one of the A.S., namely the statement S_2, is not at all known to be true. S_2 is, in fact, functioning as a low-level hypothesis which we wish to test. But the test is not an inductive one in the usual sense, because a verification of the prediction is also a verification of S_2—or rather, of the approximate truth of S_2 (which is all that is of interest in this context)—Neptune was not the only planet unknown in 1846; there was also Pluto to be later discovered. The fact is that we are interested in the above problem in 1846, because we know that if the prediction turns out to be true, then that prediction is precisely the statement S_3 that we need for the following deduction;

Theory: U.G.
A.S.: S_1, S_2, S_3

Explanandum: the orbit of Uranus

—i.e., the statement S_3 (that the planet mentioned in S_2 has precisely the orbit O)[13] is the solution to the problem with which we started. In this case we started with a problem of the Schema II type: we introduced the assumption S_2 as a simplifying assumption in the hope of solving the original problem thereby more easily; and we had the good luck to be able to deduce S_3—the solution to the original problem—from U.G. together with S_1, S_2, and the more important good luck that S_3 turned out to be true when the Berlin Observatory looked. Problems of the Schema II-type are sometimes mentioned by philosophers of science when the missing A.S. are *laws;* but the case just examined, in which the missing A.S. was just a further contingent fact about the particular system is almost never discussed. I want to suggest that Schema II exhibits the logical form of what Kuhn calls a "puzzle".

If we examine Schema II, we can see why the term "puzzle" is so appropriate. When one has a problem of this sort one is looking for something to fill a "hole"—often a thing of rather under-specified sort—and that *is* a sort of *puzzle*. Moreover, this sort of problem is extremely widespread in science. Suppose one wants to explain the fact that water is a liquid (under the standard conditions), and one is given the laws of physics; the fact is that the problem is extremely hard. In fact, quantum mechanical laws are needed. But that does not mean that from classical physics one can deduce that water is *not* a liquid; rather the classical physicist would give up this problem at a certain point as "too hard"—i.e., he would conclude that he could not find the right A.S.

The fact that Schema II is the logical form of the "puzzles" of normal science explains a number of facts. When one is tackling a Schema II-type problem there is no question of deriving a prediction from U.G. plus given A.S., the whole problem is to find the A.S. The theory—U.G., or whichever—is *unfalsifiable in the context*. It is also not up for "confirmation" any more than for "falsification"; *it is not functioning in a hypothetical role*. Failures do not falsify a theory, because the failure is not a false prediction from a theory together with known and trusted facts, but a failure to *find* something—in fact, a failure to find an A.S. Theories, during their tenure of office, are highly immune to falsification; that tenure of office is ended by the appearance on the scene of a better theory (or a whole new explanatory technique), not by a basic sentence. And successes do not "confirm" a theory, once it has become paradigmatic, because the theory is not a "hypothesis" in need of confirmation, but the basis of a whole explanatory and predictive technique, and possibly of a technology as well.

To sum up: I have suggested that standard philosophy of science, both "Popperian" and non-Popperian, has fixated on the situation in which we derive predictions from a theory, and test those predictions in order to falsify or confirm the theory—i.e., on the situation represented by Schema I. I have suggested that, by way of contrast, we see the "puzzles" of "normal science" as exhibiting the pattern represented by Schema II—the pattern in which we take a theory as fixed, take the fact to be explained as fixed, and seek further facts—frequently contingent[14] facts about the particular system—which will enable us to fill out the explanation of the particular fact on the basis of the theory. I suggest that adopting this point of view will enable us better to appreciate both the relative unfalsifiability of theories which have attained paradigm status, and the fact that the "predictions" of physical theory are frequently facts which were known beforehand, and not things which are surprising relative to background knowledge.

To take Schema II as describing everything that goes on between the introduction of a paradigm and its eventual replacement by a better paradigm would be a gross error in the opposite direction, however. The fact is that normal science exhibits a dialectic between two conflicting (at any rate, potentially conflicting) but interdependent tendencies, and that it is the conflict of these tendencies that drives normal science forward. The desire to solve a Schema II-type problem—explain the orbit of Uranus—led to a new hypothesis (albeit a very low-level one): namely, S_2. Testing S_2 involved deriving S_3 from it, and testing S_3—a Schema I-type situation. S_3 in turn served as the solution to the original problem. This illustrates the two tendencies, and also the way in which they are interdependent and the way in which their interaction drives science forward.

The tendency represented by Schema I is the *critical* tendency. Popper is right to emphasize the importance of this tendency, and doing this is certainly a contribution on his part—one that has influenced many philosophers. Scientists do want to know if their ideas are wrong, and they try to find out if their ideas are wrong by deriving predictions from them, and testing those predictions—that is, they do this *when they can*. The tendency represented by Schema II is the *explanatory* tendency. The element of conflict arises because in a Schema II-type situation one tends to regard the given theory as something *known*, whereas in a Schema I-type situation one tends to regard it as *problematic*. The interdependence is obvious: the theory which serves as the major premise in Schema II *may* itself have been the survivor of a Popperian test (although it need not have been—U.G. was accepted on the basis of its explanatory successes, not on the basis of its surviving attempted falsifications). And the solution to a Schema II-type problem must itself be confirmed, frequently by a Schema I-type test. If the solution is a general law, rather than a singular statement, that law may itself become a paradigm, leading to new Schema II-type problems. In short, attempted falsifications do "corroborate" theories—not just in Popper's sense, in which this is a tautology, but in the sense he denies, of showing that they are true, or partly true—and explanations on the basis of laws which are regarded as *known* frequently require the introduction of *hypotheses*. In this way, the tension between the attitudes of explanation and criticism drives science to progress.

11. Kuhn versus Popper

As might be expected, there are substantial differences between Kuhn and Popper on the issue of the falsifiability of scientific theories. Kuhn stresses the way in which a scientific theory may be immune from falsification, whereas Popper stresses falsifiability as the *sine qua non* of a scientific theory. Popper's answers to Kuhn depend upon two notions which must now be examined: the notion of an auxiliary hypothesis and the notion of a *conventionalist stratagem*.

Popper recognizes that the derivation of a prediction from a theory may require the use of auxiliary hypotheses (though the term "hypothesis" is perhaps misleading, in suggesting something like putative laws, rather than assumptions about, say, boundary conditions). But he regards these as part of the total "system" under test. A "conventionalist stratagem" is to save a theory from a contrary experimental result by making an *ad hoc* change in the auxiliary hypotheses. And Popper takes it as a fundamental methodological rule of the empirical method to avoid conventionalist stratagems.

Does this do as a reply to Kuhn's objections? Does it contravene our own objections, in the first part of this paper? It does not. In the first place, the "auxiliary hypotheses" A.S. are not fixed, in the case of U.G., but depend upon the context. One simply cannot think of U.G. as part of a fixed "system" whose other part is a fixed set of auxiliary hypotheses whose function is to render U.G. "highly testable".

In the second place, an alteration in one's beliefs, may be *ad hoc* without being unreasonable. "*Ad hoc*" merely means "to this specific purpose". Of course, "*ad hoc*" has acquired the connotation of "unreasonable"—but that is a different thing. The assumption that certain stars have dark companions is *ad hoc* in the literal sense: the assumption is made for the specific purpose of accounting for the fact that no companion is visible. It is also highly reasonable.

It has already been pointed out that the A.S. are not only context-dependent but highly uncertain, in the case of U.G. and in many other cases. So, changing the A.S., or even saying in a particular context "we don't know what the right A.S. are" may be *ad hoc* in the literal sense just noted, but is not "*ad hoc*" in the extended sense of "unreasonable".

12. Paradigm Change

How does a paradigm come to be accepted in the first place? Popper's view is that a theory becomes corroborated by passing severe tests: a prediction (whose truth value is not antecedently known) must be derived from the theory and the truth or falsity of that prediction must be ascertained. The severity of the test depends upon the set of basic sentences excluded by the theory, and also upon the improbability of the prediction relative to background knowledge. The ideal case is one in which a theory which rules out a great many basic sentences implies a prediction which is very improbable relative to background knowledge.

Popper points out that the notion of the number of basic sentences ruled out by a theory cannot be understood in the sense of cardinality; he proposes rather to measure it by means of concepts of *improbability* or *content*. It does not appear true to me that improbability (in the sense of logical [im]-probability)[15] measures falsifiability, in Popper's sense: U.G. excludes *no* basic sentences, for example, but has logical probability *zero*, on any standard metric. And it certainly is not true that the scientist always selects "the most improbable of the surviving hypotheses" on *any* measure of probability, except in the trivial sense that all strictly universal laws have probability zero. But my concern here is not with the technical details of Popper's scheme, but with the leading idea.

To appraise this idea, let us see how U.G. came to be accepted. Newton first derived Kepler's Laws from U.G. and the A.S. we mentioned at the outset: this was not a "test", in Popper's sense, because Kepler's Laws were already known to be true. Then he showed that U.G. would account for the tides on the basis of the gravitational pull of the moon: this also was not a "test", in Popper's sense, because the tides were already known. Then he spent many years showing that small perturbations (which were already known) in the orbits of the planets could be accounted for by U.G. By this time the whole civilized world had accepted—and, indeed, acclaimed—U.G.; but it had not been "corroborated" at all in Popper's sense!

If we look for a Popperian "test" of U.G.—a derivation of a new prediction, one risky relative to background knowledge—we do not get one until the Cavendish experiment of 1781—roughly a hundred years after the theory had been introduced! The prediction of S_3 (the orbit of Neptune) from U.G. and the auxiliary statements S_1 and S_2 can also be regarded as a confirmation of U.G. (in 1846!); although it is difficult to regard it as a severe test of U.G. in view of the fact that the assumption S_2 had a more tentative status than U.G.

It is easy to see what has gone wrong. A theory is not accepted unless it has real explanatory successes. Although a theory may legitimately be preserved by changes in the A.S. which are, in a sense, *"ad hoc"* (although not *unreasonable*), its *successes* must not be *ad hoc*. Popper requires that the predictions of a theory must not be antecedently known to be true in order to rule out *ad hoc* "successes"; but the condition is too strong.

Popper is right in thinking that a theory runs a risk during the period of its establishment. In the case of U.G., the risk was not a risk of definite falsification; it was the risk that Newton would not find reasonable A.S. with the aid of which he could obtain real (non- *ad hoc*) explanatory successes for U.G. A failure to explain the tides by the gravitational pull of the moon alone would not, for example, have falsified U.G.; but the success did strongly support U.G.

In sum, a theory is only accepted if the theory has substantial, non-*ad hoc,* explanatory successes. This is in accordance with Popper; unfortunately, it is in even better accordance with the "inductivist" accounts that Popper rejects, since these stress *support* rather than *falsification.*

13. On Practice

Popper's mistake here is no small isolated failing. What Popper consistently fails to see is that *practice is primary:* ideas are not just an end in themselves (although they are *partly* an end in themselves), nor is the selection of ideas to "criticize" just an end in itself. The primary importance of ideas is that they guide practice, that they structure whole forms of life. Scientific ideas guide practice in science, in technology, and sometimes in public and private life. We are concerned in science with trying to discover correct ideas: Popper to the contrary, this is not *obscurantism* but *responsibility*. We obtain our ideas—our correct ones, and many of our incorrect ones—by close study of the world. Popper denies that the accumulation of perceptual experience leads to theories: he is right that it does not lead to theories in a mechanical or algorithmic sense; but it does lead to theories in the sense that it is a regularity of methodological significance that (1) lack of experience with phenomena and with previous knowledge about phenomena decreases the probability of correct ideas in a marked fashion; and (2) extensive experience increases the probability of correct, or partially correct, ideas in a marked fashion. "There is no logic of discovery"—in that sense, there is no logic of *testing,* either; all the formal algorithms proposed for testing, by Carnap, by Popper, by Chomsky, etc., are, to speak impolitely, *ridiculous:* if you don't believe this, program a computer to employ one of these algorithms and see how well it does at testing theories! There are *maxims* for discovery and maxims for testing: the idea that correct ideas just come from the sky, while the methods for testing them are highly rigid and predetermined, is one of the worst legacies of the Vienna Circle.

But the correctness of an idea is not certified by the fact that it came from close and concrete study of the relevant aspects of the world; in this sense, Popper is right. We judge the correctness of our ideas by applying them and seeing if they succeed; in general, and in the long run, correct ideas lead to success, and ideas lead to failures where and insofar as they are incorrect. Failure to see the importance of practice leads directly to failure to see the importance of success.

Failure to see the primacy of practice also leads Popper to the idea of a sharp "demarcation" between science, on the one hand, and political, philosophical, and ethical ideas, on the other. This "demarcation" is pernicious, on my view; fundamentally, it corresponds to Popper's separation of theory from practice, and his related separation of the critical tendency in science from the explanatory tendency in science. Finally, the failure to see the primacy of practice leads Popper to some rather reactionary political conclusions. Marxists believe that there are laws of society; that these laws can be known; and that men can and should act on this knowledge. It is not my purpose here to argue that this Marxist view is correct; but surely any view that rules this out a priori is reactionary. Yet this is precisely what Popper does—and in the name of an *anti*-a priori philosophy of knowledge!

In general, and in the long run, true ideas are the ones that succeed—how do we know this? This statement too is a statement about the world; a statement we have come to from experience of the world; and we believe in the practice to which this idea corresponds, and in the idea as informing that kind of practice, on the basis that we believe in any good idea—it has proved successful! In this sense "induction is circular". But of course it is! Induction has no deductive justification; induction is not deduction. Circular justifications need not be totally self-protecting nor need they be totally uninformative[16]: the past success of "induction" increases our confidence in it, and its past failure tempers that confidence. The fact that a justification is circular only means that that justification has no power to serve as a *reason*, unless the person to whom it is given as a reason already has some propensity to accept the conclusion. We do have a propensity—an a priori propensity, if you like—to reason "inductively", and the past success of "induction" increases that propensity.

The method of testing ideas in practice and relying on the ones that prove successful (for that is what "induction" is) is not unjustified. That is an *empirical* statement. The method does not have a "justification"—if by a justification is meant a proof from eternal and formal principles that justifies reliance on the method. But then, nothing does—not even, in my opinion, pure mathematics and formal logic. Practice is primary.

Hilary Putnam

Department of Philosophy
Harvard University
February, 1969

Notes

[1] I have discussed positivistic meaning theory in "What Theories Are Not", published in *Logic, Methodology, and Philosophy of Science*, ed. by A. Tarski, E. Nagel, and P. Suppes (Stanford: Stanford University Press, 1962), pp. 240-51, and also in "How Not to Talk about Meaning", published in *Boston Studies in the Philosophy of Science*, Vol. II, ed. by R. S. Cohen and M.W. Wartofsky (New York: Humanities Press, 1965), pp. 205-22.

[2] For a discussion of "approximate truth", see the second of the papers mentioned in the preceding note.

[3] "Confirmation" is the term in standard use for *support* a positive experimental or observational result gives to a hypothesis; Popper uses the term "corroboration" instead, as a rule, because he objects to the connotations of "showing to be true" (or at least probable) which he sees as attaching to the former term.

[4] *Bayes's theorem* asserts, roughly, that the probability of a hypothesis H on given evidence E is directly proportional to the probability of E on the hypothesis H, and also directly proportional to the antecedent probability of H—i.e., the probability of H if one doesn't know that E. The theorem also asserts that the probability of H on the evidence E is less, other things being equal, if the probability of E on the assumption $\overline{H}$ (*not*-H) is greater. Today probability theorists are divided between those who accept the notion of "antecedent probability of a

hypothesis", which is crucial to the theorem, and those who reject this notion, and therefore the notion of the probability of a hypothesis on given evidence. The former school are called "Bayesians"; the latter "anti-Bayesians".

⁵ Cf. my paper " 'Degree of Confirmation' and Inductive Logic", in *The Philosophy of Rudolf Carnap* (The Library of Living Philosophers, Vol. 11), ed. by Paul A. Schilpp (La Salle, Ill.: Open Court Publishing Co., 1963), pp. 761-84.

⁶ Popper's reply to this sort of criticism is discussed below in the section titled "Kuhn versus Popper".

⁷ This point is made by many authors. The point that is often missed is that, in cases such as the one discussed, the auxiliary statements are much less certain than the theory under test; without this remark, the criticism that one *might* preserve a theory by revising the A.S. looks like a bit of formal logic, without real relation to scientific practice. (See below, "Kuhn versus Popper".)

⁸ I have in mind saying "the planets exert forces on each other which are more than .999 (or whatever) gravitational", rather than "the planets exert *no* non-gravitational forces on each other". Similar changes in the other A.S. could presumably turn them into true statements—though it is not methodologically unimportant that no scientist, to my knowledge, has bothered to calculate exactly what changes in the A.S. would render them true while preserving their usefulness.

⁹ Hilary Putnam, "The Analytic and the Synthetic", in *Minnesota Studies in the Philosophy of Science*, Vol. III, ed. by H. Feigl and G. Maxwell (Minneapolis: University of Minnesota Press, 1962), pp. 358-97.

¹⁰ N. R. Hanson, *In Patterns of Discovery* (Cambridge, England: Cambridge University Press, 1958).

¹¹ Thomas S. Kuhn, *The Structure of Scientific Revolutions*, Vol. II, No. 2 of *International Encyclopedia of Unified Science* (Chicago: University of Chicago Press, 1962).

¹² Louis Althusser, *Pour Marx* and *Lire le Capital* (Paris, 1965).

¹³ I use "orbit" in the sense of space-time trajectory, not just spacial path.

¹⁴ By "contingent" I mean *not physically necessary*.

¹⁵ "Logical probability" is probability assigning equal weight (in some sense) to logically possible worlds.

¹⁶ This has been emphasized by Professor Max Black in a number of papers.

5

Imre Lakatos

POPPER ON DEMARCATION AND INDUCTION*

CONTENTS

Popper's ideas represent the most important development in the philosophy of the twentieth century; an achievement in the tradition—and on the level—of Hume, Kant, or Whewell. Personally, my debt to him is immeasurable: more than anyone else, he changed my life. I was nearly forty when I got into the magnetic field of his intellect. His philosophy helped me to make a final break with the Hegelian outlook which I had held for nearly twenty years.[1] And, more important, it provided me with an immensely fertile range of problems, indeed, with a veritable research programme. Work on a research programme is, of course, a critical affair, and it is no wonder that my work on Popperian problems has frequently led me into conflict with Popper's own solutions.[2]

* I should like to thank my friends Colin Howson, Alan Musgrave, Helmut Spinner, John Worrall, Elie Zahar and especially John Watkins for their critical scrutiny of previous versions. Their comments and objections are referred to throughout the paper.

—Editors' Note:

Imre Lakatos had corrected the page proofs of the present paper shortly before his sudden death on 2 February 1974. He had urged that his notes (now to be found on pp. 263-270) be printed at the foot of each page since they form an integral part of the text. We very much regret that we were unable to meet this request. (EDS.)

In the present note I shall sketch my position on what Popper himself frequently referred to as the two main problems of his now classical *Logik der Forschung*: the problem of demarcation and the problem of induction. Popper first gave a solution of the problem of demarcation and then, having claimed that "the problem of induction is only an instance or facet of the problem of demarcation", he applied his demarcation criterion to solve the problem of induction.[3] In my view, Popper's solution of *the problem of demarcation* is a great achievement but can be improved upon, and even in its improved form opens up large problems hitherto unsolved. But I think that *the problem of induction* is definitely more than merely an "instance or facet" of the problem of demarcation. Popper, in his early philosophy, offered decisive criticisms of earlier solutions of the problem—or rather problems—of induction, and suggested a purely *negative* solution. His later philosophy (based on the idea of truth-content and verisimilitude) involved a shift of the problem and also a *positive* solution of the shifted problem; but, to my mind, he has not yet realised the *full* implications of his own achievement.

I. POPPER ON DEMARCATION

(a) Popper's Game of Science

Popper's "logic of scientific discovery" (or "methodology", or "system of appraisals" or "demarcation criterion" or "definition of science")[4] is a theory of scientific rationality; more specifically, a set of standards for scientific theories. Originally people had hoped that a "logic of discovery" would provide them with a mechanical book of rules for solving problems. This hope was given up: for Popper the logic of discovery or "methodology" consists merely of a set of (tentative and far from mechanical) rules for the appraisal of ready, articulated theories. All the rest he sees as a matter for an empirical psychology of discovery, outside the normative realm of the logic of discovery. This represents an all-important shift in the problem of normative philosophy of science. *The term "normative" no longer means rules for arriving at solutions, but merely directions for the appraisal of solutions already there.* Some philosophers are still not aware of this problem shift.[5]

Popper's logic of discovery contains "proposals", "conventions", about when a theory should be taken seriously (when a crucial experiment could, and indeed has been, devised against it) and about when a theory should be rejected (when it has failed a crucial experiment). Popper's logic of discovery gives, for the first time in the context of a major epistemological research programme, a new role to experience in science: scientific theories are not based on, established or "probabilified" by, "facts" but rather eliminated by them. For Popper, progress consists of an incessant, ruthless, revolutionary confrontation of bold, speculative theories and repeatable observations, and of the subsequent fast elimination of the defeated theories: "The method of trial and error is a *method of eliminating false theories* by observation statements".[6] "Conjectures [are] boldly put forward for trial, to be eliminated if they clash with observations".[7] Thus, the history of science is seen as a series of *duels* between theory and experiment, duels in which only experiments can score decisive victories. The theoretician proposes a scientific theory; some basic statements contradict it; if one of these becomes "accepted",[8] the theory is "refuted" and must be rejected and a new one has to take its place. "What ultimately decides the fate of a theory is the result of a test, i.e., an agreement about basic statements."[9] Popper realises, of course, that we always test large systems of theories rather than isolated ones. But he does not regard this as an insurmountable difficulty: he suggests that we should *guess*—and, indeed, *agree*—which part of such a system is responsible for the refutation (that is, which part is to be regarded as false), perhaps helped by independent tests of some portions of the system. Within Popper's philosophy this kind of guessing is absolutely indispensable: if one were allowed to blame refutations upon the initial conditions *all the time*, no major theory need ever be rejected. He is not content with tests which are designed to test large systems: he calls on the scientist to specify, beforehand, those experiments which will, if their outcome is negative, lead to the falsification of the very heart of the system.[10] He demands of the scientist that he specify in advance under what experimental conditions he would give up his *most basic* assumptions.[11] This, indeed, is the gist of Popper's "demarcation criterion" or, to use a better term, of his definition of science.[12]

Popper's definition of science can best be put in terms of "conventions" or "rules" governing the *"game of science"*.[13]

The opening move must be a *consistent, falsifiable hypothesis*; that is, a consistent hypothesis which has agreed-on potential falsifiers. A potential falsifier is a "basic statement" whose truth-value is decidable with the help of the experimental techniques of the time. The scientific jury must agree *unanimously* that there is an experimental technique which will enable them to assign a truth-value to the "basic statement". (Unanimity can, of course, be reached by expelling the minority as pseudoscientists or cranks.)[14]

The next move is the repeated performance of the test in a controlled experiment,[15] and the second decision of the jury on what actual truth-value (truth or falsehood) to attribute to the potential falsifier. (If this second decision is not unanimous there are two possible moves: either the status of "potential falsifier" must be withdrawn and, unless a replacement is found, the opening move cancelled; *or, alternatively, the dissenting minority [of the jury] must be declared cranks and excluded from the jury.*)[16]

If the second verdict is *negative*, and the potential falsifier is rejected, then the hypothesis is declared "corroborated", which only means that it invites *further* challenges. If the second verdict is *positive*, and the potential falsifier accepted, then the hypothesis is declared "falsified", which means that it is *rejected*, "overthrown", "dropped", buried with military honours.[17] (In 1960 Popper introduced a new rule: military pomp can only be awarded to an eliminated hypothesis, if, before it was falsified, it was at least once—in a different experiment—corroborated.)[18]

After the burial a new hypothesis is invited. This new hypothesis must, however, explain the partial success, if any, of its predecessor, and also something *more*. A hypothesis, however novel in its intuitive aspects, will not be allowed to be proposed, unless it has novel empirical content in excess of its predecessor. If it has no such excess content, the referee will declare it "*ad hoc*" and make the proposer withdraw it. If the new hypothesis is not *ad hoc*, the standard procedure for falsifiable hypotheses, as described above, is followed for the new hypothesis.[19]

This "scientific game", if properly played, will "progress" in the sense that the theories subsequently proposed will have increasing generality (or "empirical content"); they will pose ever deeper *questions* about the universe.[20]

Just as the rules of chess do not explain why some people should play the game and, indeed, devote their life to it, the rules of science do not explain why some people should play the game of science and, indeed, devote their life to it. The rules decide whether a particular *move* is "proper" (or "scientific") or not, but they remain silent about whether the *game as a whole* is "proper" (or "rational") or not. The rules say nothing either about the (psychological) motives of the players or about the (rational) purpose of the game. One can of course play the game as a genuine game and enjoy it for itself, without caring for its purpose or being aware of one's motives.

Note. I had endless discussions with some of my Popperian friends about the identification of Popper and "Popper₁" (the naive methodological falsificationist) in my [1968*b*] and [1970] and in this section. I should like to say that never in my life have I experienced more sharply the pains of the historian than in this analysis. My [1968*a*], especially pp. 384 f. shows that then I identified Popper with my "Popper₂", the sophisticated methodological falsificationist. In my [1968*b*] I shifted my position and then suggested that *Popper conflated the two positions.* I held the same position in the text of my [1970], but in the Appendix, *I identified Popper essentially with Popper₁*, the naive methodological falsificationist. I maintain this position in my present paper, but with the grave suspicion that I might have missed some vital ingredient in the whole analysis. Could it be that the problem of *The Logic of Scientific Discovery* was a different one from the one I reconstructed? Is *my* split of Popper into Popper₁ and Popper₂ a result of *my* problem shift? No doubt, the most characteristic Popperian₁ quotations occur in Popper's *Poverty of Historicism* and *Open Society.* Are these no more than occasional exaggerations which occur only in his passionate condemnation of social pseudosciences? But surely Popper himself describes his original problem as how to demarcate science from pseudoscience! I confess that I am now at a loss as an exegetic and only hope that Popper's reply will dissolve my puzzlement.

(b) How Can One Criticise the Rules of the Scientific Game?

The rules of the game are *conventions*, and can be formulated in terms of a *definition*.[21] How can one criticise a definition, in particular, if one interprets it nominalistically?[22] A definition is then a mere abbreviation, a tautology. What can one criticise about a tautology? Popper claims that his definition of science is "fruitful": "that a great many points can be clarified and explained with its help". He quotes Menger: "Definitions are dogmas; only the conclusions drawn from them can afford us any new insight".[23] But how can a definition have explanatory power or afford new insights? Popper's answer is this: "It is only from the consequences of my definition of empirical science, and from the methodological decisions which depend upon this definition, that the scientist will be able to see how far it conforms to his intuitive idea of the goal of his endeavours".[24]

This answer complies with Popper's general position that conventions can be criticised by discussing their "suitability" relative to some purpose: "As to the suitability of any convention opinions may differ; and a reasonable discussion of these questions is only possible between parties having some purpose in common. The choice of that purpose. . .goes beyond rational argument".[25] But Popper, in his *Logik der Forschung* never specifies a *purpose* of the game of science that would go beyond what is contained in its rules. The idea that the *aim* of science is *truth*, occurs in his writings for the first time in 1957.[26] In his *Logik der Forschung* the quest for truth may be a psychological *motive* of scientists—it is not a rational *purpose* of science.[27]

Even in Popper's later writings we find no suggestion of how to appraise one consistent set of rules (or demarcation criterion) as leading more successfully towards Truth than another.[28] Indeed, the thesis that any such argument connecting method and success is impossible, has been a cornerstone of Popper's philosophy from 1920 to 1970. Thus I conclude that Popper never offered a theory of rational criticism of consistent conventions.[29] He does not answer the question: *"Under what conditions would you give up your demarcation criterion?"*.[30]

But the question can be answered. I shall give my answer in two stages: first a naive and then a more sophisticated answer. I start by recalling how Popper, according to his own account, had arrived at his criterion. He thought, like the best scientists of his time, that Newton's theory, although refuted, was a wonderful scientific achievement; that Einstein's theory was still better; and that astrology, Freudism and twentieth-century Marxism were pseudoscientific. His problem was to find a definition of science from which these *"basic judgments"* concerning each of these theories followed; and he offered a novel solution. Now let us agree *provisionally* on the meta-criterion that *a rationality theory—or demarcation criterion—is to be rejected if it is inconsistent with accepted "basic value judgments" of the scientific community.*[31] Indeed, this metamethodological rule would seem to correspond to Popper's methodological rule that a scientific theory is to be rejected if it is inconsistent with an ("empirical") basic statement unanimously accepted by the scientific community. Popper's whole methodology rests on the contention that there exist (relatively) singular statements on whose truth-value scientists can reach unanimous agreement; without such agreement there would be a "new Babel" and "the soaring edifice of science would soon lie in ruins".[32] But, even if there is agreement about "basic" statements, if there were no agreement whatsoever about how to appraise scientific achievement relative to this "empirical basis", would not the soaring edifice of science equally soon lie in ruins? No doubt it would. Although there has been little agreement concerning a *universal* criterion of the scientific character of theories, there has been considerable agreement over the last two centuries concerning *single* achievements. While there has been no *general* agreement concerning a theory of scientific rationality, there has been considerable agreement concerning the rationality of a *particular* step in the game—was it scientific or crankish? A general definition of science thus must reconstruct the acknowledgedly best games and the most esteemed gambits as "scientific"; if it fails to do so, it has to be rejected.

Then let us propose tentatively that, *if a demarcation criterion is inconsistent with the basic appraisals of the scientific élite, it should be given up.*[33] This metacriterion was suggested to me by Popper's own description of his original problem-situation, and by his own brand of methodological falsificationism (but, I should stress, one can accept Popper's falsificationism and yet reject this metafalsificationism). However, *if* we apply this metacriterion (which I am going to reject later), Popper's demarcation criterion—that is, Popper's rules of the game of science—has to be rejected.[34]

(c) A Quasi-Polanyiite "Falsification" of Popper's Demarcation Criterion

Popper's demarcation criterion can indeed be easily "falsified" by using the metacriterion proposed in the last section; that is, by showing that in its light the best scientific achievements were unscientific and that the best scientists, in their greatest moments, broke the rules of Popper's game of science.

Popper's basic rule is that *the scientist must specify in advance under what experimental conditions he will give up even his most basic assumptions:* "Criteria of refutation have to be laid down beforehand: it must be agreed which observable situations, if actually observed, mean that the theory is refuted. But what kind of clinical responses would refute to the satisfaction of the analyst *not merely a particular clinical diagnosis but psychoanalysis itself?* And have such criteria even been discussed or agreed upon by analysts?".[35] In the case of psychoanalysis Popper was right: no answer has been forthcoming. Freudians have been nonplussed by Popper's basic challenge concerning scientific honesty. Indeed, they have refused to specify experimental conditions under which they would give up their basic assumptions. For Popper this is the hallmark of their intellectual dishonesty. But what if we put Popper's question to the Newtonian scientist: "What kind of observation would refute to the satisfaction of the Newtonian not merely a particular Newtonian explanation but Newtonian dynamics and gravitational theory itself? And have such criteria even been discussed or agreed upon by Newtonians?". The Newtonian will, alas, scarcely be able to give a positive answer.[36] But then, if psychoanalysts are to be condemned as dishonest by Popper's standards, must not Newtonians be similarly condemned?

Popper may certainly withdraw his celebrated challenge and demand falsifiability—and rejection on falsification—only for *systems* of theories, including initial conditions and all sorts of auxiliary and observational theories. This is a considerable withdrawal, for it allows the imaginative scientist to save his pet theory by suitable lucky alterations in some odd corner of the theoretical maze. But even Popper's mitigated rule will make life impossible for the most brilliant scientist. For, in large research programmes there are always known anomalies: normally the researcher puts them aside and follows the positive heuristic of the programme.[37] In general he rivets his attention on the positive heuristic rather than on the distracting anomalies, and hopes that the "recalcitrant instances" will be turned into confirming instances as the programme progresses. On Popper's terms, even great scientists use forbidden gambits, *ad hoc* stratagems: instead of regarding Mercury's anomalous perihelion as a falsification of the Newtonian theory of our planetary system and thus as a reason for its rejection, most of them shelved it as a problematic instance to be solved at some later stage—or offered *ad hoc* solutions. This methodological attitude of treating as *anomalies* what Popper would regard as counterexamples is commonly accepted by the best scientists. Some of the research programmes now held in highest esteem by the scientific community progressed in an ocean of anomalies.[38] Rejection of such work by Popper as irrational ("uncritical") implies—at least on our quasi-Polanyiite metacriterion—a falsification of his definition.

Moreover, for Popper, *an inconsistent system* does not forbid any observable state of affairs and working on it must be invariably regarded as irrational: "a self-contradictory system must be rejected. . .[because it] is uninformative. . .No statement is singled out. . .since all are derivable".[39] But some of the greatest scientific research programmes progressed on inconsistent foundations.[40] Indeed, in such cases the best scientists' rule is frequently: "Allez en avant et la foi vous viendra". This anti-Popperian rule secured a sanctuary for the infinitesimal calculus hounded by Bishop Berkeley, and for naive set theory in the period of the first paradoxes. Indeed, if the game of science had been played according to Popper's rule book, Bohr's 1913 paper would never have been published, inasmuch as it was inconsistently grafted on to Maxwell's theory, and Dirac's delta functions would have been suppressed until Schwartz.

In general, Popper stubbornly overestimates the immediate striking force of purely negative criticism. "Once a mistake, or a contradiction, is pinpointed, there can be no verbal evasion: it can be proved, and that is that."[41]

This is how some of the "basic" appraisals of the scientific *élite* "falsify" Popper's definition of science and scientific ethics.

> *Note. I do not actually hold the metacriterion described in section (b) and applied in section (c). I shall negate the theses of both sections in what follows.* I only chose this Socratic-Popperian dialectical way of developing my position because I think this is the best way of developing a complex argument: by asking a simple question, giving a simple answer and then by criticising the answer (and possibly the question), thus being led to more sophisticated questions and to more sophisticated solutions. This approach also suggests that the dialectic does not end in some "final solution".

(d) An Amended Demarcation Criterion

One can easily amend Popper's definition of science so that it no longer rules out essential gambits of actual science. I tried to bring about such an amendment, primarily by shifting the problem of appraising theories to the problem of appraising historical series of theories, or, rather, of "research programmes", and by changing Popper's rules of theory rejection.[42]

First, *one may "accept" not only basic but also universal statements as conventions: indeed, this is the most important clue to the continuity of scientific growth.*[43] The basic unit of appraisal must be not an isolated theory or conjunction of theories but rather a *research programme,* with a conventionally accepted (and thus by provisional decision "irrefutable") *hard core* and with a *positive heuristic* which defines problems, foresees anomalies and turns them victoriously into examples according to a preconceived plan. The scientist lists anomalies, but, as long as his research programme sustains its momentum, ignores them. *It is primarily the positive heuristic of his programme, not the anomalies, which dictate the choice of his problems.*[44] Only when the driving force of the positive heuristic weakens, may more attention be given to anomalies. (The methodology of research programmes can explain in this way *the relative autonomy of theoretical science*; Popper's disconnected chains of conjectures and refutations cannot.)

The *appraisal* of large units like research programmes is in one sense much more liberal and in another much more strict than Popper's appraisal of theories. This new appraisal is *more tolerant* in the sense that it allows a research programme to outgrow infantile diseases, such as inconsistent foundations and occasional *ad hoc* moves. Anomalies, inconsistencies, *ad hoc* stratagems can be consistent with progress. The old rationalist dream of a mechanical, semimechanical or at least fast-acting method for showing up falsehood, unprovenness, meaningless rubbish or even irrational choice has to be given up. It takes a long time to appraise a research programme: Minerva's owl flies at dusk. But this new appraisal is also *more strict* in that it demands not only that a research programme should successfully predict novel facts, but also that the protective belt of its auxiliary hypotheses should be largely built according to a preconceived unifying idea, laid down in advance in the positive heuristic of the research programme.[45]

It is very difficult to decide, especially if one does not demand progress at each single step, when a research programme has degenerated hopelessly; or when one of two rival programmes has achieved a decisive advantage over the other. There can be no "instant rationality". *Neither the logician's proof of inconsistency nor the experimental scientist's verdict of anomaly can defeat a research programme at one blow.* One can be "wise" only after the event. Nature may shout NO, but human ingenuity—contrary to Weyl and Popper[46]—may always be able to shout louder. With sufficient brilliance, and some luck, any theory, even if it is false, can be defended "progressively" for a long time.

But when should a particular theory, or a whole research programme, be rejected? I claim, only if there is a better one to replace it.[47] Thus I separate Popperian "falsification" and "rejection", the conflation of which turned out to be the main weakness of his "naive falsificationism".[48]

My modification, then, presents a very different picture of the game of science from Popper's. The best opening gambit is not a falsifiable (and therefore consistent) hypothesis, but a research programme. Mere "falsifications" (that is, anomalies) are recorded but not acted upon. "Crucial experiments" in Popper's sense do not exist: at best they are honorific titles conferred on certain anomalies *long after the event*, when one programme has been defeated by another one. For Popper, a crucial experiment is described by an accepted basic statement which is inconsistent with a theory. I, for one, hold that no accepted basic statement *alone* entitles us to reject a theory. Such a clash may present a problem (major or minor), but in no circumstance a "victory". No experiment is crucial at the time it is performed (except perhaps psychologically). The Popperian pattern of "conjectures and refutations", that is, the pattern of trial-by-hypothesis followed by error-shown-by-experiment breaks down.[49] A theory can only be eliminated by a *better* theory, that is, by one which has excess empirical content over its predecessors, some of which is subsequently confirmed. And for this replacement of one theory by a better one, the first theory does not even have to be "falsified" in Popper's sense of the term.[50] Thus progress is marked by instances verifying excess content rather than by falsifying instances,[51] and "falsification" and "rejection" become logically independent.[52] Popper says explicitly that "before a theory has been refuted we can never know in what way it may have to be modified".[53] In my view it is rather the opposite way around: before the modification we do not know in what way, if at all, the theory had been "refuted", and some of the most interesting modifications are motivated by the "positive heuristic" of the research programme rather than by anomalies.[54]

(e) An Amended Metacriterion

An opponent could claim that the falsification of my criterion is not much more difficult than Popper's. What about the immediate impact of great crucial experiments, like that of the falsification of the parity principle? Or the long, pedestrian, trial-and-error procedures which occasionally precede the announcement of a major research programme? Will not the judgment of the scientific *élite* go against my universal rules?

I should like to present my answer in two stages. First, I should like to amend slightly my previously announced provisional metacriterion,[55] and then replace it altogether with a better one.

First, the slight amendment. If a universal rule clashes with a particular "normative basic judgment", one should allow some time to the scientific community to ponder about the clash: they may give up their particular judgment and submit to the general rule.[56] These "second-order" falsifications must not be rushed.

Secondly, if we abandon naive falsificationism in *method*, why stick to it in *metamethod*? We can easily have a second-order methodology of scientific research programmes.

While maintaining that a theory of rationality has to try to organise basic value judgments in universal, coherent frameworks, we do not have to reject such a framework immediately merely because of some anomalies or other inconsistencies. On the other hand, a good rationality theory must anticipate further basic value judgments unexpected in the light of their predecessors or even lead to the revision of previously held basic value judgments.[57] We reject a rationality theory only for a better one, for one which, in this quasi-empirical sense, represents a *progressive shift*. Thus this new—more lenient—metacriterion enables us to compare rival logics of discovery and discern growth in "metascientific" knowledge.

For instance, Popper's theory of scientific rationality need not be seen as "falsified" simply because it clashes with some actual basic judgments of leading scientists. On the contrary, on our new criterion it represents progress over its justificationist predecessors. For, contrary to these predecessors, it rehabilitated the scientific status of falsified theories like phlogiston theory, thus reversing a value judgment which expelled the latter from the history of science proper into the history of irrational beliefs. Also, it reversed the appraisal of the falling star of the 1920s: the Bohr-Kramers-Slater theory.[58] In the light of most justificationist theories of rationality the history of science is, at its best, a history of *pre*scientific preludes to some *future* history of science.[59] Popper's methodology enabled the historian to interpret more of the *actual* basic value judgments in the history of science as rational: it constituted progress.

On the other hand, I hope that my modification of Popper's logic of discovery will be seen, in turn—on the criterion I specified—as a further step forward. For it seems to offer a coherent account of *more* old, isolated basic value judgments as rational; indeed, it has led to new and, at least for the justificationist or naive falsificationist, *surprising* basic value judgments. For instance, on Popper's theory, it becomes *irrational* to retain and further elaborate Newton's gravitational theory after the discovery of Mercury's anomalous perihelion; or it becomes *irrational* to develop Bohr's old quantum theory based on inconsistent foundations. From my point of view, these were perfectly *rational* developments. My theory, unlike Popper's, explains some rearguard skirmishes for defeated programmes as perfectly rational, and thus leads to the reversal of those standard historiographical judgments which led to the disappearance of many of these skirmishes from history of science textbooks.[60] These rearguard skirmishes were previously deleted both by the inductivist and by the naive falsificationist party histories.

Progress in the theory of rationality is thus marked by historical discoveries: by the reconstruction of a growing bulk of value-impregnated history as rational.[61] This idea may be seen as a self-application of my theory of scientific research programmes to a (nonscientific) research programme concerning scientific appraisals.[62]

I, of course, can easily answer the question when I would give up my criterion of demarcation: when another one is proposed which is better on my metacriterion. (I have not yet answered the question under what circumstances I shall give up my metacriterion; but one must always stop somewhere.)[63]

Finally let me elaborate two characteristics of my methodology and metamethodology somewhat further.

First, I advocate a primarily quasi-empirical approach instead of Popper's aprioristic approach for law-giving to science.[64] I do not lay down general rules of the game a priori, so that, if history of science turns out to violate the rules, I would have to call the business of science to start anew. The law must take into account, if not be based upon, the verdict of the scientific jury. According to the conservative doctrine of Oakeshott and Polanyi, there must be only the jury, unfettered by written law. According to Popper merely the jury—even with common law—is not enough. There must be the authority of statute law to distinguish between good and bad science and to direct the jury in periods when a good tradition is in danger of degeneration or when new bad traditions emerge.[65] But in my view, there must be a dual system of authority, because the wisdom of the scientific *jury* has not been, and cannot be, fully articulated by the philosopher's *law*. Laws need authoritative interpreters. This is why, in matters of academic autonomy and the authority of tradition, I stand, even if only slightly, to the "right" of the more "liberal" Popper, who, to my mind, has a rather naive trust in the power of his (right!) law of scientific behaviour, and forgets that until now all the "laws" proposed by the philosophers of science have turned out to be false generalising interpretations of the verdicts of the best scientists. Up to the present day it has been the scientific norms, as applied instinctively by the scientific *élite* in *particular* cases, which have constituted the main yardstick of the philosopher's *universal* laws. Methodological progress still lags behind instinctive scientific verdicts in the sense that the main problem is to find, if possible, a theory of rationality which would explain *actual* scientific rationality rather than to bring legislative interference by the philosophy of science to the most advanced sciences.[66]

Secondly, I hold that philosophy of science is more of a guide to the historian of science than to the scientist. Since I think that philosophies of rationality lag behind scientific rationality even today, I find it difficult fully to share Popper's optimism that a better philosophy of science will be of *considerable* help to the scientist;[67] although no doubt it may help—and Popper's philosophy *has* helped—those great scientists whose scientific judgment was warped by the influence of previous, worse philosophies.

All this raises a host of problems about age-old problems of the role of authority, the right balance between the law and the jury, the mechanism of constitutional change, as applied to science. Institutionalised science is not participatory democracy (as some students, American senators and British MPs seem to think).[68] Scientific decision cannot be based on majority vote. But should it then be guided by enlightened despotism? Is the scientific community an "open" society, as Popper sees it, or a "closed" one, as Polanyi and Kuhn do? And which *ought* it to be?[69]

Instead of going any further into this field of problems, where Kuhn's theory is now the centre of discussion, I shall turn to the problem of induction and its relation to the problem of demarcation.

II. NEGATIVE AND POSITIVE SOLUTIONS OF THE PROBLEM OF INDUCTION: SCEPTICISM AND FALLIBILISM

(a) The Game of Science and the Search for Truth

A "logic of discovery" in the Popperian sense, that is a system of appraisal of scientific theories, defines "rules of the scientific game".[70] These rules demarcate science from nonscience and in particular from pseudoscience, and thus offer a *demarcation criterion*. But, in one respect, this demarcation criterion is poorer than most previous criteria. Most previous criteria laid down the aim of science as the discovery of the blueprint of the universe. Each "discovery" discerns a piece of this blueprint: thus each step of the "game" is seen as a step towards the goal. But what is the aim of *Popper's* "scientific game"? In inductivism the game was strictly connected with, and subordinated to, the Aim. In Popper's philosophy this link seems to be severed. The rules of the game, the methodology, stand on their own feet; but these feet dangle in the air without philosophical support.

The problem of induction, as Popper rightly pointed out, was originally identical with the problem of demarcation. Justificationists rigorously subordinated the rules of the game to the aim of science, to the finding of the Blueprint of the Universe: a step in the scientific game was proper only if it was *proved* to be a step in reconstructing this blueprint or, as they later more modestly claimed, if it was *proved* to be a likely (or "probable") step towards it. But Popper, in the early stage of his philosophy, shifted the centre of gravity to the problem of demarcation and separated it from the problem of induction. He solved the problem of demarcation without justifying the game by subordinating it to a final *aim*; and then he claimed to have negatively solved (or, rather, dissolved) the problem of induction. He supported this latter claim with the courageous assertion that the game is *autonomous*, that one cannot—and need not—*prove* that the game actually progresses towards its aim; one may only piously *hope* that it does.

Popper's classical *Logik der Forschung* is consistent with the game of science being pursued simply for its own sake.[71] Of course it is abundantly clear that Popper's *instinctive* answer was that the aim of the science *was* indeed the pursuit of Truth; but, inasmuch as in 1934 the correspondence theory was in eclipse, he thought he could do nothing but adopt a cautious position, which, in its formulation if not in its spirit, was entirely sceptical: science could at best—tentatively—detect error. He proudly noted that "in [his] logic of science it is possible to avoid using the concepts 'true' and 'false' ".[72] If science was victorious, it was victorious in *rejecting* refuted and provisionally *accepting* corroborated theories.[73] The "success" of science was nothing but unmasking alleged successes; indeed, "those who are unwilling to expose their ideas to the hazard of refutation do not take part in the scientific game".[74] If a theory stands up to severe tests, it is awarded the honorific title "corroborated". But the *only* function of high corroboration is to challenge the ambitious scientist to overthrow the theory.[75] Scientific "progress" is increased awareness of ignorance rather than growth of knowledge. It is *"learning"* without ever *knowing*.

(Popper does not seem fully to have realised that, within the framework of his *Logik der Forschung*, he cannot even answer the question what *can* one *learn* in the game of science. One cannot learn about the world even from one's *"mistakes"*, one cannot detect genuine epistemological error unless one has a theory of truth and a theory of how one may recognise increasing or decreasing truth-content. A "dogmatic falsificationist", of course, *can* learn about the world from his mistakes; a "methodological falsificationist" *can not*, as I shall later argue, without invoking some principle of induction.)[76]

To put it more sharply: *Popper's demarcation criterion has nothing to do with epistemology.* It says nothing about the epistemological value of the scientific game.[77] One may, of course, *independently* of one's logic of discovery, *believe* that the external world exists, that there are natural laws and even that the scientific game produces propositions ever nearer to Truth; but there is nothing *rational* about these metaphysical beliefs; they are mere animal beliefs. There is nothing in the *Logik der Forschung* with which the most radical sceptic need disagree.

Tarski's rehabilitation of the correspondence theory of truth came to Popper's attention only after the publication of the *Logik der Forschung*. But, when it did, it changed radically the general tone of Popper's philosophy of science. It stimulated Popper to complement his logic of discovery with his own theory of verisimilitude and of approximation of the Truth, an achievement marvellous both in its simplicity and in its problem-solving power.[78] It became possible, for the first time, to define *progress* even for a sequence of false theories: such a sequence constitutes progress, if its truth-content, or, as Popper proposed, its verisimilitude (truth-content minus falsity-content) increases. But this is not enough: we have to *recognise* progress. This can be done easily by an inductive principle which connects realist metaphysics with methodological appraisals, verisimilitude with corroboration, which reinterprets the rules of the "scientific game" as a—conjectural—theory about the *signs* of the *growth of knowledge*, that is, about the signs of *growing verisimilitude of our scientific theories*.[79] Popper's "rules" are then no longer pursued for their own sake; victories of science are then no longer victories merely in a game; they are even more than mere detections of error and replacements of erroneous theories by ever more comprehensive errors: they become instead putative milestones in approximating the Truth. (Popper's famous "third requirement", introduced in this very paper, may also be seen against this background: *corroborations* of major theories, rather than perpetual detections of failure, become signposts of success.[80])

As a consequence, the tone of Popper's discussion of *scepticism* has changed markedly since 1960. Before 1960 he never said anything against scepticism nor did he distinguish scepticism from fallibilism. But, since 1960, Popper has shifted *towards* epistemological optimism. He now consistently separates scepticism and fallibilism; and, indeed, his celebrated first *Addendum* to the fourth edition of his *Open Society* consists almost entirely of a sermon against scepticism. Even though in his methodology *decisions* play a vital role,[81] he is now firmly and explicitly against interpreting them as "leaps in the dark". Such an interpretation would be "an exaggeration as well as an over-dramatisation",[82] it would be "nihilist ado about nothing".[83] "Philosophical dispair is not called for", he writes, for we *can* cope with the task of "getting to know the beautiful world we live in and ourselves; and, fallible though we are, we nevertheless find that our powers of understanding, surprisingly, are almost adequate for the task—more so than we ever dreamt in our wildest dreams . . .".[84]

To some of Popper's students all this looked like the betrayal of everything that Popper had stood for; it seemed to be a break with the very essence of his *Logik der Forschung*.[85]

But it is only in the light of Popper's Tarskian turn that his *Logik der Forschung* can be properly understood. For we now understand why Popper had not offered a positive solution of induction in 1934. The main achieve-ment of his *Logik der Forschung* was to show that the problem of demarcation can be solved without any "inductive principle" being involved, which in turn could only rest on some satisfactory theory of truth. This was a most important achievement. But, after the problem of demarcation has been solved *in this autonomous way*, the link has to be reestablished between the game of science on the one hand and the growth of knowledge on the other. If once one accepts Popper's problemshift, demarcation and "induction" become *separate* problems, the solution of the second becoming a possibly trivial corollary of the solution of the first. But the remainder must not be forgotten. The positive solution of the problem of induction is that the scientific game, as played by the greatest scientists, is the best extant way of increasing the verisimilitude of our knowledge, of approaching Truth; the *sign* of increasing verisimilitude is increasing degree of corroboration. I have little doubt that Popper would have started his *Logik der Forschung* with this *positive* solution of the problem of induction, had Tarski's theory of truth come in 1925 (and had Popper arrived at his idea of truth-content and verisimilitude by 1930). But, since the idea of truth was in disarray in the 1920s and, since he did not know at the time of Tarski's results, he formulated the "rules" of science in the pragmatic terms of rejection and acceptance *alone*. He did this so ingeniously that those who tried to show that his hidden, instinctive guiding idea must actually be *there* as a hidden inductive principle, were foiled.[86] In the terminology of my "Changing Problem of Inductive Logic", Popper managed to put acceptability$_1$ and acceptability$_2$ (his methodological appraisals) on their own feet and to make them *logically* independent from acceptability$_3$.[87] But philosophically, as I said before, these feet dangled in the air without the support of an underlying conjectural "inductive" metaphysics. Popper's methodological appraisals are interesting primarily because of the hidden *inductive assumption* that, if one lives up to them, one has a better chance to get nearer to the Truth than otherwise. The value of excess corroboration is that it indicates that the scientists *might* be approaching truth, just as the value of the birds above Columbus's ship was that they indicated that the discoverers *might* be approaching land.[88]

Thus, once we have the theory of verisimilitude, we can correlate methodological appraisals with genuine epistemological appraisals. Methodological appraisals are *analytic*;[89] but without a *synthetic* interpretation they remain devoid of any genuine epistemological significance, they remain part of a pure game. A new, *synthetic* interpretation must be given to Popper's methodological appraisals with the help of an inductive principle: there must be an "acceptance$_3$" based on "acceptance$_1$" and "acceptance$_2$".[90]

Only such a positive solution of the problem of induction can separate constructive fallibilism from scepticism and from all its evil consequences, like relativism, irrationalism, mysticism. Popper, however, after having provided the tools for such a positive solution in the form of his theory of verisimilitude, shrank back from stating clearly and explicitly a positive solution of the [Popperian] problem of induction, that is, of the problem of the epistemological value of his logic of discovery.

(b) A Plea to Popper for a Whiff of "Inductivism"

Popper has not fully exploited the possibilities opened up by his Tarskian turn. While he now talks freely about the metaphysical ideas of truth and falsity, he still will not say unequivocally that the positive appraisals in his scientific game may be seen as a—conjectural—sign of the growth of conjectural knowledge; that corroboration is a *synthetic*—albeit conjectural—measure of verisimilitude. He still emphasises that "science often errs and that pseudoscience may happen to stumble on the truth".[91] Although making strongly optimistic sermons in praise of human knowledge,[92] when it comes to making a precise statement he restricts his "optimism" to a classical *sceptical* thesis: "I am a metaphysical realist, and an epistemological optimist in the sense that I hold that the truthlikeness ('verisimilitude') of our scientific theories can increase: this is how our knowledge grows".[93] A sceptic, of course, may hold realist *beliefs*; but, from the statement that "the verisimilitude of our scientific theories *can* increase", it only follows that "our knowledge *can* grow—but without our knowing it". *If so, even Popper's newly found fallibilism is nothing more than scepticism together with a eulogy of the game of science.* Popper's theory of verisimilitude remains a metaphysical-logical theory which has nothing to do with epistemology.

No wonder, then, as Watkins put it, that "in critical discussion of Popper's epistemology [we usually find] the suspicion that, far from solving the problem of rational choice between competing hypotheses, his methodology really leads to thorough-going scepticism".[94]

Watkins's reply is exceptionally lucid. It is worth quoting a passage in full:

> Many philosophers who have given up the hope that any of our empirical statements about the external world are certain, cling all the more tenaciously to the hope that some of them are at least less uncertain than others. Such philosophers tend to characterize as *scepticism* the thesis that *all empirical statements about the external world are equally uncertain.* I will use ST_1 as an abbreviation for this (first) 'sceptical' thesis. Now Popper's philosophy is 'sceptical' in the sense of ST_1; but then 'scepticism' in this sense seems to me to be unavoidable.[95]

Then Watkins goes on:

> Philosophers who place their hopes, not on certainties, whether absolute or relative, but on rational argument and criticism, will prefer to characterize as *scepticism* the thesis that *we never have any good reason for preferring one empirical statement about the external world to another.* I will use ST_2 as an abbreviation for this second sceptical thesis. ST_1 and ST_2 are by no means equivalent. ST_2 implies ST_1 (on the assumption that, if one hypothesis *were* less uncertain than another, that *would*, other things being equal, be a reason for preferring it). But ST_1 does not imply ST_2: there may be reasons having nothing to do with relative certainty for preferring one hypothesis to another. Empirical scientists cannot expect to have good reasons for preferring a particular explanatory hypothesis to all the (infinitely many) *possible* alternatives to it. But they often do have good reasons for preferring one out of several competing hypotheses which have actually been proposed. How one hypothesis may be rationally appraised as better than the other hypotheses under discussion, and what a future hypothesis would need to do for it to be even better than this one—this is what Popper's methodology is about.[96]

But the "*good reasons* for preferring one empirical statement about the external world to another" are laid down in Popper's demarcation criterion, in his rules of the game of science. Preference is only a pragmatic concept *within the context* of this game. This preference can only assume epistemological significance with the help of an additional, synthetic, *inductive (or, if you wish, quasi-inductive) principle* which would somehow assert the epistemological superiority of science over pseudoscience. Such an inductive principle must be based on some sort of correlation between "degree of corroboration" and "degree of verisimilitude". But, both Popper's and

Watkins's positions are ambiguous on whether the degree of corroboration can be interpreted *synthetically*. For instance, Watkins claims: "We may have good reasons for claiming that a particular hypothesis h_2 is closer to the truth than a rival hypothesis h_1".[97] But this contradicts his previous assertion that h_1 and h_2 are *equally* uncertain, unless he uses the terms "equally uncertain" and "closer to the truth" in the Pickwickian sense that we can have good reasons for holding that h_2 is closer to the truth than h_1, even though they are equally uncertain.[98] But such paradoxes are inevitable for philosophers who want the impossible: to fight pseudoscience from a sceptical position.

Indeed, Popper recently tends to complain that some of his critics believe that he is a mere "negativist", that he is "flippant about the search for truth, and addicted to barren and destructive criticism and to the propounding of views which are clearly paradoxical".[99] Popper's answer is as beautiful as it is unconvincing:

> This mistaken picture of our views seems to result largely from the adoption of a justificationist programme, and of the mistaken subjectivist approach to truth which I have described. For the fact is that we too see science as the search for truth, and that, at least since Tarski, we are no longer afraid to say so. Indeed, it is only with respect to this aim, the discovery of truth, that we can say that though we are fallible, we hope to learn from our mistakes. It is only the idea of truth which allows us to speak sensibly of mistakes and of rational criticism, and which makes rational discussion possible—that is to say, critical discussion in search of mistakes with the serious purpose of eliminating as many of these mistakes as we can, in order to get nearer to the truth. Thus the very idea of error—and of fallibility—involves the idea of an objective truth as the standard of which we may fall short. (It is in this sense that the idea of truth is a *regulative* idea.)

There is not a word in this passage about how to recognise the *signs* of being nearer to the Truth, nothing which amounts to more than the assertion that we must play the scientific game *seriously*, in the *hope* of getting nearer to the Truth. But did Pyrrho or Hume have anything against being "serious" or entertaining "hopes"?

In order further to clarify this whole issue, I shall analyse briefly Popper's criticism of induction.

Popper's reputation is rightly that of the scourge of induction. But, as I have pointed out before,[100] in Popper's anti-inductivist campaign (at least) three logically independent issues have to be carefully distinguished.

(i) First, there is the campaign against the *inductivist logic of discovery*. This is the Baconian doctrine according to which a discovery is scientific only if it is *guided* by facts and not *misguided* by theory. The scientist must start by purging his mind of theories (or rather *bias*); nature will then become for him an open book.[101] This doctrine was already opposed by rationalists, like

Descartes and Kant; but even they demarcated misguiding bad theories from good a priori principles which intuition can recognise as true. The method of free, creative conjectures and empirical tests developed only in stages from Whewell, Bernard, through Peirce and finally the Bergsonians, to achieve unique clarity and force in Popper's "demarcation criterion", which demarcated this method of discovery and scientific progress both from inductive fact-collecting and from "metaphysical" speculation. In this campaign Popper achieved a decisive success, not only intellectually but socio-psychologically; at least among philosophers of science Baconian method is now only taken seriously by the most provincial and illiterate. In this line he also proposed a *positive* theory about the role of speculation and experience in the growth of science;[102] but this was not the last word on the subject, and I hope to have developed it one step further.[103]

(ii) The second prong of Popper's attack was directed against the programme of an a priori probabilistic inductive logic or confirmation theory. This programme postulates that it is possible to assign—with the certainty of logic—to any pair of propositions a "degree of confirmation", which characterises the evidential support that the second proposition lends to the first. The function obeys the axioms of the probability calculus. The heart of this programme is the construction of an a priori metascience (by defining a distribution function over a finite or enumerably infinite number of possible states of the universe) that enables one to compute confirmation functions. Thus certainty is shifted from the science of the actual to the metascience of the possible, which, in turn, provides a proven confirmation theory for science. This programme was initiated by Cambridge philosophers (Johnson, Broad, Keynes) and its most persistent and influential protagonists became Hans Reichenbach and then Rudolf Carnap.[104] In this campaign too Popper achieved a complete victory, although "inductive logic", displaying all the characteristics of a degenerating research programme, is still —sociologically—a booming industry.[105]

(A weakness of this second part of Popper's anti-inductivist campaign was his determination to achieve an ultimate, clear-cut victory with one single blow; either by showing that Carnap's approach was inconsistent, or by showing that, *if* inductive logic was possible, *then* the virtue of a theory was its improbability rather than its probability, given the evidence. He did not realise that fighting a research programme—in this case a nonempirical one—by showing up its degeneration and developing a rival programme, cannot be a fast process; I hope that my development also of this prong of his campaign contributed to the clarification of some of his points.)

But the second prong of Popper's anti-inductivist campaign can be interpreted in an even stronger sense. It can be said to have been directed against *any* infallible a priori metaphysical inductive principle, whether probabilistic or nonprobabilistic, which would serve to assign a *proven* metric to the field of scientific statements.[106]

Nonprobabilistic logics of confirmation are still being produced—some with great ingenuity—by philosophers of science who understood Popper's arguments against probability logic, but not this more general message.[107]

(iii) The third prong of Popper's anti-inductivist campaign is less easily discernible. It consists of a tacit but stubborn refusal to accept any *synthetic* inductive principle connecting Popperian *analytic* theory-appraisals (like content and corroboration) with verisimilitude.[108] But why should we exclude a *conjectural* inductive principle from rationality? Why relegate the *application* of science to its "animal", "biological" function?[109] Popper's master argument against a justificationist principle of induction (namely that it leads either to infinite regress or apriorism[110]) is, *in this case*, invalid; Popper's powerful argument only applies to a principle which would serve as a premise to a *proven* measure function of (spatiotemporally local)[111] verisimilitude (one like Popper's degrees of corroboration). A conjectural inductive principle would be abhorrent only to the sceptico-dogmatist,[112] for whom the combination of total lack of proof and strong assent indicated mere animal belief. For the Humean sceptical pessimist this is the end of the road; for the Kantian dogmatic optimist this is a "scandal of philosophy" to be ironed out. But to the Popperian fallibilist, for whom conjectural metaphysics can be, at least in principle, rationally appraised, it *should* be a cause neither for sceptical resignation nor for apriorism.[113] Only some such conjectural metaphysics connecting corroboration and verisimilitude would separate Popper from the sceptics and establish his point of view, in Feigl's words, "as a *tertium quid* between Hume's and Kant's epistemologies".[114]

I had long discussions with Popper in 1966-67 about these issues; I profited immensely from them. But I was left with the impression that on what I called the "third prong of his anti-inductivist campaign" we may never see eye to eye. *The reason is not that our disagreement is too big; but that it is so very small.* The difference between total scepticism and humble fallibilism is so small that one frequently feels that one is engaged in a mere verbal quibble: should the "inductive principle" I advocate[115] be referred to as a "rationally entertained speculation", which even might be seen as very weakly "vindicated"; or should it be referred to as stark "animal belief ", conditioned in the Darwinian struggle for survival? I inserted at the end of my "Changes in the Problem of Inductive Logic" a brief section of three pages on "Popper's opposition to 'acceptability₃' ". This, I am afraid, is rather a trivial section. For, although in my lengthy and pedantic discussion of "acceptability₃", I thought to offer a new, *positive* solution to the old problem of induction, the "solution" was very thin. Alas, a solution is interesting only if it is embedded in, or leads to, a major research programme;

if it creates new problems—and solutions—in turn. *But this would be the case only if such an inductive principle could be sufficiently richly formulated so that one may, say, criticise our scientific game from its point of view.* My inductive principle tries to explain why we "play" the game of science. But it does so in an *ad hoc*, not in a "fact-correcting" (or, if you wish, "basic value judgment correcting") way. *Ad hoc* explanations are very near to mere linguistic transformations; although they may be *also* happy phrases suggesting and protecting later development. Such metaphysical developments are barred by Popper when he sternly announced that: "As for inductive logic, I do not believe that it exists. There is, of course, a logic of science, but that is part of an applied deductive logic: the logic of testing theories, or the logic of the growth of knowledge".[116] I, on the contrary, hold that the "logic of the growth of knowledge" *must* include—in addition to Popper's *logico-metaphysical* theory of verisimilitude—*some* speculative *genuinely epistemological* theory connecting scientific standards with verisimilitude.

I think it is the present thinness of a conjectural inductive metaphysics that makes Popper reluctant to see anything in it, and I appreciate his point.[117] Yet, although both "tautological" appraisals and metaphysical inductive principles are equally irrefutable, there is an immense philosophical difference between interpreting an appraisal as tautologous and interpreting it as metaphysical. For *this choice—as I already indicated—is the choice between scepticism with a purely negative solution of the problem of induction and fallibilism with a—momentarily very weak—positive solution.* By refusing to accept a "thin" metaphysical principle of induction Popper fails to separate rationalism from irrationalism, weak light from total darkness. Without this principle Popper's "corroborations" or "refutations" and my "progress" or "degeneration", would remain mere honorific titles awarded in a pure game.[118] With a *positive* solution of the problem of induction, however thin, methodological theories of demarcation can be turned from arbitrary conventions into rational metaphysics.

Popper, of course, might well retort that this "positive solution" itself is merely an arbitrary convention. The rationalist wants a positive solution of the problem of induction, therefore he postulates one. But, as Russell put it: "The method of postulating what we want has many advantages; they are the same as the advantages of theft over honest toil".[119]

Yet, why should we be more sceptical about some such metaphysical postulates than we are about "accepted" basic statements? Why not extend Popperian hardheaded conventionalism from the acceptance (without belief) of some spatiotemporally singular statements to granting similar acceptance to some universal statements (in my "hard cores") and even beyond that, to some conjectural weak "inductive principle"? Why should Popper attribute high rational-scientific (although, as I have mentioned, not genuinely epistemological) status to absurd statements like "nothing can assume higher velocity than the velocity of light", or "there is attraction between two distant masses", but classify a plausible statement like "physics has higher verisimilitude than astrology" as "animal belief"? Why should only a "basic", but not a "metaphysical", statement be accepted as long as there is no serious alternative offered?

Thus the third prong of Popper's anti-inductivist campaign leads into a Humean irrationalist theory of practical human action and of applied science.[120] Indeed, only a positive solution of the problem of induction can save Popperian rationalism from Feyerabend's epistemological anarchism.[121]

Finally, let me say that, although I do think that my criticism of Popper's solution of the *problem of demarcation* is a genuine further development in the very tradition he himself set for the "logic of scientific discovery", I do not think that my "criticism" of Popper's "solution" of the *problem of induction* is more than an attempt to make explicit the *full* implications of his own theory of verisimilitude for the problem of induction, and thus make the epistemological difference between classical scepticism and his fallibilism sharp and explicit. I hope he will be able to accept my modifications on both issues.[122]

DEPARTMENT OF PHILOSOPHY, LOGIC AND SCIENTIFIC METHOD
LONDON SCHOOL OF ECONOMICS AND POLITICAL SCIENCE AND
DEPARTMENT OF PHILOSOPHY, BOSTON UNIVERSITY
1969

[*Added in 1971:*] Popper now published a major paper on induction in order to clarify his position on this subject. Large sections of Popper [1971] consist of responses to my [1968a] and to my present contribution.

I was interested to see that *on some minor points* Popper has now adopted some of my earlier suggestions. For instance, he now equates boldness with non*adhoc*ness, that is, with excess content rather than content.[123] Also, he now gave up his long held and tenaciously defended doctrine that the degree of corroboration of an unrefuted theory cannot be smaller than the degree of corroboration of any of its consequences;[124] instead of this he has now radically moved towards the position outlined in my 'Theoretical support for predictions versus evidential support for theories'.[125] Unfortunately, the one point which Popper explicitly refers to in my work he misquotes: he claims that I 'suspect that the actual attribution of numbers to [his] "degree of corroboration", if possible, would render [his theory] inductivist in the sense of a probabilistic theory of induction'. Popper 'sees no reason whatever why this should be so'.[126] Nor do I; and I said no such thing on pp. 410-12 of my paper to which he refers the reader—nor did I say anything like this anywhere else.

On the major issue—on induction—Popper's [1971] does not contain anything new.[127] His 'criticism' of a plea for an inductive principle[128] leaves my argument for such a principle completely intact.

NOTES

[1] Since Hegel each generation has unfortunately needed—and has fortunately had—philosophers to break Hegel's spell on young thinkers who so frequently fall into the trap of "impressive and all-explanatory theories [like Hegel's or Freud's] which act upon weak minds like revelations" (cp. Popper [C.&R.. 1963a] p. 39). Moore was the liberator in Cambridge before the first war, Popper in London School of Economics after the second.

[2] Cp. my [1968a], [1968b], [1970] and [1971]. In these papers I tried to explain why I think Popper's philosophy is so immensely important. The reason why I continue to criticise various aspects of Popper's philosophy is my conviction that it represents the most advanced philosophy of our time, and that philosophical progress can only be based—even if "dialectically"—on its achievements. Although the present paper is meant to be self-contained, some of its formulations had, for the sake of brevity, to be crude. The reader will find it helpful, and perhaps, at times necessary, to compare it primarily with my [1970] for more detailed expositions of some issues.

[3] Cp. e.g. Chap. I of his [L.Sc.D., 1934b]; and also Chap. I of his [C.&R., 1963a], esp. pp. 52 ff. and 58. (The phrase quoted is on p. 54.)

[4] This profusion of synonyms has proved to be rather confusing.

[5] I should like to say here that I always had *doubts* about whether this (no doubt progressive) problem-shift had not gone a bit too far. This shift had been even more pronounced in the philosophy of mathematics than in the philosophy of science. Following Pólya, I have held that there might well be a *limbo* for a "genuine" heuristic which is rational and nonpsychologistic; it was in this vein that I expressed some reservations concerning Tarski's novel use of the term "methodology"; cp. my [1963-64], p. 4, n. 4. But I cannot here pursue this matter further.

[6] Popper [C.&R., 1963a], p. 56 (Popper's italics). Cp. below n. 73.

[7] Popper [C.&R., 1963a], p. 46.

[8] For the conditions of acceptance of basic statements, cp. Popper [L.Sc.D., 1934b], Sec. 22 and my [1970], pp. 107-8.

[9] Popper, *ibid.*, Sec. 30.

[10] For references, cp. below, nn. 36 and 48.

[11] Cp. pp. 246-47, text to n. 35. Also cp. my [1970], p. 107.

[12] Cp. my [1970], p. 109. For an interesting discussion cp. also Musgrave [1968].

[13] Popper [L.Sc.D., 1934b], Secs. 11 and 85. The first paragraph in Section 11 explains why he gave the title *The Logic of Scientific Discovery* to his book and is worth quoting: "Methodological rules are here regarded as *conventions*. They might be described as the rules of the game of empirical science. They differ from the rules of pure logic rather as do the rules of chess, which few would regard as part of *pure* logic: seeing that the rules of pure logic govern transformations of linguistic formulae, the result of an inquiry into the rules of chess could perhaps be entitled 'The Logic of Chess', but hardly 'Logic' pure and simple. (Similarly, the result of an inquiry into the rules of the game of science—that is, of scientific discovery—may be entitled 'The Logic of Scientific Discovery'.)"

[14] I am afraid Popper did not spell out this implication; although he mentions, as if it were a matter of fact, that cranks do not "seriously disturb the working of the various social institutions

which have been designed to further scientific objectivity. . ." (Popper [*O.S.*, 1945*c*], Vol. II, p. 218). Then he goes on: "*Only political power*. . .can impair [their] functioning. . .". (Also cp. his [1957*g*], p. 32.) I wonder.

15 For the concept of "controlled experiment", cp. my [1970], p. 111, n. 6.

16 Cp. above n. 14.

17 Popper [*L.Sc.D.*, 1934*b*], Secs. 3 and 4. Also cp. Sec. 22 ("Falsifiability and Falsification") for "special rules. . .which determine under what conditions a system is to be regarded as falsified". It is intriguing that *at least in this particular section* (Sec. 22) there is not a word about the identification of "falsification" in the sense here described with "overthrow" or "elimination". Some of my friends used this omission as evidence that Popper did not advocate such an identification, but left the problem of elimination—as opposed to "falsification"—open. But, in other passages, especially in works related to social sciences (cp. e.g., his [1957*g*], pp. 133-34), Popper clearly identifies "falsification" with "rejection" and "elimination". And if falsification does *not* mean rejection, what *does* it mean? Popper tells us nothing about how we can continue to play the game of science with a *falsified* hypothesis.

18 Cp. his [*C.&R.*, 1963*a*], pp. 242-45.

19 Following Popper's new rule referred to in the previous footnote, the anti-*adhoc*ness rules may also be tightened; and we have to distinguish between *adhoc*₁ and *adhoc*₂, cp. my [1968*a*], pp. 375-90, esp. p. 389, n. 1.

20 Popper [*L.Sc.D.*, 1934*b*], Sec. 85, last sentence.

21 Cp. Popper [*L.Sc.D.*, 1934*b*], Secs. 4 and 11.

22 For an excellent discussion of the distinction between nominalism and realism (or, as Popper prefers to call it, "essentialism") in the theory of definitions, cp. Popper [*O.S.*, 1945*c*], Chap. 11, and [*C.&R.*, 1963*a*], p. 20. Also cp. my [1970], p. 126.

23 Popper [*L.Sc.D.*, 1934*b*], Sec. 11.

25 *Ibid.*

25 *Ibid.*, Sec. 4.

26 Cp. his [1957*i*].

27 He calls the search for truth "the strongest [unscientific] motive" ([*L.Sc.D.*, 1934*b*], Sec. 85). Also cp. above, pp. 257-58.

28 Popper's crucial arguments against various inductivist theories of science show that they are *inconsistent*. On the other hand, he admits that the conventionalist theory is consistent, "self-contained and defensible", and concludes: "My conflict with the conventionalists is not one that can be settled by a detached theoretical discussion" (Popper [*L.Sc.D.*, 1934*b*], Sec. 19). Is then the choice between *consistent* sets of rules a matter of subjective taste?

29 In the early 1960s Popper adopted Bartley's comprehensively critical rationalism. According to this theory all propositions accepted by a rational person must be open to criticism. But the basic weakness of this position is its emptiness. There is not much point in affirming the criticisability of any position we hold without concretely specifying the forms such criticism might take. (For an interesting criticism of Bartley's position cp. Watkins [1971].)

30 This flaw is the more serious since Popper himself has expressed qualifications about his criterion. For instance in his [*C.&R.*, 1963*a*] he describes "dogmatism", that is, treating anomalies as a kind of "background noise", as something that is "to some extent necessary" (p. 49). But on the next page he identifies this "dogmatism" with "pseudoscience". Is then pseudoscience "to some extent necessary"? Also, cp. my [1970], p. 177, n. 3.

31 "Basic value judgments" would sound better in German: *"normative Basissätze"*.

32 Popper [*L.Sc.D.*, 1934*b*], Sec. 29.

33 This approach, of course, does not mean that we *believe* that the scientists' "basic judgments" are unfailingly rational; it only means that we *accept* them in order to criticise uni-

versal definitions of science. (If we add that no such *universal* criterion has been found and no such *universal* criterion will ever be found, the stage is set for Polanyi's conception of the lawless closed autocracy of science.)

The idea of this metacriterion may be seen as a "quasi-empirical" self-application of Popperian falsificationism. I had introduced this "quasi-empiricalness" earlier in the context of mathematical philosophy. We may abstract from *what* flows in the logical channels of a deductive system, whether it is something certain or something fallible, whether it is truth and falsehood or probability and improbability, or even moral or scientific desirability and undesirability: it is the *how* of the flow which decides whether the system is negativist, "quasi-empirical", dominated by *modus tollens* or whether it is justificationist, "quasi-Euclidean", dominated by *modus ponens*. (Cp. my [1967].) This "quasi-empirical" approach may be applied to *any* kind of normative knowledge like ethical or aesthetic, as has already been done by Watkins in his [1963] and [1967]. But now I prefer another approach: cp. below, n. 62.

[34] It may be noted that this metacriterion does not have to be construed as psychological, or "naturalistic" in Popper's sense. (Cp. his [*L.Sc.D.*, 1934*b*], Sec. 10.) The definition of the "scientific *élite*" is not an empirical matter.

[35] Popper [*C.&R.*, 1963*a*], p. 38, n. 3 (italics mine). This, of course, is equivalent to his celebrated "demarcation criterion" between science and pseudoscience—or, as he put it, "metaphysics". (For this point, also cp. Agassi [1964], Sec. VI.)

[36] Cp. my [1970], pp. 100-101.

[37] Cp. my [1970], esp. pp. 135 ff.

[38] *Ibid.*, pp. 138 ff.

[39] Cp. Popper [*L.Sc.D.*, 1934*b*], Sec. 24.

[40] Cp. my [1970], esp. pp. 140 ff.

[41] Popper [*L.Sc.D.*, 1959*a*], p. 394. He adds: "Frege did not try evasive manoeuvres when he received Russell's criticism". But of course he did. (Cp. Frege's *Postscript* to the second edition of his *Grundgesetze*.) This historiographical mistake may also be related to Popper's earlier overconfidence in the unambiguity of mathematical reasoning. Also cp. my [1968*a*], p. 357, n. 2.

[42] Cp. my [1968*a*], [1968*b*] and [1970]. Popper always held, and in his later philosophy particularly emphasised, that 'the influence of [some] nontestable metaphysical theories upon science exceeded that of many testable theories', and even started to talk about 'metaphysical research programmes'. (Cp. my [1970], p. 183, n. 3.) But whereas Popper acknowledged the *influence* of metaphysics *upon* science, I see metaphysics as an integral part of science. For Popper—and for Agassi and Watkins—metaphysics is *merely* 'influential'; I specify concrete patterns of appraisal. And these *conflict* with Popper's earlier appraisals of "falsifiable" theories which he has not yet abandoned.

[43] Popper does not permit this: "There is a vast difference between my views and conventionalism. I hold that what characterises the empirical method is just this: our conventions determine the acceptance of the *singular*, not of *universal* statements". (Popper [*L.Sc.D.*, 1934*b*], Sec. 30.)

[44] Agassi, in some passages, seems to deny this: "Learning from experience is learning from a refuting instance. The refuting instance then becomes a problematic instance". (Agassi [1964], p. 201.) In his [1969] he attributes to Popper the statement that "we learn from experience by refutations" (p. 169), and adds that, according to Popper, one can learn *only* from refutation but not from corroboration (p. 167). But this is a very one-sided theory of learning from experience. (Cp. my [1970], p. 121, n. 1, and p. 123.)

Feyerabend, in his [1969], says that *"negative instances suffice in science"*. (He adds in a footnote that he omits Popper's "somewhat strange theory of corroboration".) These problems of demarcation are, of course, closely connected with the problem of induction; also cp. below, n. 85.

[45] In my [1970] I called patched-up developments which did not meet such criteria *ad hoc₃* stratagems. Planck's first correction of the Lummer-Pringsheim formula was *ad hoc* in *this*

sense. A particularly good example is Meehl's anomaly. (Cp. my [1970], p. 175, n. 3 and p. 176, n. 1.)

⁴⁶ Popper [L.Sc.D., 1934b], Sec. 85.

⁴⁷ Cp. my [1968a], pp. 383-86, my [1968b], pp. 162-67, and my [1970], pp. 116 ff. and pp. 155 ff.

⁴⁸ One important consequence is the difference between Popper's discussion of the "Duhem-Quine argument" and mine; cp. on the one hand Popper [L.Sc.D., 1934b], last paragraph of Sec. 18 and Sec. 19, n. 1; Popper [1957g], pp. 131-33; Popper [C.&R., 1963a], p. 112, n. 26, pp. 238-39 and p. 243; and on the other hand, my [1970], pp. 184-89.

⁴⁹ Popper, in one interesting passage, tries to define the difference between the amoeba's and Einstein's method; they both seem to pursue the method of conjectures and refutations ([C.&R., 1963a], p. 52). Popper thinks that Einstein has a "*more* critical and constructive attitude" than the amoeba (italics mine). I think that a better solution is that the amoeba has *no (articulated) research programmes.*

⁵⁰ Popper occasionally—and Feyerabend systematically—stressed the *catalytic* role of alternative theories in devising so-called "crucial experiments". But alternatives are not merely catalysts, which can be later removed in the rational reconstruction, but are *necessary* parts of the falsifying process. (Cp. my [1970], p. 121, n. 4.)

⁵¹ Cp. esp. my [1970], pp. 120-21.

⁵² Cp. esp. my [1968a], p. 385 and [1970], p. 121.

⁵³ Popper [C.&R., 1963a], p. 51.

⁵⁴ Cp. esp. my [1970], pp. 135-38.

⁵⁵ Cp. above, p. 246.

⁵⁶ There is a certain analogy between this pattern and the occasional appeal procedure of the theoretical scientist against the verdict of the experimental jury; cp. my [1970], pp. 127-31.

⁵⁷ This latter criterion is analogous to the exceptional "depth" of a theory which clashes with some basic statements available at the time and, at the end, emerges victorious. (Cf. Popper's [1957i].) Popper's example was the inconsistency between Kepler's laws and the Newtonian theory which set out to explain them.

⁵⁸ Van der Waerden thought that the Bohr-Kramers-Slater theory was bad: Popper's theory showed it to be good. Cp. van der Waerden [1967], p. 13 and Popper [C.&R., 1963a], pp. 242 ff.; for a critical discussion cp. my [1970], p. 168, n. 4 and p. 169, n. 1.

⁵⁹ The attitude of some modern logicians to the history of mathematics is a typical example; cp. my [1963-64], p. 3.

⁶⁰ Cp. my [1970], Sec. 3(c).

⁶¹ I need not say that no rationality theory can or should explain *all* history of science as rational: even the greatest scientists make wrong steps and fail in their judgment.

⁶² The methodology of research programmes may thus be applied to normative knowledge, including even ethics and aesthetics; this would then supersede the (naive falsificationist) "quasi-empirical" approach as outlined above, n. 33.

⁶³ For an interesting discussion cp. Naess [1964].

⁶⁴ Alternatively, one might claim that this quasi-empirical approach is already implicit in Popper's metamethod, and I only make it *explicit.* After all, Popper's starting point was to define "science" in such a way that it should include the refuted Newtonian theory and exclude unrefuted astrology, Marxism and Freudism. Indeed, he says in the Preface of his [L.Sc.D., 1959a] that "since we possess many detailed reports of the discussions pertaining to the problem whether a theory such as Newton's or Maxwell's or Einstein's should be accepted or rejected, we may look at these discussions as if through a microscope that allows us to study in detail, and objectively some of the more important problems of 'reasonable belief' ". Thus one might argue

that Popper's metamethod was in my sense "quasi-empiricist", even though he was not aware of it.

Kraft is very near to my quasi-empirical methodological approach. (Cp. Kraft [1925], esp. pp. 28-31.) Popper's description of Kraft's position as "naturalistic" (Popper [*L.Sc.D.*, 1934*b*], Sec. 10, n. 5) seems to be based on a misreading of some ambiguous passages. Kraft, in fact, advocates a metamethodology which *learns* primarily from historical case studies, but in a normative-critical way.

[65] The former seems to apply to modern particle physics; the latter to some of the main schools of modern sociology, psychology and social psychology.

[66] The situation may be changing now: cp. the previous footnote.

[67] Cp. Popper [*L.Sc.D.*, 1959*a*], p. 19.

[68] Cp. my [1968*c*].

[69] Cp. Watkins [1970], p. 26.

[70] Popper [*L.Sc.D.*, 1934*b*], Sec. 85.

[71] Some of my friends objected that this is not so; that the *aim* of science, according to Popper's [*L.Sc.D.*, 1934*b*], is clearly to discover ever deeper questions, and that Popper's methodology follows from this presupposition. I reject this objection: asking "ever deeper questions" is *synonymous* with the ban on "conventionalist stratagems"; that is, "asking deeper questions" is a *rule* of the game; if it is also its purpose, then the game has its purpose in itself.

[72] Popper [*L.Sc.D.*, 1934*b*], Sec. 84.

[73] The whole of *Logik der Forschung* is in an important sense a *pragmatic* treatise; it is about *acceptance* and *rejection* and not about *truth* and *falsehood*. (But it is not *pragmatist*: it does not identify acceptance with truth and rejection with falsehood.) Popper occasionally deviates from his pragmatic-methodological terminology, and he slips, no doubt unintentionally, into the language of "dogmatic falsificationism". (For this concept cp. my [1970], pp. 93 ff.) For instance, in his *Open Society* he describes the *"main point"* of his *Logik der Forschung* in these words: "We can never rationally establish the truth of scientific laws; all we can do is. . .to eliminate the *false* ones" (Vol. II, p. 363; my horrified italics).

[74] Popper [*L.Sc.D.*, 1934*b*], Sec. 85.

[75] Popper [*L.Sc.D.*, 1959*a*], p. 419.

[76] For the terms "dogmatic" and "methodological" falsificationism cp. my [1968*b*] and [1970].

[77] This is characteristic of the demarcation criterion of "methodological falsificationism". The demarcation criterion of "dogmatic falsificationism", on the other hand, is genuinely epistemological. (For the two criteria cp. my [1970], p. 93-116.)

[78] Cp. "Truth, Rationality and the Growth of Scientific Knowledge", forming Chap. 10 of his [*C.&R.*, 1963*a*].

[79] The expression *"growth of scientific knowledge"* appears characteristically as the subtitle of the *chef d'oeuvre* of his later philosophy. In his [*L.Sc.D.*, 1934*b*] he claimed that "that main problem of philosophy is the critical analysis of the appeal to the authority of experience" (Section 10). But in the new Preface to the 1959 English edition he says that "the central problem of epistemology has always been and still is the growth of knowledge". There is a marked shift from the negativist 1934 text to the optimistic 1958 Preface.

[80] For a detailed critical discussion and references, cp. my [1968*a*], pp. 379-90.

[81] This is why I called it "revolutionary conventionalism": cp. my [1970], p. 105.

[82] Popper [*O.S.*, 1962*c*], pp. 380-81.

[83] *Ibid.*, p. 383.

[84] Popper [*O.S.*, 1962*c*], p. 382.

[85] Agassi accused Popper of a "verificationist" turn. (Cp. Agassi [1959]; for Popper's reply see

Popper [C.&R., 1963a], p. 248, n. 31.) Later Agassi tried to attribute to Popper the strange view that corroboration may guide us in our "choice", but we can "learn" only from refutations (Agassi [1969]). Feyerabend too seems to think that corroboration plays no real role in science or learning from experience (cp. Feyerabend [1969]). Also, cp. above, n. 44.

86 For example, J. O. Wisdom and Ayer argued that only an inductive principle can prevent upholding refuted theories in the hope that the refutations will come to an end; only an inductive principle can explain why we hold that refuted theories stay refuted. I have shown that they were wrong. Cp. my [1968a], p. 392.

87 This is the message of Sec. 79 of Popper's [L.Sc.D., 1934b].

88 The analogy must be taken with a pinch of salt. Columbus's inference from the sighting of birds to the nearness of land was easily refutable; my "inductive principle" is not.

89 For references cp. below, n. 108.

90 Cp. my [1968a], pp. 375-90.

91 Popper [1968c], p. 91.

92 Cp. above, text to nn. 82, 83 and 84.

93 Popper [1968c], p. 93.

94 Watkins [1968], pp. 277-78.

95 Ibid.

96 Ibid., p. 279.

97 Watkins [1968], p. 280.

98 This inconsistency also occurs in the celebrated Chapter 10 of Popper's [C.&R., 1963a]. I quote Watkins only because his exposition is so clear.

99 Popper [C.&R., 1963a], p. 229.

100 Cp. my [1968a], pp. 403 ff.

101 This method may be associated—as in Descartes's case—with an intuitive-psychologistic theory of content-increasing ("inductive") logic. But one may try to dispense with such logic and search for some universal inductive principles which would turn inductive logic into a deductive system. For this programme of deductive reconstruction of induction cp. Max Black [1967], pp. 174 ff.

102 Cp. his [C.&R., 1963a], pp. 42-46. However, Popper fails to emphasise that there can be no such thing as a purely empirical theory of learning. Before studying the psychology of learning, we must agree on a normative demarcation between learning and being indoctrinated. Cp. my [1970], p. 123, text to n. 2.

103 Cp. my [1971], esp. Sec. 2(b).

104 Carnap confused the philosophical issue by his conviction that all a priori true propositions are bound to be analytic; therefore the inductive principle is analytic. This confusion was exposed by Nagel and Popper. (For references cp. my [1968a], p. 361, n. 2.)

105 It is important to realise that the introduction of an inductive principle gives "induction" a deductive structure. (Cp. above, n. 81.) Victor Kraft, for instance, proposed, in 1925, such a "deductivist" approach. To claim that this is the view that Popper adopted later (as Feyerabend puts it in his [1963]) is incorrect. Victor Kraft, in his undeservedly neglected [1925], may have anticipated Popper on many points, but not in his radical anti-inductivism. Kraft, in this work, contrary to Feyerabend's false account, proposed that an inductive assumption may provide a "logically justified" expectation for the future (p. 253), and pointed out that therefore his position differed significantly from Hume's (pp. 254-55). (Incidentally, according to Feyerabend, "Popper himself refers to Kraft as one of his predecessors". This is untrue: there are two references to Victor Kraft in the Logik der Forschung, both critical.) Today Kraft still advocates an inductive principle, which, once introduced, would make science completely "deductive" (Kraft [1966]).

[106] Popper was so much preoccupied with his fight against a priori *probabilistic* measures of confirmation that he, at least for a brief moment, seems to have faltered in his stand against a priori *nonprobabilistic* measures; cp. my [1968a], pp. 411 ff.

[107] Hintikka, L. J. Cohen and, perhaps, Levi, could be mentioned here.

[108] Popper, and following him, Agassi and Watkins have interpreted "degree of corroboration" as a strictly tautologous appraisal. (For references, cp. my [1968a], pp. 401-5, esp. p. 401, n. 3, and p. 403, n. 3.) This interpretation bears out my analysis of Popper's "third anti-inductivist campaign".

[109] Popper [*L.Sc.D.*, 1934b], Sec. 85.

[110] Popper [*L.Sc.D.*, 1934b], Sec. 1.

[111] Cp. my [1968a], p. 399.

[112] For the "dialectical unity" of dogmatism and scepticism as two poles of justificationism, cp. Popper [*C.&R.*, 1963a], p. 228; and also my [1962] and [1966].

[113] Victor Kraft seems to have come very near to such a position. He abhorred Humean scepticism which "denies rationality to empirical science and characterises it as being as irrational a phenomenon as the belief in paradise or in demons". ([1925], p. 208.) He abhorred the idea that "general knowledge about reality had no more validity than conjectural" (p. 255). On the other hand, he rejected Kantian apriorism and pointed out that Kant's very question ("how is [infallible] science possible") assumed the existence of an infallible science. In fact, he points out, science is fallible and thus the question disappears. "Then one can go on to reconstruct science as free, basisless—as completely arbitrary" (p. 31).

This is, of course, the step from Kant to LeRoy (cp. my [1970], pp. 104 ff.). But then Kraft, disappointingly, introduces "simplicity" as a *validating* criterion ([1925], pp. 257-58); and he even asserts the *absolute validity* of basic statements (p. 253).

[114] Feigl [1964], p. 47.

[115] In my [1968a] I contrasted my fallible "metaphysical principle" to "inductive principles", which then I took to be *by definition* infallible (p. 398). I chose this terminology in order not to offend Popper on a purely semantical point and to uphold the claim that he destroyed *all* possible kinds of inductive principle. Now I have changed my terminology, inasmuch as Popper himself has started to talk about a "positive solution" of the problem of induction (cp. below, n. 121); and, indeed, there is nothing wrong with preserving old time-honoured terms (like "inductive principle") even after a problem has been as radically shifted as the problem of induction was by Popper.

[116] Popper [1968c], p. 139.

[117] "Inductive principles" which use methodological appraisals (like Popper's corroboration or my problem shift appraisals as tentative measures of verisimilitude) are, I admit, sadly irrefutable. Only God can see the discrepancy between the verisimilitude and the scientific appraisal of our best theories. This is the crucial support for Popper's scepticism.

(The actual principle, as posited in the discussion of "acceptance₃" in my [1968a], is rather complicated. Now I would prefer to state it in the form that—roughly speaking—the methodology of scientific research programmes is better suited for approximating the truth in our actual universe than any other methodology; cp. my [1971].)

[118] As Feigl put it: "The problem is precisely to show what entitles us to use honorific descriptions". (Feigl [1964], p. 49.)

[119] Russell [1919], p. 71.

[120] There is, of course, an alternative: to elaborate a rational theory of practical action which is *independent* of scientific rationality. There are traces of this approach in Popper and it was explicitly advocated by Watkins. This is how Popper and Watkins, leading protagonists of the Scientific Weltanschauung landed in a position for which science as a guide of life is an anomaly. (Cp. my [1968a], pp. 402 ff.)

[121] I think that Feyerabend's transformation from the Popperian Feyerabend₁ into the anarchist darling of the New Left (Feyerabend₂) was due to his change to a radically sceptical interpretation of Popper's own philosophy of science. Also, my discussion explains Popkin's puzzlement as to whether or not Popper is a sceptic. (Cp. Popkin [1967], p. 458.)

[122] Indeed, I was pleased to learn from Popper that, in response to my [1968a], he has now inserted a short *Addendum* on p. 226 of his [*L.Sc.D.*, 1969e]. In this he says: "The logico-methodological problem of induction is not unsolvable, but has been (negatively) solved in my book: (a) *Negative solution*. We cannot justify our theories, either as true or as probable. This solution and the following solution are compatible: (b) *Positive solution*. We can *justify* the choice of certain theories in the light of their corroboration, that is, in the light of the present state of rational discussion of the rival theories from the point of view of their verisimilitude". *This is the first time Popper mentions a "positive" solution of the problem of induction.* This "positive solution" is, then, simply that we base our guess concerning which theory has higher verisimilitude on the comparison of their degrees of corroboration. (Of course, Popper here would need my *corrected* version of degree of corroboration which assigns positive degrees of corroboration or of "acceptability₂" even to refuted theories: cp. my [1968a], pp. 384-85.) Moreover, he says that this also solves the *"practical problem of induction"*: we choose the hypothesis which is estimated to have higher verisimilitude. He calls this a risky but rational choice.

But even Popper's *Addendum* does not fully clarify the queries I raised. On a careful reading of the text it transpires that Popper still has not realised that the "positive solution" which he now proposes implies the existence of a synthetic inductive principle. He still has not withdrawn his claim that his degree of corroboration is *analytic*. But, if so, then he needs an additional *synthetic* principle which will turn this analytic measure function into a synthetic function estimating verisimilitude. There remains an unresolved inconsistency between a genuine (that is, metaphysical) "positive solution" of the problem of induction and the "third prong" of his anti-inductivist campaign.

[123] Popper [1971], p. 181; cp. Lakatos [1968a], p. 375.

[124] Cp. e.g. Popper [1959a], p. 270 and Watkins [1964], p. 98.

[125] Lakatos [1968a], Sec. 3, 4 (pp. 405-408).

[126] Popper [1971], p. 184, n. 23.

[127] He repeats his well-worn tautology that 'in so far as we *have* to choose, it will be "rational" to choose the best tested theory. This will be "rational" in the most obvious sense of the word known to me: the best tested theory is the one which, in the light of our *critical discussion* appears to be the best so far, and I do not know of anything more "rational" than a well-conducted critical discussion' (p. 188). This insistence that the game of science is in no need of an extra-methodological rationale, leads him to discourage epistemologists: 'No theory of knowledge should attempt to explain why we are successful in our attempts to explain things' (p. 189). What then should a theory of knowledge attempt to explain?

[128] Cp. especially the last two paragraphs of Sec. 12 of his [1971], p. 195.

REFERENCES

Agassi, Joseph [1964]. "Scientific Problems and Their Roots in Metaphysics." *The Critical Approach to Science and Philosophy*. Edited by M. Bunge. New York: The Free Press, 1964, pp. 189-211.

_____ [1969]. "Popper on Learning from Experience." *Studies in the Philosophy of Science, American Philosophical Quarterly Monograph Series*. Edited by N. Rescher, 1969, pp. 162-71.

Black, Max [1967]. "Induction." *The Encyclopedia of Philosophy*. Edited by P. Edwards. Vol. 4. New York: Macmillan, 1967, p. 169.

Feigl, Herbert [1964]. "What Hume Might Have Said to Kant." *The Critical Approach to Science and Philosophy*. Edited by M. Bunge. New York: The Free Press, 1964, pp. 45-51.

Feyerabend, Paul [1963]. "Review of Kraft's *Erkenntnislehre.*" *British Journal for the Philosophy of Science*, **13**, pp. 319-23.

—————— [1969]. "A Note on Two 'Problems' of Induction." *British Journal for the Philosophy of Science*, **19**, pp. 251-53.

Kraft, Victor [1925]. *Die Grundformen der wissenschaftlichen Methoden.* Vienna and Leipzig: Hölder-Pichler-Tempsky A.-G., 1925.

—————— [1966]. "The Problem of Induction." *Mind, Matter and Method*. Edited by P. Feyerabend and G. Maxwell. Minneapolis: University of Minnesota Press, 1966, pp. 306-17.

Lakatos, Imre [1962]. "Infinite Regress and the Foundations of Mathematics." *Aristotelian Society Supplementary Volume*, **36** (1962), 155-84.

—————— [1963-1964]. "Proofs and Refutations." *British Journal for the Philosophy of Science*, **14**, pp. 1-25, 120-39, 221-43, 296-342.

—————— [1966]. "Popkin on Skepticism." *Physics, Logic and History.* Edited by W. Yourgrau and A. D. Breck. New York: Plenum Publishing, 1969, pp. 220-23.

—————— [1967]. "A Renaissance of Empiricism in the Recent Philosophy of Mathematics." *Problems in the Philosophy of Mathematics*. Edited by I. Lakatos. Amsterdam: North-Holland Publishing Company, 1967, pp. 199-202.

—————— [1968a]. "Changes in the Problem of Inductive Logic." *The Problem of Inductive Logic*. Edited by I. Lakatos. Amsterdam: North-Holland Publishing Co., 1968, pp. 315-417.

—————— [1968b]. "Criticism and the Methodology of Scientific Research Programmes." *Proceedings of the Aristotelian Society*, **69** (1968-69), 149-86.

—————— [1968c]. "A Letter to the Director of the London School of Economics." *Fight for Education, A Black Paper*. Edited by C. B. Cox and A. E. Dyson. London: The Critical Quarterly Society, 1968.

—————— [1970]. "Falsification and the Methodology of Scientific Research Programmes." *Criticism and the Growth of Knowledge.* Edited by I. Lakatos and A. E. Musgrave. London: Cambridge University Press, 1970, pp. 91-195.

—————— [1971]. "History of Science and its Rational Reconstructions." *Boston Studies in the Philosophy of Science*. Edited by R. C. Buck and R. S. Cohen. Vol. 8. New York: Humanities Press, 1970.

Musgrave, Alan [1968]. "On a Demarcation Dispute." *Problems in the Philosophy of Science.* Edited by I. Lakatos and A. E. Musgrave. Amsterdam: North-Holland Publishing Co., 1968, pp. 78-85.

Naess, Arne [1964]. "Reflections About Total Views." *Philosophy and Phenomenological Research,* **25** (1963-64), 16-29.

Popkin, Richard H. [1967]. "Skepticism." *The Encyclopedia of Philosophy.* Edited by P. Edwards. Vol. 7. New York: Macmillan Co., 1967, pp. 449-60.

Popper, K. R. [1934*b*]. *Logik der Forschung.* Vienna: Julius Springer, 1935. (expanded English edition: Popper [1959*a*]).

_____ [1945*c*]. *The Open Society and Its Enemies,* Vol. II. London: George Routledge & Sons, 1945.

_____ [1957*g*]. *The Poverty of Historicism.* London: Routledge & Kegan Paul, 1957; Boston: The Beacon Press, 1957.

_____ [1957*i*]. "The Aim of Science." *Ratio,* **1** (1957), 24-35.

_____ [1959*a*]. *The Logic of Scientific Discovery.* London: Hutchinson, 1959; New York: Basic Books, 1959.

_____ [1962*c*]. "Facts, Standards and Truth: Further Criticism of Relativism." *Addendum* to *The Open Society and Its Enemies.* 4th ed. London: Routledge & Kegan Paul, 1962. [1945*c*]

_____ [1963*a*]. *Conjectures and Refutations: The Growth of Scientific Knowledge.* London: Routledge & Kegan Paul, 1963; New York: Basic Books, 1963.

_____ [1968*c*]. "Remarks on the Problems of Demarcation and of Rationality." *Problems in the Philosophy of Science.* Edited by I. Lakatos and A. E. Musgrave. Amsterdam: North-Holland Publishing Co., 1968, pp. 88-102.

_____ [1969*e*]. *Logik der Forschung.* 3d ed.

_____ [1971]. "Conjectural Knowledge: My Solution of the Problem of Induction." *Revue Internationale de Philosophie,* **95-96** (1971), 167-97.

Russell, Bertrand [1919]. *Introduction to Mathematical Philosophy.* London: George Allen & Unwin; New York: Macmillan Co., 1919.

Van der Waerden, B. L. [1967]. *Sources of Quantum Mechanics.* Magnolia, Mass.: Peter Smith, 1967.

Watkins, J. W. [1963]. "Negative Utilitarianism." *Aristotelian Society Supplementary Volume,* **37**, pp. 95-114.

_____ [1964]. "Confirmation, the Paradoxes and Positivism." *The Critical Approach to Science and Philosophy.* Edited by M. Bunge. New York: The Free Press, 1964, pp. 92-115.

_____ [1967]. "Decision and Belief." *Decision Making.* Edited by R. Hughes. London: British Broadcasting Corporation, 1967.

_____ [1968]. "Hume, Carnap and Popper." *The Problem of Inductive Logic.* Edited by I. Lakatos. Amsterdam: North-Holland Publishing Co., 1968, pp. 271-82.

_____ [1970]. "Against Normal Science." *Criticism and the Growth of Knowledge.* Edited by I. Lakatos and A. E. Musgrave. London: Cambridge University Press, 1970, pp. 25-37.

_____ [1971]. "CCR: A Refutation." *Philosophy,* **47,** pp. 56-61.

6

Peter Medawar

HYPOTHESIS AND IMAGINATION*

'There is a mask of theory over the whole face of nature'

I

If an educated layman were asked to set down his understanding of what goes on in the head when scientific discoveries are made and of what it is about a scientist that qualifies him to make them, his account of the matter might go something like this: a scientist is a man who has cultivated (if indeed he was not born with) the restless, analytical, problem-seeking, problem-solving temperament that marks his possession of a Scientific Mind. Science is an immensely prosperous and successful enterprise—as religion is not, nor economics (for example), nor philosophy itself—because it is the outcome of applying a certain sure and powerful method of discovery and proof to the investigation of natural phenomena: *The Scientific Method*. The scientific method is not deductive in character: it is a well-known fallacy to regard it as such: but it is rigorous neverthelesss, and logically conclusive. Scientific laws are *in*ductive in origin. An episode of scientific discovery begins with the plain and unembroidered evidence of the senses—with innocent, unprejudiced observation, the exercise of which is one of the scientist's most precious and distinctive faculties—and slowly builds upon it a great mansion of natural law. Imagination kept within bounds may ornament a scientist's thought and intuition may bring it faster to its conclusions, but in a strictly formal sense neither is indispensable. Yet Newton was too severe upon hypotheses, for though there is indeed something *mere* about hypotheses, the best of them may look forward to a dignified middle age as Theories.[1]

A critic anxious to find fault might now raise a number of objections, among them these: (1) there is no such thing as a Scientific Mind; (2) there is no such thing as The Scientific Method; (3) the idea of naive or innocent observation is philosophers' make-believe; (4) 'induction' in the wider sense

* First published in *The Art of the Soluble* (London: Methuem & Co.; New York: Barnes & Noble, 1971).

that Mill gave it is a myth; and (5) the formulation of a natural 'law' always begins as an imaginative exploit, and without imagination scientific thought is barren. Finally (he might add) it is an unhappy usage that treats a hypothesis as an adolescent theory.

1. There is no such thing as a Scientific Mind. Scientists are people of very dissimilar temperaments doing different things in very different ways. Among scientists are collectors, classifiers and compulsive tidiers-up; many are detectives by temperament and many are explorers; some are artists and others artisans. There are poet-scientists and philosopher-scientists and even a few mystics. What sort of mind or temperament can all these people be supposed to have in common? *Obligative* scientists must be very rare, and most people who are in fact scientists could easily have been something else instead.

2. There is no such thing as The Scientific Method—as *the* scientific method, that is the point: there is no one rounded art or system of rules which stands to its subject matter as logical syntax stands towards any particular instance of reasoning by deduction. 'An art of discovery is not possible', wrote a former Master of Trinity; 'we can give no rules for the pursuit of truth which shall be universally and peremptorily applicable'. To many philosophers of science such an opinion must have seemed treasonable, and we can understand their unwillingness to accept a judgement that seems to put them out of business. The face-saving formula is that although there is indeed a Scientific Method, scientists observe its rules unconsciously and do not understand it in the sense of being able to put it clearly into words.

3. The idea of naive or innocent observation is philosophers' make-believe. To good old British empiricists it has always seemed self-evident that the mind, uncorrupted by past experience, can passively accept the imprint of sensory information from the outside world and work it into complex notions; that the candid acceptance of sense-data is the elementary or generative act in the advancement of learning and the foundation of everything we are truly sure of.[2] Alas, unprejudiced observation is mythical too. In all sensation we pick and choose, interpret, seek and impose order, and devise and test hypotheses about what we witness. Sense-data are taken, not merely given: we *learn* to perceive.[3] 'Why can't you draw what you see?' is the immemorial cry of the teacher to the student looking down the microscope for the first time at some quite unfamiliar preparation he is called upon to draw. The teacher has forgotten, and the student himself will soon forget, that what he sees conveys no information until he knows beforehand the kind of thing he is expected to see. I cite more evidence on this point below.

4. Induction is a myth. In donnish conversation we are not taken aback when someone says he has 'deduced' something or has carried out a deduction; but if he were to say he had *in*duced something or other we should think him facetious if not a pompous idiot. So it is with 'Laws': Scientists do not profess to be trying to discover laws and use the word itself only in conventional contexts (Hooke's Law, Boyle's Law). (The actual usages of scientific speech are, as I shall explain below, extremely revealing.) It is indeed a myth to suppose that scientists actually carry out inductions or that a logical autopsy upon a completed episode of scientific research reveals in it anything that could be called an inductive structure of thought.

'Induction' in the wider sense that distinguishes it from perfect or merely iterative induction (see below) is a word lacking the qualities that would justify its retention in a professional vocabulary. It is seldom, if ever, used in any sentence of which it is not itself the subject, and it has no agreed meaning. *Finding* a meaning for induction has been a philosophic pastime for more than a hundred years. Whewell used the word, but with some feeling in later years that he might have dropped it. 'There is really no such thing as a distinct process of induction', said Stanley Jevons; 'all inductive reasoning is but the inverse application of deductive reasoning'—and this was what Whewell meant when he said that induction and deduction went upstairs and downstairs on the same staircase. For Samuel Neil, however, 'induction' was confined to the act of testing a scientific conjecture or presupposition, and this was also C. S. Peirce's usage ('The operation of testing a hypothesis by experiment . . . I call induction'.)[4]. Peirce accordingly uses the words *retroduction* or *abduction* to mean what Jevons called *in*duction. Nowadays the tendency is to use 'experimentation' to stand for the acts used in testing a hypothesis, leaving 'induction' as a vague word to signify all the various ways of travelling upstream of the flow of deductive inference. (Popper, of course, is for abandoning 'induction' altogether.)

The word *experiment* has also changed its meaning. When amateurs of the history of science attribute to Bacon the advocacy of the experimental method, they are often acting under the impression that Bacon used the word as we do. But a Baconian 'experiment' had the connotation that still persists in the French *expérience* today: a Baconian experiment is a contrived experience or contrived happening as opposed to a natural experience or happening, for Bacon rightly supposed that common knowledge was not enough and that there was no relying upon luck of observation—upon 'the casual felicity of particular events'. The Philosophers of Mind took the same view: experiments were 'designed observations' intended 'to place nature in situations in which she never presents herself spontaneously to view, and to extort from her secrets over which she draws a veil to the eyes of others'.[5] Rubbing two sticks together to see what happens is an experiment in Bacon's sense; rubbing two sticks together to see if enough heat can be generated by friction to ignite them is an experiment in the modern sense. An experiment of the first kind leaves one with no answer to the question (a 'good' question: see below), 'Why on earth are you rubbing those two sticks together?'

I shall refer later to the changing connotation of 'hypothesis', a word that has grown in stature as 'induction' has declined.

The concept of induction was entrenched into scientific methodology through the formidable advocacy of John Stuart Mill. Mill, said John Venn in 1907,[6] had 'dominated the thought and study of intelligent students to an extent which many will find it hard to realize at the present day'; yet he could still take a general familiarity with Mill's views for granted, in spite of having recorded as far back as 1889 'a broadening current of dissatisfaction' on the part of physicists which had 'mostly taken the form of an ill-concealed or openly avowed contempt of the logical treatment of Induction'. It is, however, the indifference rather than the hostility of critically-minded scientists that has allowed the myth of induction to persist—combined, I believe, with the great earnestness and sincerity of Mill himself; for Mill believed, as so many good people believe today, that if only we could formulate and master The Scientific Method many of the vexed problems of modern society would vanish before its use.

Mill's was, of course, Induction in the strong, imperfect or open-ended sense. 'Induction', said Mill ('that great mental operation')

> is a process of inference; it proceeds from the known to the unknown; and any operation involving no inference, any process in which what seems the conclusion is no wider than the premises from which it is drawn, does not fall within the meaning of the term.

That would be very well if he had not also said that induction was an exact and logically rigorous process, capable of doing for empirical reasoning what logical syntax does for the process of deduction.

> The business of inductive logic is to provide rules and models (such as the syllogism and its rules are for ratiocination) to which, if inductive arguments conform, those arguments are conclusive, and not otherwise.[7]

There seems no point in mulling over the logical errors of Mill's *System*, for they are now common knowledge—for example, his failure to distinguish between the methodologies of discovery and of proof (though Whewell had insisted on the distinction), and the circularity of his attempt to justify that 'ultimate syllogism' which had 'for its major premise the principle or axiom of the uniformity of the course of nature'. But one may yet be surprised by how little he understood the methodological functions of hypotheses, and by the hopeless ambition embodied in his belief that it was possible merely by taking thought to arrive with certainty at the truth of general statements containing more information than the sum of their known instances.

The current of informed opinion was already flowing in the other direction. The probationary characer of scientific law is implicit in all of Whewell, and long before him George Campbell, in his influential and widely read *Philosophy of Rhetoric* (1776), had said of inductive generalization that there 'may be in every step, and commonly is, less certainty than in the preceding; *but in no instance whatever can there be more*' (italics mine). 'No hypothesis', said Dugald Stewart, 'can completely exclude the possibility of exceptions or limitations hitherto undiscovered'. By the latter half of the nineteenth century the point had become commonplace. 'No inductive conclusions are more than probable', said Jevons; 'we never escape the risk of error altogether'. Venn took pains to emphasize his belief 'that no ultimate objective certainty, such as Mill for instance seemed to attribute to the results of induction, is attainable by any exercise of the human reason'. 'The conclusions of science make no pretence to being more than probable', wrote C. S. Peirce.

The logical status of deduction and syllogistic reasoning had not been seriously in question since the days of Bacon. Syllogistic reasoning (an 'unnatural art', Campbell had called it, and others 'futile' or 'puerile') was indeed a logically conclusive process, but that was because it merely 'expands and unfolds', merely brings to light and makes explicit the information lying more or less deeply hidden in the premises out of which it flows. Deduction makes known to us only what the infirmity of our powers of reasoning has so far left concealed. The case had been well put by Archbishop Whateley,[8] and Mill accepted it; and so the peculiar and distinctive role of deduction in scientific reasoning came to be overlooked. Convinced nevertheless that Science had come upon irrefragable general truths by some process other than deduction, Mill had no alternative but to put his faith in induction—to believe in the existence of a valid inductive process even if his own account of it should prove faulty or incomplete.

What about Baconian induction—the painstaking assembly and classification of natural and elicited (experimental) facts of which Jevons said that it reduced the methodology of science to a kind of bookkeeping? By the sixth edition of the *Origin* in 1876, Darwin had convinced himself that he had been a good Baconian, but his correspondence tells a different story. Darwin's status as the culture-hero of induction—the great but deeply humble scientist listening attentively to Nature's lessons from her own lips—has now to be reconciled with evidence that he had the germ of the idea of natural selection before ever he had read Malthus.[9]

It is Karl Pearson whose scientific practice and theoretical professions earn him the right to be called a true Baconian. 'The classification of facts', he wrote in *The Grammar of Science*, and

. . . the recognition of their sequence and relative significance is the function of science . . . let us be quite sure that whenever we come across a conclusion in a scientific work which does not flow from the classification of facts, or which is not directly stated by the author to be an assumption, then we are dealing with bad science.[10]

Poor Pearson! His punishment was to have practised what he preached, and his general theory of heredity, of genuinely inductive origin, was in principle quite erroneous.

I have given here the conventional view of Bacon's methodology, and shall return later to the claim made on his behalf by Coleridge and others that he was fully aware of the methodological value of hypotheses.

5. The formulation of a natural law begins as an imaginative exploit and imagination is a faculty essential to the scientist's task. Most words of the philosopher's vocabulary, including 'philosopher' itself, have changed their usages over the past few hundred years.[11] 'Hypothesis' is no exception. In a modern professional vocabulary a hypothesis is an imaginative preconception of *what might be true* in the form of a declaration with verifiable deductive consequences. It no longer tows 'gratuitous', 'mere' or 'wild' behind it, and the pejorative usage ('evolution is a mere hypothesis', 'it is only a hypothesis that smoking causes lung cancer') is one of the outward signs of little learning. But in the days of Travellers' Tales and Marvels, when (as John Gregory contemptuously remarked)[12] philosophers were more interested in animals with two heads than in animals with one, 'hypothesis' carried very strongly the connotation of the wantonly fanciful and above all (we read it often) the gratuitous; nor was there any thought that a hypothesis need do more than explain the phenomena it was expressly formulated to explain. The element of *responsibility* that goes with the formulation of a hypothesis today was altogether lacking. Thomas Burnet's *Sacred Theory of the Earth* (1684-90) is a case in point—a romantic and absurd cosmology using the word 'hypothesis' in just the sense that Newton repudiated. 'Men of short thoughts and little meditation', Burnet says in self-defence, 'call such theories as these, Philosophick Romances'. But, he says

> . . . there is no surer mark of a good Hypothesis, than when it doth not only hit luckily in one or two particulars but answers all that it is to be applied to, and is adequate to Nature in her whole extent.
> But how fully or easily soever these things may answer Nature, you will say, it may be, that all this is but an Hypothesis; that is, a kind of fiction or supposition that things were so and so at first, and by the coherence and agreement of the Effects with such a supposition, you would argue and prove that this is so. This I confess is true, this is the method, and if we would know anything in Nature further than our senses go, we can know it no otherwise than by an Hypothesis . . . and if that Hypothesis be easie and intelligible, and answers all the phaenomena . . . you have done as much as a Philosopher or as Humane reason can do.

Burnet's reasoning thus ends at the very point at which scientific reasoning begins. He did not seem to realize that his hypothesis about what the Earth was like before the flood and what it would be like after the Fire was but one among a virtual infinitude of hypotheses, and that he was under a moral obligation to find out if his were preferable to any other.

Burnet's preposterous speculations were expounded in prose that earned him immortality; because they were not, many philosophic romances that must have been known to Newton are now forgotten. Thomas Reid shall be allowed to sum the prevailing situation up.[13] 'It is genius', he says, 'and not the want of it, that adulterates philosophy, and fills it with error and false theory. A creative imagination disdains the mean offices of digging for a foundation', leaving these servile employments to scientific drudges. 'The world has been so long befooled by hypotheses in all parts of philosophy', that we must learn 'to treat them with just contempt, as the reveries of vain and fanciful men'. Newton *could* have invented a hypothesis to account for gravitation, but 'his philosophy was of another complexion', for Newton had been 'taught by Lord Bacon to despise hypotheses as fictions of human fancy'.

Because Newton is cast as the hero of every scientific methodology of the past 200 years, philosophers who attached great importance to hypotheses felt it their duty to explain away Newton's famous and profoundly influential disavowal. Stanley Jevons was so sure that Newton had practised what is now often called the 'hypothetico-deductive' method that he was inclined to think *hypotheses non fingo* ironical. But for 200 years after Newton no one could advocate the use of hypotheses without an uneasy backward glance. Dugald Stewart said that an 'indiscriminate zeal against hypotheses' had been 'much encouraged by the strong and decided terms in which, on various occasions, they are reprobated by Newton'. 'Newton appears to have had a horrour of the term *hypothesis*', said William Whewell. Sir John Herschel spoke up in favour of hypotheses.[14] Samuel Neil in 1851 deplored the 'widely prevalent prejudice in the present age against hypotheses', and Thomas Henry Huxley had felt obliged to say, 'Do not allow yourselves to be misled by the common notion that a hypothesis is untrustworthy merely because it is a hypothesis'. Even George Henry Lewes found himself unable to propound his fairly sensible views on hypotheses without much prevarication and pursing of the lips.[15]

Where does Mill stand? Modern philosophers who are for various reasons 'pro-Mill' can of course find him a devotee of hypotheses. Hypotheses, Mill will be found to say, provide 'temporary aid', even 'large temporary assistance' ('temporary' because hypotheses are the larval forms of theories); hypotheses are valuable because they suggest observations and experiments, and in this respect they are indeed indispensable. However, all this had been said before, repeatedly: some instances I shall cite later. In his less conventional utterances on hypotheses Mill betrayed that he had no deep understanding of what is now thought to be their distinctive methodological function. He feared that people who used hypotheses did so under the impression that a hypothesis must be true if the inferences drawn from it were in accordance with the facts. Later therefore he says (*System* III. 14. 6):

> It seems to be thought that an hypothesis . . . is entitled to a more favourable reception, if besides accounting for all the facts previously known, it has led to the anticipation and prediction of others which experience afterwards verified.

This, he says, is 'well calculated to impress the uninformed', but will not impress thinkers 'of any degree of sobriety'.

Mill feared the imaginative element in hypotheses: 'a hypothesis being a mere supposition, there are no other limits to hypotheses than those of the human imagination'. These are Reid's fears, preying on Mill at a time when good reasons for feeling fearful had largely disappeared. Today we think the imaginative element in science one of its chief glories. Even Karl Pearson recognized it as a motive force in *great* discoveries, but of course 'imagination must not replace reason in the deduction of relation and law from classified facts'. (The belief that great discoveries and little everyday discoveries have quite different methodological origins betrays the amateur. Whewell, the professional, insisted that the bold use of the imagination was the rule in scientific discovery, not the exception: see below.) All the same, the idea that hypotheses arose by mere conjecture, by guesswork, was thought undignified. Whewell had called good hypotheses 'happy guesses', though elsewhere, as if the occasion called for something more formal, he spoke of 'felicitous strokes of inventive talent'. But philosophers like Venn did not take to it: 'It is . . . scarcely an exaggeration of Whewell's account of the inductive process to say of it, as in fact has been said, that it simply resolves itself into making guesses'.

It is the word that is at fault, not the conception. To say that Einstein formulated a theory of relativity by guesswork is on all fours with saying that Wordsworth wrote rhymes and Mozart tuneful music. It is cheeky where something grave is called for.

II

I now turn to consider the history during the eighteenth and nineteenth centuries of some of the central ideas of the hypothetico-deductive scheme of scientific reasoning, confining myself, as hitherto, almost wholly to English and Scottish philosophers and the tradition of thought they embody. Among these ideas are:

(1) the uncertainty of all 'inductive' reasoning and the probationary status of hypotheses;

(2) the role of the hypothesis in starting inquiry and giving it direction, so confining the domain of observation to something smaller than the whole universe of observables;

(3) the asymmetry of proof and disproof: only disproof is logically conclusive;

(4) the obligation to put a hypothesis to the test.

1. I have already mentioned a number of earlier opinions on the inconclusiveness of scientific reasoning (above, pp. xx 136-7).

2. It is our imaginative preconception of what might be true that gives us an incentive to seek the truth and a clue to where we might find it. 'In every useful experiment', said John Gregory, writing in 1772, 'there must be some point in view, some anticipation of a principle to be established or rejected'. Such anticipations, he went on to say, are *hypotheses:* people were suspicious of hypotheses because they did not fully understand their purpose, but without them 'there could not be useful observation, nor experiment, nor arrangement, because there would be no motive or principle in the mind to form them'. Dugald Stewart quoted passages expressing the same opinion in the writings of Boscovich, Robert Hooke, and Stephen Hales[16]—scientists all three. But on this point Coleridge sweeps everyone else aside.[17] In every advance of science, he assures us, 'a previous act and conception of the mind . . . and *initiative* is indispensably necessary', for when it comes to founding a theory on generalization,

> . . . what shall determine the mind to one point rather than another; within what limits, and from what number of individuals shall the generalization be made? *The theory must still require a prior theory for its own legitimate construction.* [Italics mine]

Coleridge (like Stewart and later Neil) managed to convince himself of the great Francis Bacon's full awareness of the need for an 'intellectual or mental *initiative*' as the 'motive and guide of every philosophical experiment . . .

> . . . namely, some well-grounded purpose, some distinct impression of the probable results, some self-consistent anticipation . . . which he affirms to be the prior *half* of the knowledge sought, *dimidium scientiae.*

The passage all three quote as evidence for this interpretation[18] is, in my reading of it, too slight to carry so great a weight of meaning.

3. Many philosophers in the older and the newer senses have spoken of the value of false hypotheses, and Stewart particularly commends the opinions of Boscovich ('the slightest of whose logical hints are entitled to particular attention'). Boscovich had said that by means of hypotheses

... we are enabled to supply the defects of our *data*, and to conjecture or divine the path to truth; always ready to abandon our hypothesis, when found to involve consequences inconsistent with fact. And, indeed, in most cases, I conceive this to be the method best adapted to physics; a science in which ... legitimate theories are generally the slow result of disappointed essays, and of errors which have led the way to their own detection.[19]

This is all right as far as it goes, but what one will not find so easily is a premonition of one of the strongest ideas in Popper's methodology, that the only act which the scientist can perform with complete logical certainty is the repudiation of what is false. It is *falsification* that has the logical stature attributed by the logical positivists to verification: 'Every experiment may be said to exist only in order to give the facts a chance of disproving the null hypothesis'.[20] The asymmetry of proof, considered as a point of logic, is of course very elementary, and it is merely slovenly or simpleminded to suppose that hypotheses are proved true if they lead to true conclusions. No logician of science has ever done so. Whewell certainly realized that refutation was methodologically a strong procedure, stronger than confirmation, an opinion that comes out more clearly in his aphorisms than in the body of the text:

> (ix) The truth of tentative hypotheses must be tested by their application to facts. The discoverer must be ready, carefully to try his hypotheses in this manner ... and to reject them if they will not bear the test.
> (x) The process of scientific discovery is cautious and rigorous, not by abstaining from hypotheses, but by rigorously comparing hypotheses with facts, and by resolutely rejecting all which the comparison does not confirm.

These opinions shocked Mill. Dr. Whewell's system, he complained, did not recognize 'any necessity for proof':

> If, after assuming an hypothesis and carefully collating it with facts, nothing is brought to light inconsistent with it, that is, if experience does not *dis*prove it, he is content; at least until a simpler hypothesis, equally consistent with experience, presents itself.

To Mill this attitude of Whewell's betrayed 'a radical misconception of the nature of the evidence of physical truths'. No wonder Venn said that a person who read both Mill and Whewell would find it hard to believe that they were discussing the same subject! The verdict must go to Whewell, 'whose acquaintance with the processes of thought of science', said Peirce, 'was incomparably greater than Mill's'.

4. The formulation of a hypothesis carries with it an obligation to test it as rigorously as we can command skills to do so. There was no sign of any such sense of obligation in Burnet's *Sacred Theory*: to explain the phenomena it was designed to explain was judged evidence enough. It satisfied curiosity in much the same way as a mother's desperately *ad hoc* answers satisfy the insistent questioning of a child. The child is not interested in the content of the

answer: he asks as if he were under an instinctual compulsion to do so, and the act of answering completes a sort of ritual of exploration. But when curiosity is satisfied it is discharged: formulation of a hypothesis may act as a deterrent rather than as a stimulus to inquiry—a danger the earlier critics of the use of hypotheses were fully aware of.

Even the more sophisticated authors of Philosophick Romances did not seem to realize that any one set of phenomena could be explained by many hypotheses other than the one they fancied. It seems a strange blindness, but I think that Dugald Stewart in a finely reasoned passage got to the bottom of it. It was a favourite conceit in eighteenth-century philosophizing—Stewart found it in Boscovich, Le Sage, D'Alembert, Gravesande and Hartley—that natural philosophy is, in David Hartley's words,[21]

> . . . the art of *decyphering* the Mysteries of Nature . . . so that . . . every Theory which can explain all the Phaenomena, has all the same Evidence in its favour, that it is possible the Key of a Cypher can have from its explaining that Cypher.

Stewart found the analogy inept for many reasons, the chief being that whereas a cypher has one key, a unique solution, physical hypotheses seldom, if ever, 'afford the *only* way of explaining the phenomena to which they are applied'.

It is all very well to say that we are under a permanent obligation to test hypotheses, but, as Peirce said,

> . . . there are some hypotheses which are of such a nature that they can never be tested at all. Whether such hypotheses ought to be entertained at all, and if so in what sense, is a serious question.

Certainly the logical positivists took the question very seriously indeed, and Popper has done so too, but I do not recollect its having been a live issue before Peirce.

III

Let me now set out the gist of the hypothetico-deductive system as it might be formulated today. ('Gist' is the right word, for there is no question of its providing an abstract formal framework which becomes a concrete example of scientific reasoning when we fill in the blanks.) First, there is a clear distinction between the acts of mind involved in discovery and in proof. The generative or elementary act in discovery is 'having an idea' or proposing a hypothesis. Although one can put oneself in the right frame of mind for having ideas and can abet the process, the process itself is outside logic and cannot be made the subject of logical rules. Hypotheses must be tested, that is criticized. These tests take the form of finding out whether or not the deductive consequences of the hypothesis or systems of hypotheses are statements that correspond to reality. As the very least we expect of a hypothesis is that it should account for the phenomena already before us, its 'extra-mural' implications, its predictions about what is not yet known to be the case, are of special and perhaps crucial importance. If the predictions are false, the hypothesis is wrong or in need of modification; if they are true, we gain confidence in it, and can, so to speak, enter it for a higher examination; but if it is of such a kind that it cannot be falsified even in principle, then the hypothesis belongs to some realm of discourse other than Science. Certainty can be aspired to, but a 'rightness' that lies beyond the possibility of future criticism cannot be achieved by any scientific theory.

The first strongly reasoned and fully argued exposition of a hypothetico-deductive system is unquestionably Karl Popper's. Quite a large part of it had been propounded at the level of learned discourse rather than of critical analysis by William Whewell, F. R. S., Master of Trinity College, in 1840. Whewell is never heard of nowadays outside the ranks of historians of science: if one mentions his name one may be asked to spell it. But his reputation in his day was formidable. Whewell wrote upon ethics, hydrostatics, political economy, astronomy, verse composition, terminology, the Platonic dialogues, mechanics, geology and the History and Philosophy of the Inductive Sciences. He was the first *scientist*, I believe, to express a lengthy and carefully thought out opinion on the nature of scientific discovery, and in a sense the first scientist of any description, for he invented the word itself.[22]

There are many inadequacies in Whewell, but the spirit is right. No general statement, he said, not even the simplest iterative generalization, can arise merely from the conjunction of raw data. The mind always makes some imaginative contribution of its own, always 'superinduces' some idea upon the bare facts. A hypothesis is an explanatory conjecture giving one of many possible explanations that might meet the case.

> A facility in devising hypotheses, therefore, is so far from being a fault in the intellectual character of a discoverer, that it is, in truth, a faculty indispensable to his task.
> To form hypotheses, and then to employ much labour and skill in refuting, if they do not succeed in establishing them, is a part of the usual process of inventive minds. Such a proceeding belongs to the rule of the genius of discovery, rather than (as has often been taught in modern times) to the *exception*.

Yet it is indispensably necessary for the discoverer to demand of his hypotheses 'an agreement with facts such as will withstand the most patient and rigid inquiry', and, if they are found wanting, to turn them resolutely down:

> Since the discoverer has thus constantly to work his way onwards by means of hypotheses, false and true, it is highly important for him to possess talents and means for rapidly *testing* each supposition as it offers itself.

> The hypotheses which we accept ought to explain phenomena which we have observed. But they ought to do more than this: our hypotheses ought to *foretell* phenomena which have not yet been observed [but which are] of the same kind as those which the hypothesis was invented to explain.

Whewell did not believe that a scientist acquired factual information by passive attention to the evidence of his senses; the idea of 'naive' or 'innocent' observation (see above, p. xx 132) he rejected altogether: 'Facts cannot be observed as Facts except in virtue of the Conceptions which the observer himself unconsciously supplies'. The distinction between fact and theory was by no means as distinct as people were accustomed to believe: 'There is a mask of theory over the whole face of nature'. Strictly speaking, no scientific discovery can be made by accident. What Whewell has to say on Man as the Interpreter of Nature[23] is a suitable prolegomenon to Popper's famous lecture *On the Sources of Knowledge and of Ignorance.*

The account of scientific method which became recognized as the official alternative and rival to Mill's was not Whewell's but Stanley Jevons's. Jevons is not as fresh as Whewell nor so boldly original; we may think he should have acknowledged Whewell more often than he did. Jevons gave it as his 'very deliberate opinion' that 'many of Mill's innovations in logical science . . . are entirely groundless and false'. As to Bacon, he took the 'extreme view of holding that Francis Bacon . . . had no correct notions as to the logical method by which from particular facts we educe laws of nature'. Jevons endeavoured to show that 'hypothetical anticipation of nature is an essential part of inductive inquiry', the method 'which has led to all the great triumphs of scientific research'. Even in the 'apparently passive observation of a phenomenon' our attention should be 'guided by theoretical anticipations'.

The three essential stages in the process which he continued with deliberate vagueness to call 'induction' were, in his own words,

(a) Framing some hypothesis as to the character of the general law.

(b) Deducing consequences from that law.

(c) Observing whether the consequences agree with the particular facts under consideration.

Hypothesis is always employed, he says, consciously or unconsciously.

This account of the matter had come to be pretty widely agreed upon during the second half of the nineteenth century. We shall find it in Neil and Adamson[24] and very clearly in Peirce. (Venn, in spite of his reputation, I find disappointing.) There are many premonitions of the hypothetico-deductive method in the eighteenth century and even earlier, particularly in the writing of scientists. The clearest known to me is Dugald Stewart's, a point worth making because of the dismissive and totally erroneous opinion that his philosophy is simply a reproduction of his master's, Thomas Reid's, voice. In answer to Reid's rhetorical challenge to name any advance in science which had arisen by the use of a hypothetical method, Stewart thought it sufficient to mention the theory of Gravitation and the Copernican system.

Stewart believed that most discoveries in science had grown out of hypothetical reasoning:

> It is by reasoning synthetically from the hypothesis, and comparing the deductions with observation and experiment, that the cautious inquirer is gradually led, either to correct it in such a manner as to reconcile it with facts, or finally to abandon it as an unfounded conjecture. Even in this latter case, an approach is made to the truth in the way of *exclusion* . . .

Stewart's own analysis of the use of those tiresome adjectives *synthetic* and *analytic* shows he is here using 'synthetically' in the sense of 'deductively'.

IV

A scientific methodology, being itself a theory about the conduct of scientific inquiry, must have grown out of an attempt to find out exactly what scientists do or ought to do. The methodology should therefore be measured against scientific practice to give us confidence in its worth. Unfortunately, this honest ambition is fraught with logical perils. If we assume for the sake of argument that the methodology is unsound, then so also will be our test of its validity. If we assume it to be sound, then there is no point in submitting it to test, for the test could not invalidate it. These difficulties I shall surmount by disregarding them entirely.

What scientists *do* has never been the subject of a scientific, that is, an ethological inquiry. It is no use looking to scientific 'papers', for they not merely conceal but actively misrepresent the reasoning that goes into the work they describe.[25] If scientific papers are to be accepted for publication, they must be written in the inductive style. The spirit of John Stuart Mill glares out of the eyes of every editor of a Learned Journal.

Nor is it much use listening to accounts of what scientists *say* they do, for their opinions vary widely enough to accommodate almost any methodological hypothesis we may care to devise. Only unstudied evidence will do—and that means listening at a keyhole. Here are some turns of speech we may hear in a biological laboratory:

> 'What gave you the idea of trying . . .?'
> 'I'm taking the view that the underlying mechanism is . . .'
> 'What happens if you assume that . . .?'
> 'Actually, your results can be accounted for on a quite different hypothesis'.
> 'It follows from what you are saying that if . . ., then . . .'
> 'Is that actually the case?'
> 'That's a good question' [i.e. a question about a true weakness, insufficiency, or ambiguity].

'That result squared with my hypothesis'.
'So obviously that idea was out'.
'At the moment I don't see any way of eliminating that possibility'.
'My results don't make a story yet'.
'I'm still at the stage of trying to find out if there is anything to be explained'.
'Obviously a great deal more work has got to be done before . . .'
'I don't seem to be getting anywhere'.

Scientific thought has already reached a pretty sophisticated professional level before it finds expression in language such as this. This is not the language of induction. It does not suggest that scientists are hunting for facts, still less that they are busy formulating 'laws'. Scientists are building explanatory structures, *telling stories* which are scrupulously tested to see if they are stories about real life.

It has been a tradition among philosophers that we should look to the physical sciences and to simple, lofty discoveries if we are to see the Scientific Method at work in its most easily intelligible form. I question this opinion. The simplicity of great discoveries is often a measure of how far they have travelled from their beginnings. Let a biologist have a turn. Here is Claude Bernard, writing just one hundred years ago:[26]

> A hypothesis is . . . the obligatory starting point of all experimental reasoning. Without it no investigation would be possible, and one would learn nothing: one could only pile up barren observations. To experiment without a preconceived idea is to wander aimlessly.

Indeed,

> Those who have condemned the use of hypotheses and preconceived ideas in the experimental method have made the mistake of confusing the contriving of the experiment with the verification of its results.

Over and over again Bernard insists that hypotheses must be of such a kind that they can be tested, that one should go out of one's way to find means of refuting them, and that 'if one proposes a hypothesis which experience cannot verify, one abandons the experimental method'. Claude Bernard is most distinctive and at his best in his insistence on the critical method, on the virtue and necessity of Doubt.

> When propounding a general theory in science, the one thing one can be sure of is that, in the strict sense, such theories are mistaken. They are only partial and provisional truths which are necessary . . . to carry the investigation forward; they represent only the current state of our understanding and are bound to be modified by the growth of science . . .

This is powerful evidence, for Claude Bernard, in creating experimental physiology, did indeed put scientific medicine on a new foundation. His philosophy *worked*.

In real life the imaginative and critical acts that unite to form the hypothetico-deductive method alternate so rapidly, at least in the earlier stages of constructing a theory, that they are not spelled out in thought. The 'process of invention, trial, and acceptance or rejection of the hypothesis goes on so rapidly', said Whewell, 'that we cannot trace it in its successive steps'. What then is the point of asking ourselves where the initiative comes from, the observation or the idea? Is it not as pointless as asking which came first, the chicken or the egg?

But this is not a pointless question: it matters terribly which came first: scientific dynasties have been overthrown by giving the wrong answer![27] It matters no less in methodology; we may collect and classify facts, we may marvel at curiosities and idly wonder what accounts for them, but the activity that is characteristically scientific begins with an explanatory conjecture which at once becomes the subject of an energetic critical analysis. It is an instance of a far more general stratagem that underlies every enlargement of general understanding and every new solution of the problem of finding our way about the world. The regulation and control of hypotheses is more usefully described as a *cybernetic* than as a logical process: the adjustment and reformulation of hypotheses through an examination of their deductive consequences is simply another setting for the ubiquitous phenomenon of negative feedback. The purely logical element in scientific discovery is a comparatively small one, and the idea of a *logic* of scientific discovery is acceptable only in an older and wider use of 'logic' than is current among formal logicians today.

The weakness of the hypothetico-deductive system, insofar as it might profess to offer a complete account of the scientific process, lies in its disclaiming any power to explain how hypotheses come into being. By 'inspiration', surely; by the 'spontaneous conjectures of instinctive reasoning', said Peirce; but what then? It has often been suggested that the act of creation is the same in the arts as it is in science:[28] certainly 'having an idea'—the formulation of a hypothesis—resembles other forms of inspirational activity in the circumstances that favour it, the suddenness with which it comes about, the wholeness of the conception it embodies, and the fact that the mental events which lead up to it happen below the surface of the mind. But there, to my mind, the resemblance ends. No one questions the inspirational character of musical or poetic invention because the delight and exaltation that go with it somehow communicate themselves to others. Something *travels*; we are carried away. But science is not an art form in this sense; scientific discovery is a private event, and the delight that accompanies it, or the despair of finding it illusory, does not travel. One scientist may get great satisfaction from another's work and admire it deeply; it may give him great intellectual pleasure; but it gives him no sense of participation in the discovery, it does

PETER MEDAWAR

not carry him away, and his appreciation of it does not depend on his being carried away. If it were otherwise the inspirational origin of scientific discovery would never have been in doubt.

SIR PETER MEDAWAR, F.R.S.

CLINICAL REASEARCH CENTRE
HARROW, ENGLAND
SEPTEMBER, 1965

NOTES

[1] *Hypotheses non sequor* runs an early draft of Newton's famous disclaimer, which we are to translate, as Whewell did, 'I feign no hypotheses': see I. Bernard Cohen, *Isis,* **51** (1960), 589. Newton did, of course, use and propound hypotheses in the modern sense of that word; the unwholesome flavour which Newton found in the word is discussed below.

[2] The fundamental axiom of empiricism—*nihil in intellectu quod non prius in sensu*—is of course mistaken. Animals *inherit* information (for example, on how to build nests, or what to sing) in the form of a sort of chromosomal tape recording. This instinctual knowledge is not arrived at by association of ideas, anyhow of sensory ideas received by the animal in its own lifetime.

[3] D. O. Hebb, *The Organization of Behavior* (New York: John Wiley & Sons, 1949), esp. p. 31.

[4] Here and hereinafter I quote from the following works of the authors cited in Part I, Sec. 4:
William Whewell, *The Philosophy of the Inductive Sciences*, 2d ed., 2 vols. (London: John W. Parker, 1847; 1st ed., 1840).
F. Stanley Jevons, *The Principles of Science*, rev. 2d ed., (London, 1877; 1st ed., 1873).
Samuel Neil, "The Art of Reasoning": twenty articles in successive issues of the first two vols. of the *British Controversialist* (1850-51) of which Neil was editor; particularly **2**, No. 11.
C. S. Peirce, *Collected Papers of Charles Sanders Peirce*, ed. by C. Hartshorne and P. Weiss (Cambridge, Mass.: Harvard University Press), Vol. 2: *Elements of Logic* (1932); Vol. 6: *Scientific Metaphysics* (1935).

[5] Dugald Stewart, *Elements of the Philosophy of the Human Mind*, 2d ed. (London, 1802-14), Vol. 1 (1802; 1st ed., 1792), Vol. 2 (1816; 1st ed., 1814).

[6] John Venn, *The Principles of Empirical or Inductive Logic*, 2d ed. (London, 1907; 1st ed., 1889).

[7] John Stuart Mill, *A System of Logic,* 8th ed. (London, 1872; 1st ed., 1843).

[8] Richard Whateley, *Elements of Logic*, 9th ed. (London, 1848; 1st ed., 1826).

[9] Gavin de Beer, *Charles Darwin* (London: Nelson, 1963), p. 98. In his Autobiography Darwin once declared that he could not resist forming a hypothesis on every subject, and his letters to Henry Fawcett and to H. W. Bates are very revealing (*More Letters of Charles Darwin*, ed. by F. Darwin and A. C. Seward (London: John Murray, 1903), pp. 176, 195.
For the origin of the idea of Natural Selection, see also L. Eisely in *Daedalus* (Summer, 1965), 588-602.

[10] Karl Pearson, *The Grammar of Science*, 3d ed. (London, 1911; 1st ed., 1892).

[11] E.g. 'science', 'art', 'pure science', 'applied science'; 'analysis', 'synthesis'; 'experiment'; and, of course, notoriously, words like *genius, creation, enthusiasm.*

[12] John Gregory, *On the Duties and Qualifications of a Physician* (London, 1820; 1st ed., 1772).

[13] Thomas Reid, *Essays on the Intellectual Powers of Man*, 1st ed. (1785); contained in *The Works of Thomas Reid*, ed. by W. Hamilton, 4th ed. (London, 1854).

[14] John Herschel, *Discourse on the Study of Natural Philosophy* (London, 1831).

[15] George Henry Lewes, *Problems of Life and Mind*, 4th ed., (London, 1883; 1st ed., 1873), esp. pp. 296, 316-17.

[16] See Stephen Hales's Preface to his *Statical Essays*, 4th ed., (London, 1769; 1st ed., 1727) and a number of passages in Robert Hooke's *Posthumous Works* (London, 1705). For Boscovich, see n. 19 below.

[17] Samuel Taylor Coleridge, *On Method*, 3d ed. (London, 1849; 1st ed., 1818).

[18] Boscovich, *De Augmentis Scientiarum*, trans. by Gilbert Wats (London, 1674), Bk. 5, Chap. 3, II.

[19] Dugald Stewart's translation of the footnotes on pp. 211-12 of Boscovich's *De Solis ac Lunae Defectibus* (London, 1760).

[20] R. A. Fisher, *The Design of Experiments* (London, 1935).

[21] David Hartley, *Observations on Man* (London, 1749), Vol. 1, pp. 15-16.

[22] And 'physicist' and many other useful words, including *eocene, miocene,* and *pliocene*: see P. J. Wexler, 'The Great Nomenclator: Whewell's Contributions to Scientific Terminology', *Notes & Queries*, N.S. **8**, p. 27, January 1961. Professor S. Ross in *Notes and Records of the Royal Society* (**16** [1961], 187) has recounted the correspondence between Whewell and Michael Faraday upon what best to call the two opposite poles of the electrolytic cell. Faraday toyed with alphode and betaode, voltaode and galvanode, zincode and platinode, dexiode and skiaode, oriode and occiode, eastode and westode, eisode and exode, orthode and anthode. 'My dear Sir,' wrote Whewell, '. . . I am disposed to recommend . . . *anode* and *cathode*', and so they came to be.

[23] *Philosophy of the Inductive Sciences*, 2d ed.; in particular see Bk. 1, Chap. 2, Secs. 9, 10.

[24] Robert Adamson in his article *Bacon, Francis* in the 9th ed. of the *Encyclopaedia Britannica* (Edinburgh, 1875). See also Augustus de Morgan's *A Budget of Paradoxes* (London, 1872): 'Modern discoveries have not been made by large collections of facts . . . A few facts have suggested an *hypothesis*, which means a *supposition*, proper to explain them. The necessary results of this supposition are worked out, and then, and not till then, other facts are examined to see if these ulterior results are found in nature. The trial of the hypothesis is the *special object* . . . Wrong hypotheses, rightly worked from, have produced more useful results than unguided observations'.

[25] See Popper's 'Science: Problems, Aims, Responsibilities', in *Federation Proceedings* (Federation of American Societies for Experimental Biology), **22** (1963), 961-72; and my own broadcast, 'Is the Scientific Paper a Fraud?' in *The Listener* (September 12, 1963). This broadcast was followed by a correspondence (issues of September 26 and October 10) illustrating the style of thought that makes scientists treat the 'philosophy of science' with exasperated contempt.

[26] Claude Bernard, *Introduction à l' Étude de la Médecine Expérimentale* (Paris, 1865).

[27] A person who believes that the egg came first, i.e. that a new kind of egg came before a new kind of chicken, is a Mendelist, a Morganist, and to our way of thinking a regular guy, though classified until recently in Russia as a fascist villain intent upon undoing the work of the Revolution; conversely a person who believes that the chicken came first is a Lamarckist, a Michurinist and a Lysenkoist, and was at one time suspected of plotting to overthrow the constitution of the United States.

[28] See for example J. Bronowski, *Science and Human Values*, rev. ed. (New York: John Wiley & Sons, 1965), esp. pp. 19, 27, 51.

*Grover Maxwell**

CORROBORATION WITHOUT DEMARCATION*

INTRODUCTION

A portion of this essay consists of criticisms of Sir Karl Popper's *criterion of demarcation* and of the solution (or disposal) of the problem of induction that he holds it to provide. But the main thrust of the paper is intended to be less negative. The *criterion of demarcation* and the emphasis upon (deductive) falsifiability are usually thought to be crucial for, and central to, Popper's approach to epistemology and philosophy of science; but I believe that this is true only for the letter and not for the spirit of his thought. The latter is concerned with *critical scrutiny* (of knowledge claims) in general and does not limit itself merely to attempts to falsify them. And it reminds the epistemologist and the philosopher of science that their primary concern must be with *what* a knowledge claim *asserts* rather than with the *language* in which it is couched. Philosophy of cognitive knowledge is of a piece with such knowledge; it seeks to add to our store of significant truths (or near truths) about the universe and is not limited to mere analysis of the concepts with which they may be expressed. With this general approach of Popper's I remain in complete agreement, and I shall try to emulate it in criticizing and attempting to modify and augment some of his more specific views, hoping to advance a small step or so, as he would say, "closer to the truth."

In Part I of the paper, it is argued that many, perhaps most, important scientific theories are not falsifiable and that, even if they were, such a fact would not provide a basis for a satisfactory epistemology and philosophy of science. It is concluded, since the *criterion of demarcation* uses falsifiability as a basis for separating "scientific" (or "empirical") propositions from "nonscientific" (or "metaphysical") ones, that it must be rejected as being much too restrictive. The implications of this conclusion for problems about confirmation, corroboration, etc., and for the traditional problem of induc-

* Support of research by the National Science Foundation, the Carnegie Corporation, and the Minnesota Center for Philosophy of Science of the University of Minnesota is gratefully acknowledged.

tion are considered in Part II; and Part III consists of an endeavor to alter and augment some of Popper's ideas in order to arrive at a constructive theory of confirmation.

I

Popper's views on the matters just mentioned are so widely known that I shall summarize them here only briefly.[1] However, careful attention must be paid to the following tenet of his, for its importance cannot be overemphasized: *he rejects the view that general knowledge is, as a rule, inferred from (observational) evidence*, in any usual sense of "infer." Rather, in order to expand our store of knowledge, we first turn our attention to *problems*. In the simplest case, which will serve as an adequate example, a problem might be to find an *explanation*[2] for some singular fact (or alleged fact) such as the fact that my roof started leaking last night—or the fact that this thing (which happens to be a crow) is black. The first step towards solving such a problem is to propose an *hypothesis* or a *theory* to *explain* the fact; this means, roughly, to propose a proposition which, when conjoined with certain other propositions, most of which we take to be known already (the "background knowledge"), yields as a logical consequence a proposition stating the fact to be explained. To repeat, the theory, or hypothesis, is not obtained by inferring it from the relevant evidence so far at hand, i.e., the fact(s) to be explained. The proposal of a theory—a possible explanation—is a *creative* response of the investigator to the problem, and this "creative leap" presumably results from as-yet-poorly-understood psychological processes; in any event, problems about the *origins* of theories and hypotheses are supposed to fall within the province of psychology (or sociology, or evolutionary theory, etc.) and not be the concern of the philosopher or logician. Once a theory has been proposed, it should be tested as severely as possible by subjecting it to varied and sincere attempts to *falsify* it. The results of such tests must be reproducible and intersubjectively attestable. So long as these attempts at falsification fail, we are justified in tentatively retaining and using the theory and always continuing, if possible, the attempts at falsification. The potential falsifiers ("basic statements") are singular observation statements of a certain kind whose exact nature need not concern us here. They, in their turn, are not *conclusively* verifiable (or falsifiable) and, in principle, may be subjected to the same kind of testing outlined above. For this reason, and since theories may be "saved" by qualifying assumptions such as *ad hoc* hypotheses, conclusive falsifiability is not required. Popper, of course, proscribes "patching up" via *ad hoc* assumption; such a proscription he calls a *methodological rule*. Such matters as this will be discussed in detail later; but even here, it should be remarked that Popper recognizes that this and certain other methodological rules must quite often be invoked before a given theory or hypothesis may be taken to be falsified.

Of much more importance than purely existential statements are statements containing both universal and existential quantifiers. Some such statements *are* falsifiable, but many interesting and important ones are not. Among these is the logic teacher's old friend, "All men are mortal," which, unpacked, asserts that, given any man, there is (will be) some time at which he dies. Clearly, the existential quantification over temporal instants (or finite temporal intervals—it does not matter) precludes the possibility of falsifying instances: no matter how long any given man lives, the logical possibility that he will die at *some* time always remains and, with it, the logical possibility for "All men are mortal" to be true. Now, surely, in any usual sense of "confirm," we would regard "All men are mortal" as being a highly confirmed generalization. This is because, although it has no falsifiable instances, *it has verifiable ones*, e.g., "Jones dies on October 5, 1969" verifies "Jones is mortal," and such instances that are actually verified are commonly regarded as confirmatory. That this is as it should be will become apparent, I hope, in Part III of this paper; but, in anticipation and because its importance cannot be overemphasized, let me just mention an important general principle of which mixed quantification provides one kind of example: there are many situations in scientific and common sense inquiry where a "negative outcome" of an experiment or observation not only would fail to falsify the theory or hypothesis of interest, but would count against or disconfirm it only very slightly, while a *"positive outcome" would be highly confirmatory.* This seems to pose, prima facie at least, an extremely serious difficulty for Popper's *falsificationism, deductivism,* and *criterion of demarcation.*[3] It is interesting to note that results analogous to those just discussed are obtained for corroboration, in Popper's technical sense;[4] the details are given in Appendix II, where it is shown that nonfalsifiable statements such as, "All men are mortal," can be given a high *degree of corroboration* on the basis of instances of death among men—*literally, corroboration without demarcation!*

A defender of the falsifiability criterion might counter all of this by maintaining that, contrary to common belief, "All men are mortal," like all other unfalsifiable theories, is metaphysical, nonempirical, and nonscientific and, moreover, that computations of degrees of corroboration are allowable only for falsifiable theories, so that instances of men dying do not really provide an acceptable basis for testing the theory that all men are mortal. Such a move, at this point, seems fair enough, and, moreover, it raises *the* fundamental question that both critics and defenders of Popper's *falsificationism* and *deductivism* must face: Are, or are not, the *methodological rules* recommended by Popper, and which are necessary in order for deductive falsification to be certified in actual cases, acceptable? A defender must, of course, hold that they are, and he should give *arguments* for their acceptability. For example, he must defend the prohibition of *ad hoc* hypotheses and the injunction to select the auxiliary hypotheses (and other statements needed to make the inference of falsifiable consequences deductive) so carefully that all of the premises in the *explanation* of the "evidence" can be certified as unproblematic *except* the hypothesis being tested.[5] As a critic of falsificationism, I shall argue that these rules are *not generally* acceptable and that, even in special cases, they are acceptable only when qualified by *ceteris paribus* clauses. I shall not only try to show that they are not generally observed in actual scientific practice but, more importantly, that they *ought not* to be so observed. *Falsifiability* will remain as an important, but usually unattainable, *regulative ideal* for theories, but it cannot serve as a basis for sharply distinguishing the scientific from the unscientific, nor can attempts at *falsification* serve as the only means for testing theories by experiment and observation.

Arguments for these conclusions will be continued by considering examples from scientific practice. Many of the theories and principles that are relevant for these matters are so firmly established and so frequently used as guides in scientific inquiry that they are taken for granted and virtually never stated explicitly.[6] Among these is 'Every solid has a melting point', or, more explicitly, 'For every solid, at a given external pressure, there is a temperature above which it becomes liquid (or gaseous)', along with similar statements about boiling points and other transition points. This is obviously not falsifiable, since we cannot subject any solid to the entire range of temperatures up to infinity degrees. A possible objection is that the last statement in quotes should be replaced by the stronger statement 'For every pure solid substance, at a given external pressure there is *exactly one* melting point', which *seems* to be falisfiable. Two comments are in order. First, the latter statement is logically equivalent to the conjunction of 'For every pure. . ., there is at least one melting point' and 'For every pure. . ., there is at most one melting point'. Since the first conjunct is not falsifiable (though it is confirmable and disconfirmable, I should say) and since it does not seem to increase the falsifiability of the "theory as a whole," it seems that, according to the criterion of demarcation, it should be eliminated from the system. Yet it seems to play a role comparable in importance to that of the second conjunct. Are we not justified in confidently trying to determine the melting point of a newly discovered compound (with a view to its characterization for future investigators) and in doing the same for an unidentified compound, in order to establish its identity, even though such endeavors are not attempts to falsify anything? The second comment is concerned with more basic issues, and it will be necessary to dwell on it at greater length.

To introduce this second difficulty, we note that if 'melting point' means simply, 'temperature at which liquefaction begins', the possibility and not infrequent actual occurrence of "metastable states" (some of which are quite *stable*) renders the *second* conjunct not only falsifiable but *false*. For example, many liquids, including water, often remain in the liquid state far below their freezing points (melting points); in such a *metastable state*, they solidify throughout almost instantaneously when disturbed mechanically. In order to retain the melting point principle, it is necessary to add the qualifying phrase 'at equilibrium', or, what amounts to the same thing and what is actually done in practice, to define 'melting point' as '*equilibrium* liquefaction (or solidifaction) point'. But now, although the new statement is highly useful and, we believe, well confirmed, it is *not* falsifiable. This is partly due to the nature of the theoretical predicate 'at equilibrium'. Suppose we tried to falsify the statement by establishing that ice has two melting points at, say, one atmosphere of pressure. And, indeed, suppose we discovered that on some occasions or with some samples melting began at 0° C. and, on others, not until 15° C. Still, in order to *falsify* the statement, it would be necessary to *verify* statements to the effect that both the 0° melting and the 15° liquefaction are *equilibrium* processes. And such statements while *confirmable*, are *not* verifiable. Since equilibrium is a necessary initial condition of all tests employed by traditional thermodynamics, it follows that none of the theories of this branch of physics are falsifiable. This calls attention to an even more important and more general principle, which has been almost entirely overlooked: *In order to derive statements that are inconsistent with the relevant observational "basic statements," in most cases it is necessary, even in the physical sciences, to use as premises not only the theory in question plus auxiliary theories, but also singular statements expressing initial conditions involving unobservables, e.g., "This system is at equilibrium."* So, strictly speaking, virtually no scientific theories are falsifiable. At best, what can be falsified is a conjunction consisting of the theory, the auxiliary theories (background knowledge), and singular statements about unobservables. The theory can always be "saved" by conjecturing that some unobservable "foul up" of initial conditions produced the observed result. Such conjectures are by no means always *ad hoc*. For, although they are generally neither verifiable nor independently falsifiable, there may well be independent means for confirming or disconfirming them. See, for example, the case of the neutrino hypothesis discussed below. To repeat this point of central importance, in testing the more interesting and important theories, it is not merely the theory plus (singular) observation statements plus auxiliary hypotheses which imply "testable" results, but, rather the theory plus all of these *and plus singular theoretical statements*, i.e., statements of initial conditions involving unobservables; and the latter are neither falsifiable nor verifiable, though they are confirmable and disconfirmable. As before, it can always be countered that these assumptions about unobservable initial conditions should be regarded as unproblematic in order to make the theory being tested vulnerable to falsification. But this rejoinder encounters grave difficulties. For although the particular assumptions made in a given case may make the theory falsifiable by a given *basic statement*, it is well known that there will always be alternative assumptions about the initial conditions that will "save" the theory from being falsified by this basic statement. Surely there are no a priori or *purely methodological* reasons for always selecting the former kind of assumption—indeed, if we are bound and determined to falsify, we can, for any *basic statement*, always "cook up" a conjunction of auxiliary hypotheses and initial conditions by virtue of which the basic statement "falsifies" the theory being "tested." We obviously require some means of selecting among alternative assumptions about unobservable initial conditions, auxiliary hypotheses, etc. On pain of circularity or infinite regress only does it seem that we can suggest passing falsification tests as providing such a criterion for selection.

Even if this difficulty can be circumvented, there is still another one. Suppose, *per impossibile*, that the statements to the effect that equilibrium was attained were verified. (Similar, though not identical, methodological considerations would arise if, *per possibile*, these statements were highly *confirmed*.) Judging from similar cases in the history of science, it is not likely that we would consider the statement in question ('. . .at most one melting point') falsified. We would believe that we had discovered *two kinds* of ice—that ice occurs in at least two *allotropic* forms, each being a distinct "pure substance" and each having its characteristic melting point. This hypothesis would *not* be *ad hoc*, for it would imply the existence of structural differences—intermolecular, intramolecular, or both—between the two forms. But, again, it is not falsifiable; failure to discover such differences might be due to lack of sufficient ingenuity or sufficiently sensitive means of detection. Since they are not falsifiable and since they detract from rather than add to, the falsifiability of the system as a whole, it seems that the criterion of demarcation would reject, as not belonging to empirical science, the statements about melting points as well as the one about allotropy. Yet it seems to me that science not only *does* use such statements but, more importantly, that it *ought* to do so. For they are confirmable and disconfirmable (in any usual sense of these terms), they play a useful role in scientific inquiry, and, if true, they state interesting and important facts about the constitution of the world. If persistent and ingenious attempts to discover differences in structure between the putatively allotropic forms of ice failed, both the hypothesis of the allotropy of ice and that of the uniqueness of melting point would be disconfirmed, whether to such a degree that we would be justified in rejecting them we need not consider here. But, if such attempts were successful, it seems to me obvious that *both* hypotheses would be highly confirmed (though not to the same extent), *even though such attempts were not attempts at falsification.*

Because of its far-reaching consequences for one of the basic principles of modern science, I shall consider one other (rather notorious) example, the neutrino hypothesis.[7] It is well known that the mass-energy loss of an atomic nucleus due to beta decay is, in general, greater than the mass-energy of the emitted beta particle. Rather than regarding this as falsifying the principle of the conservation of mass-energy, physical theory was modified by addition of (something like) the statement 'For every beta emission there is a neutrino emitted from the same nucleus'. The mass-energy of the neutrino accounted for the "observed" energy discrepancy. The statement is nonfalsifiable not so much because of its existential character but because of the nature of the neutrino. It has zero, or extremely small, rest mass; it has no charge; and the capture or interaction "cross-section" of atomic nuclei and other particles relative to the neutrino, while unknown, was postulated to be extremely small—perhaps negligible. The neutrino, it seemed, was almost, if not quite, "undetectable in principle." Was the neutrino hypothesis *ad hoc*? With respect to the mass-energy anomaly, it was not; for it also explained "observed" anomalies in momentum and particle spin. Before deciding whether it was *ad hoc* relative to the set of these three anomalies, it will be desirable to consider the general grounds for such a charge.

Whereas the epithet '*ad hoc*' is sometimes justifiably applied, I believe that this occurs less often than is commonly supposed. An hypothesis is often said to be *ad hoc* with respect to a certain fact, if and only if it explains the fact in question and no others. ('Fact' is used here in a very broad sense and may refer to "empirical" and, even, "theoretical" regularities.) But this characterization hardly seems fair, for such an hypothesis, *if it be conjoined with appropriate auxiliary hypotheses*, may lead to new predictions and its explanatory potential may extend beyond the facts initially explained. This will always be a logical *possibility* unless the putatively *ad hoc* hypothesis is logically equivalent to the *one* "fact" (or *one* set of facts) that it was originally designed to explain. To be actually *ad hoc* is to be circular—nothing more, nothing less. It might be held that we are justified in calling an hypothesis *ad hoc* when its "observable" consequences are exhausted by the explanandum for which it was originally adduced. This suggestion, if tidied up sufficiently, incorporates the sound pragmatic principle that in many cases, such an hypothesis is of little use unless it cashes some of its promissory notes—unless, for example, careful analysis of the hypothesis or enrichment of the theory of which it is a part results in additional *testable* or confirmable consequences. But, again, the *possibility* of such cashing-in will always be present unless the hypothesis is *equivalent* to the original explanandum. For these reasons, I am extremely wary when the charge, *"ad hoc"* is leveled; and the neutrino hypothesis is a beautiful case in point, for prima facie it seemed to be an excellent *paradigm* of what are intuitively labeled *"ad hoc"* hypotheses. But, certainly the hypothesis was not logically equivalent to the "facts" that the detected anomalies in mass-energy, momentum, and spin accompanying beta decay and, as will appear below, when the hypothesis was conjoined with appropriate auxiliary hypotheses, new and *confirmable*, though *not falsifiable* consequences appeared. It now appears, for example, that this prima facie *ad hoc* hypothesis has opened up an extensive and exciting new area of inquiry, neutrino astronomy.[8]

In 1956, the neutrino was "experimentally detected." The success of the experiment resulted from the fulfillment of the rather pious hope that the neutrino cross-section of the protons (hydrogen nuclei) employed as "neutrino traps" was large enough to permit some actual interaction as well as some rather dubious assumptions about auxiliary hypotheses and unobservable initial conditions. The experiment was a test of the neutrino hypothesis and, indirectly, the conservation law. The positive results highly confirmed the former and added considerably to confirmation of the latter. But a negative result would *not* have falsified (though it would have slightly disconfirmed) either the neutrino hypothesis or the conservation law or the conjunction of the two. The only thing which could have been reasonably said to be strongly disconfirmed, much less falsified, would have been the pious hope about the cross-section of the particular kind of "neutrino traps" employed or some other auxiliary assumption.

I conclude that we are sometimes justified in incorporating nonfalsifiable (though confirmable and disconfirmable) statements into a theory, even when this results in the entire theory's becoming less falsifiable. This is probably most often the case when a basic, highly confirmed principle, such as the conservation law, *seems* to be contravened. In such a case we may even be justified in introducing an hypothesis which *seems* to have a strong prima facie *ad hoc* flavor. Several writers[9] have correctly noted that such principles seem to "become nonfalsifiable" in that they cannot be overthrown by one (or a few) kind of experimental results, no matter how often repeated. But they are mistaken, I believe, in attributing this to a shift toward the quasi-analytic end of a Quinian spectrum (Putnam) or the acquisition of a kind of "necessity" (Alexander) or to their denials becoming "conceptually untenable" (Hanson).[10] It is, rather, that such principles are so well confirmed that it is more reasonable to suppose that some (essentially used) "auxiliary hypothesis" is false or that some factor in the initial conditions, such as the escape of energy via neutrinos, is responsible for the discrepancy than to suppose that the principle in question is false. Needless to say, however, such principles must not be made invulnerable (unless they are made *A-true* and thus, empty). There is always the possibility that a large variety of disconfirming evidence will make it reasonable to abandon the principle in question.

In this discussion of the general unfalsifiability of theories, examples have been chosen from the physical sciences partly because this is the area with which I am most familiar, but mostly because one would expect to find more readily falsifiable theories in these the "hard" sciences than anywhere else. From my scant knowledge of the kinds of actual theories employed in physchology, the social sciences, and even in the biological and medical sciences, those that have actually been falsified by observation and experiment (as opposed to those that are abandoned because they are inconsistent with *other* [unfalsifiable] theories) and those that *could* be so falsified, seem to be even more scarce than in the physical sciences. Consider the extremely simple example afforded by the theory that cancer is caused by a virus. This seems to have a good prima facie claim to being a respectable scientific theory and, indeed, is so regarded by a number of researchers. And surely we can easily imagine circumstances in which we would regard it as highly confirmed: means of detection and isolation might finally be developed whereby a kind (or kinds) of virus was discovered in large numbers in cancer patients, which appeared to produce cancer in animals, and for which a highly effective vaccine was eventually developed. But obviously no amount of unsuccessful but sincere and ingenious effort to discover such a virus would falsify the theory (although it might disconfirm it), for there would always be the possibility that the next such attempt would succeed. Suppose that it was "discovered" that cancer has an entirely different cause, perhaps some farfetched nutritional deficiency. Well, such a "discovery" would be expressed by a universal statement and no matter how highly confirmed it might be, it could, of course, never be deductively *verified* by any amount of experimental evidence. Thus it could not provide a refutation of the virus theory in the sense required by the *criterion of demarcation*, i.e., deductive falsification by *basic statements*.

Although a classification of the various factors that preclude falsifiability of theories will be provided later, I shall, for the present, rest the case against the *criterion of demarcation* and go on to consider some of the implications of its rejection for Popper's treatment of the problem of induction. But first a rather obvious but extremely important point should be made about the status of the falsifiability requirement. Such a requirement retains the role of a highly desirable, although often unattainable, regulative ideal for scientific theories. There seems no doubt that Popper is absolutely right in holding that the more vulnerable a theory is, vis-a-vis observation and experiment, the better the theory is (*ceteris paribus*, I would add). Theories should be made as testable as possible and if we are lucky enough to make them attain the level of the regulative ideal, actual falsifiability, so much the better. Later in the paper it will be explained how, on my view, many theories may be tested experimentally and, thus, *confirmed* or *disconfirmed* even when they are not falsifiable.

II

The treatment of the problem of induction that Popper gives in his latest publications still seems to depend crucially on the possibility of the actual fulfillment of the falsifiability requirement and thus, on the viability of the *criterion of demarcation*. His position as he gives it in Chapter I of his *Conjectures and Refutations* (see especially pp. 52-59), may be summarized briefly as follows:

Hume was entirely correct in his contention that there exists no relation of a logical character between observational "evidence," on the one hand, and our theories, hypotheses, etc., on the other, by virtue of which their truth can be established or even made likely. But, according to Popper, Hume's extreme skepticism is avoided by appreciating the significance of the fact that observational evidence may *falsify* a lawlike statement that asserts the existence of regularities. Since in science as well as in some of our everyday activities, our goal is *truth*, we should prefer a theory that has not been falsified and thus which, for all we know, may be true, to one that *has* been falsified by observation. Thus scientific practice, according to him, consists largely of vigorous and ingenious attempts to falsify the theories that have been proposed to solve the various problems that occupy the scientist. Theories that, at a given moment, have so far survived such attempts are the ones most worthy to be accepted (*tentatively only*) as solutions to these problems and for further experimental testing (end of summary of Popper's views).

With Popper's logical critique of induction, I am in complete agreement, and, I agree with Bertrand Russell that simple inductive procedures, if conducted *as logical procedures*, i.e., as he puts it, "if conducted without regard to common sense leads very much more often to error than to truth." (In Bertrand Russell, *My Philosophical Development* [New York: Simon and Schuster,1959].) There it is shown that for the more generally accepted forms of "inductive arguments," the following holds: given any such argument with its premises all true and its conclusion true (or intuitively acceptable) there can be formed an indefinitely large number of arguments, each of which has its premises all true, has a logical form identical with the original argument, and has a false (or intuitively unacceptable) conclusion; moreover, the conclusions of all the arguments including the original one, will be mutually inconsistent. Thus, unless there is more to "inductive logic" than its proponents have revealed, induction should be expected to give unacceptable results much more often (perhaps infinitely more often) than it gives acceptable ones. Unfortunately, similar difficulties arise for *hypothetico-deductive* explanation as a basis for *corroboration* on the basis of falsification attempts (successful or not). For, given any amount of observational evidence, there will always be an indefinitely large number of distinct, indeed mutually incompatible theories which, when conjoined with appropriate auxiliary hypotheses, initial conditions, etc., will *explain* the evidence at hand. Now suppose that we falsify a number of theories in a given area. It is true, as Popper points out, that this enables us to eliminate some of our errors. But does it provide any comfort to one whose goal is to obtain a theory in the area in question that is *true* or close to the truth? It is difficult to see why this should be so. For no matter how many false theories we eliminate there will always remain an indefinitely large number of theories, at most one of which is true. We could go on eliminating false theories forever without having any apparent reason for supposing that we have made any progress towards getting the true one. It might be thought that this difficulty would not arise if *closeness to the truth* is the goal rather than *truth*. Moreover, since corroboration (as *well* as verisimilitude) depends partly on the logical content of the theory, it (corroboration) is immune to the objection above. But I know of no reason to doubt that, given any finite interval on any kind of scale for *verisimilitude* (closeness to the truth), there will be an indefinitely large number of mutually incompatible theories, *within that interval*, that *explain* the evidence in question, and therefore are all equally well *corroborated* by the evidence. Because of these considerations and because, or so I have contended, many and perhaps most scientific theories are not falsifiable, and cannot be made so by viable methodological rules, I am forced to take an even more radical view of confirmation and corroboration than Popper does. *As far as logic is concerned*, we cannot have even the kind of negativistic reasons given by Popper for considering one theory better, or less bad, than its competitors. I believe that this prima facie skeptical result must be accepted. In my opinion, this is one of many illustrations of the impotence of *purely logical* or *purely* "conceptual" considerations for any kinds of constructive results for interesting or important problems—philosophical problems emphatically included.

So Popper's attempted disposal of Hume's problem, insofar as it is based on the falsifiability requirement, seems to fail. However, attempts at falsification are only one kind of critical scrutiny to which a theory may be subjected, as Popper himself has, of course, often stressed. Popper's general negativism, which he aptly calls "the critical approach," does provide, I believe, the basis for a more satisfactory resolution of the problem. As far as the general line of this approach is concerned it is best sketched by Popper himself in a fragment of an unpublished manuscript that he kindly made available to us at the *Minnesota Center for Philosophy of Science* when he was a visitor here in 1962. Again I summarize briefly but must take full responsibility for any deviation or inadvertent misrepresentation. The position is almost completely parallel to the one based on falsifiability; it is merely more general. Our theories should be subjected to *all* kinds of critical scrutiny that we are able to devise. For example, if one theory solves the relevant problems in a less simple, less general way than does another, the latter theory is preferable. A theory that not only solves the original problems but suggests new problems or suggests answers to problems in another area of inquiry is better (or less bad) than its competitors that fail to do this, *ceteris paribus*. To these examples, taken from Popper, I shall add at this point only one of my own. Given two theories, both of which are unfalsifiable but which have verifiable (or confirmable) consequences, if one theory has had such consequences verified, and the other has not, then the latter has survived critical scrutiny less well than the former. The theory that all men are mortal, though unfalsifiable, has withstood the years of scrutiny better than the theory that natural phosphorus is radioactive, for there have been many instances of verification of consequences of the former (every time a man dies) and none of the latter (no decay of the phosphorus 15 atom has ever been detected). As a general approach, I do not see how Popper's *critical approach* can be faulted. It does not assure us of success or, even, likely success in our search for knowledge, and it does not even allow us to know that we have succeeded when and if we ever do. But it is generally agreed today that no program can provide these assurances. If we take all of the theories that are available, always attempting to obtain new ones, subject them to the most severe examination available, and retain provisionally those that have fared less badly, have we not done, at a given time, the very best that we can? Is this not enough to *vindicate* (in Feigl's sense) our general approach? Perhaps the most immediate objection is that the approach is *so* general that it provides us with virtually nothing. The objector might go on to ask: What about the standards of criticism themselves? My answer, and I believe it coincides with Popper's is that, for the most part, these are to be considered as theories themselves, or rather, based on theories and are, thus, subject to further critical scrutiny. This, of course, does give rise to a regress; but it is a vicious one only for those who seek the unattainable; some solid, *logically certified* foundation of knowledge. Nothing is, in principle, immune to criticism, including any given standard of criticism. But we can do no more than the best that we can; due to limitations of time, energy, intelligence and other considerations, there are always practical restrictions to the extent of our critical assessment.

With one exception, which will be discussed later, we have come, with Popper's guidance, as far as logical or purely methodological considerations can bring us. However, those who seek to expand the frontiers of knowledge, even including, in my opinion, philosophers, need not restrict themselves to such considerations. This is fortunate; for, there remain legitimate and important questions that are so far unanswered. For example, it seems to be undeniable that most of us still "feel in our bones" that we *do* have *positive* reasons to believe that the sun will rise tomorrow or that the kinetic theory of gases is closer to the truth and, indeed, better confirmed than the theory that phosphorus 15 is radioactive with a half life of 10^{25} years. Is this "feeling" about our beliefs and are the beliefs themselves completely irrational or arational? It might be thought that Popper, in effect, gave a negative answer to this question by proposing his *degree of corroboration*. But he rightly denies this explicitly: "As to degree of corroboration, it . . . must not be interpreted, therefore, as a degree of the rationality of our belief in the *truth* of [a hypothesis] *h* . . . . Rather, it is a measure of the rationality of *accepting*, tentatively, a problematic guess, knowing that it is a guess—but one that has undergone searching examinations" (p. 415).

I shall argue that there *are* positive reasons both for the "feeling" about such beliefs and for the beliefs themselves. These reasons do not, however, by any means consist *merely* of observational evidence plus some *logical* relation that is supposed to transmit support from the evidence to our hypotheses. Popper's critique of induction is not abridged. The situation is actually quite simple. Our belief in the prediction that the sun will rise tomorrow is justified not in any purely logical manner by the evidence but by the *contingent theory* that the sun rises every day (or by a more general theory of the solar system), a theory from which the prediction follows deductively. It will immediately be asked, of course, "Does *evidence* play no *role*? And what about this '*contingent theory*' in its turn?" Well, if the latter is to be *justified* at all it must be by virtue of still another (contingent) theory. How this potential regress may be arrested and how evidence enters into the picture will be discussed in the following, final section, in which a *contingent* theory of confirmation will be sketched. Being contingent, it will not provide a *logic* of confirmation. It is contingent for two, not unrelated, reasons. First the theory of confirmation will be justified on the basis of another contingent theory and, secondly, any assertion that a given hypothesis is confirmed to such and such extent, given the specified evidence, will be a contingent assertion.

III

Rather than use terms that have already been preempted by other theories such as "degree of confirmation" or "degree of corroboration," I shall introduce a hopefully neutral term, "confirmation index." The value of the confirmation index is a measure of how well confirmed (in a sense to be explained) a theory is, given a specified amount of evidence. It satisfies the calculus of probability. It is, indeed, an objective probability in the sense of the frequency (or, perhaps, the propensity) interpretation. I shall first outline the program dogmatically and then discuss its application and justification.

For purposes of exposition only, it is convenient to begin by using the notion of the probability of the truth of an hypothesis or a theory. Many either regard this as illegitimate or hold that the value of such a probability is always zero. This will not be a problem, however; for I shall eventually discard the notion completely and replace it with the probability that the *verisimilitude* or truth-likeness of an hypothesis is above a certain desirably high level.

The lines along which I begin were suggested by attempts of Salmon[11] to apply a certain form of Bayes's theorem to obtain the probability of hypotheses in a frequency sense. According to him, if Bayes's theorem is written

$$P(B, A \cap C) = \frac{P(B,A) \times P(C, A \cap B)}{P(C,A)}$$

and the hypothesis or theory in question is abbreviated by "H," it is then convenient to introduce the class, A, as consisting of all hypotheses *like* H in certain relevant, important respects. H may be a theory or it may be a singular proposition such as a prediction. B is the class of all true hypotheses; it may be convenient to narrow it to include just the true hypotheses in a given area of inquiry. The probability that H is true is a probability of a single case (the *"weight"* to use Reichenbach's and Salmon's terminology) and, as is usual with frequency interpretations, is defined, in this case, as equal to P(B,D) where D is, hopefully, the most appropriate "reference class" to which H is to be assigned. (In this case, D will later turn out to be $A \cap C$.) If H is being subjected to a test by observing whether one of its consequences, O, obtains, then according to Salmon, C refers to whether O does or does not obtain. This seems to give rise to grave difficulties; I propose, therefore, to change the interpretation of C as follows. Consider H as being subjected to a test, call it E. If the outcome of E is O, then, by definition H *passes* E; if the outcome is ~O, H *fails* E. This stipulation holds whether or not O is a consequence of H. Now let C be the class of all hypotheses that pass tests at least as severe as E. The application of Bayes's theorem now seems straightforward. $P(B, A \cap C)$ is the relative frequency of true hypotheses among hypotheses *like* H that have passed tests as severe as E, which seems a satisfactory measure of the "posterior probability" of H. P(B,A) is the relative frequency of true hypotheses like H (irrespective of whether they pass tests like E or not), obviously a straightforward measure of the "prior probability" of H. Now if H implies O, then $P(C, A \cap B) = 1$, since this is the portion of true hypotheses like H that pass tests as severe as E, and since a true hypothesis will pass *any* (properly executed) test. $P(C,A)$ is the relative frequency of hypotheses that pass tests as severe as E among hypotheses like H. This will obviously be an *inverse* function of the severity of the test, which, in its turn, is an inverse function of the prior probability of the favorable evidence statement, O; so that $P(C,A)$ becomes a *direct* function of the prior probability of O and, thus, *ceteris paribus*, a good measure of the prior probability of the evidence. The values for $P(B,A)$ and $P(C,A)$ used in computing $P(B, A \cap C)$ may sometimes come from *previous* applications of Bayes's theorem in connection with *previous* tests but, on pain of infinite regress, eventually must come from guesses, hunches, "intuition," or some other nonevidential source. This problem will be discussed later.

Before proceeding, it is necessary to introduce the notion of *verisimilitude*, or *nearness to the truth* in something like the sense used by Popper. In some of his more recent writings he has stressed the crucially important fact that, although in science we do search for truth, "we want more than mere truth. . .we want interesting truth. . .we want more truth."[12] Moreover, for reasons that I shall not discuss here, it seems reasonable to hold that virtually any theory that we shall ever have will be, speaking strictly and literally, false. However, we should be quite pleased with a theory that affords a certain nearness to the truth, and we should prefer one that is closer to the truth than any available competitor. The notion of being close (or closer) to the truth (i.e., the notion of having high verisimilitude) finally adopted should be similar to that occurring in such intuitively comfortable examples as the following. Let us suppose that I am six feet and three and one-half inches tall. Then the proposition that I am six feet tall is fairly close to the truth; that I am six feet three inches tall is, however, closer. Since the planets move in ellipses (with low eccentricity), it is closer to the truth to say that the planets move in circles than to say that they move in rectangular paths. Presumably Newtonian mechanics is closer to the truth than Aristotelian mechanics and relativistic mechanics is even closer. Popper has developed a concept of the verisimilitude of a statement based on the difference between the *truth content* of the statement, a measure of the true logical consequences of the statement, on the one hand, and its *falsity content*, on the other. The latter is related to, though not identical with, the set of false consequences of the statement. Whether this is completely satisfactory I shall not consider. Since my program does not aim at anything like the assignment of precise quantitative values to the *confirmation index*, I believe that Popper's verisimilitude definition or even a rough intuitive notion of nearness to the truth will suffice for its purpose.

Let us now take the "B" in Bayes's theorem, as considered above, to refer *not* to the class of *true* hypotheses but to the class of hypotheses with *verisimilitude equal to or greater than a certain reasonably high value.* $P(B, A \cap C)$ will now be the relative frequency of hypotheses with verisimilitude above a certain desirably high level among hypotheses like H that have passed tests as severe as E and will thus be a measure of the posterior probability *that H has a verisimilitude above the level in question.* This we now call the *confirmation index* of H. $P(B, A)$ becomes a measure of the prior probability that H's verisimilitude is above this level, etc.

It has been emphasized above that in most cases, a theory, H, does not *logically entail* any observation O. This gives rise to the difficult problem of how to estimate the value of $P(C, A \cap B)$ on the right-hand side of Bayes's theorem. For unless H entails O, this term will no longer, in general, be equal to one. In order to attend to this it will be convenient to adopt the following (conditional) definition of "probability."

If the relative frequencies of members of the class Y remain reasonably constant among most reasonably sized, randomly sequenced subclasses of X, then the *probability* of Y on X, $P(Y, X)$, is the relative frequency of Y's among X's averaged over all such subclasses.

It might be objected that if the antecedent of this conditional definition does not obtain for a given case (or in general) then "probability" is not defined for such a case. But this seems to be a merit; for it highlights the fact that, unless the antecedent does obtain, no viable concept of probability will be applicable. Moreover, I believe that the assumption that the antecedent obtains in a great many cases should be added to the "justificatory theory" that I shall introduce later and that it can be vindicated in the same manner that will be outlined for this entire program. Incorporating the limit of the relative frequency into the definition seems neither necessary, sufficient, nor desirable for a viable concept of probability, for the difficulties of the *long run* and of the *short run* seem to me insurmountable. These arise, of course, because there is absolutely no logical relation between the limit of the frequency and the frequency in any finite subclass no matter how large. (Note, however, if the sequence of subclasses becomes infinite, the existence of the limit of the relative frequency is guaranteed if the antecedent of the definition holds.) The occurrence of the vague notions designated by *"reasonably constant"* and *"most"* in the definition seems advisable. What the exact values will be in a given case will depend at least in part on the purposes of the investigation, e.g., What degree of precision do we need or want? And, of course, the provisions built into this definition of "probability" enable us to compute (binomial law, law of large numbers, etc.) what the probability that we will get such precision will be.[13]

In the special and simple case where H is a *statistical* hypothesis *and* where O is itself a statistical assertion, an assertion about the relative frequency in a sample of the population involving the same two classes mentioned in H, then this likelihood can be computed (with special ease, given the definition of "probability" above). Incidentally, referring back to Bayes's theorem, it can be seen that these considerations show that, so long as the ratio of P(B,A) to P(C,A) remains constant, P(B,A∩C) will vary linearly with P(C,A∩B) and thus, the statistical hypothesis, H, that confers maximum likelihood on the statistical evidence, O, will have maximum probability (weight). But unless this constancy obtains or some singularly appropriate covariation of these prior probabilities occurs, these two maxima will not, in general, coincide. Thus, it cannot be allowed that maximum likelihood methods make no use of prior probabilities. For, to justify choosing the hypothesis that confers maximum likelihood, we tacitly assume that this happy kind of covariation of prior probabilities obtains. In practice, of course, in these simple statistical cases, we try to make P(B,A) and P(C,A) equal to each other and *a fortiori*, their ratio constant, by taking large samples and employing other suitable sampling techniques.[14]

The cases where H does not imply O for some other reason than those simple statistical ones are, of course, the difficult ones. They seem to be the rule rather than the exception in medicine, psychology, and the social sciences, and I have argued that they are perhaps the rule rather than the exception in the physical sciences as well. From case to case, the failure of H to imply O may be due to any one or to any combination of the following:

(1) Simplifying assumptions of many different kinds that are almost certainly false may be used, e.g., in kinetic theory, assumption that there are no forces of attraction or repulsion between molecules and that the molecules have zero diameter; or, in a problem in hydrodynamics, that the fluid is incompressible and has zero viscosity; or, in doing computations, that certain terms in a series may be dropped, etc. These may be handled as follows: H, the ideal, closer-to-the-truth theory (if only we knew it) is "replaced" by a similar, simplified theory H'. Although we believe H' to be false, we hope that it is close enough to the truth (hopefully expressed by H) so that either the preponderance of its consequences are true or the preponderance of its consequences are quite close to the truth. Thus if, say, H' implies O, the proposition that the pointer will read 0.95, and the observed reading is 0.92, we might say that O is close enough to the truth to allow that H' passed the test in question. In such cases the value of P(C,A∩B) hopefully remains near unity.

(2) In addition to H, auxiliary hypotheses, unobservable initial conditions, etc., are essentially involved in deriving O. As we have seen, this is almost always the case. In the simplest instance, when the only additional assumption, A, is *unproblematic* "background" knowledge, we can assert A

and, since $(H \cdot A) \rightarrow O$ is logically equivalent to $A \rightarrow (H \rightarrow O)$, we can *deduce* $H \rightarrow O$ ("$\rightarrow$" to be read "implies," not "entails"). Unfortunately however, an important case, discussed earlier and one that seems to obtain almost universally, arises when A or one or more of its conjuncts is an hypothesis about *unobservable* initial conditions, e.g., that the system is at thermodynamic (or chemical, or etc.) equilibrium or that the apparatus is sufficiently free of undetected contaminating substances, etc. These can, in principle, be given the same treatment recommended for other kinds of auxiliary hypotheses. In actual practice we use mostly hunches and intuitions that these initial conditions do obtain. When such hunches reach the conscious level and become explicitly formulated, what we usually do is to entertain the pious hope that they are close enough to the truth so that the works will not be too much messed up. If the experiment comes out to suit us, we tend promptly to forget this aspect of it. Usually not much is said about it in the scientific literature. The assumption that, in spite of this, nature is kind enough to let things work out pretty well, fairly often is something else that perhaps can be vindicated in the manner discussed later. Similar considerations apply when some of the auxiliary theories (as opposed to singular hypotheses) cannot be regarded as unproblematic but which, nevertheless, good scientific conscience indicates should be used—for example, recall the discussion of the "detection" of the neutrino, above. In such cases, there are two main alternatives: we can consider the hypothesis being tested to be not just H, but H', the entire (dubious) conjunction of H with auxiliary hypotheses, etc., or we can still regard H as being the hypothesis under test and estimate the value of $P(C, A \cap B)$ to be high or low depending, respectively, on whether our estimate of the prior probability of the auxiliary assumptions is high or low.

(3) H has no falsifiable consequences, or H has no falsifiable observational consequences. Here, of course, we can always keep adding auxiliary assumptions until we finally have a falsifiable conjunction. But quite often this is neither practicable, necessary, nor desirable. For it will often be the case that, due to mixed quantification of an appropriate kind, H or H·A will have verifiable consequences even though it has no falsifiable ones. Simple examples: *all men are mortal (for every man there is a time at which he dies); all crystalline solids have melting points.* Given the initial condition that Jones is a man, the former implies that Jones will die at some time which, in turn, is verified by Jones's dying August 1, 1966. And, of course, we have here the usual situation vis-à-vis Bayes's theorem: if the prior probability of the hypothesis is not too low and if that of the verifiable consequence is not *too* high, then the verification of the latter will increase the confirmation index of the hypothesis appreciably. Psychoanalytic practice is said to abound in such instances where, moreover, the prior probability of the verified consequence is extremely low. And this is why the analyst might claim that, after observ-

ing perhaps only a few such (*unreproducible*) instances, he is not too moved
by hard-nosed critics demanding predictability, falsifiability, and repro-
ducibility. However, further complications arise for psychoanalysis in considerations to follow.

(4) H (together with known initial conditions) does not imply O, nor
have we been able to *formulate* plausible auxiliary hypotheses that will do the
trick, but we have strong hunches that there exist certain true (or near true) as
yet *un*formulated hypotheses and that certain appropriate but *unknown* initial conditions obtain such that the conjunction of H and these hunches does
entail O (or statistically imply it), i.e.:

$$\text{(i)} \qquad (\exists I) \; [I{\cdot}A{\cdot}H{\cdot}(H{\cdot}I{\cdot}A{\rightarrow}O)]$$

Note first that no essential difficulty arises from the fact that we can always
trivially take A to be simply the hypothesis that H implies (*not* entails) O. Of
course we *can*, but in most cases, as practising scientists, especially in psychology and the social sciences, we do *not*. Our H's (theories, guesses,
hunches) are usually such that even if $\sim$O obtains we do not take H to be
conclusively refuted. Moreover, even if we strongly believe that H does *imply*
O we often feel that this, in turn, should be *explained*, e.g., by the fact that
$(\exists A) \; (H{\cdot}A$ *entails* O).

Obviously, as far as confirmation and disconfirmation is concerned, this
kind of situation is extremely complex and indeterminate. Nothing like a
comprehensive treatment of it can be given here. Some of the earlier considerations still apply. It might seem ridiculous to even mention Bayes's
theorem in such cases. But I feel that it still has some value both as a proposal
(not to be taken too literally) and as an account that parallels *some* important
features of actual scientific practice. As indicated earlier, I would not take
seriously any actual numerical values to be plugged in in order to make
specific computations. My attitude toward this is the same as that of Popper
toward such values for degree of corroboration and for verisimilitude. The
most interesting and most difficult factor is again $P(C, A{\cap}B)$. The scientist's
estimate of the value of this will be a *function of* (though it is *not* to be *identified with*) his estimate of something we might call *the extent to which H implies O*. Except in special cases, this will be a function of (again, not identified
with) the strength of his hunch that there exists an A that is true (or has high
verisimilitude) *and* that the correspondingly appropriate but unknown initial
conditions do obtain such that the conjunction of these with H entails O. In a
clinical situation, for example, to explain a present pathological condition,
the psychotherapist might be led to hypothesize that certain initial conditions
obtained, i.e., that there occurred certain incidents that may or may not be
specified in the patient's childhood that caused his hate for his father to exceed the normal Oedipal amount and that, moreover, there is a true auxiliary

hypothesis, A, (or one close to the truth) that would explain why these incidents had this effect. Examples from psychology and the social sciences are the most striking and the messiest, but there are numerous similar cases in medicine and biology, and from the physical sciences as well. From my own experience I should say that in workaday chemical research on everyday problems, such situations obtain more often that not. In the physical sciences it is usually easier, as research proceeds, to make reasonable guesses at specific explicitly formulated auxiliary hypotheses, i.e., to fill in some of the promissory notes by replacing '$(\exists A)$ (...A...)' with '(...A_1...)'. But the ease of doing this is a matter of degree only, and even after such a process is completed the other difficulties for falsification discussed above remain.

Falsifiability is still a *desideratum*, but more in the sense of a regulative, virtually unattainable ideal than as a means of distinguishing what is "scientific" from what is not. Do not such considerations as these reveal the undesirability and the futility of attempts to discover any set of purely methodological principles that will provide such a distinction? Everything is metaphysical, although some things are less metaphysical than others. Incidentally, it also seems that there is at most a slippery slope between the so-called "context of discovery" and the "context of justification." Perhaps we are moving away from the former and getting closer to the latter as we replace more and more components of a given theory that have the form of '$(\exists A)$ (...A...)' with those of the form of '(...A_1...)'. This concludes the discussion of the various kinds of cases that arise when falsifiability does not obtain. It is intended to be suggestive only and not to be exhaustive or comprehensive.

Whenever $\sim$O rather than O obtains, then by definition, H fails the test E and, thus is not a member of $A \cap C$ but rather of $A \cap \overline{C}$. The relevant expression for Bayes's theorem becomes

$$P(B, A \cap \overline{C}) = \frac{P(B,A)P(\overline{C}, A \cap B)}{P(\overline{C}, A)} = \frac{P(B,A)[1 - P(C, A \cap B)]}{1 - [P(C,A)]}$$

Once again this seems to provide a good "reconstruction" of our intuitive expectations. Even though H fails the test, the measure of its posterior probability, $P(B, A \cap C)$ will not be zero, of course, except in the limiting case where both of the following hold (1) the verisimilitude requirement is set at the maximum, i.e., B is taken as the class of all *true* hypotheses *and* (2) H *does* imply O. In this case $P(C, A \cap B) = 1$ and, thus, $P(B, A \cap \overline{C}) = 0$. Where H makes O quite likely (not necessarily in the simple statistical sense but because, perhaps, $H \cdot X \rightarrow O$ and the estimated probability of the auxiliary hypothesis X is fairly high) $P(C, A \cap B)$ will be high and, thus $1 - P(C, A \cap B)$ and $P(B, A \cap \overline{C})$ will be low. We will say that the confirmation index of H is quite low or that H has been disconfirmed. Analogous considerations for other cases give analogously satisfactory results. We thus have a means of estimating the extent to which failures to pass tests disconfirm hypotheses.

I shall now try to defend this theory of confirmation, first by citing some of its advantages and then by attempting to justify it on the basis of another (contingent, scientific) theory. This other theory, in turn, will not be *justified* but only *vindicated*, vindicated in a sense similar to but not identical with that of Feigl.[15] Vindication will be by Popper's *critical approach*.

One considerable advantage is due to the fact that the *confirmation index* is an objective probability in the straightforward sense of the frequency interpretation. No confusion about this should arise from the fact that we, or the scientist, eventually have to depend on guesses and hunches to estimate the values of the prior probabilities to be used in the (rough and qualitative) computations involving Bayes's theorem. For we are making guesses about the objective values of certain relative frequencies.[16] For example, the prior probability of the hypothesis H is given by the factor P(B,A), which is the relative frequency of hypotheses with high verisimilitude among hypotheses like H in the relevant respects. The fact that we have to guess at this frequency no more makes the frequency itself subjective than does our guessing about tomorrow's weather transform the actual state of the weather when it transpires into something subjective. This, of course, highlights the difference between this theory and *personalist* or *subjectivist* ones. For the latter, the prior probabilities, by definition, simply are certain actual degrees of subjective certainty. There is, therefore, not even a logical possibility of being mistaken about them once these degrees of belief are determined. But in my sense of prior probability, i.e., certain relative frequencies, my beliefs about them no matter how firmly held may be grossly in error.

By virtue of taking the *confirmation index* in terms of the probability of a theory's having a certain verisimilitude rather than the probability of its truth, any objections involving the contention that the probability of a universal hypothesis is always zero are completely removed. Moreover, Popper's paradoxes that arise from identifying the extent to which certain evidence supports a hypothesis with a probability[17] do not arise for the *confirmation index*; for it is a measure of evidential support *and* the hypothesis' prior probability rather than of the former alone. It seems so obvious as to be hardly worth mentioning that this confirmation theory completely avoids such puzzles as Hempel's "paradoxes of confirmation" and Goodman's "grue-green" riddle. These paradoxes arise from—and, indeed are legitimate *reductios* of—taking confirmation to be a purely logical—a purely syntactical—matter. The hypothesis expressed by "all crows are black" (as well as by "all non-black things are non-crows," of course) is confirmed appreciably by a black crow and only negligibly by a non-black non-crow simply because, in view of the background knowledge, the prior probability of the next crow's being black is *much* smaller than the prior probability of the next non-black object's being a non-crow, the latter, even independently of the blackness of crows, being very close to *one*. Similarly a green emerald yields a much higher confirmation index for the hypothesis that all emeralds are green than it does for the hypothesis that all emeralds are grue because the prior probability of the latter is so much smaller—indeed very close to zero. How do we know this? Well, such an hypothesis is an outrage to our scientific and commonsense intuition and, moreover, we know (from background knowledge) that being observed at a particular time should have no effect on the color of emeralds. *Of course*, hypotheses that were once considered outrages have become accepted later. But we do not claim that the prior probability of all emeralds being grue is zero but only that it is near zero and thus, *evidence* with prior probability near zero will have to turn up before we will give the hypothesis an appreciable posterior probability.

Finally, I shall sketch the (contingent, scientific) theory that justifies the adoption of my theory of confirmation (itself a contingent, scientific theory). I have already defended the legitimacy of the use of a probability in the sense of relative frequency for the confirmation index. Moreover, in any kind of frequency interpretation, the axioms and theorems of the calculus of probability become truths of arithmetic, or rather, of set theory. Therefore there can be no question about the legitimacy of the application of Bayes's theorem. The only thing that remains to be justified is the assumption that some of our guesses, hunches, and intuitions have prior probabilities appreciably greater than zero and that our *estimates of* prior probabilities are not too wide of the mark.

The (scientific) theory that I propose is designed to explain the fact that we have knowledge or, if this way of putting it offends, that we sometimes seem to make reasonably good guesses about our environment and ourselves, or, at the very least, we *do believe* strongly some of the hypotheses, guesses, etc., that we propose, and even the latter modest proposition should be *explained*. According to the theory, we have innate constitutional dispositions and innate capacities to acquire other dispositions under appropriate circumstances. Among these are dispositions to respond to certain stimuli by making certain kinds of guesses (i.e., by proposing certain hypotheses) and by testing these guesses, discarding some, replacing them by others, etc. More specifically, we have innate capacities to acquire abilities to make *some* guesses with prior probabilities appreciably greater than zero as well as abilities to order competing hypotheses on the basis of their prior probabilities, thereby acquiring a basis for selecting some hypotheses as more worthy of further testing, evaluating, etc., *and* as being more reliable as "guides of life" for predicting the future, etc.

Similar ideas about the *origin* of knowledge, or knowledge claims, (the role of such a theory in the "context of discovery") have been proposed before, e.g., by Popper himself (*C.&R.*); Bertrand Russell;[18] Donald T. Campbell (this volume); Konrad Lorenz;[19] and others. However, the point that I am making is that, if this theory about our constitutional capacities is true, or close to the truth, then it *justifies*, to some extent at least, our confidence in our claims to general knowledge; *I am using this theory in the "context of justification."* The theory entails that a significant portion of our knowledge claims are true or close to the truth; thus the justification, *assuming the theory to be true*, is obvious, straightforward, and *deductive*. More specifically, the theory *justifies* a significant portion of our knowledge claims because it entails that the (contingent) *theory of confirmation* that I have proposed is true. This theory of confirmation, in turn, entails that a significant portion of the hypotheses that we, in fact, propose have (objective) prior probabilities appreciably greater than zero, that we are often able correctly to order competing hypotheses on the basis of their prior probabilities, and that a fair portion of instances of evidence supporting our hypotheses have prior probabilities that are appreciably less than one.

Of course, I am not making the absurd claim that in practice we self-consciously ask ourselves questions such as, "Now what is the prior probability of such and such an hypothesis and what value do we get for the posterior probability when we apply Bayes's theorem?" But we often *do* do something that gives very similar results; for example, we do sometimes order competing hypotheses on the basis of their intuitive plausibilities (which may be thought of as an estimate of their prior probabilities), we do consider an hypothesis quite highly confirmed when it makes surprising predictions that are verified (which corresponds to the fact that, with Bayes's theorem, a low prior probability for the evidence gives, *ceteris paribus*, a high posterior probability for the hypothesis), etc. The theory also postulates that this kind of *implicit* estimate of prior probabilities and implicit application of Bayes's theorem occurs also at the preconscious, the unconscious, and even, perhaps, at the physiological level. The constitutional dispositions enabling us to do this in a way that often succeeds have been acquired by the processes of mutation and natural selection. The individual in acquiring improved capacities acquires the ability to get closer and closer to the truth, and thus is better equipped to survive. In short, this confirmation theory, that I am claiming we all use implicitly, gives reasonably good results as often as it does because natural selection has caused the theory to be genetically "wired into" us. The theory, thus, not only explains the fact that we have acquired knowledge in the *past* (or, at worst, it explains the fact that we strongly believe that we have acquired such knowledge), but it also explains the survival and the accomplishments of the species; a charge of even prima facie *ad hocness* is thereby avoided.

It is acknowledged, of course, that attempts to justify modes of confirmation on the basis of contingent assumptions are as old as the "problem of induction," itself, and indeed, Hume himself offered such a "solution." And it is usually objected that such attempts are of no avail, since the contingent assumptions stand as much in need of evidential support as do any other contingent propositions and we are, thus, so the objection continues, off on an infinite regress. The answer to this objection gives the core of my strategy. The theory of confirmation offered herein is *justified relative* to the theory about constitutional capacities just offered. *If* the latter is true, the former is *justified*, as is explained above. Now, of course, the question arises about the status of the latter—the status of the *justificatory* theory. For this theory, *qua* justificatory theory, no *justification* is attempted; it is acknowledged that, on pain of infinite regress or circularity, we *cannot* offer *evidence* (using Bayes's theorem, etc.) for the theory *qua* justificatory theory. But an attempt at a kind of *vindication* using something like Popper's critical approach proceeds as follows. *Some* theory or other is called for to explain the fact that we have acquired knowledge (or the fact that we *believe* that we have), the fact that the species has survived as well as it has and the fact that it has come up with such accomplishments as flush toilets, moon ships, and hydrogen bombs, etc. Now I claim that the theory that I have just proposed stands up best to critical scrutiny than any competitor that has been proposed. We are therefore *vindicated* in tentatively accepting it. Once we have done so, it, in turn, *justifies* the (contingent) theory of confirmation that I have proposed.

My difference with Popper on this issue can now be put simply. He would use the *critical approach* on every theory and, thus, he claims that no positive evidential support can be given *any* theory. I use his *critical approach* to *vindicate one theory*, which, in its turn, *justifies* a confirmation theory whereby it *is*, in principle, possible to give positive evidential support for all other contingent theories of science and everyday life.

GROVER MAXWELL

MINNESOTA CENTER FOR PHILOSOPHY OF SCIENCE
UNIVERSITY OF MINNESOTA
APRIL, 1970

APPENDIX I

Purely Existential Statements and the Criterion of Demarcation

In his discussion of purely existential propositions, Popper considers the periodic classification of the chemical elements as originally proposed by Mendeleef (pp. 69 ff.). This classification has been taken to mean that, for every "gap" in the chart, there existed an undiscovered element awaiting either detection or preparation by nuclear transformations. Specifically, he considers the discovery of Hafnium (atomic number 72) and points out (pp. 69-70) that "all attempts to find it were in vain until Bohr succeeded in predicting several of its properties by deducing them from his theory. But Bohr's theory and those of its conclusions which were relevant to this element and which helped to bring about its discovery are far from being isolated purely existential statements. They are strictly universal statements." Popper's choice of this example and his disposal of the difficulty it raises are not themselves without difficulties, however. Long before Bohr, Mendeleef himself predicted the discovery of "ekasilicon" (germanium) and several other elements and gave surprisingly accurate estimates of many of their chemical and physical properties. More seriously, a statement of the form, 'There exists an element of atomic number so-and-so (or atomic weight such and such) that has the properties, P, Q, R,. . .' is as "purely existential" and as nonfalsifiable as 'There exists an element of atomic number so-and-so'. And it certainly seems odd to rule that the answer to the question, "Does an element with atomic number 72 exist?" is metaphysical unless it includes a statement of the theory which facilitated the element's discovery. As a matter of fact, the existence of undiscovered elements is not *logically* implied by Mendeleef's classification; the statement that the "gaps" in the chart can be filled in, though *suggested by*, is logically independent of the classification itself. So that statements such as, "There exists an element with atomic number 72" or, more generally, "There exists an element for each empty space in the periodic chart" have the logical status of independent postulates in the Mendeleef theory. Now Popper adds (p. 70 n.) that an existential statement ". . .if taken *in a context* with other statements,. . .*may in some cases* [all italics are Popper's] add to the empirical content of the whole context: it may enrich the theory to which it belongs, and may add to its degree of falsifiability or testability. In this case, the theoretical system including the existential statement in question is to be described as scientific rather than metaphysical." Now I should say that the addition of the relevant existential statements to Mendeleef's bare classificatory theory *does* enrich the theory and add to its content—though not to its "empirical content" in the Popperian sense. It renders the theory more confirmable *and* more disconfirmable in the following sense. If some or all of the predicted elements are discovered, the theory would become much more highly confirmed. If all of a large number of sincere, varied, and ingenious attempts to find such elements or to prepare them failed, the theory, of course, would not be falsified, but it would be disconfirmed and we would be justified in tentatively rejecting its existential components. However, since the existential statements are logically independent of the rest of the theory, I cannot see how they add to the *falsifiability* of the theory or make it more testable in Popper's sense of "testability."

It seems that such considerations make a good prima facie case for including purely existential statements in the corpus of science, but it may be *only* a prima facie case. It may well be that the advantages of employing the *criterion of demarcation* are great enough to more than compensate for the exclusion of (logically) isolated existential statements; furthermore, the existential statements which we have been considering may be replaced by universal ones without irreparable damage. For example, the statement 'There is an element with atomic number 72 and which has the properties P, Q, R. . .' may be replaced by 'All substances composed solely of the element with atomic weight 72 have the properties P, Q, R. . .'. Attempts to falsify the latter would be very similar to attempts to verify the former. Perhaps Popper intended something like this in the passage quoted from pp. 69-70. One difficulty remains: if failures to falsify the universal statement were due to the element's nonexistence or to failure to discover it, the universal statement could still be retained as a part, though *perhaps* not as a *confirmed* (or corroborated[20]) part, of the theory (according to Popper); but the existential statement, thus disconfirmed (in the sense adumbrated above), would be tentatively rejected. This seems odd. (We are considering these statements in the context of Mendeleef's theory and *not* as derivations from modern atomic theory.) Again, I do not believe that this objection is fatal. The universal statement could remain as a sort of "dangler," but as a harmless one; for the nonexistence or nondiscovery of the element would guarantee that there are no acceptable statements of initial conditions which would enable us to derive faulty predictions from the dangler.

The following might seem to be more serious. The failure of any falsification attempt due to nonexistence or nondiscovery of the entities in question would fail to reject or to disconfirm (and, unless the "paradoxes of confirmation" are circumvented, would corroborate) *any* consistent universal statement about such entities. Thus the failure of a sincere and prolonged attempt to find unicorns would fail to falsify (and perhaps would corroborate) the statement 'All unicorns have two hearts and one lung' as well as the statement 'No unicorns have two hearts and one lung'. I regard such an objection as trifling, partly for the reasons given above and partly because I am confident that a minor modification of Popper's theory would eliminate such examples. (Perhaps he has already implicitly or explicitly done so, and I have overlooked this fact.) Furthermore, while a philosophical theory should attempt to dispose of all putative counterexamples, I do not believe that temporary failure to do so justifies rejection of the theory when the examples are farfetched and unimportant.

I conclude that the objection from purely existential statements leaves Popper's theory viable, *provided* the theory offers certain advantages. On the other hand, the objection does make a prima facie case for the desirability of seeking an alternative theory which offers comparable advantages and which admits such statements as empirical and scientific, for we have seen how they can play useful roles in science and how, according to any usual sense of "confirmation," they may be confirmed or disconfirmed. Now Popper admits, indeed *insists*, that nonempirical ("metaphysical") statements may play roles of great importance in empirical science. Why, then, should such statements be labeled "unscientific" and be placed on the "wrong" side of a line separating empirical statements from "metaphysical" ones? And since existential statements are, in general, verifiable[21] and often *verified*, this seems to be a sufficient (though by no means a necessary) condition for terming them "empirical."

APPENDIX II

The latest definition[22] given by Popper, I believe, is

$$C(t,e) = \frac{P(e,t) - P(e)}{P(e,t) - P(e.t) + P(e)}$$

where $C(t,e)$ is the degree of corroboration of the theory of interest, t, upon evidence, e, $P(e,t)$ is the logical probability of e, upon t, $P(e)$ is the ("absolute") logical probability of e, etc., and '$e.t$' is the conjunction of 'e' and 't'. In the example above, since 'Jones dies on October 5, 1969', entails, 'Jones dies', we can safely take the latter to express our evidence e. The "theory" that all men are mortal will, of course, be t. Now since t (conjoined with the *unproblematic* "initial condition" expressed by 'Jones is a man') entails e, we have from probability calculus that $P(e,t) = 1$. Also, since t unproblematically implies e, it follows that $P(e.t) = P(t)$ and the expression becomes

$$C(t,e) = \frac{1 - P(e)}{1 - P(t) + P(e)}$$

Now $P(t)$ can be assigned any consistent value and the results will be analogous, but since, for Popper the probability of a universal statement such as t is always zero, let us so take it here for simplicity.

We now have $C(t,e) = \dfrac{1 - P(e)}{1 + P(e)}$

Let us assign $P(e)$ any consistent value, say 0.90. We observe that Jones dies on October 5, which entails an instance of t — an instance that we take as evidence e *for* t. Substituting '0.90' for 'e' we compute a value of

$$\frac{0.10}{1.9} = \frac{1}{19} = 0.053 \text{ for } C(t,e).$$

Now, suppose we observe that Smith dies on October 6. We now have two instances of t as evidence. Let us call the instance entailed by Smith's death 'e''. The total evidence now is the conjunction of 'e' and 'e''. Substituting in the expression above we get

$$C(t,e.e') = \frac{1 - P(e.e')}{1 + P(e.e')}$$

assuming e and e' to be mutually independent (Popper *does* so), we get from probability calculus:

$$\begin{aligned} P(e.e') &= P(e) \times P(e') \\ &= 0.90 \times 0.90 \\ &= 0.81 \end{aligned}$$

Substituting this result into the previous expression, we have

$$C(t,e.e') = \frac{1 - 0.81}{1 + 0.81} = \frac{0.19}{1.81} = 0.11$$

We see that Smith's death raises the degree of corroboration of (the nonfalsifiable theory) t on the available evidence from 0.053 to 0.11.

NOTES

[1] In what follows in this section, the references, unless otherwise stated, are to K. R. Popper, *The Logic of Scientific Discovery* (London: Hutchinson, 1959; New York: Basic Books, 1959). Hereinafter cited as *L.Sc.D.* (The main portion of this book was originally published as *Logik der Forschung* in Vienna in 1934.)

[2] As will appear subsequently, *explanation* will, in the main, be identified with *hypothetico-deductive* explanation.

[3] The gravity of this difficulty was pointed out to me by Professor Paul E. Meehl.

[4] K. R. Popper, *Conjectures & Refutations: The Growth of Scientific Knowledge* (London: Routledge & Kegan Paul, 1963; New York: Basic Books, 1963), p. 58 n. Hereinafter cited as *C.&R.*

[5] See, e.g., *L.Sc.D.*, pp. 82-83.

[6] For still other striking examples see J. W. N. Watkins, "Confirmable and Influential Metaphysics," *Mind*, **67** (1958), 344-65. The bulk of this portion of my essay was written before I had had an opportunity to read this interesting paper.

[7] For a fascinating nontechnical account of the history of the neutrino hypothesis and its testing, see Isaac Asimov, *The Neutrino* (Garden City, N. Y.: Doubleday, 1966).

8 *Ibid.*

9 For example: H. Putnam, "The Analytic and the Synthetic," in *Minnesota Studies in the Philosophy of Science*, ed. by H. Feigl and G. Maxwell (Minneapolis: University of Minnesota Press, 1962), Vol. III; N. R. Hanson, *Patterns of Discovery* (Cambridge, England: Cambridge University Press, 1959); H. Gavin Alexander, "General Statements as Rules of Inference," in *Minnesota Studies in the Philosophy of Science*, ed. by H. Feigl, M. Scriven, and G. Maxwell (Minneapolis: University of Minnesota Press, 1958), Vol. II.

10 Sentences which at one time have a factual content (including those that express basic laws) may, in some or all contexts, be rendered necessary (and their denials conceptually untenable) by changing their meaning such that they become analytic (more exactly, *A-true*—see my "Meaning Postulates in Scientific Theories," in *Current Issues in the Philosophy of Science*, ed. by H. Feigl and G. Maxwell [New York: Holt, Rinehart and Winston, 1961]). But the price paid for such necessity is always the same: the principle becomes completely void of factual content of any kind. This is no doubt important, but once understood it becomes unexciting. If we "push in" at one point by rendering a sentence *A-true*, a corresponding bulge of factual content will appear somewhere else in the system. Thus, if 'All electrons are negatively charged' is taken as *A-true*, 'There are positive electrons' would, indeed, be self-contradictory. But there would still be the factual question as to whether there were particles in all other respects like electrons but which had a positive charge.

11 Wesley Salmon, *The Foundations of Scientific Inference* (Pittsburgh: University of Pittsburgh Press, 1967).

12 *C.&R.*, p. 229.

13 Another complication arises due to our taking B to be the class of all hypotheses with verisimilitude above a certain value. For now, even if H entails O, $P(C, A \cap B)$ will no longer be equal to one. However, if the value of the verisimilitude is fixed at a fairly high level, then the probability that propositions like O are among the relatively large number of the *true* consequences of hypotheses like H will be very high and thus the chance that hypotheses like H with high verisimilitude will pass tests like E will be correspondingly high—perhaps close enough to one so that the factor $P(C, A \cap B)$ can be neglected. Similar considerations show that, when H does not imply O, the contribution that a small deviation of the verisimilitude from the maximum makes to the variation in $P(C, A \cap B)$ is very small. It is thus legitimate to simplify and to consider B as the class of all *true* hypotheses while we are concentrating our attention on the problem that arises when H does not imply O. $P(C, A \cap B)$ now becomes, as we would expect and desire, an excellent measure of what statisticians call *the likelihood*, of H on O, for it is the portion of true hypotheses like H that pass tests like E (and by definition for H to pass E is for O to obtain) and this is obviously a direct function of the portion of cases of true propositions like O associated with true propositions like H.

14 Popper makes a different but related point about the maximum likelihood principle in *L.Sc.D.*, "New Appendix xix."

15 H. Feigl, "De Principiis Non Disputandum. . .? On the Meaning and the Limits of Justification," in *Philosophical Analysis*, ed. by M. Black (New York: Cornell University Press, 1950), pp. 119-56.

16 Salmon makes this point in *Foundations of Scientific Inference*.

17 *L.Sc.D.*, Appendix *ix.

18 Bertrand Russell, *The Analysis of Matter* (New York: Harcourt Brace, 1927; London: Kegan Paul, 1927); also *Human Knowledge: Its Scope and Limits* (George Allen & Unwin, 1948; New York: Simon and Schuster, 1948).

19 Konrad Lorenz, "Kants Lehre vom apriorischen im Lichte gegenwärtiger Biologie," trans. in Bertalanffy & Rapoport, *General Systems, Yearbook Soc. Gen. Systems Research* (1962), pp. 23-35.

20 For Popper, confirmation or corroboration requires *corroborating instances*. Roughly speaking a corroborating instance for 'All A's are B's' consists of the accepted "basic statement," 'There is an A at such and such space-time region' and the corresponding failure to falsify the universal statement due to the acceptance of 'There is an A which is a B at such and such

space-time region'. I say *"perhaps* not . . . corroborated" because it seems to me that Popper's theory is not immune to the "paradoxes of confirmation" (see C. G. Hempel, "Studies in the Logic of Confirmation (I)," *Mind,* **54** [1945], 1-26). Thus, since 'Element no. 72 has the properties P, Q, R . . .' is logically equivalent to 'All substances lacking one of the properties P, Q, R . . . are non-(element no.72)', any instance of a substance lacking P or Q or R or . . . and which was not element no. 72 *would* corroborate the original universal statement. Such instances would, of course, be plentiful even though element no. 72 remain undiscovered.

[21] If they are about unobservables, they may be only confirmable.

[22] *C.&R.,* p. 58 n.

8

Arnold Levison

POPPER, HUME, AND THE TRADITIONAL PROBLEM OF INDUCTION

I

Thus the problem of induction is solved. But nothing seems less wanted than a simple solution to an age-old philosophical problem. . . . However this may be, I am still waiting for a simple, neat and lucid criticism of the solution which I published first in 1933 . . . and later in *The Logic of Scientific Discovery*.[1]

T he purpose of this paper is to provide the criticism that Popper has here invited. If successful, it will give Popper an opportunity to clarify his position by constructing a reply which is as "simple, neat and lucid" as that which he demands from his critics. Moreover, even if we should succeed in showing that Popper has failed to solve the problem of induction, a consideration of his arguments purporting to do so will deepen our understanding of the important issues involved; in addition, we will see in just what respect Popper's theory of method does make a genuine advance beyond Hume. This will require an assessment of the extent to which Popper's attempted solution is relevant to the difficulties posed originally by Hume.

It might be objected that there is no point in discussing Popper's attempted solution to the problem of induction, if what is meant by "the problem of induction" is Hume's problem, since the latter was long ago shown to be a pseudoproblem and to be "dissolvable" if not "solvable." Besides, the objection might continue, Hume's problem has long been superseded in the interest of philosophers by Goodman's "new riddle of induction." Given that we distinguish in practice between good and bad, or better and worse, inductive arguments; and given that inductive reasoning is not merely incomplete deductive reasoning, what is required (according to this way of thinking) is not a "justification" of induction, but adequate reasons for determining the comparative tenability of hypotheses and adequate criteria for evaluating proposed inductive arguments.[2]

However, this argument for dissolving Hume's problem of induction presupposes not only that there is a form of justificatory argument which is irreducibly inductive, but also that such a form of argument necessarily is utilized in testing scientific statements. This latter presupposition is challenged by Popper's claim that only deductive forms of argument are necessary for such testing. Thus Popper denies that there is any need for introducing a notion of "inductive argument" in order to solve the problem posed by Hume.[3] The claim that the problem of justifying induction has been dissolved is therefore irrelevant to an assessment of Popper's views.

If Popper's theory were successful in solving Hume's problem then it would be necessary to consider whether it is vulnerable to Goodman's puzzles. Since I shall argue that Popper does not succeed in solving Hume's problem, there would not be much point in my considering also whether he fails to solve Goodman's problem. But it will be possible to show briefly that Goodman's puzzles constitute as much a problem for Popper as for any 'inductivist'.

II

Popper's Theory of Testing as a Solution to Hume's Problem

In one of his characterizations of the problem of induction, Popper writes:

> . . . the logical problem of induction arises from (*a*) Hume's discovery . . . that it is impossible to justify a law by observation or experiment, . . .; (*b*) the fact that science proposes and uses laws 'everywhere and all the time'. . . . [and] (*c*) *the principle of empiricism* which asserts that in science, only observation and experiment may decide upon the *acceptance or rejection* of scientific statements, including laws and theories.[4]

It is the "apparent clash" of these three principles, and not merely Hume's "discovery," that constitutes the *logical* problem of induction. The problem may be considered solved, therefore, if it can be shown that the clash is merely apparent, that the "three principles" are really compatible. Thus, instead of attempting to refute Hume's argument against induction as a form of justificatory argument, Popper proposes to seek a noninductive method of evaluating the comparative acceptability of scientific statements, including laws and theories, and to show how this noninductive method either satisfies Hume's objections against inductive methods or prevents Hume's problem from arising.

A "theory" for Popper is a system of strictly universal statements which, given appropriate initial condition statements, may explain a wide variety of phenomena if it is true, and is such that the theory as a whole (and not necessarily each individual statement belonging to it) is empirically falsifiable.[5] Given that Hume showed the impossibility of providing a non-fallacious inductive or deductive proof of a theory on the basis of premises which consist of observational statements that are positive instances of the theory, Popper argues that it may yet be possible to provide an empirical method for accepting or rejecting theories, or at any rate that the possibility of such a noninductive empirical method is not excluded by Hume's arguments.

Popper's proposal is that the acceptance or rejection of a theory can be "decided by observation and experiment or by the result of test," because "to accept a theory is nothing more than to acknowledge that it has stood up to the severest tests we can design."[6] Thus if two theories are exactly alike except that one contains a hypothesis, h, and the other its negation, $-h$, and empirical testing shows that one of the theories is false while the other is not refuted by that test, then the one that is not refuted is tentatively acceptable or corroborated, while the other should be rejected.[7]

For Popper, explanatory theories are not imposed on us by psychological conditioning, as they are for Hume; rather, experience presents us with problems to which our response is often to 'think up' a possible explanatory solution. When we first propose an explanatory theory we cannot claim to have learned anything thereby; but if the theory is such that consequences can be deduced from it which are falsifiable by testing, it becomes possible for us to begin to "learn from experience." That is, if a theory is refuted by testing, we can respond by 'thinking up' another or revised theory which is not refuted in the same way that the earlier conjecture was, and so on; the process can be repeated until a theory is found which eliminates all the faults that we have been able to find in the previous versions or theories and combines all their advantages. Popper relates this method of testing theories to the method of learning by trial and error (conjecture and refutation), which he thinks is the fundamental model of all learning from experience. For Popper, therefore, the rationality of scientific method does not depend on our being able to establish explanatory theories as the conclusions of arguments with true premises, inductive or otherwise; but in following a method of testing which will lead to better (not necessarily true) theories, in the sense that an explanatory, empirically falsifiable theory that has been severely tested and has not been refuted by observation will be preferred by scientists to a similar theory that *has* been falsified.

This theory of method presupposes that a scientist who wishes to adhere consistently to the method of testing will be willing to discard theories that have been refuted, and that he will not be willing to patch up weak theories indefinitely by *ad hoc* devices. Also, it presupposes that he should prefer the logically simpler, more easily tested theory to one that is harder to test, because it is more open to logical alternatives. These presuppositions might be regarded as analytic with respect to the concept of what it is to be an empirical scientist. Futhermore, testing a hypothesis or theory involves taking into account pragmatic factors, such as the intentions of the scientist (e.g., the test must be a sincere attempt to refute the theory) and the availability of testable theories.

Thus Popper's notion of testing involves elements that are not analyzable merely into premises, conclusion and rule of inference, but are contributory factors in accepting or rejecting a theory in accordance with the method of science. In criticizing Popper's deductivism, it may be overlooked that his strategy is to assert the sufficiency of deductive reasoning only to evaluate specifically inferential claims in the sciences, and that his analysis of the meaning of accepting or rejecting a scientific statement is not the same as that which would be given of accepting the conclusion of a valid argument. There are no rules of acceptance in Popper's account that can be formally characterized or which are sufficient for saying that a theory is true or even that it is probable. Only the *falsity* of a theory can be a valid deduction from empirical evidence; but the fact that a rival theory is falsified is never offered by Popper as a reason for accepting the favored theory.

Assuming that we have now adequately summarized Popper's views, we want to examine whether his solution to the logical problem of induction has any bearing on Hume's problem. The latter, it will be recalled, arises when Hume asks: ". . . what is the nature of that evidence which assures us of any real existence and matter of fact beyond the present testimony of our senses and the records of our memory?"[8] After first attempting to establish that it is only by means of "the relation of cause and effect" that we could hope to justify an inference from "the testimony" of our senses and memory, Hume concludes by saying: ". . . even after we have experience of the operations of cause and effect, our conclusions from that experience are *not* founded on reasoning or any process of the understanding."[9]

What Hume is asking, divested of archaic terminology and legal metaphor, is whether statements about matters of fact that we are not directly observing, or do not or cannot possibly remember, are justifiable by argument. But his question is intelligible only if we assume that "the present testimony of our senses and the records of our memory" do assure us, at least some of the time or in some manner, of "real existence and matter of fact." For otherwise, what would be the point of asking whether we are ever justified in going beyond what the senses and memory tell us?

Futhermore, the question whether we are ever justified in going beyond the present testimony of our senses and memory, if it is intelligible, presupposes that any "assurance" we may have of "real existence and matter of fact," which depends *merely* on this kind of "testimony," does not extend as such to unobserved or unexamined matters of fact. As Hume puts it, there is here "a step taken by the mind" which requires to be explained—the step, namely, from what has been observed to what either has not or cannot possibly be observed at the time the step is taken.

We thus find Hume accepting two principles as a basis for further analysis: (1) that we can extend our knowledge beyond our senses and memory only if these are means of acquaintance with "real existence and matter of fact"; (2) that no present observation or recollection is as such a source of information concerning unobserved matters of fact.[10] Given these two principles, the problem of induction arises in the following way. First, it is pointed out that we do form conclusions pertaining to "real existence and matter of fact" that fall outside the sphere of anyone's sense perception and memory; second, it is shown that these conclusions are the same as *expectations* that what has been true of all observed cases of some certain kind will also be true of future or unobserved cases of that kind. Finally, it is shown that although these expectations may arise from our "experience of the operations of cause and effect," it does not follow that such an experience can provide us with information extending to unobserved or unexamined cases. Thus Hume is justified in concluding that although our empirical expectations cannot be more securely based than on our uniform past experience, our need to use them as guides for future action can in no way be "founded on reasoning or any process of the understanding."

In considering Hume's arguments, there are two directions in which we can go. In one direction, we question whether it is necessary to give a rational justification of an empirical expectation concerning which we are willing to grant that it has arisen on the basis of our uniform past experience. This is the direction of *dissolving* Hume's problem, of saying that induction is not deduction and that an inductive justification is nothing over and above citing the past observations which support the expectation and noting the absence or proportion of negative cases. On the other hand, we can proceed in the direction taken by Popper; here we ask whether Hume's specifically *sceptical* conclusion (that there is no "foundation in reasoning" for our "conclusions from experience") really is a valid consequence of his premises. As we have seen, the problem of induction as it arises in Hume cannot be intelligibly stated unless we assume that we have some observational knowledge. But if we do make this assumption, there are grounds for saying that Hume's argument is invalid, if it is interpreted as an argument for scepticism about the possibility of there being any "conclusions from experience" which are independent of uniformity assumptions. For, granting that we can have some knowledge of an observational kind, and granting that this observational knowledge can be formulated in statements that can be logically related to other and perhaps more general statements, it follows that there is something that we can know on the basis of experience which is independent of our uniform past experience, namely we can know that some statements, hypotheses or theories are false. That is, nothing in Hume's argument excludes the possibility of there being an observational statement which implies an existential statement that is the contradictory of some universal empirical hypothesis. Under these conditions, we could correctly infer on empirical grounds that the universal hypothesis is false. This would be a "conclusion from experience" satisfying Hume's conditions but it would not be subject to his objections against inductive inference, since the premises of such an argument could be restricted to reports of "the present testimony of our senses and the records of our memory."

It will be objected perhaps that this possibility does not in any way show that Hume's argument is invalid. But if it is indeed possible to demonstrate that some conceivable state of affairs is not actual, then it is also possible to demonstrate that some conceivable empirical belief is not rationally tenable. If so, it follows that uniform past experience is not our sole guide in matters relating to empirical beliefs; for, a demonstration of the type envisaged could result in a change of our empirical beliefs on merely logical grounds. Although such a demonstration would not amount to an "extension" of our knowledge from the observed to the unobserved, it provides a criterion for regulating knowledge-claims that is quite different in character from past experience, which Hume thought was the sole basis for regulating empirical beliefs.

Statements that report what Hume calls the present testimony of our senses and the records of our memory correspond to what, in Popper's philosophy, are called basic statements. However, a basic statement, for Popper, is distinguished not by being "justifiable by sense perception or memory," but by having a certain logical form (a basic statement has the form of a "singular existential statement"), and by the fact that it is intersubjectively testable by observation or is such that competent investigators are able to reach agreement about it. The selection of statements to be denominated basic, given that they have the appropriate logical form, is essentially a matter of convention, prompted by experience.[11]

So far we have argued that there can be an argument within the framework of Hume's assumptions whose validity is wholly independent of any difficulty about justifying induction but whose conclusion may have an empirical application. Also, we have pointed out a weakness in Hume's argument that is exploited by Popper and provides the basis for the latter's claim to have solved the "age-old" problem of induction. However, at this point another objection arises which proves more difficult to deal with than the preceding one. In fact, if I am right, this objection proves insuperable if it is pressed far enough; for it shows that in the end it is not possible to dispense altogether with inductive reasoning.

The objection I have in mind is this. Let us suppose that Hume would be willing to acknowledge, on the basis of the preceding considerations, that his sceptical conclusion does not follow, strictly speaking, from his premises. He could grant this and still not be prepared to concede that Popper's theory can provide a basis for rebutting his claim that a "conclusion from experience," in the sense of a *prediction* or a forecast of what will occur, cannot be justified by reasoning or argument. He might say that although we could learn from experience that not all swans are white without utilizing any form of induction, we cannot derive from this kind of basis any reason for supposing that the next swan we see either will or will not be white. The question that needs answering, then, is whether testing a theory in Popper's sense can provide us with any reason for preferring a predictive consequence of a tested theory to any of its possible contraries. Otherwise, Hume could retort to Popper that testing a theory could not affect our "conclusions from experience" in any sense that he (Hume) would have wished to dispute. Hume might support his objection, furthermore, by pointing out that on Popper's account neither past observations nor instance confirmations nor the fact that a theory has so far survived a wide range of tests, can count as positive supporting evidence for the truth of a predictive consequence of the theory.[12]

To put the argument in another form, unless past instances that we have observed of successful prediction based on a theory give us reason to suppose that future instances will be similarly successful, we have no reason to conjecture that a prediction which follows from a well-tested theory is true rather than false, and hence no reason for preferring a given prediction to its contraries; and this is so even if the prediction is specifically identical to predictions that have been endlessly verified in the past. Some concept of inductive reasoning, or extrapolation, is needed, therefore, in order to justify supposing that an experiment can be successfully repeated.

Can Popper succeed in avoiding this conclusion? Consider the following argument, which might be offered as a last resort. Let us suppose that by "corroborating" a theory Popper means only that the theory has stood up *so far* to all the types of test that we can devise, and that he does not intend us to believe that this gives us any reason for supposing that the theory will *continue* to survive a test of one of those types, i.e., any reason for conjecturing that a numerically new predictive consequence of the theory is true. In that case, we may ask, what reason do we have for supposing that a test can be successfully repeated? Popper might reply that we can propose and test the hypothesis that the test can be successfully repeated, and that this hypothesis can be corroborated just as the original hypothesis was corroborated. Popper's claim could then be construed as the claim that our reason for preferring theories that have survived testing up to the present is *not* that "they are likely to continue to do so," but rather that the hypothesis that theories that have repeatedly survived testing continue to do so relatively to the same type of tests is one that can often be corroborated. This might be construed as an indirect way of justifying acceptance of specifically identical predictions which follow from well-tested theories. Thus, for example, the familiar prediction that a red hot poker will warm rather than cool a bucket of water is specifically identical to an uncountable number of past predictions concerning pokers, buckets of water, and things similar to them; and the second-order hypothesis that the first-order hypothesis is reliable has been corroborated. Thus it is reasonable to accept a prediction based on the first-order hypothesis.

Obviously, this way of countering the original objection entails an infinite regress of corroborating hypotheses. Is this regress necessarily vicious? One standard way of rendering an infinite regress innocuous is by claiming a shift in the burden of proof. Once we have shown that the second-order hypothesis that a certain first-order hypothesis withstands testing, has itself withstood testing so far, we might reasonably argue (or so a Popperian might say) that there is no need to justify this second-order hypothesis unless some positive reason for doubting it is forthcoming. The positive reason that would have to be given in this case would be that hypotheses which withstand testing sometimes are refuted by an identical type of test, i.e., that experiments cannot be successfully repeated. Now the hypothesis that this may happen cannot be refuted, a Popperian might say, but it can be tested. If an experiment is repeated, for example, and a theory is refuted by specifically the same prediction that previously corroborated it, then the needed positive reason would be provided. Should that happen, however (the Popperian might go on to say), we would be doubtful about the degree of scientific development of the discipline in which the original hypothesis was proposed. And we are in fact told that in the social sciences and psychology it is often difficult if not impossible to repeat experimental tests successfully. But this has not been true in general in the physical sciences. In the physical sciences repeating a test of a well-corroborated hypthesis has usually not altered the acceptability status of the hypothesis. This is not an argument which justifies the conclusion that the eventuality in question will not occur the next time the test is repeated, but at any rate (the Popperian might say) the opposite presumption necessarily lacks support also. If, therefore, the burden of proof in this case rests on the sceptic, that is, on the person who supposes that a hypothesis may be refuted on a later occasion by a type of experiment by which it was repeatedly corroborated on earlier occasions, then it may be argued that in the absence of any counterevidence, the positive presumption is tentatively acceptable, or "corroborated." In this way the regress dialectically comes to a halt. But the only reason that it enables us to give for relying on a predictive consequence of a well-tested theory is that we have no reason for not relying on it. We may doubt, however, that this reconstruction of the rationale of applying physical laws in order to build bridges or airplanes is more satisfactory than Hume's, or even very different from his.

As if replying to this objection, Popper has recently written:

> I consider the theorist's interest in *explanation*—that is, in discovering explanatory theories—as irreducible to the practical technological interest in the deduction of predictions. The theorist's interest in *predictions*, on the other hand, is explicable as due to his interest in the problem whether his theories are true; or in other words, as due to his interest in testing his theories—in trying to find out whether they cannot be shown to be false.[13]

The view expressed by this passage seems to me to be misleading. I do not think that it is true in general that "our interest in the problem whether our theories are true" is the same as our interest "in trying to find out whether they cannot be shown to be false." Theorist or not, no one would risk sending men to the moon merely in order to find out whether current physical theory cannot be shown to be false. Furthermore, there is no question here of "reducing" our interest in explanatory theories to "practical technological interest," but only in understanding how the latter, insofar as it consists in applying physical laws, can be justified as a form of knowledge, or at any rate as a form of justified statement.

Popper's difficulty is that he cannot consistently hold that successfully surviving a wide range of experiments makes it likely that a theory will continue to survive such tests. Thus, to be consistent, he must deny that the claim that a test can be successfully repeated can be justified by argument. But, if so, he cannot claim consistently that he has solved the logical problem of induction, even as he defines it. Hume's problem is not so much solved by Popper as it is transformed from the problem of justifying generalizations based on past observations to the problem of determining the comparative acceptability of explanatory theories and other scientific statements on the basis of experimental testing. The question that we are left with is why the fact that an empirical theory has survived a wide range of experimental tests, when other comparable theories have not survived those tests, gives us good reason for supposing that a predictive consequence of the former or corroborated theory is worthy of the confidence of reasonable men, while those of the latter are not worthy. The problem is not so much that of "justifying" the supposition in question but of providing an appropriate conceptual analysis of what it is to have a reason for supposing that a theory will continue to stand up to tests or that an experiment can be successfully repeated.

Finally, if Popper does modify his position in such a way as to admit the possibility of extrapolating from the success of past tests to the likely success of future ones, he is straightway confronted with Goodman's puzzles. For, let the peculiar predicate "grue" mean green and observed before A.D. 2,000 or blue and later than that. Prior to A.D. 2,000, then, the hypothesis that all emeralds are grue will stand up to exactly the same tests that the hypothesis that all emeralds are green stands up to now. Yet the two hypotheses yield incompatible predictions. One hypothesis tells us that if anything is an emerald and is observed after A.D. 2,000 it is blue, while the other tells us it is green, but nothing can be both grue and green.

ARNOLD LEVISON

DEPARTMENT OF PHILOSOPHY
UNIVERSITY OF MARYLAND, BALTIMORE COUNTY
JULY, 1966

NOTES

[1] K. R. Popper, *Conjectures and Refutations: The Growth of Scientific Knowledge* (London: Routledge & Kegan Paul, 1963; New York: Basic Books, 1963), p. 55. Hereinafter cited as *C.&R.*

[2] See "Symposium on Inductive Evidence," *American Philosophical Quarterly*, **2**, No. 4 (October, 1965). See also: Nelson Goodman, *Fact, Fiction and Forecast*, 2d ed. (Indianapolis, New York, Kansas City: Bobbs-Merrill Company, 1965), pp. 59 ff.

[3] K. R. Popper, *The Logic of Scientific Discovery*, 3d imprint rev. (New York: Science Editions, Inc., 1961). Hereinafter cited as *L.Sc.D.* "The best we can say of a hypothesis is that up to now it has been able to show its worth, and that it has been more successful than other hypotheses, although, in principle, it can never be justified, verified, or even shown to be probable. This appraisal of the hypothesis relies solely upon *deductive* consequences (predictions) which may be drawn from the hypothesis. There is no need even to mention 'induction' " (*L.Sc.D.*, p. 315).

[4] *C.&R.*, p. 54.

[5] *L.Sc.D.*, esp. Chap. III & Chap. IV.

[6] *C.&R.*, p. 55.

[7] *L.Sc.D.*, esp. Chap. X.

[8] David Hume, *Enquiry Concerning Human Understanding*, Sec. 4, Part 1.

[9] *Ibid.*, Part 2.

[10] It might be thought that Hume has another principle which should be listed, namely that it is only by means of the relation of cause and effect that we could hope to extend our knowledge beyond the senses or memory. Hume presumably would not mean by this that only causes can be reasons for p where p is a statement about the unobserved, but rather that, if what we are interested in is better reasons for p than for *not-p*, we can hope to find such reasons only in the context of causal relations.

[11] *L.Sc.D.*, pp. 100 ff.

[12] ". . .we must not look upon science as a 'body of knowledge', but rather as a system of hypotheses; that is to say, as a system of guesses or anticipations which in principle cannot be justified, but with which we work as long as they stand up to tests, and of which we are never justified in saying that we know that they are 'true' or 'more or less certain' or even 'probable' " (*L.Sc.D.*, p. 317).

[13] *Ibid.*, p. 61, starred note to footnote 1.

Y. Bar-Hillel
POPPER'S THEORY OF CORROBORATION

For many onlookers, the running controversy on the possibility and the nature of inductive logic between two of the greatest philosophers of science of our time, Karl R. Popper and Rudolf Carnap, has been a constant source of wonder, embarrassment and frustration. For one such onlooker (and occasional participant), the major consolation lies in the fact that during this controversy a considerable amount of light has been created simultaneously with the disturbing heat. It is my partly self-assigned task, in this contribution to the present volume, to stress the enlightenment which I have drawn from the protracted discussions between Popper (and the Popperians) and Carnap (and the Carnapians), and to attempt to share it with others.[1]

Not the least among the insights I have gained is that the divergencies between the two have basically been neither disagreements in belief nor disagreements in attitude, but rather differences in interest. Differences in interest, though, as we all know, may lead to feelings of real opposition, in particular when one party believes, as has happened in our case, that the pursuit of the interests of the other party might hurt its own interests.

1. After very long and protracted deliberations, and after having thrown many drafts into the wastebasket, I finally decided on the following strategy: I shall not try to describe here in detail the development of Popper's treatment of the subject during the 34 years that have passed since his first major publication dealing with it, not because this would be uninteresting, but because it would have turned out to be too exciting; so exciting, in fact, as to detract attention from what seems to me to be the major issue, and its latest stand. For myself, I have engaged in this endeavor for many hundreds of hours, during a number of years, and have tried to follow a great mind's thinking on an intricate matter, his wavering and self-criticism, his defense against criticism by others and his counterattacks, the linguistic pitfalls into which he has fallen on occasion, and the ways by which they were later partially overcome, the asides taken by polemics with thinkers of different at-

titudes, the darkness created by the shadows thrown by such polemics, and the stretches of brilliant light of insight within that darkness. I have drawn much pleasure and much pain from this endeavor. But my task is not to deal with the Psychology of Karl Popper but rather with his Philosophy, in particular since my treatment of the psychology would after all doubtlessly be highly amateurish, highly subjective and therefore open to a new round of polemics whose fruitfulness would be very much in doubt.

Neither shall I engage in philological description and text critique. I have in my possession a very large number of notes on this aspect of our problem, and again it turns out to be an exciting one. But again I am sure that the excitement would detract from the only topic in this connection which Popper himself would regard as being of decisive value: *What is the correct conception of how scientific theories are to be confirmed, corroborated, appraised, compared and accepted?* When presenting my own conception of these matters, I shall sometimes try to indicate which part of it is due to my understanding of Popper (but not how I arrived at that understanding), and which to others. I know that my interpretation will often run counter to the letter of some of Popper's own treatments. But I have tried, as hard and conscientiously as possible, to be true to what I have taken to be the spirit of his contribution. Should I have failed in this—and I have no illusions as to my chances in this respect—I hope that Popper will make this perfectly clear in his *Replies*. Should my interpretation of Popper's contribution turn out to be not only not true to his intentions but plain untrue, I am quite sure he will make this too quite clear in his *Replies*. Altogether, I am convinced that by this strategy I shall have achieved something which has always been dearest to Popper's heart: the statement of a bold hypothesis followed by its (perhaps only partial) refutation through incisive criticism, thereby opening the way for a better hypothesis that might perhaps inherit some of the nonrefuted features of the old one.

2. Before I start presenting my own conception, based on insights due to Popper and Carnap, though on occasion going beyond them and even against them, let me first try to formulate clearly the difference of interest between Popper and Carnap in their treatment of science. In a nutshell, it seems to be this: Popper is primarily interested in the *growth of scientific knowledge,* Carnap in its *rational reconstruction;* or, to borrow terms from current methodology of linguistics, Popper's philosophy of science is *diachronically* oriented, Carnap's is *synchronic;* with still other metaphors, Popper's conception is *dynamic,* Carnap's is *static.* This surely must have been trivially evident to many observers and already appears, as a matter of fact, in the titles of their first major works—compare Carnap's *Der logische Aufbau der Welt* (1928) and *Die logische Syntax der Sprache* (1934) with Popper's *Logik der Forschung* (1934)—but when I myself belatedly realized this fact, it came

to me as a revelation. In my own view, these interests are complementary, and methodology of science in its totality, though not each and every methodologist, must cherish them both. It is my impression that this view was also shared by Carnap, though he would doubtless have added that he himself, for reasons of temperament or for no particular reasons, was interested in rational reconstruction mainly or even exclusively. With regard to Popper, the situation is clearly not so simple. He seems to feel—and has said that much many times—that an (excessive?) interest in axiomatization and formalization will turn out to be detrimental to the growth of science and should therefore be opposed and discouraged. I am not sure whether Popper meant this as a potential danger for the scientist (in which case I am ready to accept his position), or for the methodologist of science (in which case I am not). I hope he will clarify this point in his *Replies*.

3. Comparison between two (or more) competing theories is certainly a task which even a working scientist, and not only a methodologist of science, might on occasion find himself facing, and it is therefore clear that methodology of science should be concerned with analyzing this activity and finding criteria and rules for it. Interestingly and strangely enough, not enough attention has been paid to what seems to me definitely to be a decisive prior question, viz., *comparison for what purpose?* Neither Popper nor Carnap have ever, to my knowledge, explicitly posed this question. This might be the main reason why both of them seem to have assumed, Carnap without much ado, Popper with some implicit argumentation, that the comparison of theories is an essentially simple and one-dimensional affair. For Carnap, at least until recently, the one and only decisive dimension for comparison was something like likelihood-to-be-true-in-view-of-extant-empirical-evidence, for Popper it was rather potential-to-bring-about-growth-of-scientific-knowledge. *For me, it seems rather obvious that scientific theories may and should be compared along both of these as well as along a large number of further dimensions, and that these dimensions will carry varying weights depending on the particular purpose under discussion.* To mention, for the moment, just one such further dimension of a "pragmatic" nature: the pedagogical simplicity of a theory, its teachability and learnability, seems to me to be of paramount importance, both historically and in actual everyday practice, and to deserve not much less careful analysis and explication than the other, "cognitive", dimensions.

I do not want to claim that these three dimensions, and the many others one could think of, are independent of each other or that they may not turn out, upon analysis, to be definable in terms of other dimensions, to be "reducible" to them. Nor would I want to exclude the possibility that, during explication, some of these dimensions might have to be split into two or more factors. On the contrary, there is every reason to expect that some or all of these possibilities will materialize upon analysis; as a matter of fact, some have already materialized.

What might be the source of the belief, shared by Popper and Carnap, in the essential unidimensionality of theory comparison? The only motive I can think of is their (subconscious) insistence on the comparability-in-principle of any competing theories, their conviction that such theories are rank-orderable, at least in principle—and rank-ordering, of course, cannot, in general, be obtained from multidimensional comparisons. And this insistence, on its part, is motivated—so it seems to me, and this in spite of a large number of quotations from both Carnap and Popper that might literally be interpreted as showing the opposite—by what is the common goal of the comparison: *rejection* of all but one of the competing theories and *acceptance* of the surviving one.

I know, of course, that the term 'acceptance' has different meanings for Carnap and Popper, and has at least two quite different meanings for Popper alone, say, in a venerable tradition, acceptance$_1$, in which a theory is accepted$_1$, when it is, at the time of its acceptance$_1$, the preferred candidate among its competitors for undergoing severe testing; and acceptance$_2$, in which a theory is (tentatively) accepted$_2$ when at the time of its acceptance$_2$, it has passed, with flying colors, the severe tests which it had undergone, after its having been accepted$_1$ at some prior time. It is only for acceptance$_1$, of course, that Popper would like all competing theories to be rank-orderable, at least in principle, so that at each time one and only one theory would turn out to be accepted$_1$, and such that, if that theory passes the severe tests it is supposed to undergo after its acceptance$_1$, it becomes accepted$_2$ and, if it fails those tests, the next theory in line will be accepted$_1$, etc., taking into consideration, of course, that, as the result of such a failure, a new theory might be proposed that would then enter the competition. At no time would two theories compete for acceptance$_2$.

Carnap, though he presents good, and in my view decisive, arguments against accepting hypotheses that lead to immediately practical decisions—cases in which he treats "accepting a theory" as "acting as if it were true"[2]—is less radical with regard to theories with no immediate practical consequences. For them, he officially regards acceptance as a first procedural approximation. That he is ready to take this approximation seriously becomes clear when we notice that he proposes, tentatively but in all seriousness, to amalgamate the two functions along which he believes, in his later conception, that theories should be compared, viz., *content* and *degree of posterior confirmation*, into one, viz., the one whose values for a given theory would be the product of the values of the two mentioned functions.[3] I can see no other motivation for this, shall we say, strange proposal than wanting by all means to rank theories in a linear order for the purpose of acceptance.

In point of fact, both Popper and Carnap each come up with exactly two functions (from theories to some subset of the set of real numbers), whose values for competing theories will be decisive for their comparison (and thereby for their acceptance). One of these two functions is common to both, viz., the *content (-measure)* of the theories. They both seem to have, at least approximately, the same *explicandum* in mind—as a matter of historical fact, Carnap has stated many times that he adopted this concept from Popper—and, moreover, have at least one *explicatum* in common. Using '$p(T)$' as the symbol for the *explicandum* "the initial (absolute) logical probability of the theory T", both Popper and Carnap are ready to work with (though not only with)

(1) $ct(T) =_{Df} 1 - p(T)$

as a measure function for the (logical, initial) content of T, thereby identifying, for very good reasons which need not be elaborated here, this function with the improbability (and for Popper also with the degree of falsifiability, the degree of testability, the degree of corroborability, sometimes even with the degree of simplicity) of that theory.

As to the second function, there does exist a difference between Popper and Carnap as to what it is supposed to be. This difference is, as a matter of fact, of a double nature. The content of a theory being, by definition, utterly independent of how the theory has fared in the light of empirical evidence, it is mandatory to employ, for almost all purposes one can think of (at least) one other function that does take this evidence into consideration. Carnap prefers *the posterior probability of the theory on the total available evidence*, its *degree of firmness under that evidence*, say,

(2) $p(T,e)$

(using, for the sake of simplicity, the same symbol 'p' for the monadic as well as for the dyadic function, a custom which, with a minimum amount of care, should create no problems), whereas Popper has always, in print since 1934, been dead set for the *degree of corroboration of the theory by the evidence established during the process of severely testing the theory*, i.e., the difference between the posterior and the initial probability of that theory, the difference between its posterior and initial firmness, the degree of relevance of the evidence for the theory, the amount by which its probability has been changed through the evidence, hence, choosing the simplest such function for the clarification of the *explicandum*, though not necessarily for the final explication, for

(3) $cn(T,e) =_{Df} p(T,e) - p(T).$[4]

Since the posterior probability of a theory on the evidence e and the degree of corroboration of that theory by that evidence differ only by a constant, namely by its initial probability $p(T)$, this difference makes little difference when two theories of equal content are compared. For such theories the following theorem holds as an immediate consequence from (3):

(4)   If $ct(T_1) = ct(T_2)$, then $cn(T_1,e) = cn(T_2,e)$ iff $p(T_1,e) = p(T_2,e)$
and $cn(T_1,e) > cn(T_2,e)$ iff $p(T_1,e) > p(T_2,e)$.

For Carnap, who makes it perfectly clear that for two competing theories with equal content the theory with the higher *degree of posterior confirmation* (which is his *explicatum* for posterior probability) should be preferred, there is no difference whatsoever insofar as this result is concerned. However, for the case where the contents of two competing theories are different, it may well turn out that the product of the content and the posterior probability of T_1 is higher than the corresponding product for T_2, whereas the opposite holds for the products of the content and the degree of corroboration. (As an illustration, consider the case: $p(T_1) = .2, p(T_1,e) = .35,\ p(T_2) = .5, p(T_2,e) = .6$.) Although this shows even more the arbitrariness of Carnap's mentioned tentative proposal, it shows nothing in particular for Popper, except, I think, that for him the simultaneous comparison of two theories along his own two dimensions or those of Carnap is not wanted under any circumstances.

I tend to believe that, for Popper, theories should first be compared exclusively along the dimension of content in order to determine which of them should be accepted$_1$, i.e., which of them should be the first to undergo severe testing. Should the chosen theory pass these tests with flying colors, then it will be accepted$_2$, and no further comparisons are wanted. Should it fail those tests, i.e., should its degree of corroboration under these tests be below some value (about which Popper has nothing to say in particular, perhaps because he is not ready to take the numerical values of his own degree of corroboration functions seriously), then the theory will be rejected and some other theory will be accepted$_1$; in other words, for Popper there is no need to compare theories except along the dimension of content. As a matter of fact, theories should never be compared as to how they fare for the same evidence. Tests are undertaken for each theory at a time. The evidence assembled while testing one theory will, when this theory has failed the test, be discarded afterwards, and a new set of severe tests will have to be devised for the next accepted$_1$ theory. This is the best sense I could make of Popper's very many remarks on this issue. I present them here tentatively in his name. Whether or not he regards my presentation as a fair one,[5] I am not ready to accept this conception as either descriptively or normatively valid.

4. Before I present my criticisms of Popper's conception, let me make it first perfectly clear that, in my view, it does not really stand in competition with Carnap's conception. At no time does Popper seem to be interested in

the problems of applied science and technology, in the use of scientific theories for practical purposes. I remember only one passage in *Logic of Scientific Discovery*, where Popper uses the term 'technology', and he makes it many times abundantly clear that he is interested in applying science to empirical situations only in order to test theories, that his philosophy of science is a philosophy of theoretical science exclusively.

This remark is, of course, by no means meant to be a criticism. In the division of labor between philosophers of science, it is Popper's as well as anybody else's privilege to want to carve out for himself any place he pleases. But it must then be perfectly clear that the problem of comparing theories from the practical-applicational point of view, applicational not for the purpose of testing but in the sense of full-blooded technological application, is equally legitimate and that it is moreover the duty of philosophers of science—not, of course, of any individual philosopher of science, but of all of them as a group—to tackle this problem. It was this problem, though not only this problem, which made Carnap develop his inductive logic and give it later on a decision-theoretical basis. Popper would do us all a great service if he made it clear whether he means his critique of Carnap's inductive logic—sometimes taking the verbal form of denying that there is such a thing—as a denial of the legitimacy of the problem Carnap sets out to solve, or as a denial of his success in solving it (to the degree that such success is at all claimed by Carnap), or whether he only wants to deny the applicability of Carnap's—or anybody else's—inductive logic for Popper's own problem, that of comparing scientific theories from a purely theoretical point of view, for the reason that "degree of corroboration is not a probability". My own view is that Carnap's problem is fully legitimate and that his inductive logic has made an enormous contribution towards attacking if not solving it; whereas I have the gravest doubts as to the applicability of pure inductive logic towards a solution of Popper's problem, though not at all for Popper's own reasons.

To present my criticism, let me formulate Popper's conception of how a theoretical scientist should go about forming, assessing, comparing and testing theories in the following advisory *schema*. (I shall make no attempt at showing that this is not at all a good description of how the theoretical scientist works; more particularly because I am not sure to what degree Popper really wants to make such a claim.)

1. At all times, try to come up, in the domain of your scientific interest, with a theory that shall be as encompassing, as content-rich, as daring as possible.
2. If you are faced with competing theories, compute which of them has the highest content, i.e., the highest degree of absolute logical im-

probability. (This is a purely logical procedure, and any available empirical evidence should be disregarded for this purpose.) Probability logic may be used, though only as a heuristic device, and no particular importance should be given to the numerical results obtained.

3. Accept₁ the theory with the highest content (hopefully your own one), and submit it to the severest tests you can imagine and carry out. Be very sincere about seeing your theory refuted, otherwise your bias might make you miss falsifying evidence obtained during these tests.

4a. Should the theory fail the tests, forget it and start again with step 1, or, should your scientific creativity not be of sufficiently high quality, continue with step 3, for the theory with next highest content.

4b. Should the theory pass the tests, accept₂ it and continue with step 1.

I very much hope that this schema does full justice to Popper's intentions and that it is neither exaggerated nor, God forbid, a caricature of these intentions. But I am prepared to stand corrected.

Whether or not this schema is true of Popper's intentions, I claim that it is enormously exaggerated as a normative theory of the scientific theorist's behavior.

Let me skip point 1. The discussion of whether science will grow more in conditions of perpetual revolution, as Popper seems to advocate, or in conditions of stychic revolutions following the breakdown of a paradigm, as Professor Thomas Kuhn tends to see it, I can safely leave for them to thrash out.[6]

But I have the gravest doubts as to point 2. I am not at all sure that the notion of standing in competition has been or could be sufficiently well defined (or, to use less ambitious terminology, clarified) to be of much use. I can think of three or four situations in the history of science where I might want to use this phrase responsibly, such as Copernicus versus Ptolemy, Einstein versus Newton, wave versus particle, but in most other situations, and perhaps in these also, I have some doubts whether the competing theories really deal with the same domain.

But even for theories that deal with the same domain, it must be a rare situation indeed when one theory contains the other as a proper part, when the content of one theory, as the class of all theorems of that theory, contains the content of the other as a subclass. For the more frequent case, when the contents are overlapping or exclusive (the latter case probably never having occurred at all), comparison of contents is only possible through some measures assigned to them. Here, however, Popper becomes ambivalent and wavering. Is it or is it not possible to assign (initial) logical probabilities to theories, if only for the purpose of comparing the numbers attained, though not taking seriously the numbers themselves? I (in this respect departing from

Carnap's views which are much more optimistic, unrealistically so, as I see it)
regard this as practically utterly and totally hopeless and have the gravest
doubts as to whether it is even a theoretically reasonable aim. I am ready to
play around, in courses on philosophy of science, with the *Gedankenexperi-
ment* of following up the consequences of the assumption that absolute
logical probabilities can be assigned to theories, but regard any advice given
to scientists on that basis as pointless.

However, even as a sheer exercise in utopian philosophy of science, point
2 seems to me wrongheaded. I see no justification whatsoever for disregarding available relevant empirical evidence prior to performing the computa-
tion. In its extreme interpretation, Popper could not even possibly have
meant this piece of advice seriously. Would he really want to advise the
theoretical scientist to disregard already existing refuting evidence? Would he
really insist that no scanning of the literature is in general mandatory before
proceeding to perform the new severe tests? But if this extreme interpretation
is out of the question, what remains? In my view, nothing. My advice would
be: Never, for no methodological consideration, disregard extant relevant
evidence (with the only exception being the case where a literature search
might turn out to be more costly, in utility units, than performing new tests).

Assume, then, that you have somehow been able to rank-order all the
competing theories in the field of your interest according to their *initial* content, or, if my advice is taken, according to their *prior* content on the then
available total relevant evidence, or rather, since it might be advisable to
reserve the term 'content' for initial degree of corroborability only, to their
prior degree of corroborability

(5) $cy(T,e) = 1 - p(T,e)$

(where e is now, for present purposes, the total available relevant evidence).
Should one then follow point 3, accept$_1$ the theory with highest rank and start
submitting it to the severest conceivable tests? What about the case when a
severe testing of the highest-ranking theory will cost a few million dollars,
whereas the next-highest-ranking theory can be tested for a few thousand
dollars only? Is it a debasement of the lofty ideals of scientific methodology
to bring in cost and monetary considerations? It is my conviction that, if
utilities are disregarded, methodology of science will remain an ivory tower
undertaking that can be safely disregarded by the practicing scientist. And
again, I can hardly believe that Popper would disagree. But if he agrees, what
remains of his point 3?

As to point 4, when does a theory fail a test? When it has been falsified
by the outcome of the test, or already when its degree of corroboration by the
test is negative, i.e., when its posterior probability on the new evidence, e', is
lower than its prior probability on e, i.e., when

(6) $cn(T,e,e') =_{\mathrm{Df}} p(T,e') - p(T,e)$

is negative? Or perhaps only when it is highly negative? And what is then 'highly'?

In the formulation of point 4, I was using the slang term, "forget it". Popper himself, of course, never uses this term in this connection. But what does he recommend should be the reaction to a theory that has failed a severe test? Repress it into one's subconsciousness? Shelve it? File it away in some drawer for "temporarily rejected theories"? Never mention it again in one's lectures, except perhaps by adding something like "but it has been refuted"? Never test it again unless new evidence shows up which might make one think that perhaps the refutation was not really final?

Theories consist, roughly speaking, of an uninterpreted part whose vocabulary is the logical vocabulary of the language in which the theory is formulated plus the specific theoretical vocabulary of the theory (to the exclusion of pretheoretical, immediately intelligible expressions), plus its interpretation, whether in the form of rules of correspondence or any other form one can think of. Though I do not believe that Popper would accept this conception of the structure of theories—he has said many times that all expressions are theoretical to some degree or other—I am reasonably sure that he will still agree that it makes sense to distinguish between an uninterpreted calculus and its interpretation(s), though an actual separation into these parts for some given theory might be difficult or impossible. If so, what happens when a theory is rejected? What if, by changing just one rule of correspondence, the test outcome not only no longer refutes the revised theory but actually positively corroborates it? And what about some minor-looking (from a formal point of view) change in the calculus without changing the rules of correspondence? When are such changes *ad hoc?* When is a change a change? Why should these semantic sophistries be of any importance? Does Popper really believe that he has some a priori criteria to tell, in the case that two different scientists offer two different reactions to a refuted theory, which of the two is *ad hoc*, if any, and which is *ad maiorem scientiae gloriam?*

As to point 4b, when does a theory pass a test? When does it pass it with flying colors? When has it proved its mettle? When is it highly corroborated? I do not think that any clear sense can be assigned these expressions; and I am moreover quite convinced that Popper would entirely agree to that (as a matter of fact, here, as in innumerable other occasions, my views are directly derived from Popper's or rather from my interpretation of his views, as the reader will often have no difficulty in finding out, if he cares to do so). But what is then the content of point 4b, beyond some *Lebensgefühl?*

What happens when you accept$_2$ a theory? Do you try to forget all other theories? Will you never mention them again in your lectures? Will you base all your research after that ominous step on the assumption that the accepted$_2$

theory is true? Will you do so even when, in concordance with the last part of point 4b, you immediately begin to search for some better theory?

I could go on in this vein, ad infinitum. But I think I have already, if not long ago, reached the point of marginal returns. It is time for an interim summary.

5. A. The locution 'accept a theory', whatever its function and usefulness in ordinary, everyday discourse, is useless in methodology of science. Though scientists may be said, or may say of themselves, that they accept a theory, believe in it or have faith in it (or in its truth), no explication of these expressions is wanted for methodology of science; though psychology and sociology of science will doubtless be greatly interested in them, and perhaps be particularly intrigued by the fact that a similar set of terms is used for scientific theories as for religions and Weltanschauungen. In particular, none of Popper's two explicata, the ones I termed here 'accept$_1$' and 'accept$_2$', are helpful. 'Accept$_1$', besides being rather poor *qua explicatum*—and I can explain for my own benefit Popper's use of this term in this sense only as a kind of joke, of which however many will have missed the point—neither is nor should be a concept exclusively in terms of which scientists would decide as to whether and when to embark upon testing some theory. Neither content nor even prior corroborability should be the only dimensions to be taken into consideration for such a decision; not to mention that any practical comparison of competing theories along these dimensions is in almost all cases out of the question and that even the theory of such a comparison is still in an extremely doubtful stage.

B. Theories can and should be compared in a large number of dimensions of which probability, corroborability, and corroboration are only a small sample. (Notice that each of these dimensions has at least three important subdimensions, viz., initial, prior and posterior, i.e., relative to no evidence, to evidence available at some stage of interest, and evidence available at some later stage of interest, perhaps with some further subclassification as to the kind of evidence, whether "total" or obtained in the process of severe testing.) Simplicity (itself consisting of a large number of subdimensions), teachability, impact of the belief in their truth within some community on that community, are some of the others. As soon as the monopoly of "acceptance"[7] is renounced, it becomes possible and mandatory to inquire into the various goals for which theories have to be compared and determine which of the mentioned (and hinted upon) dimensions will be of importance for the various goals. One might want to classify the goals into something like cognitive, pedagogical, sociological, etc., and perhaps also classify the dimensions of comparison themselves accordingly. All this is at present almost *terra incognita*, due to the *tyranny of the idol of acceptance* over the minds of even the greatest philosophers of science.

For each such dimension and subdimension, the possibility of its quantization, in theory and in practice, has to be investigated; in case of a negative answer, the possibility of working with a comparative concept has to be studied; in case of a further negative result, one will have to inquire into how many members a family of qualitative predicates should have in order to be useful. (Should one work with the two-member family consisting of 'probable' and 'improbable' or with a four-member family consisting of 'highly probable', 'probable', 'improbable' and 'highly improbable', etc.?)

C. Corroboration by evidence is doubtless one of the most important dimensions of comparison and will probably have to be taken into account in many of the various goals for which comparisons will be undertaken. For most such goals, I take it—though it requires further investigation—the evidence to be considered will have to be, at least in principle, the total available evidence, with various compromises to be struck for practical purposes; but it is conceivable that, for one or the other goal, new evidence obtained during testing will be given special consideration, perhaps even exclusive consideration.

Corroboration (or rather, to be precise—which is necessary for present purposes—degree of corroboration) by evidence is, of course, not a probability, i.e., not a function that fulfills the standard axioms of probability theory. But it seems to be universally agreed that it can be defined exclusively in terms of probability (plus, of course, standard arithmetic), though not uniquely so. How seriously the numerical values have to be taken, i.e., whether there exists a serious goal for which the exact numerical values (and not only their comparative standing) are of importance, remains to be seen. For "highly theoretical" theories, I see no such goals, and I am sure that Popper (but perhaps not Carnap) would agree. Whether, even if desirable for some important goal, a numerical corroboration function with theories as arguments has any chance of ever being adequately defined, remains again to be seen. And again, I am rather sceptical about it.

D. This skepticism of mine reflects my doubts as to the possibility of coming up with a degree of confirmation function that will assign to theories numerical values which one would be ready to take seriously. These doubts are based, among other reasons, on the fact that the very *explicandum*, logical probability, is so much less clear for theories than for molecular or generalized observational sentences, in particular in view of the now reasonably well understood "holistic" nature of scientific theories. Popper, of course, in general shares this scepticism (with some occasional remarks that express a certain wavering) but Carnap regarded it as a reasonable goal to aim for such functions. He had few illusions as to the length of time it might take to attain it—I remember him having mentioned a century on one occasion—but I take it to be remarkable that he clung to this hope at all. None of these functions will, of course, belong to his famous "continuum", since all these functions assign the value 0 to the degree of confirmation of every general synthetic sentence in an infinite universe. Since I find myself here on Popper's side (though not necessarily sharing his reasons), let me say no more about this topic.

6. I understand that Popper's recently advocated concept of verisimilitude is to be treated in another contribution to this volume.[8] Let me then only remark rather dogmatically that I regard this attempt as an almost complete failure. The only motivation I can find for Popper having made this strange attempt is that he was not really satisfied (and rightly so) with his two-stage acceptance procedure and was looking for some one function that would somehow combine content and degree of corroboration, the same motivation that made Carnap suggest that one might try the product of content (amount of information) and degree of posterior confirmation as a measure for the acceptability of a hypothesis, thereby enabling the comparison of any two competing hypotheses.

7. While I was writing this article, Lakatos was writing his extremely interesting and detailed evaluation of the problem of inductive logic.[9] He was kind enough to send me a set of proofs, which reached me just when I was about to finish the last-but-one draft of my present contribution. This gives me a welcome opportunity to compare our views. Lakatos and I had a good amount of oral discussion throughout the last years, mostly centering around inductive logic and the Popper-Carnap controversy. Our papers doubtlessly reflect this discussion, in spite of the fact that their bulk was written independently.

There are a good number of points and views on which we seem to agree, sometimes in common opposition to customary conceptions.[10] I was particularly pleased to see that Lakatos shares my misgivings against "a monolithic, all-purpose appraisal of hypotheses" (*PIL*, p. 375), a view which he regards as some "neoclassical empiricism inherited from classical empiricism". He also shares my view that this attitude is noticeable even in Popper's conception and that a "Popperian scientist makes *separate* appraisals corresponding to the separate stages of discovery". He also uses, as I do, numerical subscripts to distinguish between various conceptions of the notion of acceptability, *qua explicanda*, though he arrives at three such notions worth explication as against my two. His acceptability$_1$ and acceptability$_2$ are closely related to mine, though not identical with them (and I shall not discuss here his acceptability$_3$). Both our notions of acceptability$_1$ are appraisals of theories prior to their testing; indeed, their main purpose is to assign priorities for testing of competing theories. But I explicate 'acceptability$_1$' as 'initial content', whereas Lakatos's *explicatum* is rather what he calls '*excess content*', i.e., "excess content over its '*background theory'* (or its *'touchstone theory'*, that is, over the theory it challenges)" (*PIL*, p. 375). This does not mean that there exists an essential difference between us. "My" *explicatum* was meant to explicate Popper's conception; as a matter of fact, having presented the explication, I went on sharply to criticize the conception behind it. Lakatos's explication is not even presented as representing Popper's actual views but rather as an improved variant of them. I take it that Lakatos would accept my criticisms of Popper's "actual" view. But though Lakatos's conception is indeed an improvement and contains important insights, I do not think at all that it is defensible in the formulation it gets from him.

Similarly, whereas I explicate 'acceptability₂' in terms of degree of corroboration, Lakatos's explication is rather in terms of *'excess corroboration'* over the touchstone theory (*PIL*, p. 381). Here, I am no longer as sure as before that Lakatos would share all my misgivings against "my" *explicatum*. I am afraid, however, that my misgivings, suitably varied, hold also against Lakatos's *explicatum*. Though the *explicanda*, i.e., the bases on which theories can be compared before testing and assessed after testing, are of utmost importance and both Popper and Lakatos contributed greatly to their clarification, both "my" and Lakatos's *explicata* create more confusion than light.

To illustrate: at one point (*PIL*, p. 383), Lakatos arrives at the advice "keep testing and explaining even a refuted theory until it is superseded by a better one", where the new theory T_2 is better than the refuted old theory in having "corroborated excess content over T_1 while T_1 has no corroborated excess content over T_2". Clearly, however, if everyone were to follow Lakatos's advice to its letter all of the time, there would be no time for corroborating new theories and therefore no opportunity for finding a better one. From Lakatos's later remarks it becomes reasonably clear what he really intends to say by this unfortunate formulation. These intentions are sensitive and defensible; the explication is neither.

8. It is Popper's unforgettable merit to have clarified the decisive role played by theories and theorizing in the growth of science and to have done this in an unforgettable way.[11] The climate in which he began this lifework of his was not at all favorable to his endeavor, on occasion even plain hostile. In the early thirties, logical "positivism", operationism, behaviorism, and pragmatism were the most progressive and sprouting schools in philosophy of science, and they all shared at that time a definite atheoretical outlook (*"theorias non fingo"*), first trying to explain away theoretical concepts and theories, then grudgingly granting them a certain ("instrumental") role in the systematization of observational knowledge, the only "real" knowledge. It took a Popper to hammer it into the minds of the philosophers of science (and into the mode of speech of scientists who knew this all along) that theories are

instrumental (without quotes) in the growth of observational knowledge while
increasing our understanding. Just because theories have "surplus" content,
partly through the use of strong logics and partly through the use of
theoretical terms with "surplus" meaning that goes beyond their
"operational definitions", they have growth-inducing power, in addition to
systematizing power, by encouraging new types of observations and experiments.

I only wish Popper would realize to what degree the Carnapians of the
seventies are on his side in this respect and that their pronouncements to this
effect are meant in all sincerity. Those who nowadays promote inductive logic
are no longer "inductivists" in Popper's pejorative sense (and some never
were), nor are they all "instrumentalists".[12] Many of them continue to be interested in a better understanding of the systematizing power of scientific
theories and continue, for this purpose but not only for this purpose, to be interested in inductive logic. But I simply don't know anybody who denies the
importance of the concept of growth-inducing power. Popper's continued
feud against the "systematizers" seems to me no longer useful and a plain
waste of time, his and ours. None of us believes any more, if he ever believed
so, that theories with minimum surplus content are preferable for all purposes, though we continue to be convinced that they have their advantages,
ceteris paribus, for some purposes.

Let me finish with my *ceterum censeo:* By freeing ourselves from the
bonds of the acceptance syndrome, we shall be able to utilize the time saved
thereby, now spent on fruitless feuding after having long ago reached the
marginal returns of mutual criticism, for a better understanding of the very
dimensions along which theories can be compared and of the many purposes
theories fulfill. I am fully convinced that this appeal is entirely in Popper's
spirit. I hope he will make it accord with his letter.

YEHOSHUA BAR-HILLEL

DEPARTMENT OF LOGIC AND PHILOSOPHY OF SCIENCE
THE HEBREW UNIVERSITY OF JERUSALEM
JERUSALEM, ISRAEL
JULY, 1968

NOTES

[1] It is my good luck that the controversy around corroboration between Popper and Carnap
(and a number of Carnapians like Achinstein, Kemeny, and myself) that went on for a number of
years and a number of rounds in the late fifties has been so ably summarized and evaluated by
Henry V. Stopes-Roy in a lengthy review published in *The Journal of Symbolic Logic,* **33,** No. 1
(March, 1968), 142'ff. Having read this review, I happily discarded part of my manuscript for the
present contribution.

[2] See Rudolf Carnap, "Replies and Expositions", in *The Philosophy of Rudolf Carnap* (The

Library of Living Philosophers, Vol. XI), ed. by Paul Arthur Schilpp (La Salle, Ill.: The Open Court Publishing Co., 1963), pp. 972-73; "Probability and Content Measure", in *Mind, Matter, and Method—Essays in Philosophy and Science in Honor of Herbert Feigl*, ed. by Paul K. Feyerabend and Grover Maxwell (Minneapolis: University of Minnesota Press, 1966), pp. 248-60; "On Rules of Acceptance", in *The Problem of Inductive Logic*, Vol. II of the *Proceedings of the International Colloquium in the Philosophy of Science, London, 1965*, ed. by Imre Lakatos (Amsterdam: North-Holland Publishing Co., 1968), pp. 146-50—hereinafter cited as *PIL*.

[3] *PIL*, p. 148.

[4] I am aware of the many "simplifications" I am making here. One is that I assume, for the *explicandum*, that the initial logical probability of (noncontradictory) empirical generalizations and even of theories is positive. It seems that with respect to generalizations, adequate explications with this property are well on their way. Recent attempts along this direction have been made by both Popper and Carnap, as well as by Hintikka and his associates; see, e.g., Jaakko Hintikka, "A Two-Dimensional Continuum of Inductive Methods", in *Aspects of Inductive Logic*, ed. by Jaakko Hintikka and Patrick Suppes (Amsterdam: North-Holland Publishing Co., 1966), pp. 113-32; Risto Hilpinen, "On Inductive Generalization in Monadic First-Order Logic with Identity", *ibid.*, pp. 133-54, and Jaakko Hintikka and Risto Hilpinen, "Knowledge, Acceptance, and Inductive Logic", *ibid.*, pp. 1-20. Another simplification lies in my disregarding the many explications which Popper himself has offered over the years for degree of corroboration. At present, I am interested only in the *explicandum*, and for it, formula (3) is a good enough approximation, and certainly the simplest one.

[5] It would be of great help if Popper would commit himself on this point. For instance, it would be good to know his exact position on the question to what degree he regards it as mandatory, useful, irrelevant, or even damaging (prior to the submission of a new theory) to conduct a literature search not only with respect to the relation of the new theory to the older relevant ones (for instance, whether they are in competition with each other, complementary to each other, or what have you), but also on how the new theory fares with regard to empirical evidence collected innocently or for the purpose of testing prior theories. I think I know the answer, but I would prefer Popper to present it himself.

[6] For this thrashing out, now involving many other authors, see *Criticism and the Growth of Knowledge—Proceedings of the International Colloquium in the Philosophy of Science, London, 1965*, Vol. IV, ed. by Imre Lakatos and Alan Musgrave (Cambridge University Press, 1970).

[7] Or "the acceptance syndrome", as I dubbed this phenomenon in my second contribution, with this title, to the discussion on the rule of detachment in inductive logic published in *PIL*, pp. 150-61.

[8] Cf. especially Professor A. J. Ayer's essay on "Truth, Verification and Verisimilitude", in this volume (Essay 19).

[9] Imre Lakatos, "Changes in the Problem of Inductive Logic", in *PIL*, pp. 315-417.

[10] Some of Lakatos's remarks have a direct bearing on many of the points I tried to make in the present contribution; but it was too late to make all the changes that would have been necessitated by fully taking into account their impact. The reader is advised to read Lakatos's paper, partly as a companion, partly in counterpoint to mine.

[11] I still cannot forget that autumn day in 1936, when a copy of Popper's *Logik der Forschung* came into my hands. I started reading it at four o'clock in the afternoon and finished at four o'clock in the morning, with a five-minute break for supper. I have, of course, read it (and various subsequent editions) many times since, and each time it took me longer to finish. Just for the sake of comparison: At about the same time, I got hold of a copy of Carnap's *Die logische Syntax der Sprache*. It took me eight months (though not without interruptions) to finish the first reading of it. These two books remain till this very day the two most exciting philosophical books I have ever read, each in its own and very different way.

[12] I tried to clarify my stand in the instrumentalism-realism feud ("a plague on both houses") in "Neorealism vs. Neopositivism—A Neo-Pseudo Issue", *Proceedings of the Israel Academy*

of Sciences and Humanities, **3,** No. 3 (Jerusalem, 1964), 29-37; republished as Chap. 23 in *Aspects of Language* (Jerusalem: The Magnes Press; Amsterdam: North-Holland Publishing Co., 1970), pp. 263-72.

J. C. Eccles

THE WORLD OF OBJECTIVE KNOWLEDGE

PRELIMINARY CONSIDERATIONS

The Critical Method and the Growth of Knowledge

Discussions on scientific method among philosophers suffer only too often from a lack of actual intimate acquaintance with the work and problem of the creative scientist. Not so with Popper. My own scientific life since 1945 owes so much to my conversion (if I may call it so) to Popper's teaching that it seems appropriate if I tell here again the story of his influence on my own research experience at a critical period in 1945, and of what this conversion has meant to me ever since it took place.

Like most young scientists I had started off doing research in a rule-of-thumb manner, accepting without qualms the inductive nature of scientific method. I was very fortunate to be Sherrington's pupil in Oxford during his classical period of research on spinal reflexes. Lucky in my choice of problems, I could get on well so long as I was pursuing the direction of classical investigations. But when I ventured later into new fields, I began to recognize that I was making serious mistakes, and as a consequence suffered all the pangs that accompany the recognition of such misfortunes.

Until 1945 I held the conventional ideas about scientific research. First, hypotheses grow out of the careful and methodical collection of experimental data, according to the inductive view of science deriving from Bacon and Mill. Even today many scientists believe in this method (though more recently a somewhat rigid and oversimplified form of Popper's ideas has begun to be fairly widely accepted). Secondly, I believed that the excellence of a scientist is judged by the reliability of his developed hypotheses, and by how much they stand firm as secure foundations for further advance. Thirdly, and this was for me perhaps the most important point: it is a sign of failure and in the highest degree regrettable if a scientist espouses an hypothesis which is falsified by new data and has to be scrapped.

That was my trouble. I had long espoused an hypothesis which, I came to suspect, might have to be scrapped, and I was in a state of extreme depression about it. It was an hypothesis about synaptic transmission between nerve cells, and I had become involved in a controversy in which I took up the theory that this transmission was largely electrical rather than due to a chemical transmitter substance (as held by Dale and Loewi). I admitted the presence of a slow, chemical component, but I believed that the fast transmission across the synapse was electrical.

It was at that time that I met Popper. Among the important things which I learned from him perhaps the most important was that it was not disgraceful to have one's own favourite hypotheses falsified. That was the best news I had had for a long time. I was persuaded by Popper, in fact, to formulate my electrical hypotheses of excitatory and inhibitory synaptic transmission with sufficient precision and rigour to invite strict experimental falsification; and that is what happened to them a few years later, very largely in a cooperative venture by my colleagues and myself, when in 1951 we started to do intracellular recording from motoneurones. Thanks to my tutelage by Popper I was able to work joyfully and devotedly in bringing about the death of a brain-child which I had nurtured for nearly two decades; and I was at once able to contribute to the theory of chemical transmission which was the brain-child of Dale and Loewi.

It was in this most personal manner that I had experienced the great liberating power of Popper's teachings on scientific method.

I now firmly believe that it is of the utmost importance for scientists, and especially for the leaders of scientific research, to be illuminated and guided by a theory of scientific method. Most scientists are of course concerned with the philosophical basis of scientific discovery. I will not describe it here since I expect that this will be done elsewhere in the present volume more than once. I wish to affirm Popper's view that the growth of science is essentially due to bold theories handled "with a light hand" and yet with severest criticism. This view is often misunderstood and misinterpreted. On the contrary, I regard it as philosophically correct and of inestimable practical value. Yet in this essay I do not wish to concentrate on these matters: I rather wish to present a neurologist's reflections on some of Popper's later work, especially on what he calls "the third world" and what I will call, a little more briefly, "World 3."

In two very recent publications by Karl Popper (1968a, 1968b) I had the exciting experience of being confronted by a brilliant conceptual development that made it possible to believe in a third world and to rethink many of our intellectual problems in this new context. As against the common dualistic view that there are really two worlds, the world of matter and energy and the subjective world of conscious experience, Karl Popper has proposed three

Worlds as follows: (1) the *World of matter and energy,* which is the material world, both inorganic and organic, and including machines and all living forms—even our own bodies and brains; (2) the *World of conscious experiences*, not only our immediate perceptual experiences—visual, auditory, tactile, pain, hunger, anger, joy, fear, etc., but also our memories, imaginings, thoughts and planned actions that he refers to as our "dispositional intentions"; (3) the *World of objective knowledge,* which would include the objective contents of thoughts, as he calls it, especially of the thoughts underlying scientific and artistic and poetic expression. In particular, he stresses the World 3 status of all theoretical systems and of problems and problem situations and critical arguments. The importance of World 3 will be readily appreciated when we come to consider its relationship to Worlds 1 and 2.

In fact we can state that in World 3 are all arguments and discussions and records of human intellectual efforts, and in particular there are the records preserved in libraries and museums either as written records or as paintings, sculptures, ceramics, ornaments, tools, machines, etc. However, it is important to recognize that in World 3 there is only the objective knowledge that is coded symbolically in the actual structures that serve as vehicles for this knowledge. The material structures carrying the codes such as books, pictures, plastic art forms, films and even computer memories would be of course in World 1.

In order to illustrate the independent existence of World 3, Popper considers two "thought" experiments.

In experiment (1) all machines and tools are destroyed, also all memories of science and technology, including our subjective knowledge of machines and tools, and how to use them. But *libraries and our capacity to learn from them* survive. Clearly, after tremendous labour and much suffering, our world civilization may be restored, as men discover and learn to understand the past civilization from all the preserved documentation, i.e., from the World 3 that survives.

In experiment (2) the destruction is greater, because not only is there the destruction of World 1, but in addition *all libraries are destroyed,* so that our capacity to learn from books becomes useless. In that case men would be reduced to the barbarism of primitive man in early prehistory, and civilization could be restored only by the same slow and painful process that has characterized the story of man through Paleolithic times, a process that would take likewise tens of thousands of years.

The vastly different consequences of these two experiments establishes the reality, significance and the degree of autonomy of World 3, as well as its effects on Worlds 1 and 2. But, of course, it must be recognized that these are "thought experiments" beyond any imaginable eventuality. For example, the destruction of all subjective knowledge could occur only if all of the human race were destroyed except extremely primitive people and very young, as yet uneducated, children.

Following Popper we may consider that there are two classes of knowledge corresponding to the two senses in which the word "knowledge" can be used. There is firstly subjective knowledge, which we can regard as being stored in the neuronal mechanisms of the brain and available for recall on appropriate occasions. This class of knowledge would include all our memories insofar as they relate to the products of human intellectual efforts. Secondly, there is knowledge in an objective sense, which is of course knowledge in World 3. It consists of myths, stories, ideas, problems, theories and arguments coded in some appropriate form so that their objective existence is ensured and in fact can continue independently of anybody's claim to know them or to know about them, and even of any belief that may be held by men at any one time. However, it is important to recognize that this objective knowledge is a product of human intellectual activity. It may, for example, result from the effort to develop theoretical systems and explanations of all natural phenomena and even of problems that relate to the world of conscious experience such as occurs in some branches of the neural sciences, as for example the science of psychophysics. It also includes all the efforts of design and construction, which are motivated in part by the desire to build a better life, and in part by aesthetic and religious ideas. At any one time in history there may be much in World 3 that is only potentially capable of being known. It is largely autonomous, but not absolutely and finally autonomous. We have examples of great intellectual achievements that go virtually unrecognized in one age only to be later rediscovered, as for example Mendel's mathematical laws of genetics. As another example I can instance the whole effort of archaeology that can be considered as an attempt to uncover and discover the World 3 of ancient civilizations. Special examples of this occur in the efforts to decode written languages. For example the linear B scripts of Minoan civilization were undecipherable, probably for almost three millenia, until Michael Ventris deciphered the codes in 1954.

World 3 is essentially a world of storage. It has been the genius of man through the whole story of his civilization to have left in enduring form his imagination and his sense of design and purpose which was initially in the style and form of his fashioning of clay, of stone, of flint and of pottery, or in the delineation of his cave paintings. The surviving fragments give insight into the creativity of primitive man, and reveal the slow emergence of more sophisticated forms of symbolic expression. All of these enduring records of human creativity belong to World 3, because they can give us insight into the thoughts and imaginings of men of the remote past, that is of the contents of the World 2 of men; and this World 3 content is greatly increased as the artefacts attain the added sophistication and style made possible for work in metal—copper, bronze, gold, silver and iron. The ultimate of achievement eventually came with the development of written languages, which usher us into the presence of the great historic Civilizations.

Instinctive Behaviour

When we come to consider the nature and scope of World 3, we come up against suggestions made by Popper in relation to nonliving structures made by animals "such as spiders' webs, or nests built by wasps or ants, the burrows of badgers, dams constructed by beavers, or paths made by animals in forests." It is not clear if these structures—or rather their design features—are to be regarded merely as providing examples of animal activities analogous to those of man when he makes additions to World 3. Popper himself states that he is trying to support the autonomous existence of World 3 by a kind of biological argument. However, I think that this attempt is mistaken because the analogy between animal and human behaviours is superficial. It disappears when the problem is studied in depth.

In the first place it is remarkable that animals building some of the most elegant structures with geometrical design have relatively simple nervous systems—as for example the social insects—ants, bees, wasps—and the spiders. Other constructional animals such as birds and lower orders of mammals, the badgers and the beavers, also have nervous systems less highly developed than the higher orders of mammals, e.g., the anthropoid apes, that have virtually no constructional propensities.

Secondly, we have the amazing story of the immense time lag between man's development of a full-sized brain and his significant contributions to World 3, as I shall outline below.

As argued by Konrad Lorenz, the instinctive behaviour exhibited by the remarkable building operations of animals has a hard core of absolutely fixed and relatively complex automation. This inborn movement form is genetically determined, and can be termed a fixed-action pattern. Neurologically we can regard it as deriving from genetically determined structural and functional patterns of neurones, which of course would be of very great complexity. There must be a complexity adequate on the one hand to handle effectively all the diverse and ever-changing inputs from receptor organs and, on the other hand, to give expression to the wide variety of movements required in the constructional process. This operational complexity must even be extended to account for the remarkable skill of animals to repair, with apparent intelligence and insight, defects in the structures they have built, as for example with wasps mending their damaged nests (R. W. Hingston; quoted by Thorpe, 1956).

As neurologists we must believe that even the most complex behavioural patterns of animals are an expression of the operation of their neuronal machinery. With instinct, the crucial element is that the neuronal machinery has its performance already determined by genetic information. Modifications by learning are relatively slight or undetectable, particularly for insects and spiders. Instinctive behaviour is, however, also dependent on a suitable environment, as signalled to the nervous system by the various receptor organs, and also by the internal environment. For example, hormones can greatly influence instinctive behaviour. Well-known examples of such modifications are given by spiders that construct disordered or distorted webs when under the influence of various neuropharmacological agents, such as amphetamines, tranquilizers, barbiturates, etc. It should also be remembered that an instinctive behaviour is not fully formed as an on-going program played by command centers in the central nervous system. On the contrary, it can be recognized as a sequential operation, each stage being dependent on information fed into the central nervous system from the previously completed stages.

These comments must not be understood as belittling the wonders of instinctive behaviour by animals and the skill and imagination displayed in the investigations by ethologists. There have been the most fascinating and searching studies on the instinctive behaviours of many animals, but as yet they have been restricted almost entirely to the descriptive level. An understanding at the neurobiological level will require decades of rigorous investigation, and already many promising investigations are being essayed.

As recognized by Popper (1970), the evolutionary development of the instinctive behaviour responsible for the building of complex structures must be regarded merely as a special aspect of the evolutionary development of all animal behaviour. For example, songs and dances of birds have behaviour patterns as complex and refined as those employed in nest building. It is my contention that a quite different evolutionary process is involved in the emergence and development of World 3. It is usually called cultural evolution in order to signify its complete distinctiveness from biological evolution.

POPPER'S WORLD 3

The Origins of World 3 and the Evolution of Culture

As we survey the cultural story of mankind, the most remarkable discovery is that there were eons of incredibly slow development. For the greater part of the immensely long Paleolithic age, some 500,000 years, all we know is the slow development of stone tools—from flaked pebbles to the very gradually improved hand axe. It is generally believed that this almost unimaginable slowness demonstrates that man was greatly handicapped by not having yet an effective communication by speech. It was not until the Upper

Paleolithic era that man seemed to have achieved a new awareness and sense of purpose—as witness the remarkable progress in a few thousand years, relative to the virtual stagnation for the previous hundreds of thousands of years. One can readily imagine that a language giving clear identification of objects and actions, and the opportunity of discussing and arguing, lifted man to a new level of creativity, and that this linguistic stimulus resulted in a large variety of stone tools with greatly improved design. But the most fascinating insight into the artistic creativity of upper Paleolithic man is given by the cave paintings of southern France and northern Spain. When I saw the marvelous paintings of Lascaux, I was overwhelmed by the feeling that these artists had highly developed imagination and memory as well as a refined aesthetic sense. Undoubtedly they had a fully developed language so that they could discuss the techniques they employed and the ideas that inspired them. One has the impression that, at this period of about 15,000 B.C., man was very richly contributing to World 3—to our World 3. At the same time there were carvings and modellings of animals and of archetypal female figures that probably are representative of Mother Goddesses. Many would achieve distinction in modern sculpture exhibitions!

Jacquetta Hawkes (1965) has expressed with remarkable insight the relation of primitive man to his activities.

> It is not until the sudden appearance of art and ritual burial towards the end of the Paleolithic Age that we have anything beyond the faintest hint of man's inner, unifying existence although undoubtedly this must have been increasing and refining even while in his extraverted and practical life man went from battering pebbles to shaping a hand-axe. We can assume at the intellectual level a growing ability to categorize and to draw conclusions from the past for the benefit of the future. At the imaginative level there must have been mounting power to picture things (and particularly objects of desire such as game animals) when they were not before the eyes, comparable to the ability to visualize the completed tool within the unshaped block of stone. The beautiful shape of the hand axe itself can, indeed, be used as a proof of the early emergence of an aesthetic sense . . . their satisfying proportions show that already a quarter of a million years ago the imaginative mind had its own sense of rightness in pure form which, whatever its source, still holds good for us today.

In the subsequent Mesolithic age, man developed and perfected hunting methods and also clothing and housing, but artistically it was disappointing after the great achievements of the later Paleolithic. This technological Mesolithic period, beginning at 10,000 to 8000 B.C., was relatively brief.

The Neolithic age of settled farming communities began as early as 7000 B.C. in Jericho and at 6500 B.C. at Jarmo in Mesopotamia. The settled towns and villages soon became remarkable for their substantial houses and for the fine pottery and weaving. These developments were possible because of the prosperous farming with crops of barley and wheat and with domesticated animals, sheep, ox, goat, pig and dog. In addition, the stone tools were finely made with polished surfaces. The pottery clearly reveals that Mesopotamian man was guided by an aesthetic sense. The decorative patterns of Hasuma and Jarmo were in part abstract, but also, as with the Samarra pottery of the 5th millenium B.C., there was a very sophisticated stylization of animal forms to give designs that display a high artistic sense. This Mesopotamian pottery is remarkable for the combination of utility and elegance, so that it deserves an honoured place in World 3.

About 1000 years after its development in Mesopotamia, Neolithic culture had spread from there to Egypt, so seeding the great periods of Egyptian civilization. Later there was a wide dispersal to Europe and to Asia (first to the Indus valley and later to China) of this central feature of the Neolithic culture, namely farming with settled communities of villages and towns. Meanwhile great developments continued in Mesopotamia, which undoubtedly led the world during the magnificent periods of Sumerian civilization. The Neolithic age gave place to the Bronze age at about 4000 B.C. and, during the third millenium B.C., gold, silver and bronze workmanship was of a high order. In the third millenium B.C. there were most sensitive and appealing human sculptures, revealing that the artists had great skill and humanity. However, as Malraux (1960) comments, "The purpose of early artists is not to imitate but to reveal form enabling man to enter into communion with their gods—and so transcendent is this purpose that the artist is as unaware of it as the saint is unaware of his own sainthood."

This Malraux quotation is introduced in order to warn against a modern "arty" outlook on the craftsmen of ancient civilizations. They did not set out to make their style and to win their recognition, but rather to be immersed in the whole stream of their civilization, and to live with it and to create in harmony with it. This was the case even as recently as the Medieval civilization with the stone carvers, and the fresco and glass painters.

In this great era several sophisticated cities had grown up in Mesopotamia. Woolley (1965) has estimated that the population at Ur was about 360,000 early in the second millenium B.C. Architecture had flourished; but throughout an amazingly long period there was still no written language. The storage of all the information needed for the maintenance of much larger settled communities was apparently in the memories of the officials, of the craftsmen, of the priests, and, of course, it was coded in the objects themselves—houses, pottery, sculptures and figurines, implements, weapons, etc.

It is difficult for us to imagine how remembered tradition could cope with the complexities of such administration. This dire need was the stimulus that caused Sumerians to make their greatest of all contributions to human culture—the development of a written language. Pictograms had been used to make records of numbers of objects—sheep, cattle, cows, etc. Their purpose was to enumerate things, but they could not convey statements.

As finely expressed by Sir Leonard Woolley (1965):

> Pictorial representation ends and true writing begins at the moment when an indubitable linguistic element first comes in, and that can only happen when signs have acquired a phonetic value. The gap which divides the pictogram from the hieroglyph and ultimately from the phonetic sign is so great that for most peoples it has proved impassable. It is to the credit of the Sumerians that they were able to bridge that gap, and, as soon as they had done so, their neighbours were quick to adopt not necessarily the Sumerian system, but the Sumerian idea, and there arose a number of scripts which differed completely in form from the Sumerian, but were indebted to it for the basic conception that a written sign might represent not a thing but a sound.
>
> All the archaeological evidence available seems to prove that true writing was first developed in southern Mesopotamia.

The earliest example of this occurs at about 3300 B.C., and by 3000 B.C. it had developed a syllabary of up to 900 signs at Uruk—most of which were still ideograms of rather complex form. The usage was so complicated that it was restricted to a small body of specialists (the scribes). They progressively simplified the forms so that eventually it was completely abstract, consisting of various arrangements of tapered signs inscribed in soft clay tablets by a stylus made like a wedge, hence the name "Cuneiform" for the first written language that was fully developed by about 2800 B.C.

This must rank as one of the greatest discoveries in human history; for by means of it, man could live beyond time. Thoughts, imaginings, ideas, understandings, and explanations experienced and developed by men living in one age can be written down for distribution in that age and also for recovery in later ages. A man's creative insights need no longer die with him, but, when encoded in written language, become constituents of World 3 and can be reexperienced by later men who have the ability to decode. And so we enter into the historical epochs where the different civilizations have left records of their economic and political activities, their myths and legends, their drama, poetry, history, philosophy and religion. These are the records that we especially think of when we come to describe the contents of World 3; hence the justification for the initial statement that World 3 is a world of storage.

There is undoubtedly a feeling of bathos in the uses to which this marvellous discovery was put initially. Mostly it was used for business documents, contracts, inventories, deeds of sale! But also it was used for Royal inscriptions and at a later stage for recording religious texts. But even this limited usage gives us the first clear statements about an early civilization, so that History takes over from the Proto-history of the preceding civilization.

There is good evidence that the Sumerian idea—not the detailed scripts—was borrowed by other cultures, so that they too developed their scripts, which in Egypt was the hieroglyphic script, and in China was essentially of an ideographic character. This borrowing must have occurred at the ideographic stage of Sumerian language before the stage of abstraction to the cuneiform script. Some authorities regard the Egyptian and Chinese as independent inventions without information from Sumer. But, when we consider the long time man used a spoken language without essaying to convert it into a written form, it seems unlikely that there would be three independent discoveries, two a little later than the Sumerian. Certainly the close association between Sumer and Egypt would have facilitated the transfer of such a valuable idea.

It is more difficult to trace the development of literature than of the plastic arts; because we are almost completely dependent on late copies for our knowledge of the original literature. But in Sumer and Egypt there was fine poetry and prose as early as 3000 B.C.—the greatest period of Egyptian literature was from 2800 to 2000 B.C. After 1800 B.C. all creativity in literature virtually ceased in both Mesopotamia and Egypt. As has happened with so many more recent Civilizations, periods of great achievements come to an end. But World 3 goes on in the preserved records, the scripts and all the works in the plastic arts. In this way it was possible for the Medieval and Renaissance Civilizations to recover so much of the forgotten Classical Civilization. And, in the last century, there have been immensely successful efforts to discover the Civilizations from more remote times, such as the Sumerian briefly referred to above. These efforts must rank as some of the glorious performances of man, whereby he has recovered, organized and appreciated so much of the great creative achievements of earlier Civilizations, and so has immeasurably added to the content and richness of our World 3.

I hope that this brief survey of the origin and early development of World 3 makes it clear that it has no relationship to the constructions made by animals. This difference can further be emphasized when it is recognized that each human individual has to be educated from babyhood to be able to participate even at the simplest level in the Culture he has been born into; though of course he carries genetically the potentiality for this participation. This generalization applies to babies from all races. Their cultural development from that of the stone age culture of primitive men of today in which they may be born to that of the advanced technological cultures is entirely dependent on their opportunities to learn. A very young child from a stone age culture can be assimilated readily to our culture; and, conversely, a very young child of our culture, if immersed in a stone age culture, would carry no genetic memory of our culture, and merely be assimilated to the primitive culture of his environment. Completely different propositions obtain for all of the instinctive behaviours of animals. This behaviour is largely, if not entirely, inborn, but it is of course modified by environmental influences. Animals brought up in isolation exhibit a remarkable ability to develop the behaviour patterns of the normal adult, for example nest-building or birdsong; but with birds and mammals the finesse of the performance is dependent on having examples on display, i.e., the details of the performance have an imitative basis (Tinbergen, 1951; Thorpe, 1956).

It can be concluded that animal behaviour in constructions, on the one hand, and human purpose and design at all levels of doing and making, on the other hand, are quite distinct. The one belongs to biological evolution, the other to cultural evolution. Animals are innocent of culture and civilization, which are distinctively human. There is no trace of them in the whole of animal evolution, which is governed by trial and error acting blindly, but of course being guided by instinctive and learning behaviour. I use the word "blind" because there is no evidence that animal behaviour pattern is based on the understanding of a situation, in the way that we use the word "understanding" in respect of human behaviour.

The specific human relationship of World 3 has been very well expressed by Popper (1970).

> My central thesis. . .is that the self or the ego is anchored in the third world, and that it cannot exist without the third world. Before discussing this thesis more fully it may be necessary to remove the following apparent difficulty. As I have here so often said, the third world is, roughly, the universe of the products of our minds. How can this be if, on the other hand, our minds or our selves cannot exist without the third world? The answer to this apparent difficulty is very simple. Our selves, the higher functions of language, and the third world have evolved and emerged together, in constant interaction; thus there is no special difficulty here. To be more specific, I deny that animals have states of full consciousness or that they have a conscious self. The self evolves together with the higher functions of language, the descriptive and the argumentative functions.

The Location of World 3 and its Mode of Communication to World 2

We can illustrate these problems initially by attempting to reply to the question: In the reading of a book, how do thoughts or ideas come to my conscious experience? The patterns of black marks on white paper are in World 1, and after transmission as radiation, are transmitted by the excellent optical system of our eyes to a similar pattern of dark and light illumination on the retina. Thence it is transduced by the photochemical and synaptic mechanisms of the retina into the coded patterns of impulses in the million-or-so fibers of each optic nerve. After further integrative procedures on the way to the visual cortex and in the visual cortex, the information is still transmitted by impulse discharges from nerve cells; but it has been developed to a coding of simple geometrical configurations, the various nerve cells responding selectively to lines of specific lengths and direction, and also to angles of particular configurations.

This stage of partially developed neuronal selectivity must be much earlier in the neuronal processing than the conscious recognition of geometrical forms or of alphabetical letters, because that recognition is much more generalized, as witness the extreme range of size, shape and orientation that is still compatible with the conscious recognition of a simple geometrical form, such as a triangle or a letter of the alphabet. The concept of triangularity for example must arise from extremely complex spatiotemporal patterns of impulses in millions of neurones, not just in the visual cortex, but in the adjacent nonstriate visual areas, and also possibly in the more generalized interpretive cortex.

In some manner, completely beyond our understanding, conscious experiences emerge from these spatiotemporal patterns. However, if we do not understand the language in its coded presentation in the book, if we cannot *read* the language, the only experience we can have is of black marks on white paper. We may of course feel an aesthetic appreciation of a beautifully written language, as for example an Oriental or an Arabic script, without in any way being able to understand it; and in that way too, the World 3 coded in books may give special experiences to our World 2.

However, a still more complex neuronal process must occur when we are decoding the pattern of black marks on white paper to give us words and sentences, that is to give a phonetic and meaningful conscious experience, which we simply call reading a book with understanding. There is not merely an instantaneous and fleeting recognition, but also a short-term memory process whereby the interplay of sequential phrases and sentences is built up into more complex levels of interrelationship and understanding. The World 1 events developed in our brains gain in this way ever more complex liaison with the World 2 of conscious experience.

As a final process there is the more enduring storage of information by development of specific neuronal connectivities in the cerebral cortex. When these are read out to give again complex spatiotemporal patterns of neuronal activity resembling those originally operating during the storage, we experience long-term memories. These long-term memories are of course the basis of all our cultural life. For example, when we are reading a book in a field of scholarship with which we are familiar, the ideas that are conveyed from the printed page in the manner outlined above are compared, tested, modified and even rejected in the light of the immense long-term storage of an educated brain, which gives on read-out the relevant memories of ideas, arguments and hypotheses stored from previous experiences.

Those of us who write scholarly books recognize that we obtain a very special satisfaction of an aesthetic kind in developing clear logical stories that represent our ideas. Our enjoyment in this work derives from many sources, of which I instance three from my own experience. Firstly, I learn much in the disciplined process of writing a book. Secondly, it gives me the opportunity of making my ideas generally available for discussion, comment and criticism. Thirdly, I now have a comprehensive account of a subject that I can refer to. If it is well indexed (and I always index my own books!), it provides me with a substitute for the memory processes of my brain. I can regard this as a transfer from the memory stores that have been amassed in my brain. I have found that this increasing memory load in my brain makes retrieval more difficult and unsure—what we colloquially refer to as a failure of memory! Necessarily we must resort to storage systems with codes in an external World 1 in order to supplement the storage coded in World 1 of our brain. For example, we use notes, card indexes, punched card systems etc., and eventually the printed records of books and reviews.

It seems to me that an arbitrary distinction is made if World 3 status is restricted to the knowledge that is stored in some coded form on World 1 objects other than in the brain. The stored memories in my brain can be recovered to consciousness by a retrieval mechanism operating in my brain that in its essential terminal steps must be the same as when identical memories are retrieved by being read out from some document where it has been stored in the coded form of a written language. Initially, of course, this latter retrieval process involves as an addition the physics and physiology of the perceptual process, as outlined above; but, thereafter, the unique spatiotemporal patterns of neuronal operation can be presumed to be similar in order to present to my consciousness similar ideas.

Much that is destined for eventual impression in the appropriate coding in World 3 may be held in such memory stores in the brain and is immediately available in discussions on scientific, artistic or other cultural matters. The largest contributions to a scientific symposium usually arise in this way from the memory stores of the participants rather than from any manuscripts they may bring along. Another example would be the Homeric poems or the Icelandic Sagas that survived for generations in memory stores of successive generations of bards.

In summary, we can state that World 3 is a world of storage, for the whole of human creativity through the prehistory and the history of the cultures and civilizations. What we call in old-fashioned terminology a cultured man is a man able to retrieve from this storage and to enter into an understanding of it. But, of course, this retrieval is also right up to the contemporary scene, where critical evaluation is concerned in elimination of error or banality and in the setting of standards.

POPPER'S CONCEPTS OF THE SCIENTIFIC METHOD

Introduction

I now come to consider the concept of the world of objective knowledge (World 3) in relation to the Popperian concepts of the scientific method whereby we refine and develop more and more our understanding of the natural world.

A simple initial account of Popper's philosophy of scientific method is given in the following quotation (Popper, 1963b),

> My thesis, as I have already indicated, is that we do not start from observation but always from problems—from practical problems or from a theory which has run into difficulties; that is to say, which has raised, and disappointed, some *expectations.*
>
> Once we are faced with a problem, we proceed by two kinds of attempt: we attempt to guess, or to conjecture, a solution to our problem; and we attempt to criticize our usually somewhat feeble solutions. Sometimes a guess or a conjecture may withstand our criticism and our experimental tests for quite a time. But, as a rule, we find that our conjectures can be refuted, or that they do not solve our problem, or that they solve it only in part; and we find that even the best solutions—those able to resist the most severe criticism of the most brilliant and ingenious minds—soon give rise to new difficulties, to new problems. Thus we may say that our knowledge grows as we proceed from old problems to new problems by means of *conjectures and refutations;* by the refutation of our theories or, more generally, of our *expectations.*

The Nature of Scientific Investigation

Many scientists have some naive belief that science is concerned with the making of scientific observations with the best techniques available, and that out of all these observations there emerges some coherent story or hypothesis, which often is rather apologetically referred to as a "provisional hypothesis." This is, of course, a protective device in order that the scientist may avoid identifying himself with some hypothesis that may bring him into obloquy, if it is later disproved. But implicit in this usage of the concept "provisional hypothesis" is the concept that, in the eventual development of that scientific investigation, it will be possible to formulate a fully fledged scientific hypothesis or theory that has evolved beyond the provisional stage to take its rightful place as an integral component in the body of scientifically established knowledge.

This misunderstanding of the nature of science has serious consequences both for science itself and for individual scientists. Scientific publication becomes too much occupied with the reporting of experimental observations that achieve status because they have been carried out by the latest and most expensive techniques, and not because they are designed to test some particularly interesting scientific idea or postulate. As a consequence, scientific

literature is overwhelmed by mere reportage of observations that are published just as observations, without organic relationship to precisely formulated
hypotheses. Such observations are scientifically meaningless. They are boring
and soon to be forgotten. There is thus a great wastage in every aspect of
scientific endeavour—in the efforts of the scientists themselves, in the usage
of scientific equipment and technical personnel, and in the facilities for scientific publication.

Besides this wastage there is a real danger that the misunderstanding of
the scientific endeavour may have serious consequences on the scientist
himself. The erroneous belief that science eventually leads to the certainty of
a definitive explanation carries with it the implication that it is a grave scientific misdemeanour to have published some hypothesis that eventually is
falsified. As a consequence, scientists have often been loath to admit the
falsification of such an hypothesis, and their lives may be wasted in defending
the no longer defensible. Whereas, according to Popper, falsification in whole
or in part is the anticipated fate of all hypotheses, and we should even rejoice
in the falsification of an hypothesis that we have cherished as our brain-child.
One is thereby relieved from fears and remorse with respect to our failed
scientific theories and ideas, and science becomes an exhilarating adventure,
where imagination and vision lead to conceptual developments transcending
in generality and range the experimental evidence. The precise formulation of
these imaginative insights into hypotheses opens the way to the most rigorous
testing by experiment, it being always anticipated that the hypothesis may be
falsified and that it will be replaced in whole or in part by another hypothesis
of greater explanatory power. In this way conceptual developments lead to
experimental testing, which is always designed in relation to hypotheses. The
status of a scientific hypothesis is given by the effectiveness with which it
challenges rigorous experimental testing and by its explanatory power, which
should be far beyond present knowledge, i.e., its status may be measured by
its predictive scope.

The usual statements of Popper's views on the methodology of science
give an impression of some rigidity of operation that rarely corresponds to
the experiences of scientists—even of those who, like myself, fully subscribe
to his methodology. As I examine my procedures in the course of making
some scientific discovery, I find that it looks much more like the opportunistic tactics of guerilla warfare than the organized strategies of major
combats. For example, at the outset of a recent investigation on the input of
information into the cerebellum, it was not appreciated that the correlation of
diverse inputs of information could occur only if these inputs act directly
upon precisely the same region of the cerebellar cortex. This constraint arises
from the well-attested observations that there are no effective looping
association paths in the cerebellar cortex. In fact, there are no chains of ex-

citatory neurones that could provide a basis for circulating impulses, whereby any input could be briefly retained in some dynamic pattern of operation. Furthermore, it was not realized that, if the total information from the sensory receptors of a limb were to be fed into one particular zone of the cerebellar cortex, the integrational functioning of the neuronal machinery would be "jammed" by the overwhelming confusion of input. There must be some regional zoning of various subsets of the input, so that the same input participates in many different integrational assemblages. Integration would therefore be of piecemeal character. However, before the experimental investigation, this was not predicted, though, when discovered, it appeared so necessary and so obvious. My experience is that often I have only a very vague horizon-of-expectations (to use Popper's felicitous phrase) at the beginning of a particular investigation; but, of course, sufficient to guide me in the design of experiments; and then I am able to maintain flexibility in concepts which are developed in the light of the observations, but always of a more general character, so that the horizon-of-expectations is greatly advanced and developed and itself gives rise to much more rigorous and searching experimental testing than could have been designed at the outset.

Illustrations from Neurobiological Investigations

A key point of Popper's teaching with respect to the most effective procedures in scientific research is that it is of the utmost importance to carry out research related to an horizon-of-expectations that derives from a well-developed theory extending far into the unknown. I can illustrate the manner in which this procedure has guided and aided me by giving two examples of my experiences in the recent decade or so.

The first example is the hypothesis that in the mammalian central nervous system a nerve cell can have only one kind of action at all of its synapses, for example, that it can be an excitatory nerve cell exerting only a postsynaptic excitatory action, or it can be purely an inhibitory nerve cell. It cannot be ambivalent, having an excitatory action at some of its synapses and an inhibitory action at others. The hypothesis is thus that nerve cells can be quite sharply divided into two classes, those exciting and those inhibiting. This hypothesis was put up on the basis of a very few species of these two types of nerve cells (Eccles, 1957), but now, in the mammalian nervous system, there are almost 30 species of purely inhibitory neurones and no examples of ambivalent neurones. The full story of this hypothesis and of its testing is told in my Sherrington Lectures (Eccles, 1969). It has stimulated much experimentation and severe attack, and there have been several claims of its refutation that later have been found to be untenable. So, to date, this hypothesis has not been falsified, and in itself has led to the conceptual development of most interesting problems in neurogenesis that will be referred to later.

Nevertheless, several minor features of the original formulation have been falsified. For example, it was postulated that inhibitory neurones are all short-axoned, and now there are three examples in which the axons of inhibitory neurones are centimeters in length. Another early postulate was that this switching to an inhibitory neurone is a simple commutatorlike device in order to effect a transformation in the synaptic transmitter substance; whereas it now is known that there are more complex organizations, for example, inhibition of inhibitory interneurones, and that detailed patterns of neural activation can be transmitted by inhibitory neurones as a kind of negative image. For example, the sole output from the cerebellar cortex is via inhibitory cells—the Purkyně cells. These cells normally are firing spontaneously, and the information transmitted by them may be either an increase or decrease in firing frequency, which results respectively as a decreased or increased discharge rate from target neurones, i.e., in a mirror-image response.

A second hypothesis concerned the ionic mechanism of inhibition. A nerve impulse causes liberation of a special transmitter substance from inhibitory presynaptic terminals, and these act momentarily on the subsynaptic membrane, i.e., across the synapse causing ionic currents to flow across this membrane. These ionic currents actually are the basis of the inhibition of the postsynaptic cell. It has been shown that alterations in the electrical potential gradient across the subsynaptic membrane effect changes in the ionic currents exactly in accord with the postulate that these ionic currents are attributable simply to the movement of ions down their electrochemical gradients. The problem then was to determine the species of ions that move down this gradient. In an early investigation it was found that the injection of some species of anions into a nerve cell affected the ionic currents in a way which showed that these particular anions were moving down their electrochemical gradients and so across the subsynaptic membrane. On the other hand, some anion species caused no change in ionic current flow across the inhibitory subsynaptic membrane. Since the four anion species that were shown to move across the inhibitory membrane were all smaller in the hydrated state than the five anion species that failed to move across the membrane, it was postulated that size of the hydrated anion was the determining factor as to whether it could move across the inhibitory subsynaptic membrane or not. In other words, the inhibitory transmitter opened up "gates" of a certain critical size which only allowed the four small anion species to pass through and these were impervious to the larger anions. Thus in general, the postulate was that under the influence of the inhibitory transmitter the passage of ions through the subsynaptic membrane was a simple diffusion through pores of a rigorously standardized size, there being a net movement of any species of permeable ion along its electrochemical gradient with a consequent potential change across the postsynaptic membrane (Eccles, 1957).

This generalization, from a few examples, has now been tested by injection into nerve cells of all the possible anions (34) and there is only one exception—the formate ion—which, in the hydrated state, is slightly larger than three anions to which the membrane is impervious. The present position is that the hypothesis of critical pore size is corroborated, but with the special, as yet unsolved, problem of the formate anomaly. The formulation of this postulate, relating a critical pore size to anion permeability, has stimulated much research on the ionic mechanisms of inhibitory action (cf. Eccles, 1964, 1966).

This ionic permeability to anions below a critical size is characteristic of the postsynaptic inhibitory synapses, and serves to differentiate them sharply from excitatory synapses. Evidently in mammalian neurogenesis there is some profound biological principle that "forbids" the synapses made by any one cell to be of two classes, i.e., that its synaptic transmitter would be able to open ionic gates characteristic both of excitatory synapses ($Na^+ + K^+$ permeable) and of inhibitory synapses (K^+ and/or Cl^- permeable). The conclusion to be drawn from these various examples is that there is no known exception to two general principles which can be formulated in relation to chemically transmitting synapses in the mammalian brain.

The first principle is that, at all of the synaptic terminals of a nerve cell, there is always the liberation of the same transmitter substance or substances, examples being acetylcholine, noradrenaline, gama-amino-butyric acid, and glycine. Strictly speaking, this is Dale's Principle, and it derives from the metabolic unity of the cell.

The second principle is that, at all of the synaptic terminals of a nerve cell, the transmitter substance opens just one type of ionic gate, that characterizing either excitatory or inhibitory synapses. Otherwise stated, a nerve cell cannot be ambivalent with respect to the essential mechanism of its synaptic action on the subsynaptic membrane.

In contradistinction to the first principle, there is no simple explanation for the rigid operation of the second principle. For example, it cannot simply be derived from the first principle; because a transmitter substance such as acetylcholine acts as an excitatory type of transmitter substance at some synapses (sympathetic ganglia, neuromuscular junctions and the synapses of motor axon collaterals on the Renshaw cells in the spinal cord), and as an inhibitory type of transmitter at others (vagus on heart, synapses on H- and D-cells in Mollusca). It seems that there must be some principle of neurogenesis, whereby the outgrowing axonal branches of a neurone can make effective synaptic contacts only of an excitatory or of an inhibitory type.

Firstly, it is postulated that already at that very early stage of neural development the neurone is specified as excitatory (E) or inhibitory (I). It is possible then to formulate postulates about the way in which such a specified neurone is constrained to establish synaptic contacts exclusively of the one or the other type (Eccles, 1969).

The most probable postulate seems to be that, by chemical sensing, the growth cones of an I-neurone search out patches on the surface of a neurone that are already specified as being inhibitory, there being the consequent development of a functional inhibitory synapse—and similarly for the growth cones of E-neurones and the formation of functional E-synapses. It has been shown that the surface of a muscle fiber is covered by preformed cholinoceptive patches before the motor nerve fibers establish synaptic contacts acting by acetylcholine transmission.

An alternative postulate is that the preformed I-growth cones sense out appropriate neurone surfaces that are not yet specified with patches, but are identified by some other chemical criterion, in the way that is observed with growth of nerve fibers in tissue culture. The I-growth cones then make effective I-synapses by creating in the subsynaptic membrane of these appropriate neurones the receptor patches for the I-transmitter substance and the associated ionic gates that give the fully functional inhibitory synapses; and similarly with the E-growth cones. We have to make the additional postulate that the presynaptic terminal of an I-cell together with the I-transmitter liberated therefrom can create not only receptor patches for the I-transmitter, but also the ionic gates of inhibitory character, i.e., for K^+ and/or Cl and not for Na^+; and similarly for the E-synapses—Na plus K^+ and not Cl^-.

These postulates are as yet purely speculative, but they have the merit of defining problems susceptible to scientific experiment, and of providing new insights in relation to observations that have already been reported. Experimental investigations are now being undertaken to test these various hypotheses of morphogenesis and neurogenesis in the cerebellar cortex of the rat, where it appears that in differentiating mitoses the same primordial cells give rise to both excitatory and inhibitory neurones. This neurogenesis occurs after birth and so is readily available for experimental investigations.

These examples from my own experiences in neurophysiology illustrate the manner in which I have endeavoured to follow Popper in the formulation and in the investigation of fundamental problems in neurobiology. I hope that they illustrate the sense of liberation and adventure that I have derived from this. Furthermore, I think they have enabled me to progress much further and faster than would otherwise have been the case in my efforts to understand some operative features of the central nervous system. I am not, of course, advocating any slavish adherence to every detail of the principles formulated by Popper; but rather that our methods should be enlightened by the general

principles. Popper himself has summed up his view of the method of science
in three words: problems—theories—criticism.

Popper puts up extremely rigorous principles of operation in respect of
the testing of scientific hypotheses; but he mitigates their severity by
providing encouragement even when there are repeated failures in the
attempted solution of a problem (Popper, 1963b).

> Thus we become acquainted with a problem only when we have many times tried
> in vain to solve it. And after a long series of failures—or producing tentative
> solutions which turn out not to be acceptable solutions of the problem—we may
> even have become experts in this particular problem. We shall have become ex-
> perts in the sense that, whenever somebody else offers a new solution—for exam-
> ple, a new theory—it will be either one of those theories which we have tried out
> in vain (so that we shall be able to explain why it does not work) or it will be a
> new solution, in which case we may be able to find out quickly whether or not it
> gets over at least those standard difficulties which we know so well from our un-
> successful attempts to get over them.
>
> My point is that, even if we persistently fail in solving our problem, we shall
> have learned a great deal by having wrestled with it. The more we try, the more
> we learn about it—even if we fail every time. It is clear that, having become in
> this way utterly familiar with a problem—that is, with its difficulties—we may
> have a better chance to solve it than somebody who does not even understand the
> difficulties. But it is all a chance: in order to solve a difficult problem one needs
> not only some understanding but also some luck.

Finally I would like to quote a most wise and authoritative statement by
Popper (1963a) that summarizes so remarkably the approach we should have
in our attempts at "the understanding of nature."

> What we should do, I suggest, is to admit that all knowledge is human; that
> it is mixed with our errors, our prejudices, our dreams, and our hopes; that all we
> can do is to grope for truth even though it be beyond our reach. We may admit
> that our groping is often inspired, but we must be on our guard against the belief,
> however deeply felt, that our inspiration carries any authority, divine or
> otherwise. If we thus admit that there is no authority beyond the reach of
> criticism to be found within the whole province of our knowledge, however far it
> may have penetrated into the unknown, then we can retain, without danger, the
> idea that truth is beyond human authority. And we must retain it. For without
> this idea there can be no objective standards of inquiry; no criticism of our con-
> jectures; no groping for the unknown; no quest for knowledge.

POSTSCRIPT

At the present stage of development of civilization it can be claimed that
the scientific attempt to understand nature is the most successful of all activities in the ongoing human effort to extend the world of objective
knowledge, that is World 3. Moreover, it forms the basis of the technology

that within a few decades has transformed the conditions of life in the developed countries, and that, in its increasing application forms a measure of the progress of the developing countries. The frequent confusion in the usage of the terms science and technology has given rise to the common, but mistaken idea that science is responsible for the many disorders that arise from the uncontrolled use of technology. Hence there has been a widespread attack on civilized values and even on the whole of World 3 by the forces of irrationalism. In these times of disorder and disillusionment amongst so many academics it is essential for creative intellects to make manifest the wonderful heritage that we have in the world of objective knowledge, and that gives us all our Civilization and Culture. Without it we would be primitive barbarians. An appropriate tribute to Karl Popper is to say that he has been one of the foremost creative intellects in this century in this great enterprise of conserving and further adding to the world of objective knowledge.

SIR JOHN ECCLES

DEPARTMENT OF PHYSIOLOGY
SCHOOL OF MEDICINE
STATE UNIVERSITY OF NEW YORK, BUFFALO
SEPTEMBER, 1970

REFERENCES

Eccles, J. C. (1957). *The Physiology of Nerve Cells.* Baltimore: Johns Hopkins Press.

———— (1964). *The Physiology of Synapses.* Berlin, Göttingen, Heidelberg: Springer-Verlag.

———— (1966). "Ionic Mechanisms of Excitatory and Inhibitory Synaptic Action." *Annals of New York Academy of Science,* **137**, pp. 473-94.

———— (1969). *The Inhibitory Pathways of the Central Nervous System* (Sherrington Lectures). Liverpool, England: Liverpool University Press.

Hawkes, Jacquetta (1965). *Prehistory. History of Mankind. Cultural and Scientific Development.* Vol. 1, Part 1. UNESCO. London: New English Library.

Malraux, A. (1960). *Preface to Sumer by André Parrot.* Translated by Stuart Gilbert and James Emmons. London: Thames and Hudson.

Popper, K. R. (1963a). *Conjectures and Refutations: The Growth of Scientific Knowledge.* London: Routledge & Kegan Paul; New York: Basic Books.

———— (1963b). "Science: Problems, Aims, Responsibilities." *Federation Proceedings*, Federation of American Societies for Experimental Biology, **22**, pp. 961-72.

_____ (1968a). "Epistemology Without a Knowing Subject." *Logic, Methodology and Philosophy of Sciences.* Edited by van Rootselaar and Staal. Vol. III. Amsterdam: North-Holland Publishing Company.

_____ (1968b). "On the Theory of the Objective Mind." *Akten des XIV. Internationalen Kongresses für Philosophie* (Vienna), **1**.

_____ (1970). The Emory Lectures (in course of publication).

Thorpe, W. H. (1956). *Learning and Instinct in Animals.* London: Methuen and Co.

Tinbergen, N. (1951). *The Study of Instinct.* Oxford: Clarendon Press.

Woolley, L. (1965). *The Beginnings of Civilization. History of Mankind. Cultural and Scientific Development.* UNESCO. London: The New English Library.

J. W. N. Watkins
THE UNITY OF POPPER'S THOUGHT

Contents

1. Introduction

'Modern analytical empiricism', Russell has said, 'has the advantage, as compared with the philosophies of the system-builders, of being able to tackle its problems one at a time, instead of having to invent at one stroke a block theory of the whole universe.'[1] Agreed; but it is also a shade disappointing, surely, when an analytic philosopher's lifework adds up to a collection of separate results with no tendency to coalesce into a general view.

For there is a third possibility between system-building and piecemeal analysis. A philosopher may tackle separate problems 'one at a time'; but as his problems and ideas ramify, connections may become discernible between main ideas of his in different fields. Then, if his original problems were central ones within their respective fields, he may come close to fulfilling, but unselfconsciously and without strain or contrivance, something of the synoptic ambition of the system-builders of the past.

So far, so vague. Let me be more specific. I take as the original core of Popper's epistemology his *falsificationism*;[2] and I take his *indeterminism* to have been the most striking component of his metaphysical outlook around 1950.[3] I remember suggesting to Popper, some time in the early 1950s, that these two pillars of his philosophy, falsificationism and indeterminism, were essentially independent of one another. As I recall, he accepted this without demur. My aim, now, is to refute that old suggestion, which I made before his ideas on evolution and biology had got under way in the late 1950s. Briefly, I shall argue that his indeterminism is significantly related to his evolutionism, which in turn is significantly related to his falsificationism: the last is not, after all, independent of the first.

Thus my presentation will by no means follow the historical order in which Popper developed his ideas. What came first historically—his philosophy of scientific knowledge—will emerge last, here; and what came last historically—his biological and evolutionist ideas[4]—will come in the middle.

A word of apology about the style of this contribution: after some rereading I put Popper's writings away and set about recasting his ideas in my own order and in my own words (though I did, of course, check some points afterwards). One result is a paucity of quotations and references. Another is something I rather deplore when I meet it in someone else. In an extended commentary on an author's ideas it ought always to be clear what stance the commentator is taking: whether he is now reporting the man's ideas, or advancing views of his own either about them (for instance, about their interconnectedness) or about subjects handled by his author. I fear that in what follows I often fail to make explicit which stance I am adopting. The fact is that most of these ideas have entered more or less deeply into my own thinking—most deeply, perhaps, in the case of indeterminism (my section on this developed runaway tendencies which I had some difficulty in restraining). The reader should assume, unless there are clear indications to the contrary, both that the ideas being presented (however freely) are Popper's and that I assent to them as well. Another thing: I have on previous occasions discussed various aspects of Popper's methodology and epistemology.[5] On the present occasion I try not to retraverse old territory: I concentrate mainly on

Popper's metaphysical view of the world and of living organisms; his epistemology will be the destination rather than part of the subject matter of this paper.

At the behest of my title (which was proposed to me) I had planned to go on to examine some connections between these ideas and Popper's ideas in the fields of moral, social and political philosophy. I reluctantly dropped this plan when I realised that the existing paper was as overlong as it was overdue.

2. Indeterminism

I will begin with a distinction which will be important in what follows.

(2.1) Metaphysical determinism and scientific determinism. Metaphysical determinism, as here understood, is a doctrine about the world and does not, by itself, assert anything about science. Scientific determinism incorporates metaphysical determinism and adds that there is, in principle, no limit to scientific knowledge of the world, present, past and future.

The idea of metaphysical determinism was expressed long ago by Democritus when he said: 'from infinite time back are foreordained by necessity all things that were and are and are to come.'[6] This formulation brings out very well the idea of the symmetry of past and future: both are equally fixed; past events are not with us any more but they are still part of the world, and future events are not with us yet but they are already part of the world. (Popper uses the analogy of a cinematic film, part of which has already passed through the projector and part of which is still to come; but both parts are *there*.) Full-blooded determinism says that every tiny detail of every event is precisely predetermined.

Scientific determinism superimposes on metaphysical determinism the epistemological claim that there is, in principle, no limit to the extent to which the already fixed and determined future may be scientifically foreknown from a knowledge of present conditions and of the laws of nature. In practice, no doubt, all our scientific predictions have a penumbra of imprecision; but according to scientific determinism this could, in principle, always be reduced as much as desired by making more thorough and precise determinations of initial conditions.

Metaphysical indeterminism and scientific indeterminism are the contradictories of metaphysical determinism and scientific determinism. Metaphysical indeterminism says that there is at least one event such that there was a time prior to its occurrence at which it was *not* causally predetermined to occur. Scientific indeterminism says that there is at least one event such that there was a time prior to its occurrence at which it was in principle impossible scientifically to predict that it would occur. An indeterminist theory should, of course, go on to say what *kinds* of event are undetermined, or unpredictable, and why.

Scientific determinism is, of course, a stronger doctrine than metaphysical determinism which it incorporates and stiffens; conversely, scientific indeterminism is a weaker doctrine than metaphysical indeterminism. (The adjective 'scientific' here is to indicate, not that these doctrines are empirically testable, but that they are doctrines about the possibilities of scientific knowledge.) Scientific indeterminism asserts that there would still be gaps in the best possible scientific foreknowledge of the future. Metaphysical indeterminism makes the stronger assertion that there are 'gaps'—genuinely open possibilities—in the future-as-so-far-determined. It is possible to combine the two weaker doctrines, metaphysical determinism and scientific indeterminism; indeed, most determinists nowadays have retreated to metaphysical determinism: they admit that there are events which are in principle unpredictable by scientific methods, adding that these events are nevertheless causally determined.

Popper holds the stronger indeterminist position, metaphysical indeterminism; and the immediate target of most of his antideterminist arguments has been the stronger determinist position, scientific determinism. However, it will be a thesis of this section of the present paper that those arguments, reinforced by an argument of Landé's, also show that *metaphysical* determinism is an unreasonable doctrine.

The issues, then, are metaphysical issues. But the *arguments* which we are going to consider consist of nonmetaphysical considerations drawn from methodology, common sense, logic, probability and statistics, quantum theory, and theory of knowledge.

(2.2) The breakdown of scientific determinism. Concerning hypotheses that conflict with deep-seated convictions of common sense—such as the conviction that we can do something about the future, whereas the past is unalterable—Popper proposes the following methodological thesis: the onus is on the proponent of the hypothesis to make a case for it; and if the best case so far made for it is defeated, that suffices for the rebuttal of the hypothesis (unless a better case is made for it). In other words, it is enough to *undermine* such a hypothesis; we do not need to *refute* it (which may in any case be impossible, for the hypothesis may well be metaphysical).

Now, Newtonian physics did seem to provide powerful support for the determinist case against the commonsense belief that the future, unlike the past, is not completely fixed and unalterable. Admittedly, Newton himself introduced a certain indeterminacy with his idea that, when minor irregularities within the solar system have so accumulated as to endanger its stability, God will intervene to restore order; for Newtonian physics could not predict exactly when such divine tinkerings will occur, and exactly what forms they will take. But Laplace was able to eliminate this anomaly;[7] and he went on to give a famous formulation of the thesis of scientific determinism: for an 'intelligence' (or 'Demon', as it came to be called) able to comprehend in an instant the relative situations of all bodies and the forces which act on them and to analyse these data, 'nothing would be uncertain and the future, like the past, would be present to its eyes.'[8]

In 1950 Popper showed that scientific determinism breaks down *even in classical physics*, if the idea of a Laplacean Demon is given a physical interpretation, if the Demon is embodied in a mechanical predictor.[9] For, however powerful it may be, this predictor—call it P_1—will not be able fully to predict its *own* future states (by the 'Tristram Shandy' argument); a second predictor P_2 may be introduced to make good this deficiency; but P_2 will be able to predict P_1's future states only if P_1 is *not* attempting to predict P_2's future states (by the 'Oedipus' argument). And since P_2 is also unable to predict its own future states (by 'Tristram Shandy' again) *these* now remain unpredicted. The unpredictability has been shifted rather than eliminated; and it will again only be shifted if a third predictor is introduced to make good this new deficiency.

Thus even without invoking the indeterminacy relations of quantum theory, Popper could claim that metaphysical determinism has been deprived of its main support—viz., scientific determinism—and should therefore, according to the methodological thesis mentioned above, no longer be upheld against our commonsense convictions.

But the metaphysical determinist is unlikely to be bowled over by these considerations. He may reject that methodological thesis; or he may place determinism itself among his deepest commonsense convictions, so obvious and convincing does it seem to him. If he is at all scientifically 'with it' he is likely, in view of Heisenberg's uncertainty principle, to have abandoned scientific determinism long ago without feeling obliged thereby to abandon also the metaphysical core of his determinist position. Let us look into this.

(2.3) Objectivism, probabilistic physics, and indeterminism. A metaphysical determinist who espouses scientific indeterminism might give a popular generalisation of Heisenberg's uncertainty principle along these lines.

Measurement is always partly a physical process. So, any act of measuring will cause some physical disturbance; and this disturbance, although it proceeds in a causally determinate way in accordance with natural law, may very well affect the property being measured.[10] By using delicate measuring processes that are sensitive to variations in the thing measured while having very little disturbing effect upon it, we may succeed in making highly accurate measurements. But suppose we try to measure factors (light photons perhaps) *involved in our most delicate measuring processes* (light-ray probes perhaps): their very smallness and lightness and sensitivity is almost certain to mean that *they* will be easily disturbed if some measuring process is turned upon them. This may not destroy all possibility of measuring them. (Perhaps we could still make *some* measurements of them as accurately as we wished, but in making these very accurate measurements we might cause such disturbance that there would be other measurements we could hardly make at all.)

But it is almost certain to mean that we could not make *all* desired measurements to *any* desired degree of accuracy. It may have been reasonable in Laplace's day to assume that there is no limit to the precision and completeness with which determining factors might in principle be ascertained, but we cannot continue to make this assumption today. The idea of the perfectly univocal and determinate foreknowledge available to a Laplacean Demon can be retained as an expression of metaphysical determinism—for the Demon was imagined to use intuitive rather than disturbing physical methods of measurement. But science must use such methods; and in those fields where such 'observer-interference' creates insurmountable limits to the completeness and accuracy with which data can be ascertained, it is likely that *probabilistic* theories are the best that can be achieved.

Along some such lines as those might a metaphysical determinist reconcile himself, plausibly enough, to the probabilistic theories of modern physics. But his determinism, Popper points out, obliges him to put a special interpretation—an essentially anthropocentric interpretation—upon such theories:[11] these cannot be taken at their face value as statements about the world, for in nature (according to metaphysical determinism) nothing is chancey or merely probable; probabilities reside in the subjective world of our thinking, not in the objective world outside. A probabilistic theory must be regarded as tacitly avowing the *incompleteness* of its description of nature; and where a probabilistic theory is the best that we have been able to achieve, it must be regarded as an expression of the incompleteness of *our* knowledge, i.e., as a statement that is at least partly about *us*. If 'probability is the very guide of life' that is because we must almost always act on insufficient evidence.[12] Relative to a complete knowledge of laws and initial conditions, such as Laplace's Demon was imagined to possess, the probability of any possible event will, according to metaphysical determinism, be either one or zero. Where physics can do no better than ascribe some intermediate value, there 'probability is relative' (in the words of Laplace, who was not only a Newtonian determinist but also, of course, a great probability-theorist) 'in part to [our] *ignorance*, in part to our knowledge.'[13] And this implication of determinism remains, whether or not one adds that we are bound to be at least partially ignorant of the state of any microphysical system.

By contrast, Popper has no deterministic doctrine to *prevent* him from taking a probabilistic theory at its face value as a straightforward description of the world: a gappy theory may describe a gappy world rather than avow the gappiness of our knowledge of a gapless world. Moreover, his objectivism *encourages* him so to take it.

Popper's objectivism is an important tendency in his whole philosophy.[14] Here I will only state it briefly in order to assess its implications for indeterminism. An argument for it will be mentioned later (Sec. 4.4 below).

It combines two ideas, one a truism of common sense, the other a little more recondite. The first is realism or the assumption that the world exists 'out there', largely independent of our activities. The second is the idea that science *also* exists 'out there', largely independent of our mental processes. It is not merely that scientific hypotheses and experiments are recorded in far more publications than any one person could hope to peruse. It is rather that the *content* or objective meaning of a published scientific theory must transcend anyone's understanding of it. Of course, people are needed for the invention and transmission of a scientific theory. But they will not know of all its (infinitely many) implications, some of which may be discovered long after it was first put forward, and many of which will never be discovered. (More about this later.) A theory cannot be identified with the sum of people's partial understandings of it. And once a theory has been launched it may acquire an independent life of its own. (Consider the remarkable history of Euclidean geometry after Euclid.) On this view, science is a structure which transcends the mental processes of those who help to make it, rather as a cathedral transcends the manual processes of those who helped to build it.[15]

Combining this with realism we get: science exists objectively and it is about an objectively existing world. Mental states (feelings of certainty, doubt, etc.) are extraneous to science so conceived (though they help to determine what goes into science). A physical theory is deprived of its scientific purport when treated as an expression of a state of mind rather than as an assertion about the world; rather as a joke is no laughing matter to the psychoanalyst who treats it as a *symptom*.

This sounds innocent enough—until we come to the probabilistic and statistical theories of modern microphysics; for, as we have seen, the determinist *is* obliged to treat such theories as expressions of partial ignorance. But Popper's objectivism implies that we may treat such theories, no less than causal and deterministic ones, as statements about the world. If a theory says, for example, that the probability that a photon will pass through a half-silvered mirror is one-half, then we may cheerfully take this to mean, *not* that *our* ignorance is such that *we* have no more reason to expect the photon to pass through than to be reflected, but that *nature* is indifferent between letting it through and reflecting it back.

In short, this objectivism speaks against the gentleman's agreement between metaphysical determinism and probabilistic microphysics.

Popper's objectivism, realism and indeterminism are united in his propensity interpretation of probability. Before turning to this, however, I will present an argument of Landé's against a view that combines metaphysical determinism with scientific indeterminism. This argument is important for Popper in helping further to undermine that gentleman's agreement. Also, Landé's argument applies quite generally to probabilistic situations whether at the macrolevel or at the microlevel; so it helps to counter the soothing suggestion that indeterminacies, if they exist at all, exist

J. W. N. WATKINS

down in the microlevel basement and do not disturb the medium-sized furniture of our human world. (This can also be countered, of course, by invoking the possibility of micro-macro amplifying devices. To recall a famous imaginary experiment: whether Schroedinger's cat gets electrocuted depends on whether the photon passes through the half-silvered mirror.)[16]

(2.4) Landé's argument. The determinist will admit that we seem to be able to create, more or less at will, pockets of randomness in our causally determined world: we have only to start rattling dice or spinning coins and sequences will develop (if our setup is 'fair') that are random at least in the sense of being proof against gambling-systems.

But the metaphysical determinist will say that this sense of 'random' is only an epistemological sense: it refers to *our inability* to discover a successful gambling-system. As we saw, he may allow that some events (determined, according to him, by hidden causes) are scientifically unpredictable even in principle, and he can easily add that sequences of such events may very well be random in this epistemological sense. But he will insist that no sequence is random in any *ontological* sense: the events that constitute a 'random' sequence are not *causally* indeterminate.

Suppose our randomising setup consists of what we may call a Landé-blade arrangement.[17] This is as follows. When a lever is pulled a billiard ball rolls down a chute and on to an adjustable blade from which it falls off to left or right. The determinist will probably agree that, if we position the blade centrally and then release a large number of balls one after another down the chute, we shall generate an (epistemologically) random sequence of lefts and rights. But he will also insist that whether an individual ball will fall to the left or the right is causally predetermined in every case—namely, by various little unobserved asymmetries in our setup.

We might call this insistence an illustration of the determinist's *stock response* to random sequences. Landé's originality, here, is to *accept* this stock response for the sake of argument, and to reveal its bizarre implications.

Suppose that we are about to drop one thousand balls, one after another, on to our centrally positioned Landé-blade and that the determinist endorses the statistical prediction that approximately *five hundred* balls will land on the left.

According to determinism, the little asymmetries that determine which way a ball falls are, of course, themselves causally determined by prior conditions which in turn are causally determined, and so on. Consider, now, a succession of one thousand states of the universe—$S_1, S_2, \ldots S_{1000}$—such that S_1 obtained just n years before the first ball lands, S_2 just n years before the second ball lands, and so on. (Provided we do not exceed the age of the universe, we may make n as large as we like.) Landé's point is this. If we now combine our previous statistical prediction with the determinist's stock response, we can get the following *retrodiction*: the sequence $S_1 \ldots S_{1000}$ contained approximately *five hundred* world-states each of which (given the laws of nature) predetermined that a ball would fall off our blade to the left just n years later (call these 'left-determining states' for short).

But *why* (we now ask the determinist) should there *then* have been approximately *five hundred* left-determining states? Remember, we have not released the balls yet and do not know exactly how they will fall out. This retrodiction follows (given determinism) from a statistical *prediction* derived, in its turn, from a consideration of the symmetry of our setup and the equiprobabilities it involves. So our question is: why should the world *then* have been so nicely geared to the statistical requirements of our probabilistic setup today?

One way of dealing with this question would be to deny that a *determinist* is really entitled to derive that statistical prediction from those probabilistic considerations: hence our question does not arise. I shall argue in the next subsection that this reply is, indeed, correct. But most determinists do feel entitled to derive statistical predictions from probabilistic considerations; and, for them, only two kinds of answer to our question seem possible: one which consistently denies that there was ever any ontological indeterminacy (as opposed to mere scientific unpredictability: ontological indeterminacy would defeat the predictive powers even of a Laplacean Demon); and one which concedes that there was once some ontological indeterminacy. Let us begin with the second kind of answer (*soft* determinism, as Landé calls it).

It would run something like this. Once long ago (perhaps in the very beginning) there was cosmic chaos. Let n have a value so that the sequence of world-states, $S_1 \ldots S_{1000}$, falls within that chaotic period. Each of those world-states must have been either a left-determining or a right-determining state. With respect to these two properties, left-determining and right-determining, the sequence should (in view of the cosmic chaos), be random, and the chance that a given world-state within the sequence is left-determining equals the chance that it is right-determining. Hence, it is highly probable that the sequence comprised approximately five hundred left-determining and five hundred right-determining states. The sequence we are now about to generate by releasing balls down the chute will be a causal descendant of that ancestral random sequence.

Such an answer seems unsatisfactory for several reasons. (1) Its plausibility wanes when we turn to randomising setups that give *unequal* probabilities to the possible outcomes. Let us now adjust our Landé-blade slightly so that about three-quarters of the balls should fall to the left—now why should the original chaos have thrown up a sequence of world-states containing about three times more left-determining than right-determining states? (2) This answer ('soft determinism') can hardly satisfy the full-fledged determinist, since it merely *backdates* randomness without *reducing* it, implying that there is (in the timeless sense of 'is') as much (ontological) randomness in the world as there appears to be, though it is not where it appears to be: every epistemologically random sequence observed today is the causally necessitated descendant of . . . an ontologically random ancestral sequence. (3) Nor can it satisfy the indeterminist, who sees no point, once ontological randomness has been admitted, in trying to confine it to some disreputable cosmic epoch in the past. (4) It seems to suggest *that we can control the past*: for we now seem *free* to adjust our Landé-blade to generate varying proportions of lefts and rights; does this not mean that we are *also* free to adjust the proportion of left-determining and right-determining states in the remote past? (The determinist will answer that we are not, causally speaking, free to adjust it: whether or not we *shall* adjust it has *also* been determined in the remote past along with the sequence of lefts and rights that we shall obtain. I will revert to this point shortly.)

So let us leave 'soft' determinism and repeat our question to a 'hard' determinist: why should past conditions have conformed themselves so nicely to the exigencies of our randomising setup today? Only one answer is open to him, according to Landé: he will have to say that the harmony was *preestablished*; in other words, he will have to invoke a *theological conspiracy-theory of randomness.* 'Hard' or full-fledged metaphysical determinism turns out to call for a being more active than Laplace's Demon, one who not merely foresees all but who, foreseeing all the 'games of chance' that will ever be played (whether by nature, as in radioactive emission, or by randomising machines or human beings) skilfully manipulated the initial conditions so that pockets of 'randomness' would be predetermined to break out as occasion demanded. God, on this view, instead of playing dice with the world, has rigged our dice games for us.

But notice that even this conspiracy-theory is not yet quite conspiratorial enough to eliminate all indeterminacy. To predetermine just what numbers would be thrown up by a roulette wheel in Monte Carlo during 1977, God would have needed a gambler-proof sequence of numbers. Now it is possible, as Popper showed in 1934,[18] *to use a formula* for constructing a randomlike sequence. If God chose this method he would need to keep the formula secret from us. Determinism involves forbidden truths, a point to which I shall revert (p. 387 below).

Alternatively, God might have constructed a random sequence with the help of genuine indeterminacies—generated, perhaps, by some sort of celestial roulette wheel that threw up numbers which even he could not foresee or gamble successfully against.[19] But now we are back with soft determinism and the idea of original sequences that are ontologically random.

As well as pockets of randomness we also generate pockets of intelligible behaviour in the physical world; and Landé's argument can be extended to these. Suppose—to revert to an unfinished point—that I am now arguing with a determinist and have just claimed that determinism implies that we can control the past by adjusting our Landé-blade (see p. 380 above. I now silently and confidently predict that he will reply that past conditions determined *both* whether I shall adjust the blade *and* what sequence of lefts and rights will ensue. Then determinism implies that I can proceed from this prediction to the *retrodiction* that *n* years ago physical conditions were such as to determine, given the laws of physics, that *n* years later my determinist friend's tongue and lips would move in ways appropriate to the expression of this reply to my objection. But why should the universe *then* have been so nicely geared to the physical exigencies of our philosophical discussion today? Again, it seems that the determinist will be driven to a theological conspiracy-theory.

(2.5) The propensity interpretation. In considering Landé's argument we assumed that the following three inferences were in order for our imaginary opponent, who combines metaphysical determinism with scientific indeterminism and who recognises the fundamental role of probability and statistics in modern physics: (i) from evidence about the setup (blade centrally positioned, etc.) to a probabilistic hypothesis (the probability of a ball falling to the left equals that of its falling to the right); (ii) from this probabilistic hypothesis to a statistical prediction (approximately five hundred balls will fall to the left and five hundred to the right); (iii) from this statistical prediction to a corresponding retrodiction (approximately five hundred left-determining and five hundred right-determining states *n* years ago). It was upon this last unwanted inference that Landé dwelt. But let us now dwell a little on the second inference. Is our metaphysical determinist entitled to draw it?

Remember that he insists that how each ball will fall is causally predetermined but *by asymmetries of which we are ignorant.* His observations tell him only of the *symmetry* of the setup. It is his determinist faith that assures him of the existence of the left-causing and right-causing asymmetries. But if he has no empirical knowledge of the factors that decide which way any ball will fall, he must presumably interpret this probabilistic hypothesis as saying that *we have no more reason to suppose* that a ball will fall to the left than to the right. Now a probabilistic hypothesis understood in this subjective way becomes a statement about *us*, about our ignorance of the deciding factors. And Popper (following von Mises) points out that predictions about future events in the external world (in this case, the statistical prediction mentioned in (ii) above) cannot be derived from premises about our present ignorance.[20] A premise that is to yield conclusions about the external world must itself assert something about the external world. A determinist who affirms his ignorance of the very factors which, according to him, decide which way each ball falls surely has no warrant for predicting that about five hundred will fall to the left. Landé's point was that determinism gives the determinist something he does not want, viz., a license to job backwards from an about-to-be-generated statistical sequence of lefts and rights to an ancestral sequence of world-states. The present point is that determinism deprives the determinist of something he does want, viz., a license to job forwards from his knowledge of the (causally neutral) observed symmetry of his randomising setup, and his ignorance of the (causally decisive) unobserved asymmetries within it, to a statistical prediction.

Suppose we confront a determinist with a black box which has a push button at one end and two lamps, one red and one green, at the other. When the button is pushed one or other of the two lamps flashes on a moment later. We assure the determinist that if he could see the mechanism inside the box he could easily predict, whenever the button was pressed, which lamp would flash on. We tell him that we are about to press the button one thousand times, and we invite him to predict approximately how many reds and greens we shall get.

His correct reply, surely, would be that, since the box hides the causally decisive factors, he has no evidence on which to base a prediction; he has no reason to expect more reds than greens or vice versa; but this is *not* a reason for *expecting* approximately equal numbers of reds and greens.

But how, from a determinist point of view, does this case differ from the Landé-blade case? For here too the causally decisive factors are hidden.

The determinist may say that past experience (which gives him no guidance in the case of our black box) does tell him roughly what to expect in the case of our Landé-blade; more generally, our experience of so-called 'randomising' devices justifies the introduction of a postulate that licenses inferences (under appropriate conditions) from probabilistic hypotheses to statistical predictions.

This may be so. But consider what, according to determinism, such a postulate would implicitly claim. To repeat: where a probabilistic hypothesis is the best we have been able to achieve, it is (according to determinism) an avowal of our ignorance, whereas a statistical prediction is a statement about the world. Hence such a postulate would claim that in stochastic processes the frequency with which events recur conveniently conforms itself to our ignorance—another remarkable preestablished harmony.

A simpler way of enabling statistical conclusions to be drawn from probabilistic premises is to interpret the latter objectively, as statements about the world. Now the frequency theory provides an objective interpretation of probabilistic hypotheses; and for many years Popper accepted the frequency theory. This allows for the derivability of statistical predictions by interpreting a probabilistic hypothesis as itself a kind of statistical statement. Indeed, the adoption of the frequency theory almost seems to be *dictated* by the logical maxim that 'statistical conclusions can only be derived from statistical premisses'.[21] But in the 1950s he moved on to a propensity interpretation.

A normal statistical situation consists of a setup which generates random sequences in which attributes recur with certain frequencies. According to the propensity interpretation, to ascribe a probability of, say, 1/4 to getting a six uppermost with a certain loaded die should be understood roughly like this: in this whole die-throwing setup the six possibilities are weighted so that the setup is disposed to generate random sequences in which the six appears uppermost with a frequency that approaches 1/4 as the sequence grows longer.

When a probabilistic hypothesis is interpreted in this way, it incorporates what the same hypothesis would assert if interpreted in a frequency sense, for propensities are interpreted as tendencies to produce frequencies.[22] Thus the propensity interpretation equally permits the derivation of statistical predictions. But does this interpretation really go beyond a frequency interpretation? And if so, is not its surplus content redundant?

A frequency-theorist, even if he does not regard the introduction of propensities as obscurantist metaphysics, is likely to resist it as a redundant complication. What is needed for the ascription of a probability-value, according to him, is essentially straightforward and unmysterious: a given random sequence (or 'collective') in which a certain attribute occurs with a certain frequency. We do not need, he will say, to peer behind the sequence to the alleged propensities of the setup; moreover, these 'propensities' can hardly be anything more than reifications of frequencies.

But Popper argues that there are cases where the frequency-theorist *is* obliged to rely essentially on the propensities of the setup, if he is to ascribe the probability-value that he and everyone else would want to ascribe.[23] The argument is this. Suppose that we have a long sequence consisting almost entirely of throws with a loaded die, but including two throws with a true die; in this long sequence the six appears uppermost with a frequency of 1/4. Now we all want to say that in the case of those two throws with the true die the probability of a six appearing uppermost was 1/6. But the frequency-theorist may not say this so long as he treats those throws as members of our long, actual, impure sequence: within *this* sequence the probability of a six on any throw would, for him, be 1/4. So he must treat them as members of a different sequence. But what sequence? It cannot consist just of those two throws, for the six could not have appeared uppermost with a frequency of 1/6 in that little sequence. It must be a *virtual* sequence of throws with this true die: it is only in this virtual sequence that the six may be said to appear uppermost with a frequency of 1/6.

Assume that the true die was destroyed after it had been thrown twice. (This assumption is logically inessential and is introduced for rhetorical effect.) Now, surely, we can query the frequency-theorist's claim that frequencies are hard and real whereas propensities are ghostly hypostatizations of frequencies. For in the present case the frequency pertains to a very ghostly sequence. Moreover, if we ask the frequency-theorist *why* he supposes that in that (nonexistent) sequence the six *would* have appeared uppermost with a frequency of 1/6, he will have to appeal to the setup (the symmetry of the true die, the manner of shaking it, etc.) and its tendency, disposition or propensity—call it what you will—to generate sequences with that limiting frequency. Now, instead of the propensity being a shadowy reification of a real frequency, the frequency seems rather to be the shadowy projection of a real propensity.

Admittedly, a propensity-statement *may* be made *ad hoc* relative to a frequency-statement. Example: having found that a loaded die landed six uppermost 257 out of 1,000 throws, we declare that the die has a propensity of 0.257 to land six uppermost. But as we have seen, the boot may be on the other foot. Example: we examine a pinboard and, without releasing any balls, calculate how its propensities would alter were we to tamper with the pins in various ways. To these propensity-estimates we now attach virtual sequences each having the appropriate limiting frequency.

A probability statement about the outcome of a *single* experiment is interpreted, on both the frequency and the propensity theory, as an abbreviation of a more complex statement. But whereas the frequency-theory treats it as an abbreviated version of a statement about something counterfactual (a statement about what *would* have happened if the experiment, instead of being made only once, had been repeated an indefinitely large number of times), the propensity-theory treats it as an abbreviated version of a statement about something real, if dispositional, namely the structure of a certain setup and its weighting of possible outcomes.

A dispositional structure may, of course, be real even though it remains largely or wholly unactualised. (A fragile vase may remain unbroken.) Popper compares the idea of the propensity of a setup to generate certain frequencies with the idea of a field of force, or of an electromagnetic field. A field is a highly dispositional structure. We may actualize some of its potentialities, say by exploring it with a probe. But it is there whether we probe it or not. The propensity-theory is not obliged to invoke anything fictitious in its interpretation of probability statements about single experiments.

The propensity interpretation implies that indeterminacy is by no means incompatible with orderliness. (This is important for biology.) A setup with a propensity to generate random sequences of a certain kind may be a very stable structure; and the sequences it generates may, of course, display admirable statistical regularities. This interpretation also implies that we can, ontologically speaking, generate something like *isolated pockets* of randomness—by activating a randomising setup, we can cause random sequences to *start up*, if not *ex nihilo*, at any rate against a nonrandom background. For whereas determinism requires us to regard each element in such a sequence as fully determined by antecedent conditions, the propensity interpretation allows us to regard them as partially undetermined (though *influenced* by the weightings of the propensity setup). This frees us from what may be called the 'artesian well' view of random sequences: namely, the view that whenever we generate an empirical random sequence, we mysteriously cause a subterranean system of dispersed causal chains briefly to concentrate and surface for our inspection (Landé's point again). Here, the propensity interpretation seems only sensible. For there need be nothing random about the construction of a randomising setup. Rather to the contrary: a *good* roulette wheel, say, is precision-tooled to make it as regular and symmetrical as possible.

Popper's main reason for preferring a propensity interpretation is that it makes possible a systematically objective interpretation of quantum theory. So far as indeterminism is concerned, the chief result of such an interpretation is that, instead of trying to bring microindeterminacies into a quasi-subjective and quasi-determinist framework (attributing them to observer interference), we should accept (so long as we accept the quantum theory itself) that the world is made of elements which behave with a certain objective indeterminacy. This entitles us to invert what I call 'Spinoza's gambit', namely his attribution of the belief that we are free to our ignorance of microdeterminants. For we may now attribute the belief that a gas, say, behaves in a perfectly determinate way to ignorance of microindeterminacies; its lawlike regularities are really only statistical. To make the point as Popper makes it: some things—clocks, for instance—appear to behave in a pretty determinate manner, others—clouds, for instance—in a pretty indeterminate manner; according to classical determinism, a cloud is really a complex of interacting pieces of 'clockwork'; but according to quantum theory (objectively interpreted), a clock is really a complex of interacting micro-'clouds'.

(2.6) The future growth of science. As a last argument for indeterminism I will discuss Popper's claim that the future course of theoretical science cannot be predicted by rational or scientific methods.[24]

Imagine that we have received the following tip-off from the Angel of Truth: current indeterministic microphysical theories will be superseded during the next twenty years by a deeper physical theory which will be no less deterministic than classical physics.[25] (I want to correct any impression that may have been given in preceding pages that Popper's case for indeterminism depends essentially, or even mainly, on the current success of indeterministic physics.)

Let us refer to this theory of the future as *T*. The Angel vouchsafed neither the content of *T* nor the identity of its inventor(s). What would this tip-off imply for the determinism/indeterminism issue?

We know that the world as described by T will be deterministic, and we can assume that T will provide a pretty comprehensive description of the world. But there is, presumably, at least one thing that T will not comprehend, namely the fact of its own invention.[26]Could this fact be brought within the ambit of our scientific knowledge? Is there, in principle, any possibility of scientifically predicting the content of T (and the timing of its invention)?

Let 'K' stand for the totality of our current scientific knowledge. Now we know in advance that T will be inconsistent with K; for K includes those indeterministic microphysical theories that are going to be superseded by the deterministic T. (On Popper's theory of the growth of scientific knowledge, there is nothing untoward about such an inconsistency between old and new scientific theories; indeed, it is methodologically desirable, because a theory which is strictly inconsistent with the *explicandum* it was to explain, a theory which has the temerity to challenge and correct its well-attested *explicandum*, should be less *ad hoc* and more severely testable than a theory which is perfectly consistent with its original *explicandum*.)[27]

Now if T will be inconsistent with K, then either T will not be logically derivable from K or K will itself be internally inconsistent, in which case the denial of T will also be logically derivable from K. In either case there is no hope of predictively singling out the content of T on the basis of the totality of our present scientific knowledge.

So if there is to be any hope of scientifically predicting T it will have to be on the basis, not of K as a whole, but of some part of K. Indeed, a scientific determinist might very well insist that what is chiefly relevant for the prediction of T is *not* existing evidence and theories in what will become the domain of T, not existing scientific material for which T will make a successful take-over bid, but something very different, namely knowledge about the brain (and future causal influences upon it) of the inventor-to-be of T. So let us now consider this suggestion.

It seems to involve considerable difficulties. First, we must *catch our man*. (The Angel did not tell us who will invent T.) Second, we must acquire minutely detailed information about the state of his brain *without thereby disturbing it* in any way that would affect his process of invention. Third, having computed the future behaviour of our discoverer (however identified), we must *select* from the large number of marks that he is (according to our forecast) going to make on paper during the next twenty years just those that will express T. (*This* selection problem would be aggravated if the first selection problem—selecting the right man—had been met by casting our net widely over a number of candidates.) Fourth, we must *interpret* the marks thus selected.

But suppose all these difficulties overcome, and the prediction made. Then, of course, T would now have been discovered by the predictor, for whom three cheers![28] And if we impute an awareness of this discovery plus a horror of plagiarism to the physicist in question, then he will assuredly *not* go on putting marks on paper as forecast. The scientific process will have been speeded up, not foretold.

We usually think of scientific theories as existing apart from the world they describe; and we tend, in consequence, to regard deterministic theories as supporting a determinist view of the world. But, of course, scientific activity, including the invention and elaboration of scientific theories (whether deterministic or not), is also part of the world: indeed, within our human world it is something of great causal significance. And since scientific activity involves creativity and unpredictability, science would still provide a decisive argument for scientific indeterminism even if all its theories were deterministic.

But does science, considered as a human activity, support *metaphysical* indeterminism? Take some hypothesis first formulated at time t_1; at any earlier time t_0 it could not have been scientifically predicted that this hypothesis would first be formulated at time t_1, since to make such a prediction would have involved formulating the hypothesis at t_0. Here, as with other cases of unpredictability, the metaphysical determinist remains free to insist that the event E at t_1 (the original invention of the hypothesis) was unpredictable at t_0 *despite* the fact that at t_0 conditions C already existed which, in conjunction with the relevant laws of nature L, causally necessitated the occurrence of E at t_1.

But notice that each time the metaphysical determinist makes this move he adds to the stock of *forbidden truths* implied by his doctrine. The conditions C at t_0 were public facts and, presumably, capable in principle of being ascertained then; and so, presumably, were the laws L. Yet if we had known the truth about C and L at t_0, and if we had thereupon predicted the occurrence of E at t_1, E would *not* have occurred at t_1. On this view, what was wrong with our device of a tip-off from the Angel of Truth was that the Angel *divulged* part of the truth: it should have been kept hidden from us. There would likewise be trouble if God divulged to us the inscrutable formulas that govern our seemingly random sequences (see p. 380 above) or if a superphysiologist divulged to a human agent a prediction, based on the present state of the agent's brain, about a future decision of the agent.[29] Spinoza claimed that *in*determinism is sustained by ignorance, but it turns out that determinism requires us to remain in ignorance about ever so many truths that would cease to be truths if we knew about them.

Metaphysical indeterminism frees us from the doctrine of forbidden truths. Instead of saying that the facts about a scientific discovery due to be made in ten years' time are already there—but we must not learn about them yet—we can say that the facts just are not there yet: the future of science, as presently determined, is largely open. Instead of saying that the individual elements of sequences to be generated by an unbiassed roulette wheel are predetermined by hidden causes which no gambler could find out in advance, we can say that they are not fully predetermined; and instead of saying that the future decision of an agent who has not made up his mind is already causally predetermined by facts he must not learn about (for that would disturb him), we can say that his future decision is not fully determined yet.

I will conclude this section with a comment on how far Popper has come, not only in his methodological precepts but in his argumentative practice, from his 1934 position that metaphysical hypotheses, being irrefutable, are not rationally arguable.[30] In 1958 he sketched a theory of the criticisability of irrefutable doctrines (its moral was: assess them in relation to the problems they were intended to meet):[31] but I doubt whether this metatheory covers his own multiple criticisms of the doctrine of determinism. That he has not disproved the metaphysical core of the determinist position goes without saying. But his arguments (reinforced at a crucial point by Landé's) are strong enough, I believe, to defeat the determinist case against our commonsense Libertarianism. Of course, the debate may take a different direction in future years; but however the debate may go, one of Popper's results, here, will surely stand: an irrefutable metaphysical doctrine may, after all, be rationally debated.

3. Biology and Evolution

Popper's ideas in this area are still developing rapidly, and I will attempt no more than a nontechnical sketch of them. (Anything more ambitious would in any case be beyond my competence.)

(3.1) Indeterminacy and plastic control. To the idea of elementary particles changing state with a certain objective indeterminacy, an important idea of Popper's must now be added. But, before introducing it, I will mention his rejection of the claim (made by Hume, among others) that there is no middle possibility between sheer chance, on the one hand, and complete causal determination on the other. The denial of this claim is already implicit in the propensity-theory of probability. If we modify the propensities of a probabilistic setup, the effects of our modification will, typically, fall into neither of these extreme categories. Suppose we adjust the bias of a loaded die so that six landing uppermost becomes a little more probable. Then neither is it a matter of sheer chance whether the six will land uppermost more frequently nor is the six infallibly determined to land uppermost more frequently during the next series of throws. (It *may* chance to land uppermost with a *lower* frequency.) Rather, the propensities of our die-throwing setup have been given a new bias.

With an eye to Popper's general view of organisms I may add here that one biassable setup may be placed under the influence (or 'plastic' control—see below) of a superior biassable setup. Propensities may be superimposed on propensities.[32] (Indeed, we might have a whole hierarchy of propensities.) For instance, the pins of a pinboard might be adjusted in certain ways according to the falls of our variably loaded die. Then, by varying its loading, we should indirectly influence the way the balls fall out on the pinboard without, of course, being able to determine where the individual balls shall go.

Gas molecules bottled up inside a cylinder might be said to be under 'iron' control: their movement is subject to overall limits that are well-nigh rigid. If the gas is released into the atmosphere, we have the opposite extreme: the dispersing molecules cease to be under any overall control. There is also a kind of control intermediate between 'iron' control and no control, which Popper calls *plastic control*. He illustrates this with the example of a soap bubble. Here, the outer film is *responsive* to the motion of the molecules within it: it will expand if the bubble is warmed, for instance. (Of course, the bubble will burst, just as the cylinder will explode, if the molecules grow overexcited; but we are primarily interested, here, in cases where control is maintained.) In cases of plastic control there is a certain give and take between that part or aspect of the system which is more controlling than controlled and those parts which are more controlled than controlling.

Such a system may itself be a component of a larger system which is itself plastically controlled. If we regard such a hierarchical system as a unitary whole, we can expect its overall behaviour to be far more determinate than that of its smallest parts—but not completely determinate, in view of the give-and-take nature of plastic control. Variations in the behaviour of components at the lowest level might significantly affect their local control-system, and a change in it might significantly affect the control-system above it, and so on. Indeed, it might even happen that the influence of the original variations, instead of being progressively muffled as it spreads upwards, was actually amplified, leading to a significant change in the overall behaviour of the whole unit.

We now introduce three suppositions concerning organisms generally. (1) An organism comprises a complex of plastic controls. (2) An organism is a polycentric[33] system in which controls operate simultaneously at various levels, and in which a control may shift from one locus to another. For instance, control may be pushed down to a deeper level (as when a consciously learned skill becomes largely unconscious and physiological). (3) Despite this polycentricity, we can roughly distinguish an organism's *central* control-system (which may itself have a polycentric structure[34]) from its executive or 'motor' parts.[35] As an acknowledgement of this, we might call an organism a quasi-hierarchical system of plastic controls.

(3.2) Pilots of evolutionary change. Given this rough dualism between controlling and executive parts, we can now present an evolutionary hypothesis of Popper's which seems to me convincing and important. Sup-

pose that a prima facie favourable mutation occurs within an executive part, so that the organism's 'motor' power is enhanced. But suppose, also, that there is no corresponding improvement in control and that the increased motor-power now outruns the organism's central control. Then this mutation should be *disadvantageous*. (Popper illustrates this idea with a fighter-plane controlled by an automatic pilot: if its engine-power were to increase beyond the controlling capacity of the pilot it would be more likely to crash.) Now suppose, conversely, that a mutation occurs in the central control-system that results in control-skill outrunning motor-power. *This* would not be disadvantageous; and, should an appropriate increase in motor-power subsequently be brought about by mutation, then the organism would be altogether more powerful and effective. The important moral that Popper draws from this is that in evolutionary progress it is (favourable) *mutations in the central control system that lead the way*.[36] Motor-developments are improvements only if they are in line with prior control-developments.

He claims that this idea suggests a solution for the following problem within neo-Darwinian theory. According to the latter, the evolution of a complicated organ, such as the eye, involves an immense sequence of favourable mutations, each of which was (a) *rare* (it is very unlikely to have occurred independently in more than a tiny minority of the members of a species), and (b) conferred only a *tiny advantage*, from a survival point of view, on those in whom it occurred (for instance, the mutation might have brought about a very slight improvement in the focussing of the eye). Yet, if the characteristic associated with this mutation subsequently became a standard part of the physical endowment of the species, it must have spread, eventually, through the whole species. After a time, all surviving members of the species would be descendants of one or more of those individuals in which the mutation originally occurred. Those unlucky enough not to have acquired the characteristic either by mutation or by inheritance would eventually die out.

There would be no problem if a significant advantage had originally been bestowed upon a tiny minority, or if a tiny advantage had originally been bestowed upon a significantly large number. What seems rather astonishing is the sweeping success, heredity-wise, of a mutation that originally brought such a slight advantage to so few individuals.

Briefly, Popper's answer is that this is a serious difficulty only for those evolutionists who adopt (explicitly or implicitly) a monistic view in which an organism's control-system is completely merged with its motor-abilities. But the problem can be solved if we adopt a dualistic view that allows us, not merely to distinguish control-skill from motor-power, but to impute a certain quasi-autonomy or partial independence to the former. (This dualism is not identical with a mind-body dualism; rather, the former dualism is put forward as something like a biological forerunner of the latter. More about this later.) A dualistic view allows us to suppose that control-skill can exceed motor-power.[37] (On a monistic view these would merely be two *aspects* of *one* system and thus automatically aligned, Spinoza-wise.) And this in turn allows us to suppose that an organism may be *ready to make good use* of any mutation in its motor-power that fits in with its preexisting aim-structure and control-skill. By itself, a very slight improvement in eye focus (to revert to our previous example) could hardly be expected to have much survival value; but if a hawk, say, or some other organism that is already making something like optimum use of its eyes—if such an organism were to gain even a very slight improvement in eye-power, then we could expect this to have *significant* survival value for it (rather as a racing driver, unlike an ordinary motorist, might be significantly helped by a slight increase in engine-power).[38]

Consider a woodpecker (one of Popper's own examples)—or rather, some distant ancestor of the modern woodpecker, an ancestor not yet equipped with a beak suitable for getting at insects in the bark of trees. To this bird, which got its food in other ways, the gift of a stronger beak would probably, by itself, have been of no advantage (it might even have made the bird a clumsier and less efficient food-gatherer). But now suppose that some change in its environment engendered in it an interest in additional sources of food supply. Suppose, moreover, that the bird's central nervous system was already capable of controlling a more powerful beak. *Now* a beak-strengthening mutation could constitute a significant step towards the modern woodpecker.

(3.3) Organisms' problems. To the ideas already introduced—indeterminacy, plastic control, the piloting role of favourable mutations in the central control-system—we must now add Popper's thesis that 'all organisms are constantly, day and night, *engaged in problem-solving.*'[39]

Popper's objectivism (see p. 377 above) applies to problems also. Problems may exist unperceived, or partially perceived, or misperceived. An organism may deal successfully with a problem of which it is not conscious. (It may become conscious of the problem if it *fails* to cope with it.) A sleeping organism still has various problems to deal with. (One may be to *sleep on* through an unwelcome disturbance—a problem which, according to Freud, the sleeper may temporarily solve by incorporating the disturbance into his dream. Another may be to *wake up* at the silent approach of danger.) A lecturer dealing articulately on the blackboard with some theoretical problem is also dealing unthinkingly with a host of other problems—for instance, that of keeping his balance.[40] And the problem to which he is addressing himself on the blackboard may be much larger and deeper than he realizes. (Popper holds that the only way to try to get a realistic estimate of a problem is to try to solve what you now take the problem to be; when your first attempt fails, you may begin to see how naive was your original estimate, and you may now attempt to solve a revised and enlarged version of the problem; when this too fails. . . . This view implies that a problem may be adequately characterized only with hindsight, *after* it has at last been successfully solved.[41])

A soap bubble presumably has no problems—it does not seek food or try to avoid punctures. With an amoeba the case is different. It has food problems and will display great pertinacity in solving them.[42]

Thus for Popper the transition from the merely physical to the biological is marked, not merely by the orthodox criteria for living matter (duplication, mutation, self-repair, etc.) but by the emergence of problem-solving at the biological level. This throws a new light on the ideas of indeterminacy and plastic control in the biological domain. A series of more or less random movements made by an organism may now be regarded as a series of *trial solutions* for the problem it confronts; and the control element may now be understood as a selective capacity for discarding unrewarding trial solutions and pursuing the more rewarding ones. A floating amoeba which throws out pseudopods more or less at random may be regarded as essaying possible solutions for its nutrition-problem; and its ability, when one of its pseudopods touches something solid, to regather its dispersed protoplasm and concentrate itself around the newly found matter, may be attributed to some rudimentary selective control.[43]

In solving one problem an organism creates a new problem-situation for itself. The process is unending—until the organism reverts to the problem-free condition of dead matter.

I will conclude this section with a final look at the question of biological indeterminism. The present view allows that, in the case of a higher organism engaging in some standard activity, where the control is more or or less continuous, rapid and precise, the sequence of trial-and-error movements may be so smoothed out that it appears to be *one smooth and determinate action*. Thus a person raising a glass to his lips will be unaware—if he is not suffering from cerebellar disease—of the tiny oscillations in his arm-movement, so quickly and nicely are these checked by negative feedback.[44]

The biological determinist will concede that we cannot, in practice, predict with as much precision as we might desire just *when* a particular cat will spring at the mouse before it and just *where* its paws will land; but he will probably add that an analogous inexactitude is likely, in practice, to infect predictions about billiard ball tracks and other mechanical processes.

Against this Popper has argued that there is an important asymmetry between the inexactitude of our biological predictions and that of our mechanical predictions.[45] According to classical mechanics we know very well which initial conditions we should have to ascertain more precisely in order to obtain a more precise mechanical prediction. But in biology the corresponding claim breaks down: we do not know what we *should* have to ascertain more precisely in order to make more precise predictions about the cat's movements. And this is just what one would expect if organisms consist, essentially, of more or less indeterminate elements plastically controlled. If it is the controlling part which endows the organism with whatever predictability its movements have, and if this is not an 'iron' control, but a plastic control under which indeterminacy is not entirely stifled, then it is to be expected that predictions will in principle be possible only within rather tolerant limits.

4. Bodies, Minds, Ideas[46]

Since Descartes, nearly every philosopher has assumed that a solution for 'the' body-mind problem would be unobtainable while dualism and interactionism were both retained. It seemed that if dualism were retained, it would have to be combined with some kind of parallelism, and that if interactionism were retained, it would have to be combined with some form of monism. Or monism might be combined with *linguistic* parallelism (there are not two categories, physical processes and mental processes; rather, a given process may be described in either of two languages, a physicalist language and a mentalist language).

Popper, however, is as convinced of the reality of interaction as Descartes was; and he is a kind of dualist. Of course, he rejects Descartes's idea of *substance*; and he could not accept a two-category ontology that makes no provision for distinctively *biological* processes (or for the *objective contents* of mental processes—see Sec. 4.4 below). But he does hold, in line both with Descartes and with common sense, that someone may, for instance, be persuaded by argument to do something he would not otherwise have done, in which case his bodily behaviour is causally influenced by something extraphysical which is not reducible to its physical accompaniments.

According to the prevailing view, this neo-Cartesianism should put Popper under a crippling handicap, here. Actually, part of his 'solution' of the mind-body problem consists in exposing the inadequacy of the grounds on which dualist interactionism has been dismissed as impossible (see Sec. 4.1 below).

I put scare quotes round the word 'solution' just now, because it is one of Popper's characteristic theses that we seldom, if ever, come up with a complete and final solution of a problem: an excellent solution is almost certain to raise fresh problems, in which case we can say either that the old problem has been replaced by new problems, or that the old problem has been *shifted* in a progressive way, the success of the solution varying with the extent of the shift.[47]

It might seem that physicalist reductionism promises a progressive problem-shift of the old body-mind problem. However, from Popper's account of scientific reductions I shall (in Sec. 4.2) draw the conclusion (not actually drawn by Popper himself) that there cannot be a genuine scientific reduction of mental processes to physical processes, and hence that physicalist reductionism is doomed to remain a mere unfulfilled *programme*. In Sec. 4.3 I will sketch Popper's positive view. Now I turn to his diagnosis of the belief, so widespread among philosophers, that dualist interactionism is an impossible position.

(4.1) Interactionism. As Popper sees it, interactionism (the thesis that extraphysical factors like arguments, moral considerations, etc., can influence people's bodily behaviour) has suffered a philosophical fate very similar to that of indeterminism (the thesis that future developments are to some extent open and determinable).

The two theses are, of course, closely connected. Given the temporal priority of matter over the emergence of consciousness, determinism implies that human decisions, etc., never *initiate* causal processes: they must be regarded, either as nonphysical links in a *mixed* but uninterrupted causal process, or (more tidily) as the shadowy accompaniments of brain movements that are part of an uninterrupted and uniformly *physical* process. Physical indeterminism allows room for extraphysical initiatives; but it needs to be reinforced by interactionism if it is to allow for our taking advantage of the *Spielraum* it offers.

Both indeterminism and interactionism are deeply embedded in our commonsense world view; and both have, according to Popper, been repudiated at the behest of naive philosophical theories which, though originally instigated by scientific considerations, have long since lost any scientific justification they may once have had.

If Newtonian physics provided the chief scientific argument against physical indeterminism, Descartes's surprisingly popular push-theory of physical causation (his action-by-contact theory) provided the chief argument against interactionism: if mental events, such as decisions, have (as Descartes insisted) an intensity but no extension, then his push-theory surely implies (however reluctant Descartes himself may have been to admit the implication) that a man's decisions cannot causally affect his bodily movements.

This *simpliste* theory of physical causation is, of course, quite obsolete today; yet many philosophers cling to its negative implications for mind-body interaction, despite the fact that both common sense and physics admit many kinds of causal interaction between essentially different kinds of thing. One of Popper's examples, here, is light and matter, light being essentially differentiated from matter by its velocity. Another example, which has been adduced in this connection by J. O. Wisdom, is electricity and magnetism, which seem radically different and mutually irreducible: yet there is electromagnetic interaction.[48] (Philosophers seem never to have asked in *this* context embarrassing questions like, Just *where* in a dynamo does the interaction take place? Electromagnetic theory has had no pineal gland trouble.)

Descartes's push-theory (only extended bodies act on extended bodies) is a special case of the old idea that only like acts on like. I remember Popper making two points about this old idea. First, there seems to be a mass of evidence against it. (Consider sunburn: in what way is a sunburnt face *like* the rays of the sun? Or consider the tides and the moon.) Second, Aristotle gave it a twist that perhaps rendered it compatible even with mind-body interaction: he said that when *A* acts on *B*, *A* makes *B* more like *A* than it was before. This means that, if *A* makes a *big* difference to *B*, then *B* must originally have been *very* unlike *A*. But a man's soul seems to make a very big difference to his body. . . .

But perhaps the most decisive point, in Popper's case against allowing ourselves to be bullied by an obsolete theory of physical causation into regarding mind-body interaction as impossible, is this. Descartes's push-theory was found by the young Leibniz to be internally incoherent: lacking any concept of *force* it could not explain why two extended volumes *resist* mutual penetration.[49] But forces are physical intensities, and are not extended in Descartes's sense. If body-body interaction involves forces, then there is certainly some kind of interaction between *physical* intensities and extended bodies. But if there is interaction between (physical) *intensities* and bodies,[50] if something can act on a body without itself being extended, then there is no longer any compelling reason to deny mind-body interaction. The alleged impossibility of mind-body interaction is not God-given but only Descartes-given (or rather, Descartes-implied).

(4.2) Reductionism. Philosophical reductionists are often surprisingly deprecatory towards scientific reductions.[51] It is as if they felt that Occam's Razor is safe only in philosophical hands. Let science seem to call for some revision of commonsense categories and they reach for a Paradigm-Case or Polar-Contrast argument to show that common sense never multiplies entities unnecessarily.

Popper may also be called a defender of common sense (though he defends it with different weapons).[52] But he is also a defender of *scientific* realism, and an admirer of scientific *reductions*.

What is a scientific reduction? It is something more than the straightforward subsumption of one theory under a larger theory. Let S_1 be that which undergoes reduction and S_2 that to which S_1 gets reduced. Let us first consider S_1 on its own, prior to the advent of S_2. Typically, S_1 will comprise a considerable body of theories, experimental laws, and associated experimental evidence; it will have had a great deal of empirical success (but it may have had an occasional setback too); and it will, when realistically interpreted, involve a distinctive physical ontology (for instance, if S_1 had the old caloric theory of heat at its centre, then its ontology would include the idea of a fluid heat-substance obeying deterministic laws).

Now comes S_2. Its relation to S_1 is a mixture of conflict and near-continuity. The commercial analogy would be a take-over bid leading to the dismissal of the old management but leaving much of the subordinate organisation of the old firm little changed. The main conflict between S_2 and S_1 will be at the ontological or 'theoretical entities' level. Typically, S_2 will more or less flatly *repudiate* the ontology of S_1 (for instance, if S_2 were the kinetic theory of heat, then it flatly denies that heat is a fluidlike substance obeying deterministic laws). At the empirical level there will be near-continuity between the predictive implications of the old S_1 and those of the new S_2. We can expect S_2 to make predictions in domains outside the predictive scope of S_1 (for the superseding S_2 should have more empirical content than S_1). We can also hope that a few crucial experiments between S_2 and S_1 will be possible; and this means that there should be some empirically significant discrepancies between their respective predictive implications in their common domain. But very slight discrepancies may be sufficient for this. And if S_2 is to make a successful take-over bid for S_1 which had itself been well tested and empirically successful in its heyday, we can hardly expect more than small discrepancies at the experimental level.

Thus, in the case of a *reduction* of S_1 to S_2, as opposed to a mere subsumption of S_1 under S_2, the old ontology is dissolved and replaced by something else. (Fluid heat-substance, for instance, is replaced by molecular bombardment, etc.) But this will be accompanied by a near-reproduction of S_1's empirical content by S_2. This dual character of a scientific reduction allows Popper to say that a world as described by S_2 would *simulate* that world as described by S_1. For example, the kinetic theory of heat says (a) that there is no such thing as a fluid heat-substance, temperature changes being due to molecular bombardment etc., and (b) that such molecular activity has statistical effects (dispersion, levelling out, etc.) that behave very much *as if* they were the observable manifestations of an underlying fluidlike substance. Or to give one of Popper's own examples, Darwinian theory both *denies* that there is inheritance of acquired characteristics and *explains* how an evolutionary development nevertheless *simulates* a Lamarckian development.

In the case of a scientific reduction, then, to explain *is* to explain away; *but* the explanation provides a sufficient *substitute* for what is explained away (or eliminated, or 'reduced').

The situation is very different in the case of what may be called, rather insultingly, a philosopher's 'stroke-of-the-pen' (or perhaps 'sweep-of-the-razor') reduction. Of course, the materialist can *declare* that mental events are really physical events, just as the idealist can declare that physical phenomena are really mental phenomena. But such verbal ping-pong gets us nowhere. Moreover, a philosophical pseudoreduction actually tends rather to *impede* than to encourage a scientific reduction in the same area.[53] A scientific reduction begins by *taking very seriously* the S_1-like characteristics that will be 'explained away' by S_2. (Darwin did not pooh-pooh the appearance of design displayed by higher organisms; rather, he showed how their marvellous biological organisation could nevertheless be explained in an essentially nontheological and nonteleological way.) But a merely philosophical 'reduction' is all too likely to obscure, by a process of persuasive redefinition, those obstinately S_1-like characteristics which need rather to be highlighted if the *explicandum* for a scientific reduction is to be well specified.

A positivist would presumably say that if a new scientific system S_2 leads to only very *slight* revisions of the predictive implications of S_1, then S_2 can hardly be said to *revolutionise* our understanding of its subject matter, since its cognitive content is nothing more than the sum of its predictive implications. But a scientific realist, who holds that the content of a scientific theory also includes a certain ontology (fluid substance, bouncing molecules, forces, magnetic fields, electrons, photons or whatever) can regard S_2 as effecting a major ontological revision even though it may cause relatively little empirical disturbance. If I watch what I take to be a tortoise finding its way round obstacles to regain its lair, and if later I learn that I was actually watching one of Professor Grey Walter's cunningly contrived feedback mechanisms, I would have to admit that I was seriously wrong in taking it to be a real, live, goal-seeking organism—though I might console myself by adding that the mistake was understandable because the simulation was so good. Rather similarly, someone who accepts the reduction of S_1 to S_2 would agree that the world *appears* in many ways to be an S_1-world; but he would add that this appearance is deceptive: it is an S_2-world *simulating* an S_1-world.

What is the bearing of all this on the question of the scientific reducibility of psychology to physiology and finally, perhaps, to physics? Popper concedes that it is at least conceivable that such a reduction might eventually be carried out,[54] though he obviously doubts that it ever will be. But it seems to me that his general account of scientific reductions means that *this* reductionist programme *cannot* be carried out. For let us try to suppose that it will be carried out. Then those phenomena which we now regard as *experiences* are going to stand revealed as physical processes that *simulate* experiences but are *not* experiences. But it seems to me to be nonsense, and not just false, to say of somebody's toothache that it is not really an experience but only something simulating an experience.

Now I turn to Popper's positive view of the mind-body relationship.

(4.3) The evolution of mind. Darwin did not try to explain the origin of life; rather, he offered an explanation for the origin of species, *given* some original, lowly form of life, in terms of fecundity, variations, etc. Popper has not tried to explain the origin of consciousness; rather, he offered an explanation for the emergence of conscious control, given the emergence of incipient consciousness somewhere along the evolutionary trail, in terms of: the quasi-interactionist idea of plastic control;[55] the quasi-dualist distinction between the central control system of an organism and its motor-system and the idea that it is mutations in control-systems that lead the way in evolutionary

development;[56] and the idea that a control system is a quasi-hierarchical system,[57] so that higher levels of control should come into operation in the course of evolutionary progress.

Suppose that some species, as yet without consciousness, had acquired, through natural selection, a propensity to withdraw on touching a certain kind of poisonous vegetation. Now suppose that some rudimentary kind of consciousness supervenes, and that brief contact with the vegetation now causes a sensation of irritation. This would be biologically useless if it were a *mere accompaniment* (or epiphenomenon) of already existing physiological processes. But it would be biologically useful if it reinforced the organism's central control system in its propensity to organise the withdrawal of its body from the vegetation. If, later, mere proximity to the stuff came to cause unpleasant sensations of smell, that again would be biologically useless unless it exerted a controlling influence, tending to deter the organism before it had touched the stuff.

An organism that retreats from something poisonous because it gives off an unpleasant smell may be said to have 'learnt', through evolutionary trial and error, to 'decode' a certain kind of danger signal. (More about this in Sec. 5.4 below.) A zebra that starts running when its ears pick up sound waves caused by a lion's roar, and a man who starts running on seeing the word 'BULL', have learnt more sophisticated forms of decoding.

This evolutionist view, whereby consciousness emerges at the upper levels of a quasi-hierarchical control-system, suggests that consciousness itself should develop a quasi-hierarchical organisation. An 'expectation' may be physiological, or subconscious;[58] and a conscious expectation may sink into subconsciousness, though liable to be jolted into consciousness if disappointed.

It may be objected that all this leaves mind-body interaction a miracle, though one accredited now to evolution rather than to God. So be it; but then, evolution has wrought millions of other 'miracles', millions of structures and processes which would seem to call for some supernatural explanation if an evolutionist explanation were not available.

(4.4) Minds and ideas. Popper's objectivism (see pp. 376-77 above) suggests, to put it picturesquely, that a person's mind interacts not only with the body 'beneath' it but with ideas 'above' it.

Let me illustrate. A certain physicist, let us suppose, knows a certain physical theory inside out. He knows, too, the criticisms that have been levelled against it and the alternatives to it that have been proposed. But he finds that all these criticisms can be met, and that there are cogent objections to each of those alternatives. So the case for the theory is about as good as it could be. And yet, he 'accepts' it only in a very tentative way. Why? He knows that it has infinitely many logical consequences; so that, although he understands it well, humanly speaking, there is much—infinitely much—of it, logically speaking, of which he is ignorant. There may be nasty surprises lurking among its unexamined consequences. He knows, too, that there are many—infinitely many—possible alternatives to it, some of which may be superior to it.

His attitude of critical acceptance, versus belief or commitment, is a consequence of his recognition (caused largely by logical considerations) that his understanding of this objective theoretical structure can only be partial. Its objectivity helps to determine his psychological attitude towards it.

Someone with a horror of Platonism (however mitigated) may declare that it was our physicist's *belief* in its objectivity and transcendence that caused his *half-belief* [59] in the theory: the interactions were all within the psychological domain.

One may say with a show of truth that it is not the traffic light turning red but the motorist's *perception* of its turning red that causes him to pull up. But if one adds or insinuates that the physical traffic light had nothing to do with it, or even that there is no such thing as a physical traffic light but only a set of perceptions, one of course creates the problem of accounting for the *coordination* among the perceptions of the various motorists who would ordinarily be regarded as responding to the same traffic signals.

Our physicist, we may suppose, is in the habit of discussing that theory with other competent physicists. No doubt, there are differences among their respective understandings of the theory, just because each has only a partial understanding of it. (Each motorist gets only a partial view of the traffic lights.) And they may sometimes talk at cross-purposes about it. But, by and large, in their discussions, they all take themselves to be discussing *the same thing*. How is this (rough and imperfect but undeniable) coordination of their understandings of the theory to be explained if *it* is not there to be understood, there being nothing but their respective subjective conceptions? The theory cannot be identified with its associated chalk marks, ink marks, etc. It is what these marks *express* that our physicists discuss. It seems to me that a thoroughgoing anti-Platonist will have to call in God, or subliminal advertising, to account for this sort of coordination.

Anyway, for Popper a person may be seen as a quasi-hierarchical system of plastic controls that extends from the physicochemical level to the psychological level *and beyond* to the level of objective ideas. (It seems to me that this view allows a perfectly good construction to be placed on certain phrases, such as 'There was a genuine meeting of minds', at which a subjectivist would look askance.) That objective ideas exert no more than a plastic control is obvious from the fact that a man's logical canons may be good but his reasoning sloppy.

I indicated that Popper's objectivism is a very mitigated version of Platonism. For one thing, Popper's 'third world' (as he rather alarmingly calls it) contains as many false ideas as true ones. For another, it is man made (though in making it men have built greater than they knew: their abstract artefacts turn out to have various unexpected properties which may or may not be discovered). There is a two-way, not just a one-way, interaction between minds and ideas.

Spinoza shifted the mind-body problem by regarding the mind-body relation as a special case of the one-to-one correspondence between parallel attributes of the universe. Popper has shifted the problem by regarding the relation as a special kind of plastic control within a system of plastic controls.

5. Evolutionism and Falsificationism

It might be supposed that my attempt to relate Popper's falsificationism to his indeterminism via his evolutionism is bound to fail for a very simple reason: His falsificationist methodology is essentially *normative*: it proposes an *aim* for science (*not* certainty or high probability, but increasing explanatory content and verisimilitude), from which it derives *rules* for playing the scientific game well (roughly: *don't* play for safety; make your conjectures as easily testable as you can; make your responses to objections and counterevidence as little *ad hoc* as you can). His indeterminism and evolutionism, on the other hand, are *not* normative doctrines; so his methodological 'oughts' cannot derive from those metaphysical 'isms'.

To this the short answer is that whereas an 'is' does not imply an 'ought', 'ought' does imply 'can'. But there is a longer answer which is more interesting.

(5.1) Scientific rationality. Popper's methodology is a theory of scientific rationality, or of scientific progress, or of rational appraisal of scientific hypotheses, in the absence of anything like empirical verification. What distinguishes this theory from most theories of confirmation or induction is that the only relations between hypotheses and observation reports (or basic statements) that it takes into account are *deductive* relations.[60] Like Hume, Popper holds that an inductive 'inference' is simply an invalid inference—despite the huge literature on 'inductive logic', there is no such thing as inductive *logic*. There *is* such a thing as probability logic; but probability logic cannot do what inductivists want inductive logic to do.[61]

But there is a crucial difference, here, between Hume and Popper. Hume combined his thesis concerning the essential illogicality of induction with the thesis that induction is psychologically unavoidable and biologically indispensable: it is as natural for men to make inductive inferences as it is for them to breathe; if a man were, *per impossibile,* to abstain from making them, he would be paralysed and would soon die.[62]

If Hume had been right on the psychological as well as on the logical issue of induction, we should have to conclude, either that there is no such thing as scientific rationality, or that scientific 'rationality' is essentially illogical. Now Popper has offered an empirical-*cum*-logical refutation of

Hume's psychological thesis.[63] Rather than reproduce this, however, I shall argue (in the next subsection) that Popper's evolutionism sanctions the contrary psychological thesis that it is rather the method of trial and error (or of conjectures and refutations) that is as natural as breathing.[64]

(5.2) Inborn expectations. There is a good passage in Arthur Koestler's *The Ghost in the Machine*, where he protests against the popular view that organisms are passively conditioned by their environment:

> . . . the moment it is hatched or born the creature lashes out at the environment, be it liquid or solid, with cilia, flagellae, or contractile muscle fibre. . . . It does not merely adapt to the environment, but constantly adapts the environment to itself—it eats and drinks its environment, fights and mates with it, burrows and builds in it. [P. 153]

In Popper's philosophy this *attacking* attitude is given an epistemological dimension: an attitude that reaches its highest expression in science, it is already present in a primitive form in young animals. A newborn animal does not patiently wait to have beliefs instilled into it via its sense organs by the environment; rather, it 'lashes out at the environment' with inborn expectations.

The idea of inborn expectations develops naturally out of Popper's idea of an organism's central control system.[65] An animal is born equipped with a central control system already sufficiently developed to enable it, under normal conditions, to cope successfully with the initial problems of its life. It owes its inheritance of such a system to the long evolutionary process of trial and error whereby its ancestors have succeeded gradually better in coping with similar conditions. Of course, the system will probably break down if conditions change significantly: it presupposes fairly stable conditions. But, if conditions *are* stable, the animal may be said to be born endowed with a lot of physiologically incorporated 'foreknowledge' of them. A newborn baby 'expects' to have air to breathe; it also 'expects' to be fed and 'knows' what to do when presented with a nipple.

Inborn expectations are logically important for Popper in halting the regress of hypotheses preceded by more primitive hypotheses, with sense experience playing a mainly negative and corrective role.[66] Let us now turn to his account of sense experience.

(5.3) Sense experience. Locke allowed that an observer may actively direct his attention this way or that; but having directed his gaze, say, upon an object, an image of it will be 'obtruded' into his mind in a way that is just as causal and automatic as the way in which objects produce images in mirrors.[67]

Kant saw very clearly that the empiricist account of sense experience creates and cannot solve the problem of how the *manifold* and very various data which reach a man's mind from his various senses get *unified* into a coherent experience.

Kant's solution consisted, essentially, in leaving the old quasi-mechanistic account of sense organs intact, and endowing the mind with a powerful set of organising categories—fixed, universal, and necessary—which unify and structure what would otherwise be a mere jumble.

Popper's evolutionist view modifies Kant's view at both ends: inter-pretative principles lose their fixed and necessary character, and sense organs lose their merely causal and mechanistic character. Here I will deal only with the latter point.

As we saw, a favourable mutation, for Popper, is one that fits in with preexisting interests and control-skills. A hawk is interested in *prey* and a favourable mutation in a hawk's eye will, typically, be one that enhances its skill in detecting prey. A favourable mutation in a mouse's eye, on the other hand, will typically be one that enhances its skill in detecting escape routes and refuges.[68]

On this evolutionist view, what an animal's sense organs provide it with is not raw sense-data that require mental processing before they become perceptions; rather, they provide it with the sorts of predigested *information* the animal needs in its practical problem-solving. Of course, such sensory information is open to ever more theoretical interpretation; the present point is simply that the process of interpretation begins already at the physiological level in the sense organs themselves.[69]

(5.4) Fallibilism and realism. On Popper's evolutionist view, then, *it is physiologically impossible to obtain a pure sense-datum*: we cannot entirely inhibit our built-in interpretative propensities.

How reliable may we assume these interpretative propensities to be? We know that it is rather easy to devise *trompe l'oeil* situations by exploiting the assumptions we unnoticingly rely upon in our observations of things. And sense-deceiving situations sometimes occur without anyone devising them. The fallibilist view of basic statements (like 'This is a glass of water') that Popper originally took for logical reasons[70] is hereby reinforced: if we are always interpreting, we are always liable to misinterpret.

But there is another side to it. I mentioned earlier the notion of an animal's sense organs *decoding* signals reaching it from its environment. We may now add that evolutionism suggests that they should be, by and large, *pretty good* at such decoding.

The idea of sensory decoding seems to me of considerable philosophical value, especially with regard to the serious division that has existed within the realist camp since the days of Galileo, Descartes and Locke. It has seemed to many would-be realists that if science were true, then much of our ordinary, commonsensical, observational knowledge must be false, or at any rate systematically misleading. To put it in seventeenth-century terms: if we accept what science tells us about the 'primary' qualities of things, then we must radically revise our commonsense view of their 'secondary' qualities. Thus realists seemed to be faced with a painful choice: either cling to commonsense realism (grass really is green, etc.) and interpret science in some nonrealist way (for instance, instrumentally) or interpret science realistically and adopt a nonrealist view of experience (grass is not really green, we mentally 'paint' it green).

The evolutionist idea of sensory decoding helps to dissolve this dilemma: it supports commonsense realism, and it undermines the main argument for the irreconcilability of commonsense realism and scientific realism.[71] I will take the second point first.

That argument goes roughly like this: I am, let us say, perceiving an orange. If I am a scientific realist I must assume that some causal process has led to my having this perception. I now ask for a scientific inventory, as complete as possible, of all the physical factors and elements that enter into this process. I am told on the best scientific authority that such an inventory would include molecules, atoms, photons, neurons, etc., but would *not* include any *orange*. Thus *if we take science seriously* we must conclude that, although my perception of an orange is indeed caused by external realities, these are about as different as they could be from my idea of an orange—colourless, tasteless, and very small. The *orange* exists only in my mind.

Let us transpose this argument to another setting. After watching a play on television I ask for a scientific inventory of the physical elements of the television set's input. I am told about electronic impulses etc., but not about dialogue, actors, plot, etc. Why am I not thereby obliged to conclude that the *play* did not reach the set from outside and must, therefore, have been the work of the set itself? Because a television set is a device for *decoding* the electronic impulses that reach it.

But (it will be objected) *those* signals had been encoded at the transmitting end: it makes no sense to speak of an eye decoding 'signals' emanating from a *natural* source.

Evolutionism suggests a different answer. For it has taught us that an animal's organs may, as a result of natural selection, be so very well adapted that it is *as if* they had been designed: there is generally a remarkably good 'fit', given its needs, between an animal's organs and its environment.

Consider the 'fit' between dogs' noses and pieces of meat. It may not be quite on a par with that between a television receiver and a transmitter, but it is very good. Fresh meat gives out certain 'signals' that ordinarily enable a dog in its vicinity to find it. Bad meat gives out rather different 'signals'. And natural selection has so attuned dogs' noses to these various signals that they are able, in effect, to *perceive* the badness of a bad piece of meat.

No doubt, a nose is a somewhat crude instrument. It tells its owner nothing about the swarm of odourless, etc., particles that continually bombard it. But just imagine, for a moment, that one could swap one's nose for an artificial proboscis, a veritable marvel of scientific technology which would inform its owner very fully about the nature of the particles bombarding it—and *only* about these. Someone who made the swap might afterwards complain that his new nose *is not crude enough:* it does not warn him when he is about to eat bad meat.

Landé proposes (with acknowledgements to Dr. Johnson) to regard something as physically real if it is kickable[72] (Popper adds: and if it can kick back). By this criterion, "the average plumber" is not physically real; but plumbers are; so are particles (they can be kicked around in cyclotrons, etc.) and fields of force; and so is bad meat (which has a vicious kickback).

Evolutionism suggests that the information about the physical realities of our near-environment that our sense organs provide is generally rather reliable, otherwise we would not be here. (The fact that so many pedestrians survive in our car-ridden cities argues for considerable skill in perceiving the speeds and distances of motorcars.) Of course, they under-inform us. (Our eyes do not inform us of the existence—to give one of Popper's examples—of infra-red light.) And they sometimes misinform us. But we can be confident that they do not systematically misinform us about those features of the world realistic appraisals of which are sometimes a matter of life or death.

(5.5) Conclusion. I will wind up this lengthy reconstruction of Popper's philosophy with a brief recapitulation in the reverse order, from his falsificationism to his indeterminism.

For present purposes, his falsificationist view of science may be summarised thus. Science attacks the world with hypotheses. (It is a continuation of that attacking attitude so characteristic of living creatures.)[73] Scientific hypotheses have a one-sided relation to evidence: they may be knocked out by evidence, but cannot get verified, or even confirmed in any quasi-verificationist sense (such as probabilified). For scientific hypotheses typically go far beyond the evidence, not only in their universality, but in their exactitude;[74] and they typically involve highly theoretical ideas that have no analogue in experience.[75] However, the absence of anything like verifiability does not mean the end of scientific rationality; for scientific progress can be assessed without invoking (illusory) verifications.[76]

This falsificationist view makes hypotheses essentially prior to observations. A new hypothesis shows the way to new observations, but new observations do not show the way to an explanatory scientific hypothesis. Of course, very many observations will already have been made in the domain of a new hypothesis before it was introduced, but these will have been prompted by earlier hypotheses, for there is no such thing as pure observation.[77] Past observations, especially ones that told against earlier hypotheses, help to constitute the problem-situation for the new hypothesis, but they give no positive indications as to what the new hypothesis should be. A path-breaking new scientific hypothesis is a free creation relative to existing observational knowledge (though the latter puts constraints upon it, of course). It will also be a free creation relative to the entire body of current scientific knowledge, with which it may very well conflict.[78] This view brings out the genuine *novelty* of new ideas in science, a kind of novelty that goes far beyond recombination of existing elements into new patterns, the maximum novelty allowed by classical empiricism.

Having argued the point earlier, I now assume that the unpredictable process of thinking up and developing new ideas in science is not a fully determined, causal process (though causal factors may affect it, of course): such scientific inventiveness has, I shall assume, a certain freedom and autonomy. The question now is, what sort of psychological or psychobiological view can adequately accommodate such intellectual creativity?

Formally, there seem to be two main alternatives. One is to treat it (together, perhaps, with artistic and other kinds of creativity) as entirely *sui generis* and to try to accommodate it within a psychobiological setting that is otherwise essentially causal and deterministic. The other alternative is to accommodate it within a psychobiological system which already displays some spontaneity and initiative at lower levels and in more rudimentary forms.

Descartes could be said (with due qualifications) to have tried the first alternative. (His concept of free will is by no means equivalent to the kind of intellectual inventiveness being considered here; but they are alike in their causal indeterminacy.) His mind-body dualism involved an indeterminism-determinism dualism also. But this latter dualism *could not be sustained, given Descartes's two-way interactionism:* if bodily motions are frequently being deflected by something that is not causally determinate, then they are not causally determinate either. If we agree with Broad that for Descartes a man is a machine haunted by an angel,[79] we must add that the machine is loose enough to allow the angel to influence its workings.

Thus, if interactionism is retained—and who, after Hiroshima, would deny that scientific thinking interacts with the world?—the first alternative turns out to be no alternative: the indeterminacy of that which we would accommodate within a deterministic setting will infect that setting with its own indeterminacy. Instead of grudgingly conceding a minimal psychobiological indeterminacy, it would be less *ad hoc* to introduce physical indeterminacies at the outset.

Physical indeterminacies as such have no biological or psychological significance. However, in a system where they are under some sort of selective control, physical indeterminacies may graduate into exploratory movements or random trials, the selection process discarding or eliminating those trials which turn out to be 'errors' (say, from a survival point of view). Roughly: physical indeterminacy plus selective control equals trial-and-error organism.

The *evolution* of trial-and-error organisms already displays something like a trial-and-error pattern. Indeed, there is an obvious analogy between the relation of mutations to environment according to neo-Darwinism, and that of conjectures to experience according to Popper. It is misleading to say that evolutionary developments are *induced* by ecological pressures. According to neo-Darwinism, what evolutionary developments take place depends essentially on what mutations occur; and it seems that genetic mutations are associated with microphysical indeterminacies;[80] in any case they certainly are not triggered by *ecological* factors: relative to the ecological environment, mutations are incalculable 'acts of God'. What the ecological environment determines is whether a mutation that has somehow occurred passes or (far more probably) fails survival-tests.

Happily, the analogy between biological and scientific evolution breaks down in one important respect: scientists do not perish with their hypotheses: 'the critical or rational method consists in letting our hypotheses die in our stead.'[81]

One last point. It is remarkable how many classical theories of knowledge are hit *either* by the fact that theoretical science exists at all *or* by the fact that it is far from coextensive with the human race (it is something of a 'sport', or a series of 'sports', in our intellectual history). For instance, Humean empiricism with its key dogma 'that all our ideas are deriv'd from correspondent impressions', can hardly be squared with those highly theoretical, experience-transcending ideas that are so characteristic of modern science and cosmology.[82] But in 'answering' Hume, Kant went too far in the other direction: by displaying contemporary (i.e., Newtonian) physics, not as a possible conjectural system, but as a *necessary* product of our organising categories, he made the problem 'no longer how Newton would make his discovery but how everybody else could have failed to make it.'[83]

Popper's philosophy of science is in no danger of implying that science should be ubiquitous and uniform. For one thing, hypotheses are put forward as solutions to *problems*, and problem-situations change. Also, although different people may independently hit upon similar solutions for the same problem, there is no general reason to expect such simultaneous discoveries. The developing experimental situation will tolerate a variety of rival hypotheses; indeed, it will tolerate rival *traditions*. Again, there is a rough analogy with biological evolution. Similar mutations *may* occur independently in different regions. On the other hand, different regions that are ecologically pretty similar may tolerate pretty diverse species. The marsupials of Australia are, one might say, in a different evolutionary tradition from the placentals of North America.

Determinism and inductivism, although not bound logically together, are natural coalition partners; for, of all extant epistemologies, it is inductivism that most readily furnishes a causal account of belief-formation. There is likewise, as we have seen, a natural coalition between indeterminism and falsificationism (whereby scientific knowledge is seen as growing through conjectures and refutations). There seems to me no doubt as to which pair of doctrines offers the more cheerful picture. The first depicts man as an induction machine nudged along by external pressures, and deprived of all initiative and spontaneity. The second gives him the *Spielraum* to originate ideas and try them out. Learning about the world means, on the first view, being conditioned by it; on the second view, it means adventuring within it.

J. W. N. WATKINS

DEPARTMENT OF PHILOSOPHY, LOGIC AND SCIENTIFIC METHOD
LONDON SCHOOL OF ECONOMICS AND POLITICAL SCIENCE
JANUARY, 1969

NOTES

[1] Bertrand Russell, *The History of Western Philosophy* (New York: Simon & Shuster, 1946), p. 862. It seems that Russell had not always found analytical methods entirely satisfying. In 1902 he had written to Gilbert Murray: 'If only one had lived in the days of Spinoza, when systems were still possible' (*The Autobiography of Bertrand Russell, 1872-1914* [Boston: Atlantic Monthly Press, 1967], p. 163). And see *The Philosophy of Bertrand Russell* (The Library of Living Philosophers, Vol. 5), ed. by Paul A. Schilpp (La Salle, Ill.: The Open Court Publishing Co., 1944), p. 11.

[2] See Popper's 1933 letter to *Erkenntnis*, reprinted as Appendix *1 in *The Logic of Scientific Discovery* (London: Hutchinson, 1959; New York: Basic Books, 1959). Hereinafter cited as *L.Sc.D.*

[3] K. R. Popper, 'Indeterminism in Quantum Physics and in Classical Physics', *British Journal for the Philosophy of Science,* 1, Nos. 2 & 3 (August and November, 1950). The *British Journal for the Philosophy of Science* will hereinafter be cited as *B.J.P.S.*

[4] In 1957 Popper added a 'Metaphysical Epilogue' containing, I believe, the first statement of some of these ideas, to the *Postscript* (still unpublished, alas) to *L.Sc.D.* In 1961 he developed them further in a Herbert Spencer Lecture ('Evolution and the Tree of Knowledge') which for some reason was not published. [Now Chap. 7 of *Objective Knowledge: An Evolutionary Approach* (London: Oxford University Press, 1972).—EDITOR] His first published work in this field was *Of Clouds and Clocks: An Approach to the Problem of Rationality and the Freedom of Man* (St. Louis: Washington University, 1966). Hereinafter cited as *CC.*

[5] Perhaps I may be forgiven for drawing attention to just one of these previous papers. In my more megalomaniac moments I like to think that the unending stream of papers on the so-called 'paradoxes of confirmation' would dry up if account were taken of my 'Confirmation, the Paradoxes, and Positivism', in *The Critical Approach to Science and Philosophy: Essays in Honor of Karl R. Popper*, ed. by Mario Bunge (New York: The Free Press, 1964).

[6] As reported by Plutarch; see Cyril Bailey, *The Greek Atomists and Epicurus* (Oxford, 1928; New York: Russell & Russell Publishers, 1964), p. 120.

[7] Pierre Simon de Laplace, *Oeuvres Complètes* (Paris, 1878-1884), Vol. VI, pp. 479 f.

[8] *Ibid.*, Vol. VII, pp. vi-vii. Laplace adds that astronomy gives us a feeble idea of such an intelligence.

[9] Popper, 'Indeterminism in Quantum Physics and Classical Physics'. (See n. 3 above.)

[10] Popper has often mentioned that one *alters* the temperature of a liquid by inserting into it a

thermometer at a different temperature. Allan M. Munn has independently put the same point very clearly: 'Even at the macroscopic level of classical physics we recognize that every act of measurement disturbs a system to some extent. . . . As one example, take the apparently simple operation of placing a meter stick alongside an object. . . . If the meter stick is at a different temperature from the object, it will change the latter's temperature and hence its length. This could be avoided if the meter stick were at the same temperature as the object, but to ascertain this it would be necessary to take the temperature of the object, and this measurement in turn would affect the object' (*Freewill and Determinism* [London, 1960; Toronto: University of Toronto Press, 1961], p. 149).

11 This point is made very clearly in the still unpublished *Postscript* to Popper's *L.Sc.D.*

12 As Bishop Butler himself agreed: 'For nothing which is the possible object of knowledge . . . can be probable to an infinite Intelligence; since it cannot but be discerned absolutely as it is in itself—certainly true, or certainly false. But *to us*, probability is the very guide of life' (*Analogy and Sermons*, Bohn Library [1889], p. 73; italics mine).

13 Laplace, *Oeuvres Complètes*, Vol. VII, p. viii (italics mine).

14 See Popper's 'Epistemology without a Knowing Subject', *Proceedings of the 3d International Congress for Logic, Methodology and Philosophy of Science* (Amsterdam, 1968), pp. 333-73.

15 One of the few things Popper finds valuable in Hegel is the latter's idea of the objectification of mind, the embodiment of transient ideas in relatively stable and public forms (buildings, social customs, political organizations, etc.); unfortunately, after taking the human psyche out of objective mind, Hegel pumped a superhuman psyche into it.

16 In his interesting paper, 'Between Micro and Macro', *B.J.P.S.*, **14**, No. 53 (May, 1963), Joseph Agassi raises various objections (including the amplifiability of quantum effects) to the claim that quantum theory applies only to the microdomain and classical physics only to the macrodomain (in which Planck's constant may be neglected). His conclusion is that *according to quantum theory* the two-slit experiment could be performed, and an interference pattern created, using billiard balls—if the billiard balls moved *very* slowly and we had millions of years in which to perform the experiment.

17 See Alfred Landé: 'Indeterminism and Continuity', *Mind*, **67** (April, 1958); 'The Case for Indeterminism' in *Determinism and Freedom in the Age of Modern Science*, ed. by Sidney Hook (New York: New York University Press, 1958); 'Causality and Dualism on Trial', in *Philosophy of Science, The Delaware Seminar*, Vol. 1, ed. by B. Baumrin (New York: John Wiley & Sons, 1963); and Alfred Landé, *New Foundations of Quantum Mechanics* (New York: Cambridge University Press, 1965), pp. 27 f.

18 *L.Sc.D.*, Appendix iv.

19 This would be an example of what I have called a 'haunted-universe' doctrine: the behavior of terrestrial roulette wheels is ultimately controlled by ghostly celestial roulette wheels. *Mind*, **67** (July, 1958).

20 See Popper's *L.Sc.D.*, p. 151, and 'Probability Magic or Knowledge out of Ignorance', *Dialectica*, **11**, No. 3/4 (1957). For R. von Mises's criticism of the subjective conception of probability see, for example, his *Probability, Statistics and Truth* (2d ed.; New York: Humanities Press, 1957), pp. 75 f.

21 *L.Sc.D.*, p. 208. Einstein disputed this maxim.

22 See, e.g., K. R. Popper, 'Quantum Mechanics without "The Observer" ', in *Quantum Mechanics and Reality*, ed. by Mario Bunge (Berlin, Heidelberg, New York: Springer-Verlag, 1967), p. 33.

23 See Popper's 'The Propensity Interpretation of Probability', *B.J.P.S.*, **10**, No. 37 (May, 1959), esp. pp. 31 f.

24 K. R. Popper, *The Poverty of Historicism* (London: Routledge & Kegan Paul, 1957), Preface, pp. ix-x. Hereinafter cited as *PH*.

25 This puts D. Bohm and J. P. Vigier pretty well on the side of the Angel.

Actually, the Angel could hardly claim that current theory will be superseded by a *purely* deterministic theory with no statistical assumptions. For current theory and the evidence associated with it contains a massive amount of statistical material, and statistical conclusions can be derived only from premises of which some are statistical (see above, n. 21).

I notice that Bohm and Vigier—perhaps with this point in mind—are careful to say that they are aiming at a theory that is *more* deterministic than quantum mechanics, not at one that is *completely* deterministic. See, for instance, *Observation & Interpretation: A Symposium of Philosophus and Physicist,* Colston Papers, ed. by S. Körner (Hamden, Conn.: Shoe String Press, 1957), Vol. 9, pp. 47, 60, 73, 77.

[26] The lines along which this might be proved were suggested over thirty years ago by P. W. Bridgman when he claimed that a theory comprehensive enough to comprehend the fact of its own existence would involve an infinite regress. See his *The Nature of Physical Theory* (Princeton, N. J.: Princeton University Press, 1936), p. 118.

[27] K. R. Popper, 'The Aim of Science', *Ratio,* **1,** No. 1 (December, 1957), 24-35.

[28] His triumph would be the more remarkable if he were a physiologist who was ignorant of the branch of science to which T belongs. As Popper has mentioned, this determinist idea of physiological predictability means that a deaf physiologist might have written a wonderful symphony by studying Beethoven's body (*CC*, p. 11).

[29] This is a topic which D. M. MacKay has often analysed. See, for instance, his 'On the Logical Indeterminacy of a Free Choice', *Mind,* **69** (January, 1960). MacKay makes acknowledgements to Popper's analysis of the 'Oedipus Effect' (see above, p. 375). (Added in 1971: see now my 'Freedom and Predictability: an Amendment to MacKay', *B.J.P.S.,* **22,** No. 3 [August, 1971].)

[30] See, for instance, *L.Sc.D.*, p. 206, n. *2.

[31] K. R. Popper, *Conjectures and Refutations: The Growth of Scientific Knowledge* (London: Routledge & Kegan Paul, 1963; New York: Basic Books, 1963), pp. 193-200. Hereinafter cited as *C.&R.*

[32] I am drawing, here, on the 'Metaphysical Epilogue' in Popper's unpublished *Postscript* to *L.Sc.D.*

[33] This term is due to M. Polanyi; see his *The Logic of Liberty* (London, 1951; Chicago: University of Chicago Press, 1951), pp. 170 f.

[34] As F. A. Hayek has emphasized: '. . . the brain of an organism . . . is itself in turn a polycentric order' (*Studies in Philosophy, Politics and Economics* [London, 1967; Chicago: University of Chicago Press, 1967], p. 73).

[35] See Popper's 'Evolution and the Tree of Knowledge'. [See n. 4 above.—EDITOR]

[36] *Ibid.*

[37] I understand that we use only a small part of our overgrown brains.

[38] A similar hypothesis has been independently advanced by Arthur Koestler in his *The Ghost in the Machine* (London, 1967; New York: Macmillan, 1968), pp. 152-58. He summarises it thus: ' "Fortune favours the prepared mind," wrote Pasteur, and we may add: fortunate mutations favour the prepared animal' (p. 156).

[39] *CC,* p. 23 (italics in the original).

[40] 'If I am standing quietly . . . then . . . my muscles are constantly at work, contracting and relaxing in an almost random fashion . . . , but controlled, without my being aware of it, by error-elimination . . . so that every little deviation from my posture is almost at once corrected. So I am kept standing, quietly, by more or less the same method by which an automatic pilot keeps an aircraft steadily on its course' (*CC*, p. 25).

[41] *Ibid.*, p. 26. This idea that one cannot properly understand the problem one is currently working on fits in with Koestler's idea that great scientists are 'sleepwalkers'.

[42] An amoeba has been known to pursue an elusive ball of food for ten minutes or more. Its method is to grasp the food by throwing out pseudopods, to smother the food with its

protoplasmic body, and then to try to ingest it. See, e.g., H. S. Jennings, *Behavior of the Lower Organisms* (New York, 1906; Bloomington: Indiana University Press, 1962), p. 15; and E. S. Russell, *Directiveness of Organic Activities* (Cambridge: Cambridge University Press, 1945), p. 122.

43 'The response mechanism of amoeba's one cell is activated basically in the same way as each one of the ten thousand million cells in our brain' (W. Grey Walter, *The Living Brain*, 2d ed. [Baltimore: Penguin, 1961], p. 29).

44 See J. O. Wisdom, 'The Hypothesis of Cybernetics', *B.J.P.S.*, **2**, No. 5 (1951), p. 10. Wisdom quoted from A. Rosenblueth, N. Wiener, and J. Bigelow, 'Behavior, Purpose, and Teleology', *Philosophy of Science*, **10** (1943), 20.

45 In the chapter on 'Indeterminism' in Popper's unpublished *Postscript* to *L.Sc.D.*

46 In this section I shall draw freely on some of Popper's unpublished writings, lectures, seminar talks, and discussions.

47 Problems may also be shifted in a retrogressive way, of course. Imre Lakatos calls these 'degenerating problem-shifts'.

48 J. O. Wisdom, 'A New Model for the Mind-Body Relationship', *B.J.P.S.*, **2**, No. 8 (February, 1952).

49 For references see K. R. Popper, 'Philosophy and Physics', *Proceedings of the XIIth International Congress for Philosophy* (Florence, 1960), **2**, pp. 367-74; see also my *Hobbes's System of Ideas* (London, 1965; New York: Hutchinson University Library, 1965), pp. 122 f.

50 Already in 1600 William Gilbert in *De Magnete* had compared the interaction between magnetic force and a loadstone to that between soul and body.

51 Thus Gilbert Ryle's *The Concept of Mind* is an essay in philosophical reductionism, whereas his *Dilemmas* is largely a defence of the plain man's ontology against any depredations of modern science.

52 See the methodological thesis mentioned on p. 374 above; and see Sec. 5.4.

53 I am drawing here on an unpublished address of Popper's entitled 'A Realist View of Logic, Physics, and History'. (Added in 1971: now Chap. 1 in *Physics, Logic, and History*, ed. by Wolfgang Yourgrau and Allen D. Breck [New York and London: Plenum Press, 1970].)

54 *Ibid.*

55 See Sec. 3.1 above.

56 See Sec. 3.2 above.

57 See p. 389 above.

58 See Sec. 5.2.

59 See H. H. Price and R. B. Braithwaite on 'A Half-Belief ', *The Aristotelian Society*, Supp. Vol. **38** (1964), 149-74.

60 This point is elaborated in my 'Non-inductive Corroboration', in *The Problem of Inductive Logic*, ed. by I. Lakatos (Amsterdam: North-Holland Publishing Co., 1968), pp. 61-66.

61 See, e.g., *L.Sc.D.*, Sec. 80.

62 In Hume's *Treatise* this idea emerges at the end of Section I and beginning of Section II of Part IV, Book I: ' 'Tis happy, therefore, that *nature breaks the force of all sceptical arguments* in time, and keeps them from having any considerable influence on the understanding. . . . Thus the sceptic still continues to reason and believe, even tho' he asserts, that he cannot defend his reason by reason; and by the same rule he must assent to the principle concerning the existence of body, tho' he cannot pretend by any arguments to maintain its veracity. *Nature has not left this to his choice*, and has doubtless esteem'd it an affair of too great importance to be trusted to our uncertain reasonings and speculations' (italics mine).

In the *Enquiry* the same idea emerges even more clearly towards the end of Part II of Section XII: 'The sceptic . . . justly insists, that all our evidence for any matter of fact, which lies beyond the testimony of sense or memory, is derived entirely from the relation of cause and effect; that we have no other idea of this relation than that of two objects, which have been frequently conjoined together; that we have no argument to convince us, that objects, which have, in our experience, been frequently conjoined, will likewise, in other instances, be conjoined in the same manner; and that *nothing leads us to this inference but custom or a certain instinct of our nature*; . . . But . . . he must acknowledge, if he will acknowledge anything, that all human life must perish, were his principles universally and steadily to prevail. All discourse, all action would immediately cease; and men remain in a total lethargy, till the necessities of nature, unsatisfied, put an end to their miserable existence. It is true; so fatal an event is very little to be dreaded. *Nature is always too strong* for principle' (italics mine; Hume's italics omitted).

[63] *C.&R.*, pp. 42-46.

[64] I have pointed out elsewhere (in *The Problem of Inductive Logic*, p. 277, n. 1) that *Hume himself* was, at one point, nudged by awkward psychological facts into something like a trial-and-error theory of belief-formation.

[65] See p. 389 above.

[66] *C.&R.*, p. 47.

[67] John Locke, *An Essay Concerning Human Understanding*, II, i, 25.

[68] There was a time when my household contained three cats and three mice. The cats' problem—how to get the mice out of their cage—was solved (whether accidentally or purposefully I cannot say) one afternoon by a cat jumping on the cage so that it fell on the floor with the lid open. The mice now had the urgent problem of finding and reaching, in unfamiliar territory, places where the cats could not reach them. They solved it in a flash, and sped unerringly to safe refuges, one down the toe of a shoe, another under a low armchair, another under the wardrobe—three brilliant perceptual-motor performances. The cats tried the same solution on several subsequent occasions, but the mice always reached safe refuges.

[69] Alerted by Popper's idea I have since learnt of some recent evidence that goes some way to corroborate it. (This evidence was obtained after an important advance in experimental neurophysiology which made it possible to record the excitation and discharge of *individual* nerve cells.)

I heard from Dr. R. Jung, of the University of Freiburg, that a cat's eye, as well as having cells that are excited by light and cells that are excited by darkness, has *cells that are excited by edges or borders*—so that a cat's retinal images are, presumably, rather like photographs with profiles picked out in ink.

Professor A. Uttley and B. Delisle Burns reported a rather similar finding to the 1967 conference of the British Society for the Philosophy of Science: cat's eyes have cells that are excited by *differences* of light and shade. If we look at a uniformly grey vertical strip against a background that shades from black at the top to white at the bottom, we see the strip as shading from light grey at the top to dark grey at the bottom. Uttley and Burns suggested a physiological explanation for this optical illusion. Even an eye that is steadily focussed is continually making rapid little scanning movements. (If scanning is artifically inhibited, the retinal image fades away.) If our eyes are similar to cat's eyes, then some of our optical nerve-cells are excited by the relative *lightness* of the upper part of the grey strip, and others by the relative darkness of the lower part.

[70] See Popper, *L.Sc.D.*, pp. 94-95.

[71] Popper himself has not, I think, discussed sensory decoding in print. The importance of the idea was brought home to me in the following way.

Grover Maxwell argued from scientific realism against commonsense realism in his 'Scientific Methodology and the Causal Theory of Perception' (*Problems in the Philosophy of Science*, ed. by I. Lakatos & A. E. Musgrave [Amsterdam: North-Holland Publishing Co., 1968], pp. 148-60).

W. V. Quine, in a comment on Maxwell's paper (*ibid.*, pp. 161-63), suggested that, rather as an observer's spoken testimony about, say, the contents of a room he has been inspecting may be regarded as an encoding of his observational knowledge of those contents, so may his observational knowledge be regarded as an encoding of selected traits of those contents.

Maxwell discussed the comments on his paper by Quine, Popper and others at Popper's seminar at the London School of Economics in 1967. During the ensuing discussion, in which Popper vigorously defended the compatibility of scientific realism with commonsense realism, I began to see the importance for this issue of the idea of sensory decoding. The idea fits naturally into Popper's evolutionist view of an organism's sensory equipment.

[72] A. Landé, *New Foundations*, p. 17.

[73] See the quotation from Koestler on p. 401 above.

[74] See Popper, 'The Aim of Science', *Ratio,* **1**, No. 1 (1957).

[75] An early example of such an idea to which Popper has drawn attention is Anaximander's hypothesis that the earth 'is held up by nothing, but remains stationary owing to the fact that it is equally distant from all other things'. (See *C.&R.*, p. 138.)

[76] 'We have learned not to be disappointed any longer if our scientific theories are overthrown; for we can, in most cases, determine with great confidence which of any two theories is the better one. We can therefore know that we are making progress; and it is this knowledge that to most of us atones for the loss of the illusion of finality and certainty' (K. R. Popper, *The Open Society and Its Enemies* [London: Routledge & Kegan Paul, 1952], Vol. II, p. 12).

[77] See above, p. 402.

[78] See p. 386 above.

[79] C. D. Broad, *Ethics and the History of Philosophy* (London: Routledge & Kegan Paul, 1952), p. 167.

[80] This would fit in nicely with Popper's indeterminism. In this connection Hermann Weyl has written: 'One is tempted to complete the picture by interpreting mutation as a rare quantum jump' (*Philosophy of Mathematics and Natural Science* [Princeton: Princeton University Press, 1949], p. 278).

[81] *CC*, p. 27.

[82] And of some ancient cosmology, too. See n. 75 above.

[83] *C.&R.*, p. 95.

Donald T. Campbell
EVOLUTIONARY EPISTEMOLOGY*

A n evolutionary epistemology would be at minimum an epistemology taking cognizance of and compatible with man's status as a product of biological and social evolution. In the present essay it is also argued that evolution—even in its biological aspects—is a knowledge process, and that the natural-selection paradigm for such knowledge increments can be generalized to other epistemic activities, such as learning, thought, and science. Such an epistemology has been neglected in the dominant philosophic traditions. It is primarily through the works of Karl Popper that a natural selection epistemology is available today.

Much of what follows may be characterized as "descriptive epistemology," descriptive of man as knower. However, a correct descriptive epistemology must also be analytically consistent. Or, vice versa, of all of the analytically coherent epistemologies possible, we are interested in those (or that one) compatible with the description of man and of the world provided by contemporary science. Modern biology teaches us that man has evolved from some simple unicellular or virus-like ancestor and its still simpler progenitors. In the course of that evolution, there have been tremendous gains in adaptive adequacy, in stored templates modeling the useful stabilities of the environment, in memory and innate wisdom. Still more dramatic have been the great gains in mechanisms for knowing, in visual perception, learning, imitation, language and science. At no stage has there been any transfusion of knowledge from the outside, nor of mechanisms of knowing, nor of fundamental certainties.

* Prepared during the author's tenure as a Fellow of the Center for Advanced Study in the Behavioral Sciences, under USPHS Special Fellowship 1-F3-MH-30, 416-01, 1965-66. Revised with the support of N.S.F. Grant GS32073X. The author has had the opportunity to profit from the suggestions of D. M. Armstrong, W. Ross Ashby, H. J. Barr, Gregory Bateson, John Birmingham, Henry W. Brosin, Robert W. Browning, Milič Čapek, Arthur Child, Michael Cullen, Jan Dick, Michael T. Ghiselin, Moltke Gram, R. J. Hirst, Donald D. Jensen, Harry J. Jerison, Gary Koeske, Thomas S. Kuhn, Joseph LaLumia, Arnold Levison, Mark Lipsey, Konrad Lorenz, D. M. MacKay, Wolfe Mays, Earl R. MacCormac, Grover Maxwell, Theodore Mischel, Charles Morris, Thomas Natsoulas, F. S. C. Northrop, Stephen C. Pepper, Burton Perrin, Hugh G. Petrie, John R. Platt, Henryk Skolimowski, Herman Tennessen, William Todd, Stephen E. Toulmin, C. F. Wallraff, Robert I. Watson, Philip P. Wiener, and William C. Wimsatt.

An analytically coherent epistemology could perhaps be based upon a revelation to Adam of true axioms and deductive logic, from which might be derived, perhaps in conjunction with observations, man's true knowledge. Such an epistemology would not be compatible with the evolutionary model. Nor, would be a direct realism, an epistemology assuming veridical visual perception, unless that epistemology were also compatible with the evolution of the eye from a series of less adequate prior stages back to a light-sensitive granule of pigment. Also incompatible would be a founding of certainty on the obviously great efficacy of ordinary language. In the evolutionary perspective, this would either commit one to a comparable faith in the evolutionary prestages to modern language, or to a discontinuity and point of special creation. Better to recognize the approximate and only pragmatic character of language at all stages, including the best. An analytic epistemology appropriate to man's evolved status must be appropriate to these evolutionary advances and to these prior stages, as well as to modern man.

We once "saw" as through the fumblings of a blind protozoan, and no revelation has been given to us since. Vision represents an opportunistic exploitation of a coincidence which no deductive operations on a protozoan's knowledge of the world could have anticipated. This is the coincidence of locomotor impenetrability with opaqueness, for a narrow band of electromagnetic waves. For this band, substances like water and air are transparent, in coincidental parallel with their locomotor penetrability. For other wave lengths, the coincidence, and hence the cue value, disappears. The accidental encountering and systematic cumulations around this coincidence have provided in vision a wonderful substitute for blind exploration. In this perspective, clear glass and fog are paradoxical—glass being impenetrable but transparent, fog being the reverse. Glass was certainly lacking in the ecology of evolution. Fog was rare or nonexistent in the aqueous environment of the fish where most of this evolution took place. (Modern man corrects the paradoxical opacity of fog through exploiting another coincidence in the radar wave bands.) The visual system is furthermore far from perfect, with usually overlooked inconsistencies such as double images for nonfixated objects, blind spots, optical illusions, chromatic aberration, astigmatism, venous shadows, etc.

In all of this opportunistic exploitation of coincidence in vision there is no logical necessity, no absolute ground for certainty, but instead a most back-handed indirectness. From this perspective, Hume's achievement in showing that the best of scientific laws have neither analytic truth nor any other kind of absolute truth seems quite reasonable and appropriate. Here description and analysis agree.

1. The Selective Elimination Model

The advances produced in the course of evolution are now seen as due to natural-selection, operating upon the pool of self-perpetuating variations which the genetics of the breeding group provide, and from within this pool, differentially propagating some variations at the expense of others. The supply of variations comes both from mutations providing new semistable molecular arrangements of the genetic material and from new combinations of existing genes. Considered as improvements or solutions, none of these variations has any a priori validity. None has the status of revealed truth nor of analytic deduction. Whatever degree of validation emerges comes from the differential surviving of a winnowing, weeding-out, process.

Popper's first contribution to an evolutionary epistemology is to recognize the process of the succession of theories in science as a similar selective elimination process. The theme is expressed clearly, if but in passing, in the 1934 *Logik der Forschung*. Here are two relevant passages:

> According to my proposal, what characterizes the empirical method is its manner of exposing to falsification, in every conceivable way, the system to be tested. Its aim is not to save the lives of untenable systems but, on the contrary, to select the one which is by comparison the fittest, by exposing them all to the fiercest struggle for survival.[1]
> ... How and why do we accept one theory in preference to others?
> The preference is certainly not due to anything like an experiential justification of the statements composing the theory; it is not due to a logical reduction of the theory to experience. We choose the theory which best holds its own in competition with other theories; the one which, by natural selection, proves itself the fittest to survive. This will be the one which not only has hitherto stood up to the severest tests, but the one which is also testable in the most rigorous way. A theory is a tool which we test by applying it, and which we judge as to its fitness by the results of its applications.[2]

Fuller expressions of this evolutionary epistemology were contained in his unpublished manuscript of 1932, *Die beiden Grundprobleme der Erkenntnistheorie* (subsequently titled *Das Problem: die Erkenntnistheorie der Naturgesetzlichkeit*). In later publications, especially as collected in *Conjectures and Refutations*,[3] the theme is more explicitly presented and elaborated.

These additions add trial-and-error learning by man and animals to the prototypic illustrations of his basic logic of inference (logic of discovery, logic of the expansion of knowledge). They make explicit his willingness to identify the process of knowledge with the whole evolutionary sequence.

> Without waiting, passively, for repetitions to impress or impose regularities upon us, we actively try to impose regularities upon the world. We try to discover similarities in it, and to interpret it in terms of laws invented by us. Without waiting for premises we jump to conclusions. These may have to be discarded later, should observation show that they are wrong.

This was a theory of trial and error—of *conjectures and refutations*. It made it possible to understand why our attempts to force interpretations upon the world were logically prior to the observation of similarities. Since there were logical reasons behind this procedure, I thought that it would apply in the field of science also; that scientific theories were not the digest of observations, but that they were inventions—conjectures boldly put forward for trial, to be eliminated if they clashed with observations; with observations which were rarely accidental but as a rule undertaken with the definite intention of testing a theory by obtaining, if possible, a decisive refutation.[4]

Hume was right in stressing that our theories cannot be validly inferred from what we can know to be true—neither from observations nor from anything else. He concluded from this that our belief in them was irrational. If 'belief' means here our inability to doubt our natural laws, and the constancy of natural regularities, then Hume is again right: this kind of dogmatic belief has, one might say, a physiological rather than a rational basis. If, however, the term 'belief' is taken to cover our critical acceptance of scientific theories—a *tentative* acceptance combined with an eagerness to revise the theory if we succeed in designing a test which it cannot pass—then Hume was wrong. In such an acceptance of theories there is nothing irrational. There is not even anything irrational in relying for practical purposes upon well-tested theories, for no more rational course of action is open to us.

Assume that we have deliberately made it our task to live in this unknown world of ours; to adjust ourselves to it as well as we can; to take advantage of the opportunities we can find in it; and to explain it, if possible (we need not assume that it is), and as far as possible, with the help of laws and explanatory theories. *If we have made this our task, then there is no more rational procedure than the method of trial and error—of conjecture and refutation:* of boldly proposing theories; of trying our best to show that these are erroneous; and of accepting them tentatively if our critical efforts are unsuccessful.[5]

The method of trial and error is not, of course, simply identical with the scientific or critical approach—with the method of conjecture and refutation. The method of trial and error is applied not only by Einstein but, in a more dogmatic fashion, by the amoeba also. The difference lies not so much in the trials as in a critical and constructive attitude towards errors; errors which the scientist consciously and cautiously tries to uncover in order to refute his theories with searching arguments, including appeals to the most severe experimental tests which his theories and his ingenuity permit him to design.[6]

In the process, Popper has effectively rejected the model of passive induction even for animal learning, and advocated that here too the typical process involves broad generalizations from single specific initial experiences, generalizations which subsequent experiences edit.[7] It is noteworthy that the best of modern mathematical learning theories posit just such a one-trial learning process, as opposed to older theories which implied inductive accumulation of evidence on all possible stimulus contingencies.[8]

Most noteworthy, Popper is unusual among modern epistemologists in taking Hume's criticism of induction seriously, as more than an embarrassment, tautology, or a definitional technicality. It is the logic of variation and selective elimination which has made him able to accept Hume's contribution to analysis (while rejecting Hume's contribution to the psychology of learning and inference) and to go on to describe that sense in which animal and scientific knowledge is yet possible.

2. Locating the Problem of Knowledge

It is well to be explicit that involved in Popper's achievement is a recentering of the epistemological problem. As with Hume, the status of scientific knowledge remains important. The conscious cognitive contents of an individual thinker also remain relevant. But these no longer set the bounds of the problem. The central requirement becomes an epistemology capable of handling *expansions* of knowledge, *breakouts* from the limits of prior wisdom, *scientific discovery*. While one aspect of this general interest is descriptive, central to Popper's requirement is a logical epistemology which is compatible with such growth.

> The central problem of epistemology has always been and still is the problem of the growth of knowledge. And the growth of knowledge can be studied best by studying the growth of scientific knowledge . . . .A little reflection will show that most problems connected with the growth of our knowledge must necessarily transcend any study which is confined to common-sense knowledge as opposed to scientific knowledge. For the most important way in which common-sense knowledge grows is, precisely, by turning into scientific knowledge. Moreover, it seems clear that the growth of scientific knowledge is the most important and interesting case of the growth of knowledge.
>
> It should be remembered, in this context, that almost all the problems of traditional epistemology are connected with the problem of the growth of knowledge. I am inclined to say even more: from Plato to Descartes, Leibnitz, Kant, Duhem, and Poincaré; and from Bacon, Hobbes, and Locke to Hume, Mill, and Russell, the theory of knowledge was inspired by the hope that it would enable us not only to know more about knowledge, but also to contribute to the advance of knowledge—of scientific knowledge, that is.[9]
>
> I now turn to the last group of epistemologists—those who do not pledge themselves in advance to any philosophical method, and who make use, in epistemology, of the analysis of scientific problems, theories, and procedures, and, most important, of scientific discussions. This group can claim, among its ancestors, almost all the great philosophers of the West. (It can claim even the ancestry of Berkeley despite the fact that he was, in an important sense, an enemy of the very idea of rational scientific knowledge, and that he feared its advance.) Its most important representatives during the last two hundred years were Kant, Whewell, Mill, Peirce, Duhem, Poincaré, Meyerson, Russell, and—at least in some of his phases—Whitehead. Most of those who belong to this group would agree that scientific knowledge is the result of the growth of common-sense knowledge. But all of them discovered that scientific knowledge can be more easily studied than common-sense knowledge. For it is *common-sense knowledge writ large*, as it were. Its very problems are enlargements of the problems of common-sense knowledge. For example, it replaces the Humean problem of 'reasonable belief' by the problem of the reasons for accepting or rejecting scientific theories. And since we possess many detailed reports of the discussions pertaining to the problem whether a theory such as Newton's or Maxwell's or Einstein's should be accepted or rejected, we may look at these dis-

cussions as if through a microscope that allows us to study in detail, and objectively, some of the more important problems of 'reasonable belief'.

This approach to the problems of epistemology gets rid. . . of the pseudo-
psychological or 'subjective' method of the new way of ideas (a method still used
by Kant). But it also allows us to analyse scientific problem-situations and scientific discussions. And it can help us to understand the history of scientific
thought.[10]

A focus on the growth of knowledge, on acquisition of knowledge,
makes it appropriate to include learning as well as perception as a knowledge
process. Such an inclusion makes relevant the learning processes of animals.
However primitive these may be, they too must conform to an adequate
logical epistemology. Animal learning must not be ruled out as impossible by
the logic of knowing.[11] Popper notes these broader bounds to the
epistemological problem in numerous places in *Conjectures and Refutations*,
for example:

> Although I shall confine my discussion to the growth of knowledge in
> science, my remarks are applicable without much change, I believe, to the growth
> of pre-scientific knowledge also—that is to say, to the general way in which men,
> and even animals, acquire new factual knowledge about the world. The method
> of learning by trial and error—of learning from our mistakes—seems to be fun-
> damentally the same whether it is practised by lower or by higher animals, by
> chimpanzees or by men of science. My interest is not merely in the theory of
> scientific knowledge, but rather in the theory of knowledge in general. Yet the
> study of the growth of scientific knowledge is, I believe, the most fruitful way of
> studying the growth of knowledge in general. For the growth of scientific
> knowledge may be said to be the growth of ordinary human knowledge *writ
> large*.[12]

Such a location of the epistemological problem differs strikingly from
traditional views, even though overlapping them. Given up is the effort to
hold all knowledge in abeyance until the possibility of knowledge is first
logically established, until indubitable first principles or incorrigible sense
data are established upon which to build. Rather, the cumulative achievement
of logical analysis is accepted: such grounds are logically unavailable. No
nonpresumptive knowledge and no nonpresumptive modes of knowing are
possible to us. The difference between science and fiction, or between truth
and error, must lie elsewhere, as in the tests and outcomes of testing of the
logical implications of the presumptions. No claims to the refutation of a
consistent (and therefore unspoken) solipsism is made. The logical
irrefutability of such a possibility is accepted. The problem of knowledge,
however, is elsewhere—in truth claims descriptive of a more than now-
phenomenal world. This presumptive descriptive character is as inextricable
in "direct" observation as in the statement of laws. The interest in the
primitive fundamentals of knowledge does not begin or end with the conscious contents or sense-data of the philosopher himself.

Another older and also more current statement of the epistemological problem is also eschewed. This is the identification of "knowledge" not as "true belief" but as "true belief" which is also "rationally justified" or "well-grounded." Though widely used in linguistic analysis, this point of view implicitly accepts as valid an inductivist epistemology (giving but superficial lip service to Hume in recognizing such induction as providing only approximate validity). Popper does not limit truth to those statements which have rational support or are well-grounded before they are asserted. Truth rather lies in the outcome of subsequent tests.

> *We do not know: we can only guess.* And our guesses are guided by the un-scientific, the metaphysical (though biologically explicable) faith in laws, in regularities which we can uncover—discover. Like Bacon, we might describe our own contemporary science—'the method of reasoning which men now ordinarily apply to nature'—as consisting of 'anticipations, rash and premature' and as 'prejudices'.
>
> But these marvelously imaginative and bold conjectures or 'anticipations' of ours are carefully and soberly controlled by systematic tests. Once put forward, nòne of our 'anticipations' are dogmatically upheld. Our method of research is not to defend them, in order to prove how right we were. On the contrary, we try to overthrow them. Using all the weapons of our logical, mathematical, and technical armory we try to prove that our anticipations were false—in order to put forward, in their stead, new unjustified and unjustifiable anticipations, new 'rash and premature prejudices'.[13]

3. A Nested Hierarchy of Selective-Retention Processes

Human knowledge processes, when examined in continuity with the evolutionary sequence, turn out to involve numerous mechanisms at various levels of substitute functioning, hierarchically related, and with some form of selective retention process at each level. While Popper has for most of his career been more interested in the logic of knowing than in a descriptive epistemology, in *Of Clouds and Clocks* he has expanded his evolutionary perspective along these lines. This is a paper which should be read by both epistemologists and those interested in problems of purpose and teleology. A few brief quotations from it will serve to introduce the present section.

> My theory may be described as an attempt to apply to the whole of evolution what we learned when we analysed the evolution from animal language to human language. And it consists of a certain *view of evolution* as a growing hierarchical system of plastic controls, and of a certain *view of organisms* as incorporating—or in the case of man, evolving exosomatically—this growing hierarchical system of plastic controls. The Neo-Darwinist theory of evolution is assumed; but it is restated by pointing out that its 'mutations' may be interpreted as more or less accidental trial-and-error gambits, and 'natural selection' as one way of controlling them by error-elimination.[14]

He also emphasizes what are called here vicarious selectors:

Error-elimination may proceed either by the complete elimination of unsuccessful forms (the killing-off of unsuccessful forms by natural selection) or by
the (tentative) evolution of controls which modify or suppress unsuccessful
organs, or forms of behavior, or hypotheses.[15]

Our schema allows for the development of error-eliminating controls (warning organs like the eye; feed-back mechanisms); that is, controls which can
eliminate errors without killing the organism; and it makes it possible, ultimately, for our hypotheses to die in our stead.[16]

Also important is his emphasis on the multiplicity of trials needed at each
error-elimination level, the necessity for the profuse generation of
"mistakes."

More generally, in *Clouds and Clocks,* Popper has spoken for that
emerging position in biology and control theory which sees the natural selection paradigm as the universal nonteleological explanation of teleological
achievements, of ends-guided processes, of "fit."[17] Thus crystal formation is
seen as the result of a chaotic permutation of molecular adjacencies, some of
which are much more difficult to dislodge than others. At temperatures warm
enough to provide general change, but not so warm as to disrupt the few
stable adjacencies, the number of stable adjacencies will steadily grow even if
their occurrence is but a random affair. In crystal formation the material
forms its own template. In the genetic control of growth, the DNA provides
the initial template selectively accumulating chance fitting RNA molecules,
which in turn provide the selective template selectively cumulating from
among chaotic permutations of proteins. These molecules of course fit multiple selective criteria: of that finite set of semistable combinations of protein
material, they are the subset fitting the template. The template guides by
selecting from among the mostly unstable, mostly worthless possibilities
offered by thermal noise operating on the materials in solution. Turning the
model to still lower levels of organization, elements and subatomic particles
are seen as but nodes of stability which at certain temperatures transiently
select adjacencies among still more elementary stuff.

Turning to higher levels, the model can be applied to such dramatically
teleological achievements as embryological growth and wound healing.
Within each cell, genetic templates for all types of body proteins are
simultaneously available, competing as it were for the raw material present.
Which ones propagate most depends upon the surrounds. Transplantation of
embryonic material changes the surroundings and hence the selective system.
Wounds and amputations produce analogous changes in the "natural selection" of protein possibilities. Spiegelman[18] has specifically noted the Darwinian analogy and its advantages over vitalistic teleological pseudoexplanations which even concepts of force fields and excitatory gradients may par-
take of.

Regeneration provides an illustration of the nested hierarchical nature of
biological selection systems. The salamander's amputated leg regrows to a

length optimal for locomotion and survival. The ecological selection system does not operate directly on the leg length however. Instead, the leg length is selected to conform to an internal control built into the developmental system which vicariously represents the ecological selective system. This control was itself selected by the trial and error of whole mutant organisms.[19] If the ecology has recently undergone change, the vicarious selective criterion will correspondingly be in error. This larger, encompassing selection system is the organism-environment interaction. Nested in a hierarchial way within it is the selective system directly operating on leg length, the "settings" or criteria for which are themselves subject to change by natural selection. What are criteria at one level are but "trials" of the criteria of the next higher, more fundamental, more encompassing, less frequently invoked level.

In other writings[20] the present author has advocated a systematic extrapolation of this nested hierarchy selective retention paradigm to *all* knowledge processes, in a way which, although basically compatible with Popper's orientation, may go farther than he would find reasonable in extremity, dogmatism and claims for generality. It may on these same grounds alienate the reader. (Disagreement at this point will not rule out accepting later propositions.)

1. A blind-variation-and-selective-retention process is fundamental to all inductive achievements,[21] to all genuine increases in knowledge, to all imcreases in fit of system to environment.

2. In such a process there are three essentials: (a) Mechanisms for introducing variation; (b) Consistent selection processes; and (c) Mechanisms for preserving and/or propagating the selected variations. Note that in general the preservation and generation mechanisms are inherently at odds, and each must be compromised.

3. The many processes which shortcut a more full blind-variation-and-selective-retention process are in themselves inductive achievements, containing wisdom about the environment achieved originally by blind variation and selective retention.

4. In addition, such shortcut processes contain in their own operation a blind-variation-and-selective-retention process at some level, substituting for overt locomotor exploration or the life-and-death winnowing of organic evolution.

The word "blind" is used rather than the more ususal "random" for a variety of reasons. It seems likely that Ashby[22] unnecessarily limited the generality of his mechanism in Homeostat by an effort fully to represent all of the modern connotations of random. Equiprobability is not needed, and is definitely lacking in the mutations which lay the variation base for organic evolution. Statistical independence between one variation and the next, although frequently desirable, can also be spared: in particular, for the generalizations essayed here, certain processes involving systematic sweep scanning are recognized as blind, insofar as variations are produced without prior knowledge of which ones, if any, will furnish a selectworthy encounter. An essential connotation of blind is that the variations emitted be independent of the environmental conditions of the occasion of their occurrence. A second important connotation is that the occurrence of trials individually be uncorrelated with the solution, in that specific correct trials are no more likely to occur at any one point in a series of trials than another, nor than specific incorrect trials. A third essential connotation of blind is rejection of the notion that a variation subsequent to an incorrect trial is a "correction" of the previous trial or makes use of the direction of error of the previous one. (Insofar as mechanisms do seem to operate in this fashion, there must be operating a substitute process carrying on the blind search at another level, feedback circuits selecting "partially" adequate variations, providing information to the effect that "you're getting warm," etc.)[23]

While most descriptions of discovery and creative processes recognize the need for variation, the present author's dogmatic insistence on the blindness of such variation seems generally unacceptable. As will be seen in what follows, particularly in the discussions of vision and thought, there is no real descriptive disagreement. The present writer agrees that the overt responses of a problem-solving animal in a puzzle box are far from random, and this for several reasons: 1. Already achieved wisdom of a general sort which limits the range of trials (such wisdom due to inheritance and learning). 2. Maladaptive restriction on the range of trials. (Such biases due to structural limitations and to past habit and instinct inappropriate in a novel environment.) But these first two reasons will characterize the wrong responses as well as the correct ones, and offer no explanation of the correctness of the correct one. 3. Vicarious selection, appropriate to the immediate problem, achieved through vision. (See the subsequent section on this topic.) When, in considering creative thought, Poincaré is followed, allowing for unconscious variation-and-selection processes, opportunity for descriptive disagreement is further reduced. The point is not empirically empty, however, as it sets essential limits and requirements for any problem-solving computer (discussed under Thought, below). But the point is also analytic. In going beyond what is already known, one cannot but go blindly. If one can go wisely, this indicates already achieved wisdom of some general sort.

Expanding this orientation and applying it to the setting of biological and social evolution, a set of ten more or less discrete levels can be distinguished, and these are elaborated in the following sections.

1. *Nonmnemonic problem solving.* At the level of Jennings's[24] paramecium, stentor, and Ashby's[25] Homeostat, there is a blind variation of locomotor activity until a setting that is nourishing or nonnoxious is found. Such problem-solutions are then retained as a cessation of locomotion, as a cessation of variation. There is, however, no memory, no using of old

solutions over again. Ashby deliberately took Jennings's paramecium as his model, and describes the natural selection analogy at this level as follows:

> The work also in a sense develops a theory of the "natural selection" of behaviour-patterns. Just as in the species the truism that the dead cannot breed implies that there is a fundamental tendency for the successful to replace the unsuccessful, so in the nervous system does the truism that the unstable tends to destroy itself imply that there is a fundamental tendency for the stable to replace the unstable. Just as the gene pattern in its encounters with the environment tends toward ever better adaptation of the inherited form and function, so does a system of step- and part-functions tend toward ever better adaptation of learned behavior.[26]

In a world with only benign or neutral states, an adaptive organism might operate at this level without exteroceptors. Wherever it is, it is trying to ingest the immediate environment. When starvation approaches, blind locomotor activity is initiated, ingestion being attempted at all locations. Even at this level, however, there is needed an interoceptive sense organ which monitors nutritional level, and substitutes for the whole organism's death. In the actual case of Jennings's stentor, chemoreceptors for noxious conditions are present, vicarious representatives of the lethal character of the environment, operating on nonlethal samples or signs of that environment. It is these chemoreceptors and comparable organs which in fact provide the immediate selection of responses. Only indirectly, through selecting the selectors, does life-and-death relevance select the responses.

At this level of knowing, however, the responses may be regarded as direct rather than vicarious. And, as to presuppositions about the nature of the world (the ontology guiding epistemology), perhaps all that is assumed is spatial discontinuity somewhat greater than temporal discontinuity in the distribution of environmental substances: moving around is judged to bring changes more rapidly than staying put. At this level the species has discovered that the environment is discontinuous, consisting of penetrable regions and impenetrable ones, and that impenetrability is to some extent a stable characteristic. The animal has "learned" that there are some solvable problems. Already the machinery of knowing is biasedly focused upon the small segment of the world which is knowable, as natural selection makes inevitable.

2. *Vicarious locomotor devices.* Substituting for spatial exploration by locomotor trial and error are a variety of distance receptors of which a ship's radar is an example. An automated ship could explore the environment of landfalls, harbors and other ships by a trial and error of full movements and collisions. Instead, it sends out substitute locomotions in the form of a radar beam. These are selectively reflected from nearby objects, the reflective opaqueness to this wave band vicariouly representing the locomotor impenetrability of the objects. This vicarious representability is a contingent dis-

covery, and is in fact only approximate. The knowledge received is recon-
firmed as acted upon by the full ship's locomotion. The process removes the
trial-and-error component from the overt locomotion, locating it instead in
the blindly emitted radar beam. (The radar beam is not emitted randomly,
but it could be so emitted and still work. The radar beam is, however, emitted
in a blind exploration, albeit a systematic sweep.) Analogous to radar and to
sonar are several echolocation devices in animals. Pumphrey has described
the lateral-line organ of fish as a receiver for the reflected pulses of the broadcast pressure waves emitted by the fish's own swimming movements. The all-
directional exploring of the wave front is selectively reflected by nearby objects, pressure wave substituting for locomotor exploration. The echolocation
devices of porpoises, bats, and cave birds have a similar epistemology.[27]

Assimilating vision to the blind-variation-and-selective-retention model
is a more difficult task.[28] It seems important, however, to make vision
palpably problematic, in correction of the common sense realism or the direct
realism of many contemporary philosophers which leads them to an uncritical assumption of directness and certainty for the visual process. The
vividness and phenomenal directness of vision needs to be corrected in any
complete epistemology, which also has to make comprehensible how such an
indirect, coincidence-exploiting mechanism could work at all. Were visual
percepts as vague and incoherent as the phosphors on a radar screen, many
epistemological problems would be avoided. From the point of view of an
evolutionary epistemology, vision is just as indirect as radar.

Consider a one-photocell substitute eye such as was once distributed for
the use of the blind. To an earphone, the cell transmitted a note of varying
pitch depending upon the brightness of the light received. In blind search with
this photocell, one could locate some objects and some painted boundaries on
flat surfaces, all boundaries being indicated by a shift in tone. One can imagine an extension of this blind search device to a multiple photocell model,
each photocell of fixed direction, boundaries being located by a comparison
of emitted tones or energies perhaps in some central sweep scanning of out-
puts. To be sure, boundaries would be doubly confirmed if the whole set were
oscillated slightly, so that a boundary stood out not only as comparison
across adjacent receptors at one time, but also as a comparision across times
for the same receptors. (The eye has just such a physiological nystagmus, essential to its function.) Similarly, one could build a radar with multiple fixed-
directional emitters and receivers. It would search just as blindly, just as
openmindedly, as the single beam and sweep scanner. In such multiple receptor devices, the opportunities for excitation are blindly made available and
are selectively activated.

Blind locomotor search is the more primary, the more direct exploration. A blind man's cane is a vicarious search process. The less expensive cane
movements substitute for blind trials and wasted movements by the whole

body, removing costly search from the full locomotor effort, making that seem smooth, purposeful, insightful.[29] The single photocell device seems equally blind, although utilizing a more unlikely substitute, one still cheaper in effort and time. The multiple photocell device, or the eye, uses the multiplicity of cells instead of a multiplicity of focusings of one cell, resulting in a search process equally blind and open-minded, equally dependent upon a selection-from-variety epistemology. The substitutability of cane locomotion for body locomotion, the equivalence of opaque-to-cane and opaque-to-body, is a contingent discovery, although one which seems more nearly "entailed," or to involve a less complex, less presumptive model of the physical world than does the substitutability of light waves or radar waves for body locomotion.

This is, of course, a skeletonized model of vision, emphasizing its kinship to blind fumbling, and its much greater indirectness than blind fumbling, phenomenal directness notwithstanding. Neglected is the presumptive achievement of the visual system in reifying stable discrete objects, stable over a heterogeneity of points of viewing; neglected is the fundamental epistemological achievement of "identifying" new and partially different sets of sense data as "the same" so that habit or instinct or knowledge can be appropriately applied even though there be no logically entailed identity.[30]

3. *Habit* and 4. *Instinct.* Habit, instinct, and visual diagnosis of objects are so interlocked and interdependent that no simple ordering of the three is possible. Much more detailed work is needed on the evolution of knowledge processes, and such an examination would no doubt describe many more stages than are outlined here. Such a study could also profitably describe the "presumptions" about the nature of the world, or the "knowledge" about the nature of the world, underlying each stage. Certainly the extent of these presumptions is greater at the more advanced levels.

The visual diagnosis of reindentifiable objects is basic to most instinctive response patterns in insects and vertebrates, both for instigation of the adaptive pattern and for eliminating the trial-and-error component from the overt response elements. In a crude way, instinct development can be seen as involving a trial and error of whole mutant animals, whereas trial-and-error learning involves the much cheaper wastage of responses within the lifetime of a single animal.[31] The same environment is editing habit and instinct development in most cases, the editing process is analogous, and the epistemological status of the knowledge, innate or learned, no different. Thus the great resistance of the empiricists to innate knowledge is made irrelevant, but in the form of a more encompassing empiricism. It can be noted that all comprehensive learning theories, including those of Gestalt inspiration, contain a trial-and-error component, be it a trial and error of "hypotheses" or "recenterings."[32]

These general conclusions may be acceptable, but the evolutionary discreteness of the two processes is not as clear as implied nor should instinct necessarily be regarded as more primitive than habit. Complex adaptive instincts typically involve multiple movements and must inevitably involve a multiplicity of mutations at least as great in number as the obvious movement segments. Furthermore, it is typical that the fragmentary movement segments, or the effects of single component mutations, would represent no adaptive gain at all apart from the remainder of the total sequence. The joint likelihood of the simultaneous occurrence of the adaptive form of the many mutations involved is so infinitesimal that the blind-mutation-and-selective-retention model seems inadequate. This argument was used effectively by both Lamarckians and those arguing for an intelligently guided evolution or creation. Baldwin, Morgan, Osborn, and Poulton[33] believing that natural selection was the adequate and only mechamism, proposed that for such instincts, learned adaptive patterns, recurrently discovered in similar form within a species by trial-and-error learning, preceded the instincts. The adaptive pattern being thus piloted by learning, any mutations that accelerated the learning, made it more certain to occur, or predisposed the animal to certain component responses, would be adaptive and selected no matter which component, or in what order affected. The habit thus provided a selective template around which the instinctive components could be assembled. (Stating it in other terms, learned habits make a new ecological niche available which niche then selects instinct components.) It is furthermore typical of such instincts that they involve learned components, as of nest and raw material location, etc.

This can be conceived as an evolution of increasingly specific selection-criteria, which at each level select or terminate visual search and trial-and-error learning. In what we call learning, these are very general drive states and reinforcing conditions. In the service of these general reinforcers, specific objects and situations become learned goals and subgoals, learned selectors of more specific responses. (Even for drives and reinforcers, of course, the environment's selective relevance is represented indirectly, as in the pleasureableness of sweet foods, the vicariousness of which is shown by an animal's willingness to learn for the reward of nonnutritive saccharine.) In the habit-to-instinct evolution, the once-learned goals and subgoals become innate at a more and more specific response-fragment level. For such an evolutionary development to take place, very stable environments over long evolutionary periods are required.

Popper in his Herbert Spencer Lecture of 1961[33a] makes a creative analysis of the evolution of purposeful behavior which in some ways parallels Baldwin's, but is more explicit on the hierarchial selection of selectors. Using a servomechanism model of an automated aeroplane, he suggests that mutations of "aim-structure" precede and subsequently select mutations in "skill structure."

5. *Visually supported thought.* The dominant form of insightful problem solving in animals, e.g., as described by Köhler,[34] requires the support of a visually present environment. With the environment represented vicariously through visual search, there is a substitute trial and error of potential locomotions in thought. The "successful" locomotions at this substitute level, with its substitute selective criteria, are then put into overt locomotion, where they appear "intelligent," "purposeful," "insightful," even if still subject to further editing in the more direct contact with the environment.

6. *Mnemonically supported thought.* At this level the environment being searched is vicariously represented in memory or "knowledge," rather than visually, the blindly emitted vicarious thought trials being selected by a vicarious criterion substituting for an external state of affairs. The net result is the "intelligent," "creative," and "foresightful" product of thought, our admiration of which makes us extremely reluctant to subsume it under the blind-variation-and-selective-retention model. Yet it is in the description of this model that the trial-and-error theme, the blind permutation theme, has been most persistently invoked. When Mach in 1895 was called back to Vienna to assume the newly created professorship in "The History and Theory of Inductive Sciences," he chose this topic:

> The disclosure of new provinces of facts before unknown can only be brought about by accidental circumstances . . .[35]
> . . . In such [other] cases it is a psychical accident to which the person owes his discovery—a discovery which is here made "deductively" by means of mental copies of the world, instead of experimentally.[36]
> . . . After the repeated survey of a field has afforded opportunity for the interposition of advantageous accidents, has rendered all the traits that suit with the word or the dominant thought more vivid, and has gradually relegated to the background all things that are inappropriate, making their future appearance impossible; then, from the teeming, swelling host of fancies which a free and high-flown imagination calls forth, suddenly that particular form arises to the light which harmonizes perfectly with the ruling idea, mood, or design. Then it is that that which has resulted slowly as the result of a gradual selection, appears as if it were the outcome of a deliberate act of creation. Thus are to be explained the statements of Newton, Mozart, Richard Wagner, and others, when they say that thoughts, melodies, and harmonies had poured in upon them, and that they had simply retained the right ones.[37]

Poincaré's famous essay on mathematical creativity espouses such a view at length, arguing that it is mathematical beauty which provides the selective criteria for a blind permuting process usually unconscious:

> One evening, contrary to my custom, I drank black coffee and could not sleep. Ideas rose in crowds; I felt them collide until pairs interlocked, so to speak, making a stable combination.[38]
> . . . What happens then? Among the great numbers of combinations blindly formed by the subliminal self, almost all are without interest and without utility; but just for that reason they are also without effect upon the esthetic sensibility.

Consciousness will never know them; only certain ones are harmonious, and, consequently, at once useful and beautiful.[39]

. . . Perhaps we ought to seek the explanation in that preliminary period of conscious work which always precedes all fruitful unconscious labor. Permit me a rough comparison. Figure the future elements of our combinations as something like the hooked atoms of Epicurus. During the complete repose of the mind, these atoms are motionless, they are, so to speak, hooked to the wall; so this complete rest may be indefinitely prolonged without the atoms meeting, and consequently without any combination between them.

On the other hand, during a period of apparent rest and unconscious work, certain of them are detached from the wall and put in motion. They flash in every direction through the space (I was about to say the room) where they are enclosed, as would, for example, a swarm of gnats or, if you prefer a more learned comparison, like the molecules of gas in the kinematic theory of gases. Then their mutual impacts may produce new combinations.[40]

. . . In the subliminal self, on the contrary, reigns what I should call liberty, if we might give this name to the simple absence of discipline and to the disorder born of chance. Only this disorder itself permits unexpected combinations.[41]

Alexander Bain was proposing a trial-and-error model of invention and thought as early as 1855.[42] Jevons in 1874[43] was advocating a similar model in the context of a rejection of Bacon's principle of induction on grounds similar to Popper's.

I hold that in all cases of inductive inference we must invent hypotheses until we fall upon some hypothesis which yields deductive results in accordance with experience.[44]

It would be an error to suppose that the great discoverer seizes at once upon the truth or has any unerring method of divining it. In all probability the errors of the great mind exceed in number those of the less vigorous one. Fertility of imagination and abundance of guesses at truth are among the first requisites of discovery; but the erroneous guesses must be many times as numerous as those which prove well founded. The weakest analogies, the most whimsical notions, the most apparently absurd theories, may pass through the teeming brain, and no record remain of more than the hundredth part. There is nothing really absurd except that which proves contrary to logic and experience. The truest theories involve suppositions which are inconceivable, and no limit can really be placed to the freedom of hypothesis.[45]

In his very modern and almost totally neglected *Theory of Invention* of 1881, Souriau effectively criticizes deduction, induction, and *"la methode"* as models for advances in thought and knowledge. His recurrent theme is *"le principe de l'invention est le hazard"*:

A problem is posed for which we must invent a solution. We know the conditions to be met by the sought idea; but we do not know what series of ideas will lead us there. In other words, we know how the series of our thoughts must end, but not how it should begin. In this case it is evident that there is no way to begin except at random. Our mind takes up the first path that it finds open before it, perceives that it is a false route, retraces its steps and takes another direction.

Perhaps it will arrive immediately at the sought idea, perhaps it will arrive very belatedly: it is entirely impossible to know in advance. In these conditions we are reduced to dependence upon chance.[46]

By a kind of artificial selection, we can in addition substantially perfect our thought and make it more and more logical. Of all the ideas which present themselves to our mind, we note only those which have some value and can be utilized in reasoning. For every single idea of a judicious and reasonable nature which offers itself to us, what hosts of frivolous, bizarre, and absurd ideas cross our mind. Those persons who, upon considering the marvelous results at which knowledge has arrived, cannot imagine that the human mind could achieve this by a simple fumbling, do not bear in mind the great number of scholars working at the same time on the same problem, and how much time even the smallest discovery costs them. Even genius has need of patience. It is after hours and years of meditation that the sought-after idea presents itself to the inventor. He does not succeed without going astray many times; and if he thinks himself to have succeeded without effort, it is only because the joy of having succeeded has made him forget all the fatigues, all of the false leads, all of the agonies, with which he has paid for his success.[47]

... If his memory is strong enough to retain all of the amassed details, he evokes them in turn with such rapidity that they seem to appear simultaneously; he groups them by chance in all the possible ways; his ideas, thus shaken up and agitated in his mind, form numerous unstable aggregates which destroy themselves, and finish up by stopping on the most simple and solid combination.[48]

Note the similarity of the imagery in the final paragraph with that of Ashby as cited under level 1, above, and that of Poincaré, Mach and Jevons.

In Souriau's use of the phrase "artificial selection," he seems to refer to the analogy with Darwin's theory of natural selection, but we cannot be certain. Souriau's book is totally devoid of citations or even mentions of the works of any other. William James, however, is completely explicit on the analogy in an article published in 1880.[49] Arguing against Spencer's model of a perfectly passive mind, he says:

And I can easily show that throughout the whole extent of those mental departments which are highest, which are most characteristically human, Spencer's law is violated at every step; and that, as a matter of fact, the new conceptions, emotions, and active tendencies which evolve are orginally *produced* in the shape of random images, fancies, accidental outbirths of spontaneous variation in the functional activity of the excessively unstable human brain, which the outer environment simply confirms or refutes, preserves or destroys—selects, in short, just as it selects morphological and social variations due to molecular accidents of an analogous sort.[50]

.... The conception of the [scientific] law is a spontaneous variation in the strictest sense of the term. It flashes out of one brain, and no other, because the instability of that brain is such as to tip and upset itself in just that particular direction. But the important thing to notice is that the good flashes and the bad flashes, the triumphant hypotheses and the absurd conceits, are on an exact equality in respect of their origin.[51]

James departs from the more complete model presented in Poincaré,[52] Mach,[53] and Campbell[54] by seemingly having the full range of mental variations selected by the external environment rather than recognizing the existence of mental selectors, which vicariously represent the external environment. (The selected products, of course, being subject to further validation in overt locomotion, etc.)

Among the many others who have advocated such a view are Baldwin, Fouillé, Pillsbury, Woodworth, Rignano, Thurstone, Lowes, Tolman, Hull, Muenzinger, Miller and Dollard, Boring, Humphrey, Mowrer, Sluckin, Pólya and Bonsack.[55] One presentation which has reached the attention of some philosophers is that of Kenneth J. W. Craik, in his fragmentary work of genius, *The Nature of Explanation*,[56] a work which in many other ways also espouses an evolutionary epistemology.

The resultant process of thought is a very effective one, and a main pillar of man's high estate. Yet it must be emphasized again that the vicarious representations involved—both environmental realities and potential locomotions being represented in mind-brain processes—are discovered contingent relationships, achieving no logical entailment, and in fine detail incomplete and imperfect. This same vicarious, contingent, discovered, marginally imperfect representativeness holds for the highly selected formal logics and mathematics which we utilize in the processes of science.

Computer problem solving is a highly relevant topic, and is perhaps best introduced at this point. Like thinking, it requires vicarious explorations of a vicarious representation of the environment, with the exploratory trials being selected by criteria which are vicarious representatives of solution requirements or external realities. The present writer would insist here too, that if discovery or expansions of knowledge are achieved, blind variation is requisite. This being the case, it is only fair to note that Herbert Simon, both a leading computer simulator of thought and an epistemologically sophisticated scholar, rejects this point of view, at least in the extreme form advocated here. For example, he says "The more difficult and novel the problem, the greater is likely to be the amount of trial and error required to find a solution. At the same time, the trial and error is not completely random or blind; it is, in fact, highly selective."[57] Earlier statements on this have been still more rejective.[58] The present writer has attempted elsewhere to answer in more detail than space here permits,[59] but a brief summary is in order. The "selectivity," insofar as it is appropriate, represents already achieved wisdom of a more general sort, and as such, selectivity does not in any sense explain an innovative solution. Insofar as the selectivity is inappropriate, it limits areas of search in which a solution might be found, and rules out classes of possible solutions. Insofar as the selectivity represents a partial general truth, some unusual solutions are ruled out. Simon's "heuristics" are such partial truths, and a computer which would generate its own heuristics would have to do so by a blind trial and error of heuristic principles, selection from which would represent achieved general knowledge. The principle of hierarchy in problem solving depends upon such discoveries, and once achieved, can, of course, greatly reduce the total search space, but without at all violating the requirement of blindness as here conceived. For example, one of the heuristics used in Simon's "Logic Theorist" program[60] is that any substitution or transformation which will increase the "similarity" between a proposition and the desired outcome should be retained as a stem on which further variations are to be tried. Any transformation decreasing similarity should be discarded. Similarity is crudely scored by counting the number of identical terms, with more points for similarity of location. This rule enables selection to be introduced at each transformational stage, greatly reducing the total search space. It employs an already achieved partial truth. It produces computer search similar to human problem solving in failing to discover roundabout solutions requiring initial decreases in similarity. Beyond thus applying what is already known, albeit only a partial truth, the new discoveries must be produced by a blind generation of alternatives.

7. *Socially vicarious exploration: observational learning and imitation.*
The survival value of the eye is obviously related to an economy of cognition—the economy of eliminating all of the wasted locomotions which would otherwise be needed. An analogous economy of cognition helps account for the great survival advantage of the truly social forms of animal life, which in evolutionary sequences are regularly found subsequent to rather than prior to solitary forms. In this, the trial-and-error exploration of one member of a group substitutes for, renders unnecessary, trial-and-error exploration on the part of other members. The use of trial and error by scouts on the part of migrating social insects and human bands illustrates this general knowledge process. At the simplest level in social animals are procedures whereby one animal can profit from observing the consequences to another of that other's acts, even or especially when these acts are fatal to the model. The aversion which apes show to dismembered ape bodies, and their avoidance of the associated locations, illustrates such a process.[61] In ants and termites the back tracking on the tracks of foragers who have come back heavy laden illustrates such a process for knowledge of attractive goal objects. The presumptions involved in this epistemology include the belief that the model, the vicar, is exploring the same world in which the observer is living and locomoting, as well as those assumptions about the lawfulness of that world which underlie all learning.

Also noted in social animals, perhaps particularly in their young, is a tendency to imitate the actions of models even when the outcomes of those actions cannot be observed. This is a much more presumptive, but still "rational" procedure. It involves the assumptions that the model animal is capable of learning and is living in a learnable world. If this is so, then the model has probably eliminated punished responses and has increased its tendencies to make rewarded responses, resulting in a net output of predominantly rewarded responses (the more so the longer the learning period and the stabler the environment).[62]

But even in imitation, there is no "direct" infusion or transference of knowledge or habit, just as there is no "direct" acquisition of knowledge by observation or induction. As Baldwin[63] analyzes the process, what the child acquires is a criterion image, which he learns to match by a trial and error of matchings. He hears a tune, for example, and then learns to make that sound by a trial and error of vocalizations, which he checks against the memory of the sound pattern. Recent studies of the learning of bird song confirm and elaborate the same model.[64]

8. *Language.* Overlapping with levels 6 and 7 above is language, in which the outcome of explorations can be relayed from scout to follower with neither the illustrative locomotion nor the environment explored being present, not even visually-vicariously present. From the social-functional point of view, it is quite appropriate to speak of the "language" of bees, even though the wagging dance by which the scout bee conveys the direction, distance, and richness of his find is an innate response tendency automatically elicited without conscious intent to communicate. This bee language has the social function of economy of cognition in a way quite analogous to human language. The vicarious representabilities of geographical direction (relative to the sun and plane of polarization of sunlight), of distance, and of richness by features of the dance such as direction on a vertical wall, length of to-and-fro movements, rapidity of movements, etc., are all invented and contingent equivalences, neither entailed nor perfect, but tremendously reductive of flight lengths on the part of the observing or listening worker bees.[65] The details of von Frisch's analysis are currently being both challenged and extended. Perhaps the dance language does not communicate as precisely as he thought. Perhaps sonic, supersonic, and odor-trail means are also involved. It seems certain, however, that there are effective means of transmitting to other bees the successful outcomes of scout bee explorations in such a manner as to greatly reduce the total wasted exploratory effort over that required of solitary bees.

Given the present controversy over "bee language," it may be well to make the point of a functional-linguistic feature in social insects at a more primitive level. Ants and termites have independently discovered the use of pheromones for this purpose: an explorer who has encountered food exudes a special external hormone on his walk back to the nest. The other workers backtrack on this special scent. If they too are successful, if the food supply remains plentiful, they keep the pheromone track renewed. The "knowledge" of the environment upon which the worker bases his trip is profoundly indirect. This "knowledge" is more directly confirmed if and when the worker finds food (although the also implied information that food is more prevalent in this direction than in most others is not tested at all). But even this confirmation is profoundly indirect at the individual system level, for it involves sense-organ criteria for nourishingness rather than nourishingness itself. These criteria turn out to be approximate within limits set by the prior ecology. Nonnourishing saccharin and ant poison illustrate the indirectness and proneness to illusion in novel ecologies.

For human language too, the representability of things and actions by words is a contingent discovery, a nonentailed relationship, and only approximate. We need a Popperian model of language learning in the child and of language development in the race. Regarding the child, this would emphasize that word meanings cannot be directly transferred to the child. Rather, the child must discover these by a presumptive trial and error of meanings, which the initial instance only limits but does not determine. Rather than logically complete ostensive definitions being possible, there are instead extended, incomplete sets of ostensive instances, each instance of which equivocally leaves possible multiple interpretations, although the whole series edits out many wrong trial meanings. The "logical" nature of children's errors in word usage amply testifies to such a process, and testifies against an inductionist version of a child's passively observing adult usage contingencies. This trial and error of meanings requires more than the communication of mentor and child. It requires a third party of objects referred to. Language cannot be taught by telephone, but requires visually or tactually present ostensive referents stimulating and editing the trial meanings.

Moving to the evolution of human language, a social trial and error of meanings and namings can be envisaged. Trial words designating referents which the other speakers in the community rarely guess "correctly" either fail to become common coinage or are vulgarized toward commonly guessed designations. All words have to go through the teaching sieve, have to be usefully if incompletely communicable by finite sets of ostensive instances. Stable, sharp, striking object-boundaries useful in manipulating the environment have a greater likelihood of utilization in word meanings than do subtler designations, and when used, achieve a greater universality of meaning within the community of speakers. Such natural boundaries for words exist in much greater number than are actually used, and alternate boundaries for highly overlapping concepts abound. Just as certain knowledge is never achieved in science, so certain equivalence of word meanings is never achieved in the iterative trial and error of meanings in language learning. This equivocality and heterogeneity of meanings is more than trivial logical technicality; it is a practical fringe imperfection. And even were meanings uniform, the word-to-object equivalence is a corrigible contingent relationship, a product of a trial and error of metaphors of greater and greater appropriateness, but never complete perfection, never a formal nor entailed isomorphism.[66]

9. *Cultural cumulation.* In sociocultural evolution there are a variety of variation and selective retention processes leading to advances or changes in technology and culture. Most direct, but probably of minor importance, is the selective survival of complete social organizations, differentially as a function of cultural features. More important is selective borrowing, a process which probably leads to increased adaptation as far as easily tested aspects of technology are concerned, but could involve adaptive irrelevance in areas of culture where reality testing is more difficult. Differential imitation of a heterogeneity of models from within the culture is also a selective system that could lead to cultural advance. The learning process, selective repetition from among a set of temporal variations in cultural practice, also produces cultural advance. Selective elevation of different persons to leadership and educational roles is no doubt involved. Such selective criteria are highly vicarious, and could readily become disfunctional in a changing environment.[67]

10. *Science.* With the level of science, which is but an aspect of sociocultural evolution, we return to Popper's home ground. The demarcation of science from other speculations is that the knowledge claims be testable, and that there be available mechanisms for testing or selecting which are more than social. In theology and the humanities there is certainly differential propagation among advocated beliefs, and there result sustained developmental trends, if only at the level of fads and fashions. What is characteristic of science is that the selective system which weeds out among the variety of conjectures involves deliberate contact with the environment through experiment and quantified prediction, designed so that outcomes quite independent of the preferences of the investigator are possible. It is preeminently this feature that gives science its greater objectivity and its claim to a cumulative increase in the accuracy with which it describes the world.

An emphasis on the trial-and-error nature of science is a recurrent one, perhaps more characteristic of scientists describing scientific method than of philosophers. Agassi attributes such a view to William Whewell as early as 1840: "Whewell's [is] in retrospect a Darwinian view: we must invent many hypotheses because only a few of them survive tests, and these are the ones that matter, the hard core around which research develops."[68] James, Huxley, Boltzmann, Ritchie, Jennings, Cannon, Northrop, Beveridge, Pepper, Auger, Holton, Roller, Gillispie, Caws, Ghiselin, and Monod are also among those espousing such a view,[69] along with Toulmin, Kuhn, and Ackermann, to be discussed in more detail below.

There are a number of aspects of science which point in this direction. The opportunism of science, the rushing in and rapid development following new breakthroughs, are very like the rapid exploitation of a newly entered ecological niche. Science grows rapidly around laboratories, around discoveries which make the testing of hypotheses easier, which provide sharp and consistent selective systems. Thus the barometer, microscope, telescope, galvanometer, cloud chamber, and chromatograph all have stimulated rapid scientific growth. The necessity for the editing action of the experiment explains why a research tradition working with a trivial topic for which predictions can be checked advances more rapidly than research focused upon a more important problem but lacking a machinery for weeding out hypotheses.

A major empirical achievement of the sociology of science is the evidence of the ubiquity of simultaneous invention. If many scientists are trying variations on the same corpus of current scientific knowledge, and if their trials are being edited by the same stable external reality, then the selected variants are apt to be similar, the same discovery encountered independently by numerous workers. This process is no more mysterious than that all of a set of blind rats, each starting with quite different patterns of initial responses, learn the same maze pattern, under the maze's common editorship of the varied response repertoires. Their learning is actually their independent invention or discovery of the same response pattern. In doubly reflexively appropriateness, the theory of natural selection was itself multiply independently invented, not only by Wallace but by many others. Moreover, the ubiquity of independent invention in science has itself been independently discovered.[70]

Placing science within the selective retention theme only begins the analysis that will eventually be required, for there are within science a variety of trial-and-error processes of varying degrees of vicariousness and interdependence. At one extreme is the blindly exploratory experimentalist who within a given laboratory setting introduces variations on every parameter and combination he can think of, without attention to theory. While such activity does not epitomize science, such research often provides the empirical puzzles that motivate and discipline the efforts of theoreticians. A multiple opportunism of selective systems (or "problems") needs also to be emphasized. Whereas the mass explorations of pharmaceutical houses for new antibiotics may be single-problem oriented, "basic" research is, like biological evolution, opportunistic not only in solutions, but also in problems. The research worker encountering a new phenomenon may change his research problem to one which is thereby solved. Serendipity as described by Cannon and Merton,[71] and the recurrent theme of "chance" discovery, emphasize this double opportunism. Its occurrence implies that the scientist has an available agenda of problems, hypotheses, or expectations much larger than the specific problem on which he works, and that he is in some sense continually scanning or winnowing outcomes, particularly unexpected ones, with this larger set of sieves.

At the opposite extreme from this blind laboratory exploration is Popper's view of the natural selection of scientific theories, a trial and error of mathematical and logical models in competition with each other in the adequacy with which they solve empirical puzzles, that is, in the adequacy with which they fit the totality of scientific data and also meet the separate requirements of being theories or solutions. Popper[72] has, in fact, disparaged the common belief in "chance" discoveries in science as partaking of the inductivist belief in directly learning from experience. Although there is probably no fundamental disagreement, that issue, and the more general problem of spelling out in detail the way in which a natural selection of scientific *theories* is compatible with a dogmatic blind-variation-and-selective retention epistemology remain high priority tasks for the future.

Intermediate perhaps, is Toulmin's[73] evolutionary model of scientific development, which makes explicit analogue to population genetics and the concept of evolution as a shift in the composition of gene pool shared by a population, rather than specified in an individual. In his analogy, for genes are substituted "competing intellectual variants," concepts, beliefs, interpretations of specific fact, facts given special importance, etc. The individual scientists are the carriers. Through selective diffusion and selective retention processes some intellectual variants eventually become predominant, some completely eliminated. Some new mutants barely survive until their time is ripe.

The selective systems operating on the variations need also to be specified. As Baldwin and Peirce emphasized, the selective system of science is ultimately socially distributed in a way which any individualistic epistemology fails to describe adequately. Vicarious selectors also must be specified. Whereas the meter readings in experiments may seem to be direct selectors, this is only relatively so, and most of the proximal selection is done on the basis of vicarious criteria, including the background presumptions required to interpret the meter readings, some of which are very general in nature. In keeping with the nested hierarchy evolutionary perspective, a trial and error of such presuppositions, would be expected as part of the overall process. Both Toulmin's interpretation of the history of science in terms of shifts in what does not need to be explained and Kuhn's paradigm shifts can be interpreted in this light.[74] This is consistent with Toulmin's own evolutionary orientation. Although Kuhn also uses natural selection analogues, a natural selection of paradigms imputes to surviving paradigms a superiority over their predecessors which he explicitly questions. Ackermann has extended the evolutionary perspectives of Kuhn, Popper, and Toulmin, viewing experimental evidence as providing ecologies or niches to which theories adapt, i.e., which select theories.[75]

4. Historical Perspectives on Evolutionary Epistemology

What we find in Popper, and what has been elaborated so far, is but one type of evolutionary epistemology, perhaps best called a natural selection epistemology. As we have seen, there were both implicit and explicit forerunners of this in the nineteenth century, but they did not provide the dominant theme. Instead, theories of pre-Darwinian type generated the major evolutionary input into epistemology, even though their acceptance was furthered by the authority of Darwin's work. Herbert Spencer was the major spokesman for this school. Although he was an enthusiastic recipient of Darwin's theory of natural selection (and may even have coined the phrase "survival of the fittest"), he was a vigorous evolutionist before he read Darwin, and his thinking remained dominated by two pre-Darwinian inputs. The first was the model of embryological development, and the second was a version of Lamarckian theory in which the animal mind was a passive mirror of environmental realities. Čapek has provided three excellent historical reviews[76] of Spencer's epistemology and its influence. Among his positive contributions was his insistence that knowing had evolved along with the other aspects of life. Also valuable was his concept of the "range of correspondences," the range becoming broader at higher evolutionary stages as manifest both in distance-receptor depth and range of environmental utilization. (His evolutionary Kantianism will be discussed below.)

What Spencer missed was the profound indirectness of knowing necessitated by the natural selection paradigm, and the inevitable imperfection and approximate character of both perceptual and scientific knowledge at any stage. Instead, believing that an infinitely refinable and sensitive human cognitive apparatus had in the course of evolution adapted perfectly to the external environment, he became a naive realist accepting the givens of the cognitive processes as fundamentally valid. He also viewed human cognition as validly encompassing all reality, rather than just those aspects behaviorally relevant in the course of human evolution. Čapek sees the major limitations of Mach's and Poincaré's evolutionary epistemologies as stemming from their residual tendency to follow Spencer in accepting the completeness of cognitive evolution. It was against the Spencerian version of evolutionarily produced cognitive perfection and completeness that Bergson rebelled.[77]   The Spencerian evolutionary epistemology had become a quite dominant view by 1890, a fact difficult to believe so absent has been any evolutionary epistemology in the major philosophical discussions of the last fifty years. William James, in 1890, speaks of the pervasive "evolutionary empiricists."[78] Georg Simmel, in 1890, was able to write,

> It has been presumed for some time that human knowing has evolved from the practical needs of preserving and providing for life. The common underlying presupposition is this: there exists objective truth, the content of which is not influenced by the practical needs of the knower. This truth is grasped only because of its utility, correct conceptions being more useful than wrong ones. This view is common to various schools of epistemology, in realism where knowing is an inevitable grasping of an absolute reality, in idealism, where knowing is directed by *a priori* forms of thought.[79]

While accepting a natural selection epistemology, Simmel argues that, for the evolving animal, truth and usefulness are historically one. Anticipating von Uexküll and Bergson, he notes that the phenomenal worlds of animals differ from one to the other, according to the particular aspects of the world they are adapted to and the different sense organs they have.

Pragmatism's relation to natural selection and other evolutionary theories is mixed. In William James's prepragmatism writings, he clearly espoused a natural-selection fallibilism of thought, social evolution, and science, in explicit opposition to Spencer's passive-omniscient Lamarckianism.[80] A vague social-evolutionary orientation appears in his writings on pragmatism, but nowhere as explicit on the issues of importance here. John Dewey's faith in experimentalism was never explicitly related to the variation-and-selective-retention epistemology, and his only reference to natural selection in his book, *The Influence of Darwin on Philosophy*, is in refutation of the argument for God's existence from the wondrous adapted complexity of organisms.[81] In his chapter of that book on the problem of knowledge, no mention of natural selection or trial and error occurs.

Charles Sanders Peirce is profoundly ambivalent in this regard. His concept of truth as "the opinion which is fated to be ultimately agreed to by all who investigate"[82] partakes of the "left-overs" or winnowing model of knowledge which is the particular achievement of the selective retention perspective. Here is another fragment with this flavor:

> ... it may be conceived, and often is conceived, that induction lends a probability to its conclusion. Now that is not the way in which induction leads to the truth. It lends no definite probability to its conclusion. It is nonsense to talk of the probability of a law, as if we could pick universes out of a grab-bag and find in what proportion of them the law held good. Therefore, such an induction is not valid; for it does not do what it professes to do, namely make its conclusion probable. But yet if it had only professed to do what induction does (namely, to commence a proceeding which must in the long run approximate to the truth), which is infinitely more to the purpose than what it professes, it would have been valid.[83]

Another Peirceian imagery that is quite sympathetic is that of a primeval chaos of chance, within which nodes of order emerged, nodes which grew but never exhausted the chaos, a background of chance and indeterminacy remaining. This imagery is preminiscent of that of Ashby.[84] But the mechanism which is used to explain the emergence is not selective retention, but a mentalistic, anthropomorphic, "tendency to habit" on the part of physical matter:

> ... a Cosmogonic Philosophy. It would suppose that in the beginning—infinitely remote—there was a chaos of unpersonalized feeling, which being without connection or regularity would properly be without existence. This feeling, sporting here and there in pure arbitrariness, would have started the germ of a generalizing tendency. Its other sportings would be evanescent, but this would have a growing virtue. Thus the tendency to habit would be started; and from this, with the other principles of evolution, all the regularities of the universe would be evolved. At any time, however, an element of pure chance survives and will remain until the world becomes an absolutely perfect, rational, and symmetrical system, in which mind is at last crystallized in the infinitely distant future.[85]

Peirce was thoroughly conversant with the concept of natural selection and recognized it as Darwin's central contribution. Certainly he had in his creative exploration all of the ingredients for a selective retention evolutionary epistemology. Yet, the perspective if ever clearly conceived was also ambivalently rejected, and compatible statements such as those above are few and far between, overshadowed by dissimilar and incompatible elements. Wiener[86] has carefully documented his ambivalence on the issue. In spite of all of his emphasis on evolution, and on the ontological status of chance, Peirce was not a Darwinian evolutionist. Rather he favored the views of both Lamarck and Agassiz, or at least gave them equal status. Wiener is able to quote Peirce as describing Darwin's theory as one which "barely commands scientific respect," and "did not appear at first at all near to being proved, and to a sober mind its case looks less hopeful now [1893] than it did twenty years ago."[87] While later expressing much more Darwinian positions, he hedged by regarding sports (and trial thoughts) as being initiated by lack of environmental fit, and as being formed "not wildly but in ways having some sort of relation to the change needed."[88] Peirce's evolutionism was nostalgic for if not consistently committed to a God-guided evolution:

> ... a genuine evolutionary philosophy, that is one that makes the principle of growth a primordial element of the universe, is so far from being antagonistic to the idea of a personal creator that it is really inseparable from that idea; while a necessitarian religion is in an altogether false position and is destined to become disintegrated. But a pseudo-evolutionism which enthrones mechanical law is at once scientifically unsatisfactory, as giving no possible hint of how the universe has come about, and hostile to all hopes of personal relations to God.[89]

In connection with such a view, however, he had the important insight that natural laws (and perhaps even God Himself) are evolutionary products and are still evolving.[90]

James Mark Baldwin is known to philosophers today only as the editor of the 1901-1905 *Dictionary of Philosophy* for which Peirce wrote a number of entries. Professionally a psychologist, he is perhaps today better remembered by sociologists of the Cooley tradition, or as a contender for the dubious honor of writing the first social psychology text (that by subtitle and preface) in 1897. Always a vigorous evolutionist, Darwinist-Weismannian and anti-Lamarckian, he turned to epistemology in his later years in his several volumes on *Thought and Things or Genetic Logic*.[91] In 1909 he published casually a brief book on *Darwin and the Humanities*[92] which stands in marked contrast with Dewey's contemporaneous *The Influence of Darwin on Philosophy*[93] for its pervasive use of the natural selection and generalized selective retention theme. In this volume Baldwin summarized more concisely points he had made elsewhere, some of which have been cited above:

> ... My favorite doctrines, and those in which my larger books have been in some measure original, seem now, when woven together, to have been consciously inspired by the theory of Natural Selection: I need only mention 'Organic Selection,' 'Functional Selection,' 'Social Heredity,' 'Selective Thinking,' 'Experimental Logic,' thoroughgoing 'Naturalism of Method,' etc. Such views as these all illustrate or extend the principle of selection as Darwin conceived it—that is, the principle of survival from varied cases—as over against any vitalistic or formal principle.[94]
>
> ... Natural selection is in principle the universal law of genetic organization and progress in nature—human nature no less than physical nature.[95]
>
> ... Summing up our conclusions so far with reference to Darwinism in Psychology we may say:
>
> (1) The individual's learning processes are by a method of functional 'trial and error' which illustrates 'natural' in the form of 'functional selection.'
>
> (2) Such acquisitions, taken jointly with his endowment, give him the chance of survival through 'natural,' in the form of 'organic selection.'
>
> (3) By his learning, he brings himself into the traditions of his group, thus coming into possession of his social heritage, which is the means of his individual survival in the processes of 'social and group selection.'
>
> (4) Thus preserved the individual's endowment or physical heredity is, through variation, directed in intelligent and gregarious lines through 'natural' as 'organic selection.'
>
> (5) Individuals become congenitally either more gregarious or more intelligent for the maintenance of the group life, according as the greater utility attaches to one or the other in the continued operation of these modes of selection.[96]

His distinction between pragmatism and his version of instrumentalism deserves quoting at some length:

> The theory of truth becomes either one of extreme 'Pragmatism' or one

merely of 'Instrumentalism.'

Instrumentalism holds that all truth is tentatively arrived at and experimentally verified. The method of knowledge is the now familiar Darwinian procedure of 'trial and error.' The thinker, whether working in the laboratory with things or among the products of his own imaginative thought, *tries out hypotheses*; and only by trying out hypotheses does he establish truth. The knowledge already possessed is used instrumentally in the form of a hypothesis or conjecture, for the discovery of further facts or truths. This reinstates in the sphere of thinking the method of Darwinian selection.

Here Darwinism gives support to the empiricism of Hume and Mill and forwards the sober British philosophical tradition. And no one illustrates better than Darwin, in his own scientific method, the soberness, caution, and soundness of this procedure.

But a more radical point of view is possible. What is now known as Pragmatism proceeds out from this point. It is pertinent to notice it here, for it offers a link of transition to the philosophical views with which we must briefly concern ourselves.

Pragmatism turns instrumentalism into a system of metaphysics. It claims that apart from its tentative instrumental value, its value as guide to life, its value as measured by utility, seen in the consequences of its following out, truth has no further meaning. Not only is all truth selected for its utility, but apart from its utility *it is not truth*. There is no reality then to which truth is still true, whether humanly discovered or not; on the contrary, reality is only the content of the system of beliefs found useful as a guide to life.

I wish to point out that, in such a conclusion, not only is the experimental conception left behind, but the advantages of the Darwinian principle of adjustment to actual situations, physical and social, is lost; and if so interpreted, instrumentalism defeats itself. This clearly appears when we analyze a situation involving trial and error. Trial implies a problematical and alternative result: either the success of the assumption put to trial or its failure. When we ask why this is so, we hit upon the presence of some 'controlling' condition or circumstance in the situation—some stable physical or social fact—whose character renders the hypothesis or suggested solution either adequate or vain, as the case may be. The instrumental idea or thought, then, has its merit in enabling us to find out or locate facts and conditions which are to be allowed for thereafter. These constitute a *control upon knowledge and action*, a system of 'things'.[97]

5. *Kant's Categories of Perception and Thought as Evolutionary Products*

The evolutionary perspective is of course at odds with any view of an *ipso facto* necessarily valid synthetic a priori. But it provides a perspective under which Kant's categories of thought and intuition can be seen as a descriptive contribution to psychological epistemology. Though we reject Kant's claims of a necessary a priori validity for the categories, we can in evolutionary perspective see the categories as highly edited, much tested presumptions, "validated" only as scientific truth is validated, synthetic a posteriori from the point of view of species-history, synthetic and in several way a priori (but not in terms of necessary validity) from the point of view of an individual organism. Popper makes this point in the following quotation:

The problem 'Which comes first, the hypothesis (H) or the observation (O),' is soluble; as in the problem, 'Which comes first, the hen (H) or the egg (O)'. The reply to the latter is, 'An earlier kind of egg'; to the former, 'An earlier kind of hypothesis'. It is quite true that any particular hypothesis we choose will have been preceded by observations—the observations, for example, which it is designed to explain. But these observations, in their turn, presupposed the adoption of a frame of reference: a frame of expectations: a frame of theories. If they were significant, if they created a need for explanation and thus gave rise to the invention of a hypothesis, it was because they could not be explained within the old theoretical framework, the old horizon of expectations. There is no danger here of an infinite regress. Going back to more and more primitive theories and myths we shall in the end find unconscious, *inborn* expectations.

The theory of inborn *ideas* is absurd, I think; but every organism has inborn *reactions* or *responses*; and among them, responses adapted to impending events. These responses we may describe as 'expectations' without implying that these 'expectations' are conscious. The new-born baby 'expects', in this sense, to be fed (and, one could even argue, to be protected and loved). In view of the close relation between expectation and knowledge we may even speak in quite a reasonable sense of 'inborn knowledge'. This 'knowledge' is not, however, *valid a priori*; an inborn expectation, no matter how strong and specific, may be mistaken. (The newborn child may be abandoned, and starve.)

Thus we are born with expectations; with 'knowledge' which, although not *valid a priori*, is *psychologically or genetically a priori*, i.e. prior to all observational experience. One of the most important of these expectations is the expectation of finding a regularity. It is connected with an inborn propensity to look out for regularities, or with a *need* to *find* regularities, as we may see from the pleasure of the child who satisfies this need.

This 'instinctive' expectation of finding regularities, which is psychologically *a priori*, corresponds very closely to the 'law of causality' which Kant believed to be part of our mental outfit and to be *a priori* valid. One might thus be inclined to say that Kant failed to distinguish between psychologically *a priori* ways of thinking or responding and *a priori* valid beliefs. But I do not think that his mistake was quite as crude as that. For the expectation of finding regularities is not only psychologically *a priori*, but also logically *a priori*: it is logically prior to all observational experience, for it is prior to any recognition of similarities, as we have seen; and all observation involves the recognition of similarities (or dissimilarities). But in spite of being logically *a priori* in this sense the expectation is not valid *a priori*. For it may fail: we can easily construct an environment (it would be a lethal one) which, compared with our ordinary environment, is so chaotic that we completely fail to find regularities. . . .

Thus Kant's reply to Hume came near to being right; for the distinction between an *a priori* valid expectation and one which is both genetically and logically prior to observation, but not *a priori* valid, is really somewhat subtle. But Kant proved too much. In trying to show how knowledge is possible, he proposed a theory which had the unavoidable consequence that our quest for knowledge must necessarily succeed, which is clearly mistaken. When Kant said, "Our intellect does not draw its laws from nature but imposes its laws upon nature", he was right. But in thinking that these laws are necessarily true, or that we necessarily succeed in imposing them upon nature, he was wrong. Nature very often resists quite successfully, forcing us to discard our laws as refuted; but if we live we may try again.

Kant believed that Newton's dynamics was *a priori* valid. (See his *Metaphysical Foundations of Natural Science*, published between the first and the second editions of the *Critique of Pure Reason*.) But if, as he thought, we can explain the validity of Newton's theory by the fact that our intellect imposes its laws upon nature, it follows, I think, that our intellect *must succeed* in this; which makes it hard to understand why *a priori* knowledge such as Newton's should be so hard to come by.[98]

This insight is the earliest and most frequently noted aspect of an evolutionary epistemology, perhaps because it can be achieved from a Lamarckian point of view, as well as from the natural selection model which is absolutely essential to the previous points. Herbert Spencer, a Lamarckian for these purposes, achieved this insight, as Höffding conveniently summarizes:

> With regard to the question of the origin of knowledge Spencer makes front on the one hand against Leibniz and Kant, on the other against Locke and Mill. He quarrels with empiricism for two reasons:—firstly, because it does not see that the matter of experience is always taken up and elaborated in a definite manner, which is determined by the original nature of the individual; secondly, because it is lacking in a criterion of truth. We must assume an original organisation if we are to understand the influence exercised by stimuli on different individuals, and the criterion by means of which alone a proposition can be established is the fact that its opposite would contain a contradiction. In the inborn nature of the individual then, and in the logical principle on which we depend every time we make an inference, we have an *a priori* element; something which cannot be deduced from experience. To this extent Spencer upholds Leibniz and Kant against Locke and Mill; but he does so only as long as he is restricting his considerations to the experience of the individual. *What is a priori for the individual is not so for the race.* For those conditions and forms of knowledge and of feeling which are original in the individual, and hence cannot be derived from his experience, have been transmitted by earlier generations. The forms of thought correspond to the collective and inherited modifications of structure which are latent in every new-born individual, and are gradually developed through his experiences. Their first origin, then, is empirical: the fixed and universal relation of things to one another must, in the course of development, form fixed and universal conjunctions in the organism; by perpetual repetition of absolutely external uniformities there arise in the race necessary forms of knowledge, indissoluble thought associations which express the net results of the experience of perhaps several millions of generations down to the present. The individual cannot sunder a conjunction thus deeply rooted in the organisation of the race; hence, he is born into the world with those psychical connections which form the substrata of "necessary truths" (see *Principles of Psychology*, pp. 208, 216; cf. *First Principles*, p. 53. "Absolute uniformities of experience generate absolute uniformities of thought"). Although Spencer is of opinion that the inductive school went too far when they attempted to arrive at everything by way of induction (for, if we adopt this method, induction itself is left hanging in the air), yet, if he had to choose between Locke and Kant, he would avow himself a disciple of the former; for, *in the long run, Spencer too thinks that all knowledge and all forms of thought spring from experience.* His admission that there is

something in our mind which is not the product of our own *a posteriori* experience led Max Müller to call him a "thoroughgoing Kantian," to which Spencer replied: "The Evolution-view is completely experiential. It differs from the original view of the experimentalists by containing a great extension of that view.—*But this view of Kant is avowedly and utterly unexperiential.*"[99]

It is of no small interest to notice that John Stuart Mill, who at first demurred at Spencer's evolutionary psychology, afterwards declared himself convinced that mental development takes place not only in the individual but also in the race by means of inherited dispositions. He expressed this modification of his view a year before his death in a letter to Carpenter, the physiologist (quoted in the latter's *Mental Physiology*).[100]

As Wallraff[101] has documented, the demoting of Kant's categories to the level of descriptive rather than prescriptive epistemology began in 1807 with Jacob Fries's effort to interpret the categories as having only a psychological base, as but descriptive of human reason. While such a position was typically accompanied by a thoroughgoing dualism and was purely mentalistic, by 1866 Frederick A. Lange was able to discuss the a priori as aspects of a "physicopsychological" organization of the mind,[102] and to posit, with Mill, the possibility of "erroneous *a priori* knowledge." He also wrote:

Perhaps some day the basis of the idea of cause may be found in the mechanism of reflex action and sympathetic excitation; we should then have translated Kant's pure reason into physiology, and so made it more easily conceivable.[103]

All that was lacking here was an explicit statement of the kind of validation of such physiological biases which a natural-selection evolution provides. Helmholtz's biological interpretation of the Kantian a priori categories is similar.[104]

Baldwin had the insight in 1902 and earlier:

As Kant claimed, knowledge is a process of categorizing, and to know a thing is to say that it illustrates or stimulates, or functions as, a category. But a category is a mental habit; that is all a category can be allowed to be—a habit broadly defined as a disposition, whether congenital or acquired, to act upon or to treat, items of any sort in certain general ways. These habits or categories arise either from actual accommodations with 'functional' or some other form of utility selection, or by natural endowment secured by selection from variations.[105]

In the tradition of pragmatism, the categories were seen as but pragmatically useful ways of thinking, usually products of culture history rather than biological evolution,[106] although in espousing such a viewpoint, Wright was able to say in passing:

In a certain sense, therefore, the distinctions involved in some, at least, of the categories, *viz.*, space, time, thing, and person, are present in the sense percepts of animals. . . .It is clear that historically and phylogenetically perceptual elements anticipatory of some of the categories existed prior to the genesis of thought.[107]

Wright's position is extended explicitly by Child[108] who posits both "biotic categories," biological functions shared with animals and of biological survival value, and "sociotic categories" which are cultural products. He says in passing "Since Kant, the term 'category' has primarily referred to the presumably pervasive structures of racial mind."[109]

A great many other scholars have considered some kind of an evolutionary interpretation of Kant's categories, usually very briefly and without citing others. In approximately chronological order these include James, Morgan, Mach, Poincaré, Boltzmann, Fouillé, Cassirer, Shelton, Reichenbach, R. W. Sellars, Uexküll, Meyerson, Northrop, Magnus, Lorenz, Piaget, Waddington, Bertalanffy, Whitrow, Platt, Pepper, Merleau-Ponty, Simpson, W. S. Sellars, Hawkins, Barr, Toulmin, Wartofsky, and Watanabe. Quine, Maxwell, Shimony, Yilmaz, and Stemmer have made much the same point without explicit reference to the Kantian catagories.[110] Of these, many are essentially biologists generalizing into philosophy. This brief quote from Waddington epitomizes their message:

> The faculties by which we arrive at a world view have been selected so as to be, at least, efficient in dealing with other existents. They may, in Kantian terms, not give us direct contact with the thing-in-itself, but they have been moulded by things-in-themselves so as to be competent in coping with them."[111]

Most of the passages cited are very brief, noting the insight only in passing. In marked contrast is the rich exposition provided by Lorenz.

In his essay, "Kant's Doctrine of the *A Priori* in the Light of Contemporary Biology," Lorenz[112] accepts Kant's insight as to some degree of fit between innate categories of thought and the *Ding an sich*. He accepts Kant's claim that without such prior-fitting categories, no one could achieve in his own lifetime the empirical, experiential, knowledge of the world which he does achieve. He accepts in some sense Kant's skepticism as to the form of knowledge. While to Lorenz more than Kant the *Ding an sich* is knowable, it certainly is only known in the knower's categories, not in those of the *Ding an sich* itself. Thus he accepts Kant as psychologist if not as epistemologist. As with all of those we have cited above, from Spencer on, any validity or appropriateness of the categories to the *Ding an sich* is due to their status as a product of an evolution in which the *Ding an sich* has acted in the editorial role of discarding misleading categories.

Lorenz, like Popper[113] recognizes that it was to Kant's great disadvantage to believe Newton's physics perfectly true. When Kant then recognized the a priori human intuitions of space, time, and causality as fitting Newton's physics (which they do to a lesser degree than Kant thought), he had a greater puzzle on his hands than a modern epistemologist has. From our viewpoint, both Newton's laws of dynamics and the intuitive categories of space perception can be seen as but approximations to a later more complete physics (or to the *Ding an sich*).

The realization that all laws of "pure reason" are based on highly physical or mechanical structures of the human central nervous system which have developed through many eons like any other organ, on the one hand shakes our confidence in the laws of pure reason and on the other hand substantially raises our confidence in them. Kant's statement that the laws of pure reason have absolute validity, nay that every imaginable rational being, even if it were an angel, must obey the same laws of thought, appears as an anthropocentric presumption. Surely the "keyboard" provided by the forms of intuition and categories—Kant himself calls it that—is something definitely located on the physicostructural side of the psychophysical unity of the human organism. . . . But surely these clumsy categorical boxes into which we have to pack our external world "in order to be able to spell them as experiences" (Kant) can claim no autonomous and absolute validity whatsoever. This is certain for us the moment we conceive them as evolutionary adaptations. . . .At the same time, however, the nature of their adaptation shows that the categorical forms of intuition and categories have proved themselves as working hypotheses in the coping of our species with the absolute reality of the environment (in spite of their validity being only approximate and relative). Thus is clarified the paradoxical fact that the laws of "pure reason" which break down at every step in modern theoretical science, nonetheless have stood (and still stand) the test in the practical biological matters of the struggle for the preservation of the species.

The 'dots' produced by the coarse 'screens' used in the reproductions of photographs in our daily papers are satisfactory representations when looked at superficially, but cannot stand closer inspection with a magnifying glass. So, too, the reproductions of the world by our forms of intuition and categories break down as soon as they are required to give a somewhat closer representation of their objects, as in the case in wave mechanics and nuclear physics. All the knowledge an individual can wrest from the empirical reality of the 'physical world-picture' is essentially only a working hypothesis. And, as far as their species-preserving function goes, all those innate structures of the mind which we call 'a priori' are likewise only working hypotheses. Nothing is absolute except that which hides in and behind the phenomena. Nothing that our brain can think has absolute, *a priori* validity in the true sense of the word, not even mathematics with all its laws.[114]

Lorenz portrays for the concepts of space and causality their analogues in water shrew, greylag goose, and man, arguing for each an "objectivity," yet limitedness and imperfection. For a weak microscope, we assume that the homogeneous texture provided at its limit of resolution is a function of those limits, not an attribute of reality. We do this because through more powerful scopes this homogeneity becomes differentiated. By analogy, we extend this assumption even to the most powerful scope. Seeing our human categories of thought and intuition as but the best in such an evolutionary series, even though we might have no better scope to compare it with, generates a parallel skepticism. Actually we do have a better scope, modern physics, which today, at least, if not in Kant's time, provides a much finer grained view of reality. There is a two-sided message in this literature: there is an "objective" reflection of the *Ding an sich* which, however, does not achieve expression in the *Ding an sich's* own terms. Lorenz, and many of the others, have argued that the mind has been shaped by evolution to fit those aspects of the world with which it deals, just as have other body parts:

> This central nervous apparatus does not prescribe the laws of nature any more than the hoof of the horse prescribes the form of the ground. Just as the hoof of the horse, this central nervous apparatus stumbles over unforeseen changes in its task. But just as the hoof of the horse is adapted to the ground of the steppe which it copes with, so our central nervous apparatus for organizing the image of the world is adapted to the real world with which man has to cope. Just like any organ, this apparatus has attained its expedient species-preserving form through this coping of real with the real during a species history many eons long.[115]

The shape of a horse's hoof certainly expresses "knowledge" of the steppe in a very odd and partial language, and in an end product mixed with "knowledge" of other contingencies. Our visual, tactual, and several modes of scientific knowledge of the steppe are each expressed in quite different languages, but are comparably objective. The hydrodynamics of sea water, plus the ecological value of locomotion, have independently shaped fish, whale, and walrus in a quite similar fashion. Their shapes represent independent discoveries of this same "knowledge," expressed in this case in similar "languages." But the jet-propelled squid reflects the same hydrodynamic principles in a quite different, but perhaps equally "accurate" and "objective" shape. The *Ding an sich* is always known indirectly, always in the language of the knower's posits, be these mutations governing bodily form, or visual percepts, or scientific theories. In this sense it is unknowable. But there is an objectivity in the reflection, however indirect, an objectivity in the selection from innumerable less adequate posits.

6. Pragmatism, Utilitarianism, and Objectivity

For both Popper and the present writer the *goal of objectivity* in science is a noble one, and dearly to be cherished. It is in true worship of this goal that we remind ourselves that our current views of reality are partial and imperfect. We recoil at a view of science which recommends we give up the search for ultimate truth and settle for practical computational recipes making no pretense at truly describing a real world. Thus our sentiment is to reject pragmatism, utilitarian nominalism, utilitarian subjectivism, utilitarian conventionalsim, or instrumentalism,[116] in favor of a critical hypothetical realism. Yet our evolutionary epistemology, with its basis in natural selection for survival relevance, may seem to commit us to pragmatism or utilitarianism. Simmel in 1895[117] presents the problem forcibly, as also do Mach and Poincaré.

This profound difference in sentiment deserves much more attention than can be given here, but brief comments from a variety of perspectives may be in order. These are based on the assumption that neither Popper nor the present writer intend to relinquish the goal of objectivity, and must therefore reconcile it with the natural selection epistemology to which that very quest for objective truth has led us.

Where the emphasis on utilitarian selectivity is to counter the epistemic arrogance of a naive or phenomenal realism, we can join it unambivalently. The critical realist has no wish to identify the real with the phenomenally given. Thus the visual and tactual solidity of ordinary objects represents a phenomenal emphasis on the one physical discontinuity most usable by man and his ancestors, to the neglect of other discontinuities identifiable by the probes of modern experimental physics. Perceived solidity is not illusory for its ordinary uses: what it diagnoses is one of the "surfaces" modern physics also describes. But when reified as exclusive, when creating expectations of opaqueness and impermeability to all types of probes, it becomes illusory. The different *Umwelten* of different animals do represent in part the differential utilities of their specific ecological niches, as well as differential limitations. But each of the separate contours diagnosed in these *Umwelten* are also diagnosable by a complete physics, which in addition provides many differentia unused and unperceived by any organism.[118]

Nor do we claim any firmer grounding of the scientific theory and fact of today than do the pragmatists and utilitarians. Indeed, Popper's emphasis on criticism may produce an even greater skepticism as to the realism of present-day science. There is, however, a difference in what it is that is being grounded. Consider a graph of observational points relating the volume of water to its temperature. An extreme punctiform pragmatism or definitional operationism would regard the observations themselves as the scientific truth. A more presumptive pragmatism would fit a least squares curve with minimum parameters to the data, and regard the values of the points on the fitted curve as the scientific facts, thus deviating from some of the original observations. Even at this stage, degrees of pragmatism occur. The departure may be justified purely on the grounds of computational efficiency, or the discrepant observations may be regarded as "errorful," with the anticipation that, were the experiment repeated, the new observations would on the average fall nearer to the "theoretical" values than to the original observations. Most scientific practice is still less pragmatic, more realistic than this: Of all mathematical formulae that fit the data equally well with the same number of parameters, scientists choose that one or those whose parameters can be used in other formulae subsuming other observations. While the search for such parameters may most often be done as a search for physically interpretable parameters, it can also be justified on purely utilitarian grounds. In extending this series, were Popper's position to be classified as a pragmatism at all it would have to be as pragmatic selection from among formal theories claiming to be universally descriptive of the real world, but not identified as the real world. Even this degree of pragmatism needs to be qualified.

The extremes of pragmatism, definitional operationism, and phenomenalism would equate theory and data in a true epistemological monism. But as elaborated in actual philosophies of science, the dualism of data and theory just described is accepted. Adequately to handle the issues raised in discussions of epistemological monism and dualism[119] we need to expand the framework to an epistemological trinism (trialism, triadism, trimondism) of data, theory, and real world (approximately corresponding to Popper's "second world," "third world," and "first world").[120] The controversial issue is the conceptual inclusion of the real world, defining the problem of knowledge as the fit of data and theory to that real world.

Such a critical realism involves presumptions going beyond the data, needless to say. But since Hume we should have known that nonpresumptive knowledge is impossible. As Petrie[121] has pointed out, most modern epistemologies recognize that scientific beliefs are radically underjustified. The question is thus a matter of which presumptions, not whether or not presumptions. Biological theories of evolution, whether Lamarckian or Darwinian, are profoundly committed to an organism-environment dualism, which when extended into the evolution of sense organ, perceptual and learning functions, becomes a dualism of an organism's knowledge of the environment versus the environment itself. An evolutionary epistemologist is at this level doing "epistemology of the other one,"[122] studying the relationship of an animal's cognitive capacities and the environment they are designed to cognize, both of which the epistemologist knows only in the hypothetical-contingent manner of science. Thus he may study the relationship between the shape of a rat's running pattern ("cognitive map") and the shape of the maze it runs in. Or he may study the polarization of sunlight (using scientific instruments since his own eyes are insensitive to such nuances) and the bee's sensitivity to plane of polarization. At this level he has no hesitancy to include a "real world" concept, even though he may recognize that his own knowledge of that world even with instrumental augmentation is partial and limited in ways analogous to the limitations of the animal whose epistemology he studies. Having thus made the real-world assumption in this part of his evolutionary epistemology, he is not adding an unneeded assumption when he assumes the same predicament for man and science as knowers.

It is true, of course, that in an epistemology of other animals he has independent data on the "knowledge" and "the world to be known," and thus studying the degree of fit involves no tautology. It is true that in extending this "epistemology of the other one" to knowledge of modern physics, no separate information on the world-to-be-known is available with which to compare current physical theory. But this practical limitation does not necessitate abandoning an ontology one is already employing. (This argument is of course only compelling vis-à-vis those of such as Simmel, Mach, and Poincaré, who base their utilitarian nominalism and conventionalism on an evolutionary perspective.)

We can also examine utilitarian specificity versus realism in the evolution of knowing. Consider the spatial knowledge of some primitive locomotor animal, perhaps Konrad Lorenz's [123] water shrew. It may have a thirst space it uses when thirsty, a separate hunger space, a separate space for escape from each predator, a mate-finding space, etc. In its utilitarianism, there is a separate space for every utility. In a higher stage of evolution, the hypothesis has emerged that all these spaces are the same, or overlap. The realistic hypothesis of an all-purpose space has developed. There is abundant evidence that white rat, cat, dog and chimpanzee are at or beyond this stage: that spatial learning achieved in the service of one motive is immediately available for other motives. Along with this goes spatial curiosity, the exploring of novel spaces and objects when all utilitarian motives (thirst, food, sex, safety, etc.) are sated and the exploration has no momentary usefulness. Such disinterested curiosity for "objective," all-possible-purpose spatial knowledge-for-its-own-sake has obvious survival value, even though it may transcend the sum of all specific utilities. Scientific curiosity of course goes beyond the specifically utilitarian to a much greater extent. Survival relevant criteria are rare among the criteria actually used in deciding questions of scientific truth. The science Mach was attempting to epitomize had made most of its crucial selections from among competing theories on the basis of evidence (such as on the phases of the moons of Jupiter) of no contemporary or past utility. And in the history of science, those who took their theories as real, rather than their contemporary conventionalists, have repeatedly emerged in the main stream for future developments.

These several disparate comments scarcely begin the task of relating the critical-realist, natural-selection epistemology to the recurrent issues in the history of the theory of knowledge. Potentially it can provide a dialectic resolution to many old controversies. But spelling out the points of articulation with the main body of epistemological concerns remains for the most part yet to be done.

Summary

This essay has identified Popper as the modern founder and leading advocate of a natural-selection epistemology. The characteristic focus is on the growth of knowledge. The problem of knowledge is so defined that the knowing of other animals than man is included. The variation and selective retention process of evolutionary adaptation is generalized to cover a nested hierarchy of vicarious knowledge processes, including vision, thought, imitation, linguistic instruction, and science.

Historical attention is paid not only to those employing the natural-selection paradigm, but also to the Spencerian-Lamarckian school of evolutionary epistemologists, and to the ubiquitous evolutionary interpretation of the Kantian categories. It is argued that, whereas the evolutionary perspective has often led to a pragmatic, utilitarian conventionalism, it is fully compatible with an advocacy of the goals of realism and objectivity in science.

DONALD T. CAMPBELL

DEPARTMENT OF PSYCHOLOGY
NORTHWESTERN UNIVERSITY
OCTOBER, 1970

NOTES

[1] K. R. Popper, *The Logic of Scientific Discovery* (London: Hutchinson; New York: Basic Books, 1959), p. 42. Hereinafter cited as *L.Sc.D.* Reprinted by permission of the author and publishers.

[2] *L.Sc.D.*, p. 108.

[3] K. R. Popper, *Conjectures and Refutations* (London: Routledge & Kegan Paul; New York: Basic Books, 1963). Hereinafter cited as *C.&R.*

[4] *C.&R.*, p. 46. Reprinted by permission of the author and publishers.

[5] *C.&R.*, p. 51.

[6] *C.&R.*, p. 52. (See also *C.&R.*, pp. 216, 312-13, 383, and *ad passim*.)

[7] For example, *C.&R.*, p. 44.

[8] W. K. Estes, "All-or-None Processes in Learning and Retention," *American Psychologist,* **19** (1964), 16-25; F. Restle, "The Selection of Strategies in Cue Learning," *Psychological Review,* **69** (1962), 329-43; R. C. Atkinson and E. J. Crothers, "A Comparison of Paired-Associate Learning Models Having Different Acquisition and Retention Axioms," *Journal of Mathematical Psychology,* **1** (1964), 285-312.

[9] *L.Sc.D.*, pp. 17-19.

[10] *L.Sc.D.*, p. 22.

[11] Russell has made a similar point in identifying himself with an evolutionary epistemology: "There is another thing which it is important to remember whenever mental concepts are being discussed, and that is our evolutionary continuity with the lower animals. Knowledge, in particular, must not be defined in a manner which assumes an impassable gulf between ourselves and our ancestors who had not the advantage of language," Bertrand Russell, *Human Knowledge: Its Scope and Limits* (New York: Simon and Schuster, 1948), p. 421.

[12] *C.&R.*, p. 216.

[13] *L.Sc.D.*, pp. 278-79.

[14] K. R. Popper, *Of Clouds and Clocks: An Approach to the Problem of Rationality and the Freedom of Man* (St. Louis, Missouri: Washington University, 1966), p. 23. This is the Arthur Holly Compton Memorial Lecture, presented at Washington University on April 21, 1965, and printed as a 38-page booklet; reprinted in K. R. Popper, *Objective Knowledge: An Evolutionary Approach* (Oxford: Clarendon Press; New York: Oxford University Press, 1972). This excerpt reprinted by permission of the author and publishers.

[15] *OCC*, p. 23.

[16] *OCC*, p. 25.

[17] The most complete recent review of this voluminous literature is William Church Wimsatt, "Modern Science and the New Teleology" (unpublished Ph.D. diss., University of Pittsburgh, 1971); and W. C. Wimsatt, "Teleology and the Logical Structure of Function Statements," *Studies in History and Philosophy of Science*, **3**, No. 1 (April, 1972). He recognizes the proper understanding of this problem as inextricably involved with an evolutionary epistemology.

[18] S. Spiegelman, "Differentiation as the Controlled Production of Unique Enzymatic Patterns," *Symposia of the Society for Experimental Biology, II:Growth in Relation to Differentiation and Morphogenesis* (New York: Academic Press, 1948).

[19] H. J. Barr, "Regeneration and Natural Selection," *American Naturalist,* **98** (1964), 183-86.

[20] D. T. Campbell, "Methodological Suggestions from a Comparative Psychology of Knowledge Processes," *Inquiry,* **2** (1959), 152-82: and D. T. Campbell, "Blind Variation and Selective Retention in Creative Thought as in Other Knowledge Processes," *Psychological Review,* **67** (1960), 380-400.

[21] The use of the phrase "inductive achievements" is for convenience in communicating and does not in the least imply advocacy of the Bacon-Hume-Mill explanation of those achievements nor disagreement with Popper's brilliant criticisms of induction.

[22] W. R. Ashby, *Design for a Brain* (New York: John Wiley & Sons, 1952).

[23] The above five paragraphs have been quoted with some rearrangement and transitional modifications from pp. 380 and 381 of Campbell, "Blind Variation" (note 20).

[24] H. S. Jennings, *The Behavior of the Lower Organisms* (New York: Columbia University Press, 1906).

[25] *Design for a Brain* (note 22).

[26] *Ibid.*, p. vi (note 22).

[27] R. J. Pumphrey, "Hearing," *In Symposia of the Society for Experimental Biology, IV: Physiological Mechanism in Animal Behavior* (New York: Academic Press, 1950) pp. 1-18; W. N. Kellogg, "Echo-Ranging in the Porpoise," *Science,* **128** (1958), 982-88; and D. R. Griffin, *Listening in the Dark* (New Haven: Yale University Press, 1958).

[28] D. T. Campbell, "Perception as Substitute Trial and Error," *Psychological Review,* **63** (1956), 331-42.

[29] *Ibid.*, pp. 334-335. Note also the example of left-hand search substituting for right-hand exploration in a blind sorting task.

[30] Beginnings on this problem of pattern matching are to be found in Bertrand Russell's discussion of the "structural postulate," pp. 460-72, and 492, of *Human Knowledge: Its Scope and Limits* (New York: Simon & Schuster, 1948); in Konrad Lorenz, "Gestaltwarnehmung als

Quelle wissenschaftliche Erkenntnis," *Zeitschrift für experimentelle und angewandte Psychologie*, **6** (1959), 118-65, translated as "Gestalt Perception as Fundamental to Scientific Knowledge," *General Systems*, **7** (1962), 37-56; and in D. T. Campbell, "Pattern Matching as Essential in Distal Knowing," in *The Psychology of Egon Brunswik*, ed. by K. R. Hammond (New York: Holt, Rinehart & Winston, 1966), pp. 81-106.

[31] The formal analogy between natural selection and trial-and-error learning has been noted by many, including James M. Baldwin, *Mental Development in the Child and Race* (New York: Macmillan, 1900); Samuel Jackson Holmes, *Studies in Animal Behavior* (Boston: Gorham Press, 1916); Ashby, *Design for a Brain;* and J. W. S. Pringle, "On the Parallel Between Learning and Evolution," *Behaviour*, **3** (1951), 175-215.

[32] D. T. Campbell, "Adaptive Behavior from Random Response," *Behavioral Science*, **1** (1956), 105-10.

[33] James M. Baldwin perhaps first proposed the idea. He reprints relevant papers by C. Lloyd Morgan, H. F. Osborn, E. B. Poulton, and himself in *Development and Evolution* (New York: Macmillan, 1902), using the terms "orthoplasy" and "organic selection" to cover the concept.

[33a] In *Objective Knowledge*, pp. 256-80 (note 14).

[34] Wolfgang Köhler, *The Mentality of Apes* (New York: Harcourt, Brace, 1925).

[35] Ernst Mach, "On the Part Played by Accident in Invention and Discovery," *Monist*, **6** (1896), 161-75.

[36] *Ibid.*, p. 171.

[37] *Ibid.*, p. 174.

[38] Henri Poincaré, "Mathematical Creation," in H. Poincaré, *The Foundations of Science* (New York: Science Press, 1913), p. 387.

[39] *Ibid.*, p. 392.

[40] *Ibid.*, p. 393.

[41] *Ibid.*, p. 394.

[42] 1855 is the date of the first edition of Alexander Bain, *The Senses and the Intellect.* The quotations are from the 3d ed. (New York: Appleton, 1874), pp. 593-95.

[43] Stanley Jevons, *The Principles of Science* (London: Macmillan, 1892). (1st ed., 1874; 2d ed., 1877; reprinted with corrections, 1892.)

[44] *Ibid.*, p. 228.

[45] *Ibid.*, p. 577.

[46] Paul Souriau, *Theorie de l'Invention* (Paris: Hachette, 1881), p. 17.

[47] *Ibid.*, p. 43.

[48] *Ibid.*, pp. 114-15.

[49] William James, "Great Men, Great Thoughts, and the Environment," *The Atlantic Monthly*, **46**, No. 276 (October, 1880), 441-59. See also William James, *Principles of Psychology* (New York: Henry Holt, 1890), Vol. II, pp. 617-79.

[50] *Ibid.*, p. 456.

[51] *Ibid.*, p. 457.

[52] "Mathematical Creation" (note 38).

[53] "Part Played by Accident" (note 35).

[54] "Blind Variation" (note 20).

[55] See Appendix I.

[56] See Appendix I.

[57] Herbert A. Simon, *The Sciences of the Artificial* (Cambridge, Mass.: The MIT Press, 1969), p. 95.

[58] A. Newell, J. C. Shaw & H. A. Simon, "Elements of a Theory of Human Problem Solving," *Psychological Review,* **65** (1958), 151-66.

[59] "Blind Variation," pp. 392-95 (note 20).

[60] Newell, Shaw & Simon, "Human Problem Solving" (note 58).

[61] D. O. Hebb, "On the Nature of Fear," *Psychological Review,* **53** (1946), 259-76.

[62] Solomon E. Asch in *Social Psychology* (New York: Prentice-Hall, 1952) has argued the rationality of such imitative or conformant behavior, and the social nature of man's cognition of the world. See also D. T. Campbell, "Conformity in Psychology's Theories of Acquired Behavioral Dispositions," in *Conformity and Deviation,* ed. by I. A. Berg and B. M. Bass (New York: Harper & Row, 1961), pp. 101-42; D. T. Campbell, "Social Attitudes and Other Acquired Behavioral Dispositions," in *Psychology: A Study of a Science,* Vol. 6: *Investigations of Man as Socius,* ed. by S. Koch (New York: McGraw-Hill, 1963), pp. 94-172, and A. Bandura, *Principles of Behavior Modification* (New York: Holt, Rinehart & Winston, 1969).

[63] James M. Baldwin, *Thought and Things, or Genetic Logic* (New York: Macmillan, 1906), Vol. I, p. 169. Popper has also emphasized this, in Sec. 3-V, galleys 5-7 of his unpublished *Postscript.*

[64] R. A. Hinde, ed., *Bird Vocalizations* (Cambridge, England and New York: Cambridge University Press, 1969). See especially the chapters by Lorenz and Immelman.

[65] Karl von Frisch, *Bees, Their Vision, Chemical Sense, and Language* (Ithaca:Cornell University Press, 1950); T. A. Sebeok, ed., *Animal Communication: Techniques of Study and Results of Research* (Bloomington, Ind.: Indiana University Press, 1968); and T. A. Sebeok & A. Ramsay, eds., *Approaches to Animal Communication* (The Hague, Netherlands: Mouton & Company, 1969). Note especially the elegant new confirmation of von Frisch by J. L. Gould, M. Henerey, and M. C. MacLeod, "Communication of Direction by the Honey Bee," *Science,* **169** (1970), 544-54.

[66] The above two paragraphs are condensed from D. T. Campbell, "Ostensive Instances and Entitativity in Language Learning," in *Unity through Diversity,* ed. by N. D. Rizzo (New York: Gordon and Breach, forthcoming in 1973). See also E. R. MacCormac, "Ostensive Instances in Language Learning," *Foundations of Language,* **7** (1971), 199-210. Quine has presented a quite similar view, except for his employment of a passive conditioning learning theory in place of a trial and error of meanings, although his trial and error of "slicings" or abstractions is probably equivalent. See W. V. Quine, *Word and Object* (Cambridge, Mass.: MIT Press, 1960), and especially pp. 26-39 of W. V. Quine, *Ontological Relativity* (New York: Columbia University Press, 1969). Austin's faith that distinctions preserved in ordinary language have as referents distinctions in the world referred to, is justified by a similar model of language evolution.

[67] For a review of this literature, see Margaret Mead, *Continuities in Cultural Evolution* (New Haven: Yale University Press, 1964); and D. T. Campbell, "Variation and Selective Retention in Sociocultural Evolution," in *Social Change in Developing Areas: A Reinterpretation of Evolutionary Theory,* ed. by H. R. Barringer, G. I. Blanksten, and R. W. Mack (Cambridge, Mass.: Schenkman, 1965), pp. 19-49. Perhaps the first to consider social evolution in explicitly natural selection terms was William James, "Great Men, Great Thoughts" (note 49). Louis Rougier has explicitly posited a competition of and a natural selection from among culturally diverse modes of thought in explaining the development of logical and scientific thinking, in *Traité de la Connaissance* (Paris: Gauthier-Villars, 1955), pp. 426-28. See also Pierre Auger (Appendix II).

[68] Joseph Agassi, "Comment: Theoretical Entities Versus Theories," in *Boston Studies in the Philosophy of Science,* ed. by R. S. Cohen and M. W. Wartofsky (Dordrecht, Holland: D. Reidel, 1969), Vol. V.

[69] See Appendix II.

[70] See Appendix III.

[71] W. B. Cannon, *The Way of An Investigator* (New York: W. W. Norton & Co., 1945); R. K. Merton, *Social Theory and Social Structure* (Glencoe: Free Press, 1949).

[72] K. R. Popper, *Postscript*, unpublished, galleys 5-7, Secs. 3-V and 3-IX.

[73] S. E.Toulmin,"The Evolutionary Development of Natural Science," *American Scientist*, **55** (1967), 456-71. See also S. E. Toulmin, *Foresight and Understanding: An Inquiry Into the Aims of Science* (Bloomington, Indiana: Indiana University Press, 1961); S. E. Toulmin, "Neuroscience and Human Understanding," in *The Neurosciences*, ed. by Frank Schmitt (New York: Rockefeller University Press, 1968); S. E. Toulmin, *Human Understanding*, Vol. I: *The Evolution of Collective Understanding* (Princeton, N. J.: Princeton University Press, 1972).

[74] *Foresight and Understanding* (note 73); T. S. Kuhn, *The Structure of Scientific Revolutions* (Chicago: University of Chicago Press, 1962).

[75] Robert Ackermann, *The Philosophy of Science* (New York: Pegasus, 1970).

[76] Milič Čapek, "The Development of Reichenbach's Epistemology," *Review of Metaphysics*, **11** (1957), 42-67; Milič Čapek, "La Théorie Biologique de la Connaissance chez Bergson et sa Signification Actuelle," *Revue de Metaphysique et de Morale* (April-June, 1959), 194-211; and Milič Čapek, "Ernst Mach's Biological Theory of Knowledge," *Synthese*, **18** (1968), 171-91, reprinted in *Boston Studies in the Philosophy of Science*, ed. by R. S. Cohen and M. W. Wartofsky (Dordrecht, Holland: D. Reidel, 1969), Vol. V, pp. 400-21.

[77] Bergson also rejected the Darwinian blind mutation and natural selection model of cognitive evolution. However, his emphasis on the utility-perspectival, partial, oversimplified, nature of human cognition, and its inappropriateness when extended into the subatomic and galactic areas is in agreement with the natural selection epistemology advocated here ("La Théorie Biologique"). That Mach and Poincaré were explicitly natural-selectionist rather than Lamarckian both in their perspective on cognitive evolution and in their treatment of creative thought indicates the need for further analysis. Čapek's attribution to Mach of Spencer's belief in the completeness and perfection of the evolutionary process is contradicted by this quotation from Mach's contemporary, Boltzmann, "Mach himself has shown in a most ingenious way that no theory is either absolutely true or absolutely false, and that, moreover, every theory is constantly being improved just as are organisms as described by Darwin." *Populäre Schriften*, p. 339 (Appendix II).

[78] *Principles of Psychology*, p. 617 (note 49).

[79] Georg Simmel, "Über eine Beziehung der Selectionslehre zur Erkenntnis-theorie," *Archiv für systematische Philosophie*, **1**, No. 1 (1895), 34-45. The present writer has had the benefit of access to two unpublished papers, the first is Herman Tennessen, "Brief Summary of Georg Simmel's Evolutionary Epistemology," June, 1968, being an abstract of Herman Tennessen "Georg Simmel's tillemping av selecksjonslaeren pa erkjennelsesteorier," in *Filosofiske Problemer* (Oslo: Norwegian University Press, 1955), pp. 23-30. The second is a preliminary translation of Simmel's paper by Irene L. Jerison. Simmel does not, in fact, cite Spencer, nor any other on this point.

[80] *Principles of Psychology* and "Great Men, Great Thoughts" (note 49).

[81] John Dewey, *The Influence of Darwin on Philosophy* (New York: Henry Holt & Co., 1910; Bloomington: Indiana University Press, 1965), pp. 11-12.

[82] *Collected Papers of Charles Sanders Peirce*, ed. by Charles Hartshorne and Paul Weiss (Cambridge, Mass.: Harvard University Press, 1931-58), 5.407. (All references to Peirce in this paper follow the standard practice of designating volume and paragraph in the *Collected Papers*.) Also quoted in Manley Thompson, *The Pragmatic Philosophy of C. S. Peirce* (Chicago: University of Chicago Press, 1953), p. 83, and in Philip P.Wiener, *Evolution and the Founders of Pragmatism* (Cambridge, Mass.: Harvard University Press, 1949), p. 93.

[83] *Collected Papers*, 2.780.

[84] *Design for a Brain* (note 26).

[85] *Collected Papers*, 6.33. See also 5.436, 6.200, 6.262, 6.606, 6.611.

[86] *Founders of Pragmatism*, Chap. 4, pp. 70-96 (note 82).

[87] *Ibid.*, p. 77.

[88] *Ibid.*, pp. 87-88.

[89] *Collected Papers*, 6.157, original date 1892.

[90] Wiener, *Founders of Pragmatism*, pp. 94-95 (note 82); Peirce, *Collected Papers*, 1.348.

[91] James M. Baldwin, *Thought and Things, A Study of the Development and Meaning of Thought, or Genetic Logic*, Volume I: *Functional Logic or Genetic Theory of Knowledge;* Volume II: *Experimental Logic or Genetic Theory of Thought;* Volume III: *Genetic Epistemology* (London: Swan Sonnenschein [in Muirhead's Library of Philosophy]; New York: Macmillan, 1906, 1908, 1911). If these volumes left any impact at all, it was in the French tradition out of which Jean Piaget's recent work on genetic epistemology emerges.

[92] James M. Baldwin, *Darwin and the Humanities* (Baltimore: Review Publishing Co., 1909; London: Allen & Unwin, 1910).

[93] *Influence of Darwin* (note 81).

[94] *Darwin and Humanities*, p. viii (note 92). Reprinted by permission of the American Psychological Association.

[95] *Ibid.*, p. ix.

[96] *Ibid.*, pp. 32-33.

[97] *Ibid.*, pp. 68-73.

[98] *C.&R.*, pp. 47-48.

[99] Harold Höffding, *A History of Modern Philosophy* (London: Macmillan, 1900; New York: Dover, 1955), Vol. II, pp. 475-76.

[100] *Ibid.*, pp. 457-58.

[101] Charles F. Wallraff, *Philosophical Theory and Psychological Fact* (Tucson: University of Arizona Press, 1961), pp. 10-11.

[102] *Ibid.*, p. 11; Frederick Albert Lange, *The History of Materialism* (New York: Humanities Press, 1950), Vol. 2, p. 193. (Reprinting of a translation first published in 1890.)

[103] *History of Materialism*, p. 211 (note 102).

[104] Čapek, "Mach's Theory of Knowledge" (note 76).

[105] The quotation is from James M. Baldwin, *Development and Evolution* (New York: Macmillan, 1902), p. 309. See also his *Mental Development* (Macmillan, 1900), and *Darwin and the Humanities* (note 97).

[106] E.g., William James, *Pragmatism* (New York: Longmans-Green, 1907), pp. 170, 182, 193. This is also Rougier's position, *Traité de la Connaissance* (note 67). Marx Wartofsky also emphasizes primarily the social evolution of the Kantian a priori, in "Metaphysics as Heuristic for Science," in *Boston Studies in the Philosophy of Science*, ed. by R. S. Cohen and M. W. Wartofsky (Dordrecht, Holland: D. Reidel, 1968), Vol. III, pp. 164-70.

[107] William K. Wright, "The Genesis of the Categories," *The Journal of Philosophy, Psychology and Scientific Methods*, **10** (1913), 645-57, esp. 646.

[108] Arthur Child, "On the Theory of the Categories," *Philosophy and Phenomenological Research*, **7** (1946), 316-35.

[109] Child, "Theory of Categories," p. 320.

[110] See Appendix IV.

[111] "Evolution and Epistemology" (Appendix IV).

[112] "Kants Lehre vom apriorischen" (Appendix IV).

[113] *C.&R.*, p. 48, quoted above note 98. See also Hans Reichenbach, as reported by Čapek, "Reichenbach's Epistemology" (note 76).

[114] Lorenz, "Kants Lehre vom apriorischen," pp. 103-4, translation pp. 26-27 (Appendix IV). Reprinted by permission of the author.

[115] *Ibid.*, pp. 98-99, translation p. 25 (Appendix IV).

[116] Note that James M. Baldwin as quoted above, *Darwin and the Humanities*, pp. 68-73 (note 97), uses the term instrumentalism in a unique way, in making the very point against pragmatism being made here.

[117] "Beziehung der Selectionslehre" (note 79).

[118] von Bertalanffy, "Relativity of Categories" (Appendix IV).

[119] A. O. Lovejoy, *The Revolt Against Dualism* (La Salle, Ill.: Open Court, 1930); W. Köhler, *The Place of Value in a World of Facts* (New York: Liveright, 1938).

[120] K. R. Popper, "Epistemology without a Knowing Subject," in *Logic, Methodology, and Philosophy of Sciences*, ed. by B. van Rootselaar and J. E. Staal (Amsterdam: North-Holland, 1968), Vol. III, pp. 333-73; K. R. Popper, "On the Theory of the Objective Mind," *Akten des XIV internationalen Kongresses für Philosophie*, 1 (Vienna, 1968), 25-53. Both are reprinted in *Objective Knowledge* (note 14), pp. 106-52 and 153-90.

[121] H. G. Petrie, "The Logical Effects of Theory on Observational Categories and Methodology," duplicated (Northwestern University, June 20, 1969).

[122] D. T. Campbell, "Methodological Suggestions from a Comparative Psychology of Knowledge Processes," *Inquiry*, 2 (1959), 157; D. T. Campbell, "A Phenomenology of the Other One: Corrigible, Hypothetical, and Critical," in *Human Action*, ed. by T. Mischel (New York: Academic Press, 1969), pp. 41-69.

[123] "Kants Lehre vom apriorischen" (Appendix IV).

APPENDIX I: TRIAL-ERROR AND NATURAL-SELECTION MODELS FOR CREATIVE THOUGHT

Alexander Bain, *The Senses and the Intellect*, 3d ed. (New York: Appleton, 1874), pp. 593-95. (1st ed., 1855.)

Stanley Jevons, *The Principles of Science* (London: Macmillan Co., 1892). (1st ed., 1874.)

William James, "Great Men, Great Thoughts, and the Environment," *The Atlantic Monthly*, **46**, No. 276 (October, 1880), 441-59.

Paul Souriau, *Theorie de l'Invention* (Paris: Hachette, 1881).

Ernst Mach, "On the Part Played by Accident in Invention and Discovery," *Monist*, **6** (1896), 161-75.

James M. Baldwin, *Mental Development in the Child and the Race* (New York: Macmillan, 1900).

A. Fouillé, *L'Evolutionisme des Idées-Forces* (Paris: Alcan, 1906), pp. 276-77. (Note that his emphasis on *conscience* as providing a goal-directed "artificial selection," in contrast with the aimless natural selection, deserves separate treatment.)

Henri Poincaré, "Mathematical Creation," in H. Poincaré, *The Foundations of Science* (New York: Science Press, 1913), pp. 383-94. (First published in 1908.)

W. B. Pillsbury, *The Psychology of Reasoning* (New York: Appleton-Century-Crofts, 1910).

E. Rignano, *The Psychology of Reasoning* (New York: Harcourt, Brace, 1923). (French ed. 1920.)

R. S. Woodworth, *Psychology* (New York: Henry Holt and Co., 1921).

L. L. Thurstone, *The Nature of Intelligence* (New York: Harcourt, Brace, 1924).

E. C. Tolman, "A Behavioristic Theory of Ideas," *Psychological Review*, **33** (1926), 352-69.

John L. Lowes, *The Road to Xanadu* (New York: Houghton Mifflin, 1927; New York: Vintage Books, 1959).

C. L. Hull, "Knowledge and Purpose as Habit Mechanisms," *Psychological Review*, **37** (1930), 511-25.

K. F. Muenzinger, "Vicarious Trial and Error at a Point of Choice: I. A General Survey of Its Relation to Learning Efficiency," *Journal of Genetic Psychology*, **53** (1938), 75-86.

N. E. Miller and J. Dollard, *Social Learning and Imitation* (New Haven: Yale University Press, 1941).

Kenneth J. W. Craik, *The Nature of Explanation* (New York: Cambridge University Press, 1943).

E. G. Boring, "Great Men and Scientific Progress," *Proceedings of the American Philosophical Society*, **94** (1950), 339-51.

G. Humphrey, *Thinking* (London: Methuen & Co., 1951).

W. R. Ashby, *Design for a Brain* (New York: John Wiley & Sons, 1952).

O. H. Mowrer, "Ego Psychology, Cybernetics and Learning Theory," in *Kentucky Symposium: Learning Theory, Personality Theory, and Clinical Research* (New York: John Wiley & Sons, 1954), pp. 81-90.

W. Sluckin, *Minds and Machines* (Harmondsworth: Penguin Books, 1954).

G. Pólya, *Mathematics and Plausible Reasoning*, Vol. I: *Induction and Analogy in Mathematics;* Vol. II: *Patterns of Plausible Inference* (Princeton, N. J.: Princeton University Press, 1954).

Donald T. Campbell, "Blind Variation and Selective Retention in Creative Thought as in Other Knowledge Processes," *Psychological Review*, **67** (1960), 380-400.

F. Bonsack, *Information, Thermodynamique, vie, et pensée* (Paris: Gauthier-Villars, 1961).

APPENDIX II: NATURAL SELECTION AS A MODEL FOR THE EVOLUTION OF SCIENCE

William James, "Great Men, Great Thoughts, and the Environment," *The Atlantic Monthly*, **46**, No. 276 (October, 1880), 441-59.

Thomas H. Huxley, *Collected Essays*: Vol. II, *Darwiniana* (New York: D.

Appleton, 1897), p. 299. (Original date of essay, 1880.)

For Mach and Poincaré, see Čapek "Mach's Theory of Knowledge" (note 76).

L. Boltzmann, *Populäre Schriften* (Leipzig: Barth, 1905), pp. 338-44 and *ad passim*.

A. D. Ritchie, *Scientific Method* (London: Kegan Paul, Trench & Trubner, 1923).

H. S. Jennings, *The Behavior of the Lower Organisms* (New York: Columbia University Press, 1906).

Karl R. Popper, *Logik der Forschung* (Vienna: Julius Springer, 1935).

W. B. Cannon, *The Way of An Investigator* (New York: W. W. Norton & Co., 1945).

F. S. C. Northrop, *The Logic of the Sciences and the Humanities* (New York: Macmillian Co., 1947), pp. 119-31.

W. I. B. Beveridge, *The Art of Scientific Investigation* (New York: W. W. Norton & Co., 1950).

S. C. Pepper, *The Sources of Value* (Berkeley: University of California Press, 1958), pp. 106-8.

Pierre Auger, *L'Homme Microscopique: Essai de Monodologie* (Paris: Flammarion, 1952).

Pierre Auger, "The Methods and Limits of Scientific Knowledge," in *On Modern Physics* (New York: Collier Books, 1962), pp. 93-125.

Gerald Holton, and Duane H. D. Roller, *Foundations of Modern Physical Science* (Reading, Mass.: Addison-Wesley, 1958), pp. 232-34, 241-42, 245.

S. E. Toulmin, *Foresight and Understanding: An Inquiry Into the Aims of Science* (Bloomington, Indiana: Indiana University Press, 1961).

S. E. Toulmin, "The Evolutionary Development of Natural Science," *American Scientist,* **55** (1967), 456-71.

T. S. Kuhn, *The Structure of Scientific Revolutions* (Chicago: University of Chicago Press, 1962).

C. C. Gillispie, "Remarks on Social Selection as a Factor in the Progressivism of Science," *American Scientist,* **56** (1968), 439-50.

Peter Caws, "The Structure of Discovery," *Science,* **166** (1969), 1375-80.

Michael T. Ghiselin, *The Triumph of the Darwinian Method* (Berkeley: University of California Press, 1969).

Robert Ackermann, *The Philosophy of Science* (New York: Pegasus, 1970).

Jacques Monod, *Chance and Necessity* (New York: Alfred H. Knopf, 1971), pp. 165 ff.

APPENDIX III: ON THE UBIQUITY OF MULTIPLE
INDEPENDENT INVENTION

Paul Souriau, *Theorie de l'Invention* (Paris: Hachette, 1881).

A. L. Kroeber, "The Superorganic," *American Anthropologist,* **19** (1917), 163-214.

W. F. Ogburn and D. Thomas, "Are Inventions Inevitable?" *Political Science Quarterly,* **37** (1922), 83-93.

E. G. Boring, "The Problem of Originality in Science," *American Journal of Psychology,* **39** (1927), 70-90.

Conrad Zirkle, "Natural Selection before the Origin," *Proceedings of the American Philosophical Society,* **84** (1941), 71-123.

B. Barber, *Science and the Social Order* (Glencoe, Illinois: Free Press, 1952).

R. K. Merton, "Priorities in Scientific Discovery: A Chapter in the Sociology of Science," *American Sociological Review,* **22** (1957), 635-59.

R. K. Merton, "Singletons and Multiples in Scientific Discovery: A Chapter in the Sociology of Science," *Proceedings of the American Philosophical Society,* **105** (1961), 470-86.

Donald T. Campbell, "Methodological Suggestions from a Comparative Psychology of Knowledge Processes," *Inquiry,* **2** (1959), 152-82.

Donald T. Campbell and Herman Tauscher, "Schopenhauer, Seguin, Lubinoff, and Zehender as Anticipators of Emmert's Law: With Comments on the Uses of Eponymy," *Journal of the History of the Behavioral Sciences,* **2,** No. 1 (January, 1966), 58-63.

C. Limoges, *La Selection Naturelle* (Paris: Presses Universitaire de France, 1970).

APPENDIX IV: BIOLOGICAL EVOLUTION AS THE
ORIGIN OF THE A PRIORI CATEGORIES OF
THOUGHT AND PERCEPTION IN MAN

Herbert Spencer, *Principles of Psychology* (New York: D. Appleton and Co., 1897). (1st ed., 1855.)

William James, *Principles of Psychology* (New York: Henry Holt and Co., 1890), Vol. II, pp. 617-79.

C. L. Morgan, "The Law of Psychogenesis," *Mind,* **1** (1892), 81.

Georg Simmel, "Über eine Beziehung der Selectionslehre zur Erkenntnistheorie," *Archiv für systematische Philosophie,* **1,** No. 1 (1895), 34-45.

James M. Baldwin, *Development and Evolution* (New York: Macmillan Co., 1902).

For Ernst Mach and Henri Poincaré, see Milič Čapek, "Mach's Theory of Knowledge" (note 76).

L. Boltzmann, "Über eine These Schopenhauer," in *Populäre Schriften* (Leipzig: Barth, 1905), pp. 385-402, esp. p. 398.

A. Fouillé, *L'Evolutionisme des Idées-Forces* (Paris: Alcan, 1906).

Ernst Cassirer, *Substance and Function* (La Salle, Illinois: Open Court Publishing Co., 1923; Dover, 1953), pp. 269-70. (German original, 1910.)

H. S. Shelton, "On Evolutionary Empiricism," *Mind*, **19** (1910), 49.

William K. Wright, "The Genesis of the Categories," *The Journal of Philosophy, Psychology and Scientific Methods*, **10** (1913), 645-57, esp. 646.

R. W. Sellars, *Evolutionary Naturalism* (La Salle, Illinois: Open Court Publishing Co., 1922).

For Hans Reichenbach, see Čapek, "Reichenbach's Epistemology" (note 76).

J. von Uexküll, *Theoretical Biology* (New York: Harcourt, Brace, 1926).

E. Meyerson, *Identity and Reality* (London: Allen and Unwin, 1930), p. 39. Regarding Meyerson, see Joseph LaLumia, *The Ways of Reason* (New York: Humanities Press, 1966).

F. S. C. Northrop, *Science and First Principles* (New York: Macmillan Co., 1931). (This book contains a remarkable early statement of the natural-selection, steady-state, feed-back model of biological organization.)

F. S. C. Northrop, *Philosophical Anthropology and Practical Politics* (New York: Macmillan Co., 1960), p. 46.

Rudolph Magnus, "The Physiological *A Priori*," in *Lane Lectures on Experimental Pharmacology and Medicine* (Stanford University Press, 1930), pp. 97-102; Stanford University Publications, University Series, Medical Sciences, Vol. II, No. 3, pp. 331-37.

Konrad Lorenz, "Kants Lehre vom apriorischen im Lichte gegenwärtiger Biologie," *Blätter für Deutsche Philosophie*, **15** (1941), 94-125; also translated in *General Systems*, ed. by L. von Bertalanffy and A. Rapoport (Ann Arbor: Society for General Systems Research, 1962), Vol. VII, pp. 23-35.

Konrad Lorenz, "Die angeborenen Formen möglicher Erfahrung," *Zeitschrift für Tierpsychologie*, **5** (1943), 235-409.

Arthur Child, "On the Theory of the Categories," *Philosophy and Phenomenological Research*, **7** (1946), 316-35.

Jean Piaget, *Introduction a l'Epistemologie Genetique*, 3 vols. (Paris: Presses Universitaire de France, 1950).

Jean Piaget, *The Origins of Intelligence in Children* (New York: International University Press, 1952), pp. 2-3. See also John H. Flavell, *The Developmental Psychology of Jean Piaget* (Princeton: Van Nostrand, 1963), for relevant citations back to 1924. Note Piaget's full-fledged evolutionary epistemology which explicitly rejects both Darwinism-mutationism and trial-and-error-concepts in favor of an ac-comodationism lying intermediate between that and Lamarckianism, also rejected.

C. H. Waddington, "Evolution and Epistemology," *Nature*, 173 (1954), 880-81.

C. H. Waddington, *The Nature of Life* (London: Allen and Unwin, 1961), pp. 123-25.

Ludwig von Bertalanffy, "An Essay on the Relativity of Categories," *Philosophy of Science*, 22 (1955), 243-63.

G. J. Whitrow, "Why Physical Space Has Three Dimensions," *British Journal of the Philosophy of Science*, 6 (1956), 13-31.

John Platt, "Amplification Aspects of Biological Response and Mental Activity," *American Scientist*, 44 (1956), 181-97.

John Platt, "Functional Geometry and the Determination of Pattern in Mosaic Receptors," in *Symposium on Information Theory in Biology*, ed. by H. P. Yockey, R. L. Platzman, and H. Quastler (New York: Pergamon, 1958), pp. 371-98.

S. C. Pepper, *The Sources of Value* (Berkeley: University of California Press, 1958), pp. 106-8.

M. Merleau-Ponty, *Sense and Nonsense* (Evanston, Illinois: Northwestern University Press, 1964), p. 84.

George Gaylord Simpson, "Biology and the Nature of Science," *Science*, 139 (1963), 84-85.

W. S. Sellars, *Science, Perception and Reality* (London: Routledge & Kegan Paul, 1963), p. 90.

David Hawkins, *The Language of Nature: An Essay in the Philosophy of Science* (San Francisco: Freeman, 1964), pp. 46-52, 252-54.

H. J. Barr, "The Epistemology of Causality from the Point of View of Evolutionary Biology," *Philosophy of Science*, 31 (1964), 286-88.

S. Watanabe, "Une explication mathématique due classement d'objects," in *Information and Prediction in Science*, ed. by S. Dockx and P. Bernays (New York: Academic Press, 1965), pp. 39-45.

H. Yilmaz, "A Theory of Speech Perception," *Bulletin of Mathematical Biophysics*, 29 (1967), 793-825.

H. Yilmaz, "Perception and Philosophy of Science," presented to the Boston Colloquium for the Philosophy of Science, October 28, 1969, and to appear in *Boston Studies in the Philosophy of Science*, ed. by R. S. Cohen and M. W. Wartofsky.

S. E. Toulmin, "Neuroscience and Human Understanding," in *The Neurosciences*, ed. by Frank Schmitt (New York: Rockefeller University Press, 1968).

Marx Wartofsky, "Metaphysics as Heuristic for Science," in *Boston Studies in the Philosophy of Science,* ed. by R. S. Cohen and M. W. Wartofsky (Dordrecht, Holland: D. Reidel, 1968), Vol. III, pp. 164-70.

W. V. Quine, *Ontological Relativity* (New York: Columbia University Press, 1969), pp. 126-28.

Abner Shimony, "Scientific Inference," in *Pittsburgh Studies in the Philosophy of Science,* ed. by R. Colodny (Pittsburgh: University of Pittsburgh Press, 1970), Vol. IV, pp. 79-172.

Abner Shimony, "Perception from an Evolutionary Point of View," *Journal of Philosophy,* **68** (1971), 571-83.

Nathan Stemmer, "Three Problems in Induction," *Synthese,* **23**, Nos. 2/3 (1971), 287-308.

Grover Maxwell, "Corroboration without Demarcation," in this volume.

Jacques Monod, *Chance and Necessity* (New York: Alfred A. Knopf, 1971), pp. 149-59.

Michael T. Ghiselin, "Darwin and Evolutionary Psychology," *Science,* **179** (1973), 964-68, has discovered that Darwin belongs in this list, giving an evolutionary explanation of Plato's necessary ideas preexisting in the soul. The evidence is to be found in Cambridge University's collection of Darwin's papers, Notebooks N and M 1838-39.

Anyone attempting a review in this area should also examine the remarkable use of the concept of trial and error for resolving Kant's problems by A. D. Lindsay, "Introduction," in Immanuel Kant, *Critique of Pure Reason* (London: J. M. Dent, Everyman's Library, 1934).

13

Eugene Freeman and Henryk Skolimowski
THE SEARCH FOR OBJECTIVITY
IN PEIRCE AND POPPER*

CONTENTS

I. CHARLES PEIRCE AND OBJECTIVITY IN PHILOSOPHY

The Meaning of Objectivity

I make a distinction between what I call *factual objectivity* and what I call *rule objectivity*. The former is ontological and involves *conformity to reality* or facts. The latter is epistemological and involves *conformity to rules* which establish objectivity by fiat and social agreement. Factual objectivity is closely related to the ordinary language sense of objectivity, which presupposes the (uncritical) realistic distinction between mutually exclusive 'subjects' (or selves) and 'objects' (or not-selves). If we disregard for the moment the practical difficulties of reaching ontological and epistemological agreement as to where the demarcation line between the self and the not-self is to be drawn, we find the ordinary language meaning of 'objectivity', as given for example in Webster's unabridged dictionary, quite instructive. 'Object' is defined in one context as "The totality of external phenomena consituting the not-self "; 'objectivity' is defined derivatively as "the quality,

---

*Part I of this paper was written by Eugene Freeman, Part II by Henryk Skolimowski, and Part III by both authors.

state, or relation of being objective"; and objective, in turn, is defined as "something that is external to the mind." Here 'subject' (or self, or mind) is the basic undefined term, in terms of which we can define objectivity as non-subjectivity, in polar contrast to 'subjective', which means 'that which is part of or inside of the self'. To be objective thus means to be other than the self, or external to the self (we do not raise here, of course, the interesting problems of the possible differences between the self and the mind, but merely include the latter as part of the former). The test of objectivity and subjectivity, on this view, is whether something is inside or outside of the self, i.e., part of the self or not. This ordinary language notion of objects and subjects presupposes the (uncritical) realistic view that we perceive *chairs,* not *percepts* of chairs, and that chairs are outside of our minds and thus our selves, even though the percepts of the chairs we perceive are not.

We cannot, however, be satisfied with a distinction between subject and object which is unambiguous only to the extent that it remains purely formal without empirical content. In order for objectivity to be factual objectivity, i.e., to have factual content, the demarcation between the self and the not-self must be ontologically correct—the line must be drawn between them in what as a matter of fact is the *right* place. It must also meet whatever epistemological requirements are necessary to give us the requisite assurance that we *know* that it is correct. But, whereas philosophers are able to agree that what is 'inside' the self is subjective and what is 'outside' is objective, they are not always able to agree on where the line of demarcation between the self and the not-self is to be drawn, because of the enormous variation in their ontological and epistemological presuppositions and assumptions. Thus what is objective for one philosopher may be a mere figment for another.

This account places high demands on what is expected of objectivity for it to be factual objectivity. Perhaps the demands are too high. What we expect of objectivity for it to be factual is that it should be genuine—that it should be veridical—we might almost say that it should be factually factual, or objectively objective, that it should attain absolute verisimilitude.

But of course it should be apparent that terms like genuine objectivity, or objective objectivity, and even the very term factual objectivity, beg the question of genuineness in much the same almost desperate table-pounding fashion as is involved in referring to perception as veridical, that is, as not merely true, but *truly* true. Such verbal devices only show the absurdity of trying to express ourselves by using old words whose meanings have become too blurred and ambiguous to fit our needs, to say nothing of the futility of raising our voices or repeating ourselves in frustration when our words carry no conviction, as is so often the case when we try to express the inexpressible—the absolute that is forever beyond the reach of our knowledge—the truth that is truly true, the reality that is really real, the objectivity that is objectively objective.

What I call 'rule objectivity', on the other hand, makes much less pretentious claims, as it is concerned only with the practical questions relating to *the rules of what constitutes acceptable evidence* on the basis of which claims for objectivity are validated. Validation of a claim to objectivity begins with individual replications by independent observers of the crucial observations (and arguments) on which a particular claim to objectivity depends. Each such replication is insofar a test of the *factual* objectivity of the original claim, a test in which negative results are categorical refutations, whereas positive results yield confirmations which are only tentative.

It is well known that positive confirmation in science is hardly more than an unattainable ideal limit. However, when replications are pooled, whereas in a strict logical sense they still do not categorically furnish absolute confirmation, they become in James's term, "practical absolutes" which furnish us with sufficient confirmation to permit us to continue our investigation as though (*als ob*) the confirmations were *absolute*. Thus pooled replications on which there is intersubjective agreement furnish a collective confirmation which has *rule* objectivity. The individual observers who replicate the appropriate tests and arguments are like a collective jury, or a collective umpire, and wherever questions of fact or judgment are decided by juries or umpires, whatever they are able to agree upon as *being in their opinion* objectively valid is defined *by the rules under which they operate* as *being* objectively valid, i.e., as rule objective validity. It is evident that rule objectivity is thoroughly pragmatic—it is objectivity as it affects human behavior. In a word, we behave toward that which has rule objectivity as though (*als ob*) it were true in fact instead of by agreement, and 'intersubjective agreement' is seen to be the translation into pragmatic or operational language of the term 'objectivity'.

The rules of science, by a similar fiat, grant rule objectivity to a claim for objectivity which is confirmed by the pooled replications of *competent,* independent observers. Science does not claim factual objectivity for its claims of the moment—to do so would in a sense reduce the method of science to the absurdity of making an endless series of factual claims which are always fated to be contradicted by new evidence. Rule objectivity, on the other hand, does not directly claim to be factual, but only that there is adequate intersubjective agreement to prove that the claim has not yet been falsified. Accordingly, a claim validated by rule objectivity can be revoked without contradicting the previous validation, which did not claim factuality, but only that all the replications made up to that date were in agreement as confirmatory of the claim. Should subsequent replications fail to agree, then the claim that the replications agree can be withdrawn without the embarrassment of confessing that what I claimed yesterday as the truth today I admit as false. In a word, rule objectivity testifies to social agreement, not to factuality. Furthermore, not only is a claim which has gained its validation on the basis of rule objectivity treated *as though* it had gained its validation on the basis of factual objectivity, but this fiction (and that it is a fiction is never denied) is carried still further in behaving toward all claims which are granted rule objective validity as though they were all *equal* in their factuality, even when we are convinced on other grounds that this is not the case.[1]

Science ostensibly accepts, in the absence of any immediate evidence to the contrary, all rule objective validations as equally valid, and treats them as though they had been equally validated *factually*. However, it does not accept its own verdict as final, but continues to make a vigorous and sustained search to find the very evidence to the contrary which would refute its own validation. This is because even though all rule objective validations are equally valid as rule validations, they may each have a different degree of truth content. Accordingly, our conviction about the reliability of a hypothesis is increased by three factors (of which the least powerful is the first), namely:

1. the competence and skill of the persons involved in proposing and testing the hypothesis on the basis of whose agreement rule objective validity is granted;
2. the total number of replications made; and
3. the total number of tentatively confirmed but independently established claims which mutually support each other.

It is obvious that on all three counts rule objective validity has a far greater probability of being factually valid in science than in any other enterprise. The almost limitless opportunity for continued replication and retesting in science persuades Peirce that in the long run science is *predestined* to hit on the truth (5.407).[2] This is one of the fundamental disagreements between Peirce and Popper. For Peirce seems on some occasions,[3] but not on others (5.590-604), to adhere to the "manifest theory of truth," as Popper calls it: it is the nature of truth that it will hit us sooner or later, given enough time. Popper, on the other hand, emphatically denies this: we may never hit on the truth, it is very hard to come by—and even if we were to hit upon it, we can never know with certainty that we have done so. Hence the greatest emphasis is placed on error elimination. The more successful we are in purging error, the closer we can hope to approach the truth.[4]

The Problem of Objectivity in Peirce's Philosophy

The problem of objectivity in Peirce's philosophy was the problem of establishing the objective validity in experience of the categories which Peirce had proposed as the fundamental categories of logic. The apparently formal and empty names which Peirce uses to identify his categories are not merely numerical labels. Rather, they are *descriptive* names[5] for various fundamental categories of logic which at the same time are ontological categories. In their pure form, as abstract ideal limits, *Firstness* is the category, for which the prototype in logic is the monad, of those entities which are what they are in and of themselves alone—thus they are *originals*. *Secondness* is the category of those things which would not be what they are if they were not *constitutively* related to one other thing—e.g., causes or effects. *Thirdness* is the category of those things which would not be what they are if they were not *constitutively* related to two other things—e.g., a mediator, or an interpreter. The essential claim of Peirce's logic of relations was that there are three unique and irreducible kinds of relations, monadic, dyadic, and triadic (or polyadic). He then argued that they must have been derived from three irreducibly different kinds of logical thought processes, and thus by some stretch of logic, they are fundamental categories of being.

> . . . When the notation which suffices for exhibiting one inference is found inadequate for explaining another, it is clear that the latter involves an inferential element not present to the former. Accordingly, the procedure contemplated [that of discovering the irreducible types of notation] should result in a list of categories of reasoning, the interest of which is not dependent upon the algebraic way of considering the subject. [3.428]

However, even if we grant that Peirce, through his logic of relations has discovered the ultimate categories of reasoning, it seems to me that we are still far from having demonstrated how or why these categories are transformed into objective categories of all being. Where does the objectivity of Peirce's categories come from? As nearly as I can make out, through the affirmation of a purely metaphysical presupposition which in an earlier study (in 1934) I called Peirce's *Ontological Postulate*, namely, "that the principles of formal logic and epistemology are directly related to the principles of Being, that the structure of logic is the key to the structure of Reality."[6] This postulate was the foundation of Peirce's ontology, which was "simply the hypostatization of a logic into a categorial system without argument" (*CCP*, p. 1). Peirce defines the categories as "a table of conceptions drawn from the logical analysis of thought and regarded as applicable to being" (1.300). "I shall not here inquire," Peirce writes, "how far it is justifiable to apply the conceptions of logic to metaphysics. For I hold the importance of that question, great as it is, to be perhaps secondary, . . ." (1.301).

But a set of categories derived from formal abstract principles of logic must also be formal and abstract. In order to get to categories which have factual objective validity, we must start from concrete factual experience, rather than from an abstract logic. However, concrete experience is always particular, and categories to be adequate must be universal, not merely particular. Some happy combination of the universality, afforded only by abstract logical principles, and the applicability to nature, afforded only by concrete particular experience, is required as the minimum necessary attribute of categories in order for them to be at the same time, as Whitehead would have required,[7] sufficiently factual to be "applicable" and sufficiently general (universal) to be "adequate" for the understanding and the explanation of human experience.

Peirce's Method: Mathematical Empiricism

Peirce's concern to ensure for his categories both the universality of mathematics and the applicability of empirical science led him to formulate a method which Charles Hartshorne has termed 'mathematical empiricism' (*CCP*, p. 3n.). This method is the philosophical counterpart of the method of empirical science. The latter consists essentially of the proposing of a speculative hypothesis (which Popper aptly refers to as a conjecture) to solve a problem which has meaningful consequences in human experience—i.e., one which is testable (or as Popper aptly puts it, is falsifiable) by observation. Testable predicted consequences of the hypothesis are then checked by making appropriate observations and the hypothesis is thereby either refuted or tentatively retained.

Perhaps the greatest similarity in the methods of Peirce and Popper appears in their accounts of the nature and origin of the hypothesis. For both men, the hypothesis is a conjecture, and for both, it is the outcome of a shower of wild imaginative guesses, one of which survives. For Peirce the process whereby the thinker is led from the examination of unexplained facts to a theory which explains them is called 'retroduction' or 'abduction'. For Popper, the examination of a knowledge situation suggests *problems*, which we attempt to solve by putting forth tentative theories (imaginative guesses). The procedures of testing hypotheses or solving problems may start as logical exercises when we test them for coherence, congruence, and noncontradiction, but must always terminate in empirical testing. Popper points out that we always place our problems into what he calls a "third world background" (i.e., a background of objective ideas which are neither physical things nor merely subjective mental entities but independent knowables—like Plato's ideas—thus *objects* for knowledge).[8] This third world background, Popper adds, "consists of at least a *language*, which always incorporates many theories in the very structure of its usages . . . and many other theoretical assumptions, unchallenged at least for the time being" ("Obj. Mind," pp. 22-32).

Nor does Peirce, any more than Popper, challenge the theoretical assumptions on which he rests his philosophy. One of Peirce's most memorable remarks is his eloquent "let us not pretend to doubt in our

philosophies what we do not doubt in our hearts." Peirce followed this advice
devotedly, even to the point of letting his heart make his eyes see things that
were not there, such as the observations he fancied were made by
philosophers by virtue of which philosophy becomes a positive (i.e., an empirical) science.

> Mathematics . . . makes no external observations, nor asserts anything as real
> fact. . . . Philosophy is not quite so abstract. For though it makes no *special*
> observations, as every other positive science does, yet it does deal with reality. It
> confines itself, however, to the universal phenomena of experience; and these are,
> generally speaking, sufficiently revealed in the ordinary observations of every-
> day life. [3.428]

Like the disappointed father who gives his new-born daughter the name of the
son he had longed for, Peirce cannot accept the fact that philosophy is not an
empirical science, so he gives it the name he had hoped it would bear. He
grants, and then attempts to brush away, the crucial objection that
philosophers do not make special observations as all other empirical scientists do, and that without specific empirical content philosophy could hardly
claim to be a positive science. Peirce contends that philosophers *do* deal with
empirical reality, but that their observations are limited to "the universal
phenomena of experience," as "revealed in the ordinary observations of
every-day life" (3.428).

A similar contention is found in Popper, who writes that ". . . scientific
knowledge is merely a development of ordinary knowledge or common sense
knowledge . . . " (*L.Sc.D.*, p. 18). At this point, however, it seems to me that
Peirce has stretched the meaning of either the term 'observation' or 'universal' beyond recognition. 'Observations', in the ordinary language sense in
which the term refers to the results of a crucial procedure in empirical
science, are, of course, *sensory* observations, i.e., observations mediated by
one or more of the special sense organs. Whereas 'universal' means 'infinitely
boundless' and infinite boundlessness is obviously beyond the reach of ordinary observations, which cannot extend outside of the limited confines of
the space and time in which they are made. I know of no kinds of "ordinary
observations of every-day life" which will disclose anything but particular
phenomena. If by chance an observer were actually to observe phenomena
which were indeed manifestations or instantiations of something or some
things which were indeed universal, the observer could not know their universality, if all he knew about them came from his ordinary observations of
them. The knowledge of their universality would have to come to him from
some other way of knowing.

I do not quarrel with Peirce's contention that his categories are objective—rather, I share his heartfelt conviction on this. What I do question is
Peirce's paradoxical claim about the universality of what can be known

through *observation*, thus, about the objectivity of Thirdness as given directly in *perception*. That Thirdness is "perceived" is the basic contention of Peirce's strikingly original and subtle Phenomenology, which he invents in the vain hope that it will furnish him with an epistemological tool powerful enough to give the abstractions of logic the concrete content required to transform them into objective principles applicable to all being. The Phenomenology "treats of the Universal Qualities of phenomena in their immediate phenomenal character"[9] (5.122).

In some ways Peirce's Phenomenology reminds me of the 'nail soup' made in the old folk tale by stirring a pot of boiling water with a magic nail. The gypsy who owned the nail would persuade a housewife to let him demonstrate his magic in return for his dinner. They would go to the kitchen and a pot of water would soon be boiling briskly on the stove. The gypsy would then stir the pot slowly with his magic nail, while the housewife watched him carefully. After a while he would say, "Plain nail soup is very good. But it is even better with a pinch of salt." The housewife would nod her head, and add some salt. The stirring and the watching would be resumed. Then the gypsy would mention another way to improve nail soup. In due course the soup would be finished, and the housewife would be surprised to discover that the soup made by using the magic nail tasted exactly like the soup she made herself without it.

It happens that I do think that Peirce's categories are genuinely objective and universal, just as I think that nail soup would be genuinely nutritious. But I am no more convinced that the universality which I grant I find in the categories comes from perception than I am convinced that the nutriments in the soup come from the nail. Murray Murphey, who holds a similar view, puts it this way: "It is impossible to regard Peirce's phenomenological treatment of the categories as anything more than a quite unsuccessful sleight of hand."[10] But even though Peirce is unsuccessful here in what he set out to do, I think Murphey's metaphor is hardly appropriate. Sleight of hand implies deliberate deception by a kind of skilled trickery, and Peirce was not trying to trick his reader into accepting something that Peirce himself knew was not true. On the contrary, although Peirce's arguments may not have been correct, nevertheless he believed in them with all his heart. Thus the deception was not sleight of hand, but self-deception, like nail soup made by a cook who believed in the magic of the nail.

Murphey points out that it is essential to Peirce's position that in order to avoid subjectivism, and at the same time to account for orderly experience, it is necessary for Peirce to maintain that Thirdness is directly perceived, since he accepts the empirical axiom that nothing can be in the intellect which was not first known through the senses, from which it follows that unless generality is given in perception, it can never be known at all (*DPP*, pp. 376

ff.). I think that Peirce is right in holding, as Kant does, that we are able to account for orderly experience through our knowledge of universals, but as I have already stated, I think that Peirce was mistaken in his contention that such universals are given in perception.

Peirce's nail soup, which he calls his phenomenology, instead of containing nothing but sensory observation, is enriched by the addition of *illicitly added ontological ingredients which give the phenomenology all the universality and generality that perception can never give it.* Peirce is able to add the illicit ingredients to his nail soup by using the word 'observation' in four different senses, three of which are specialized whereas the fourth is general, combining the other three ambiguously and vaguely. These four senses of the term 'observation', which may be symbolized as O_s, O_i, O_H, and O_g, are the following:

1. O_s is observation in the narrow literal sense where it means sense perception.
2. O_i is observation in its broader metaphorical sense where it means rational insight or intuition.
3. O_H is observation in an intriguing Hegel-like synthesis of the preceding two senses, where it designates the simultaneous observation (O_s) of icons of abstract entities and the observation (O_i) of the entities themselves as mirrored in their icons.
4. O_g is observation in the conveniently ambiguous general sense which includes the foregoing three senses without distinguishing between them.

It is O_H which adds the ontological richness to observation which O_s can never bring. Formal mathematical and logical entities and relationships are on my view forever beyond the grasp of O_s. But they are within easy reach of O_H, which begins with a genuinely phenomenological step in which icons of abstract entities are observed by O_s. This is followed by a wholly ontological step required for the validation of O_H. This consists of the acceptance of a presupposition or postulate the truth of which guarantees the correctness of the procedure of knowing abstract entities by observing their icons. This presupposed postulate is not put into words by Peirce. As I would reconstruct it, the postulate might be expressed as follows:

Whatever is true of an icon as observed by O_s, is true of the abstract entity for which the icon is a visible sign.

The postulate is seen to be true by intuition or rational insight, i.e., O_i, whereas the abstract entity is known 'observationally' through the complex synthesis of empirical and rational observation which I have called O_H.

In summary, the abstract entities are not directly observable (O_s), but the icons which are constructed to mirror them are directly observable (O_s).

However, the abstract entities are observable in a sort of indirect fashion through O$_H$. Accordingly, the paradoxical claim can be made that we can observe the 'unobservable', by observing the icons which mirror the unobservable—very much as Perseus, by looking at the reflection mirrored in his shield, was able to view with impunity the forbidden sight of the face of Medusa.

Another subtle variation from ordinary language notions of perception is Peirce's important distinction between a perception and a perceptual judgment. This distinction affords Peirce the grounds for introducing an additional amount of interpretation into the essence of perception (he had already pointed out that some degree of interpretation is involved from the outset in perception). Like the perception itself, the perceptual judgment, on Peirce's view, retains its objectivity despite its being to some extent an interpretation by the subject, inasmuch as the subject has no control over the process, any more than he has over the prior process of perceiving (2.140-41).

Peirce defines a perceptual judgment as "a judgment absolutely forced upon my acceptance, and that by a process which I am utterly unable to control and consequently am unable to criticize" (5.157). This is very much like Descartes's notion of ideas which are so clear and simple that we cannot resist them. A critical case of the kind of perceptual judgments involved in Peirce's so-called perception of universals is afforded by the perception of the relationship between events which are apparently successive in time, i.e., the relationship of apparent subsequence. As difficult as the notion can be from a logical point of view, Peirce found it quite acceptable to assume that "Thirdness pours in upon us through every avenue of sense" (5.157).

> Now consider the judgment that one event C *appears to be* subsequent to another event A. Certainly, I may have inferred this; because I may have remarked that C was subsequent to a third event B which was itself subsequent to A. But then these premises are judgments of the same description. It does not seem possible that I can have performed an infinite series of acts of criticism each of which must require a distinct effort. The case is quite different from that of Achilles and the tortoise because Achilles does not require to make an infinite series of distinct efforts. It therefore appears that I must have made some judgment that one event *appeared to be* subsequent to another without that judgment having been inferred from any premiss [i.e.] without any *controlled* and *criticized* action of reasoning. If this be so, it is a perceptual judgment in the only sense that the logician can recognize.

The crucial claim here is Peirce's identification of 'perceptual judgment' and perception.

> But from that proposition that one event, Z, is subsequent to another event, J, I can at once deduce by necessary reasoning a universal proposition. Namely, the definition of the relation of apparent subsequence is well known, or sufficiently so for our purpose. Z will appear to be subsequent to Y if and only if A appears

to stand in a peculiar relation, R, to Y such that nothing can stand in the relation R to itself, and if, furthermore, whatever event, X, there may be to which Y stands in the relation R, to that same X, Z also stands in the relation R. [Cf. 3.562B] This being implied in the meaning of subsequence, concerning which there is no room for doubt, it easily follows that whatever is subsequent to C is subsequent to anything, A, to which C is subsequent—which is a universal proposition.

Thus my assertion at the end of the last lecture appears to be most amply justified. Thirdness pours in upon us through every avenue of sense. [5.157]

What Peirce does here is illicitly to include intuition and deduction along with perception as being necessarily involved in the so-called perceptual procedure, from which Peirce "can at once deduce by necessary reasoning a universal proposition." But a procedure which involves as an essential step "deduction by necessary reasoning" can hardly be asserted to be sense perception. And that Peirce intended us to interpret his words as referring to some kind of perception other than sense perception is hardly consistent with his proclamation at the end of the paragraph just quoted in which he writes that "Thirdness pours in upon us through every avenue of sense" (5.157).

The exact place where Peirce goes wrong is in his defintion of perceptual judgment (5.157) quoted above, in which he defines perceptual judgment in terms of necessary but not sufficient characteristics. That perceptual judgments are forced upon us, that we have no control over them, and thus cannot criticize them, I grant is quite true. But I would say that this is equally true of many of the judgments we make in logic and mathematics through 'insight' or 'rational intuition', where we 'see' that a proposition is true, but only in a metaphorical and not in the perceptual sense of seeing, O_i and not O_s.

In a word, Peirce's basic mistake is to use the metaphorical sense of 'perceiving' or 'seeing' as though it were the literal sense. In the metaphorical sense of seeing, we 'see' that something is true by insight or intuition (cf. 6.493). In the literal sense of seeing, we see by looking at something with our eyes and perceiving it. If we broaden the term 'perception' to include the metaphorical sense, which of course includes 'rational insight', there is no difficulty in agreeing with Peirce's contention that we can know universals (Thirdness) through 'perception'. But, although this dissolves the difficulties which would confront us if we were to have used the term perception in its literal sense, it also dissolves that part of the claim that Thirdness is objective which rests on Thirdness being perceived. Things which are *perceived* have a prima facie claim to objectivity, but only if they are perceived through sensory perception (O_s). If they are known through some way other than through sensory perception, the claim that they are objective because they are *perceived* is a misrepresentation, unless it is explicitly made clear that the term 'perception' is not being used in its ordinary sense of 'sense perception', but as a figure of speech.

Thus we have gone full circle, and we return to Peirce's starting point, the Ontological Postulate, that the ultimate categories of logic *must be* the objective categories of being.[11] This postulate is the foundation on which the *objectivity* of Peirce's categories rests, and I cannot accept his claim that he is able to validate the objectivity of his categories by means of perception. It is only by rational intuition that we can know this postulate. By pooling the efforts of independent competent observers who are able to replicate the act of seeing by their own rational intuition that the postulate is self-evident for them, their agreement grants rule objective validity to the postulate, to the extent that they can agree.

Objectivity in Philosophy on Peirce's Terms: His Sign Theory

Peirce, who was typically a scientist in his rejection of absolutistic claims in philosophy, makes no pretense of offering us absolute truth or absolute factual objectivity. For those who are content with rule objectivity and degrees of truth content, Peirce's philosophy, when accepted on his own terms, is extraordinarily successful.

The principles and criteria for objectivity in philosophy which can be developed from Peirce's philosophy rest ultimately on two presuppositions[12] which are basic to his theory of the categories:

1. Peirce's Ontological Postulate—that the structure of logic is the mirror of the structure of reality;
2. That Peirce's three categories of logic are ultimate categories of metaphysics and of reality.

From the monad, dyad, and triad of Peirce's logic are derived not only his categories of Firstness, Secondness, and Thirdness, but his theory of signs as well. For Peirce there are three basic types of signs, the icon, the index, and the token (or symbol), and these are not merely variations on the theme of his three categories, but, to use the same figure, the categories themselves played in a different key.

In Peirce's theory of signs, the monad, or Firstness, is present in the form of the *icon*; the dyad, or Secondness, as the *index*; and the triad, or Thirdness, as the *token* (or symbol). An icon is a monadic sign which stands for something else, its object, by resembling it—thus by being itself, it is also (figuratively) its object. For example, an iconic sign of whiteness is a patch of white chalk on a blackboard, which stands for whiteness by (figuratively) being whiteness. Or a diagram of a relationship, such as the inclusion of one class within another, is an iconic sign of the relationship, which stands for the relationship by (figuratively) being the relationship.

An index is a dyadic sign which stands for its object by pointing to it, through some connection with its object that denotes it without describing it—e.g., demonstrative and relative pronouns, pointing fingers, weather-vanes, indicators on instruments, etc.

Peirce has one of the most clear-headed and convincing accounts of the factual objectivity and existential reality of the 'external' world in the entire history of philosophy. For Peirce as an empirical scientist as well as a philosopher, objectivity meant replication by an independent observer of the testimony on the basis of which a claim for objectivity is made. But here the critical first step is to communicate successfully to the would-be replicator *where and how he is to look* if he is to see what the subject sees. This is done by demonstration, and while not infallible, there is no better method of demonstration than the directing of the attention by means of a pointing finger and an indexical pronoun, or by a 'pointer reading' on a scientific instrument. If no replicator is able to see anything at the end of the pointing finger, e.g., the pink elephants to which the victim of delirium tremens points, we know that the subject is describing a world of fiction and not fact. Peirce points out that *the only way* that we can distinguish the real world from the world of fiction is by using indexes (2.337, 3.363, 8.39 ff.).[13]

Peirce uses Duns Scotus's term "haecceities" to designate the *thisness* to which attention is directed by a gesture accompanied by a demonstrative (or indexical) pronoun, e.g., "Look at *this*." 'This' names a something for which objective reality is claimed, a claim which can be confirmed by intersubjective testing. Thus from the category of Secondness, from which Peirce's indexical signs are derived, Peirce is able to establish the factual objectivity of the external world by *denotation*.

A token or symbol is a triadic sign, which stands for its object through the intervention of a mind or interpreter which connects sign and object through its own fiat, e.g., "let the word 'dog' stand for dog in the English language." All conventional 'symbols' (in the ordinary language sense) are triadic signs (or tokens), thus all meaning is triadic.

Peirce's clarification of the nature of signs, and of meaning in general led directly to his doctrine of pragmatism, which for him was essentially a theory of meaning rather than an epistemology or metaphysics. This theory throws a flood of new light on traditional epistemological and metaphysical problems. By defining the meaning of any concept as 'the conceivable consequences in experience which the affirmation or denial of that concept implies', Peirce excludes as without meaning all claims which are beyond the theoretically possible reach of intersubjective testing, and thus limits the bounds of the objective world to the bounds of the *rule objective* world. By setting attainable limits for his goals, Peirce is thus able to achieve them admirably well—perhaps as well as any philosopher who ever lived.

General Requirements for Objectivity

A set of three general requirements for objectivity can be formulated on the basis of Peirce's theory of signs:

1. all reasoning is diagrammatic;
2. the ultimate test of objectivity is denotation;
3. meaning must be defined pragmatically.

(1) From the category of Firstness, as expressed in the icon, we can formulate the following requirement. As Peirce himself stipulated, since reasoning consists of experimentation upon relations expressed by icons, ultimately *all reasoning must be diagrammatic.* "For reasoning," in Peirce's words, "consists in the observation that where certain relations subsist certain others are found, and it accordingly requires the exhibition of the relations reasoned within an icon" (3.363). When the relations involved in a piece of reasoning are expressed by means of diagrams or icons, such as, e.g., mathematical formulae or diagrams, the formulae of symbolic logic or logical diagrams such as those of Euler or Venn, the reasoning can accurately be replicated by intersubjective testing, and is thus objective.

(2) From the category of Secondness, as expressed in the index, we can formulate the requirement that the *ultimate test of reality consists of denotative procedures*, the final links of which are ostensive identifications by means of *indexes* (thus, demonstrative pronouns) and *gestures*. This is hard-headed realism. We attempt to establish correspondence between our descriptions and haecceities, and we identify the haecceities by pointing to them. When astronomers first pointed their telescopes at exactly the place indicated by the calculations of Leverrier and Adams, they transformed a theoretical Neptune into an 'objectively real' *haecceity*.

(3) From the category of Thirdness, as expressed in the token, we can formulate the requirement that *meaning must be defined pragmatically.* That is to say, meaning is the relating of a sign to its referent by an interpreter.

Interpreter (or Interpretant)[14]

Sign   Referent

A sign is *something* that stands for *something else* for an *interpreter*. Meaning is always triadic and always involves the *purposes of the interpreter*, who attaches the referent to the sign as its meaning *for him*. Thus, meaning is essentially pragmatic, that is, in the sense that it involves human purposes. It is only when we introduce the third element, the interpreter, who relates the referent and the sign vehicle as constituting meaning for him, that meaning arises.

Built into the criterion which defines meaning triadically, in terms of the fiat of the interpreter (which of course is determined by his purposes) is the famous restriction that the interpreter must be a radical empiricist. Meaning can be found only in "conceivable consequences in human experience."

Secondness is the acknowledgment of a brute external reality which is in no way dependent on the thinking of the knower for its existence. The objectively real is the "that" or "this" pointed to by the index. On the level of Secondness it is known only as a brute fact without meaning—an "other" or an "object" as distinguished from the subject who knows it. But what it *means* is known only through Thirdness, through its *pragmatic meaning*, as defined by the fiat of the interpreter, who limits its meaning entirely to the conceivable consequences it can have in human experience, and thus to human purposes.

Thus Peirce's theory of pragmatism, conceived as a *theory of meaning*, developed from the logical implications of the category of Thirdness. *The essence of pragmatism is identical with the category of Thirdness*, namely the recognition that meaning and purpose are inseparable, that meaning must be interpreted in terms of human purposes and conduct.[15]

The general requirements for objectivity discussed above enable us to draw the following conclusions from what we can term the pragmatic criterion of objectivity (pragmatic in the sense just stipulated).

1. The criterion rules out as meaningless any purported aspects of meaning which are not "confirmable" by sensory observation of empirical phenomena. It thus eliminates all supranatural metaphysics and all absolutes from science, and insofar as philosophers follow suit, from philosophy as well.
2. It ensures that the independent observers who participate in the intersubjective testing will all agree on what crucial observations need to be made to replicate a claim for objectivity, since each of the observations to be made is precisely specified beforehand, and thus the testimony of the participants will be uniformly precise in its relevance.
3. It ensures that the skills required of the participants will be well within the reach of each of them, since only basic perceptual skills, and no highly specialized qualities of intelligence or good judgment are called upon. Thus this ensures that the rule objective validity established by the pooled judgment of the participants has the highest possible reliability.

Popper's criterion of falsifiability is congruent with the above three consequences of the pragmatic criterion for objectivity. So much so that at first glance Popper's criterion of falsifiability may seem to be equivalent to the pragmatic criterion of meaning, differing only in that it is expressed in its logically equivalent negative rather than positive form. However, even though the principles are logical equivalents, an enormous conceptual advance is made by Popper in this deceptively simple but brilliantly original turn from the positive to the negative form of the pragmatic principle. It is to Popper, and to Popper alone, to whom we are indebted for recognizing the importance of the negative form of the principle as expressing most adequately what (rule) objectivity means in science; and once this has been pointed out, simple as it may seem, we can never go back to the positive principle without seeing that it does not quite capture the essence of scientific objectivity.

The germ of the Popperian notion of falsification is actually expressed by Peirce—"the best hypothesis, in the sense of the one most recommending itself to the inquirer, is the one which can be the most readily refuted if it is false" (1.120). But the idea remained a relatively dormant seed until it reached full flower in Popper's philosophy of science.

I am reminded here not only of Columbus and the egg, but of the brilliant and paradoxical reversal of Occam's principle of parsimony by Karl Menger, who points out[16] that the simplicity which is so prized in science and mathematics is sometimes a pseudosimplicity, and that we should be as ready to use what he calls his "prism" to disperse an oversimplified complexity (like the concept of function) into its individually important consitituent concepts, as we are ready to use Occam's razor to prune away an overcomplicated simplicity.

Methodology and Metaphysics: Tychism and Platonic Realism

Peirce is a resolute champion of the doctrine of fallibilism and indeterminism in science and philosophy. In a famous remark, Peirce observes that

> the most refined comparisons of masses, lengths, and angles, far surpassing in precision all other measurements, . . . fall behind the accuracy of bank accounts, and . . . the ordinary determinations of physical constants, such as appear from month to month in the journals, are about on a par with an upholsterer's measurements of carpets and curtains. . . . [6.44]

Similarly, Popper, as Skolimowski has noted in Part II of the present paper (p. 488), holds that there is no secure foundation for knowledge—that we can build only on piles driven into a swamp.

Popper reaches this conclusion from his insistence that to be scientific means to be falsifiable—to be falsifiable means that we can never have absolute truth (which of course could not be falsified). Popper's argument is primarily methodological or epistemological.

Tychism

From similar grounds, Peirce derives a similar conclusion—but he continues beyond science to spin out a metaphysical doctrine which, although it is consistent with fallibilism in the sense in which the term is used above, is neither a necessary nor the only plausible one which would be consistent with it: namely, his doctrine of *Tychism*, or the doctrine that in the world, there is to be found freedom, originality, creativity, indeterminism—which are not dependent on our thinking, and are thus real. These are manifestations, or schemata, of Peirce's important category of Firstness—for which these terms are each in a sense question-begging affirmations of Peirce's faith in their objectivity—a faith which is as cardiac as it is cortical, and which, in the best of company, e.g., Bergson, Whitehead, Boutroux, William James, Hartshorne, and others, I share with Peirce.

Peirce's Tychism is a fully developed metaphysical position which affirms his personal conviction that there are certain manifestations of Firstness in nature, such as real chance, real possiblity, real freedom, real creativity—thus real indeterminism, which would be logically impossible and thus could not even be conceived unless the laws of nature wiggled. And, on Peirce's terms, the conclusion that the laws of nature do in fact wiggle, even if the amount of wiggling is less than we could actually observe, is inescapable; if they did not, there would be no Firstness in the world, no originality, no freedom, no indeterminism, nothing but events inexorably fated to occur, through laws that were absolutely uniform, and thus permitted no exceptions to wiggle out from under their rule.

Accordingly, Peirce *begins* his argument with his metaphysical conclusion, his affirmation of the reality of freedom, spontaneity, creativity, possibility, chance (thus indeterminism), to which he fits the only premise that could support such a conclusion, namely, that the laws of nature are sufficiently irregular to provide for freedom and spontaneity, i.e., that they wiggle.

This despite the fact that (for me) his premise appears to be counterintuitive in at least two respects:

1. The complexity required of laws which could wiggle is so enormous as to make them counterintuitive in their complexity alone, in contrast to the intuitive clarity and simplicity of laws which are perfectly regular and do not wiggle; and
2. Even on the wiggle theory, a certain amount of extrapolation and smoothing of the imperfections of the data is mandatory—some of the discrepancies between our predictions and our results still need to be attributed to imperfections in our measurements.

But for anyone with a cardiac faith in a tychistic metaphysics which affirms the reality of freedom, chance, creativity, indeterminism, counterintuitive though it may be to hold that the laws of nature wiggle—even a minute (unobservable) amount—the counterintuitivity must be ignored and the wiggling of the laws must be postulated as a premise. Otherwise there can be no freedom, chance, spontaneity, creativity, etc. in the universe. Or the argument can be reversed, as I think was the case with Peirce, with the elements of a tychistic indeterminism being postulated as the premises from which it follows, necessarily, that the laws do wiggle.

The major difference between Peirce and Popper here is that Popper remains consistent in his denial of the possibility of ever reaching or knowing absolute laws on strictly methodological and epistemological grounds, and thus does not, as far as I can tell, commit himself to any statement which affirms or denies that the laws wiggle. What his conclusion comes to is that *we can never know, on scientific grounds, that they do not.*

Platonic Realism

What is in some respects the most striking similarity in the metaphysics of both Peirce and Popper is their realistic ontology. For Peirce, whose original formulations of his position were nominalistic, it took many years of sustained reflection and revision for him to move to a consistently realistic ontology. In a recent issue of *The Monist,* Max Fisch points out, in a definitive study of Peirce's progress towards realism,[17] that it was not until 1897 that Peirce can be said to have been successful in moving from nominalism to realism on the important issue of the reality of *possibility.* As late as 1902, Paul Carus, then editor of *The Monist,* charged that Peirce was extremely nominalistic in his views on *necessity,* but in his reply Peirce showed clearly that his ontology was on the contrary thoroughly realistic. The last doubts were dispelled, however, in Peirce's third series of *Monist* articles, which began in 1905. Here Peirce finally purged his pragmatism of the "nominalistic dross" which had tainted its earlier forms by unequivocally rejecting the nominalistic error that "the potential, or possible, is nothing but what the actual makes it to be" (1.422), and affirming instead the objective reality of "real modality, including real necessity and real possibility" (5.457), the objective reality of "real *vagues,* and especially real possibilities" (5.453).

With his fully matured realistic insight, Peirce was then able to solve the famous question about the hardness of the diamond which was kept in a wad of cotton and then burnt in a furnace before it had ever been tested for hardness. His solution, which is implied by his ontology, was that the meaning of 'hardness' is to be understood in terms of the *possible* test that *might have been* made rather than the actual test that never was made. Thus by defining pragmatic meaning in terms of conceivable consequences in experience, rather than by merely actual ones, Peirce was able to make a basic contribution to modal logic which unfortunately seems to have been overlooked by the contemporary logicians who are currently investigating conditional definitions, reduction sentences, and dispositional concepts (cf., the essay by Pap, and Carnap's replies to Pap, in the Schilpp volume on Carnap's philosophy).[18]

Popper's realistic ontology, although it is fundamentally in agreement with Peirce's in accepting the objective reality of the Platonic Forms (which Popper designates as "third world entities" or "intelligibles") contains a striking variation from orthodox forms of Platonism, in his contention that

> the third world is (together with human language) the product of men, just as honey is the product of bees. *Like Language* (and like honey) *it is an unintended and thus an unplanned product of human action*. . . . even the natural numbers are the work of men, the products of human language and of human thought. Yet there is an infinity of such numbers, more than will ever be pronounced by men, or used by computers. And there is an infinite number of true equations between such numbers, and of false equations; more than we can ever pronounce as true, or as false. . . . unexpected new problems arise as an unintended by-product of the sequence of natural numbers; for instance the unsolved problems of the theory of prime numbers. . . . These problems are *autonomous*. They are in no sense made by us; they are discovered by us; and in this sense they exist, undiscovered, prior to their discovery. ["Obj. Mind," pp. 29-30]

Thus in much the same fashion as there was a paradoxical nominalistic ingredient in Peirce's early avowedly realistic ontology, so there is presently a paradoxical subjectivistic ingredient in Popper's avowedly realistic ontology. That the Platonic forms are *man made* is a fascinating conjecture which glows with a spark of plausibility until the question is raised as to how man-made forms differ (except for the accident of their birth) from either (a) forms made by the Deity or (b) forms that never were made but always were. For myself, I can see no difference between them—if there is no trace of subjectivity in the forms after they have come into being, then how they came into being has no operational significance and their subjectivity is vacuous. Thus Popper's interesting variation from orthodoxy seems to me to be provocative and paradoxical but in the end much more in agreement with Peirce's position than different from it. Perhaps as Popper continues to develop his ontology a new shower of Popperian conjectures will produce a new speculation about the Forms that will be less paradoxical and less vacuous—I will wait for it with great interest.

EUGENE FREEMAN

DEPARTMENT OF PHILOSOPHY
SAN JOSE STATE UNIVERSITY
DECEMBER, 1969

II. KARL POPPER AND THE OBJECTIVITY
OF SCIENTIFIC KNOWLEDGE

1. Popper's Problem

> We are not students of some subject matter but students *of problems*. . . . I fail to understand the attraction of philosophy without problems. . . . Only if he [the student of philosophy] understands the contemporary problem-situation in the sciences can the student of the great philosophers understand that they tried to solve urgent and concrete problems. . . . in philosophy methods are unimportant; *any* method is legitimate if it leads to results capable of being rationally discussed. What matters is not methods or techniques but a sensitivity to problems.[19]

So speaks Sir Karl Popper. It will be quite in order therefore to discuss his philosophy in terms of the problems that have preoccupied and perhaps haunted him.[20] Since the reconstruction of all his problems would be beyond the scope of one essay, we shall concentrate on one particular problem which, in our opinion, is crucial for the understanding of his other problems. What is then this crucial problem? The defence and justification of the objectivity and rationality of science and of all human knowledge. Is this the sole characteristic of his philosophy? Certainly not. Was he the first or the only one to defend the rationality and objectivity of scientific knowledge? The answer is again: no. Now, if Popper was not the first and not alone in defending the rationality and objectivity of science, and furthermore if this defence cannot be regarded as the sufficient characterization of his philosophy, why should we insist that this was his main problem? The point is that this was his main problem although he shared it with many others. What he did not share with others, what was unique and original in his philosophy was the manner in which he saw his problem and the way he attempted to solve it.

I contend that in order to understand the work of an original philosopher we must comprehend:

I. the background knowledge-situation which was the source of his reflection;
II. philosophical schools and doctrines against which he developed his own doctrines.

We must thus reconstruct the knowledge-situation within which he was enveloped. But equally importantly we must reconstruct the philosophical battlefield, the theatre of operations within which a given philosopher worked out his ideas. Without reconstructing both we shall be unable to explain specific developments of a given philosopher; we shall be unable to decipher in depth various subtleties of his doctrines; and much of the content may escape us too.

We know very well, from Popper's own writings[21] the background knowledge-situation which was the source of inspiration for his methodological and epistemological views. On the one hand there was Einstein whose theories convinced Popper about the tentative character of all human knowledge, about the fallibility of the most entrenched theories, about the fact that no knowledge is absolute. On the other hand, there were the theories of Freud, Adler and Marx, the examination of which convinced Popper that a theory which cannot be refuted by any empirical test should not be treated on a par with theories which can be tested and refuted by experience. Most if not all theories of "hard" science (physics and chemistry) are testable and refutable by empirical evidence. Hence the criteria was formulated that in order to count as scientific, a given theory must, at least in principle, be refutable. This part of Popper's methodology is very well known and I shall not belabor it any further. But we should never lose sight of the fact that Popper's methodology and his philosophy of science have not merely been refinements of some existing theories, although their anticipation can be traced to various previous thinkers; Popper provided a new methodology which attempts to meet the challenge of a new knowledge situation, Einstein's eclipse of Newton in particular.

Now, what was the philosophical tradition or the school of thought which Popper was primarily fighting against? The philosophers from the Vienna Circle, no doubt. He called them the positivists. And since then this name stuck to the philosophical movement known otherwise as The Vienna Circle. To distinguish them from nineteenth-century positivists, the positivists of the Vienna Circle received the name 'logical positivists' and later—'logical empiricists'.

The first point I wish to make is that Popper's main epistemological and methodological conceptions were worked out and formulated in his conscious opposition to the philosophy of the Vienna Circle. All Popper's doctrines bear the seal, so to speak, of his struggles against the logical empiricists.

The second point I wish to make is that thirty years later Popper acquired new opponents. These opponents derived their initial inspiration from Popper's works, or at any rate shared with Popper some important assumptions as to the nature of science not shared by logical empiricists. But they went too far in 'subjectivizing science'. For this reason Popper started to evolve his philosophy along new lines to combat the peril of subjectivism. By 1960 the controversy between the Vienna Circle and Popper died down. Yet

Popper's ideas underwent during the last decade a new and surprising development. Should we assume that it was an internal development of his former doctrines? Such an assumption would leave us with a perplexing question: why has this development occurred along these specific lines and not others? We must notice at once that Popper's recent doctrines are startling in some respects and do need an explanation if they are to be considered a continuation of his original programme. However, if we assume that Popper reacted to a new knowledge-situation, to new proposals in the philosophy of science, his developments become at once quite clear. It is thus my contention that we must become aware of Popper's new philosophical opponents in order to grasp the essence of his new metaphysics and in order to appreciate the edge of his argument. These new opponents in the 1960s appeared to be Michael Polanyi with his *Personal Kowledge* and above all Thomas Kuhn with his *The Structure of Scientific Revolutions*.[22]

There is one important difference, however. In the 1930s Popper formulated his theories in open, conscious and explicit opposition to the pronouncements of the Vienna Circle. In the 1960s the relation of his new metaphysics and epistemology to the doctrines of his new opponents is much more opaque, elusive and implicit, and consequently is more difficult to trace.

I shall divide Popper's philosophy into two periods. This has mainly an heuristic function. No claim is made that Karl Popper in the first period and Popper in the second period were two different philosophers. The first period lasted until roughly 1960; the second began with the early 1960s and continues. I shall refer to these two periods as:

I. The methodological period,
II. The metaphysical period.

Further examination of Popper's philosophy I trust will justify my terminology.

2. The Methodological Period

Why should we call Popper's first period methodological? Because the methods of the acquisition of knowledge, the logic of scientific discovery, the growth of scientific knowledge are his central concerns.

His worthy opponents, the philosophers from the Vienna Circle, were no less concerned with the objectivity and rationality of scientific knowledge than Popper was. But their approach to science and scientific knowledge was quite different. They studied the *structure* of science. This meant a logical reconstruction of the statements of which science is made. They were interested in the criteria of meaning. These criteria gave them the key to the recognition of the basic cognitive elements which make up science. They also searched for the ultimate components of the structure of knowledge. These components they found in protocol statements depicting the ultimate components of the structure of the empirical world. In pursuing their programme, they were of necessity concerned with the justification of induction. In their view induction was an essential part of the scientific method: from basic facts (ultimate constituents of reality) as expressed by protocol statements, we purportedly arrive at scientific theories via induction.

Now, I contend that Popper's disagreement with logical empiricists was not about this or that particular issue, but was a disagreement about the whole conception of science and thereby the whole conception of human knowledge. The kernel of this disagreement can be expressed by the question: *which is the best road to understanding science—the study of its structure, or the study of its growth*? It is in relation to this question that all the differences between Popper and the logical empiricists should be seen. It is in opposition to the structuralist conception of the Vienna Circle that Popper developed his specific views on the nature of scientific knowledge. It is in this context that we must consider his original ideas about the objectivity and rationality of scientific knowledge.

I shall now contrast Popper's views on various aspects of scientific knowledge with the corresponding views of philosophers from the Vienna Circle.

The contrast here is essentially between the evolutionary or dynamic concept of science and the static or mechanistic concept of science; the former is concerned with the evolutionary growth of science, the latter with the logical structure of science. The justification of the objectivity of science within the static concept of knowledge means the establishment of the firm core of indubitable knowledge (basic protocol statements), and then the logical reduction of other knowledge to this firm core. The justification for the objectivity of science within the dynamic concept of knowledge means the establishment of rational criteria for the acquisition of knowledge and for the understanding of accumulated knowledge. Within the framework of the dynamic concept, which accentuates the acquisition of knowledge, there is no place for absolute knowledge; there is no place for the privileged class of statements which represent the core of indubitable knowledge; there is no place for sense data as the basis of certainty. All these are aspects of the justification of the objectivity of knowledge as can be found in the logical empiricists who represent a prima facie case of a static conception of science.

By contrast, Popper defines objectivity almost in opposite terms. "Now I hold," Popper writes, "that scientific theories are never fully justifiable or verifiable, but that they are nevertheless testable. I shall therefore say that the *objectivity* of scientific statements lies in the fact that they can be *intersubjectively tested*."

My use of the terms 'objective' and 'subjective' is not unlike Kant's. He uses the

ISSUE	LOGICAL POSITIVISTS	POPPER
What should we study in order to understand science?	The structure of science	The growth of science
What is the starting point of our inquiries?	Facts and observation	Problems
What are our basic conceptual units?	Protocol statements	Tentative hypotheses
How do we arrive at scientific theories? Alternatively, what is the process of the acquisition of knowledge?	Simplifying the matter—Induction	The process of conjecture and refutations, that is bold guessing followed by relentless criticism.
What are the foundations of knowledge? Is there indubitable knowledge?	The rock bottom of knowledge are the basic facts given to us in immediate experience and expressible through protocol statements.	There is no rock bottom of knowledge. All knowledge is tentative. The foundations of knowledge are piles driven into a swamp deep enough to carry the edifice of our present knowledge.
How do we distinguish scientific knowledge from nonscientific?	The verifiability principle of meaning enables us to delineate the realm of scientific knowledge from nonscientific.	The principle of demarcation delineates falsifiable theories which are scientific from nonfalsifiable which are not.

word 'objective' to indicate that scientific knowledge should be *justifiable*, independently of anybody's whim: a justification is 'objective' if in principle it can be tested and understood by anybody. If something is valid for anybody in possession of his reason, then its grounds are objective and sufficient.[23]

Against objectivity as grounded in the ultimate components, that is in protocol statements, Popper argues in the following way:

> . . . if we adhere to our demand that scientific statements must be objective, then those statements which belong to the empirical basis of science must also be objective, i.e. intersubjectively testable. Yet intersubjective testability always implies that from the statements which are to be tested, other testable statements can be deduced. Thus if the basic statements in their turn are to be inter-subjectively testable, *there can be no ultimate statements in science:* there can be no statements in science which cannot be tested, and therefore none which cannot in principle be refuted, by falsifying some of the conclusions which can be deduced from them.[24]

And here is a famous statement concerning the foundations of objective knowledge.

> The empirical basis of objective science has thus nothing 'absolute' about it. Science does not rest upon rock-bottom. The bold structure of its theories rises, as it were, above a swamp. It is like a building erected on piles. The piles are driven down from above into the swamp, but not down to any natural or 'given' base; and when we cease our attempts to drive our piles into a deeper layer, it is not because we have reached firm ground. We simply stop when we are satisfied that they are firm enough to carry the structure, at least for the time being.[25]

All the characteristics of objective knowledge, as formulated in *Logik der Forschung* of 1934 (translated as *The Logic of Scientific Discovery* in 1959), are inverse images as it were of the characteristics ascribed to objective knowledge by logical empiricists. In the 1940s, in the period of the *Open Society and Its Enemies*, the conception of objectivity as intersubjective testability was, as Popper puts it, "generalized" and replaced by the more general idea of intersubjective *criticism*, or in other words by "the idea of mutual rational control by critical discussion."[26] Later, in the 1960s, some radical changes occurred in his concept of objectivity; they were radically new formulations, when Popper obviously turned his attention from the Vienna Circle to his new opponents. Before we examine this period, some parallels will be in order.

Traditionally, the objectivity of scientific knowledge implied the recognition of the absolute character of knowledge. In Popper's philosophy the objectivity of knowledge excludes the absoluteness of knowledge: no knowledge which is objective can be absolute. Objective knowledge must be testable; testable means refutable; refutable means nonabsolute.

Traditionally, the certainty of objective knowledge was guaranteed either by an infallible method (as for example in Descartes), or by discovering in nature some ultimate components (for logical empiricists these were 'basic facts'). Popper's conception affirms on the other hand that no objective knowledge can be certain; and hence no ultimate components of any sort can be accepted; on the other hand, it implies that there is no supreme method, no royal road to truth.

Thus, in the fallibilistic concept of knowledge objectivity is divorced from absoluteness, is divorced from certainty, is divorced from the 'hard' facts and 'unbiased' observation, all of which are usually interwoven into one pattern in traditional concepts of objective knowledge.

Now, it appears that during the last decade or so the battle over the nature of science has been resolved in favor of the dynamic, evolutionary concept of knowledge.[27] Leading structuralists, that is the leading adherents to the structural concept of knowledge such as Carnap, Hempel and Nagel, have been able to add some fine finishing touches to their original ideas of how science should be reconstructed in order to form a neat logical edifice. But they were unable to suggest any major novel ideas. Indeed, some structuralists have implicitly and sometimes explicity admitted that the approach they adopted has proved insufficient.[28]

It is therefore quite natural that the most interesting and novel ideas in the philosophy of science during the last decade came from the adherents of the dynamic concept of knowledge. I have in mind here such people as Feyerabend, Kuhn, Lakatos, Polanyi, Toulmin. They have in a way carried on and developed various aspects of Popper's dynamic programme. But sometimes they carried some of these aspects so far, radicalized some of the positions so much that Popper found it necessary to defend himself against other dynamic concepts of science.

Before we proceed further, one final word summarizing the methodological period. Whatever differences can be perceived between Popper and the logical empiricists, and whatever significance we attach to these differences, we must not overlook some fundamental similarities. One was the belief, tenaciously held by both Carnap and Popper, in the rational and objective character of science; another was the idea that a sharp distinction can and should be drawn between science and *non*science. The differences were about *how* to draw this distinction, *how* to define the rationality and objectivity of science.

In the later, metaphysical period the issues are quite different. The growth of science, the bone of contention between Popper and the Vienna Circle, is now taken for granted. What is at stake is the very rationality and objectivity of science, the legitimacy of the distinction between science and *non*science. The issue is no longer how to draw this distinction, but whether there is such a distinction to be drawn at all, whether rationality is an attribute of science, whether there are intersubjective procedures peculiar to science.

Thus, the whole focus has been shifted to problems of greater generality. Science is no longer taken for granted as a clearly discerned and discernable part of human experience. The determination of the nature of science is now seen as inextricably tied to the examination of conceptual frameworks. Conceptual frameworks are now seen as originating cognitive units of science and as determining the character of the problems of science. The conceptual frameworks themselves, however, are now seen as at least partly determined by the nature of language which we find more complex than we had ever imagined. Furthermore, conceptual frameworks are seen in the context of the interaction between existing science and the scientific community which attempts to extend this science, in the context of the interaction of existing science with the minds of particular scientists, and also in the context of the interaction of science with the whole intellectual heritage of the civilisation. Karl Popper has not been swept aside by these developments; on the contrary, he has entered into the main stream of them.

3. The Metaphysical Period

Now, in the 1930s Popper was clearly in the minority and the odd man out when he insisted that no knowledge is absolute, that all knowledge is the product of the *human agent* and as such is fallible (the operative term here is 'human agent'); that the criteria of objective knowledge are to be sought in intersubjective testability which is *social* in character (the operative term here is 'social'); that we do not start with hard facts and pure observation but rely on *larger conceptual units* such as problems and conjectures (the operative term here is 'larger conceptual units'). All these characteristics of human knowledge—its subjective components as related to the human agent, its social character, and the importance of larger conceptual units—became in the course of time radicalized by other adherents of the dynamic concept of knowledge.

The most formidable ally-opponent proved to be Thomas Kuhn with his *The Structure of Scientific Revolutions*. He has provided a paradigm for a dynamic concept of science which has eclipsed all the previous ones. I use the term 'paradigm' here in the Kuhnian sense in all its plasticity and ambiguity. Kuhn's model of science is based on the idea of paradigms. The paradigm of all paradigms is Newtonian physics. Every scientific revolution introduces a new paradigm, a new way of viewing problems, a new way of viewing the universe. After the introduction of a new paradigm there follows a period of routine work called 'normal science': the filling in of all kinds of gaps and little holes predetermined by the paradigm.

I shall not elaborate the Kuhnian model which is well known. And I shall not dwell on the ambiguities of the term 'paradigm'. Most if not all of Kuhn's critics fail to notice that the multiplicity of meanings of the term 'paradigm' is not only its weakness; it is also its forte. One may wonder whether Kuhn's model of science would have become so popular and indeed so challenging to the philosophers of science if the term 'paradigm' had been given one precise meaning.

Now, both Popper's and Kuhn's models of science are evolutionary, are concerned with the growth of science, with the acquisition of new knowledge, with the methodology of scientific research. But there are some important consequences following from Kuhn's ideas which are incompatible with or flatly contradictory to some important contentions of Popper's philosophy of science.

1. Conceptual units which are of primary importance in the rational reconstruction of the growth of knowledge, particularly when the most significant changes occur in science, that is when scientific revolutions happen—are not conjectures and refutations, but something larger, that is paradigms. Paradigms thus provide the framework and the basis and in a sense they originate and determine theories as conceived by Popper. From this it follows that conjectures and refutations as conceptual units of a certain kind are subordinated to more important conceptual units.
2. Scientific theories are hardly ever refuted in actual scientific practice. Kuhn as a matter of fact does not say as some impute it to him that scientific theories are *born refuted*.[29] He says that like old soldiers they fade away. If a discrepancy appears between a theory and empirical evidence, it is hardly ever treated as a refutation of the theory under examination, but rather as an anomaly. The conclusion from this argument thus follows that if theories are not refuted, they are not refutable; if they are not refutable, they are not testable; if they are not testable, there is no criterion (no rational intersubjective criterion at any rate) to distinguish science from nonscience. Such a conclusion not only undermines the criterion of refutability and thus testability of scientific theories, but also the very criterion of rationality and the distinction between science and nonscience.
3. The third argument which can be found in Kuhn is that the acceptance and thus the validity of scientific theories is a matter of the consensus of scientists of a given epoch. From this it follows that there are no universal intersubjective criteria for scientific knowledge, but only criteria which are determined by a social group. This is sociologism.

Before we go any further, I shall distinguish three different kinds of conceptual units corresponding to three different levels of inquiry:

I. facts and observation, of primary importance to logical empiricists and most empiricists;

II. problems, conjectures (theories), and refutations, of primary importance to Popper; on this level 'facts' and 'observation' are guided
and determined by our problems and theories;

III. paradigms, of primary importance to Kuhn. They determine at least
partially not only the content of our theories, but also the comprehension of our 'facts'.

Now, in order to exhibit the limitations of the logical empiricist
programme as a methodology of science, Popper did not argue on the same
level as they did, *within* their framework, with their conceptual units, but he
ascended one level higher and showed so to speak from above that facts and
observation are determined by the structure of theories, by the content of our
problems.

In order to exhibit the limitations of Popper's methodology, Kuhn went
a step higher, to a framework of a higher degree of generality. He disclaimed
theories as basic conceptual units and instead ascended to the framework in
which paradigms are basic units.

In order to counteract Kuhn, Popper had to ascend to a still higher level,
he had to develop a conceptual framework of a still higher degree of generality. The story outlined here is a fascinating one because it involves not so
much a competition of theories but a clash of frameworks. Framework F_2
may be judged "better" than framework F_1 if F_2 subordinates the conceptual
units of F_1 to F_2, and also subordinates the problems of F_1 to the more fundamental problems of F_2.

The crucial debates in the philosophy of science of the last decade has
with increasing sharpness and clarity focussed on conceptual frameworks;
clashes of frameworks, constructions of alternative research programmes
through reformulating basic conceptual units have become the central arena
of the philosophy of science. These debates have been of a fundamental
nature because the framework not only provides conceptual tools and determines the nature of problems, but usually spells out what counts as genuine
science, thereby determining the scope of science; in so doing it implicitly or
explicitly defines the meaning of rationality and the objectivity of science and
not infrequently it suggests the concept of truth. This is why debates over
frameworks are so fascinating and fundamental.

The conclusion that emerges from my remarks is that we have considerable liberty to choose the framework we consider best for our cognitive
purposes. The consequence of this is a form of radical conventionalism:
through different conceptual frameworks, more or less arbitrarily chosen, we
investigate and indeed in some respect constitute different aspects of reality.
A similar thesis was already advanced in the early 1930s by the late Polish
philosopher, Kasimir Ajdukiewicz. The consequences of this version of conventionalism for recent controversies in the philosophy of science are too

numerous and too far-reaching to be discussed here. I shall attempt to deal with them in another place.

Popper's thought, as I have mentioned, has undergone, in recent years, a conspicuous development. His new metaphysical doctrine, which we are to discuss shortly and which he calls interestingly enough "the third world theory," is in fact a new epistemology. It clearly opposes the psychological and the sociological approach to the philosophy of science, in order to restore the objectivity (that is intersubjectivity) and rationality of scientific knowledge apparently undermined by these approaches. Now, even if the three world doctrine was not directly induced by those concepts of knowledge, it remarkably counteracts their consequences.

Popper's doctrine concerning the three worlds has only recently been published, and consequently is not very well known. For this reason I shall sketch it in some detail.

4. The Three Worlds of Karl Popper

What are the three worlds distinguished by Popper? The first is the physical world or the world of physical states. The second is the mental world or the world of mental states. And the third is the world of intelligibles or of ideas in the objective sense, that is the world of possible objects of thoughts or the world of objective contents of thought. All these formulations are Popper's. As we can see, Popper establishes a pluralistic universe. From an epistemological point of view, and particularly from a methodological point of view, the third world (of intelligibles) is all-important.

The third world, and Popper admits this, has much in common with Plato's theory of forms and ideas, and therefore also with Hegel's objective spirit. Popper argues, however, that his theory differs radically in some decisive respects from Plato's and Hegel's, that "it has more in common still with Bolzano's theory of a universe of propositions in themselves and of truths in themselves though it differs from Bolzano's also. My third world resembles most closely the universe of Frege's objective contents of thought."[30]

Now, the three worlds are related to each other. The first two can interact, and the last two can interact as well; but the first and the third cannot. Thus, the second world, the world of subjective or personal experience, interacts on the one hand with the objective physical world, and on the other hand with the world of objective ideas. The division of the three worlds: into the world of material entities, the world of mental entities and the world of cognitive entities, although ontological in character, serves epistemological ends. It is to enable Popper to provide a new justification of the objectivity of scientific knowledge. This justification consists in demonstrating that all knowledge is human invention, but that nevertheless it is in a sense superhuman, that it transcends the social and subjective spheres of particular human beings or groups of human beings.

The third world is the defining characteristic of Popper's new epistemology. "My central thesis is," Popper says, "that any intellectually significant analysis of the activity of understanding has mainly, if not entirely, to proceed by analyzing our handling of third-world structural units and tools."[31] The formulation is a bit clumsy but the intention is quite clear. What are these structural units of which the third world is made? They are intelligibles, that is possible or actual objects of understanding. "Theories, or propositions, or statements," Popper tells us, "are the most important third world linguistic entities." The emphasis that they are *linguistic* is quite characteristic here. The period in which everything "linguistic" was considered an anathema and was exorcised with great gusto is now over. References to Benjamin Lee Whorf are made; he showed, as Popper admits, that language always incorporates many theories in the very structure of its usage.

To repeat, the activity of understanding consists essentially in operating with third world objects, the intelligibles. The *intelligibilia* are "as objective as *visibilia* which are physical bodies and virtual or possible objects of sight."

Now, the justification of the objectivity of scientific knowledge and of all knowledge lies in the fact that the third world is *autonomous*, but not autonomous in the traditional Platonic sense in which the autonomy of ideal forms (third-world entities) entails their absolute transhuman character. Popper's third world is autonomous but at the same time a product of the human mind.

> One can accept the reality, or as it may be called, the autonomy of the third world, and at the same time admit that the third world is a product of human activity. One can even admit that the third world is man-made and, in a very clear sense, superhuman at the same time.[32]

Genetically speaking the third world is a human product; its ontological status is, however, now autonomous. We can act upon this world and contribute to its growth, but all our individual contributions are "vanishingly small." The autonomy of the third world consists also of the fact that it has grown far beyond the grasp of any man, even of all men. "Its action upon us has become at least as important for its growth as our creative action upon it."

Thus, the objectivity of scientific knowledge is no longer sought in intersubjective criticizability, in the testability of theories by the enlightened, critical and rational scientific community, but in the autonomy of the third-world entities. The independent status of these entities is the guarantee of the objectivity of scientific research and of scientific theories. This new objectivism, as J. W. N. Watkins calls it (under no circumstances to be confused with the "objectivism" of Ayn Rand!), may be regarded as a mitigated version of Platonism (see section 4.4 of Watkins's paper in this volume).

Now, whether a very mitigated version of Platonism is Platonism or not I shall not dispute here. But we shall notice that this justification of the objectivity of scientific knowledge (within the third-world doctrine) is *quite* different from the one formulated and defended in *The Logic of Scientific Discovery* and in *Conjectures and Refutations*. As I have suggested, different conceptual frameworks constitute different concepts of objectivity and different extensions for science.

Popper's new objectivism on the one hand effectively combats psychologism and sociologism in contemporary philosophy of science, but on the other invites serious criticism. I shall discuss these two points in their stead. Before I do that, a few words of comment about other conceptual schemes will be in order.

In the era when entire conceptual frameworks are radically manipulated, it is customary not to discuss the opponent's views within his own framework, but to translate them into one's own. The more flexible and open-ended is our framework, the more room it leaves for manoeuvre. Hence a tendency has developed to make our frameworks as plastic and open-ended as possible. Paul Feyerabend and Imre Lakatos represent extreme examples of this tendency. They are allegedly concerned with methodological research programmes which would be most effective in the acquisition of new scientific knowledge. In the quest for a fruitful methodology, they become insensitive to the requirements of conceptual consistency. The result is a stark conceptual chaos; in their frameworks there is *no* possibility of distinguishing science from nonscience, of defining science, of formulating the criterion of rationality and objectivity for scientific knowledge. We are thus offered very interesting methodological schemes for the effective acquisition of scientific knowledge, but the point is that we are not at all certain that what we are going to acquire is *scientific* knowledge.

But Karl Popper, for whom scientific knowledge, in spite of its fallible character, has been the supreme accomplishment of mankind, and as such had to be separated from other realms of human experience, would not tolerate its characteristics being blurred for the sake of acquiring a fruitful methodology. The third-world doctrine, as I have mentioned, is an attempt to preserve the objectivity of science from the onslaughts of sociologism and psychologism. Science is thus saved from sociological relativism because scientific theories are not at the mercy of the community of scholars of a given epoch. On the contrary, this community itself is only a fragment of the whole process of the development of the autonomous third world. And it is also saved from psychological individualism (a la Polanyi) because individual scientists do *not* create science at will or according to their whims, but they are all of them little workers working on a vast assembly line and their contributions, however great individually and however idiosyncratic in their nature, are "vanishingly small" from the standpoint of the entire third world.

Now, the difficulty of Popper's position and hence his vulnerability to criticism lies in the relation between the third and the second worlds. The third-world entities (intelligibilia) are autonomous; and so are the second-world entities (mental acts) because the three worlds exist independently of each other, although related to one another. The term 'related' is crucial here; particularly as far as the second and the third worlds are concerned. The third world is entirely a human creation; it is autonomous but a product of the human mind. The activity of an individual mind belongs to the second world (of mental entities, of *acts* of comprehension). But on the other hand, the products of this activity become the third-world entities: meanings of statements, contents of thought. Now, how is it possible that mental activity (all the acts of which belong to the second world) may result in products which are a part of the third world if there is no similarity whatever between entities of these two worlds? Popper does not explain. In his framework this is a very mysterious occurrence. It seems that unless we postulate a superhuman third world in the classical Platonic sense (independent for its existence from human beings), we shall be in constant difficulty when we maintain that cognitive acts do take place in the second world, but that nevertheless cognitive results (so to speak a by-product of these acts) are a part of the autonomous third world.

I shall thus advance a thesis that unless we are able to demonstrate that the *process of understanding*, that is the mental activity which takes place within the minds of particular individuals, *has its roots in the third world of intersubjective entities*, the ghost of nineteenth-century psychologism will haunt the edifices of objective knowledge. Popper is perfectly aware of this ghost of psychologism. He makes strenuous efforts to "objectify" the second world. Indeed, the title of the paper he delivered to the XIVth International Congress of Philosophy in Vienna in 1968 bears the conspicuous title "On the Theory of the Objective Mind." Although the effort is strenuous, it is not successful.

I shall now examine the relationship between the second and the third worlds as conceived by Popper, and attempt to demonstrate that he has failed to provide a theory of *objective* mind. As an alternative, in the last section of this part of our essay, I shall suggest my own theory of objective mind. This theory develops Popper's program of objective knowledge beyond Popper's own position.

What then are the relationships between the second and the third worlds according to Popper? I shall let Popper speak.

It seems to me important to describe the relationships of the three worlds in this way; that is with the second world as the mediator between the first and the third. Although rarely stated, this view seems to me clearly involved in the three world theory. According to this theory, the human mind can see a physical body in the *literal sense* of 'see' in which the eyes participate in the process. It can also 'see' or 'grasp' an arithmetical or a geometrical object; a number, or a geometrical figure. But although in this sense 'see' or 'grasp' is used in a *metaphorical way*, it nevertheless denotes a real relationship between the mind and its intelligible object, the arithmetical or geometrical object; and the relationship is *closely analogous* to 'seeing' in the literal sense. Thus the mind *may be linked* with objects of both the first and the third world.[33] [Italics mine]

We have here in one passage four different relationships ascribed to the activity of the mind in grasping objects of the third world: (i) 'seeing' in the literal sense, (ii) 'seeing' in the metaphorical sense, (iii) a relationship closely analogous to seeing, and (iv) the assertion that the mind may be linked with objects of the third world. It should not be assumed that it is easy to describe the relationship between any two cognitive orders. All the same, Popper's description is very unilluminating. We still do not know how subjective cognitive acts lead to intersubjective cognitive results. All Popper's difficulties on this issue stem, in my opinion, from one source, namely from Popper's insistence that there is no similarity *whatsoever* "on any level of problems between contents and the corresponding processes," that is between the entities of the second and the third world. This is emphatically pronounced on more than one occasion. Popper seems to assume that the recognition of any such similarity is a concession to psychologism. It seems to follow for him that to recognize such a similarity is to identify intelligibles with thought processes. To make this identification is to dissolve the autonomy of the third world, is to remove the objective grounds for our knowledge, is simply to dissolve the objectivity of knowledge.

Such a consequence would indeed be pernicious. But there is no cause for alarm. For to recognize a *similarity* between two kinds of entities is not the same as identifying one with the other. But even in the process of identification of objects (entities), shall we say A and B, we do not obliterate B if we identify it with A. Only in mathematics, if A is identified with B, is it indistinguishable from B. In epistemology we do not operate with formal identities of the sort we use in mathematics.

Furthermore, even if we do identify (in some sense of 'identify') entities of the second and the third world, it is not necessarily the case that we identify entities of the third world with entities of the second world and thereby, as Popper seems to suggest, reduce the third world to the second one and consequently deprive the third world of its autonomy. We have another possibility, however, namely to identify (in one sense of the term 'identify') the second world with the third world, to establish in other words that entities of the second world in some important sense resemble entities of the third world, to demonstrate that *the processes of thinking in the individual mind become cognitive processes if and only if they are carried on through structural units of the third world.* This will be the line of my argument.

5. Language and Mind

I suggest that there is not only a similarity but a strict parallelism between the structure of the mind and the structure of our knowledge, between the structural units of the third world and the structural units of the second world.

Now, let us suppose that there is no similarity, no parallelism of any kind, as Popper contends, between the entities of the third world and the entities of the second world. How then can the mind handle knowledge? How can it grasp intelligibles—". . . it is one of the main functions of the second world to *grasp* [italics mine] the objects of the third world," says Popper. And he adds "This is something we all do: it is part of being human to learn language and this means, essentially to learn to grasp *objective thought contents* (as Frege called them)."[34] To repeat again, how can the mind participate in knowledge which belongs to the third world if, in the process of thinking, there is neither parallelism nor any kind of resemblance to the structural units which express the results of these thoughts? How can such a mind extend existing knowledge?

It is clear that if there is no similarity between these two worlds, between entities characteristic of these worlds, then there is no possibility for the mind to comprehend knowledge which belongs to the third world. If on the other hand the mind does comprehend it, and furthermore does extend this knowledge, it is because somewhere between the second and the third world there occurs a calibration of mental acts of the mind into cognitive structures which express the content of these acts.

Assuming the validity of Popper's contention that all knowledge is man made, but that it nevertheless transcends particular men, and indeed all men, and that its action upon us is no less important than our action upon it, I shall argue that objective mind is an aspect of objective knowledge; that it is, in other words, an aspect of the third world. Put differently, I shall argue that we can talk about the mind as a "subjective instrument" through which an individual grasps universal knowledge and at the same time to treat this "instrument," and all its cognitive functions as a component of objective knowledge.

Popper has emphasized that "it is part of being human to learn language and this means essentially to grasp objective thought content," that "language always incorporates many theories in the very structure of its usage." These are very interesting and revealing statements. Putting his case in this manner Popper invites us to examine the entire issues (of the objectivity of knowledge and of the mind) through the medium of language.

In recent years, Noam Chomsky has been a foremost champion of the view that an appropriate investigation of the structure of language may lead to far-reaching epistemological consequences. Chomsky is specifically concerned with the process of the acquisition of language. And his main question is: What kind of structure must our mind possess to make the acquisition of language, especially by the child, possible?

What is primarily at stake is to determine the so-called 'deep structures' which are innate structures. These structures are responsible for the diversity of linguistic forms characteristic of the 'surface structures' dealt with by ordinary grammars. But "a consideration of the nature of linguistic structure can shed some light on certain classical questions concerning the origin of ideas."[35] "This investigation may reveal to us some of the specific mechanisms that enable us to acquire knowledge from experience, specific mechanisms that provide a certain structure and organization, and no doubt certain limits and constraints on human knowledge and systems of belief . . . we can hope to learn [from this investigation] some important things about the nature of human intelligence and the products of human intelligence."[36]

Thus Chomsky's theory of language, which he calls *generative grammar* (as it is concerned with the structures that enable mind to generate new linguistic forms and new knowledge), embraces a large field and implies a number of important consequences.

One of them is a doctrine of innate ideas, and another is psychologism. In Chomsky the two are related to each other: psychologism, which he calls 'mentalism', seems to 'follow' from the doctrine of innate ideas. Now, Chomsky's merit in revealing the bewildering complexity of the structure of language cannot be overrated. We shall return later to the concept of the linguistic mind implied in his theory. Chomsky's mentalism and his doctrine concerning innate ideas, on the other hand, are questionable, if not entirely spurious.

Chomsky says ". . . it is natural to expect a close relation between innate properties of the mind and features of linguistic structure: *for language*, after all, *has no existence apart from its mental representation*"[37] (italics mine). Thus, mentalism implies the reduction, to use Popper's terminology, of the autonomous third world of cognitive entities to the second world of mental entities. The doctrine of innateness, on the other hand, if it is to include a hypothesis about linguistic universals, implies the denial of the growth of scientific concepts. We shall discuss these two issues in some detail.

First, one more general point. I have already mentioned that Popper stubbornly resists the idea of a close relationship between mental entities and cognitive entities. Chomsky on the other hand goes overboard in the other

direction: he 'mentalizes' the autonomous third world of Popper. The consequence of the first (Popper's) position is that the function of the mind in
'grasping' cognitive content and in extending knowledge is mysterious. The
consequence of the second (Chomsky's) position is that it undermines the objectivity of scientific knowledge.

Now, Chomsky's mentalism, if it is meant to be a resurrection of
nineteenth-century psychologism, is open to all the objections to which psychologism is vulnerable; particularly to the objections related to the distinction between the *act* of cognition being mental and thus subjective, and the
result of cognition being intersubjective content meaningful in virtue of the
language in which it has been expressed.[38] Thus, all the epistemological perils
inherent in psychologism: its subjectivization of science and in the final
analysis its subjective idealism are hidden in the concept of mentalism. If
mentalism, on the other hand, is not meant to be a resurrection of psychologism, then it is a misnamed doctrine whose obscurity will have to be
considerably clarified.

What are the linguistic universals allegedly planted in the structure of
our mind? Chomsky is tantalizingly evasive in describing them in detail.[39]
Their general characteristics follow from a rationalist conception of the nature of language and a rationalist conception of the acquisition of knowledge.
The essence of both is the view that "the general character of knowledge, the
categories in which it is expressed or internally represented, and the basic
principles that underlie it, are determined by the nature of the mind." From
which it follows that "The role of experience is only to cause the innate
schematicism to be activated and then to be differentiated and specified in a
particular manner."[40] Thus, "Experience serves to elicit, not to form, these
innate structures." Or in still another manner, the stimulation "provides the
occasion for the mind to apply certain innate interpretive principles, certain
concepts that proceed from 'the power of understanding' itself. . . ."[41]
Chomsky thus postulates innate 'categories', 'concepts', 'linguistic universals'
(". . . a characteristic feature of current work in linguistics is its concern for
linguistic universals. . . . ").

We can discern two distinctive theses in Chomsky's contentions: (i) that
there are cognitive structures of the mind; and (ii) that these structures are innate. Clearly, we can assert (i) without asserting (ii); in other words, (ii) does
not follow logically or epistemologically from (i).

I shall now argue that 'linguistic universals', 'innate concepts', 'inborn
categories', in sum all those phrases which purport to denote inborn,
specifically linguistic structures are either used in a figurative sense, or, if
used in the literal sense, are refuted by the actual growth of scientific
knowledge.

The shortest possible form of our argument can be presented as follows:

if there are innate *concepts* (categories, linguistic universals), then there is no *growth* of concepts; if there *is* growth of concepts, then there are no *innate* concepts; but in fact there *is* growth of concepts, therefore there are no innate concepts. This growth of concepts is exemplified particularly in the history of scientific knowledge; these concepts, it must be emphatically stressed, are not trivial or marginal, but essential for our understanding of the universe.

I shall, of course, disallow that innate concepts (categories) can change their nature, can, in other words, 'grow'; if they are innate, they do not change; if they do change, they are not innate. Chomsky might argue at this point that what is innate are *ideas*, not concepts or categories. I may then retort: how are these ideas related to concepts and categories? What part or aspect of the concept is the 'idea' supposed to be? How does an idea become a concept? And furthermore, how are these 'innate ideas' related to the growth of concepts? Unless the relation of 'innate ideas' to concepts and the categories of science is made clear, I shall have to regard them as mysterious or devoid of meaning.

Now, what kind of arguments are left for rescuing the doctrine of innate concepts? Can we question the notion of the *growth* of concepts? Hardly, for the history of science is the history of the growth of concepts. The extensions of knowledge and the refinements of scientific theories are inseparably linked with the growth of concepts. Concepts thus grow, change, undergo metamorphosis. It is sufficient to mention the evolution of such concepts as 'force' and 'gravity' to realize at once that their pre-Newtonian meaning was different from the meaning they acquired in Newtonian mechanics, and still different within the system of Einstein's physics: extensions and refinements of scientific knowledge are responsible for these consecutive metamorphoses. If this is so, then there are no innate concepts of 'force' or 'gravity', for if there were, which ought to be considered innate: pre-Newtonian, Newtonian, or Einsteinian? Or consider the extraordinary evolution of the concept of 'matter'. Which of its successive embodiments (and there were dozens usually reflecting the state of scientific knowledge at a given time) is to be considered the innate one? It must be observed at the same time that the concept of *matter* is not a marginal one. If there were innate concepts, this concept ought to be among them. Or finally, let us take the concept of 'innate ideas' itself. It means something different now from what it meant in Locke's time. We do not attach different meanings to concepts because we have become bored with their existing meaning. They acquire different meanings because they grow and evolve. And this is so in relation to all important concepts making up the corpus of scientific knowledge. Thus, if we admit that concepts do grow and change, we *cannot* uphold the thesis of innate concepts, in its classical sense at least.

Now, is it still possible to maintain any sort of doctrine of innate concepts (ideas) *after* we have recognized the evolution of scientific knowledge? It is indeed, if we are prepared to bear the consequences. There are at least two courses left to us.

We may postulate an innate, permanent and unalterable programming in our mind (involving specific concepts and categories) which is compatible with the changes in scientific knowledge. But then we shall have to assume, as Plato did, that various stages in the evolution of science are not really the result of the *evolution* of science, but rather they represent the process of the unfolding of constant, unalterable categories. Evolution does not concern the growth of concepts in this case because we are committed to the universe of constant concepts which do not change. This is a logical possibility, but a rather far-fetched one.

Another possibility is to assume that the innate programming, innate concepts and categories *change* during the process of the growth of knowledge. Such a doctrine no doubt would be burdened with perplexing enigmas. We would have to explain *why* the changes in the innate programming fit the changes in scientific knowledge so remarkably. In order to maintain that this cognitive programming is innate, that is to say is not caused by external circumstances such as the growth of science, we would have to assume that this 'fit' is coincidental. If we were to assume that it is not, that is that it might have been caused by external circumstances, then we would in fact renounce the doctrine of innate ideas.

To conclude our discussion. The growth of scientific knowledge forces upon us the following alternatives regarding the doctrine of innate ideas:

(i) to abandon the doctrine of innate ideas;

(ii) to build into our innate doctrine a stipulation that innate concepts can evolve, a rather peculiar doctrine of innateness;

(iii) to assume that there are innate elements in the cognitive structure of the mind, cognitive dispositions of the mind which facilitate the emergence of concepts and ideas.

6. On the Concept of the Linguistic Mind

It is clear that Chomsky's impetuous antibehaviorist campaign led him to an untenable position in regard to the concept of mind. One can uphold a rationalist conception of mind, in the traditional sense of the term, that is, one can maintain that the mind is an active organ in the acquisition of language and of knowledge, and specifically that the cognitive structure of mind is a linguistic one, *without* at the same time being committed to the doctrine of innate ideas.

In the pages that follow I shall propose a model for science and the mind that combines the rationalist conception of mind with an evolutionary conception of science. This model stems from the conviction that the rationalist conception of mind cannot be systematically developed if the evolutionary conception of science is totally disregarded; on the other hand, the evolutionary conception of science cannot be consistently maintained without assuming a rationalist conception of mind. Furthermore, it appears that only if we combine the two can we arrive at a satisfactory justification of the objectivity of scientific knowledge and of objective mind.

Now, to reiterate and emphasize some of the points that have been already mentioned in relation to the concept of the linguistic mind. The increase of our knowledge does not consist merely in the accumulation of more and more facts of the same kind, which is the quantitative growth of knowledge, but consists also in the comprehension of these facts with increasing depth which is the qualitative growth of knowledge. The latter is achieved through the construction of more powerful theories which give a more penetrating and more complete account of phenomena, and which reveal relationships not dreamt of before. The explanation of the growth of knowledge in depth is inconceivable if the mind were just a passive receptor, postulated by the behaviorists; on the other hand, this is entirely conceivable if we think of the mind as endowed with cognitive structures which can originate new cognitive structures. How do these new cognitive structures come into being? In other words, how do we extend existing knowledge? By articulating theories and explanations which have been only half-articulated, ambiguous, incoherent before. How does this articulation occur? There is no articulation without elucidations of language. Thus the growth of knowledge is inseparable from the growth of language which means introducing new concepts, splitting existing concepts, discovering in language hidden ambiguities, clarifying the multitude of meanings compressed in one term, refining the penumbra of uncertainty surrounding concepts. These elucidations of language—the discovery of new concepts for new contents, and the endowment of old concepts with new meanings—are essential for that function of the mind which is called creativeness and which is indispensible for extending existing knowledge.

Thus, the growth of science means increasing the content of scientific theories and enriching the language of science. This growth has neither been smooth nor linear, and its convulsions are reflected in the twists of language with its conceptual shifts, changes in meaning, metamorphoses of concepts. Changes in language follow like a shadow the changes in the content of science. But it must also be remembered that new content of science can only be expressed through new concepts.

The human mind is a linguistic mind. Human knowledge is linguistic knowledge. Knowledge, particularly scientific knowledge, must possess content. Content must be expressible through symbols. Symbols organized in coherent wholes are languages. Language is thus understood here in a broad sense. Any coherent system of symbols may be considered as language. It is a condition *sine qua non* of objective knowledge that it must be expressed by means of intersubjective symbols. It is thus in this sense that human knowledge is linguistic knowledge.

The growth of the language of science reflects the growth of science. But at the same time the growth of the language of science is a reflection of our mental growth. Thus in the second sense, the growth of the language of science reflects the growth of our mind—that is, the cognitive structure of mind. In language we witness the culmination and crystallization of two aspects of the same cognitive development: one aspect related to the content of science; the other aspect related to our *acts* of comprehension of this content. Since it is inconceivable to express any of these two aspects without language—because language unites them both—we are bound to conclude that there is a parallel conceptual development of the content of science, as expressed through the outer language of science, and the inner mental structures of the mind, as expressed through inner acts of understanding. Since fundamental concepts through which we grasp and express our knowledge of the world have changed and evolved, it is fair to conclude that the structure of our mind has changed and evolved as well. The conclusion that our examination leads us to is that the structure of the mind, the conceptual arrangement of the mind mirrors the structure and the limitations of the knowledge by which they have been shaped. Mental structures depend for what they are on the corresponding development of science and of all knowledge. Thus *the conceptual structure of the mind changes with shifts and developments in the structure of our knowledge.*

At this point we must assume that there is a parallel conceptual development of our knowledge and of the mind. Knowledge forms the mind. The mind formed by knowledge develops and extends knowledge still further which in turn continues to develop the mind. Thus there is a continuous process of interaction between the two. Although they are independent categories as far as their meaning is concerned, viewed in the overall cognitive development, knowledge and mind are functionally dependent on each other and indeed inseparable from each other. They are two sides of the same coin; two representations of the same cognitive order. The concept of mind must include knowledge which has formed it and which it possesses.

The mind without knowledge is like an unprogrammed computer. The analogy with the computer enables us to see another peculiar characteristic of the mind. While the computer can operate only with the knowledge programmed into it, the mind on the contrary can, so to speak, up-programme itself. While it functions, it can arrive at results which transcend its original programming. This process of up-programming during problem solving is absolutely essential for both the growth of knowledge and the

growth of the mind. If the mind did not possess this ability, it would be exactly like a computer, retrieving and transforming knowledge according to the
patterns built into it, according to its strictly formalized programming. We
may carry the parallels between the two a step further and say that the mind
is a very peculiar kind of computer, a computer which has programmed into
it the ability to go beyond the limits of its programming, beyond the limits of
itself, which is in a way a contradiction in terms. This is why the mind is *not* a
computer.

7. The Conceptual Net of Science and the Conceptual Structure of the Mind

The changing state of science means the changing content of science.
The total content of science is expressed by the totality of concepts and their
relationships. This totality of concepts is sometimes called the conceptual apparatus of science. I shall call this totality of concepts, using Popper's phrase,
"the conceptual net" of science. We can talk about the net of science *in toto*
as well as about the conceptual net of a particular science, for example
physics. The net of Newtonian physics includes Newton's laws and other laws
following from them, as well as the philosophical presuppositions concerning
the absoluteness of space and time and the constancy of matter. But it also includes terms and concepts which belong basically to other sciences, such as
chemistry and biology. And in addition it includes many terms and expressions of ordinary language.

Now, the three expressions "the conceptual net," "the conceptual
framework," and "the conceptual apparatus" are akin in their meanings and
can often be used interchangeably. The conceptual framework usually
describes the outline, the skeleton within which other concepts are located
and to which they are related. By "the conceptual apparatus" we usually
mean an aggregate of all technical terms specific to a given science. "The
conceptual net" of a science, as the term is used here, comprises them both
and also includes many expressions which are, strictly speaking, not expressions of this science, but which nevertheless are necessary to account for
its content. For example, the logical particles, such as "or," "and,"
"if . . . then," "not" are included in the language of every science. And so are
many expressions of ordinary language.

To repeat, by the conceptual net of science I shall understand the totality
of concepts by means of which the content of science is expressed. Such a
totality cannot be formalized. To formalize it would require explicating its
formalism in terms which do not belong to it. Such an explication would require a still larger conceptual framework which in turn could not be formalized in its own terms. The conceptual net of a given science is thus not an
easily definable entity because (i) it merges with the nets of other sciences, (ii)
because it merges with ordinary language, and (iii) most significant of all,

because it changes historically. We may attempt to formalize a part of the content of science either for aesthetic reasons or for the sake of logical clarity. But we must be aware that it is only a part of the content that has been formalized.

The development of the conceptual net with its complicated mesh of interrelationships is thus an inseparable element in the growth of science. But this is only a part of the history of science, of the history of human cognition. This part may be called *external*. It is external because our knowledge, once formulated in language, could in theory be assimilated by nonhumans. We may imagine that, after a holocaust which annihilates all human beings, some extraterrestrial intelligences visit our planet and discover our learned treatises and thus assimilate our knowledge. In assimilating this knowledge they would have to decipher the conceptual net within which our knowledge is situated. Briefly, if formulated by means of concepts and expressed through intersubjective language, knowledge becomes external to the mind. In theory nonhumans can learn and assimilate it. Needless to say, the external part of objective knowledge corresponds to Popper's third world.

Now, the other part of human cognition is internal. It is internal because it takes place in the mind. We ought to distinguish here between cognitive *acts* and cognitive *results*. Cognitive acts occur in the mind. They are the internal part of the process of cognition. The internal part thus corresponds to Popper's second world. But with a difference, because Popper contends that there is no similarity between structural units of the third world and the processes of comprehension through which we grasp the content of these third-world units; while we insist that there is a very close similarity between these two levels. Cognitive acts represent the structure of the mind which has been formed by the third-world units. Cognitive results on the other hand are theories and statements—linguistic utterances or other symbolic representations which express the content of these acts; they are the external part. Expressed by means of intersubjective language congnitive acts become externalized. Their content becomes independent of particular minds.

Now, in order to develop science the mind must possess concepts through which it can grasp the content of science. Kant called these basic concepts through which knowledge is apprehended "the schemata of the mind." We need not accept Kant's notion of the schemata and his model of the mind in order to recognize that the mind follows certain prestructured patterns in apprehending knowledge. I shall call these patterns *the patterns of thought*. We have an inherent tendency to think about certain subject matters in specific categories and specific patterns of thought.

Patterns of thought are the units in which knowledge is organized. They correspond to Popper's intelligibilia, structural units of the third world. I thus extend the idea of structural units to both the third and the second worlds. Scientific knowledge is highly organized. Organizing units or patterns of thought enable us to structure knowledge into intelligible forms. Patterns of thought are thus forms through which knowledge becomes intelligible. Again, we do not have to assume absolute forms of intelligibility and absolute categories of the mind in order to recognize that some patterns of thought are more crucial for the growth and comprehension of knowledge than others.

Every new hypothesis is an invention of a new possible world. The development of science during the last century has proved that so many of these inventions fit nature beautifully (although at first they appeared to be bizarre and impossible) that there seems to be no limit to the imagination. The consequence following from this contention is that in the future the human mind may organize knowledge of the world in such fantastic and "impossible" units (patterns, categories, forms), that is to say fantastic and impossible from our contemporary point of view, that whatever presupposition we lay down as necessary for today will be shattered tomorrow. Radically new ways of organizing knowledge may not only bring changes in our picture of the world, but also in our understanding of such concepts as *rationality* and *intelligibility*. After all, the concepts of rationality and intelligibility are by-products of the development of our knowledge.

Now, specific patterns of thought are not given to us *deus ex machina*. My central thesis is that there is an isomorphism between the conceptual network of science and the conceptual order of the mind, that is to say that *the conceptual development of science is paralleled by the conceptual development of the mind*. Science, that is the conceptual network of science, forms the mind. But the mind does not remain passive. It interacts and transforms the network. The conceptual arrangement of the mind with its specific patterns of thought and its specific categories thus mirrors the development of the conceptual net of science with its complicated mesh of concepts and their relationships. These continuous interactions between the mind and science are in actual fact interactions between the mind of an individual scientist and a particular science. But the result of these individual interactions constitutes a new stage in the development of science and a new stage in the conceptual development of the mind. Science and the mind are thus historical entities. An historical approach is required to do justice to various phases of the development of science and mind. Our criteria for appraisal must be situated in an historical context.

To reiterate: the arguments concerning the relationship between Popper's third and second worlds: there is and there must be a parallelism between the structural units of the third world (the intelligibles) and the entities of the second world through which we grasp and comprehend the content of scientific statements and theories. We comprehend them because the cognitive order is as it were grafted onto the mind. It is only by recognizing the mind as a part of the growth of knowledge that we can arrive at a consistent idea of objective knowledge and thereby a consistent justification of the objectivity of knowledge.

Like the computer the mind can only function if it has knowledge stored in it. If there is no knowledge stored in it, that is knowledge in the objective sense as exemplified by scientific knowledge, there is no comprehension of the content of statements and theories. But unlike the computer, as we have emphasized, the mind can go beyond the limits of its original cognitive programming and produce new knowledge. New knowledge means a new cognitive programming.

In summary, the notion of objectivity here proposed is based on the recognition that there is a parallelism between the conceptual development of knowledge and the conceptual development of mind: they depend on each other and limit each other. The mind cannot transcend existing knowledge too far because it mirrors the conceptual limitations of knowledge. If a mind makes too revolutionary a leap and goes far beyond existing knowledge, then the person possessing this mind is at worst confined to a lunatic asylum, and at best is considered a crackpot. Why? Because other minds conditioned by the current knowledge cannot comprehend the validity of his leap. Occasionally such a crackpot is rediscovered later. It may happen, when we have updated our conceptual net in the light of our later knowledge, that such a leap fits perfectly into the structure of the more recent knowledge.

The justification for the objectivity of scientific knowledge given above is that (1) it accepts Kuhn's historical and social approach, but it escapes the dangers of irrationality inherent in Kuhn's conception; (2) it accepts Popper's conception of the third world of intelligible entities which are man made and yet transhuman, but it escapes the difficulties in which Popper found himself by denying that there is any resemblance between the entities of the second and the third world; (3) it accepts Chomsky's idea of the structures of mind, being responsible for the acquisition of language and of knowledge, but it avoids the pitfalls of Chomsky's innatism which is incompatible with the growth of scientific knowledge.

Henryk Skolimowski

Department of Humanities
The University of Michigan, Ann Arbor
December, 1969

III. Peirce and Popper — Similarities and Differences

1. The Conception of Science

There is no novel idea in modern and contemporary philosophy which could not ultimately be traced to ancient Greece.

To find an anticipation of a novel thought or a doctrine is not difficult. The roots of all important doctrines are as long as our intellectual tradition. To find a *striking* anticipation of a doctrine or thought is another matter. For a striking anticipation means that two thinkers quite independently arrived at very similar positions. Such is the case we believe with Peirce and Popper.

Popper was first alerted to the writings of Peirce by reading Gallie's Commentary in 1952. By this time Popper's own philosophy was for the most part fully formed, so that the striking similarities which are here and there found between his philosophy and that of Peirce are evidence that they were caught up in the same conceptual net, and that their philosophic temperaments were sufficiently alike, so that they responded in similar fashion to similar influences.

We have already mentioned some of the similarities between Peirce and Popper. We shall now summarize the most relevant points of their philosophies of science. The first no doubt is their conception of science. In a very nontrivial sense they shared the same notion of science: science as inseparable from its growth, to be understood in its growth, and through its growth. It is thus an evolutionary, dynamic and historical conception of science.

Peirce explicitly says:

> Let us remember that science is a pursuit of living men, and that its most marked characteristic is that when it is genuine, it is in an *incessant state of metabolism and growth*. . . . Most of the classifications of the sciences have been classifications of systematized and established knowledge—which is nothing but the exudation of *living science*. . . . [1.232] [Italics ours]

And in the same vein,

> Let us look upon science—the science of today—as a *living* thing. [6.302] . . . by science we all habitually mean a *living and growing* body of truth. [6.304] [Italics ours]

The crucial role of conjecture in science is noted by Peirce in the following (Popperian) observation, " . . . science itself, the living process, is busied mainly with conjectures, which are either getting framed or getting tested" (1.234).

The current fashion of defining philosophy as that which philosophers do when they are doing philosophy is anticipated by Peirce in some similar remarks he makes in defining science:

> If we are to define science, not in the sense of stuffing it into an artificial pigeonhole where it may be found again by some insignificant mark, but in the sense of characterizing it as a living historic entity, we must conceive it as that about which such men as I have described busy themselves. [1.44]

I have already remarked that a definition of science in general which shall express a really intelligent conception of it as a living historic entity must regard it as the occupation of that peculiar class of men, the scientific men. [1.99]

Here is what Popper has to say about the nature of science as rooted in its growth.

I assert that continued growth is essential to the rational and empirical character of scientific knowledge; that if science ceases to grow it must lose that character. [C.&R., 215]

Or in the as yet unpublished 1961 Herbert Spencer Lecture, "Evolution and the Tree of Knowledge,"

All this may be expressed by saying that the growth of our knowledge is the result of something like a natural selection of hypotheses: our knowledge consists, at every moment, of those hypotheses which have shown their fitness by surviving so far in their struggle for existence; a struggle which eliminates those hypotheses which are unfit.

This interpretation may be applied to animal knowledge, pre-scientific knowledge, and scientific knowledge. What is peculiar to scientific knowledge is this: that the struggle for existence is made harder by the conscious and systematic criticism of our theories. Thus while animal knowledge and pre-scientific knowledge grow mainly through the elimination of those who hold the unfit hypothesis, scientific criticism often makes our theories perish in our stead, eliminating our mistaken beliefs before such beliefs lead to our own elimination.

This statement of the situation is meant to describe how knowledge really grows. [P. 6, mimeographed prepublication draft][42]

This is a conception of science which explicitly and consciously opposes the Baconian tradition—science being an enterprise based on facts and induction, general laws being induced from particular facts. The philosophy of science of John Stuart Mill is the nineteenth-century embodiment of Baconianism. Of Mill's philosophy Peirce caustically remarked:

John Stuart Mill endeavored to explain the reasonings of science by the nominalistic metaphysics of his father. The superficial perspicuity of that kind of metaphysics rendered his logic extremely popular with those who think, but do not think profoundly. . . . [1.70]

Then Peirce went on to analyze Kepler's achievement to show how Mill's account of Kepler utterly trivializes Kepler and indeed makes a caricature of him.

But so to characterize Kepler's work [in the manner Mill does] is to betray total ignorance of it. Mill certainly never read the *De Motu* [*Motibus*] *Stellae Martis*, which is not easy reading. The reason it is not easy is that it calls for the most vigorous exercise of all the powers of reasoning from beginning to end. [1.71]

Peirce painstakingly reconstructs Kepler's w ɔrk and points out the imaginative hypotheses which had to be conceived at various junctures of Kepler's great work.[43] "This (Kepler's work) is the greatest piece of retroductive reasoning ever performed" (1.74).

This anticipates Popper in the style, spirit, and language of the argument. What is lacking in Peirce's arguments to make it entirely Popperian is to point out at various junctures the way in which various hypotheses have been *refuted* to give rise to new hypotheses, which after a further process of error elimination led to the successful hypothesis.

Popper's archenemy is Francis Bacon himself. Although sensitive to the history of science and fully aware of Bacon's achievement, Popper never misses the opportunity to criticize the Baconian inductive model of science. The 'dogma' of observation, "the myth of a scientific method that starts from observation and experiment" are stock phrases which Popper uses when discussing Bacon's concept of science.

Popper's reconstruction of Kepler's work,[44] while constantly denouncing the myth of observation, does not essentially differ from Peirce's reconstruction. Thus Peirce's and Popper's conceptions of science are not only strikingly similar as far as their formulations are concerned, but they render the same historical picture of science when applied to important excerpts in the history of science. This of course has its explanation in the logic of discovery they both ascribe to.

2. Logic of Discovery

From the historical—evolutionary—conception of science follows a specific methodology, a logic of discovery. Indeed, the logic of discovery is an integral part of this historical evolutionary conception of science, and conversely, Popper's logic of discovery implies as its ultimate consequence the evolutionary concept of science. The essence of this logic of discovery could be formulated in Peirce's words, "Do not block the way of inquiry" (1.135).

Peirce called his methodology abduction, or retroduction, and sometimes, indeed, fallibilism. Fallibilism is, of course, one of the labels which Popper also uses on occasion to identify his philosophy. (That this label is not quite a happy one we shall show below.)

> *Retroduction* is the provisional adoption of a hypothesis, because every possible consequence of it is capable of experimental verification, so that the persevering application of the same method may be expected to reveal its disagreement with facts, if it does so disagree. [1.68]

Retroduction, we are told in another context, goes upon the hope that there is a sufficient affinity between the reasoner's mind and nature's to render guessing not altogether hopeless—this is very much in harmony with

Chomsky's rationalist conception of mind. Peirce continues: "It is true that agreement does not show the guess is right; but *if it is wrong it must ultimately get found out*" (1.121; italics ours).

The most striking of Peirce's formulations is perhaps this: "The best hypothesis, in the sense of the one most recommending itself to the inquirer, is the one which can be the most readily refuted if it is false" (1.120). Could we have anything more Popperian than this?

> He [the scientist] . . . entertains hypotheses which are almost wildly incredible, and treats them with respect for the time being. Why does he do this? Simply because any scientific proposition whatever is always liable to be refuted and dropped at short notice. [1.120]

For Popper, as we have argued at length in Part II, falsifiability is the criterion of demarcation of science from nonscience, is the basis for the criterion of objectivity and rationality of science and is, in a word, the cornerstone of science. The method of conjectures and refutations is the surest and most effective method for the acquisition of new and important truths, though we must remember that these are only tentative truths.

> . . . it is not the accumulation of observations which I have in mind when I speak of the growth of scientific knowledge, but the repeated overthrow of scientific theories and their replacement by better or more satisfactory ones. [*C.&R.*, p. 215]

And in the previously mentioned Herbert Spencer Lecture, *"the growth of knowledge proceeds from old problems to new problems by means of conjectures and refutations"* (p. 3).

Both Peirce and Popper had rigorous scientific training. Yet both envisage in "wild imagination" an indispensable prelude to scientific discovery. Peirce observes that "A pretty wild play of the imagination is, it cannot be doubted, an inevitable and probably even a useful prelude to science proper" (1.235). And in the same vein, he adds

> It is not too much to say that next after the passion to learn there is no quality so indispensable to the successful prosecution of science as imagination. Find me a people whose early medicine is not mixed up with magic and incantations, and I will find you a people devoid of all scientific ability. [1.47] . . . The scientific imagination *dreams* of explanations and laws. [1.48]

And here is Popper: "The history of science, like the history of all human ideas, is a history of irresponsible dreams, of obstinacy, and of error" (*C.&R.*, p. 216). *"We do not know: we can only guess"* (*L.Sc.D.*, p. 278).

3. Science as a Human Enterprise

Both Peirce and Popper agree that science is a human enterprise, that, like any inquiry, to be meaningful it must be conceived in terms of human ends and purposes. Science is not a world of abstract entities above and beyond the human world, but is an inherently human enterprise, conducted by human beings for human purposes. Peirce writes:

> The question is what theories and conceptions we *ought* to entertain. Now the word "ought" has no meaning except relatively to an *end*. That ought to be done which is conducive to a certain end. The inquiry therefore should begin with searching for the *end* of thinking. [5.594]

For Popper, science is essentially an activity of problem-solving, not just intellectual problems, but all kinds of problems. "From the amoeba to Einstein, the growth of knowledge is always the same: we try to solve our problems, and to obtain, by a process of elimination, something approaching adequacy in our tentative solutions" (Herbert Spencer Lecture, p. 6).

Traditionally, the reliability of science was gained from its strict exclusion of chance and freedom, from its being a strict determinism. But, for Popper as well as for Peirce, science has changed from a determinism to an indeterminism. Its goal is no longer *certainty* but only *tentative reliability*, and it provides a place for freedom, spontaneity, and creativity in the world.

With so many fundamental similarities between Peirce's thought and Popper's, why are there nevertheless such striking differences between them? The answer lies partly in the fact that, in spite of his originality, Peirce's ideas were neglected except by James and Royce and Dewey. Consequently, whatever influence his philosophy of science had in the early decades of this century, and thus upon Popper, was exerted only indirectly.

Another important reason for the lack of continuity between Peirce and Popper[45] lies in the way they philosophize. Popper exhibits an extraordinary degree of consistency in relating all aspects of his epistemology and methodology to the single idea of refutability, particularly in his classical period of *The Logic of Scientific Discovery* and *Conjectures and Refutations*. There is no center of gravity in Peirce. Ayer has suggested that Peirce's theories suffered a split of personality because they are an unsuccessful blend of two rival strains in his philosophy: the scholasticism which leads to the proliferation of abstract entities and the pragmatism which aims at their removal.[46] Here are some of the incongruities of Peirce's philosophy of science.

1. On the one hand he maintained that all knowledge is tentative, that "any scientific proposition whatever is always liable to be refuted and dropped at short notice" (1.120). On the other hand he maintained that we can and ultimately will arrive at absolute truth.
2. On the one hand he contended that new knowledge can be acquired only by means of abduction, "Every single item of scientific theory which stands established today has been due to abduction" (5.172).

On the other hand he maintained that *induction* is the way to new knowledge.

3. On the one hand he considered observation as only a part of the testing procedure of an hypothesis which is in harmony with his fallibilism; and, on the other hand, he asserted that "Every inquiry whatsoever takes its rise in the observation . . ." (6.469). "It thus appears that all knowledge comes to us by observation" (2.444).

These discrepancies are not as severe when the whole context is carefully examined as they may appear at first glance. However, explicit statements can be found in Peirce for and against many classical positions. The sign of a good thinker is consistency; but the sign of a truly original one, we might argue, is inconsistency. Peirce's work is like the Bible: so all-embracing that it yields itself to diametrically opposed interpretations. The fruitfulness of Peirce's thought can be seen in the whole spectrum of philosophical inquiries—from myth and symbol to formal logic. Nowhere is the fertility of his thought greater than in the philosophy of science.

It is perhaps unfortunate that the methodologies of both Peirce and Popper should be called by so inapt a term as 'fallibilism'. According to *Webster's Unabridged Dictionary*, the term 'fallibilism' denotes "the theory that it is impossible to attain absolutely certain empirical knowledge because the statements constituting it cannot be utimately and completely verified—opposed to infallibilism." Fallibilism, according to the above definition, is best understood in negative terms as the denial or rejection of any claims to infallibility. The term fallibilism is also obviously related to the adjective 'fallible'—which means the human propensity to make mistakes, or to quote the same dictionary again, means "liable to err" or "liable to be erroneous or inaccurate."

If "fallibilism" is understood in either of these two senses, the term is singularly inapt, almost to the point of caricature, as a name for the method of science. For the root sense of fallibilism, on either interpretation, suggests that what scientists do when they are doing science is simply "making mistakes"—that science is an enterprise which consists in making one mistake after another, and that it is foredoomed by fate always to err, and like Sisyphus, it must always struggle in vain against its fate.

But this misses the main point about what science is doing when it is making its mistakes—and that is, not that it makes them, but that (a) it *recognizes* them, and (b) it *eliminates* them, and (c) it *advances* beyond them, and thus, asymptotically, gets closer and closer to the truth. Accordingly, if one were arbitrarily to attempt to describe the method of the scientist entirely in terms of his mistakes, even then it would obviously be a better description to say that what the scientist is doing is that he is *recognizing* and *eliminating* and *advancing* beyond his mistakes rather than merely to say that what he is doing is *making* them.

Like Peirce, Popper also on occasion labels his philosophy "fallibilism." But a much happier designation for identifying the methodology of both Peirce and Popper is found in Popper's inspired phrase, "conjectures and refutations," which comes much closer to capturing the essence of Scientific Method.

E. F. AND H. S.

DECEMBER, 1969

NOTES

[1] Thus, even though we know that some innocent men are hanged and some guilty men are set free by our courts, all verdicts of 'guilty' are equally (rule) objectively valid and all verdicts of 'innocent' are equally (rule) objectively valid. But we know that they are not equally (factually) objectively valid. On occasion, for example, an appeal and a new trial will disclose evidence which will prove that the previous verdict distorted the facts and was a miscarriage of justice. Or a photograph will belatedly show that an umpire was mistaken when he ruled that a runner was out because he did not touch second base, or that the judges of a race called the wrong winner. Juries and umpires and referees, in short, are fallible, and, although some of their mistakes can be corrected, the machinery available for correcting mistakes is sharply limited and quickly exhausted in contrast to the almost endless opportunity for correction and revision in science.

[2] All references to Peirce in this paper follow the standard practice of designating volume and paragraph in the *Collected Papers of Charles Sanders Peirce*, edited by Charles Hartshorne and **Paul Weiss (Cambridge: Harvard University Press, 1931-58).**

[3] Actually, Peirce himself denied his own 'manifest theory of truth' in his more fundamental metaphysics of 'Tychism' and his generally fallibilistic philosophy of science.

[4] Recently Popper has proposed a schema for the acquisition of knowledge as follows:

$$P_1 \rightarrow TT \rightarrow EE \rightarrow P_2$$

Here P_1 is the *problem* from which we start, TT (the 'tentative theory') is the imaginative conjectural solution which we first reach, for example our first *tentative interpretation*. EE ('*error elimination*') consists of a severe critical examination of our conjecture, our tentative interpretation: it consists, for example, of the critical use of documentary evidence and, if we have at this early stage more than one conjecture at our disposal, it will also consist of a discussion and comparative evaluation of the competing conjectures. P_2 is the problem situation as it emerges from our first attempt to solve our problem. It leads up to our second attempt (*and so on*). A satisfactory understanding (to say nothing of finality) will be reached if the interpretation, the conjectural theory, finds support in the fact that it can throw new light on new problems—on more problems than we expected; or if it finds support in the fact that it explains many subproblems, some of which were not seen to start with. Thus we may say that we can gauge the progress made by comparing P_1 with one of our later problems (Pn, say). Karl Popper, "On the Theory of the Objective Mind," in *Proceedings of the Fourteenth International Congress for Philosophy* (Vienna, 1968), p. 32. Hereinafter cited as "Obj. Mind."

[5] They are *descriptive* names inasmuch as the essence of the number 'one' is constitutively involved in 'Firstness'; the essence of the number 'two' is constitutively involved in 'Secondness'; the essence of the number three is constitutively involved in 'Thirdness'.

[6] Eugene Freeman, *The Categories of Charles Peirce* (La Salle, Ill.: The Open Court Publishing Co., 1934), p. 1. Hereinafter cited as *CCP*.

[7] Alfred North Whitehead, *Process and Reality* (New York: Macmillan and Co., 1929), p. 4.

[8] This is one of Popper's most recent doctrines, and is not to be found in the treatises of his classical period (*The Logic of Scientific Discovery* and *Conjectures and Refutations*). It is considered at some length by Skolimowski in Part II of the present paper.

[9] Here Peirce puts himself into a predicament from which he cannot easily (if at all) escape.

[10] Murray G. Murphey, *The Development of Peirce's Philosophy* (Cambridge: Harvard University Press, 1961), p. 368. Hereinafter cited as *DPP*.

[11] Cf. p. 468 above.

[12] For myself, I am quite ready to accept without reservations both of these presuppositions, and to reserve for discussion elsewhere the question I raised in a previous study as to whether or not there are alternative categories (*CCP*, p. 20). To this question Father W. P. Haas has responded by pointing out that Peirce described many other categories which were "more or less variations on the theme of the basic three": William Paul Haas, O.P., *The Conception of Law and the Unity of Peirce's Philosophy* (Notre Dame, Indiana: The University of Notre Dame Press, 1964), p. 33. This does not answer my question, which was concerned with the possibility that there may be other ultimate categories which are *not* variations on Peirce's basic three. However, I do not think that it would be required of Peirce's categories that they be the *only* categories of philosophy (ultimate or otherwise) for them to be of first rank in their importance (as I am convinced that they are), and for them to serve as the foundations for a philosophy that will offer us rule objectivity.

[13] This claim is echoed in Bridgman's doctrine of operationalism.

[14] Peirce uses the term interpretant as a broader term than interpreter to designate the context in which interpretation occurs—as e.g., the rules and usages of a language—but for the present purpose the simpler notion of interpreter will suffice.

[15] *CCP*, p. 41.

[16] Karl Menger, "A Counterpart of Occam's Razor in Pure and Applied Mathematics—Ontological Uses," *Synthese*, **12**, No. 4 (1960), 415-29.

[17] Max Fisch, "Peirce's Progress from Nominalism Toward Realism," *The Monist*, **51**, No. 2 (April, 1967), 159-78.

[18] *The Philosophy of Rudolf Carnap*, ed. by Paul A. Schilpp (La Salle, Ill.: The Open Court Publishing Co., 1963).

[19] K. R. Popper, *Conjectures and Refutations* (London: Routledge & Kegan Paul Ltd., 1962; New York: Basic Books, 1963), pp. 67, 70, 72, 73,. Hereinafter cited as *C.&R.*

[20] Although Popper has always been emphatic in underlining the primacy of problems, he is not the only contemporary philosopher to grasp the significance of problems for philosophy. From quite different quarters we hear the same appeal. "To understand the work of an original philosopher it is necessary to see—and not merely to see but to feel—the logical *impasse* by which he was held up. We should always be asking the question just what was the conceptual fix he was in? What dilemma was pinching him?" And I quote again the same philosopher:

> From Transatlantic journals I gather that at this very moment British philosophy is dominated by some people called 'linguistic analysts' . . . It falsely suggests, for one thing, that any sort of careful elucidation of any sort of complex or subtle ideas will be a piece of philosophizing. . . . But ever worse, it suggests that philosophical problems are like the chemist's or the detective's problems in this respect, namely that they can and should be tackled piecemeal. Finish problem A this morning, file the answer, and go to problem B this afternoon. This suggestion does violence to the vital fact that philosophical problems inevitably interlock in all sorts of ways.

These are the opinions of no one else but Professor Gilbert Ryle of Oxford (as expressed in *Dilemmas*, p. 125, and "The Theory of Meaning" in *British Philosophy in Mid-Century* (New

York: Humanities Press, 1957, pp. 263, 264) who is considered to be an archetype of the linguistic philosopher. The paradox here is this: Popper, in spite of his fruitful and long lasting encounter with methodology, did not hesitate to denounce explicitly methods and techniques in philosophy. Ryle, on the other hand, in spite of his life long search for the world purged of unnecessary entities (there is no question that almost all Ryle's philosophical endeavours converged to one positive point which is a kind of radical nominalism), he did not hesitate to say "Ontologizing is out". Thus, on the one hand a methodologist is denouncing methods, and on the other an ontologist is denouncing ontologizing.

[21] See particularly "Philosophy of Science: a Personal Report" in *British Philosophy in Mid-Century*. This essay is also to be found in *Conjectures and Refutations* under the slightly changed title, "Science: Conjectures and Refutations."

[22] Michael Polanyi's *Personal Knowledge* (Chicago: University of Chicago Press, 1958) and Thomas Kuhn's *The Structure of Scientific Revolutions* (Chicago: Chicago University Press, 1962) mark the beginning of the period in which Popper's position has been radicalized by his followers.

Polanyi's concept of personal knowledge, as formulated in his book under the same title, is a radical subjectivization of science and of all cognitive knowledge. The subjective functions of the human agent in the process of acquisition of knowledge (Polanyi wants to demonstrate) are unrestricted by any universally accepted criteria of intersubjectivity. The rationality of science as Popper conceives it is thus undermined. Science, as presented by Polanyi, is a subjective affair of particular scientists, and the term 'affair' seems to be particularly appropriate here.

[23] K. R. Popper, *The Logic of Scientific Discovery* (London: Hutchinson, 1959; New York: Basic Books, 1959), p. 44.

[24] *Ibid.*, p. 47.

[25] *Ibid.*, p. 111.

[26] In another place in *Open Society and its Enemies* (Princeton: Princeton University Press, 1966), Popper writes:

We could then say that rationalism is an attitude of readiness to listen to critical arguments and to learn from experience. It is fundamentally an attitude of admitting that *"I may be wrong and you may be right, and by an effort, we may get nearer to the truth"*. It is an attitude which does not lightly give up hope that by such means as argument and careful observation, people may reach some kind of agreement on most problems of importance. [P. 213]

[27] John Passmore writes in *The Encyclopedia of Philosophy* about logical positivism: "Logical positivism is dead; is as dead as philosophical doctrine can be." The exhaustion of logical positivism as a viable and fruitful philosophy had naturally its consequences for the philosophy of science.

[28] Carnap admitted this explicitly in his autobiographical essay in *The Philosophy of Rudolf Carnap* (The Library of Living Philosophers, La Salle, Illinois: Open Court Publishing Co., 1967); and Hempel in *Aspects of Scientific Explanation* (New York: Free Press, 1965).

[29] Imre Lakatos, in his characteristically flamboyant style, made this allegation in "Criticism and the Methodology of Scientific Research Programmes," *The Proceedings of the Aristotelian Society* (1968), p. 163. The idea that theories could be born refuted is really nonsensical and is indefensible in any philosophy of science.

[30] Karl Popper, "Epistemology Without a Knowing Subject," *Logic, Methodology of Sciences III*, ed. van Rootselaar and Staal (Amsterdam: North-Holland Publishing Co., 1968), p. 333.

[31] Popper, "Obj. Mind," p. 33.

[32] *Ibid.*, p. 29.

[33] *Ibid.*, p. 26.

[34] *Ibid.*, p. 27.

[35] Noam Chomsky, "Recent Contributions to the Theory of Innate Ideas," in *Boston Studies*

in the Philosophy of Science, Vol. III (New York: The Humanities Press, 1968), p. 81. Hereinafter cited as "Theory of Innate Ideas."

[36] Noam Chomsky, "Knowledge of Language," *Times Literary Supplement* (May 15, 1969), p. 523.

[37] Noam Chomsky, *Language and Mind* (New York: Harcourt, Brace & World, 1968), p. 81.

[38] After all Husserl's demolishing of psychologism should not be treated lightly. If we do recognize that language possesses intersubjective meanings, then *results* of thinking acts are *not* mental processes; and then it is not the case, as Chomsky astonishingly claims, that "language has no existence apart from its mental representation."

[39] The deep structure "is the underlining abstract structure of a sentence that determines its semantic interpretation." Put in other words, "it is the deep structure underlining the actual utterance, a structure that is purely mental, that conveys the semantic content of the sentence." "Deep structures," we are told, "are fundamentally the same across languages, although the means for their expression may be quite diverse." Quite consistently, Chomsky is unwilling to commit himself to say something more specific about these structures.

[40] Chomsky, "Theory of Innate Ideas," p. 88.

[41] *Ibid.,* p. 89.

[42] [Now Chap. 7 of *Objective Knowledge: An Evolutionary Approach* (London: Oxford University Press, 1972).—EDITOR]

[43] Peirce's reconstruction of Kepler is such a model of excellence in demonstrating abductive reasoning as an integral part of science that we quote his account in full:

"What Kepler had given was a large collection of observations of the apparent places of Mars at different times. He also knew that, in a general way, the Ptolemaic theory agrees with the appearances, although there were various difficulties in making it fit exactly. He was furthermore convinced that the hypothesis of Copernicus ought to be accepted. Now this hypothesis, as Copernicus himself understood its first outline, merely modifies the theory of Ptolemy so far as [to] impart to all the bodies of the solar system one common motion, just what is required to annul the mean motion of the sun. It would seem, therefore, at first sight, that it ought not to affect the appearances at all. If Mill had called the work of Copernicus mere description he would not have been *so very far* from the truth as he was. But Kepler did not understand the matter quite as Copernicus did. Because the sun was so near the centre of the system, and was of vast size (even Kepler knew its diameter must be at least fifteen times that of the earth), Kepler, looking at the matter dynamically, thought it must have something to do with causing the planets to move in their orbits. This retroduction, vague as it was, cost great intellectual labor, and was most important in its bearings upon all of Kepler's work. Now Kepler remarked that the lines of apsides of the orbits of Mars and of the earth are not parallel; and he utilized various observations most ingeniously to infer that they probably intersected in the sun. Consequently, it must be supposed that a general description of the motion would be simpler when referred to the sun as a fixed point of reference than when referred to any other point. Thence it followed that the proper times at which to take the observations of Mars for determining its orbit were when it appeared just opposite the sun—the true sun—instead of when it was opposite the *mean* sun, as had been the practice. Carrying out this idea, he obtained a theory of Mars which satisfied the longitudes at all the oppositions observed by Tycho and himself, thirteen in number, to perfection. But unfortunately, it did not satisfy the latitudes at all and was totally irreconcilable with observations of Mars when far from opposition. [1.72]

"At each stage of his long investigation, Kepler has a theory which is approximately true, since it approximately satisfied the observations (that is, within 8′, which is less than any but Tycho's observations could decisively pronounce an error), and he proceeds to modify this theory, after the most careful and judicious reflection, in such a way as to render it more rational or closer to the observed fact. Thus, having found that the centre of the orbit bisects the eccentricity, he finds in this an indication of the falsity of the theory of the equant and substitutes, for this artificial device, the principle of the equable description of areas. Subsequently, finding that the planet moves faster at ninety degrees from its apsides than it ought to do, the question is whether this is owing to an error in the law of areas or to a compression of the orbit. He in-geniously proves that the latter is the case. [1.73]

"Thus, never modifying his theory capriciously, but always with a sound and rational motive for just the modification he makes, it follows that when he finally reaches a modification—of most striking simplicity and rationality—which exactly satisfies the obser-vations, it stands upon a totally different logical footing from what it would if it had been struck out at random, or the reader knows not how, and had been found to satisfy the observation. Kepler shows his keenly logical sense in detailing the whole process by which he finally arrived at the true orbit. This is the greatest piece of Retroductive reasoning ever performed." [1.74]

[44] Popper, *C.&R.*, pp. 188 ff.

[45] It was only recently that Popper discovered Peirce and came to appreciate him to the point of calling him "one of the greatest philosophers of all times." (Karl Popper, *Of Clouds and Clocks* [St. Louis: Washington University, 1966], p. 5.)

[46] A. J. Ayer, *The Origins of Pragmatism* (London, 1968), p. 179. Cf. the two rival strains first pointed out by Eugene Freeman in 1934 as the unresolved dualism of the ontology and the phenomenology of Peirce. *CCP*, pp. 5-6.

14

Herbert Feigl and *Paul E. Meehl*

THE DETERMINISM-FREEDOM AND
BODY-MIND PROBLEMS

O ur cherished friend, Sir Karl, has very penetratingly and challengingly dealt in several essays[1] with two of the most difficult and controversial issues of modern philosophy and science. In accordance with Popper's own designations we shall speak of "Compton's problem" and "Descartes's problem". Compton's problem is how to account for free choice and genuine (artistic or scientific) creativity; Descartes's problem concerns the relation of the mental to the physical. These problems are closely related, and both are viewed by Popper in the light of modern physics, biology, psychology and of the theory of language. Although we do not pretend to know of any definitive solutions of either problem, and although we tend to agree with several important points made by Popper, we propose to submit to him a number of critical reflections. What we hope to show is that the "plastic" (or "cloud-like") control stressed by Popper does not necessarily require a basic indeterminism; and that the role of meanings and reasons in the representative and argumentative functions of language does not necessarily imply a dualism of mind and body.

I

Popper's "nightmare of determinism"—very much like the dread of the "block universe" of William James—seems to us to rest on identifying determinism with strict predictability. We can hardly believe that Popper regards these terms as synonymous. If so, this could only be due to an unrelinquished remnant of positivistic thinking in the keenest and most outstanding contemporary critic of positivism. It seems quite unlikely that Popper, for once, and quite contrary to his general enlightened attitude, has fallen victim to a verificationist prejudice. This would indeed be inconsistent with his pronouncements in other places on the *metaphysical*, i.e., untestable nature of the doctrine of determinism. In any case, we think that complete predetermination becomes a "nightmare" only if one assumes that some sort of Laplacean World Formula could ever be produced by scientists. Such a World Formula would then—inserting the total set of specific numerical values for the initial and boundary conditions—furnish a World Calendar. In such a calendar one could look up one's own future, the future of mankind and of our planet in general, etc., in perfect detail; and if the basic laws are temporally symmetrical (as they are at least in classical physics), one could also reconstruct any phase of the historical, prehistorical, or cosmological past. It is the attainability of a World Formula thus understood which leads to absurdly paradoxical and abhorrently unpalatable consequences. Fatalism would then seem the only possible attitude. Any avoidance reaction to predictions of unpleasant or disastrous events would itself have to be derivable from the World Formula, and the well-known phenomenon of a self-annulling prediction would be logically impossible—as long as we assume the World Formula to be correct. Precise and detailed predictions of future works of art, of scientific theories, of the rise or decline of civilizations, etc., would all be attainable in terms of an accurate physicalistic description of every and all spatiotemporal events—indeed including the "putting of ink marks on paper"—be it a future composer's symphonic score, or the manuscript of a great mathematician or theoretical physicist of the year 2500! If such precise predictions were possible, then we might have full knowledge of scientific theories, or achievements of works of art, long before they were—respectively—invented or created. This is surely as logically incoherent an idea as is that of H. G. Wells's time machine! Furthermore, if the World Formula permitted the prediction of a fatal automobile accident which someone is to suffer at a definite place and a precise date—in the future, then he could not succeed in conveniently staying at home, and thus avoid the disaster. By a curious and intricate concatenation of circumstances he would nevertheless be "destined" to die in precisely the predicted circumstances, and in the specified space-time region. If the World Calendar contained a prediction of even some highly desired event, one could not—merely for the sake of disproving the World Formula—change the course of events such that the predicted one would not take place.

Considerations such as these have often been adduced as a reductio ad absurdum of determinism. But it should be clear that it is rather the attainability of the World Formula which the foregoing arguments refute. Now, as is agreed on all hands, the idea of the World Formula is to be understood as a logical conjunction of *three* propositions: (1) The doctrine of the deterministic form of all basic natural laws. (2) The precise, complete (and simultaneous) ascertainability of all initial and boundary conditions. (3) The mathematical feasibility of the hopelessly complex computations necessary for precise and complete predictions (or retrodictions). Now, as no one knows better than Popper (though this is really a matter of the most elementary propositional logic), if a conjunction of several independent propositions entails a false or absurd conclusion, not every one of the conjuncts is (necessarily) false. In the empirical sciences there are experimental or statistical methods to pinpoint the "culprit" (or culprits) among the conjoined premises. In our problem this is obviously impossible. Nevertheless, there are excellent reasons for regarding propositions (2) and (3) as false at any rate; thus leaving the hypothesis of determinism at least open for further consideration.

We should make it quite clear immediately that neither in the above remarks, nor in what follows, are we pleading for the doctrines of determinism. We consider it quite possible that the indeterminism of present quantum mechanics (or something akin to it) may never be overcome. On the other hand, it is conceivable that a future theory regarding a further substratum of micro-microevents might have deterministic form and be nonemergentist. The question as to what form—deterministic or statistical—the "rock bottom" laws of the universe have, is indeed never conclusively decidable; and this for the simple reason that there is not and could not be a criterion by which to recognize the "rock bottom" of nature. As David Bohm has suggested, it is logically conceivable that our universe may be "infinitely deep"—layer upon layer without end. Hence, the only sensible question to ask is whether at a given stage of scientific (experimental and theoretical) investigation the (on that level) basic laws are strictly causal (deterministic) or statistical (probabilistic). Hence, while we agree with Popper that neither the doctrine of determinism nor that of indeterminism is conclusively decidable,[2] we think that empirical evidence, that is reasons, can be adduced that justify a tentative endorsement of one or the other doctrine. Surely, if the triumphant successes of classical mechanics, and of the nineteenth-century field theories had continued to furnish adequate explanations in every domain of the empirical sciences, determinism would have remained a highly plausible frame hypothesis.

Since it is imperative for our conception of determinism to separate it quite radically from all references to prediction and predictability, perhaps an explicit formulation of "strict lawfulness" is needed. We suggest the following definition: Any event in the world (as described in the four-dimensional representation) instantiates a nomological proposition—i.e., either a basic or a derived law. Thus understood, the frame hypothesis of determinism is not hopelessly untestable. Indeed, it was the unexpected development of quantum physics in our century that for the first time cast *serious* doubt upon the determinism doctrine. But before we turn to the implications of indeterminism for "Compton's problem", let us show that the two other conjuncts in the World

Formula doctrine are much more vulnerable than the idea of determinism. As Popper himself has shown,[3] even under the presupposition of the determinism of classical physics, there is a fundamental (we should think set-theoretical) impossibility in ascertaining and recording the initial and boundary conditions of a closed system. As long as the observing-measuring instrument and/or observer is part of the system under scrutiny, not all of the system can be "mapped" on to part of itself. This would indeed seem a *logical* impossibility as regards proposition (2), i.e., of the full ascertainability of the total set of conditions. To this might be added the basic physical impossibility of knowing about incoming "inputs" before they have arrived. According to the extremely well-corroborated principles of the special theory of relativity, any "messages", "information" (really any sort of propagation of causal influences) cannot occur at a velocity greater than the speed of electromagnetic waves. Hence—strictly speaking—there can be only ex post facto explanations of events—but no rigorous and completely reliable predictions of them. Only the events in Minkowski's "passive light cone of the past" can be adduced for predictions. Any events "outside that cone" can become known only after a certain time has elapsed. While Bergson (who never quite understood Einstein's theory) did not base his early pronouncement of free will (in the sense of prior unpredictability of action) on relativistic principles, he was, nevertheless, correct in claiming that most actions could be causally explained only after they had occurred. Hence, we agree with Popper that even on the basis of the theories of classical physics (including the special and general theories of relativity) complete and precise prediction is logically and physically impossible.

We disagree with Popper, however, if he views these impossibilities of prediction as arguments against determinism. (They are, we insist, decisive arguments only against the feasibility of the World Formula.) We view the doctrine of determinism as meaningful, coherent, though, of course, only very inconclusively testable. Perhaps this merely reveals that—Popper's critique to the contrary notwithstanding—we are not as radically anti-inductivistic as he is. The very fact that one could *reason* from the successes of classical physics to the (then) plausible assumption of determinism; and that the laws of classical physics are deterministic in their mathematical formulation;—all this indicates that one can understand the meaning of determinism even if this doctrine is operationally and practically inconsequential. We do understand the counterfactual proposition: "If the totality of initial and boundary conditions could be precisely ascertained; and if the laws are deterministic; and if the immensely complex computations could be accomplished, then every event in the universe could be exactly predicted (or retrodicted)". This is the conjunction of our three propositions all over again. The idea of determinism by itself need not be wrong. It could—as it has for a long time—still serve as the guiding maxim of scientific research. It is merely "sour grapes" policy of scientists or philosophers of science, if they maintain that "statistical causality" is just as good as fully deterministic lawfulness. Einstein's well-known opposition to regarding quantum mechanics as complete, emphatically expressed his conviction that nature "at rockbottom" (?) is strictly deterministic. Having succeeded twice (viz., in his special and general theory of relativity) in a "geometrization" of physics, he hoped to succeed once more—in his attempts towards a unified field theory—to design a new fundamental account, and thus to eliminate the idea of "absolute chance" conclusively from all future science. To his great disappointment he failed in this ambitious endeavor.

On a much lower level of sophistication this "faith" in determinism is clearly exemplified by the traditional view of the games of chance. Which way spinning coins, or dice, or roulette balls, will come to rest is considered a matter of *relative chance*. The thought here is that the—no matter how complex and delicate—initial and boundary conditions strictly determine the outcome. And if we only knew their precise total constellation, we could predict the outcomes with full certainty and precision. The very concept of relative chance then presupposes determinism. Chance in this sense is relative in a twofold way: (1) Relative to our knowledge (or ignorance) the event in question is not precisely predictable. (2) The many factors or conditions relevant for the outcome have a high degree of causal independence from each other. This is the way we customarily view "accidents" or "coincidences", be it a cosmic collision of stars, or an automobile accident. Essentially this rests on the causally contingent relations of events that occur at a distance from one another and are (roughly) simultaneous. In the well known four-dimensional representations this is indicated by the crossing of world-lines. In the games of chance (and as we shall see in a moment, also in the kinetics of molecules), there is the further very important aspect of the most "delicate" dependence of outcomes upon extremely small variations in the initial conditions. As to whether, for example, a coin will come up heads or tails; or as to whether a ball on the Galton board will turn left or right after impinging on a given nail, will often depend—according to classical mechanics—on minimal differences in original positions, speeds, friction encountered, etc. Surely, here is one more extremely powerful argument for the impossibility of precise and certain predictions even under the presupposition of strict determinism.

Ascertaining by measurement of the initial conditions would have to be *completely* exact, for even infinitesimally small differences in the causal antecedents may result (by various amplification processes) in enormous differences in the ensuing effects. In other words, continuous variations in the initial conditions can bring about discontinuous changes in highly relevant features of the causal results. The ball coming down from a nail on the Galton board may finally reach one electric relay that brings about the ringing of a bell; or it may trigger off another relay, and thereby cause the explosion of a bomb. And if the initial conditions were such that the ball were coming down exactly vertically upon the nail, it should—after a few dampened bouncings—come to rest, in unstable equilibrium right on top of the nail. This latter—unheard of—event would however, be excluded by the random (heat) motion of the molecules, both in the surface of the ball and in that of the nail. Since all measurements—even from the classical-deterministic point of view—are achieved by using macroinstruments, and since molecular motion (at least at temperatures above absolute zero) is unavoidable, there is even in the classical theory an ineluctable inaccuracy (i.e., an element of chance) in the results of even the most refined measurements.

There is no need, we are sure, for any elaborate argument regarding the overwhelming complexity of the calculations that would be required for precise predictions for any but the most simple (and idealized) systems and their "development". As all the world knows, this is the *raison d'être* of the statistical approach—be it in the games of chance, in matters of insurance, or in the kinetic theories of molecular motions. The sort of system of equations that would be required for detailed and precise predictions would obviously involve difficulties far surpassing those of the astronomical n-body problem. It is, moreover, quite conceivable that the pure mathematics of such calculations might run up against insoluble mathematical problems—in the sense of the undecidability discovered by Kurt Gödel.

All these considerations, we repeat, do not however establish conclusive argument against determinism as such. To illustrate in terms of Popper's own example, the "behavior" of soap bubbles can be explained, as Ludwig Boltzmann might well have claimed, within a deterministic point of view. To be sure, precise predictions (e.g., of the moment of the bubble's bursting) are impossible—for the reasons already mentioned. Yet, according to Boltzmann's convictions, the kinetics of the air molecules inside and outside the bubble, as well as of the molecules constituting the thin "skin" of the bubble, might be construed in the light of Newtonian determinism. Boltzmann might have said that we have very good reasons for assuming such an "underlying" determinism, in spite of the hopelessness of detailed and exact predictability. Classical determinism (involving, of course, only concepts of *relative* chance) thus would provide a perfectly intelligible basis for the "plastic control" that Popper emphasizes. As he admits, "clouds" may well be "clocks" in this sense, after all. Very much, however, depends on what one means here by "in this sense". As Popper rightly sees, there is a continuum of degrees that lies between extreme cases of "clouds" and extreme cases of "clocks".

Analogous considerations apply to the differences of organisms and machines. Admittedly, there are tremendous differences between a simple mechanical machine (such as a system of levers and pulleys, or of cog wheels) and even the simplest organism, such as a protozoan. Perhaps even a difference in kind must be admitted between noncybernetic mechanisms and mechanism involving self-regulation. We must not prejudge the issue by any simplistic "man a machine" conceptions. We are inclined to think that in any case machines made of hardware (vacuum tubes, transistors, wires, transmission gears) no matter how ingeniously constructed, will, at best, simulate (or perhaps even "outdo") only certain segments of human activities. Very likely only a structure composed of the proteins of the nervous system can function in the "creative" manner of the highest human achievements. An anecdote about a conversation between a brilliant avant-garde engineer and a great musician poignantly illustrates the issue. The engineer said: "Now we can build machines that compose works of music". The musician replied: "Then you should also build some machines that will appreciate that sort of music". The point is well taken. Electronic "music" of the "aleatory" type is one of the atrocities of our age of technology. We agree wholeheartedly with Popper that human creativity cannot be explained on the basis of a "clock" (simple machine) theory of cerebral functioning.[4] We also agree that the combination of a machine with a built-in randomizer will not suffice either. But it has become increasingly clear that systems with "organismic" structures, i.e., involving Gestalt and cybernetic features, may well exemplify the typically "teleological" aspects of a great variety of physiological processes. This, together with whatever "randomizing" factors may be at play, could go a long way toward a deterministic explanation of the delicately attuned, but never fully predictable biological and psychological functions and occurrences.

As we understand Popper's views (especially in *Of Clouds and Clocks*), he rejects determinism in order to make room for an (unfortunately none too explicitly formulated) *emergentism*. Here again it seems imperative to us to distinguish between emergence in the sense of unpredictability, and emergence as involving a basic indeterminism. As has often been pointed out,[5] the impossibility of prediction in the cases of emergent novelty does not necessarily imply a denial of determinism. The familiar examples of the impossibility of predicting the properties of complexes (e.g., chemical compounds; organisms; social groups) on the basis of the properties of their constituent parts or components (e.g., chemical elements, cells, individual persons), do not establish an argument against the possibility of deterministic theories that would explain the properties of the "organic wholes". The arguments for "genuine emergence", along with the arguments for ("irreducible") holism appear plausible only as long as they are couched in *epistemic* terms. That is to say, if the properties of the parts or components have been explored only in "splendid isolation", there would hardly be any clue as to what sort of wholes (compounds, organisms, etc.) they might form when brought into interactions with each other. This is strikingly true even on the most elementary level of modern microphysics. A study of the behavior of "free" electrons (as in the cathode rays) would never suggest their "configurational behavior" in the context of even the simplest atoms. Pauli's exclusion principle (which is an independent postulate of quantum mechanics), may be considered a fundamental composition law; just as in classical mechanics the law of vectorial addition (i.e., the well-known parallelogram of forces) is a basic empirical law, logically independent of the other Newtonian laws of motion and of gravitation.

Just how far we have to explore more and more complex situations, constellations and configurations in order to "glean" (pardon the "inductivism"!) the total set of laws sufficient for purely computational (i.e., mathematical, including geometrical) inference of the regularities of complexes (wholes) cannot be decided in an a priori manner. By and large, the extant evidence encourages the view that chemistry is in principle reducible to atomic and quantum physics; and that biology (especially since the recent advances in the knowledge of the molecular structure of the nucleic acids) is equally—in principle(!)—reducible to modern physics. (This is not to deny that there are still grave unsolved problems in connection with the specifics of evolution, and other biological problems.)

The doctrine of "genuine emergence" is incompatible with the sort of reductionism just sketched only if new sorts of regularity were to crop up indefinitely at levels of higher complexity, and if these new regularities were absolutely underivable from the laws of some level of lower complexity. As we see it, there is no reason for such pessimism about the possibility of unitary scientific explanation. Quite to the contrary, there are important instances of the prediction of novel features on the basis of theories that were formulated *before* the resultant features of "compounded wholes" had been empirically known: Consider Mendeleev's predictions of new chemical elements, their properties, and the properties of their compounds; or the prediction of (artificial) fission and fusion of atomic nuclei; predictions of the phenotypical characteristics of organisms on the basis of the theory of genes, etc.

Even if such striking feats of prediction had not been achieved, the very possibility of *theories* from which the properties of "wholes" can be derived, can certainly not be denied on a priori grounds; and, as just indicated, that possibility is becoming increasingly plausible in the light of empirical evidence. This is at least one type of argument for the compatibility of (epistemic) emergence with (theoretical or "ontological") determinism. And even disregarding high-level theories, the conditions and consequences of "emergence" could be stated in the form of empirical laws. Once the resultants of compounding processes have been observed, laws formulating antecedents as causally implying their consequents would be subject to corroboration. Of course, these laws may have deterministic form (as in most cases of chemical compounding) or they may be statistical (as in genetics). If they are ineluctably statistical, then a certain measure of indeterminacy would be characteristic of emergence. If they are deterministic, then one could always (retrospectively) formulate the regularities in terms of dispositional properties of the components. (For example, sodium and chlorine are "apt" to combine into ordinary salt.)

In general, the logical situation in regard to emergence seems to be as follows: Only if the concepts of the theories (or laws) which are to be reduced (i.e., derived, explained) are explicitly definable in terms of the concepts of the reducing theory, can the reduction (derivation) be accomplished. But, since this is merely a necessary and not a sufficient condition, emergence in the sense of nonderivability may yet obtain, even if the definability condition is fulfilled. Hence, we regard the problem of emergence as an empirical question.

It is generally agreed that, e.g., laws of electromagnetism are not derivable from the laws of classical mechanics. Thus one could say that the phenomena of electromagnetism are "emergent" with respect to mechanical phenomena. It is even tempting to say that a sort of "interaction" between the electromagnetic forces and the (mechanical) masses takes place—as in the cases of "ponderomotoric" electric forces or in the phenomena of light pressure. But it is highly questionable as to whether an analogous interaction may be assumed between mental states (once they have emerged—be it in the course of phylogenetic evolution—or in the course of ontogenetic development) and the respective nervous systems. The resistance to this sort of doctrine among natural scientists and physicalistically oriented philosophers is not merely due to its "spookiness". The idea that "immaterial" mental factors somehow interact with, or intervene in, the physiological processes is not necessarily untestable, let alone meaningless. Of course, one would want to know more precisely what is meant by "immaterial" or "nonphysical". But once that is at least in outline specified, the remaining question is whether a hypothesis of this kind is needed. If some sort of nonphysical agent (let us call it "psychoid") is required in order to account for free choice and creativity, how are we to square this with all that is known about the factors that are relevant for the formation of the character, personality and intelligence of human beings? Hereditary constitution as based on the genetic makeup, together with all the influences of maturation, education (positive and/or negative reinforcements in the physical and social environments), emulation of "father figures" (or oedipal reactions against them), etc., seems to offer a sufficient basis—and one that may well be—in principle—susceptible of a physicalistic account.

The repudiation of dualistic-interactionistic explanations can be understood, if not justified, in the light of all the accumulated scientific evidence that speaks for a view of causality that is "closed" in the physical world, i.e., not open to "miraculous" interventions by nonphysical causes. The retreat of animism and vitalism is surely due to the ever growing scope of physical explanations. Driesch, the well-known vitalist, some forty years ago postulated entelechies which, though not in space, were assumed to "act into space". And anyone who assumes that the indeterminism of modern physics allows for "loopholes" or a "leeway" for the intervention of nonphysical forces, proposes in our century a doctrine homologous to the one proposed by Descartes in the seventeenth century. Descartes had to postulate a "breach" in the mechanical laws in the case of mental-physical interaction. Similarly, if there is to be anything testable in the twentieth-century idea that quantum indeterminism allows for (at least slight) influences of immaterial mental states upon the ongoing atomic processes in human brains, some sort of "breach" in, or deviation from, the statistical regularities would have to be assumed. Perhaps this sort of "violation" could be made more palatable by assuming that the local frequencies of quantum transitions (or the like) would be in keeping with the physical theory, but that a sort of "patterning" in the firing of neurons takes place which is not derivable from physical theory alone, and would thus require the intervention of a "psychoid". Hence, both Descartes and Compton alike make assumptions, which—if testable—deviate from what the physics of their respective times (seventeenth and twentieth centuries) would imply.

Naturally, all the remarks just made are merely the results of logical analyses. It does not seem likely that an experimental test will be forthcoming in the foreseeable future. Physicalistically oriented thinkers will insist that Compton merely repeated Descartes's mistaken reasoning on the more sophisticated level of twentieth-century science. Thinkers opposed to physicalism find this type of interactionism not so terribly "strange" after all. What we intended to point out is merely that some "tampering" with physical laws is unavoidable—even if the laws are partly (or largely) statistical, as they are in quantum mechanics.

Before turning to the role of meaning, rules and norms in human behavior—and thus to "Descartes's problem", a few more remarks on free will are in order. Let us candidly admit that we, too, can feel the sting of this perennial puzzle. Surely, if we human beings are solely the products of "nature and nurture", i.e., of our inherited constitutions and all the influences that have impinged upon us ever since the fertilization of the ovum from which we developed—how are we to understand the sentence asserting "in the given life situation we *could have acted differently* from the way we actually did". G. E. Moore's well-known answer "we could have acted differently, had we wanted to" merely shifts the vexing question to the freedom of "wanting". Some misguided thinkers even went so far as to question the very idea of moral responsibility by pointing out that we did not make or choose our character or personality. The current revolt against the Hume-Mill-Schlick-Hobart "dissolution" of the free will versus determinism issue indicates that perhaps we latter-day "compatibilists" should add a few further clarifying observations to the old issue. Surely it must be admitted that, for example, Schlick, despite the great clarity of his thought on the issue, did, in part, misdiagnose its roots. Schlick was very likely wrong in thinking that the trouble stems from confusing descriptive (natural) law with prescriptive (judicial) law. We are not aware of any important philosopher who committed this error. But the "compatibilist" school of thought seems to us to have provided some very important and very illuminating considerations. There is first, the obvious distinction between voluntary and compelled action. Both can be understood on the basis of deterministic assumptions. Even purely behaviorally there are (almost in the sense of physics) "degrees of freedom" with respect to the environmental context of our voluntary action. The ball on the inclined plane is "bound to" roll down. But the rabbit on the hillside might well go up or sideways. And a human being on that same hillside may sing a song, write a letter or poem, do gymnastic exercises, or eat his lunch, etc. While this is only a beginning in the explication of "freedom of choice", it is an indispensable first step. It could be formulated in terms of the comparative predominance of the internal (intradermal) factors over the external (extradermal) ones in the causal determination of behavior. However, to define "free choice" merely negatively by the absence of compulsion, coercion or constraint, though stating necessary conditions, is not by itself sufficient. Positively, there is the undeniable fact that in voluntary action, we are the doers of our deeds. Our character and personality, and our desires, express themselves in our deliberations, decisions and actions. And although the causal account cannot as yet be given in all of its detail, it should be clear that we are essential links in the causal chains of such voluntary actions. Any choice we make after surveying and contemplating the possible avenues of actions reflects our character, our momentary attitudes, sentiments, and moods. Of course, any precise and fully reliable predictions are precarious, if not impossible. Nevertheless, even the very incomplete and inexact knowledge we have acquired of our relatives, friends, and close acquaintances, often enables us to foretell, with a high success frequency, their reactions to various life situations. We know what will please, amuse, or annoy them; we know their preferences—be it in the choice of foods or drinks, or in voting for political candidates. We know that employees practically always cash their salary checks (sooner or later—usually sooner).

The ascription of responsibility for an action necessarily involves (in addition to any moral-normative considerations) causal imputation. In common language this manifests itself even in locutions that have nothing to do with moral judgments. We say, e.g., "the earthquake is responsible for the devastation", "the landslide is responsible for the change in the river's course", etc. The work of a great artist or scientist is *his*, for the simple reason that *he* produced it—never mind in that context what "produced him"! If the music of Beethoven in his late quartets (Op. 127 to Op. 135) "reflects" something of his personality of that period, does this not mean that there is a causal relation between the composer and his work? To be sure, one must not be so naive as to expect any simple and predictable relation here. Mozart produced some of his most serene and happy-sounding music in periods of great stress—if not distress. Nevertheless, there is no reason for abandoning the scientific approach which—no matter how qualified by probabilistic considerations—is after all *causal* analysis. And causal analysis, in modern interpretation, amounts to nothing else but the search for relevant variables and their lawful functional relationships. Surely coincidences of all sorts may have to be taken into account. Beethoven is reported to have been stimulated occasionally by hearing a popular tune whistled by someone in the streets of Vienna. Is this *fundamentally* different from the changes brought about in planetary motions by an "accidental" approach of a comet?

Summing up, we submit that what we know, cherish, and designate as "free choice" is not only compatible with determinism, but actually presupposes a large measure of it for the processes constituting human actions. As Popper rightly stresses, nothing is gained by the assumption of absolute chance—i.e., of completely uncaused action. What, then, could indeterminism do for genuine freedom? All it could do, we recapitulate, is to give us one more (and we admit, of course, fully decisive) argument against the attainability of the World Formula. It seems to us that the "nightmare" of the World Formula is indeed—on all counts—a chimera, a fantasy gone wild. It is in this sense on a par with theological doctrines of predestination. Divine omniscience poses exactly the same problem, and some brilliant theologians (like Jonathan Edwards) have seen quite clearly that this is perfectly compatible with human free will and moral responsibility.

Now let us face the free will perplexity once more in its most poignant form: If strict determinism were true then there are no genuine alternatives for human action. "I could have done otherwise" can mean only that if I had been different (e.g., wiser or better) I would have acted differently. But precisely because human nature is "'flexible'", i.e., capable of learning from the lessons of experience, it can change from one occasion to the next. This is certainly a most important feature in which human beings (but also many species of animals) differ from *simple* automata whose internal structure is rigidly fixed, and thus not responsive to the "lessons of experience". The sentiment of regret, while phenomenologically directed upon the past act ("I wish I had not done it"), finds its pragmatic significance in the resolution to "reform" ("Next time I'll behave differently"). Moral responsibility presupposes responsiveness to the sanctions of society. The severely insane are therefore not held responsible. Does "making an effort" make a difference? It certainly does, at least sometimes. Why not view the human conscience (somewhat as Freud suggested in his "anatomy of the personality") as a subsystem of the person (physicalistically: the organism)? As such the superego is indeed involved in highly subtle interactions with other subsystems (the ego and the id). Hence, if for example, a certain type of education results in the formation of a powerful superego, this may well manifest itself in the type of conduct a person displays.

We repudiate the idea that such free will as we possess is an illusion, arising from the ignorance of the causal conditions of our actions. There are situations in which we know the relevant antecedents quite well, and nevertheless do what we do "of our own free will". For example, we know that we are very fond of our great friend, Sir Karl; hence we quite voluntarily try to write in a manner that will not offend him. Only a detailed, complete foreknowledge such as the chimerical World Formula could provide, would deprive us of our feeling of free choice.

If all of the foregoing considerations do not remove the sting of the free will versus determinism problem, then perhaps only a word of practical wisdom can help. It is morbid to contemplate universal causation while engaged in making decisions in the context of practical urgencies. Fortunately, it is rather difficult, if not psychologically impossible, simultaneously to combine the attitude of the spectator and causal analyst with that of the goal-pursuing agent. (To the complementarity philosophers a word of warning: this has nothing whatever to do—except for a very remote analogy—with the complementarity formulated in the Copenhagen interpretation of quantum mechanics!)

We conclude that the testimony of introspection, as well as the objective observation of behavior at "choice points" quite clearly reveals the efficacy of deliberation and effort. Even if deliberation, preference, choice and action were completely determined by causal antecedents, it is still *free* choice (as contrasted with decisions imposed on us by any form of compulsion—from the normal cases of coercion to the peculiar cases of hypnosis or "brainwashing"). If "classically" oriented scientists—from Laplace to Einstein—after careful consideration of all relevant reasons—came to accept and defend a deterministic point of view, their convictions are "rational" only to the extent that they responded to the available evidence, and with their mastery of a variety of theoretical schemes, in a manner that might well be ultimately explainable in causal terms. This seems basically not different from the trial and error-elimination process involved in all cases of learning. In fact, it seems to us that (to use Sir Karl's way of formulating the matter) the refutation or the corroboration of theories had better be intelligible in causal-psychological terms, if it is not to consist of "snap judgments".

Although we grant, of course, that in many contexts the words "cause" and "reason" are used (and should be used) in categorially different ways, we submit that there are contexts in which they are practically synonymous. And even where they are not—there are subtle relations between them. This is one of the main points to be discussed in the following section.

II

Turning now to Popper's views regarding Descartes's problem, i.e., the "body-mind" problem, it will be well to point out the primary issues in the cluster of questions that are traditionally and controversially discussed under that heading. We think it useful to distinguish three major parts of that cluster: Sentience, Sapience and Selfhood. Of these it is *sapience* which is in the foreground, both for Descartes and for Popper. The problems of sapience concern the intellectual capacities and activities of human beings—in relation to the processes occurring in their nervous systems, particularly in the cortices of their brains. Everything that is relevant for perceiving, knowing, reasoning, problem solving, and the like is here comprised under "sapience". "Sentience", by contrast, designates the qualities of immediate experience, and the problem here also is to give a consistent, coherent and scientifically acceptable account of its relation to the neurophysiological process. "Selfhood", in turn designates the "identity" of the human person—among other persons—and as a continuant throughout a span of time. Here, too, there are questions as to the relationships between both the introspective and the common-life descriptions of a person, and the (ultimately physical) scientific account of the organism as the "embodiment of a mind". Popper, most understandably and justifiably, focuses on the problem of sapience. We can best set the stage for our critical examination of his position (that human sapience is incompatible with determinism) by gathering together the chief passages in *Of Clouds and Clocks* which most explicitly assert and argue this incompatibility. Popper writes:[6]

> [Quoting Compton] "If. . .the atoms of our bodies follow physical laws as immutable as the motions of the planets, why try? What difference can it make how great the effort if our actions are already predetermined by mechanical laws. . .?
>   Compton describes here what I shall call *'the nightmare of the physical determinist'*. A deterministic physical clockwork mechanism is, above all, completely self-contained: in the perfect deterministic physical world there is simply

no room for any outside intervention. Everything that happens in such a world is physically predetermined, including all our movements and therefore all our actions. Thus all our thoughts, feelings, and efforts can have no practical influence upon what happens in the physical world: they are, if not mere illusions, at best superfluous by-products ('epiphenomena') of physical events. [Pp. 8]

I believe that the only form of the problem of determinism which is worth discussing seriously is exactly that problem which worried Compton: the problem which arises from a physical theory which describes the world as a *physically complete* or a *physically closed* system [29]. By a physically closed system I mean a set or system of physical entities, such as atoms or elementary particles or physical forces or fields of forces, which interact with each other—and *only* with each other—in accordance with definite laws of interaction that do not leave any room for interaction with, or interference by, anything outside that closed set or system of physical entities. It is this 'closure' of the system that creates the deterministic nightmare [30]. [P. 8]

For according to determinism, any theories—such as, say, determinism—are held because of a certain physical structure of the holder (perhaps of his brain). Accordingly we are deceiving ourselves (and are physically so determined as to deceive ourselves) whenever we believe that there are such things as arguments or reasons which make us accept determinism. Or in other words, physical determinism is a theory which, if it is true, is not arguable, since it must explain all our reactions, including what appear to us as beliefs based on arguments, as due to *purely physical conditions*. Purely physical conditions, including our physical environment, make us say or accept whatever we say or accept; and a well-trained physicist who does not know any French, and who has never heard of determinism, would be able to predict what a French determinist would say in a French discussion on determinism; and, of course, also what his indeterminist opponent would say. But this means that if we believe that we have accepted a theory like determinism because we were swayed by the logical force of certain arguments, then we are deceiving ourselves, according to physical determinism; or more precisely, we are in a physical condition which determines us to deceive ourselves. [P. 11]

For if we accept a theory of evolution (such as Darwin's) then even if we remain sceptical about the theory that life emerged from inorganic matter we can hardly deny that there must have been a time when abstract and non-physical entities, such as reasons and arguments and scientific knowledge, and abstract rules, such as rules for building railways or bulldozers or sputniks or, say, rules of grammar or of counterpoint, did not exist, or at any rate had no effect upon the physical universe. It is difficult to understand how the physical universe could produce abstract entities such as rules, and then could come under the influence of these rules, so that these rules in their turn could exert very palpable effects upon the physical universe.

There is, however, at least one perhaps somewhat evasive but at any rate easy way out of this difficulty. We can simply deny that these abstract entities exist and that they can influence the physical universe. And we can assert that what do exist are our brains, and that these are machines like computers; that the allegedly abstract rules are physical entities, exactly like the concrete physical punch-cards by which we 'program' our computers; and that the existence of anything non-physical is just 'an illusion', perhaps, and at any rate unimportant, since everything would go on as it does even if there were no such illusions. [P. 12]

For obviously what we want is to understand how such non-physical things as *purposes, deliberations, plans, decisions, theories, intentions,* and *values,* can play a part in bringing about physical changes in the physical world. [P. 15]

Retaining Compton's own behaviorist terminology, Compton's problem may be described as the problem of the influence of the *universe of abstract meanings* upon human behavior (and thereby upon the physical universe). Here 'universe of meanings' is a shortand term comprising such diverse things as promises, aims, and various kinds of rules, such as rules of grammar, or of polite behavior, or of logic, or of chess, or of counterpoint; also such things as scientific publications (and other publications); appeals to our sense of justice or generosity; or to our artistic appreciation; and so on, almost *ad infinitum.* [P. 16]

These passages mention several distinguishable components of human mental life (e.g., our feelings, our desires, our reasonings) some of which are more clearly sapient (= cognitive) than others. Thus, for example, a person's "desire for water" would ordinarily be viewed by the psychologist as a fairly complex state of the organism, including such component aspects as water depletion in the peripheral body tissues, afferent nerve impulses arising from local dryness of the throat and mouth, chemical conditions of the extracellular fluid surrounding and bathing nerve cells in the thirst-specific and drinking control centers of the hypothalamus, a heightened "arousal" of the generalized sort associated with any strong biological drive, selective perceptual sensitization to water-related exteroceptive cues, differential activation of acquired instrumental habits (including verbal ones!) that have been strengthened by water reinforcement in the past, and so on. It seems safe to assume, on present evidence (both scientific and commonsense) that those states of the organism that we ordinarily subsume under such generic state-terms as "desire", "feeling", "motive" and the like are partly sapient, partly sentient, and partly neither. For example, unconscious wishes are, by definition, not sentient, and they are (quasi-) sapient only by a complicated—and still disputed—extension of familiar meanings.[7]

It is not our intention to consider separately each of the distinguishable kinds of mental events to which Sir Karl alludes in these passages. We do not believe this is necessary, even if our limited space permitted it. We suggest that the core philosophical objection is best represented by the "pure case" of human sapience, to wit, *rational inference* by a calm, nonhungry, nonthirsty, sexually satisfied, unfrightened, nonangry scholar, whose regnant motive is that upon which Aristotle relies in the first sentence of the *Metaphysics*.[8] We are confident that if ratiocination can be reconciled with psychological determinism, none of the other less "pure" cases, such as involve means-end selections based upon the combination of "knowledge" and "desire", will present insuperable difficulties. On the other hand, a satisfactory deterministic analysis of motivational ("goal-oriented") behavior, such as the mechanism for selecting instrumental responses tending to find sexual gratification or avoid social anxiety, might leave us with persistent doubts about the compatibility of determinism with rationality. One could put it succinctly thus: If ratiocination is compatible with determinism, then, so are purposiveness, goal-directedness, motivated choice, contemplation of alternative, means-end appropriateness, the "influence of our desires on events", and so forth. Whereas, if determinism is *in*compatible with ratiocination, Popper's case is proved, whatever might be shown about any or all of these. We therefore submit that the issue will not be prejudiced by our concentrating on the single question, "Is the doctrine of psychological determinism compatible with the existence of human rationality?"

A common ground with Professor Popper can perhaps be found in the following noncontroversial observation: "It is frequently the case that we influence other persons, and find ourselves influenced by them, through the giving of *reasons*". We employ the weak verb "influence", where many determinist psychologists would prefer to say "determine" or "control", since these stronger words beg the (empirical) question as to precisely how rigidly "clocklike" human behavior is. We do not here enter into the substantive issue, which is qualitatively no different in psychology from that presented by the other biological and social sciences (or, for that matter, as Professor Popper himself emphasizes, the physical sciences) as to whether certain systems are or are not plausibly viewed, on the basis of all available theory and evidence, as ontologically deterministic apart from the question of our "instrumental" ability to predict and control them. As pointed out earlier in this chapter, it is sometimes a rational extrapolation for the scientist to postulate that a system obeys strict laws, i.e., that all the events of a domain are instantiations of nomologicals, even though the limitations of his measuring technology are such that the determination of the initial and boundary conditions of the system make it unfeasible to predict other than statistically. For example, staying away from the human case for the moment, the animal psychologist observes a steady trend toward increased order and regularity in learning curves as he increases his control of the organism's previous history and, especially, his control of the current stimulating field. The smoothness and high-confidence predictability of cumulative response curves obtained in the "Skinner box" is the main reason for its increased use in the study of learning, emotion, psychopharmacology, etc., in preference to the previously popular maze. The lawfulness of the rat's behavior in the Skinner box is sufficiently great (better, for example, than most "physiological" research data) so that a psychologist is sometimes in the position of being able to instruct his research assistant, "See what's the matter with the apparatus", because the curve purportedly produced by a particular rat is one which he can confidently say is *psychologically impossible*, given the animal's previous training and present stimulating conditions. To quote our colleague, Professor Kenneth

MacCorquodale, "These data are impossible; God is a better engineer than Foringer (manufacturer of Skinner-boxes and associated programming and recording apparatus)". It is a matter of degree, not of kind, when the experimental psychologist—or, for that matter, the clinical psychologist, relying upon Freud's investigations—makes the usual scientific extrapolation and assumes until further notice that this fact of increased control (or even well-knit retrospective understanding) suggests that, in the limit, the system would be predictable or, putting it ontologically, that "in itself" the system is deterministic. Again, we do not propose to argue the empirical merits of the substantive questions here (especially the vexed issue, "how do persons differ from rats?").[9]

It is worth noting that there are *non*experimental occasions on which an extremely high degree of predictability, as high as we can normally obtain in an ordinary undergraduate physics laboratory experiment, is present even in the case of complex human behavior involving rational processes. If I take certain rather elementary steps to ascertain that a colleague is in a "normal" state of mind, i.e., that he is not hypnotized or psychotic or drugged or the like, I can predict his answer to certain questions (putting it another way, I can therefore, by asking these questions, control his verbal output) with essentially 100 percent certainty. Thus, we know that, if we present to Professor Popper a certain sort of invalid syllogistic argument and ask him to "comment on this *qua* logician", he will reply, "Illicit distribution of the major", or some synonymous expression. The predictability of this kind of "rational" human behavior is considerably higher than that which obtains in other areas of human behavior (e.g., falling in love, disliking a political figure) and it is also considerably higher than that which obtains in, say, organic medicine, or even in certain domains of the physical sciences (e.g., meteorology).

Furthermore, what appears from the behavioristic standpoint as a practically perfect predictability or controllability of verbal behavior can also be observed introspectively by a nonbehaviorist philosopher of, say, dualist persuasion; and the subjective experience of an individual in this type of situation is consonant with the behaviorist's impression of it, i.e., *one feels subjectively that he is completely powerless to think otherwise.* Of course, he is capable of *speaking* otherwise, and will do so if certain other motivating conditions are provided. For example, one might (as a nefarious Svengali-type psychologist) inform Professor Popper that somebody was going to put a logician's question to him in an effort to "prove the thesis of psychological determinism", and as a result of such instruction Professor Popper might be motivated to show that his behavior is *not* thus neatly predictable, and as an "act of counterwill" refuse to classify the obviously fallacious syllogism as an Illicit distribution of the Major, calling it instead an Undistributed Middle, or saying that it was all right. Here the predictability of what he *would* say is rather low, but (knowing his position on determinism) the predictability that he *would not* say what we would ordinarily expect him to say as a logician might be very high indeed. But these questions involve his overt speech output. In either case, from the subjective standpoint, he would find himself incapable—we do not say "unwilling", we mean literally *incapable*—of cognizing a fallacious syllogism as being valid. If we, as behavior-engineers, told him, "Sir Karl, we are now going to determine your thought for the next few seconds, provided you are willing to listen to what we say next. Consider the following argument. . .", he might refuse to listen to us, or decline to read an argument on a sheet of paper (i.e., we might lack adequate control of his orienting and attending behaviors). But *if* he met these conditions, i.e., if he listened to us and thought about what we were telling him, we would have attained substantially perfect control of *what* he would think about what we said. It is worthwhile emphasizing this subjective aspect, because there is a tendency, when philosophers and psychologists quarrel about this matter, to identify *determinism* with *behaviorism*. And while unquestionably these positions show certain historical connections (and temperamental affinities?) they are related by no logical necessity, as Professor Popper has been careful to remind us.

One source of philosophical (and, even more, of one's personal, "existential") rejection of the idea of psychological determinism is our tendency to associate it with those theorists and ideologists that have laid emphasis upon the *irrational* determiners of human thought and action. If you ask the typical cultivated, educated nonpsychologist for his immediate associations to the idea of psychological determinism, he will usually mention Freud, and with fair probability will add Marx, Pavlov, and—depending upon how much he has kept up with the controversy or how recent his formal education—Skinner. Now whereas Freud was a complete psychological determinist and therefore held that the "rational, reality-testing functions of the ego" were determined as much as anything else, he seemed to feel no tension, let alone logical contradiction, between his own very high valuation of rationality in the scientist's thinking, and the notion that such thinking, as much as the scientist's knee-jerk reflex or digestion, was completely determined. The main thrust of Freud's contribution was the *extent* to which irrational forces control "the surface", and the *extent* to which we are often deceived in giving a purportedly rational account of our conduct. Thus one of the Freudian Mechanisms—contributed not by Freud himself but by Ernest Jones—has the title "Rationalization", the process of giving reasons (perhaps even objectively valid reasons) for actions or beliefs that were, in fact, psychologically produced by internal forces of a very different, nonrational character. It was, of course, no *qualitatively* new discovery on Freud's part that people deceive themselves about their own beliefs and conduct; but the working out of some of the details of the machinery by which this self-deception is carried out, the *quantitative* emphasis upon its being more frequent and more powerful than had generally been supposed, and the elaboration of the *content* of the unconscious processes (e.g., what kinds of impulses are being defended against) have had an impact upon our culture which can hardly be exaggerated. The same is true of Marx who, although he never denied that rational calculation occurred (e.g., when the capitalist asks himself how he can maximize his profits), nevertheless saw a great deal of both individual mental life and cultural development as primarily reflecting economic forces which did not always appear on the surface. Thus we have the stereotype of the kind of vulgar Marxism which would "explain" Darwinism as nothing but the biologist's rationalization of Victorian competitive capitalism, or would "explain" the rise and decline of cubism in terms of the pig iron production of French industry.

Now, without entering into the empirical question whether Freud somewhat exaggerated this (admittedly) pervasive influence of the irrational, what we wish to emphasize here is the following: Whether one describes the mind in psychoanalytic terminology, or in the terminology of an experimental psychology of perception and learning, the most deterministic psychologist does not deny the existence of specific cognitive dispositions—of "habits" or "ego-structures"—that are rational in nature. Thus, for example, in Freudian theory we distinguish between the so-called "primary" and "secondary" processes, between the "pleasure principle" and the "reality principle" of mental functioning, between a relatively strong ego—that means, in large part, a realistic or rational one—and a weak ego, as is found in a young child or a regressed psychotic. One should avoid the very common temptation to think immediately, when psychological determinism is under discussion, of such determiners as one's unconscious hatred for his father or the subtle influence of a blood chemistry attributable partly to the fried eggs one had for breakfast. Popper himself succumbs to this temptation, in discussing the theoretical predictability of Mozart's or Beethoven's composing, in terms of whether they "had eaten lamb, say, instead of chicken, or drunk tea instead of coffee" (*CC*, p. 11). Sometimes unconscious conflicts or fried eggs are strong enough to impair the ego's rational functions; sometimes, fortunately for the conduct of ordinary affairs as well as the advancement of science, the fried eggs simply produce the necessary biological energy to keep the machine working, but do not, in any psychologically or philosophically important way, determine the *direction* or *content* of the ego's cognitive processes. One should not, in contemplating the social and existential implications of psychological determinism, think only of the fact that a man had a permissive mother or an authoritarian father or a vitamin deficiency, to the neglect of such equally important factors as that he inherited a high conceptual intelligence, that he read many books during his teens, that he was exposed to an excellent undergraduate course in logic, and the like.

In this connection it is important to keep in mind the distinction between object language habits and metalanguage habits. Not only do we learn by a complicated mixture of (a) direct reinforcement ("reward") for thinking straight (or, alas, crooked, as the case may be) and (b) by identification with significant figures in our environment who present models of straight or crooked thinking, and (c) by formal precept in school and university, to obey logical rules; we *also* learn a set of powerful metahabits, *such as talking to oneself about the rationality of one's own arguments* (which in the case of philosophically disposed persons may maintain the ascendency in behavior control over many and strong competitive forces). It must be confessed that tendencies of this sort are not as widespread in humankind as one might desire, and it is a presently unsolved question to what extent this sad fact is a matter of poor education or limitations on basic intelligence and temperament. But even the uncultivated layman of low education does possess a rudimentary set of such metahabits, which can be successfully appealed to, if the counterforces are not too great, to control his behavior along rational lines.

Finally, we all acquire certain *self-concepts* in the process of acculturation. For some persons, the self-concept "I am a reasonable fellow, I do not go around committing gross fallacies" is as fundamental and important a part of their personality organization as those kinds of self-concepts more familiar in the literature of psychotherapy, such as "I am an unlovable person" or "I am strong, I do not need to depend upon anybody", or "Nobody can tell me what to do!" or "I am a beautiful woman, all men are attracted to me", and so forth. Here again, while the social and clinical psychologists have attempted, with arguable success, to fill in many details about the mental *machinery*, and the family constellation that contribute to mental *content*, it is noteworthy that the basic situation in such matters has always been understood (in its essentials) by thoughtful men. Everyone knows that in discussing controversial matters, say of politics or economics or sexual morality or foreign policy, we often find ourselves trying to judge whether we can successfully appeal to a person's "need to be rational" when that second-order need, involving the possibility of a threat to his self-concept, is, on a particular substantive issue, placed in opposition to what we (from the outside) view as nonrational or irrational commitments. So we may say of a person, "He's a straight thinking, sensible, fair-minded fellow, and you can almost always learn something from him, and teach him something in a discussion; but I must warn you that he admires his father very much, and his father is a classical representative of the old Southern Bourbon type. So on the race question, you have to handle him with kid gloves; there is one issue where he can sometimes become rather illogical when pressed".

It may be objected that, when the psychologist employs locutions such as "self-concept of being a rational person", he is surreptitiously plugging a nondeterministic concept (i.e., that of *rationality*) into a behavioristic-mechanistic-deterministic theoretical framework in which such meta-categories have no place. One of us (Meehl, 1968) has examined this question at length elsewhere, and the reader may be referred to that[10] for elaboration of the position we adopt on this question. Over against the dualistic, antireductionist philosopher, we hold that there is no contradiction involved in saying, "Jones's thinking is logical [on such and such an occasion]" and saying, "Jones's thinking [including its logicality] is strictly determined by his present neurophysiological state, together with the momentary stimulus inputs; and his current neurophysiological state is in turn completely determined by his antecedents, i.e., genetic equipment interacting with his life experiences".

On the other hand, we must say (against certain kinds of neo-behaviorists) that the psychologist's scientific task—whether its explanatory, predictive, or controlling aspects are emphasized—cannot be carried out *at a molar level of analysis*, unless the psychologist employs certain of the logician's concepts and rubrics in his, the psychologist's, object language. This is not the place to develop that argument in detail, for which development the reader is referred to the article cited above by Meehl. Briefly, the position is that, in order to explain, predict, and control, let us say, the verbal behavior of a logic professor when presented with a formal fallacy such as Illicit Distribution, the psychologist must be able to *characterize the stimulus side*, i.e., the perceptual input to which the logician responds with such an utterance as "Illicit Major". And the point is that the psychologist's use of such concepts as "stimulus equivalence" or "verbal generalizations" must not be employed by him to hide a very important fact: When the psychologist is forced to make explicit the *configural* properties of a stimulus input that will render it "stimulus-equivalent" to the subject logician, so that, for example, the logician can properly classify a syllogism whose terms—except for the logical constants—are terms of which he does not know the meaning, and to which he has never been previously exposed; the only way to characterize this stimulus input is in terms of its *formal structure*. An adequate characterization of that stimulus class, regardless of what terminology the psychologist might employ in describing it, will, of course, turn out upon careful analysis to correspond to the characterization found in a logic text. It is of no substantive interest whether the behaviorist psychologist actually employs the logician's sign vehicle "Illicit Major", since it must be admitted that whatever (nonphilosophical) sign vehicle the psychologist employs, his *definition* of it will involve specifying the very same formal features which the logician specifies in defining the term "Illicit Major". For this reason we hold that when Skinner[11] speaks of logic being "embraced by our [the radical behaviorist's] analysis", although he is literally correct if he means that reasonable behavior, and the tokening of metalinguistic terms belonging to logic, have a causal history in the learning process; he is incorrect if he means that this behaviorist "embracing" involves the liquidation, or a showing of irrelevancy, of the logician's *categories* in a psychological analysis of "reasonable verbal behavior". *The molar behaviorist psychologist who concerns himself with language and with rational, cognitive, ego-functions must reconcile himself to the fact that he cannot dispense with the logician's formal categories.*

We mean by this something much stronger than what would be meant if we said it about a physicist or a botanist. Every scientist has to come to terms with the logician in two ways, namely, (a) He must exemplify logical processes in his object-linguistic discourse, i.e., he must think rationally about his subject matter; and (b) Since a great deal of scientific discussion and scholarly writing is not simply reports of observations, or formulation of theory, but is critical discussion of theories (their relationship to one another and to observations, the validity of one's own and other people's inferences, and the like), the scientist must also make use of the logician's categories in his metalinguistic discourse, i.e., in the process of scientific criticism. In respects (a)-(b) psychology is not essentially different from the other sciences. However, there are no other sciences in Comte's pyramid of the sciences below the level of psychology (we are assuming economics, sociology, anthropology and political science all appear "above" psychology in this well-known pyramid) which are forced to employ the categories of the logician or philosopher in their object language.

It is not clear why this necessity should be distressing to a biological or social scientist, but for some reason it often seems to be. Whether it should distress the philosopher depends upon whether there is some kind of paradox or contradiction involved in *meta*linguistic terms, such as "valid", or "Illicit Distribution", appearing in the *object* language discourse of an empirical science. But, if this represents a problem for the philosopher, it represents a technical problem in logical theory, so we content ourselves with merely calling attention to the oddity. (Our colleague, Professor Keith Gunderson, suggests that, since this unavoidable reference by the molar behaviorist to formal categories is so evident, any logician's theory about object language/metalanguage relationships that precludes it is, *ipso facto*, suspect.)

A final question concerning any reductionist-determinist view of the psychology of beliefs, arguments, inquiry, criticism, and the like is the question, "Would a complete causal account, *formulated in terms of the microlevel* (e.g., electrical and chemical events at neural synapses) be incompatible with our intuitive conviction that our beliefs and actions are influenced by reasons?" It is our contention, as opposed to Sir Karl's, that there is no such incompatibility, although at first impression it does appear that there must be. Suppose one takes the expression "a valid reason" as designating a kind of abstract Platonic universal which *in some sense* "exists", and would exist even if there were no thinking brains (a position we are not here espousing, but will adopt as a premise *arguendo*, since it is the one most unfavorable to the determinist analysis of human thought and action); then we hold that "the existence of a valid reason" (in some such abstract, metaphysical, Platonic sense) is a question belonging to the critical domain of logic, broadly conceived. But the *thinking* of such a reason by a living, concrete human person, the *stating* of a reason, the *hearing* of a reason, the *mentioning* of a reason, *the tokening of a sentence which expresses a proposition which is a good reason for another proposition*—these are all events very much "in the world" and "belonging to the causal order". And we maintain that one does not have to conflate reasons with causes, or to commit the fallacy of psychologism in logic (or the naturalistic fallacy in ethics), to be justified in saying that, although the validity of an argument, or the soundness and cogency of a reason, is an abstract Platonic truth about universals, nevertheless the thinking of a reason is an event, is a something which happens in space-time, in a living brain (just as the uttering of a valid reason happens in a human larynx), and instantiates nomologicals.

Admittedly there is something initially strange about the notion that a man's beliefs or actions are influenced by reasons, i.e., as we say a man is to this extent and in this matter "reasonable", and nevertheless hypothesizing—as a promissory note, until further notice, as an orienting "faith" of the scientific investigator—that the brain processes involved could, in principle, be formulated by Omniscient Jones *at a level of causal analysis which would dispense with the logician's categories*. But, although this does seem to us a bit odd, and to some readers will doubtless be highly paradoxical, we are not persuaded by Professor Popper's paper, or by any arguments that have been thus far brought to our attention, that there is anything contradictory in it. What must be understood, if we are right in our view of the matter, is that when one gives a complete causal account of a physical process at a certain level of analysis, *he does not thereby claim*, in making a metaclaim to "causal completeness", *that he has asserted everything true that could properly be asserted about the system*. In other words, it is the difference between telling the truth and telling the *whole* truth.

It is important to notice here that, whereas Professor Popper's distinction between "Compton's problem" (puzzles about determinism) and "Descartes's problem" (puzzles about the mind-body relationship) is a valid and useful one, at this stage of our discussion they are seen to be intimately related; and if the reader will turn back to the series of quotations from Popper at the beginning of this section, he will notice that Professor Popper himself has at times conflated them, we think perhaps unintentionally but unavoidably. Although the (Compton) question "How can I be rational and purposive if determined?" can be seen as presenting a philosophical problem even within a framework of radical (ontological) mind-body dualism, its bite is greatly sharpened if, instead, the determining (and determined) events are all set in a purely physicalistic ontology. Roughly put, it is bad enough if my "mind" is determined; but it is worse if my "mind" is nothing but a complex configuration of events or states, a sequence of occurrents that deterministically befall continuants that are themselves "nonmental" in nature. This fusion of the Compton problem and the Descartes problem has, of course, a venerable history, being already formulated clearly and powerfully by Plato (in the *Phaedo*, 98c - 99b) and Aristotle (in the *Metaphysics*, Book 9, Chap. 6, 1048b—18-30). It has received considerable attention from several contemporary Oxford philosophers, and from the Americans A. I. Melden and Richard Taylor, to mention only notable examples. It is perhaps foolhardy for us in this limited space to attempt a resolution of such an ancient and recondite question, to which so many able thinkers have addressed themselves (and, on the current scene, emerged with answers very different from ours). But we are satisfied that no one has formulated the determinist-monist analysis of rationality (or purposive action) *quite* in the manner we propose, and that our kind of "levels" picture of the situation, whether ultimately refutable or not, will at least constitute a contribution to the ongoing philosophical discussion of this venerable controversy.

Consider first a nonpsychological example. If I give a detailed, blow-by-blow mechanical account of a sequence of operations carried on by an ordinary desk calculator, I can properly say, in conclusion, that "causally speaking, nothing has been 'left out' of this account". But it is evident that such a detailed account in terms of the laws of mechanics (as applied to the structure-dependent properties of the machine in respect to its inner workings) does not *have* to contain such (true) statements as, "The machine is dividing 3,746 by 125". Yet that is, quite literally, what the machine is doing. It does not occur to us, in such simple, inanimate system cases, to postulate the existence of some kind of an "arithmetical" *deus ex machina* as a necessary addition to the causal system first described. Nevertheless, one can shift the level of description upward to a more "molar" level, as an instructor in a statistics laboratory would do in talking to a student about how to operate the machine. At that (more "molar"-behaviorist) level of analysis, the instructor formulates quasi-causal laws (they are tight nomologicals, as long as the machine is not broken or worn out) in which such concepts as addition, division, multiplication and the like occur in the formulation.

We think that there is a temptation, when philosophers consider the implications of psychological determinism for the possibility of human rationality and genuine criticism, to move from the (correct) statement, "At level L_c of causal analysis, not everything which might truly be said has been said" to the false (as we think) statement, "Therefore, at level L_c of analysis, the causal account is radically incomplete". If certain definitions are given at one level of analysis, and then certain reductions are carried out (given acceptance of a suitable theoretical network), it will then be clear that the things which were left unsaid follow necessarily from those things which were said, when the latter are taken together with the explicit definitions. So that, whether or not it is literally correct to say of a microphysiological account of a complicated human thought process that the account "leaves something out", depends upon a clarification of what is meant. If the speaker means to say that something has been left unsaid which could truly be said, he is right; but if he means that the causal account will not be complete unless some additional *theoretical entity* is introduced into the causal chain, then—assuming that the reductionist thesis is empirically correct—he is wrong.

In speaking of "reduction" and "definition" in the preceding paragraph, we are perhaps inviting a major misunderstanding which we shall now endeavor to forestall. Our position is not, we trust, a surreptitious reduction of the *logical* to the *physical*, as if to say that conceptual relations (e.g., class-inclusion, formal deducibility, contradiction) could be defined in terms of "nonlogical" notions (e.g., mass, rigidity, proximity, protoplasm, synaptic resistance). We take it that everyone—whether philosopher, physicist, psychologist, computer engineer, and whether determinist or not, "physicalist" or not—would agree with Sir Karl that any such reduction is impossible in principle. Logical and arithemetical relationships are *sui generis*, not definable in terms of physical or biological categories or dimensions, and we wish to make it crystal clear that we accept this truth unqualifiedly and without equivocation.

In what sense, then, can we properly speak of "explicit definition" in the preceding line of argument? Reflect again upon the desk calculator problem. Replying to an imagined critic (one who has Cartesian, antibehaviorist, antiphysicalist or emergentist views about these machines), and who complains that our detailed microaccount of the machine's transitions "leaves out the main point, namely, that the calculator is adding the numbers 4 and 3 to get the (valid) answer 7", we say the following: "It is a true statement that you offer as supplementary to our mechanical account; the machine is, quite literally, 'adding numbers', and, furthermore, it is 'getting the correct answer'. And it is true that our mechanical description did not anywhere include this arithmetical assertion. You are therefore entirely right in saying that our account does not 'say everything that can properly be said'. What we deny is that we have 'left something out' in the causal sense; specifically, we deny that there occurs any event, state, or process involving any *theoretical entity* [= entity playing an explanatory role in the nomological net, possessing causal efficacy] over and above the physical entities included in our 'nonarithmetical' account". We wish to maintain that the following statements are jointly compatible:

1. Our causal account A_c of "how the calculator works", as a physical mechanism, is complete.
2. The words "sum", "addition", "integer", etc., do not occur in A_c. (Names *of* integers may, of course, occur in the account A_c; mathematics is part of the object language of mechanics, of course. We do not talk metamathematics in describing the machine's physical operations; we do not even *mention* arithmetical theorems. We do, however, *rely upon* such theorems; and, of course, we use numerical *concepts* [e.g., "the second gear underwent three forward tooth-displacements"].)
3. "Number" is not a theoretical (causal) entity contained in, or acting upon, the machine.
4. The machine (literally) *adds numbers*.

We invite the reader to try developing a genuine contradiction from these four statements. We think there is none. What there is, is a kind of oddity—the kind of oddity that wears off, however, with sufficient familiarity. Not that we would for a moment countenance invoking oddity as a negative criterion, especially in these deep matters.

On the positive side, perhaps the shortest formulation (aimed at therapeutic erosion of the oddity-response) would be something like the following: Abstract "entities", such as formal (numerical, logical, set-theoretical) relations considered as Platonic universals, are not "in" the machine, in the sense that its *parts* are *in* it. Nor are they "in" the *event*-sequence, as, say, a wheel displacement is. But the physical entities (whether continuants or occurrents) which *are*, literally, *in* the machine, do (in some respects) exemplify those abstract universals. The cardinal number 3 is not, obviously, in the machine. But sets of structures and events of cardinality 3 are there.

In discussing with colleagues our approach to this aspect of Popper's problem, we were once met with the objection that our analysis really consisted of saying that the desk calculator (or a "logic machine", or the human brain) is a physical model satisfying the laws of arithmetic, which *all* physical entities necessarily satisfy; from which, the critic argued, it would follow that no calculators (or brains) can err. This complaint rests upon a confusion among physical levels. We must be clear about *which* physical entities and

processes are taken as elements and relations of the physical model corresponding to the elements and relations of the calculus. It is, of course, true
that the physical set formed by conjunction of a set of three iron atoms and a
set of two iron atoms is a set having cardinality 5, even though the gear in
which these five atoms lie is part of a worn-out calculator (which "makes
arithmetical mistakes"). But the cardinal number of interest is not that of the
constituent atoms, it is the number of tooth-displacements. Or, treating the
machine "molar-behavioristically", the cardinal number of interest is either
(a) The number of punch-and-cumulate operations or (b) The cardinal
number designated in English, by the numeral [= "3"] on a key punched and
cumulated once. And it is obvious that *these* (= "molar") physical events do
not necessarily satisfy the laws of arithmetic. *If* the wheels are not worn out,
prone to slippage, etc., then three punchings and cumulations of key labeled
"1" will result in a state of three-tooth-displacement; this state will persist until two further unit-additions occur. It being a theorem of arithmetic that
$3 + 2 = 5$, we know that 3 physical displacements "plus" 2 physical displacements leads to a terminal state of 5 net displacements. It is (trivially)
analytic to say that "If the machine satisfies the axioms, it satisfies the
theorems". But the point is that, whereas its constituent atoms satisfy the axioms, the "molar"-level parts and processes may fail to be a model of
arithmetic, when the physical operations occur in time and the numbers are
used to characterize resulting positions rather than historical facts. The
statements S_1: "Gear G has undergone three forward displacement events
during interval $(t_1 - t_0)$" and S_2: "Gear G has undergone two forward displacement events during interval $(t_2 - t_1)$" jointly entails S_3: "Gear G has undergone five forward displacement events during interval $(t_2 - t_0)$". This truth
of arithmetic, that $S_1.S_2 \rightarrow S_3$, cannot fail to be satisfied by the machine, worn- ·
out or not. But the conjunction S_1. S_2 does *not* entail S_4: "At t_2, Gear G is in a
state displaced five steps from its state at t_0". Gear G may have "slipped"
backward at some time during the interval. And similar considerations apply
a fortiori when a causal interaction between different gears is supposed to
model arithmetical operations.

Unavoidably, any causal reconstruction of rational mental processes in
terms of brain events will suffer, at the present state of our knowledge, either
from extreme generality—amounting to little more than a restatement in
pseudo-brain-language of such general formal concepts as "model"—or, if it
becomes more specific than this and attempts to deliver the goods, so to
speak, *scientifically*, it will be on the fringe of current empirical knowledge
and readily objected to by the critic as not only unproved but excessively
speculative. We do not take it as our task, in examining Professor Popper's
objections, to present a brain model. And since his objection is essentially
philosophical (rather than directed at what is wrong with any specific sub-

stantive theory of learning, perception, or thinking in the present state of the behavior sciences) we are confident he will not complain in either of these two ways, so long as we make quite clear which enterprise we are engaged in, i.e., a highly generalized statement of the conditions for the brain to think rationally although determined, or, on the other hand, a specific physicalistic *example* which exhibits the philosophical point we wish to make but lays no claim at all to scientific correctness.

Returning to the question of the sense in which a physicalistic account in brain language is "complete" *even though it does not say all that could truly be said*, we suggest the following as a first approximation to an account which, while maintaining the distinction between logical categories and the categories of physics or physiology, nevertheless insists that a physicalistic microaccount is nomologically complete. We have a calculus, such as arithmetic or the rules of the categorical syllogism. We have a class of brain events which are identified by appropriate physical properties—these, of course, may be highly "configural" in character—at, say, an intermediate level of molarity (i.e., the events involve less than the whole brain or some molar feature of the whole acting and thinking person, but are at a "higher" level in the hierarchy of physical subsystems than, say, the discharge of a single neuron, or the alteration of microstructure at a synapse). Considered in their functioning as inner tokenings—that is, however peripherally or behavioralistically they were originally acquired by social conditioning, considering them as now playing the role of Sellars's *mental word*[12]—there is a physically identifiable brain event b_M which "corresponds" (in the mental word sense) to the subject term in the first premise of a syllogism in Barbara. There is a second tokening event b_P which is a token of the type that designates the predicate term of the conclusion; a brain event b_S which corresponds to a tokening of the type that designates the subject term of the conclusion of the syllogism; and finally a brain event b_C corresponding to the copula. (These expository remarks are offered with pedagogic intent only. We do not underestimate the enormous complexity of adequately explaining the words "correspond" and "designate" in the immediately preceding text.)

A physically-omniscient neurophysiologist [=Omniscient Jones estopped from metatalk about logic] can, we assume, identify these four brain events b_M, b_P, b_S, b_C on the basis of their respective conjunction of physical properties, which presumably are some combination of *locus* (where in the brain? which cell assemblies?) and *quantitative properties of function* (peak level of activation of an assembly, decay rate, pulse frequency of driving the next assembly in a causal chain, mean number of activated elements participating). For present purposes we may neglect any problem of extensional vagueness, which is not relevant to the present line of argument, although it is of considerable interest in its own right.

Our physically-omniscient neurophysiologist is in possession of a finite set of statements which are the nomologicals (or quasi-nomologicals) of neurophysiology, which we shall designate collectively by L_{phys} [= neurophysiological laws]. He is also in possession of a very large, unwieldy, but finite set of statements about structure, including (a) macrostructure, (b) structure of intermediate levels, e.g., architectonics and cell-type areas such as studied microscopically in a brain-histology course, and (c) microstructural statements including microstructural statements about functional connections. We take it for granted that "learned functional connections" *must* be embodied in microstructure (although its exact nature is still a matter for research) since there is otherwise no explanation of the continuity of memory when organisms, human or animal, are put into such deep anesthesia that all nerve cell discharge is totally suspended for considerable time periods, or when normal functional activity is dramatically interrupted by such a cerebral storm as a *grand mal* seizure induced in electroshock treatment. Thus the class of structural statements S_t includes two major subclasses of statements, one being about the inherited "wiring diagram" of a human brain, and the other being the acquired functional synaptic connections resulting from the learning process.

Our omniscient neurophysiologist can derive, from the conjunction $(L_{phys} \cdot S_t)$, a "brain theorem" T_b, which, to an approximation adequate for present purposes, may be put this way: Brain-state theorem T_b: "Whenever the composite brain events $(b_M b_C b_P)$ and $(b_S b_C b_M)$ are temporally contiguous, a brain event $(b_S b_C b_P)$ follows immediately." This brain theorem is formulated solely in terms of the states b_i which are physicalistically identifiable, and without reference to any such metaconcept as class, syllogism, inference, or the like. The derivation of T_b is one of strict deducibility in the object language of neurophysiology. That is, neurophysiology tells us that a brain initially wired in such and such a way, and then subsequently "programmed" by social learning to have such and such functional connections (dispositions), will necessarily [nomological necessity] undergo the event $(b_S b_C b_P)$ whenever it has just previously undergone the events $(b_M b_C b_P)$ and $(b_S b_C b_M)$ in close temporal contiguity.

But, whereas for the neurophysiologist this brain theorem is a theorem about certain physical events *and nothing more*, a logician would surely discern an interesting formal feature revealed in the descriptive notation—the subscripts—of the b's. It would hardly require the intellectual powers of a Carnap or Gödel to notice, *qua* logician, that these brain events constitute a physical model of a subcalculus of logic, i.e., that these physical entities $[b_M, b_P, b_S, b_C]$ "satisfy" the formal structure of the syllogism in Barbara, if we interpret

b_M = tokening of middle term b_S = tokening of subject term

b_P = tokening of predicate term b_C = tokening of copula.

The "brain theorem" T_b can be derived nomologically from the structural statements S_t together with the microphysiological law-set L_{phys} given explicit definitions of the events $[b_M, b_P, b_S, b_C]$. These explicit definitions are not the model-interpretations, nor are they "psycholinguistic" characterizations. We can identify a case of b_P by its physical microproperties, without knowing that it is a tokening event, i.e., without knowing that it plays a certain role in the linguistic system which the individual who owns this brain has socially acquired. But brain theorem T_b has itself a formal structure, which is "shown forth" in one way, namely, by the syntactical configuration of the b-subscripts [M,P,S,C]. In this notation, "which subscript goes with what" is determinable, so long as the events b_i are physically identifiable. There is nothing physically arbitrary in this, and there is nothing in it that requires the physically-omniscient neurophysiologist to be thinking about syllogisms, or even, for that matter, to know that there is any such thing as a syllogism. Although again, it goes without saying that he himself must reason logically in order to derive the brain theorem. But he does not have to metatalk about rules, or about his own rule-obedience, in order to token rule conformably in his scientific object language, and this suffices to derive T_b.

One near-literal metaphor which we find helpful in conveying the essence of the "syllogistic brain theorem" situation, as we see it, is that the sequence of brain events $(b_i b_j b_k)$ $(b_j b_k b_l)$ . . . embodies the syllogistic rules. Their defined physical structure plus the physical laws of brains function causally necessitate that they exemplify syllogistic transitions, a fact revealed when the notation designating them is considered in its formal aspects. In the usual terminology of thinking processes and logic, the brain theorem T_b says, in effect, that the existence of a formal relation of deducibility (truth of logic) provides, in a brain for which the theorem obtains, the necessary and sufficient causal condition for a factual transition of inference (a mental process). This assertion may appear to "mix the languages", to "commit the sin of psychologism", to "Conflate causes with reasons"; but we maintain that none of these blunders is involved. It is a physical fact that a certain formal relation is physically embodied. If the formal features of the initial physical state were otherwise, the ensuing physical result would have been otherwise. Hence the physical embodiment of the formal relation—a fact, which is "in the world" as concretely as the height, in meters, of Mount Everest—is literally a condition for the inference to occur.

Comes now the emergentist or Cartesian dualist advancing an objection as follows: "Even granting, which I do not, that there are any such strictly deterministic brain nomologicals as L_{phys}, and assuming arguendo that your concept of a physically-omniscient neurophysiologist (who is ignorant of metastatements in logic) could actually carry out the derivation of T_b from $(L_{phys} \cdot S_t)$, I must interpose a philosophical objection which is surely available to us upon present knowledge, and does not rely upon speculations, whether optimistic or pessimistic, about the future development of brain science. My philosophical objection is a very simple one, and it is this. While you, in your imaginary reconstruction of the derivation possibility for the physically-omniscient neurophysiologist, can carefully avoid any reference to the syllogism, or to the formal validity of the inference which is 'embodied' in these brain events, *you yourself* do have in mind that this is the brain of a thinking human being, and you do intend me to understand that these brain events are his valid thinkings. Yet you say that you give an exhaustive account of what happens, and that you can explain, i.e., derive nomologically, given the structural statements S_t, all that went on. Now if it is true that you can derive everything that goes on within the object language of the physically-omniscient neurophysiologist, then the fact that this brain event sequence is [known to you and me but not to him] a process of valid inference, that the individual whose brain we are studying is *correctly thinking a syllogism in Barbara*, turns out to be an irrelevant fact, a supernumerary, something that dosen't make any difference at all. Whereas I want to hold that this is the most important fact about these happenings. How can you say that you have given a complete account of what is taking place in this person, that you have 'explained everything' about the happenings under consideration, when you have not anywhere said the most important thing there is to say, namely, *that he is making a valid inference?* If the physically-omniscient neurophysiologist can derive the brain theorem T_b without even knowing that inference is going on in this person's brain (I should of course prefer to say 'mind', but I will make concessions to your strange materialist verbal habits), then the validity of the inference makes no difference. Whereas, of course, I know perfectly well, brain physiology aside, that whether a certain inference is permissible makes all the difference in the world, and you yourself have said the same thing earlier in the present discourse. I simply do not understand how you can say that the account is causally complete when it leaves out the most important fact, which is a *logical* fact, namely, that a valid inference is being made when the person passes from tokening 'M is P' and 'S is M' to tokening 'S is P'."

Now the first thing to see about this Cartesian or emergentist objection is that it contains an important element of truth, which it is both dishonest and unnecessary for the determinist-materialist to deny. The objector points out that, in the microphysiological account of the brain events which is assumed to be offered by the physically-omniscient neurophysiologist, something that is literally true has not been said, to wit, *that a valid syllogism is being tokened*. Having freely admitted this, our next question is, does it follow from the fact that something which could be truly literally said has not been said, that the causal account is incomplete? This is the crucial issue, and we want to urge that the proper answer to this question is in the negative. But, of course, in order to examine this question, one has to arrive at some suitable convention for the use of the metalinguistic expressions "everything that can be said" and "a complete causal account of the events".

Let us first point out that there are many obvious and noncontroversial cases, lying quite outside the realm of the mind-body problem (or the determinism problem, or the intentionality problem) where it is clear that a complete causal account of a series of events can be given without explicitly saying everything that would, if said, be literally true. Examples are so numerous as to be almost pointless, so we will mention only one. Suppose that I give a causal account of the displacement of the piston in a cylinder by an expanding gas, and this account is given at the microlevel—in the extreme case, by the long, but finite, set of sentences describing the components of momenta, the positions, the impacts on the wall of the container, etc., of the individual gas molecules. Nothing is left out of this account from the standpoint of physical understanding. I do not, however, mention that the number of molecules in this batch of gas is prime. Let it not be objected that this is a silly instance. That the number of these molecules is prime is just as much a physical fact as is the set of numbers characterizing the components of their respective momenta. It is not, however, a fact we find it necessary to *mention* in giving a complete causal account of how the gas displaces the piston. This example suffices at least to show, what is really a rather trivial and unexciting truth, that one can say everything that is causally relevant in accounting (at all levels of causal analysis) for a certain phenomenon, without saying everything that is literally true about it.

But we will readily concede to the Cartesian critic that this example is, while sufficient to prove the just stated general thesis, not a fair analogy to the brain theorem problem. Because what he is objecting to in our brain theorem case is not only that we have left out something that is literally true (that the brain is thinking about a syllogism in Barbara), but that the *outcome* of the thinking is critically influenced by the *logical fact* that the inference is valid. And while it is literally true that the number of molecules in the gas is prime, this is not a fact which makes any difference to the outcome.

This last locution, the phrase "makes any difference to the outcome", contains, we think, the core of the objection, and also provides us with the essence of our answer to it. What do we mean when we say that something's being the case, or not the case, "makes any difference"? Depending upon one's views concerning causality, a number of things might be meant; but we assume that at least a minimum condition for its being appropriate to say that "such and such makes no difference" is that if such and such *had not* obtained, the outcome *would have been* the same as the outcome in fact was when such and such *did* obtain. Whatever else one might mean about something "making no difference", he surely must mean at least this counterfactual. Now is it literally correct to say, as the critic does here, that the causal account provided by the physically-omniscient neurophysiologist shows that the validity of the inference, as a formal truth, makes no difference? That is, does it follow, from the metafact that the physical microaccount provided by the neurophysiologist does not contain any reference to the formal structure (revealed by the subscripts on the b's), that *if this formal structure were not present, the terminating brain event* $(b_S b_C b_P)$ *would occur nevertheless?* Clearly not. The brain theorem is stated in terms of b's with distinguishable subscripts, and these subscripts are formally related, *within the theorem* T_b, in a certain way. Thus, we do not have a brain theorem stating the following: "Whenever brain events $(b_S b_C b_M)$ and $(b_P b_C b_M)$ occur in close temporal contiguity, they are immediately followed by brain event $(b_S b_C b_P)$". In fact, if the brain under study is that of an always-rational man, we will instead have a countertheorem here, which states that this particular contiguity will never be immediately followed by the third event, i.e., this being the brain of a perfectly rational man, he never commits the fallacy of Undistributed Middle. Now the point is that the physically-omniscient neurophysiologist *does not have to mention* this formal feature about the b-subscripts in order for his account to be causally complete, because the statements he *does* mention jointly entail, as a matter of nomological necessity, that the brain events will be related in such and such a way, i.e., that they will in fact be models of the syllogism in Barbara, a consequence which is revealed by the syntactical configuration of the subscripts. And it is literally false to say that the same "conclusion" $(b_S b_C b_P)$ would be tokened in this brain if the subscripts designating the physical events preceding this conclusion-tokening had been different from what they in fact were. In a way, the point is really quite trivial, being essentially no more than to say that if any set of properties makes a causal difference, then any other set which can be explicitly defined in terms of the first set also "makes a difference", for if those higher-level properties were not in fact what they are on a particular occasion, then, since they are defined explicitly in terms of the lower-level properties, it follows that the lower-level properties could not have been what they in fact are; and therefore the outcome would have been physically different.

It still seems admittedly a little strange that one does not have to mention the validity of the syllogism thus exemplified or embodied by the brain processes in giving a complete physical-causal account. We believe that this strangeness arises mainly from the fact that the causal account offered by the physically-omniscient neurophysiologist *begins* with certain microstructural premises contained in the collection of sentences S_t and that *these sentences collectively constitute the physical description of the microstates which embody the dispositions to compute rationally in this brain,* dispositions that have been socially learned when the individual acquired the habits of "thinking straight". That is the historical account of why these microstructural facts are what they are. But we may start our explanation of the brain theorem T_b at a given moment in time, forgetting about the learning history; then we represent only the *results* of social learning (to think straight) by statements about microstructures at the synapse, considered neuron by neuron. This way of describing the matter of course yields a paradoxical effect, because it now appears that the all-important "fact of rationality" has been left out of the picture. But the point is that the all-important fact of rationality has not really been left out of the picture, *it has instead been stated* (admittedly opaquely) *by referring to the microstructures which embody the "rational dispositions".* There is, of course, a familiar sense in which one may be considered to have expressed everything in a theoretical system when he expresses the postulates, in that he is considered to "assert" implicitly all of the theorems that follow therefrom. From this point of view, our physically-omniscient neurophysiologist therefore "asserts" the brain theorem T_b, and he therefore "asserts" the syntactical relationships holding among the b-subscripts in the terms that are contained in the brain theorem. And he therefore "asserts", although not expressly (since he speaks no metalanguage), the crucial fact that this brain is a rationally reasoning brain.

Whether a purportedly complete causal account deserves criticism because of its failure to assert explicitly one or more of the necessary consequences of what it *does* assert, depends upon several considerations such as human social interest, level of analysis as defined by the pragmatic context of one's investigation, and the like. Therefore to leave out a statement that follows from the conjunction of other statements, to the effect that the number of molecules in a contained gas is prime, would not ordinarily strike us as a very serious omission, although it would be a valid comment that "a true statement was left unsaid". But even if we remain at the level of inorganic processes, where purpose and knowledge are not attributable to the system under study, it is easy to think of instances in which something is left unsaid that one would normally think of as a very serious omission, yet that something is not something that one *must* say in giving a complete causal account of what took place. Example: I drop an ice cube in a cup of boiling tea, and physically-Omniscient Jones gives a detailed microaccount of the ensuing process of its dissolution. That is, he considers the tea, molecule by molecule, and considers the face of the ice, molecule by molecule, describing each molecular collision, the interplay between the mechanical forces of impact and the intermolecular forces tending to maintain the solid state of the ice

crystal, etc. We end up with all of the water molecules that were in the ice being dispersed among the water molecules in the tea, and our story is closed.
Here is a situation where, unlike the silly case of the prime numbered gas
molecules, we are strongly impelled to say, at the close of the account, "Well,
that's all very fine, but you know you never said once that the main thing going on here was that hot tea was losing heat to cold ice and cold ice was taking
up heat from hot tea, and the result of this whole process is that an ice cube in
a cup of hot tea has dissolved and disappeared. You didn't say that. You left
that out. *And what you left out is the most important thing that went on*".
Our point is that the question of "importance" refers to a number of considerations, which collectively may or may not lead us to be critical of an account which omits to mention something that is literally true and that in fact
follows deductively—given certain already available nomologicals and explicit definitions—from the statements that were made in the account.

In the case of the human brain thinking syllogistically, it is obvious that
there are at least two kinds of things that could be said that are not said in
stating and deriving the "brain theorem" T_b, and which make us critical of
the account. The first is the role of "purpose" (motivation, intention, goal-
orientation) in the thought processes, which we might express either with
reference to the reinforcement history of this individual (as a consequence of
which his brain cells have acquired the syllogistic dispositions that they have);
or, alternatively, by reference to the state of distress (surprise, disconfirmed
expectancy, shame or guilt, or whatever) that the individual is disposed to experience if he finds himself committing a formal fallacy. This motivational
feature is one that has not until recently engaged the attention of computer-
simulation investigators, and it will unquestionably come in for a great deal
of systematic attention in the near future. See, for example, Simon.[13] It was,
of course, not our intention to pretend that such goal-oriented factors are absent in the above account, but we presume that Sir Karl will agree that, in
spite of their intimate relations to human thought, *intentionality* and *intention* are different concepts; that one thinks rationally and that one desires to
think rationally are two different facts, although they are intimately related.

Secondly, we also omitted reference to those metatalk dispositions of the
sort that we imagined our physically-omniscient neurophysiologist to lack.
We restricted his omniscience to physical events, and kept him out of the
metalanguage of logic for our purpose in discussing the physical derivability
of the "brain theorem". But it does not appear to us that any new issue of
principle concerning determinism and rationality is raised by the introduction
of the metalanguage. Whether there are any insuperable set-theoretical or
Gödel-related difficulties in computer-hardware analogs to the human mind
is not the province of this paper and is beyond our scholarly competence. Fortunately for us Sir Karl has not made such considerations the focus of his

attention (except insofar as there is a set-theoretical problem involved in the world-calendar idea, dealt with in Section I above).

Of course, in the real world no such "brain theorem" as T_b will be validly deducible from realized conditions S_t together with the cerebral nomologicals L_{phys}, inasmuch as all actual human thinkers (even philosophers!) do at times commit formal fallacies. It does not appear to us that this qualification is germane to the analysis we are proposing, however; it merely indicates that the human brain is, as we readily agree with Sir Karl, not a complete "clock" but a mechanism having some "cloudy" properties. For expository purposes we have considered the idealized case, that is, the brain of a thinker who never reasons fallaciously. The necessary modifications are easy and obvious ones which do not, as we think, affect the point of our line of argument. There are two ways to modify the above brain theorem example which would render it more realistic, one of which accepts a determinist picture of the world and the other a quasi-determinist picture with "random" components included as part of the system. On a completely determinist view, the conjunction $S_t L_{phys}$ is explained in such a way that the various causal *sources* of fallacious reasoning, e.g., of failure to conclude validly in Barbara, are ruled out as initial conditions by restrictively characterizing S_t in sufficient microdetail. (Another way of doing this, still preserving the determinist position, is to consider three classes of determiners, one of which is the structural determiners, the second of which is again L_{phys}, but the third of which is "momentary state-variables" such as emotion, or the presence of some kind of unconscious Freudian dynamism, or unusual stimulus input or the like.) Alternatively, however, we may choose to do justice to what we, like Popper, suppose to be a certain cloudlike feature in the cerebral quasi-clock (even as causally understood by Omniscient Jones) in which case we must replace the brain theorem T_b in its nomological form by a brain theorem T'_b in stochastic form. In this case, the relationship between the stochastic brain theorem T'_b and the formal structure of the syllogism in Barbara (as shown forth in the subscripts on notation designating the brain states about which the theorem speaks) would be analogous to the familiar distinction between the statistical data that constitute an anthropologist's or a psycholinguist's "descriptive semantics" of a language, and the idealized semantical rules (*prescriptive* sense of "rule") which the dictionary writer, semantician, or logician sets down on the basis of this descriptive survey. Obviously, the overwhelming preponderance of successor states to the "premise-tokening" brain states will, in an intelligent nonpsychotic brain, be such as to reveal the same formal structure as in our idealized example. So that a perspicacious logician would have no more difficulty discerning the formal structure in the stochastically formulated theorem than he would in the nomological form, since he would immediately notice the high probability outcome (b_S b_C b_P) and then discern that its subscripts are Barbara-related to the subscripts on the antecedent cerebral events. But, of course, while identifying the usual (valid, "rational") sequence would take care of the needs of the logician who is attempting to understand whether, and how, this particular brain "thinks correctly"; the molar psychologist has an equally great interest—whether Freudian or less clinical in bent—in understanding causally why the brain theorem is merely stochastic, and in identifying the major classes of interfering factors which operate to produce departures from "validity" on certain occasions.

CONCLUSION

We must leave to the reader to judge, in the light of Sir Karl's rejoinder at the end of this volume, as to whether our criticisms of his argument are sound or not. In either case, we anticipate that his reply, like the papers to which we have reacted herein, will be stimulating and illuminating. We have not taken the reader's time nor the volume's limited space to emphasize our numerous points of agreement with Sir Karl (as, e.g., the untenability of those muddled and malignant varieties of societal determinism he so brilliantly refutes in *The Poverty of Historicism* and *The Open Society and Its Enemies*). Nor have we bestowed superfluous encomiums upon this great man. We have been engaged in an attempt to control his, and the reader's, cognitive processes—but by the method Sir Karl has so well defended in all of his writings, the method of rational criticism. We are confident that his own position will grow in clarity and depth by reaction to these criticisms of ours, as we have been moved (quasi-determined) to think afresh about the determinist position as a result of his objections.

It is perhaps unnecessary to add some final disclaimers as to what we have *not* been doing in the preceding essay. We have not been trying to make the positive case for radical determinism, which neither of us can presently hold for physics, and which is a methodological prescription as well as a promissory note, for molar psychology—the latter unlikely, for reasons Sir Karl persuasively adduces, ever to be fully paid. We have not been engaged in making a positive case for materialist monism (the "identity thesis" as a solution of the ontological mind-body problem), regarding which we both entertain doubts, mainly because of semantic difficulties with sentience (raw feels) but also, in part, due to the puzzling data on telepathy and precognition. We have not attempted to reduce the categories of logic or semantics to those of physics or biology, knowing as we do that all such efforts necessarily involve philosophical mistakes of the most fundamental kind. Finally, we have not been so foolish as to offer a specific brain model, or to propound a molar theory of cognition, which is one of the most primitive and least understood domains of scientific psychology. Our purposes have been much more modest and limited in aim, namely, to criticize the philosophical arguments by which Sir Karl has tried to show—thus far unsuccessfully, as we think—that a doctrine of determinism or quasi-determinism (=physiological determinism qualified by cerebral randomizing systems) is *incompatible* with the admitted facts of (a) practical unpredictability, (b) creative novelty, and (c) rationality (insofar as it exists) in human affairs. If our critique contributes constructively to the development of Sir Karl's thought and to further clarification of the profound and difficult issues involved, we shall be satisfied.

HERBERT FEIGL AND
PAUL E. MEEHL

MINNESOTA CENTER FOR PHILOSOPHY OF SCIENCE
UNIVERSITY OF MINNESOTA
SEPTEMBER, 1968

NOTES

[1] K. R. Popper, *Of Clouds and Clocks: An Approach to the Problem of Rationality and the Freedom of Man* (St. Louis, Missouri: Washington University, 1966.)
Also: "Indeterminism in Quantum Physics and in Classical Physics, I and II", *The British Journal for the Philosophy of Science*, 1, No. 2 (1950), 117-33, and No. 3, 173-95.
Conjectures and Refutations: The Growth of Scientific Knowledge (London: Routledge & Kegan Paul, 1963; New York: Basic Books, 1963), esp., "On the Status of Science and of Metaphysics", pp. 184-200; "Language and the Body-Mind Problem", pp. 293-98; "A Note on the Body-Mind Problem", pp. 299-303.

[2] They are not decidable for the simple reason that their formulation requires universal as well as existential quantifiers. (But many scientific propositions have this form.)

[3] K. R. Popper, "Indeterminism in Quantum Physics and in Classical Physics", Part I, *The British Journal for the Philosophy of Science*, 1, No. 2 (August, 1950), 117-33; *Ibid.*, Part II, 1, No. 3 (November, 1950), 173-95.

[4] Although it is worth mentioning that the very clocklike electronic computer, programmed to discover proofs in the elementary propositional calculus by heuristic means (i.e., without the use of a systematic algorithm or decision procedure) succeeded in finding a proof for Theorem *2.85 of *Principia Mathematica* which required three steps and relied upon five earlier theorems, whereas Russell and Whitehead's proof required nine steps and relied upon seven additional theorems, including a lemma whose only use in *PM* is to help prove Theorem *2.85 (and which in turn required eleven steps, yielding a total of twenty steps needed by these human logicians). This strikes us as a rather impressive display of rational creativity by the clocklike computer, and those with expertise in the field assure us that they have hardly begun to tap the machine's resources. Prophecy by two nonexperts: A next major advance might well be metaprogramming for a wide class of mathematical structures, with a randomizer, so that the machine will *invent* theories. It will still have its built-in plus programmed limitations—there will be "theories which it cannot think". But then, as Kant would emphasize, the same is true of us. See A. Newell and H. A. Simon, "The Logic Theory Machine: a Complex Information Processing System", *Transactions on Information Theory* (Institute of Radio Engineers, September, 1956), Vol. IT-2, No. 3, pp. 61-79; A. Newell, J. C. Shaw, and H. A. Simon, "Empirical Explorations of the Logic Theory Machine", *Proceedings of the Western Joint Computer Conference* (Institute of Radio Engineers, February, 1957), pp. 218-30; A. Newell and J. C. Shaw, "Programming the Logic Theory Machine", *ibid.*, pp. 230-40; A. Newell, J. C. Shaw, and H. A. Simon, "Elements of a

Theory of Human Problem Solving", *Psychological Review,* **65** (1958), 151-66; L. T. Allen Newell, J. C. Shaw, and H. A. Simon, "Note: Improvement of a Proof of a Theorem in the Elementary Propositional Calculus" (unpublished Carnegie Institute Proceedings Working Paper No. 8, Carnegie-Mellon University, January 13, 1958).

[5] K. F. Schaffner, "Approaches to Reduction", *Philosophy of Science,* **34**, No. 2 (1967), 137-47.

John Kekes, "Physicalism, the Identity Theory and the Doctrine of Emergence", *Philosophy of Science,* **33**, No. 4 (1966), 360-75.

C. G. Hempel, *Aspects of Scientific Explanation* (New York: The Free Press; London: Collier-Macmillan, 1965), pp. 259-64.

J. J. C. Smart, *Philosophy and Scientific Realism* (New York: Humanities Press, 1963).

Ernest Nagel, *The Structure of Science* (New York: Harcourt, Brace & World, 1961), pp. 367-80, 433-35.

Gustav Bergmann, *Philosophy of Science* (Madison: University of Wisconsin Press, 1957), pp. 140-71.

[6] K. R. Popper, *Of Clouds and Clocks: An Approach to the Problem of Rationality and the Freedom of Man* (St. Louis: Washington University, 1966). Hereinafter cited as *CC.*

[7] For a remarkably sophisticated treatment of this issue, cf. S. Freud, *The Unconscious* (1915, Standard Edition, XIV, pp. 161-215; [London: Horgarth Press, 1957]). The *locus classicus* for a molar-behavioristic defense of "cognitions" as inferred theoretical entities in infrahuman animals (and, hence, not known to have a subjective, phenomenal aspect), is, of course, Edward Chace Tolman's great *Purposive Behavior in Animals and Men* (New York: Century Company, 1932).

[8] "All men by nature desire to know".

[9] The interested reader is referred to such sources as W. Honig, ed., *Operant Behavior: Areas of Research and Application* (New York: Appleton-Century-Crofts, 1966); L. P. Ullmann and L. Krasner, eds., *Case Studies in Behavior Modification* (New York: Holt, Rinehart & Winston, 1965); L. Krasner and L. P. Ullmann, eds., *Research in Behavior Modification* (New York: Holt, Rinehart & Winston, 1965); R. Ulrich, T. Stachnik, and J. Mabry, eds., *Control of Human Behavior* (Glenview, Ill.: Scott, Foresman, 1966).

[10] Paul E. Meehl, "Psychological Determinism and Human Rationality; a Psychologist's Reactions to Professor Karl Popper's '*Of Clouds and Clocks*'", *Minnesota Studies in the Philosophy of Science* (Minneapolis: University of Minnesota Press, 1970), Vol. IV, pp. 310-12.

[11] B. F. Skinner, "The Operational Analysis of Psychological Terms", *Psychological Review,* **52** (1945), 270-77.

[12] W. Sellars, "Empiricism and the Philosophy of Mind", *Minnesota Studies in the Philosophy of Science,* Vol. I, p. 328. Also in *Science, Perception, and Reality* (New York: The Humanities Press, 1963).

W. Sellars, "Thought and Action", in *Freedom & Determinism,* ed. by K. Lehrer (New York: Random House, 1966).

W. Sellars, "Intentionality and the Mental", *Minnesota Studies in the Philosophy of Science,* Vol. II (Appendix).

[13] Herbert A. Simon, "Motivational and Emotional Controls of Cognition", *Psychological Review,* **74** (1967), 29-39.

15

Alan E. Musgrave
THE OBJECTIVISM OF POPPER'S EPISTEMOLOGY

CONTENTS

1. Knowledge as Justified True Belief

2. Popper's Elimination of Psychologism

3. Elimination of Popper's Psychologism

4. Objective Knowledge and the Knowing Subject

"The main philosophical malady of our time", writes Popper,[1] "is an intellectual and moral relativism, the latter being at least in part based upon the former". Popper's cure for this malady is to combine an insistence upon absolute or objective standards with an equal insistence upon our fallibility in trying to achieve these standards. He has called this position *fallibilistic absolutism*.[2] I had better make it clear from the outset that I accept both Popper's diagnosis and his cure—indeed, I regard them as one of the most important themes of his philosophy. My paper will, therefore, be almost entirely expository. I should like to think that it will help to clarify Popper's views on this problem, and that it contains a few further applications and developments of these views. Only on a very minor point have I been able to criticise them.

I shall now outline the way in which I will proceed. If we are to appreciate Popper's cure for relativism, then we must understand the sources from which relativism springs. Section 1 tries to isolate one such source. This is a conception of knowledge as consisting of certain or established or justified beliefs, a conception which is traditional in the theory of knowledge. I shall argue that this overoptimistic conception of knowledge leads, albeit unintentionally, to intellectual relativism and subjectivism and also to a deprecation of our best knowledge, the theories of natural science. Scientific knowledge and the traditional theory of knowledge make uneasy bedfellows. So Popper, whose first concern is with our scientific knowledge and its growth, begins by rejecting the conception of knowledge which lay at the heart of the traditional theory of knowledge.

How, then, does Popper overcome the relativism and subjectivism to which the traditional theory of knowledge often led? In Section 2, I shall try to explain how he does this, so far as our scientific knowledge is concerned, by combining an absolutism of standards with fallibilism in achieving them. In Section 3, I shall ask whether Popper's theory of science is entirely free from subjectivist blemishes. I shall argue that on one small point it is not, but that it can easily be made so using Popper's own ideas. In Section 4, I shall return to the traditional problem of rational belief, and show that Popper's fallibilistic absolutism transforms, and then solves, this problem. I shall conclude by summarizing Popper's recent writings upon the significance of human knowledge from an evolutionary and metaphysical point of view.

1. Knowledge as Justified True Belief

At the basis of the traditional theory of knowledge is the assumption that knowledge is a special kind of *belief*: knowledge consists of those beliefs which can be justified. According to this conception of knowledge, to say 'I know *X*' means something like 'I believe *X*, I can justify my belief in *X*, and *X* is true'. This conception of knowledge as justified true belief probably stems, in part, from the religious background of epistemological controversy in the seventeenth century; and by now it has even become enshrined in ordinary English usage.

The history of the theory of knowledge is in large measure the history of a great debate about whether man could know anything, in this sense of 'know'. One party to this debate, the dogmatists, as we might call them, asserted that man could know, and tried to specify what he could know and how he could come to know it. Dogmatists tried, that is, to specify those beliefs which can be justified or established or proved or verified, either totally or perhaps only partially. The opposing party, or the sceptics, as we might call them, tried to destroy the claims and arguments of the dogmatists. Sceptics tried, that is, to show that man knows nothing, that no belief is entitled to be called 'knowledge', that all are *mere* beliefs or opinions.

The story of this great battle, of the successive advances and retreats of the contenders, each backed by ingenious arguments, is a truly fascinating one. What follows can hardly aim to do justice to it.[3] Instead, it aims to isolate assumptions shared by both dogmatists and sceptics, and to outline the way in which these shared assumptions led to relativism and subjectivism and had implications, often unwelcome ones, for our understanding of science. Then, I hope, we will be able to appreciate how Popper's theory of science, and his cure for relativism, rest upon his rejection of the traditional theory of knowledge as justified true belief.

Dogmatists and sceptics agreed that knowledge, if it exists, is justified true belief. They disagreed only about whether knowledge is attainable. They agreed, in other words, that talk of absolute or objective truth makes sense only if that truth can be known—that a belief is 'objective' only if it is true and known to be true. They disagreed only about whether anything can be *known to be true*, and hence about whether any belief can be 'objective'.

Dogmatists were the champions of 'objectivity': they insisted that objective truth can be known, that we do have a means of proving it. Now the chief weapon in the sceptic's armoury was the infinite regress of proofs, discovered already by the Greeks. To prove that a statement X is true we must produce other statement(s) Y from which X logically follows: Y then establishes X in the sense that, given that Y is true, X must be true also. But obviously the truth of Y needs in its turn to be established, and so on ad infinitum. Sceptics concluded that it is impossible really to establish the objective truth of any statement, and therefore that knowledge, in the traditional sense of that term, is impossible.

Some dogmatists could not accept this drastic conclusion; to avoid it they resorted to subjectivism. They renounced the idea that one statement can be justified only by another. Instead, they argued that some fundamental beliefs must be known 'immediately', and took some subjective property of these beliefs to guarantee, perhaps even to define, the objective truth of what was believed. They resorted, that is, to a subjective theory of truth, and used it to stop the infinite regress of proofs at some privileged beliefs, or 'first principles', whose truth is guaranteed subjectively. The justification of all other beliefs was then relative to these 'first principles'.

Dogmatists disagreed amongst themselves about what the 'first principles' actually were and about how their objective truth was to be guaranteed. Intellectualists chose abstract a priori first principles, and tried to guarantee their truth by invoking the feelings of obviousness or conviction or self-evidence or clarity and distinctness or indubitability produced by undergoing certain intellectual experiences. Empiricists chose observation or perception statements, and tried to guarantee their truth by invoking the similar feelings of 'perceptual assurance' produced by undergoing certain perceptual experiences.

Now feelings of assurance are private affairs: a feeling, unlike an argument, cannot be produced for others to inspect. Reporting my feelings of conviction is like thumping the table (or my opponent!): though its rhetorical or persuasive power may be great, it can hardly be called a *rational* argumentative device. If rational discussion involves justification, and if the ultimate justification is subjective, then it is impossible to have a rational discussion with someone who disagrees over first principles.[4] All one can do in this case is to reassert and try to establish your authority. It follows that rational discussion never reflects *genuine* disagreement at all: for the discussion to be rational both parties must agree on fundamental premises ('first principles'), and any 'disagreement' must be due to somebody's failure correctly to reach the right conclusions. Dogmatists sought to defend rationality, but end up by narrowly circumscribing the role of rational argument: it consists merely in drawing conclusions from commonly 'known' premises, agreement upon which can be reached only by nonrational, authoritarian means.

Moreover, as sceptics were not slow to point out, dogmatic authoritarianism soon collapses into relativism. For the dogmatist cannot guarantee that his subjective criterion of truth will produce universal agreement on 'first principles', nor can he guarantee that he will be able to exert his authority over dissenters. Is it not notorious, said the sceptics, that different people, schools, and epochs, find *different* things to be clear and distinct, self-evident, indubitable? And does this not hold, they asked, regardless of whether these feelings of assurance are produced by intellectual experiences or perceptual ones? Does not this divergence of opinion mean that no one opinion is better than another, that none is entitled to be called 'knowledge', that all are 'mere opinions' ?

Dogmatists could only respond to this charge of relativism by insisting that their subjective guarantees of the truth of 'first principles' were, in fact, universal. All of us *ought*, they said, to find the same things evident or clear and distinct—all observers *ought* to experience the same feelings of 'perceptual assurance' in similar circumstances. "God has given to each of us some light with which to distinguish truth from error".[5] The proliferation of opinions must be due, said the dogmatists, to bias or prejudice by one or both parties. Thus they propped up their subjective criterion of truth with a *psychotherapy*: methods were proposed to cleanse the mind of bias and prejudice so that it could receive the truth, i.e., so that their subjective criteria should never deceive. Hence we have Bacon ridding us of the 'Idols that beset men's minds', so that our perceptual experience should never deceive; or Descartes purifying us by the method of doubt, so that our intellectual experience should never deceive. Dogmatists then claimed that it was only the *purified* souls who would find the same things certain. Those who disagreed must be impure: an opponent is either in need of further mental purification, or mentally defective, or plain mad.[6] Or, as Popper puts it, dogmatism leads to a *conspiracy theory of error*.[7]

Another typical dogmatist response to the diversity of 'self-evident' principles was to deny that everyone who *thinks* he has applied the criterion of truth has in fact done so. The genuine self-evidence, clarity and distinctness, indubitability, perceptual assurance, or what you will, of an assertion guarantees its objective truth. So, if two people's *experiences* of self-evidence, clarity and distinctness, indubitability, perceptual assurance, etc., lead them to disagree, then one of these experiences cannot be genuine. But then, said the sceptics, we need a criterion to tell us when our feelings of truth are genuine and therefore veridical—the feelings alone provide no criterion of objective truth at all.

It will now be clear, I hope, how dogmatists, to ensure known truth, adopted some subjective criterion of it, and as a result tended to collapse into relativism and irrationalism. Each subject (or school, or epoch) had its own subjective criterion, which defined what was 'true for' that subject (school, epoch). This criterion could establish a body of 'immediate knowledge' or 'first principles', and then other statements could be rationally known, that is, justified by reference to the first principles. But, if two subjects (schools, epochs) disagree on these immediately known 'first principles', rational discussion between them is impossible. Each subject (school or epoch) has its own framework, makes its own 'truth', and all are equally 'right', since none is *provably* better than the other.

Dogmatists usually had too much respect for objective truth to face these unpleasant consequences squarely: driven against their wishes into a relativistic impasse, they tried desperately to extricate themselves. Sceptics, who were relativists and often subjectivists by inclination, ridiculed these vacillations. But, while denying all dogmatist claims to know the objective truth, sceptics agreed with dogmatists that, if absolute or objective truth cannot be known, it is a useless fiction. Since we cannot know objective truth, they said, let us give up all pretence to objective knowledge. If we must have *some* beliefs, and we surely must, let us admit that the criteria by which we select them are purely subjective. Each subject (school, epoch) will believe what appears certain to it, what it finds 'natural' to believe (Hume), or what it finds 'useful' to believe (James). Relativism and the resulting limitations on rationality are simply facts of life, since no person (school, epoch) can *prove* to another, who does not share his framework, that his provides 'objective' knowledge.

The main question which emerges from this potted history of epistemology[8] is this: can the idea of objective truth play any role if we have no means of *knowing* it? Or, to put it more generally: does it only make sense to speak of knowledge being subject to objective standards if it is possible to *apply* these standards infallibly? The central point of Popper's fallibilistic absolutism is to reject the affirmative answer to these questions which was presupposed by both dogmatists and sceptics. Popper agrees with the sceptic, **against the dogmatist, that we cannot infallibly know objective or absolute** truth—but he agrees with the dogmatist, against the sceptic, that the notion of objective or absolute truth plays an important role as a regulative standard. In this way he tries to eschew dogmatism without succumbing to subjectivism, relativism, and irrationalism.

Popper's *Logik der Forschung* of 1934 can be regarded, I think, as an attempt to carry out this programme as regards our scientific knowledge. But, before turning to this, let me dwell for a moment upon the fact that Popper *began* his epistemological investigations by considering *scientific* knowledge. This fact is itself instructive, for it contrasts sharply with the tradition in the theory of knowledge. And this brings me to the second consequence of the traditional exclusive concern with knowledge as a species of belief, with certain or justified belief.

Natural science does, on the face of it, contain the best, the most interesting and informative, knowledge that we possess. But scientific knowledge could hardly be called 'knowledge' in the traditional sense of that term. Epistemologists interested in certainty, in justified true belief, were bound to find the rich speculations of natural science extraordinarily problematic. In the vain pursuit of certainty, epistemologists were forced to withdraw from the world of natural science and into their selves. The speculations of a Newton or a Descartes are not knowledge—what is knowledge is perhaps 'orange-looking object here now' solemnly pronounced on the occasion of an epistemologist's inspection of an orange, or 'I think, therefore I am' solemnly pronounced on the occasion of his inspection of himself. What we can know, it seems, is not much, and is supremely uninteresting to boot.

It was no accident, therefore, that some of those interested in knowledge in the traditional sense of that term gave short shrift to our best knowledge, the theories of natural science. Some failed to consider it at all.[9] Others arrived at natural science only to consign it to the limbo of the 'unknowable'. Even Locke, the great admirer of Boyle and of "the incomparable Mr. Newton", is forced to conclude that since "*natural philosophy is not capable of being made into a science* . . . it will become us, as rational creatures, to employ those faculties we have about what they are most adapted to", which is morality.[10] Others save natural science from the sad fate of being unknowable by reinterpreting it phenomenologically—since we know only our own ideas and sensations, knowable science must merely describe present sensations and give useful rules for predicting new ones.[11]

The preceding two paragraphs call for an important qualification. Though it *ought* to have been apparent that scientific theories could not be known in the traditional sense of that term, the tremendous success of Newton's theory obscured this. Newton, after all, claimed to know, and his authority could be evoked as a powerful rebuke to sceptics. It was, of course,

a problem to explain how we *could* know Newtonian physics—hence
positivist or phenomenological reinterpretations of it (for which, incidentally,
Newton's authority could also be invoked). But it was not until after the
Einsteinian revolution that the clash between science and the traditional
theory of knowledge could become fully apparent.

That clash is, fundamentally, a clash between content and certainty: the
more we say, the less certain can we be that *what* we say is true. It became apparent, after the Einsteinian revolution, that the content of our scientific
knowledge is far too rich and interesting for us to know it, in the traditional
sense of 'know'. Popper learned the epistemological lesson of the Einsteinian
revolution in physics.[12] He was the first philosopher of science, so far as I
know, to recognise that science aims, above all, to say a lot; he analysed what
'saying a lot' involves, and based an entire philosophy of science upon it. This
emphasis upon high content has far-reaching implications for the traditional
theory of knowledge.

It involves, first of all, an important distinction between contents or
statements or theories, on the one hand, and, on the other hand, the various
psychological attitudes or feelings or responses which people may have
towards these contents. The traditional idea of knowledge as justified true
belief obscured this distinction: the term 'belief' ambiguously denotes both
a particular mental act or attitude, and that which is believed, the content
towards which the act or attitude of believing is directed. But it is important
not to obscure the distinction, simply because epistemological acts, such as
the act of believing, possess very different properties and relationships from
those possessed by their contents. And this means that the kind of question
we can properly ask about an epistemological act may be very different from
the kind of question we can properly ask about its content.

For example, contents or statements or theories are either true or false,
and stand in logical relationships with each other. So we might ask of the content of some belief whether it is true, or self-consistent, or consistent with
other contents also perhaps believed, or whether it follows logically from
another possibly believed content, or whether some other possibly believed
content follows from it. All these questions are *objective* ones, in the sense
that in answering them we need take no cognizance of facts about the mental
acts or attitudes which may or may not be adopted, by all, some, or no persons, towards the contents involved. Psychological acts or attitudes, on the
other hand, stand in factual, psychological relationships to each other, rather
than in logical ones. So we might ask of an act of believing whether it is
strong or weak, or what produced it, whether it was thoughtful, arrived at by
considering arguments and evidence, rational, or whether it was rash,
careless, irrational. All these questions are *subjective* ones, in the sense that
personal or psychological considerations about the believer are essential in

order to answer them. Every epistemological act, then, has an objective and a subjective dimension, and can therefore be approached from either a subjective or an objective point of view.

Each of these approaches, or better, sets of questions, is of course a legitimate one. What is not legitimate is to confound the objective dimension with the subjective, and to imagine that exclusive concern with the latter will suffice. This was, however, often done by those concerned with knowledge as justified true belief—the result was *subjectivism*. We have already seen an extreme example of this, subjective theories of truth, which abolish the objective truth of (the content of) a belief in favour of such things as the self-evidence, indubitability, clarity and distinctness, or usefulness of (the act of) believing that content.[13] More subtle than subjectivism, though also arising out of a confusion of the objective dimension of knowledge with its subjective dimension, is the doctrine that an act of believing can be justified (i.e., shown to be reasonable) only if the content towards which that act is directed can be justified (i.e., shown to be true, or proved). I shall have more to say about this doctrine later.

The traditional theory of knowledge begins with the subjective dimension of knowledge: its main concern is not the contents of (possible) beliefs, but rather the feelings of conviction we have, or are entitled to have, towards those contents. If we begin, with Popper, from the objective dimension of knowledge, a very different perspective results. Our main problems now concern the *content* of knowledge—beliefs, *qua* feelings of certainty or conviction, become secondary. The traditional conception of knowledge and the great dogmatist/sceptic controversy about it are left far behind. I shall now discuss in more detail what results from Popper's new perspective.

2. Popper's Elimination of Psychologism

Two features of *Logik der Forschung* are especially relevant in this connection. The first is Popper's emphasis on what he calls the 'logic' of scientific knowledge as opposed to its psychology. The second is his nonpsychologistic doctrine of the 'empirical basis' of science.

In the first section of *Logik der Forschung* Popper distinguishes between "the *psychology of knowledge* which deals with empirical facts, and the *logic of knowledge* which is concerned only with logical relations". In the next section, entitled 'Elimination of Psychologism', Popper uses this distinction to eliminate from the philosophy of science analysis of how discoveries are made, which belongs to the 'psychology of knowledge': ". . .the act of conceiving or inventing a theory", he says, "seems to me neither to call for logical analysis nor to be susceptible of it". Instead he concentrates upon the analysis and evaluation of scientific theories once they have been made (the 'logic of knowledge'). And he stresses that the logical analysis of finished discoveries cannot provide a method of making discoveries. It seems, then, that, despite his title, Popper does not advocate a real 'logic of *discovery*'.[14]

Here Popper separates logical analysis of a contribution to science from psychological analysis of its contributor. He assumes that scientists analyse and evaluate contributions to science independently of personal or psychological facts about the scientist who produced it, or indeed, about anybody else. This assumption does, I think, square with scientific practice—but it hardly squares with the traditional conception of knowledge. The latter demands that any item of putative knowledge be analysed with reference to *who* claims to 'know' it. One man's 'knowledge' may be another's vain superstition: we must ask whether the alleged 'knower' really does know the item of knowledge in question.[15]

It is fundamentally this same separation which governs Popper's treatment of the problem of the 'empirical basis' of science. Traditional empiricists attempted to show that scientific knowledge could be 'known' by reference to the perceptual experiences of the knower. Perceptual experiences justified or established perception or observation statements—the rest of science could be 'known' only insofar as it could be logically inferred (deductively or, more often, inductively) from justified perception or observation statements.

Popper steers clear of subjectivism. He insists that statements can be justified only by other statements; the truth of an observation statement cannot be established by appealing to the psychological fact that you have had certain perceptual experiences, and that these experiences have caused you to feel 'perceptual assurance' that the observation statement is true. He reinforces this by pointing out that even so-called 'observation-statements' transcend experience, since they contain universal terms which presuppose universal theories.

Popper's 'empirical basis' does not, then, consist of statements whose truth is established by experience. It consists rather of those easily testable experimental statements about whose truth or falsehood the community of scientists happens to agree at some time. A scientist may be caused to accept such a statement by his perceptual experiences. But, though experiences may motivate decisions, they cannot establish the truth of the accepted statement:

> And finally, as to *psychologism*: I admit, again, that the decision to accept a basic statement, and to be satisfied with it, is causally connected with our experiences—especially with our *perceptual experiences*. But we do not attempt to *justify* basic statements by these experiences. Experiences can *motivate a decision*, and hence an acceptance or rejection of a statement, but a basic statement cannot be *justified* by them—no more than by thumping the table.[16]

Popper's 'empirical basis' does accord, I think, with scientific practice. And in doing so, it bears little resemblance to the empirical basis of traditional empiricism (hence his quotation marks). In particular, Popper does not follow traditional empiricists who, in the vain search for *certainty*, moved from "Here is a table" to "I am now having a table-like sense-datum". Popper moves in the opposite direction. Since the search for certainty is in any case a vain search, Popper is not squeamish about including in his 'empirical basis' relatively rich basic statements like "The current passing through this wire is 15 amperes". This statement is, of course, highly theoretical. But, if scientists accept the relevant instrumental techniques, and the theories involved in them, there is no reason to withdraw from it to "The pointer on my ammeter reads 15"; and there is still less reason to withdraw into the psyche of the experimenter to the statement "I am now having an ammeter-like sense-datum showing the reading 15". (If a scientist does *not* accept the relevant theory, others may discuss this theory with him directly; and statements about pointer-readings, or about 'pointer-reading-like sense-data', will again usually be irrelevant.)[17]

Popper's 'empirical basis', then, unlike the traditional one, does not play a justificatory role. Fallible premises cannot justify or prove the conclusions which follow from them, even if these conclusions do follow validly. Moreover Popper, following Hume, argues that inductive arguments from the empirical basis to scientific theories are not valid.[18] For Popper, all empirical statements are fallible, none can be justified or established as true. His 'empirical basis' plays only a *critical* role—valid deductive arguments can lead from components of his (fallible) empirical basis to the negations of those systems of hypotheses which exclude these components. But even experimental criticism in science is fallible, since the premises from which it proceeds are fallible.

At any time, the (fallible) results of the critical evaluation of a theory with respect to this 'empirical basis' can be given in its *degree of corroboration*. This is simply a summary of the tests to which that theory has been subjected, their severity, and whether the theory withstood them or not. To estimate the degrees of corroboration of two rival theories at any time is simply to summarize the empirical part of the critical discussion of these theories at that time.[19] Such estimates are (a) backward-looking,[20] and (b) objective, that is, they refer to theories, deductions, experiments, rather than to states of mind or beliefs. It is clear that a theory which is corroborated is not thereby justified or established in any sense, for in the future different tests may falsify it, or more precise repetitions of the same test may falsify it, or repetitions of the same test which are not more precise may falsify it.[21]

So much for the *negative* part of Popper's 'elimination of psychologism'. Scientific knowledge is shown not to be knowledge in the traditional epistemological sense. The subjectivist doctrines upon which that traditional idea was based are eschewed, and scientific knowledge emerges as a system of fallible conjectures or hypotheses. But can one fallible hypothesis be better than another? Can we rationally evaluate contributions to science *without* trying to justify them? Is there a middle way between dogmatist subjectivism and sceptical relativism?

These questions bring us to the *positive* part of Popper's 'elimination of psychologism', or to the absolutist aspect of his 'fallibilistic absolutism'. His logic of scientific knowledge aims to analyse the objective or nonpsychological properties of scientific knowledge, and to formulate *objective standards* in the light of which the critical appraisal of that knowledge may take place. I shall now briefly consider some examples of this, and will use them to illustrate the superiority of the objective approach to knowledge over the subjective approach.

Perhaps the most fundamental idea in the philosophy of science is the idea of *scientific explanation*, for the problems of theoretical science are explanatory ones, and their putative solutions are explanations. Popper's objective approach leads him to the well-known hypothetico-deductive analysis of explanation, according to which:

> To give a *causal explanation* of an event means to deduce a statement which describes it, using as premises of the deduction one or more universal laws, together with certain singular statements, the initial conditions.[22]

This is an objective or logical analysis: it speaks of statements or contents, and of logical relations between them. And if we are to discuss whether or not something is an explanation in this sense, and whether it is a good explanation, we must discuss whether the contents involved possess certain objective properties, that is, whether they conform to certain objective standards. As is well known, Popper has suggested the following standards: (a) deducibility of the *explanandum* from the *explanans*, (b) high explanatory power or empirical content or independent testability of the *explanans*, and (c) truth of the *explanans*.[23] Notice that all these standards are interpersonal, or better, *impersonal* ones: how well an explanation conforms to them does not depend upon any personal or psychological facts about the people who propose or contemplate it.

Contrast this with the notion of explanation which results from a subjective approach to knowledge. This might run as follows: A explains B (to person X) if A removes (X's) feelings of perplexity or puzzlement concerning B, thus rendering B unproblematic (to X).[24] This is a subjective or psychological analysis: it speaks of feelings of puzzlement, and of the psychological relations between these feelings and things which may cause them to disappear. Of course, one of the things which may relieve a person's puzzlement is his contemplation of an explanation in the objective sense of the term. But this is by no means essential, nor is it very likely (especially if the objective explanation in question is a good one).[25] Feelings of puzzlement are more effectively relieved by drugs, sleep, boredom, and old age (or by awareness of explanations which, objectively considered, are inadequate).[26] Whether something is an explanation in this subjective sense, and whether it is a good explanation, are personal or psychological questions: one man's puzzlement-reliever can be another's puzzlement-enhancer.[27]

Now this subjective idea of explanation does, perhaps, correspond to an everyday use of the word 'explain'—if so, ordinary language philosophers will warm to it. It may even be that the idea of objective explanation has evolved out of it. The two ideas are, however, very different. And if we are interested in the growth of human knowledge, and especially in scientific knowledge, it is explanation in the objective sense which is all-important. When a scientist proposes an explanation, he proposes an autonomous, impersonal structure—he seeks, that is, to explain in the objective sense of that term. And when others try to assess his contribution, they do so in the light of objective or impersonal standards: they do not, for example, count it as a valid criticism of a proposed explanation that it fails to relieve someone's puzzlement.

These are, no doubt, commonplaces for the working scientist, and they may all seem pretty obvious even to philosophers. Yet some philosophers, and even some scientists-turned-philosophers, appear to ignore them. Consider, for example, the widespread demand (emphasized, for example, by Bridgman) that a good explanation must reduce the unknown or unfamiliar to the known or familiar; or the demand that an intuitively visualizable model must be provided for the *explanans*.[28] These demands stem, it seems to me, from a subjective notion of explanation; and we must admit that reference to the familiar, or to a visualizable model, may indeed be necessary before some people's puzzlement is relieved. But these are personal or subjective matters: what is familiar or visualizable to one man may not be to another. They should, I think, have nothing to do with the adequacy of an explanation in the objective sense.

Conversely, things which happen to relieve puzzlement cannot, on that ground *alone*, be said to constitute adequate explanations. In this connection I have already mentioned 'explanation' by appeal to supernatural agencies, entelechies and vital forces. Some want to acknowledge 'historical narratives' and 'purposive explanations' as alternative 'forms of explanation' on the *sole* ground that they can set the curiosity of some historians and some ordinary Englishmen at rest.[29,30] But once we do this, we cease to discuss the intersubjective aspects of knowledge, and turn it instead into a glorified tranquilizer. If we wish to do justice to the public or intersubjective dimension of human knowledge, then it is the objective sense of explanation which must be paramount.

This has one important corollary. Since explanations are putative solutions to explanatory problems, these problems have an objective or logical dimension as well as a subjective or psychological one. A problem, subjectively considered, is a feeling of puzzlement or perplexity; objectively considered, it may be posed by logical interrelations between extant knowledge (e.g., the problem of unifying terrestrial and celestial mechanics, or the problem of the equivalence between inertial and gravitational mass). Problems can, after all, be explained to others and formulated in books—but this would not be possible if problems consisted *merely* of feelings of puzzlement. The objective dimension of problems means that at any time an individual scientist is confronted with a structure of problems, or a problem-situation, his subjective awareness of which may be more or less complete.

Problems, then, have both a subjective and an objective dimension; and again it is the latter which is paramount. Feelings of puzzlement may have nothing to do with genuine problems (in which case we could speak of 'pseudoproblems'). And, though feelings of puzzlement may play a decisive role in the psychology of discovery, they interest the epistemologist, above all, when they correspond to a genuine problem in the objective sense. Moreover, genuine problems, as we all know, can fail to provoke feelings of puzzlement for centuries: one mark of a scientific genius is to *discover* a new and important problem which had previously lain undetected.[31] All this would be lost to one who attended primarily or exclusively to the subjective dimension.[32]

A further example of Popper's objectivist approach is his discussion of the problem of *simplicity* in science. His very formulation of the problem reflects his general programme. If simplicity, so often invoked by scientists, is a merely intuitive or subjective property of a theory, then why, he asks, is the simpler theory more desirable from an epistemological point of view? His answer is that if the simpler theory is to be the better one, its simplicity cannot be analysed merely in terms of the feelings of simplicity or naturalness which contemplation of it may provoke. The main point of his analysis of appeals to simplicity is that they are usually not merely subjective: by relating simplicity to falsifiability, his analysis makes the more simple theory objectively preferable to the less simple one.[33] Now it may, of course, happen that a person may feel that one theory is intuitively more 'simple', elegant, or easy to work with, than another, and yet, at the same time, not be able to specify any objective difference between them (such as paucity of parameters or symmetry properties). In this case that person's feelings, important though they may be in guiding his own practice, will hardly be taken into account in assessing the merits of the two theories—especially if another person's feelings work in the opposite direction.

These examples illustrate the differences between the logic of knowledge and its psychology—they show, I think, that it is the former which is fundamental for our understanding of scientific knowledge. Now the logical or objective approach to knowledge depends, fundamentally, upon the objectivity of logical relations like deducibility or contradictoriness. Subjectivists used to abolish logical relations too in favour of psychological ones: they replaced the validity of an inference by the feelings of necessity or psychological compulsion which may accompany the act of drawing that inference, or 'expressed' the Law of Contradiction as "It is impossible (as a matter of psychological fact) simultaneously to believe both p and not-p". These days few commit such grave subjectivist crimes—Frege taught us better. And Popper's objectivist epistemology takes for granted the demise of psychologism in logic.[34]

Objective epistemology is also heavily dependent upon the objective or absolute concept of truth. Now this notion, though crucial, has so far hardly been mentioned in the present section, despite the important role it played in my first section. This anomaly occurs also in Popper's *Logik der Forschung*. In 1934, Popper was reticent about using the objective or correspondence theory of truth, because philosophers had made a mystery out of the idea of correspondence, and perhaps because for Popper high empirical content was, after all, more important in science than mere truth alone.[35] Yet Popper's account of science risks presenting it as a sort of instrumentalist game, unless it incorporates the idea of objective truth. No wonder, then, that as soon as he learned of Tarski's investigations Popper eagerly seized upon them as a rehabilitation of the old objective or absolute or correspondence theory of truth.[36]

No wonder too, that he has recently combined the two crucial objectivist notions of truth and of logical consequence in his theory of *verisimilitude*, which is based upon the fact that every false statement has true logical consequences. This theory allows us to speak meaningfully of one false theory being, in virtue of its greater 'truth-content', *nearer* to the truth than another false theory. It allows us also to solder the two fundamental aims of science, truth and high content, into one: high verisimilitude. And in the light of this single aim we can say that a false theory may be better than a true one simply because the former, though false, has greater verisimilitude than the latter.[37]

Popper's 'logic of knowledge' is concerned, then, with logical or objective features like truth and falsehood, deducibility, contradictoriness, deductive explanation, explanatory power or empirical content, simplicity, verisimilitude. The psychology of knowledge is concerned with psychological or subjective features which may (or may not) be *correlated* with these objective ones when some subject considers the statement in question—features like believing and doubting, inferring, feeling puzzled and being relieved of puzzlement, finding complex and difficult or finding simple. Subjectivism (or psychologism) attempts to abolish objective features in favour of their subjective correlates. But subjective features of knowledge vary from person to person and from time to time, whereas the objective properties which are supposed to 'correspond' to them do not. And as a matter of fact men have often believed what is false, and doubted what is true (the truth is not, after all, manifest). They have often made errors in deduction, and have even believed contradictory statements (logic is not, *pace* Locke, a useless subject, and it can, *pace* Wittgenstein, surprise us). Their puzzlement has typically been removed only by pseudoexplanations, and has fortunately been enhanced rather than relieved by good scientific ones. Subjectivism would be bad enough even if the correlations between objective features and subjective ones were invariable and correct; it is disastrous since, as is notorious, they are *not*.

To avoid subjectivism, we must admit that the objective dimension of knowledge is autonomous. A corollary of this autonomy is that, in his dealings with the objective dimension, man is always fallible. But, if so, can this objective dimension have any practical significance? Can these autonomous, objective features of knowledge play any role in concrete deliberations and discussions?

I shall try to answer these questions in the affirmative, by showing that the objective dimension of knowledge can play a very important role: it can embody the *standards* or *aims* which govern debates and discussions about our knowledge. In a critical debate we argue *with* an opponent, but we do not usually argue *about* him—what we argue about is almost always some objective feature of knowledge. For example, suppose I argue with someone about a statement S, which he believes to be true. If I think my opponent sincere then I accept from the outset the psychological fact that he does believe S, and that this psychological fact motivates his disagreement with me. What I argue about is only whether S is in fact true. Or, suppose a person accepts a putative explanation because it relieves his puzzlement, and I argue with him. Again, I will not deny that the explanation produces in him this psychological effect—what I will question is whether it is a good explanation. Or, suppose a person accepts a hypothesis because he finds it to be intuitively simple. In arguing with him I will not question this, but discuss rather whether the hypothesis is simple in some objective sense. The importance, then, of the objective features of knowledge is that it is these features which are usually at issue in a rational debate.

Of course, in order for us to discuss the objective dimension of our knowledge, we have to be *aware* of the items of knowledge in question. We cannot discuss whether a theory is true without being aware of the theory; we cannot discuss the merits of an explanation until that explanation has been proposed by somebody and we have learned of it. To stress the objective dimension of knowledge is not to lose sight of the fact that human knowledge is created, discussed, and evaluated by human beings. But, if man creates, discusses and evaluates his knowledge in the light of objective standards, then we will hardly be able to understand its creation, discussion and evaluation if we ignore these standards.

The autonomy of aims and standards is essential if they are to play the role of aims and standards. Traditional epistemology assumed that only if we have an infallible criterion of objective truth can that idea play any significant role in our discussions. But our estimates of truth and falsehood, though fallible and conjectural, are always estimates of an objective property. We cannot, therefore, dispense with objective truth and falsehood and consider only subjective acceptance and rejection. Again, we may estimate the comparative verisimilitude of two possibly false theories by considering their respective degrees of corroboration.[38] These estimates, though they may always be mistaken, remain estimates *of* an objective property which cannot, therefore, be ignored.[39]

Popper's 'logic of scientific knowledge' seeks, then, to specify the aims and standards in the light of which the creation and evaluation of scientific knowledge proceeds. His *methodology* is heavily dependent upon this logical analysis, since it is a system of methodological rules designed to aid the achievement of these aims. For example, having shown high explanatory power or empirical content to be a desirable property of a scientific theory, and identified it with testability, Popper formulates a methodological rule against the use of *ad hoc* hypotheses. This rule tells us not to modify a theoretical system, for example, in order to avoid a refutation, by employing an auxiliary hypothesis which reduces the testability of the system as a whole. A further example is Popper's famous demarcation criterion, according to which the theories of science are characterized by their refutability or testability, their being able to be criticised using experimental tests. Testability is partly a logical affair: to be testable a theory must possess consequences which could be checked experimentally. It is also partly methodological: a theory which might have been testable can cease to be so if a certain method of interpreting it or dealing with it is adopted.[40] Logical analysis of scientific knowledge must, if it is to give an adequate theory of science, be supplemented by *methodology*.

This raises the following questions. Since methodological rules have to be *applied* by scientists, are psychological considerations indispensable not only in discussing the production of scientific knowledge, but also in discussing its reception and assessment by scientists? In particular, must Popper's critical philosophy of science rely, for its effective application, upon the presence of critical attitudes or states of mind among scientists? Have we, therefore, to supplement it with a 'psychotherapy', not so different from traditional Baconian or Cartesian psychotherapies, and designed, like them, to bring about the requisite open, undogmatic, critical minds? Must fallibilism rely upon 'critical minds', just as inductivism relied upon the open, unprejudiced, empty minds of true Baconian scientists?

An affirmative answer to these questions would mean that, in a very important sense, not even the theory of scientific knowledge can be 'epistemology without a knowing subject'. It would also lay Popper's philosophy of science open to criticism on the grounds that the requisite completely critical, open mind does not, and cannot, exist. I shall try to answer these questions in the negative.

3. Elimination of Popper's Psychologism

I shall begin by showing that some remarks of Popper's imply, on the face of it, that he would answer them in the affirmative. In particular, he says in several places that for a severe test of a theory to be performed the tester must be *sincere* in attempting to overthrow the theory in question. I shall argue that this is foreign to the general tenor of Popper's epistemology and that his own more recent analysis of the severity of tests enables us to dispense with it. Then there are his remarks about the desirability of 'critical attitudes' among scientists. I shall argue that, despite their psychological flavour, such remarks can and should be interpreted in a nonpsychological way. The upshot of all this will be, I hope, to free Popper's position from what, at first sight, appear to be rather dubious psychological presuppositions and recommendations.

Let me turn first to the problem of the *severity of tests*. As is well known, the severity of tests plays a crucial role in Popper's philosophy of science, because the degree of corroboration of a hypothesis depends upon the severity of the tests to which it has been subjected. But what is a severe test? Having defined degree of corroboration, Popper warns us that "one cannot completely formalize the idea of a sincere and ingenious attempt [to refute a hypothesis]".[41] He explains that his formula $C(x, y)$ for the degree of corroboration of x by y "must not be interpreted as degree of corroboration, and must not be applied to problems of acceptability, unless y represents the (total) results of sincere attempts to refute x".[42] The same point is developed later:

> . . .I must insist that $C(h,e)$ can be interpreted as degree of corroboration only if e is a *report on the severest tests we have been able to design*. It is this point that marks the difference between the attitude of the inductivist, or verificationist, and my own attitude. The inductivist or verificationist wants affirmation for his hypothesis. He wants to make it firmer by his evidence e. . . .In opposition to this inductivist attitude, I assert that $C(h,e)$ must not be interpreted as degree of corroboration of h by e, unless e reports the results of *our sincere efforts to*

overthrow h. The requirement of sincerity cannot be formalized. . . .Yet if *e* is *not* a report about the results of our sincere attempts to overthrow *h*, then we shall simply deceive ourselves if we think we can interpret *C(h,e)* as degree of corroboration, or anything like it.[43]

These passages seem to make the severity of a test depend in part upon the psyche of the tester. For the *sincerity* with which a test is devised and performed seems to be distinctively psychological, to depend upon the state of mind of him who performs it. Evidence which corroborates a hypothesis must not be taken into account, says Popper, unless the tester was sincerely trying to refute the hypothesis in question. The same applies, though Popper obviously did not intend this, to evidence which *refutes* the hypothesis *h* (i.e., evidence which gives *C(h,e)* a negative value): Popper must discount this evidence too when his 'requirement of sincerity' is not met. But how are we to find out that this requirement *is* met? A report of an experimental test would, it seems, have to be accompanied by a psychological report that the tester was sincere before it could be taken seriously as an argument!

Such reports would be difficult to come by, and with psychology in its present state, pretty unreliable to boot. They do not, of course, actually figure in experimental science. And it is strange to find them appearing to play such an essential role in an epistemology dedicated, as Popper's is, to the elimination of psychologism.[44] They would infect Popper's philosophy of science with an admittedly mild form of a dangerous subjectivist disease—the disease of supposing that the value of an assertion or an argument depends upon personal or psychological facts about the person who happens to produce it.[45] Fortunately a remedy is at hand: Popper also gives an *objective* analysis of the severity of tests, an analysis which needs no recourse to the sincerity of testers.

The intuitive idea behind this objective analysis is that the more unlikely or unexpected (in the light of what we already know, of our 'background knowledge' *b*) is a prediction *p* from a hypothesis *h*, then the more severe will be the test of *h* provided by testing *p*.[46] Thus, for example, if we can predict from *h* a 'new effect' (that is, something completely unexpected in the light of *b*), then to test this prediction will constitute a severe test of *h*.[47] Or, the more precise the prediction *p*, the more severe can be a test of it, since a more precise prediction is less likely to be true, given *b*, than a less precise one.[48]

Popper himself has taken pains to emphasise the objectivity of this analysis. For example, his most recent account (and the most elaborate) of the severity of tests begins "The severity of our tests can be objectively compared. . .", and contains no reference to the sincerity of the tester.[49] It seems, therefore, that Popper would no longer defend a psychological 'requirement of sincerity' which says that a sincere tester is essential for a severe test.[50] And this is, I think, a step forward, for the idea itself is an unacceptable one.

It is pretty clear that an experimenter's sincerely wanting to overthrow a theory cannot be a *sufficient* condition for his experiment to constitute a severe test of that theory in the objective sense; the sincerest of critics may lack the imagination to produce a severe test. Is sincerity, then, only a *necessary* condition for severity? This is an *empirical* question: is it the case that whenever a test is severe the tester was sincere? Notice that the very formulation of this question presupposes that we can assess the severity of tests *independently* of the sincerity of testers. The answer to it must, I think, be negative. It is perfectly possible for a severe test to be performed by one who does not sincerely want to refute the theory in question. The tester may hope, and try, to confirm the theory—he may try to do so in a spectacular way, by showing that the theory successfully predicts a new effect. His test will be a severe one (whatever its outcome). It is probable that sincere critics will be more *likely* to produce severe tests, but sincerity is neither necessary for severity nor sufficient. I conclude, therefore, that appeals to the sincerity of testers can be dispensed with entirely in favour of Popper's objective analysis of severity of tests.

Having said this, however, a disclaimer is called for. I do not maintain that *all* important aspects of tests are captured in this objective analysis of their severity, and especially not in the *formula* in which the bare bones of this analysis are summarized. There remains, as Popper stressed, an unformalizable residue, consisting of things like the conceptual and practical *ingenuity* of the experiment or the care taken to exclude interfering factors. (There is also the requirement that in assessing the degree of corroboration of a hypothesis, we consider *all* the available evidence.) But to say that such things cannot be captured in a formula is not to relegate them to psychology: they are nonpsychological matters which can be publicly discussed, and are, in fact, continually discussed by scientists. Again, an experimenter who does not sincerely wish to refute some theory may be more likely to overlook possible interfering factors—but these can also be overlooked by the sincerest critic of the theory. And when the ingenuity or carefulness of an experiment is discussed, it is not psychological facts about the experimenter which are at issue.

Finally, I shall consider a serious problem to which Popper's 'requirement of sincerity' was a response. I refer to the fact, which Popper has repeatedly emphasised in connection with Marxism, psychoanalysis and Adlerian psychology, that it "is easy to find confirmations, or verifications, for nearly every theory—if we look for confirmations".[51] This is both true and important—but invoking a 'requirement of sincerity' to deal with it is not, I think, very satisfactory. A theory can lack genuine confirmations without lacking sincere critics; a theory which does not yield any precise and improbable predictions cannot be severely tested, no matter how sincere its critics may be. A better response to this problem of easy confirmation is to point out that easy 'confirmations' are usually spurious ones, not because they are consciously sought after, but because they do not result from severe tests in the objective sense of that term.[52]

I now turn to some more general remarks of Popper's which seem to suggest that his methodology depends essentially upon the presence of certain psychological attitudes among scientists. For example, having shown how refutations can always be evaded, Popper remarks that ". . .those who uphold [a system] dogmatically—believing, perhaps, that it is their business to defend. . .a successful system against criticism as long as it is not *conclusively disproved*—are adopting the very reverse of that critical attitude which in my view is the proper one for the scientist".[53] This could be taken to mean that the evasion of refutations is to be met merely by recommending "that critical attitude which is the proper one for the scientist".

But it would be a mistake, I think, to take too seriously the psychological flavour of the term 'attitude'. We can quite naturally read 'attitude' in a nonpsychological way, to mean 'policy' or 'method'. Popper clearly intends us to do this: in the passage just quoted, to adopt a dogmatic attitude means to "defend a system against criticism", and to defend a system involves more than getting oneself into a certain frame of mind towards it—it also involves carrying out a certain argumentative policy. This is made even more explicit when, lower down on the same page, Popper says he will solve the problem posed by the possibility of evading refutations by proposing, not a critical attitude per se, but a critical *policy* or *method* concerned with our "manner of dealing with scientific systems", or "what we do with them and what we do to them".[54]

A similar nonpsychological (or perhaps not *purely* psychological) reading should be given to the many other places in which Popper extols what he calls the critical or rational or scientific *attitude*.[55] This psychological way of speaking, though traditional, is rather misleading: it suggests that a certain state of mind is necessary, or even sufficient, for a certain argumentative policy to be adopted. But this is not the case.

Again we have here an empirical question, which presupposes that the critical character of a policy (not to mention the value of the arguments produced in carrying out that policy) can be assessed independently of the state of mind of him who adopts the policy. Those who have a critical attitude towards a hypothesis will, no doubt, be more likely to carry out a critical policy towards it. But it is perfectly possible for a person to adopt a critical policy towards a hypothesis without hoping, or thinking, that his criticisms will succeed. Conversely, one could have doubts about the satisfactoriness of a hypothesis, and yet adopt a defensive policy towards it (doubting and criticising are not the same).

It seems, then, that we must interpret the term 'critical attitude' in a primarily nonpsychological way, as referring to explicit argumentative policy rather than to implicit subjective states of mind. If we do this, then Popper's remarks about the desirability of a 'critical attitude' call for some important qualifications. As Popper himself has emphasized, it is impossible for us to adopt a critical policy towards everything at once. Each critical discussion takes a good deal for granted, assumes a great deal to be unproblematic for the purpose of that particular discussion. No part of this 'background knowledge' is immune from being made the focus of a different discussion. But remarks about the 'critical attitude which is the proper one for the scientist' cannot be interpreted as requiring that every scientist should always be criticising everything, never taking anything for granted.

If the foregoing is correct, then the difference between a critical and a dogmatic policy towards some particular hypothesis may lie simply in different conceptions of the area of the problematic. A person can try to defend the hypothesis against a refutation by criticising some of the statements involved in that refutation. It is true that Popper formulates methodological rules to *prevent* the defence of a hypothesis using what he calls 'conventionalist strategems'. But if we inspect these stratagems closely, they turn out to rescue hypotheses *without* adopting a critical policy elsewhere (they include, for example, *ignoring* or merely *dismissing as unreliable* a conflicting experimental report, or weakening the theory by reinterpreting it or by introducing an *ad hoc* auxiliary hypothesis). Popper forbids these tactics—but nothing in his methodology forbids us to defend a hypothesis by criticising the experimental arrangements or the network of hypotheses underlying the alleged refutation, or criticising some initial condition and introducing an auxiliary hypothesis which is not *ad hoc*.[56] We might call this, in contradistinction to conventionalist stratagems, the *critical defence* of a hypothesis.[57]

The 'critical defence' of a hypothesis provides, I suggest, the rationale of two remarks of Popper's which might otherwise sound rather strange coming from him. He says that:

> The dogmatic attitude of sticking to a theory as long as possible is of considerable significance. Without it we could never find out what is in a theory—we should give it up before we had a real opportunity of finding out its strength. . .[58]

This might seem to conflict with his more frequent emphasis on the desirability of a critical attitude. The apparent conflict is heightened by the psychologicist terminology—to resolve it, we must read 'attitude' in a nonpsychological way in both places. But then what is of 'considerable significance' is not a dogmatic attitude *as such*: a dogmatic attitude towards T will only be fruitful if it leads a scientist to improve T, to articulate and elaborate it so that it can deal with counterarguments; it will be unfruitful if it means merely that a scientist sticks to T without improving it. Similarly, a critical attitude towards T will be fruitful if it leads to a better theory; it will be unfruitful if it means merely that a scientist ceases to accept T, without putting something better in its place. Attitudes per se cannot be evaluated and one kind deemed to be always preferable to another. Attitudes can be evaluated only by what they *produce*, and methodology concerns the *products* of various attitudes, rather than the desirability of those attitudes in themselves.

It remains true, of course, that critical discussions are conducted by scientists, and that scientists will be motivated by their various psychological attitudes. But it is not necessary, for the critical method to be practised effectively, that scientists be the objective, open-minded paragons of virtue that inductivist mystique would have us believe.[59] Something far less dramatic is required: that in any particular dispute, the spectrum of attitudes will not be such that one side of that dispute will have no champions at all. Given this, the only further requirement is that both sides *argue* instead of merely expressing their rival attitudes. A critical philosophy of science can then analyse the intersubjective standards governing arguments in science, and try to delimit in methodological rules the sorts of arguments which are fruitful.

Moreover, whether a particular scientist abides by these standards and rules is not a purely personal affair. For science is a social institution, with definite traditions and codes of practice to which its members are socially induced to conform. Therefore, the question of whether a set of methodological rules is actually followed is as much a sociological question as a psychological one.[60] The *objectivity of science* need not rely upon the impartiality or objectivity of scientists. More important are the traditions and social institutions of science, for these may embody methodological rules which focus the attentions of scientists upon certain objective aspects of their knowledge.

The main point of this section has been that Popper's critical philosophy of science can dispense with 'critical psychologism'. It is rendered stronger and free from apparent contradictions in the process, and ceases to be vulnerable to counterclaims that not all scientists are always open-minded, undogmatic, sincere critics of all items of current scientific knowledge.

4. Objective Knowledge and the Knowing Subject

Popper's objectivist epistemology is based upon the distinction between the knowing subject and his objective knowledge, a distinction neglected in traditional epistemology. By insisting upon this distinction, we can handle problems concerning both the objective and the subjective realms in a much more satisfactory way than is traditional. This will be the theme of this last section.

Let us first return briefly to the traditional conception of knowledge as justified true belief. We can see immediately that this conception *conflated two problems which ought to be kept distinct*, and thereby gave unsatisfactory solutions to both of them. The first problem is whether we can justify, that is, establish the truth of, the content of any belief. The second problem is whether we can justify, that is, establish the reasonableness of, psychological attitudes (including that of believing) towards that content. The conflation of **these two problems leads to the dogma (already mentioned above, p. 567)** that it is reasonable to believe X if and only if X can be established as true.

If we separate these two problems, each of them is transformed. Consider first the problem of whether the content of any belief can be justified or established as true, ignoring the question of psychological attitudes towards that content. Since one statement could be established as true only by logical derivation from another one already established as true, and since this leads to an infinite regress, we must conclude that no statement can be proved (unless it is a statement of logic itself). All that we can say is that if X follows from Y, then if Y is true so is X; or if X contradicts Y, then if Y is true X cannot be true also. But if we avoid the subjectivist confusions discussed above (Section 1), then we must conclude that the sceptics are right: the traditional 'problem of knowledge' cannot be solved in a positive way, for justified knowledge is impossible.

Sceptical irrationalists concluded, from the impossibility of justifying statements, that the only rational attitude is a permanent 'suspense of judgement' and that, since we must do more than this, we must be irrational. There is, I think, much to be said for sceptical 'suspense of judgement'. But sceptical irrationalism is based upon the dogma that we may rationally believe (accept, choose) only statements which can be justified or established as true. If we give up this dogma, and divorce the problem of the justifiability of psychological attitudes from that of the justifiability of theories, then the problem of rational psychological attitudes is transformed.

It becomes, first of all, a relatively *unimportant* problem. Psychological attitudes are fleeting affairs, which can quite reasonably vary from person to person and from time to time according to circumstances. For example, my attitude to the statement 'This is a two-shilling piece' may reasonably change from uncritical reliance upon it if I am about to buy a bus ticket in quite ordinary circumstances, through institutionalized scepticism if I am employed as an inspector by the Royal Mint, to extreme wariness if, in some macabre game, my life depends upon whether the statement is true or not. These changes have nothing to do with finding new evidence, but depend solely upon the circumstances of the person considered. But these circumstances will be ignored if we conflate justification of attitudes towards theories with justification of theories, simply because they are irrelevant to the latter.

But is it ever rational to *believe* that a theory is true, when we can never prove it? Popper says not. He condemns as unreasonable strong *belief* that a theory is true, together with all its more extreme versions, such as *commitment* to the truth of a theory, and affirms, following E. M. Forster, that he does not 'believe in belief'.[61]

But can we manage without belief? And, in particular, can the scientist practise his vocation without belief? Must the scientist too be a man of faith, albeit of a faith different from that of the religious believer? Polanyi and Kuhn answer these questions in the affirmative. According to them, most if not all scientific research needs not only to be guided by an *awareness* of a prior theory, but must, if it is to be 'adequately motivated', be based upon a semireligious irrational *commitment* to that theory.[62] Popper, on the other hand, claims that the scientist need not believe: what he may sometimes need to do is to choose a theory as the best one available in the light of the critical discussion, and use it to guide his future research. Here Popper follows Russell, who argued long ago (against William James's *The Will to Believe*) that "A man of science who considers it worth while to devise experimental tests of an hypothesis, and to construct elaborate theories which use the hypothesis, is not on that account to be regarded as *believing* the hypothesis".[63]

Here what is not at issue is that much scientific work, especially experimental work, is *guided* by prior theory. What is at issue is a psychological question: is *commitment* to the prior theory necessary to provide adequate motivation for theory-guided work? And I wonder whether, for example, Eddington needed to be committed to the truth of the general theory of relativity before he undertook his eclipse experiment—surely 'adequate motivation' was provided simply by his conviction that the proposed experiment was an *important* one, and his curiosity about its outcome.

Psychological questions like this are, admittedly, difficult to decide. And the reason for this provides, at the same time, the reason why they are of secondary importance. An experimenter may be motivated by a dogmatic commitment to some theory, and despite this his investigation, which alone is open to inspection, may result in a critical argument *against* that theory. As we have already seen, this point holds also in reverse: an experimenter may be privately motivated by a deep desire to refute some theory, and nonetheless succeed only in publicly corroborating it. In short, the public argumentative status of an experimental investigation is independent of the private psychological motivation for undertaking it. Private motivations are therefore less important than they might appear to be. Let us suppose that Polanyi and Kuhn are right, as well they might be, about some scientist's need to commit himself. Popper can cheerfully respond that, irrational though his commitment is, that scientist should be left with it—he could make this response, since an irrational commitment might stimulate important work.

According to Popper, then, scientists constantly operate with theories. They constantly need to 'accept' or 'choose' or 'prefer' one theory over some others. And they may, according to Popper, use the degrees of corroboration of the various theories to guide their choices. Now we have already empha-sised that the degree of corroboration of a theory is both fallible and backward-looking (see above, p. 569). If this is so, can a positive degree of corroboration ever justify us in accepting or choosing one theory rather than another?

The answer must clearly be negative if we can make a *justified choice* of a theory only if that theory has *itself been justified*. But here again we must separate the justification of a *choice* of a theory from the justification of the *theory* itself. A scientist chooses a theory for many different purposes: to test it, to develop it further, to see if it can be applied in some new area, to analyse its logical relations with other theories, and so on. For none of these typical purposes does the theory involved need to be a justified one. Therefore a scientist can make justified choices, and may quite rationally use corrobora-tion to guide these choices.

But a scientist need not *always* 'choose' that theory with the highest degree of corroboration. He may rationally choose (that is, work on or try to develop) a falsified theory, thinking that it affords a more promising line of research than some rival theory which has not yet been falsified. (Traditional epistemology ignores such choices, thinking that one can only rationally choose a theory which is true and *believed* to be true.) While such choices may be decisive for the course of a particular scientist's research, they are very transitory affairs—the state of the critical discussion is always changing and different choices becoming reasonable.

Let us now turn briefly to the vexed question of the choice of theory for use in practice. Can degrees of corroboration guide such choices—can cor-roboration be a 'guide of life'? To use a hypothesis in practical applications is, fundamentally, to use it to predict future events. And, if corroboration is backward-looking, then it would seem that it is irrelevant to these choices, for its past success in making predictions does not render its future predictions any more secure. Yet Popper tells us that "There is not even anything irrational in relying for practical purposes upon well-tested theories, for no more rational course of action is open to us".[64] Now it has been argued that if corroboration is backward-looking then it cannot be a 'guide of life'; con-versely, if it is to be a 'guide of life' then it cannot be merely backward-looking but must also involve some inductivist assumption linking the past to the future.[65]

Popper rejects this argument, if I read him right, because it ignores the fact that what needs justification if we are to use corroboration as a guide of life is neither the corroborated theory nor any of its future predictions (in which case some inductivist assumption would be needed), but rather some person's present choice of the theory to guide his practical actions. We live in an uncertain world, we have to act, and all we have to help us are present hypotheses and our critical discussion of them: so, for Popper the most rational course open to us in these circumstances may be to act upon the best corroborated hypothesis.[66] Here again, justifiably to choose the best-corroborated hypothesis to guide one's actions involves no assumption that the best-corroborated hypothesis is itself justified. Once we have chosen some hypothesis, we may then proceed to deduce from it a prediction about the practical situation in which we are interested (the hypothesis *itself* acts as the needed link between past and future). If a precise numerical prediction is involved, we may then *act*, not upon this prediction, but upon the statement constructed from it by placing 'safety margins' around the predicted value (the *width* of these margins will depend upon the seriousness for us of being mistaken).[67]

So much, then, for problems concerning the choice or 'acceptance' of theories by individuals, and concerning the psychological attitudes individuals adopt towards knowledge. I have tried to show that if, with Popper, we divorce questions about the personal or subjective dimension of knowledge from questions about the objective dimension, then the former questions lose some of their importance and also *benefit* from the divorce. For we can reintroduce into their discussion all the vital time-dependent and personal factors which were excluded so long as justification of attitudes to theories was conflated with justification of theories (to which they were rightly thought to be irrelevant). Once such factors are reintroduced, we will find many different kinds of 'acceptance', appropriate to different situations, a diversity which has been obscured by the traditional conflation.[68]

I shall conclude by turning from the subjective dimension of knowledge to its objective dimension, which is, for Popper, the more important dimension. He argues that the fundamental distinction between the knowing or thinking subject and the object of his activities, the contents known or thought, means that there is a sort of 'third world' of objective knowledge. For objective contents possess various properties and relationships independently of any subject's awareness of them. For example, any scientific theory possesses, in a nontrivial sense, infinitely many logical consequences; yet the number of these consequences of which we can be aware at any time is necessarily finite. Facts like this mean that the 'third world' of objective contents must be distinguished both from the psychological world (where we have various kinds of awareness of objective contents) and from the physical world (where objective contents find various forms of expression in written or spoken utterances). In three recent papers, Popper has discussed this 'third world' not only from an epistemological point of view, but also from an evolutionary and metaphysical one.[69]

Popper remarks that the idea has a long prehistory in Plato's 'world of ideas', in the Stoics' world of *lekta*, in Hegel's 'objective mind', in Bolzano's realm of the 'statement-in-itself' (*Satz-an-sich*), in Brentano's realm of the 'intentional objects' of mental acts, and, above all, in Frege's 'third realm' of (objective contents of) 'thoughts'. There are, however, several important differences between these earlier doctrines and Popper's.[70] We might, at the risk of mixing metaphors, summarize these by saying that Popper tries to bring his 'third world' down to earth, and to analyse the relationships between his 'third world' and the mental and physical worlds.

For example, Plato's 'world of ideas' was divine, inhabited by unchanging, true, and perfect concepts or essences. Popper's third world is man-made and imperfect, and consists not of concepts but of theories—false theories as well as true ones. Hegel's 'objective mind', unlike Plato's world of ideas, does change: but it does so under its own steam, following the dialectical law according to which contradictions between theses and antitheses produce their syntheses. Popper's 'third world' also changes: but it does so only because of the efforts of its creators, human beings, who notice contradictions in the extant body of knowledge and in trying to eliminate them, produce new theories.[71] Bolzano and Frege made the main inhabitants of their 'third world' statements or propositions or theories, as opposed to ideas or concepts. Popper follows them, but he also allows his 'third world' to contain *arguments* and *problems*.[72]

Perhaps the most important difference is that Popper regards the 'third world' as an evolutionary product or effect of intelligent human behaviour, rather than a realm of eternal truths and falsehoods. His third world is produced by our linguistic behaviour, and especially by our using language to *describe* and to *argue*, to produce descriptions and arguments. Now descriptions and arguments possess objective properties like truth or falsehood and validity or invalidity. Popper assimilates the autonomy of these evolutionary products, their possessing properties which are independent of facts about their producers, to that of other evolutionary products (e.g., birds' nests, or beaver dams, or coral reefs).

Now it is possible, by emphasising the *eternal* character of the objective properties of knowledge, to wax metaphysical on the 'third world'. For example, if it is true that Mount Everest is now the highest mountain in the world, then the truth of this is eternal, and even before anybody was around to think of Mount Everest, it was still true that it would now be the highest mountain in the world. So, long ago there must have 'been' in the 'third world' an unthought, unuttered proposition to act as the bearer of this eternal truth.

Though possible, such doctrines and the problems to which they give rise are hardly very fruitful. They are especially unfruitful for one interested in the *growth* of knowledge, since an eternal 'third world' cannot grow. Popper's 'third world', on the other hand, does grow: new elements are put into it by the epistemological activities of human beings. For him, Newton's theory did not 'exist' in any relevant sense before Newton. But, once created, Newton's theory possessed various relationships to which temporal questions are inappropriate (it hardly makes sense to ask *when* it began to contradict Kepler's Laws). In this sense, then, Popper claims that temporal products have eternal properties.

It seems, therefore, that it is Popper's overriding interest in the growth of knowledge which has dictated his evolutionary approach to the 'third world'. The growth of knowledge depends upon the activities of human subjects. If we wish to consider human knowledge as an evolutionary product, it might seem more natural, therefore, to approach it from the point of view of the subjects who produce it. For without men to propose them there can be no statements to be true or false. Without men to draw them, there can be no inferences to be valid or invalid. Surely, it may plausibly be said, we must begin with the subject, the cause, before we turn to his objective knowledge, the effect. Do we not put the cart before the horse, the effect before the cause, in approaching human knowledge from an objective point of view? And why assume that there is a cart at all—can we not reduce the so-called objective dimension of knowledge to the subjective one?

Subjectivism, implicit in the second of these questions, has already been criticised, and I shall say no more about it. As to the first question, Popper defends the primacy of the objective approach. He points out that scientific enquiry typically proceeds from effects to their causes, and insists that "we can learn more about production behaviour by studying the products themselves than we can learn about the products by studying production behaviour".[73] For him an adequate psychology of knowledge must recognise that 'knowing subjects' deal all the time with objective contents which are in many respects autonomous, and which therefore can exert important feedback effects upon our mental life (and, via the mental world, occasionally upon the physical world itself).[74] Suppose, for example, that one physicist proposes a theory *T*. Any general theory has (nontrivial) consequences of which its author was unaware, which may raise problems of which he did not dream. Another person may discover one of these, and invent a criticism of it. A third may be induced by this valid argument against theory *T* to think that *T* is false, and thereby stimulated to invent another theory. Yet a fourth may recognise that the new theory has certain consequences relevant to technology. A fifth may use these to construct some physical artefact which has effects in the physical world (these effects can be rather dramatic). It would be difficult, if not impossible, to describe such a sequence of events adequately if we confined ourselves to *pure* psychology, and eschewed mention of the objective contents with which the different subjects were dealing. Hence Popper claims that "all the important things we can say about an act of knowledge consist in pointing out the third-world object of the act. . .and its relation to other third-world objects. . ."[75]

This applies especially to the growth of knowledge, which has taken place only through the combined efforts of innumerable subjects, pursuing common aims. But our knowledge will continue to grow only so long as those who produce it recognise its objective aspects, and utilise them as common *standards* to which they seek to conform. If objective standards are eschewed, and *pure* self-expression becomes the only aim, then the growth of knowledge will itself be in jeopardy. The growth of knowledge is itself threatened nowadays by a tide of subjectivist relativism—and if knowledge ceases to grow, its subjective dimension will, indeed, become the more important one. Subjectivism may yet succeed in vindicating itself—but only at a price.

It has often been said that it is his possession of language which distinguishes man from other animals, and this is no doubt true. But man's special place in the evolutionary scale would perhaps better be explained by saying that he has *used* language to create a body of objective knowledge. This evolutionary artefact, stored in libraries and handed down from generation to generation, enables a man to profit, in a way in which no other animal can, from the trials and errors of his ancestors. The evolution of a man has become, above all, the evolution of his knowledge, through the production of novel ideas and their struggle for survival.

ALAN E. MUSGRAVE

DEPARTMENT OF PHILOSOPHY
UNIVERSITY OF OTAGO, NEW ZEALAND
JULY, 1970

NOTES

[1] K. R. Popper (1945), *Addendum* (1961), 4th ed., Vol. II, p. 369.

[2] *Ibid.*, p. 377.

[3] More justice is done to it in Popper's British Academy Lecture of 1958, 'On the Sources of Knowledge and of Ignorance', which now forms the Introduction to his (1963). And the main points of the present section are elaborated in my (1969).

[4] Popper calls this 'framework philosophy': the doctrine that rational argument must proceed from a common 'framework' of assumptions. This doctrine is, I think, part and parcel of the idea that rational argument = justification, and thus of the traditional theory of knowledge as justified belief.

[5] René Descartes, *Discourse on Method*, 1637, Part III; cf. (1911), Vol. I, p. 98. For dogmatic empiricists it was God's creation, Nature, which could induce all minds to experience the same feelings of 'perceptual assurance'.

[6] The first two responses were used by Descartes against those who did not find the same things indubitable or clear and distinct as he did (cf. (1911), Vol. II, pp. 34-35; see also Vol. I, p. 239, and Vol. II, p. 55). The third response was used by Leonard Nelson, who remarked that anyone who doubted his 'first principles' should 'engage the services of a psychiatrist and leave the philosophers alone' ((1949), p. 128).

[7] Cf. Popper (1963), pp. 7 f.

[8] The degree to which the foregoing is rational reconstruction should be emphasized. What are called 'dogmatism' and 'scepticism' are extreme *positions*, not sects of people. Actual historical figures often switched back and forth, sometimes with bewildering rapidity, between dogmatism and scepticism in these senses, and usually settled at one of the great variety of possible intermediate positions. I still think, however, that the conflict of extremes can illuminate much traditional epistemology.

[9] This applies to contemporary language analysts. Popper aptly describes them as having replaced Locke's 'new way of ideas' with a 'new way of words' (cf. the 1959 Preface to his (1934), p. 17). This 'revolution in philosophy' is revolutionary only on the surface—the traditional problems remain, being merely transcribed into linguistic terms. For example, the traditional problem of distinguishing between genuine knowledge and mere belief now becomes the problem of elucidating the differences in ordinary English between 'I know p' and 'I believe p'. This is merely old psychologistic wine in new linguistic bottles; the quality of the wine has, I fear, not been improved by the rebottling.

[10] John Locke (1690), 'Epistle to the Reader', Vol. I, p. 14, and Book IV, Chap. 12, Sec. 10-11, Vol. II, pp. 350-51. Locke goes on, not very consistently, to recommend the study of nature—but he does so chiefly, as his examples show, for its pragmatic value.

[11] This was suggested by Berkeley, Hume, and Mach (Kant suggested a very different and more subtle form of the same doctrine). Berkeley, who knew the science of his day as well as any philosopher before or since, remarked: "I need not say, how many *hypotheses* and speculations are left out, and how much the study of nature is abridged by this doctrine". (George Berkeley, *Principles of Human Knowledge*, 1710, Part I, Sec. 102; (1948), Vol. II, p. 85.)

[12] I remember him putting the matter this way in his hitherto unpublished Shearman Memorial Lectures in London in 1961.

[13] Further examples of subjectivism, to be discussed in what follows, arise in connection with logic (see p. 573), explanation (see pp. 570-72), simplicity (see p. 572), and the severity of tests (see pp. 576-78).

[14] Logical positivists also distinguished between the psychological 'context of discovery' and the logical 'context of justification' (see, for example, Hans Reichenbach (1938), Chap. I, Sec. 1). They wanted to limit *induction* to the latter 'context', whereas originally it had been applied to both. Popper agreed that there was no inductive logic of discovery; but he did not agree that there could be an inductive logic of justification. He remarked that "the belief in inductive logic is largely due to the confusion of psychological problems with epistemological ones. It may be worth noticing, by the way, that this confusion spells trouble not only for the logic of knowledge but for its psychology as well" (Popper (1934), p. 30). The idea of a 'logic of justification' conflates the justification (i.e., proof) of the contents of theories with the justification of attitudes towards those contents (see above, pp. 567 and 582).

[15] As Locke put it: "I think we may as rationally hope to see with other men's eyes, as to know by other men's understandings. . . .The floating of other men's opinions in our brains, makes us not one jot the more knowing, though they happen to be true. What in them was science, is in us but opiniatrety. . .". See Locke (1690), Book I, Chap. iii, Sec. 24 (Vol. I, p. 115); see also, for example, Bertrand Russell (1940), p. 136.

[16] Popper (1934), p. 105 (see also pp. 43-44 and 46-47). Popper rejects psychologism in the context of Fries's *Trilemma*: infinite regress (of justification of statements by other statements) versus dogmatism versus psychologism. The difference between dogmatism and psychologism is here only slight: the dogmatist simply stops the regress at his 'first principles', but refuses to ex-

plain why he stops at one place rather than another; tne 'psychologist' does attempt to justify his 'first principles' with reference to his feelings of certainty. Dogmatism and psychologism in this sense are, for me, two names for fundamentally the same position.

[17] Exceptions are cases in which the varying 'reaction times' of experimenters affect the results of experiments. Hence the importance in these cases of substituting mechanical recorders whose records do not vary from person to person.

[18] Carnap acknowledges that observational premises cannot conclusively prove theories. He aims, therefore, to assign degrees of confirmation or partial justification to synthetic statements in the light of observation statements or 'evidence'. This programme would, if it could be carried out, also be subject to Fries's *Trilemma*. The 'evidence' cannot be assigned a degree of confirmation with respect to other 'evidence', on pain of infinite regress. Carnap himself seems to adopt a version of dogmatist psychologism: he says that we can only apply his theory of confirmation to "evidence that is *known*, i.e., *well-established by observation*" (Rudolf Carnap (1950), p. 202; see also pp. 194, 201, 206). Richard Jeffrey acknowledges that evidence is always uncertain. He proposes to stop the infinite regress at statements which, because of our perceptual experiences, we simply *cannot help* believing; yet he admits that these 'compulsory beliefs' may not be 'sound or appropriate' (Jeffrey (1968), p. 176; see also (1965), p. 156). This is explicit subjectivist relativism: what is a 'compulsory belief' for one man may not be for another; degrees of confirmation no longer aim at an objective or interpersonal evaluation of empirical knowledge, but instead represent empirical facts about the compulsions (and perhaps also the compulsion neuroses) of observers.

[19] Popper's formula for corroboration has severe limitations in this regard: see n. 38 and p. 579 above.

[20] A point stressed by J. W. N. Watkins (1968), p. 63. See also above, pp. 584-85.

[21] To rule out this last possibility is to say that repeatable experiments always give the same result, or that experimentally the future will be like the past. This *hypothesis* may lead the scientist to accept the universal statement describing the typical test result, and not to repeat the same test indefinitely; but no such universal statement can be established by experiment. (Once such a low-level universal statement is incorporated into 'background knowledge', future tests of instances of it will not be severe ones; see Popper (1963), p. 240.)

[22] Popper (1934), p. 59; a simple example is given there, and in an improved form in (1957a), pp. 122-23. As Carl G. Hempel has shown, there are several more or less vague anticipations of this analysis; for references see Hempel (1965), pp. 251, n. 7, and 337, n. 2.

[23] See especially K. R. Popper (1957b).

[24] This is the only sense of 'explanation' discussed, for example, by Percy Bridgman (1927): "the essence of an explanation consists in reducing a situation to elements with which we are so familiar that we accept them as a matter of course, so that our curiosity rests" (p. 37). Hempel calls the subjective sense of explanation the 'pragmatic' sense, and in distinguishing it from the logical sense elaborates many of the points which follow (cf. Hempel (1965), pp. 425-33).

[25] A good objective explanation typically *transcends* the *explanandum* by invoking highly speculative laws about unobservable entities or forces—with luck, this will enhance puzzlement rather than relieve it.

[26] The trouble with 'explanations' in terms of the actions and intentions of supernatural agencies, or of entelechies or vital forces, is not that they fail to relieve puzzlement, but that they do not conform to objective standards like that of independent testability.

[27] As Bridgman (1927) says: "an explanation is not an absolute sort of thing, but what is satisfactory for one man will not be for another" (p. 38).

[28] Demanded, for example, by Sir William Thomson (later Lord Kelvin) and Sir Oliver Lodge: see Hempel (1965), pp. 434-35.

[29] As to 'historical narratives', their adherents take pains to stress that historians usually provide them, and that they find them an adequate alternative *form* of explanation to the deduc-

tive one. Their adherents seem less concerned to tell us what, if any, are the objective standards in the light of which the 'adequacy' of narratives can be evaluated and one deemed objectively preferable to another. (See, for example, Arthur C. Danto (1965), esp. pp. 211 and 248-51.) My guess is that if attention is focussed upon this, narratives will emerge as series of partial deductive explanations.

[30] As to 'purposive explanations', Richard Taylor tells us that they are "usually sought in almost every aspect of life", and insists that they "differ radically from other types" of explanation. He then raises the question of their "adequacy", and his reply is merely that they are "sometimes adequate; they set curiosity at rest, they render the behaviour enquired about intelligible" (cf. Taylor (1966), p. 218).

[31] The standard use of the term 'discover' in this context, instead of 'invent', testifies to the objective character of problems. Further testimony is provided by the many simultaneous discoveries which have taken place in science. Notice, incidentally, that we need not invoke the 'social determination of thought' to explain the phenomenon of simultaneous discovery, as is done by Marx-inspired 'sociologists of knowledge'. Subjectivists explain away the objective dimension of knowledge in *psychological* terms (psychologism)—sociologists of knowledge try to achieve the same result in *sociological* terms (sociologism). Popper incisively criticised this in (1945), Vol. II, Chap. 23. The main defect which Popper exposed there was, alas, transmitted from the sociology of knowledge to its thriving intellectual offspring, the sociology of science; unfortunately, lack of space prevents me from discussing this here (see also below, p. 593, footnote 60).

[32] As Michael Polanyi (1958) appears to do, when he writes that ". . .nothing is a problem or discovery in itself; it can be a problem only if it puzzles or worries somebody, and a discovery only if it relieves somebody from the burden of a problem" (p. 122).

[33] See Popper (1934), Chap. 7.

[34] See *ibid.*, p. 98.

[35] See *ibid.*, Sec. 84, and (1963), pp. 223 and 229-30.

[36] See Popper (1934), p. 274, n. *1; (1963), pp. 223-24; and the *Addendum* (1961) to *Open Society*, esp. Sec. 1-3. In view of all this, there is really no excuse for the last sentence of the following: "Popper sometimes maintains that we can never *know* the truth. The best that we can do is to put forward hypotheses and subject them to rigorous test, for this is the way in which science progresses. Truth itself is just an illusion". (See D. W. Hamlyn (1967), p. 37.)

[37] For the theory of verisimilitude see Popper (1963), Chap. 10 and Appendices 3, 4, and 6. [Cf. also Professor Ayer's essay in this volume.—EDITOR]

[38] Unfortunately, if the two theories have both been falsified, their degrees of corroboration will, according to Popper's formulas, be the same, namely, -1 (see Imre Lakatos (1968a), p. 385. Thus in this very important case, Popper's formulas for degree of corroboration are of little use in helping us to assess comparative verisimilitudes. Such assessments can still be made in the light of the critical discussion of the two falsified theories—but for some purposes Popper's formulas for degree of corroboration turn out to be a poor summary of the state of that discussion.

[39] See Popper (1963), pp. 234-35. Thomas S. Kuhn points out, rightly, that we have no infallible means of detecting verisimilitude. He seems to conclude, wrongly in my view, that the idea of verisimilitude plays no role in the evaluation of scientific theories. (See Kuhn (1970), p. 16.) This simply applies to objective truth-likeness (verisimilitude) the standard objection to objective truth—that, since it cannot be infallibly known, it is a useless 'illusion'.

[40] See Popper (1934), esp. Sec. 19-20. The point is also discussed in my (1968).

[41] Cf. Popper's note on 'Degree of Confirmation', first published in 1954, and now reprinted in Appendix *ix of (1934); see p. 402.

[42] In an addition of 1958 to the footnote to the above passage: see Popper (1934), p. 402, n. 8.

[43] (1934), p. 418. For further statements in the same vein see (1934), p. 414; (1963), pp. 36; 58, n. 24; 279, n. 60; and 287-88; and (1957a), pp. 87-88.

[44] See, for example, the three theses of Popper (1968b), esp. in the formulations given on p. 340.

[45] More dangerous forms of this disease are rampant nowadays. It is often claimed that only those who have been psychoanalysed can understand psychoanalysis, so that the criticisms of others can be discounted a priori since they are bound to be based upon misunderstandings. It is also claimed that you must be a Marxist before you can have anything valuable to say about Marx. Or it is proposed that only those who happen to have black skins can say anything serious about the problem of race, or are competent to teach (or to learn) on so-called 'Black Studies' programmes.

[46] See Popper (1963), pp. 112 (par. 2), 240 (par. 3), 288.

[47] See Popper (1963), p. 220. Whether or not a predicted effect is a 'new' one is, of course, an objective question: it depends upon the extant body of science, not upon correlated subjective feelings of surprise or 'unexpectedness' among scientists.

[48] See Popper (1963), pp. 256 (last par.) and 287. We can, if we so wish, summarize these ideas in a formula: $S(e,h,b) = p(e,hb) / p(e,b)$, where e is the evidence, h the hypothesis under test, b background knowledge, p is conditional probability, and S severity. (Cf. Popper (1963), Appendix 2, formula (6), p. 391.) This formula is already implicit in Popper's earlier formulas for degree of corroboration ((1934), p. 401, formulas 10.1 and 10.2); but Popper did not then explain how these formulas involved an objective notion of severity of tests.

[49] Popper (1963), Appendix 2, p. 388; see also p. 220, where Popper says that we can "compare the severity of tests objectively" and *before these tests are undertaken.*

[50] Although this can hardly be what he had in mind when he wrote in 1955 (now in (1963), p. 289) that the theory of confirmation presented then "goes very considerably beyond" the theory of (1934); for the sincerity of testers remained a vital ingredient even then (see (1963), pp. 287-88).

[51] Popper (1963), p. 36.

[52] David Stove (1959) claimed that it was only by appealing to an inadmissable psychological idea of severity of tests that Popper could avoid the 'paradox of the ravens'. But, as J. W. N. Watkins (1959) pointed out, this so-called 'paradox' can be avoided using Popper's objective analysis of severity of tests (he elaborated the point in his (1960), and in Section V of his (1964)). Despite this, Stove insisted (in his (1960) on Popper's (1934)) that Popper's theory of the severity of tests was an inadmissable psychological one; he claimed (with some justice: see footnote 48 above) that in his (1934) Popper had given no nonpsychological analysis of severity; and he proceeded to provide one for him. But the main idea of Stove's objective analysis seems to be identical with that of Popper's (which had previously been explained by Watkins).

[53] Popper (1934), p. 50.

[54] *Ibid.*, p. 50.

[55] See, for example, the following remarks: "Rationalism is an attitude of readiness to listen to critical arguments and to learn from experience" (Popper (1945), Vol. II, p. 225); "What I shall call the 'true rationalism'. . .is the awareness of one's limitations. . .intellectual modesty. . ." (*ibid.*, p. 227). See also, for example, Popper (1963), pp. 50, 229, 256; (1968a), p. 296.

[56] Introducing an auxiliary hypothesis into a theoretical system can evade a refutation only if we also modify or replace one of the original premises—for, by elementary logic, merely to add an extra premise does not eliminate any of the original consequences, and in particular, not the falsified one. A famous example is the addition to Newton's theory of the (non-*ad hoc*) hypothesis of the existence of Neptune, which negated the existing premise about the number of the planets.

[57] Although Popper would not, I think, condemn the 'critical defence' of a hypothesis (*pace* Joseph Agassi (1966), p. 17), he has not analysed it in detail. Detailed analysis of it forms the heart of Imre Lakatos's idea of scientific research-programmes. Lakatos argues that empirical 'refutations' usually produce, not the complete overthrow of a theory, but rather a modified ver-

sion of what is in essentials the same theory. Fundamental ideas in science (what Lakatos terms the 'hard core' of a research programme) show remarkable tenacity, persisting through various articulated and falsifiable attempts to apply them to the world, and being abandoned only when a genuine rival is available. Lakatos argues that some of Popper's falsificationist maxims become unacceptable in the light of his analysis. For details see Lakatos's papers cited in the bibliography. [And also Lakatos's essay in this volume.—EDITOR]

⁵⁸ Popper (1963), p. 312, n. 1; for the other, similar, remark see *ibid.*, p. 49.

⁵⁹ See Popper (1945), Vol. II, pp. 216-18, where Popper criticises the myth of the 'objective scientist'.

⁶⁰ Hence the importance of a genuine sociology of science which enquires how far aims and standards given by the objective dimension of scientific knowledge are reflected in the actual operations of the 'social system of science'. Unfortunately, too much of our present sociology of science ignores the objective dimension of scientific knowledge altogether (see above, p. 591, footnote 31) and, as a result, gives at best ridiculously superficial accounts of the social dimension of science.

⁶¹ See E. M. Forster (1951), p. 75; and Popper (1968a), p. 293.

⁶² See, for example, Michael Polanyi (1946), pp. 54, 76; and Thomas S. Kuhn (1963), pp. 349, 362, or Kuhn (1962), pp. 18, 25, 162-63. This point is, in essentials, an application to scientists of the central thesis of William James (1897).

⁶³ Cf. Bertrand Russell (1910), p. 84.

⁶⁴ Popper (1963), p. 51; see also p. 57.

⁶⁵ For the most recent statement of this argument see Lakatos (1968a), Sec. 3.3, and his paper in this volume.

⁶⁶ The word 'may' needs emphasis. For there may be practical circumstances in which it would not be rational to work with the best-corroborated hypothesis because the *costs* of doing so, in terms of time and effort, are too high.

⁶⁷ See Lakatos (1968a), p. 393.

⁶⁸ Bar-Hillel (1968) has criticised the idea that there is only one kind of rational acceptance appropriate to all situations both outside and inside science. Bar-Hillel does not, however, regard the syndrome as resulting from the conflation of justification of attitudes and justification of theories. This conflation even infects our terminology. To say that a theory is 'scientifically acceptable' is often only a way of saying that it has certain objective merits. (This applies to the various kinds of scientific acceptability described by Lakatos (1968a), Sec. 3.1 - 3.3.) The terminology is misleading because we tend to think that if a theory is 'acceptable' (in this objective sense) then it ought to be accepted (in the subjective sense) by all scientists at all times for all purposes; and this ignores the importance, for considerations about subjective acceptance, of temporal and personal factors.

⁶⁹ Popper (1968b), (1968c), (1968d).

⁷⁰ See Popper (1968b), Sec. 5.

⁷¹ On this point see Popper (1963), pp. 316-17.

⁷² It may also contain works of art, designs, poems, etc., since these too, once created, acquire a certain *autonomy*. This is enough to show the triviality of the *expressionist theory of art* (art = self-expression), which ignores the objective dimension altogether. Popper has often pointed out (in lectures) that art is much more than self-expression: for if it were nothing but self-expression it would be like blowing one's nose, which also expresses the 'self'. But all sorts of things can be (truly or falsely) said about a work of art *in itself*, without referring either to the psychology of its producer or to anybody else's psychology. Ian C. Jarvie (1967) has distinguished between *responses* to a work of art (reports about how it affects people psychologically) and *evaluations* of a work of art (statements about the work of art as such, rather than its psychological origins or effects). He argues that art criticism cannot be merely a matter of taste,

594 ALAN E. MUSGRAVE

since it does not consist exclusively of the former. For excellent examples of the evaluation of works of art *qua* solutions to artistic problems, see Gombrich (1961).

⁷³ Popper (1968b), p. 340.

⁷⁴ The third world cannot, of course, exert such effects *by itself*—its effects are exerted only through one or more subject's being aware (perhaps mistakenly aware) of third-world phenomena. Cp. Popper (1968b), p. 336.

⁷⁵ Popper (1968c), p. 31.

BIBLIOGRAPHY

Agassi, Joseph (1966). 'Sensationalism'. *Mind,* **65** (1966), 1-24.

Bar-Hillel, Y. (1968). 'The Acceptance Syndrome'. *The Problem of Inductive Logic.* Edited by I. Lakatos. Amsterdam: North-Holland Publishing Company, 1968, pp. 150-161.

Berkeley, George (1948). *The Works of George Berkeley, Bishop of Cloyne.* Edited by A. A. Luce and T. E. Jessop. 9 Vols. Edinburgh: Thomas Nelson and Sons, 1948-1957.

Bridgman, Percy (1927). *The Logic of Modern Physics.* New York: Macmillan and Company, 1927.

Carnap, Rudolf (1950). *Logical Foundations of Probability.* Chicago: University of Chicago Press, 1950; 2d ed., 1962.

Danto, Arthur C. (1965). *Analytical Philosophy of History.* London: Cambridge University Press, 1965.

Descartes, René (1911). *The Philosophical Works of Descartes.* Translated by Elizabeth S. Haldane and G. R. T. Ross. 2 Vols. New York: Dover Publications, 1955 (translation first published in 1911).

Forster, E. M. (1951). *Two Cheers for Democracy.* Harmondsworth, Middlesex: Penguin Books, 1965 (first published in 1951).

Gombrich, Ernst (1961). *Art and Illusion.* 2d ed. London: Phaidon Press, 1961.

Hamlyn, D. W. (1967). 'History of Epistemology'. Article in *The Encyclopaedia of Philosophy.* Edited by Paul Edwards. Vol. 3. London: Collier-Macmillan; New York: Macmillan Company and Free Press, 1967.

Hempel, Carl G. (1965). *Aspects of Scientific Explanation and Other Essays in the Philosophy of Science.* New York: Free Press; London: Collier-Macmillan, 1965.

James, William (1897). *The Will to Believe, and Other Essays in Popular Philosophy.* London: Longmans, Green & Co., 1897.

Jarvie, Ian C. (1967). 'The Objectivity of Criticism in the Arts'. *Ratio,* **9** (1967), 67-83.

Jeffrey, Richard (1965). *The Logic of Decision.* New York: McGraw-Hill Publishing Company, 1965.

_____ (1968). 'Probable Knowledge'. *The Problem of Inductive Logic.* Edited by I. Lakatos. Amsterdam: North-Holland Publishing Company, 1968, pp. 166-80.

Kuhn, Thomas S. (1962). *The Structure of Scientific Revolutions.* Chicago: University of Chicago Press, 1962.

_____ (1963). 'The Function of Dogma in Scientific Research'. *Scientific Change.* Edited by A. C. Crombie. London: Heinemann and Co., 1963, pp. 347-69 and 386-95. (Kuhn's 'Reply' to the discussion.)

_____ (1970). 'Logic of Discovery or Psychology of Research'. *Criticism and the Growth of Knowledge.* Edited by I. Lakatos and A. E. Musgrave. London: Cambridge University Press, 1970, pp. 1-23.

Lakatos, Imre (1968a). 'Changes in the Problem of Inductive Logic'. *The Problem of Inductive Logic.* Edited by I. Lakatos. Amsterdam: North-Holland Publishing Company, 1968, pp. 315-417.

_____ (1968b). 'Criticism and the Methodology of Scientific Research Programmes'. *Proceedings of the Aristotelian Society,* **69** (1968-69), 149-86.

_____ (1970). 'Falsification and the Methodology of Scientific Research Programmes'. *Criticism and the Growth of Knowledge.* Edited by I. Lakatos and A. E. Musgrave. London: Cambridge University Press, 1970, pp. 91-195.

Locke, John (1690). *An Essay Concerning Human Understanding.* Collated and annotated, with Prolegomena, Biographical, Critical, and Historical, by Alexander Campbell Fraser. 2 Vols. New York: Dover Publications, 1959.

Musgrave, Alan E. (1968). 'On a Demarcation Dispute'. *Problems in the Philosophy of Science.* Edited by I. Lakatos and A. E. Musgrave. Amsterdam: North-Holland Publishing Company, 1968, pp. 78-88.

_____ (1969). 'Impersonal Knowledge: A Criticism of Subjectivism in Epistemology'. Ph.D. thesis, University of London, 1969 (unpublished).

Nelson, Leonard (1949). *Socratic Method and Critical Philosophy: Selected Essays.* Translated by Thomas K. Brown III. New York: Dover Publications, 1965 (first published in 1949).

Polanyi, Michael (1946). *Science, Faith and Society.* Chicago: University of Chicago Press, 1946; rev. ed., 1964.

_____ (1958). *Personal Knowledge: Towards a Post-Critical Philosophy.* London: Routledge and Kegan Paul, 1958.

Popper, K. R. (1934). *The Logic of Scientific Discovery.* English translation of *Logik der Forschung* (first published in 1934). London: Hutchinson and Company, 1959; 2d ed., 1968.

——————— (1945). *The Open Society and Its Enemies.* 2 Vols. London: Routledge and Kegan Paul, 1945; 5th ed., 1966.

——————— (1957a). *The Poverty of Historicism.* London: Routledge and Kegan Paul, 1957; 2d ed., 1960.

——————— (1957b). 'The Aim of Science'. *Ratio,* **1** (1957), 24-35.

——————— (1963). *Conjectures and Refutations: The Growth of Scientific Knowledge.* London: Routledge and Kegan Paul; New York: Basic Books, 1963; 2d ed., 1965.

——————— (1968a). 'Theories, Experience and Probabilistic Intuitions'. *The Problem of Inductive Logic.* Edited by I. Lakatos. Amsterdam: North-Holland Publishing Company, 1968, pp. 285-303.

——————— (1968b). 'Epistemology without a Knowing Subject'. *Logic, Methodology and Philosophy of Science III.* Edited by B. van Rootselar and J. F. Staal. Amsterdam: North-Holland Publishing Company, 1968, pp. 333-73.

——————— (1968c). 'On the Theory of the Objective Mind'. *Proceedings of the XIV International Congress of Philosophy* (Vienna), **1** (1968), 25-53.

——————— (1968d). 'A Realist View of Logic, Physics and History'. *Physics, Logic and History: Proceedings of the International Colloquium, Denver, 1966.* Edited by W. Yourgrau. New York: Plenum Publishing Company, 1968.

Reichenbach, Hans (1938). *Experience and Prediction.* Chicago: University of Chicago Press, 1938.

Russell, Bertrand (1910). *Philosophical Essays.* London: George Allen and Unwin, 1910; 2d ed., 1966.

——————— (1940). *An Inquiry into Meaning and Truth.* London: George Allen and Unwin, 1940.

Stove, David (1959). 'Popperian Confirmation and the Paradox of the Ravens'. *Australasian Journal of Philosophy,* **37**, No. 2 (1959), 149-51.

——————— (1960). 'Critical Notice' [On Popper's (1934)]. *Australasian Journal of Philosophy,* **38**, No. 2 (1960), 173-87.

Taylor, Richard (1966). *Action and Purpose.* Englewood Cliffs, N. J.: Prentice-Hall, 1966.

Watkins, John W. N. (1959). 'Mr. Stove's Blunders'. *Australasian Journal of Philosophy,* **37**, No. 3 (1959), 240-41.

——————— (1960). 'Reply to Mr Stove's Reply'. *Australasian Journal of Philosophy,* **38**, No. 1 (1960), 54-58.

——————— (1964). 'Confirmation, the Paradoxes, and Positivism'. *The Critical Approach to Science and Philosophy.* Edited by Mario Bunge. New York: Free Press; London: Collier-Macmillan, 1964.

——————— (1968). 'Non-inductive Corroboration'. *The Problem of Inductive Logic.* Edited by I. Lakatos. Amsterdam: North-Holland Publishing Company, 1968, pp. 61-66.

16

Paul Bernays

CONCERNING RATIONALITY

I

The following considerations, which may be regarded as a kind of comment on the philosophy of Sir Karl Popper, concern only one point of his doctrine, a doctrine explained by him in many highly instructive discourses and lectures. In these Professor Popper is not content to present his philosophical views, and his arguments in favour of them; he also lets us know how he came to adopt these views, thus giving his heuristic motivation.

One of the papers in which he reports on the development of his philosophical views has the title "The Demarcation Between Science and Metaphysics".[1] In this paper Popper explains the main point of his highly effective criticism of positivism. Positivist philosophy declares to be meaningless everything that is not scientific. In a convincing argument Popper insists that it will not do to identify the distinguishing criterion of what is scientific with the criterion of what is meaningful. The restricting criteria for meaningfulness proposed by the positivists are all shown to be inadequate, and Popper presents a criterion of demarcation between scientific and unscientific statements which is quite independent of the question of meaning, namely the criterion of "refutability" or "falsifiability". The idea of this criterion may be expressed as follows: a theoretical system which is of such a kind that, whatever the facts in its domain, there is a method of bringing the theory into agreement with the facts, cannot be regarded as scientific.

Of course, Popper does not mean that every scientific statement can actually be refuted; this indeed would be a catastrophe. He means, and expressly says, "refutability in principle"; that is, the theory or statement in question must have consequences which by their form and character admit the possibility of being false. A law in physics can (in general) be tested by experiments, and whether the result is in agreement with the law depends on the values which have been found for the quantities in question. In an analogous way an elementary law of number theory—whether proved or not—may be checked by numerical instances. (Here we are even free from the complications caused by the inaccuracy of observations.)

The preference for refutation over verification in Popper's criterion is a result of the circumstance that in science, and in particular in natural science, we are mainly concerned with general laws (natural laws); and such laws, by their lógical structure, cannot be proved to hold by one instance, whereas they can well be refuted by one instance.

The impossibility of inferring a general law, or even the probability of such a law, from instances, is put forward by Popper as the decisive argument against the "verificationists" who "demand that we should accept a belief *only if it can be justified by positive evidence*; that is to say, *shown* to be true, or, at least, to be highly probable".[2]

In opposition to this view Popper says that the most important characteristic of science is the *critical approach*: "a system is to be considered as scientific only if it makes assertions which may clash with observations; and a system is, in fact, tested by attempts to produce such clashes, that is to say by attempts to refute it".[3]

Popper regards the growth of scientific knowledge not as consisting mainly in the "accumulation of observations", but in the "repeated overthrow of scientific theories and their replacement by better or more satisfactory ones . . . For our critical examination of our theories leads us to attempts to test and to overthrow them".[4]

In order to avoid misunderstandings we have to add here Popper's views concerning what he calls *background knowledge*: "criticism", he observes, "never starts from nothing, even though every one of its starting points *may* be challenged, one at a time, in the course of the critical debate . . . all criticism must be piecemeal. . . . While discussing a problem we always accept (if only temporarily) all kinds of things as *unproblematic*: they constitute . . . for the discussion of this particular problem . . . our background knowledge."[5]

In discussing our attempts to overthrow our theories Popper certainly does not mean this as a description of the actual attitude of every experimenting physicist. He says: "From a logical point of view, all empirical tests are . . . attempted refutations."[6] At all events they can be regarded as attempted refutations. As to the actual intentions of the experimenting scientist there are however various possibilities; for instance, a scientist may have instinctive confidence in a new theory, and, in order to establish it, he may set up experiments in order to decide between this theory and previous ones. Heinrich Hertz certainly did not attempt to overthrow Maxwell's theory in the experiments by which he showed that electromagnetic waves, whose existence follows from this theory, really do exist. Or, to take another instance, the famous Michelson interference experiment, which played a decisive role in the refutation of the hypothesis of a material ether: Michelson himself did not at all intend such a refutation; even after the result of his experiment, he continued to favour this hypothesis.

Indeed, Popper himself repeatedly mentions the fact that there often is a difference between what a man intends and the significance of his work. In his Compton Memorial Lecture, *Of Clouds and Clocks,*[7] he says: "A man who works on a problem can seldom say clearly what his problem is . . . ; and even if he can explain his problem, he may mistake it. And this may even hold of scientists. . . ."

II

In regarding experiments as attempted refutations, Popper is able to survey the development of natural science from the point of view of the theory of evolution. There is a Darwinistic element in his philosophy of science which Popper himself explicitly brings to light. Indeed he says: "The critical attitude may be described as the conscious attempt to make our theories, our conjectures, suffer in our stead in the struggle for the survival of the fittest. It gives us a chance to survive the elimination of an inadequate hypothesis—when a more dogmatic attitude would eliminate it by eliminating us."[8] This Darwinistic aspect of science is impressively maintained also in Popper's lecture, just mentioned, *Of Clouds and Clocks.*

As the theory of evolution is presented there, the whole process of evolution is an ever iterated application of the method of trial and error elimination. The schema of neo-Darwinism is widened here in so far as more than *one* way of error elimination—the killing of the organism—is assumed. "In our system", Popper writes, "not all problems are survival problems: there are many very specific problems and sub-problems. . . . Our schema allows for the development of error-eliminating controls . . . ; that is, controls which can eliminate errors without killing the organism; and it makes it possible, ultimately, for our hypotheses to die in our stead."[9]

Popper describes the "fundamental evolutionary sequence of events"[10] by this schema:

$$P_1 \rightarrow TS \rightarrow EE \rightarrow P_2,$$

(where P_1 is the starting problem situation, TS a tentative solution or a multiplicity of such solutions, EE is error elimination, P_2 the problem situation at the end). This schema has an analogy with the schema of the four phases in scientific progress that Ferdinand Gonseth has presented in several of his more recent publications; but Gonseth does not speak of error elimination, but of testing an hypothesis, and there is, in his presentation, no Darwinistic element. The common characteristic is that in the passage from the third stage of the process to the fourth there usually occurs an alteration of the problem situation.

In Popper's schema this is expressed by the distinction between P_1 and P_2; this shows "that the problems (or the problem situations) which the organism is trying to deal with are often *new*, and arise themselves as products of the evolution".[11]

Besides, in speaking here of problems, Popper means "problems in an objective [or nonpsychological] sense".[12] "All *organisms*", he says, "are constantly, day and night, *engaged in problem-solving*; and so are all the evolutionary *sequences of organisms*".[13] The objective problems "can be, hypothetically, reconstructed by hindsight".[14] Thus we have here not a naturalistic, but rather an objectivizing description, in the way it is used in the history of science and of literature.

The method of problem solving is said to proceed always as a method of trial and error: "new reactions, new forms, new organs, new modes of behavior, new hypotheses, are tentatively put forward and controlled by error-elimination".[15]

III

Here it might be questioned whether all these novelties occur purely at random, so that the properly formative element is all to be ascribed to the error elimination. If one admits that this is not the case, then the biggest part of evolution remains unexplained.

A special difficulty for any explanation seems to lie in the fact that phylogenesis depends on heredity, which in turn is produced by the highly complicated and very specific hereditary apparatus. According to neo-Darwinism and, as it seems, also according to Popper's theory, we should have to assume that this apparatus also is the result of random variations and error elimination. The particular difficulty here is that the various problems solved by the hereditary apparatus are not immediate needs, but appear only if further evolution is, so to speak, anticipated as a goal.

IV

Popper's evolutionary theory is closely connected with his theory of knowledge. In opposition to the view that our theories are obtained from observations by means of a priori principles (as rationalist philosophers think), or by probability inferences (as empiricists hold), Popper states that "knowledge proceeds by way of conjectures and refutations. . . . There is [he says] only one element of rationality in our attempts to know the world: it is the critical examination of our theories. These theories themselves are guesswork. We do not know, we only guess."[16]

Now Popper repeatedly characterizes this method of conjecture and refutation also as a more consciously developed form of the method of trial and error.[17] In this developed form, the guess-character of the theories corresponds to the tentative character of the trials.

Here it seems that at the bottom of the opposition of rationality and guesswork there is the hidden assumption that rationality must be *knowing* and that therefore anything that may be refuted or may require modification cannot be rational.

However, it may be asked if it is suitable thus to restrict the concept of rationality. Shall we not admit that guessing can proceed in a more or less rational way? Rationality in guessing is indeed the object of heuristics. Concerning the examination of our theories we need to be reminded of the fact that a theory is to be evaluated in two respects: on the one hand, according to its inner merits; and, on the other, according to its explanatory power. Now, do not the inner merits of a theory constitute for it something like its rational character?

What distinguishes guessing from proving is in fact not the absence of rationality, but the kind of problem. Indeed, to set up a suitable theory of some scope is a problem in itself. Popper, in his paper, "Truth, Rationality, and the Growth of Scientific Knowledge", considers the requirements such a theory has to satisfy in order to produce real progress. Among these requirements he mentions that the theory should "resolve . . . some theoretical difficulties", that it should "proceed from some *simple, new, and powerful, unifying idea* about some connection or relation . . . between hitherto unconnected things . . . or facts".[18] But are not these required qualities of a theory precisely aspects of rationality?

V

One may now ask: what is to be regarded as the proper characteristic of rationality? It seems that it is to be found in the *conceptual element*, which transcends perceiving and (sensual) imagining and which produces a kind of *understanding*. This is a wide concept of rationality. One may restrict it by requiring a certain degree of abstractness.

Let us recall some familiar cases of rationality brought about by the formation of concepts.

(1) In pure logic rationality consists in clearly understanding what we

mean by such terms as "and", "or", "not", "if . . . then", "all", "some". The principles of logic may be regarded as "meaning postulates" (as Carnap's school calls them).[19]

(2) In pure arithmetic and algebra the rationalizing effect of the use of abstract concepts is very clear, and especially in modern mathematics it is explicitly emphasized.

(3) A particular type of rationality is involved in the way we conceive "ideal figures" in geometry. Here we have a kind of concept suggested, as it were, by visual objects. Moreover, these concepts react in a certain way upon our perception of these objects, and this is important for the theoretical study of their structural properties. In this way a threefold significance of geometrical concepts emerges. They are significant (a) for the physical theory of concrete figures and concrete bodies, and for the physics of space; (b) for the constitution of an important domain of pure mathematics; and (c) for a phenomenological theory of intuitive spatial relations.[20] In all three respects the rationality of our understanding is brought about by the application of geometrical concepts.

(4) The rationalizing effect of the formation of concepts is especially clear in theoretical physics. An outstanding instance is the imposing development of classical mechanics, which can be traced from Newton's fundamental work through the contributions of numerous eminent mathematicians to the form it assumed in the nineteenth century. Here the growth of rationality came about not mainly by criticisms but by conceptual elaboration.

(5) A sort of conceptual rationality is contained in our "background knowlege" (to use Popper's term) which already contains conceptual distinctions of kinds of objects, and in particular also of kinds of materials. (Indeed, it includes very much more!) All empirical investigations of nature are based on this fundamental stock of concepts contained in our background knowledge. Popper has repeatedly stressed the circumstance that the statements which we ordinarily regard as simply observational already presuppose this conceptual basis, so that in a proper sense we cannot say that natural science starts from observations.[21]

(6) Whereas in our primitive attitude we ascribe the connections and regularities of nature to properties of things, in science we take such regularities as something to be more closely understood; this is a critical attitude. But there is in addition a positive leading idea—*the idea of natural law.*

As is well known, David Hume, who indeed insisted that we cannot infer the validity of a law from observed cases, concluded from this that there can be no rationality (no character of reason) in the assumption of a natural law. But what he really showed was that we cannot have rational certainty of a natural law. Yet, rationality need not be interpreted as certainty. It can be a characteristic of *our ways of trying to reach understanding*. In fact, the idea of natural law is a rational conception: it could not arise in a being devoid of reason; moreover, it transcends primitive concepts.

VI

Some general remarks may be added here. In the more abstract rationality of natural science we can discern a general feature—what Gonseth calls the schematic character of all theoretical description.

The description or characterization which we attain here is not to be understood in the sense of full adequacy, but only of a schematic correspondence. The schemata set up by the theories have their inner structures, which cannot be fully identified with the constitution of physical nature. This fact shows itself in the practice of physical science by the necessity of applying in each particular problem a peculiar kind of approximation, which can be totally different for different problems.[22]

The inner structures of the theoretical schemata have a purely mathematical character; they are idealized structures. And mathematics can be regarded as the science of possible idealized structures. These idealized structures and their interrelations constitute an open domain of objectivity—an objectivity *sui generis*, different from the one we have to deal with in physics as natural science, but indeed, connected with it in the way that by a physical theory some section of physical nature is described as an approximate realization of some mathematical structure.

VII

So far we have considered only abstract scientific rationality. But one may speak of rationality also in a widened sense, so as to include prescientific rationality. In particular three types of prescientific rationality are to be mentioned.[23]

The first is the concept of life, which is an aspect of nature fundamentally distinct from the purely structural one.

The second is a variety of concepts by which the feelings and motives of psychic beings are comprehended; these are concepts like "wanting", "wishing", "love", "pride", "ambition", "jealousy", "shame", "anger".[24] By these concepts a distinct kind of understanding is achieved, which in some respects cannot be replaced by any structural explanation, however elaborate it may be.

The third consists of the concepts used to describe meaningful interactions and interrelations between individuals, like: "communication", "agreement", "promise", "order", "obedience", "claim", "privilege", "duty".

Some of these concepts are connected with the *regulative idea of justice*, which is a prominent element of rationality, and which again constitutes a domain of objectivity. An analogy can be made between, on the one hand, the relatedness of a theoretical system of physics to the domain of physical nature that it approximately describes and, on the other, the relatedness of a system of positive law to an intended objectivity of justice to which it approximates in a lower or higher degree.

Of course, all the types of rationality mentioned here have their place in Popper's philosophy; only they do not figure in his characterization of rationality. The suggestions contained in the foregoing may be found to amount merely to a shade of alteration in his philosophy. I am quite agreeable to this point of view. In fact, I should want to preserve Popper's main thesis: that, in our exploring nature, reason does not provide us with fixed a priori principles to start from, but that we are obliged to proceed by trials. The change that has been proposed here concerns Popper's assertion that in our attempts to understand the world the *only* rational element is contained in the critical attitude. This restriction of rationality to a *merely selective function* is not a consequence of Popper's thesis. Rather we can, in full agreement with it, ascribe to rationality a *creativity*: not a creativity of principles, but a creativity of concepts.

PAUL BERNAYS

ZÜRICH, SWITZERLAND
APRIL 1, 1967

NOTES

[1] K. R. Popper, *Conjectures and Refutations: The Growth of Scientific Knowledge* (London: Routledge & Kegan Paul, 1963; New York: Basic Books, 1963), pp. 253-92. Hereinafter cited as *C.&R.*

[2] "Truth, Rationality, and the Growth of Scientific Knowledge", in *C.&R.*, Sec. IX, p. 228.

[3] "The Demarcation between Science and Metaphysics", in *C.&R.*, Sec. 2, p. 256.

[4] "Truth, Rationality", Sec. I, p. 215.

[5] *Ibid.*, Sec. XV, p. 238.

[6] "On the Status of Science and Metaphysics", in *C.&R.*, Sec. I, p. 192.

[7] K. R. Popper, *Of Clouds and Clocks: An Approach to the Problem of Rationality and the Freedom of Man* (St. Louis, Missouri: Washington University, 1965), p. 26.

[8] "Science: Conjectures and Refutations", in *C.&R.*, Sec. VII, p. 52.

[9] *Of Clouds and Clocks*, pp. 24 ff.

[10] *Ibid.*, p. 24; see also *C.&R.*, p. 313 (a passage from a talk given in 1937).

[11] *Ibid.*, p. 25.

[12] *Ibid.*, p. 23; see also pp. 25 ff.

[13] *Ibid.*, p. 23; see also pp. 25 ff.

[14] *Ibid.*, p. 23; see also pp. 25 ff.

[15] *Ibid.*, p. 23; see also pp. 25 ff.

[16] "Back to the Presocratics", in *C.&R.*, Sec. XII, p. 152.

[17] Cp. "What is Dialectic?", in *C.&R.*, Sec. I, pp. 312 ff.; and "Science: Conjectures and Refutations", Sec. VII, pp. 51 ff.

[18] See *C.&R.*, p. 241.

[19] In the formalization of logic, purely logical principles are mixed with rules of a combinatorial character. It seems hardly possible, in formalizing logic, fully to separate what is purely logical.

[20] The three aspects of geometry, the experimental, the theoretical, and the intuitive, have been especially rendered prominent in Gonseth's treatise, *La Géométrie et le problème de l'espace*, Bibliothèque scientifique, Griffon, Neuchâtel, in particular Part II.

[21] See especially *The Logic of Scientific Discovery* (London: Hutchinson, 1959; New York: Basic Books, 1959), Sec. 25, pp. 94 ff.

[22] By the way, in speaking of the schematic character of the theoretical descriptions, we have to beware of a misunderstanding: the word "schematic" might suggest something rough. This is not meant here. We have, in fact, between the objects of nature and the schematic representatives a reciprocity of approximation: the schemata do not fully attain the ample multiplicity of determinations of the natural objects; on the other hand, the natural objects do not attain the mathematical perfection and precision of the schemata.

[23] One kind of prescientific rationality—that which is involved in our background knowledge—has been mentioned before.

[24] The current view that we have to deal here simply with qualities given by an inner sensation, seems on closer inspection to be somewhat doubtful. Already John Locke, who adhered in some way to this view, nevertheless preferred to use the term "reflection", instead of "internal sensation". He explained this by saying that "the ideas it affords being such only, as the mind gets by reflecting on its own operations within itself ". (*Essay Concerning Human Understanding*, Book II, Chap. I, Sec. 4.)

17

J. Bronowski

HUMANISM AND
THE GROWTH OF KNOWLEDGE

I

O ne of the pleasures of writing an essay of retrospect and appreciation is that it makes an occasion to read afresh the books that one has been taking for granted for many years. So I have been reading again in a leisurely way *The Logic of Scientific Discovery*,[1] which in one form or another is now well over thirty years old. I could not have found a more delightful task; the book reads as freshly today—and strikes as deeply and as directly—as when I first held it in my hand. There cannot be many books, at least in philosophy, which begin to become classics while they still surprise the reader with an unforced air of exhilaration and intellectual urgency. The only thing that makes *The Logic of Scientific Discovery* more pedestrian now than it was thirty years ago is the weight of notes and appendices that has been added; it was livelier to read, and more challenging to the reader, before it was cushioned in an apparatus half as long (and twice as solemn) as the text itself.

Before I review the content of *The Logic of Scientific Discovery* I ought to recall something of the setting of the 1930s in which the book appeared. The climate of the time in England (where I had just finished college) is still vivid to me—both the philosophical climate and the political climate. What Karl Popper had to say was very timely, because it came when the climate was changing, and it helped to change it; we were conscious of that at the time, in philosophy as well as in politics. Let me begin with the climate then.

II

In 1930 the model of the philosophical method in Cambridge was still the *Principia Mathematica*[2] by Alfred North Whitehead and Bertrand Russell, and the *Tractatus Logico-Philosophicus*[3] by Ludwig Wittgenstein.

That is, the main current of English philosophy was indeed preoccupied (as it had always been) with the problems of science; and it was then convinced that the empirical content of science could be expressed in the formulae of classical mathematics, and would therefore be arranged ultimately in a closed system of axioms like the *Principia*—or like the system of Spinoza, on whose *Tractatus Theologico-Politicus*[4] Wittgenstein had modeled his title. The final task of philosophy in science would be to establish a universal system of axioms from which all the phenomena of nature could be derived.

There were of course a number of grounds for suspecting even then that this program took too rigid a view of the machinery of nature. In the first place, it was already doubtful whether mathematics could be made quite as tidy as Whitehead and Russell had tried. Jan Brouwer long ago had thrown doubt on their approach to mathematics; and though he was shrugged off as a maverick, the doubt remained. Now David Hilbert had posed some unexpected and awkward questions, among which the *Entscheidungsproblem* in particular gave signs that it might become very uncomfortable. And so it turned out quite soon, when first, Kurt Gödel[5] in Vienna in 1931, and then A. M. Turing[6] in Cambridge in 1936 proved what Hilbert had suspected, that even arithmetic could not be contained in a closed system of the kind that science was supposed to be looking for.

In the second place, it seemed perverse to lay down grand rules for the conduct of science and (by implication) of nature, at the very time when physicists were discovering every day that the traditional forms of natural law would not fit their findings. Physics on the atomic scale was manifestly in flux—a flux of concepts as much as of models. Louis de Broglie and Max Born were trying to reconcile the particulate properties of electrons with their wavelike behavior. Erwin Schrödinger and Paul Dirac were creating wave mechanics. Wolfgang Pauli had enunciated the exclusion principle for some particles, Bose-Einstein statistics had been proposed for others, liquid helium was displaying its first disconcerting properties, and Werner Heisenberg had recently announced the principle of uncertainty. In such busy times, it was natural to speculate about the laws of nature, but it was peculiarly unlikely that a universal formula would be found for them. Most scientists felt in 1930 that philosophers had just caught up with nineteenth-century physics, and were trying to make it the model for all knowledge, at the very moment when physicists had painfully discovered its shortcomings. (In the same way, biologists feel today that philosophers have at last understood quantum physics, and are anxious to make it the model for all processes in nature, just when the problems of method and concept in science are shifting to biology.)

In the third place, there were doubts even among philosophers whether the entities of empirical science could be formalized as rigidly as had been supposed. Russell had made it fashionable to define the number 2 as the class of all pairs; but could such logical and, so to say, operational constructions also suffice to define the units which we suppose to underlie the mechanics of nature? Could the electron really be treated with resolute punctilio as the class of all the observations from which its properties (and therefore its existence) were inferred, as a shorthand of organization? Does not this form of scientific behaviorism close the door to speculation, and (as it were) forbid us in advance to find unexpected extensions to the concept of an electron? Frank Ramsey, who had been my teacher, and who died in 1930 before he was twenty-seven, had shown[7] that this was indeed so: if the inferred units of a science are all defined as logical constructions, then the system which connects them cannot accomodate any new relations among them. In a less exact way, many young scientists felt that logical positivism was trying to make a closed system of science, when to them the charm and the adventure of science was that it was perpetually open.

the charm and the adventure of science was that it was perpetually open.

But the first place, and the second place, and the third place too, had no influence at all on the program that philosophers of science doggedly went on following after 1930. Percy Bridgman as the apostle of operationalism, and Rudolf Carnap as the St. Paul among the survivors of the Vienna Circle, still planned a millennium in which everything worth saying would be reduced to positive matters of fact, in a universal language of science that had been scrubbed clean of all ambiguities. Carnap in particular left no doubt that (like Wittgenstein at the opening of the *Tractatus*) he thought of the world as a collection of facts, of science as the description of these facts, and thought that the ideal description would specify the coordinates in space and time of every factual event. Since this is essentially the plan that Pierre Laplace had made famous[8] and infamous more than a hundred years earlier, it is not surprising that young scientists were indifferent to philosophy, and regarded it (for all its talk about probability) as solidly stuck in the last century.

III

The political climate among English scientists in 1930 and the following years, which is also relevant to my history, had some of the same sense of disappointment and impatience. There had been a time when Cambridge philosophers had set a standard of high liberal conscience which had inspired their students: G. E. Moore had done so in his writing and teaching, and Bertrand Russell in his unswerving conduct as a pacifist. But that had been in another age, almost in another world, which had run out a decade before. Now the world of 1930 was deep in economic depression; England had two million unemployed; in continental Europe private armies were sniping in the streets; and all the starched phrases about personal freedom and humane values were becoming more unreal every day. It was a time when young men knew in their bones that politics could no longer be left to gentlemen, or to mobs either, and that they would have to commit themselves to some canons of social right and wrong. To be told that nowadays philosophy did not trade in these chattels, that logical analysis offered no guide to conduct or even to conscience, and that any prescription for them was strictly nonsense, did not heighten the respect of working scientists for the philosophers of science. Scientists were actively trying to break out from the aura of impersonality and even inhumanity with which tradition had hallowed their work and awed the public. And here they were to be herded back to the ancient postures, because philosophers were trying to construct a system of science which positively aspired to be impersonal and inhuman.

Since young men yearn for a philosophy, most of the young scientists at Cambridge turned to dialectical materialism. This is really too grand a name to give to their new beliefs, which were rather what William Blake long ago[9] had called "a refuge from unbelief—from Bacon, Newton and Locke." They were looking for some coherent ground on which to build a consistent code of personal actions in face of a mounting set of social disasters—the Wall Street crash, the hunger marches, war in Manchuria, the rise of Hitler, Stalin's crusade against Trotsky, the civil war in Spain, the *Anschluss* with Austria, and the surrender of the *Sudetenland.*

I ought to quote a characteristic instance, and I will choose one which surprised me at the time. Wittgenstein had come back to Cambridge in 1929, and at first many scientists went to his lectures. But after a while it became plain that he was no longer tackling the systematic problems of the *Tractatus.* Instead, his lectures turned literally into what he called them, a language game, which seemed to us more and more formless and devoid of method. One of the best of the philosophy students who remained loyal to him was Maurice Cornforth, and he seemed to be chosen by Wittgenstein to become his future spokesman and interpreter. But then Cornforth broke with Wittgenstein abruptly and became a Marxist. This was the most dramatic and (it was said) violent desertion from the camp of philosophic contemplation in Cambridge. The break had almost a symbolic quality; from now on the following of Wittgenstein took little interest in science. When Maurice Cornforth wrote a book of philosophy[10] many years later, he called it *Science versus Idealism,* and aimed it specifically at Wittgenstein and Carnap as the two Janus faces of idealism.

Of course none of us supposed that philosophers were indifferent to tyranny, or to the fate of those whom it threatened. After war broke out in 1939, Wittgenstein went from Cambridge to work as an orderly in Guy's Hospital in London. But that was not the light that we looked for from philosophy. We did not ask philosophers to be martyrs, or to seek purification (as T. E. Lawrence of Arabia had done) in manual labor and monastic anonymity. We wanted philosophy to be engaged in the living world, and we were shocked that we got no human gesture from the philosophers of science: no sign that philosophy and science might express more of man than his rational intellect alone.

Instead, the works that brought science to life for us came from history. An essay by a Russian, B. Hessen, called "The Social and Economic Roots of Newton's *Principia*"[11] opened our eyes to a new view of science. Although it patently overstated its case, its effect on young scientists and philosophers alike was electric. From that time, the history and philosophy of science came to be spoken of in one phrase, almost as a single subject. The Chichele professor of Economic History at Oxford, G. N. Clark, replied to Hessen in 1937 in a book[12] called *Science and Social Welfare in the Age of Newton;* yet the very form of the title shows that science was now acknowledged to have social roots. The most influential book[13] published in England came at the end of the decade, and was boldly called *The Social Function of Science.* Much of its influence (and its merit) certainly derived from the fact that its author, Desmond Bernal, was an active and original scientist.

IV

I begin with this historical preamble because it describes the status of scientific philosophy when Karl Popper began to publish. And I describe how matters stood then in England, because in the long run that is where his reputation was made. *The Logic of Scientific Discovery* was published towards the end of 1934 and, though it was published in German (it was not translated into English for almost twenty-five years), its main points began to be known in England in the next few years. There is a reference to one of them in *Language, Truth, and Logic*,[14] in which A. J. Ayer gave currency to the ideas of the Vienna Circle in 1936. Popper is an indefatigable writer, and he started to publish papers in English as early as 1938. His views became fairly well known, as well as respected, by the end of the war. Considering what else was then going on in the world, that now seems a very short time.

The Logic of Scientific Discovery is at first sight a rather dense and forbidding package of ideas. I shall exhibit some of them one by one; yet I ought to say at the outset that one of the things which made them attractive to my generation is that they are patently the expressions of a single personality. I do not think that the personality struck us as attractive in itself; on the contrary, it seemed (if anything) a little tense and touchy; but it was a genuine personality, it breathed and argued and struggled with its thoughts (and its second thoughts, and its afterthoughts). There was no doubt that *The Logic of Scientific Discovery* was written by a human being, and that it treated science as a communal activity among human beings.

The sense of humanity will be the recurrent theme of my essay: more than anything else, it is what humanism means to me. It is implied from the outset in Popper's conception of the growth of knowledge. He does not write of science as a finished enterprise, and he does not think of it (even unconsciously) as an enterprise that could conceivably be finished. In his exposition science is systematic, yet it is a perpetually open system; it is constantly changed and enlarged, year by year it grows to embrace more of nature, and yet there is no vision of an ideal system that might embrace the whole of nature. Here Popper's outlook differs radically from the vision of the positivist philosophers. Their eyes were always fixed (somewhere on the horizon) on a finished scientific system, and their analysis was always colored by the ideal relation between the parts that would be found on the day when the system was finished. Popper has no such God's eye view. He sees science simply as a going concern—a growing concern, and very much the concern of everybody. Knowledge grows because human minds work at that, and it is a workaday job which we have to get on with; no stroke of luck will find knowledge for us; for it is not there to be stumbled on, ready-made, like a lost corridor. It is not even there to be put together from its parts like a prefabricated building. None of these metaphors describes the reality of scientific knowledge, because all of them suppose that there is somewhere a structure of knowledge which is closed. But knowledge is not a structure in this sense at all; it is not a building, or any piece of architecture; you could not put the roof on it, or close it with a keystone.

Popper was so anxious to disavow the idealized view of scientific knowledge that he excluded any issue that might raise it from *The Logic of Scientific Discovery.* This is most striking in the pains which he takes to avoid discussing the *truth* of a theory in science. The last section of the book (before the peroration) points this out with a note of triumph: since Popper has discarded the test by verification, and looks askance at most criteria of corroboration or confirmation, he can get along pretty well (he explains) without a formal demand that a scientific theory should be true. We shall see that, in the long run, he has not sustained this act of self-denial. Yet we can also see why Popper worked so strenuously (and ingeniously) to achieve it in his first book, at a time when the vision of science as a closed system dominated the formalism of other philosophers of science.

V

It is well known that Popper discarded the crucial stipulation made by the Vienna Circle, namely that we should confine philosophy to the discussion of statements which can be verified, at least in principle. In its place Popper put the requirement that our statements should be capable of being falsified. On the face of it that looks like a formal difference only: but, of course, it is not, for two reasons. First, Popper's requirement is meant to apply to general laws, such as Newton's laws of motion, which can never be verified in every instance, but which could be falsified by a single instance. And, second, the demand that we should be able to find a statement false has a different function from the positivist demand that it ought to be verifiable. The potential of being verifiable was put forward by logical positivists as a criterion of meaning; it was supposed to separate meaningful statements from utterances which are essentially meaningless. Popper did not claim to have a criterion of meaning; he proposed the requirement that a statement should be capable of being found false in fact only as a criterion of *demarcation*. Its function, he says, is to mark off statements that can be used in science from statements that cannot.

In a narrow sense, the distinction between demarcation and meaning is something of an artifice here, and it has accordingly given rise to a good deal of artificial debate. For the requirement that a statement should be verifiable, or that it should be falsifiable, is at bottom a demand that it should have factual consequences, and therefore a factual content. Obviously this is a sound demand to make of a statement that purports to be scientific, on any modern characterization of science. But then the logical positivists who called it a criterion of meaning were, in essence, not saying anything different from this. In essence, they were proposing that the requirements of science should be applied to all human discourse. Their thesis was that discussion is only meaningful if it meets the criterion for rational argument in science—otherwise it is merely emotional chatter or nonsense. This is a very grand claim, because it implies that logical positivism has the key to the underlying reality in all human problems; and positivism lost its hold on us in the troubled thirties' because it failed to make the claim good. But, in the strict application to science, there is not much to choose between the words 'demarcation' and 'meaning'; the advantage that Popper's word has is simply its firm clarity; and there would be no difference in principle if he had chosen instead to call his criterion a criterion of *scientific* meaning.

The appeal of Popper's formulation, and its strength, must therefore be seen in the broad sense of its human application; and here it is surprisingly and engagingly more modest than the program of positivism. It does not claim to be a system of life, or even a system of science; it is presented tidily as a book of practical rules for the conduct and interpretation of scientific research—the word *Forschung* in the German title, research, is even more modest than the phrase *Scientific Discovery* which translates it in the English title. What Popper puts forward is a method to guide our theorizing and help assess our experiments, so that knowledge will be genuinely gained by them. For example, he carries on a running fight with induction as Francis Bacon pictured it; and, though I think his objections miss the point of the inductive stratagem (say, in Mendeleef's periodic table), they express his constant concern—induction alone does not yield any genuine advance in knowledge. *The Logic of Scientific Discovery* is an account of scientific method. As a method, the demand that a statement should be falsifiable, and the use of this demand as a criterion of demarcation, belong together as a unit, for they are two parts in a single description of how a scientific theory is debated in practice. In this broad sense, demarcation is an important idea in Popper's methodology.

VI

After what I have said about scientists in the thirties searching their souls, it may seem odd that Popper's philosophy should have appealed to them. I think that there were two separate grounds for this. One is that, having taken science for his subject, he treats it with the practical absorption of a professional. What he has to say is sensible, informed, enlightening, and (above all) realistic; it carries conviction because scientists recognize in it both what they do and what they conclude. They are therefore attentive and sympathetic to the reasoning by which Popper justifies the conclusions; for they know that these are indeed the conclusions that they draw.

The second ground for the respect which Popper earned among the scientists of my generation is that he does not claim too much for science. Consider again (for example) his demand that a statement is only scientific if it could be proved to be false. Popper stresses that this is to be treated as a criterion of demarcation and not of meaning; statements that fail this test are not scientific, but it is not asserted that they are meaningless; we therefore retain the right to believe that there can be meaningful statements which do not have a scientific content. Of course, there are scientists whom that reservation would outrage; but I imagine that they did not have the experience of philosophy in the thirties that we had. We learned then to be sceptical of the pretensions, and the reach, of scientific philosophy. In Popper we caught the sense that science is a marvelous mode of knowledge, but that at no stage does it claim to be the final or the only mode to guide human conduct. What we read in him most deeply was a passion for science, not as a system but as an activity—a method to foster the growth of knowledge.

The tone of *The Logic of Scientific Discovery* is one to catch the ear of a man actively working at research. It is systematic but not formalist—nor at the other extreme, does it move in a zigzag of happy improvisations, as the later work of Wittgenstein seems to do. It is concerned with scientific theories as intellectual entities, and not as heaps of instances: the way Popper takes fire at the word 'induction' is testimony to that. It treats experiments as a good experimenter tries to plan them, not as items of evidence, but as decisive tests: this is why Popper insists that their practical aim must be to falsify a theory (or better, one of two alternative theories); and his advice is very practical, because the best experiments are classics in the history of science exactly because they fulfill this aim. It does not shirk the central difficulty in modern science, which is that this decisive aim cannot be wholly met when the theory under test does not predict an unique outcome for an experiment, but only one of several probable outcomes. It ventures unafraid into fields of contemporary science which are still in disarray, such as quantum mechanics, and says both wise and foolish things about them. It implies, not very loudly but persistently, that an original theory is a work of imagination, and is formed more in the mind than on the bench. In short, *The Logic of Scientific Discovery* is a book to quicken the mind (and I think the heart) of every research scientist who loves his work, and I believe that they have learned more from it about scientific method than from any formal treatise on the subject.

I must not end my assessment of the book, however, without taking note of one criticism which I shall be making later. The strength of *The Logic of Scientific Discovery* is that it is, robustly, a manual of scientific method; and yet, of necessity, that is also its weakness. The book outdistances the more formal attempts (say, by logical empiricists) to analyze the content of science, because it makes no such attempt. It gives advice to guide our reasoning and to make our experiments productive, but in the end the advice is always about the testing of theories and not about their content. This is very timely and practical, but somehow it bypasses the question, why science deserves our attention—why it deserves even the small attention of these pages. The philosophers who tried to wrestle with such questions of principle have been less instructive than Popper, because they did not understand the practice of science as he does; and it is manifest now that we cannot divorce the content of science from its practice. But that does not make the questions about content irrelevant, and I shall pose them towards the end of this essay.

VII

There are several problems which relate to the growth of knowledge to which Popper has returned since 1934. Indeed, his book of collected essays *Conjectures and Refutations*[15] of 1963 has as its descriptive subtitle the phrase "The Growth of Scientific Knowledge." I shall single out the most important of these problems, in the discussion of which Popper has gone well beyond his first book, before I turn to what seems to me the central essay (and the central issue) in the collection.

The Logic of Scientific Discovery had contained a long and thoughtful analysis of the uses and abuses of the idea of probability, and the subject has rightly preoccupied Popper ever since. His main view here seems to me clear, steadfast, and wholly right. Probability on this view is a concrete property of physical systems in which the events overall come out in a consistent way, but not in an unique way. In such systems, probability is an inferred or theoretical entity which we do not observe directly, much as an electron is—and it is real in the same sense. I share this view of probability as a physical property, and so I think do most physicists now; though I prefer to express it by saying that probability can only be ascribed to events which have a *distribution,* and must be read as a symbol for the distribution as a whole. On Popper's view and mine, then, probability is not a description of a state of mind, or a subjective expectation of how a future event will turn out: and in fact these personal experiences cannot be marshalled as distributions. More important, the status or plausibility of a scientific theory cannot be described by a probability, because there is no unique distribution in which it has its place. Of course, the status of a theory goes up and down with the evidence for it; but this is not the same as having an assignable probability.

The concept of probability, therefore, cannot be separated from a probability calculus, and Popper has continued to work to give the sharpest possible form to both. The formal definition of probability which he now advances is not relevant to my purpose here, since in my view the content of probability lies in the distributions that the calculus generates. My purpose is to examine Popper's use of probability at two crucial places: in the testing of theories which predict events that are only probable, and in the formation and assessment of theories of any kind.

When a theory predicts several possible outcomes for an experiment, it is hard to tell what set of outcomes is different enough from a predicted set to falsify the theory. Strictly speaking, we should no doubt say that it is impossible to tell. The predicted outcomes of a string of experiments are all the possible samples of that size from the postulated distribution; and whatever the actual outcomes are, they certainly form a possible sample. Of course, the samples of a given size from the postulated distribution have a known distribution in their turn, and we can therefore calculate how improbable it is that we should have drawn our actual sample by bad luck alone. But this regress does not help us to make an absolute decision that the theory is false, yes or no, however far we continue it. The sample that we have drawn may be wildly improbable, but it is not impossible. How long ought we to watch a tossed penny come down heads before we can be sure that we are being cheated—the penny is bad? Strictly speaking, for ever.

The Logic of Scientific Discovery met this difficulty (which it did not hide) by fixing an arbitrary limit to the process of decision. In effect, Popper proposed that, if the collective outcome of a string of experiments is too improbable, we treat that as equivalent to falsification. (The mathematics is more elaborate, but this[16] is what it says: "that extreme improbabilities have to be neglected.") This is a sensible way to interpret experiments in practice, and it is in fact the way scientists use. But in principle it removes the test by falsification from the singular eminence to which Popper had raised it. In the first place, it makes the test arbitrary, by leaving us to fix the range of improbability that is to be accepted as zero. In the second place, it suffers from the usual regress implicit in such ranges (and in all measures of the probability of a probability), because the end points of the range have to be surrounded in turn by their own ranges, and so on. And in the third and chief place, it invites the same privilege for the test by verification that we have just allowed to the test by falsification. We can hardly make a scheme of approximate falsification, and elevate it (in effect) to a principle of sufficient falsification, without granting the same liberty to verification. Of course verification is only provisional; but the point is that in this scheme, falsification is also only provisional. In the language of mathematical statistics, as Jerzy Neyman and Egon Pearson have formulated it,[17] we cannot escape errors of both kinds: errors of acceptance in verification, and also errors of rejection in falsification.

VIII

A theory that makes only probable predictions cannot be strictly falsified by any run of its alternative outcomes. For such theories (that is, for most modern theories) the test by falsification is therefore no more decisive than a test by verification. Popper rightly criticized verification because it must be inconclusive; but in the fundamental theories of modern science, falsification can do no better—and no worse. Both offer evidence, for or against a theory, and no more.

Thus the difficulties that I have exhibited undermine the unique character of falsification. Nature provides no decisive test to prove a theory false if it makes only probable predictions. We can only sharpen the test as Popper does, by doctoring it: by stipulating for ourselves that, say, tossing ten heads in a row is too bad to be true, and the game cannot be fair—no doubt the penny is loaded. But 'no doubt' does not resolve the doubt; our rejection of the hypothesis that the game is fair remains open to doubt, and we must treat it as provisional; and if rejection is provisional, its standing is no better than that of acceptance. That is, the test by falsification has a privileged place only because it is decisive, and therefore only so long as it is decisive. Once it fails in this, it is back on all fours with the test by verification, and there is nothing to choose between them.

So, if we have to fly in the face of nature, and choose (because we have no other choice) to make falsification decisive by doctoring the test—then we must do the same for verification. If we are allowed to decide, by a test that we have made for ourselves, that ten heads in a row is too bad to be true, then we cannot be forbidden to say that some other severe requirement (say, exactly $1/2 \times 10^n$ heads in 10^n tosses) is too good to be false, and to conclude that we are not being cheated: the game is fair and the penny unloaded. (I ought to say, the game is sufficiently fair and the penny is effectively unloaded.) "The rule that extreme improbabilities have to be neglected" is[18] exactly as reasonable, or as unreasonable, for positive assertions as for negative.

In practice, scientists do act in this way, and statistical tests in general (and sequential tests in particular) use the same kind of criterion for acceptance as they do for rejection. It may be argued that this is reasonable only because the hypotheses they are testing contain statements of probability. On such a view, then, we should not be entitled to use a doctored criterion of verification when we are testing a theory whose predictions are unique—since here the criterion of falsification does not need to be doctored. I would be willing to respect this argument only if it were backed by the assertion that all theories ought to be free from statements of probability, and will be found to be so in the long run. Otherwise the distinction is an artifice, and the argument is casuistic. So long as we are allowed to doctor the criterion of falsification when we need, we cannot (I think) be forbidden to doctor the criterion of verification when we choose.

All this is very human and natural, and it is indeed how scientists behave, in accepting theories as well as in rejecting them—because there is no other practical way to behave. There is a limit to precision in all our actions, and if we are not to allow it to bring science lamely to a standstill, we must be willing to be decisive in the face of uncertainty. But what we have then is no longer a rigorous and foolproof method uniquely based on falsification. It is a stratagem for decision, but not a prescription.

Accordingly, Popper in his later work has more and more moved away from the sharp issues of scientific decision. He writes less about falsification and more about evidence; less about theories or hypotheses and more about problems; and he stresses the part played in science by argument and criticism. His picture of the scientist is no longer that of a young man with an audacious theory, devising an experiment that challenges nature to prove him wrong. Rather he is pictured now as a sceptical but benign Socratic elder (no doubt looking a little like an Austrian professor) discussing a problem with his staff, and unraveling it strand by strand until they are rationally persuaded to prefer his explanation to another. The critical steps in the discussion which lead them to reject another explanation still rely on experiments, of course, but now the experimental results are accepted as convincing without being decisive.

IX

What I have been saying implies that the proposal to test theories by falsification is powerful and original, but it does not relieve us of the need to attend to the positive evidence for a theory also. And we cannot avoid discussing this if we are to be practical, because in their practice scientists do it all the time. So it is not strange that Popper does discuss the confirmation of theories—or, as he rightly prefers to call it, their corroboration. As time has gone on, he has given more attention to it; and in the essay which I am going to single out from *Conjectures and Refutations* he states two unexpected requirements. It is indispensable (the word is his)[19] that a good theory when it is first proposed "must lead to the prediction of phenomena which have not so far been observed"; and—the other requirement—some of the phenomena must then be observed. There is a footnote[20] defending "a whiff of verification here" which would strike the practicing scientist as pedantic and indeed comic, were it not that respected writers on probability and confirmation (J. M. Keynes[21] and Rudolf Carnap[22] among them) have said that we give too much weight to prediction. Popper is on the side of the practicing scientist: he is not content to accept a theory as a passive register of known facts or effects.

A theory is an intellectual construction and not a passive register of known facts or effects. Since, like Popper, I am inveighing against all passive views of science here, I should explain my usage. I think it is misleading (and a perennial source of misunderstanding) even to say that science describes facts. Statements in science do not have the factual form of a predication, 'snow *is* white'. Such statements belong to natural history, not to science. The statements in science have the form 'snow *melts* at such and such a temperature'; and this is different in kind: it is an active statement and not a predication, it asserts that something changes, and often it derives the change from an action on our part—'when you heat snow, such and such happens'. (But when you look at snow, nothing happens so long as you stick to the predication 'is white'; something happens only when you take off from that to say 'snow *reflects* white light'—which is to say, whatever color of light you shine on it.) In short, science does not deal in predicates but in actions; and to have a fixed melting point or a wide band of reflection is not a predicate or property in the same sense in which to be white is. In my view and usage, even a singular statement in science describes a dynamic effect, 'when *u* then *v*', and not a static fact, '*A* has the property *b*'.

A theory, then, is an intellectual construction and not a register of known effects. Nevertheless, when we form a theory we take account of the known effects, and in time we look for new effects which flow from the theory. The known effects are evidence for the theory, and indispensable evidence; and when a new effect which is predicted by the theory is confirmed, it adds a measure of evidence or corroboration.

Philosophers who have tried to quantify the weight of new evidence have often said that it increases the probability of the theory. But I have already remarked that Popper insists, and rightly insists, that we cannot assign a probability to a theory: for probabilities have to conform to a calculus which (he holds, and I hold) can only be made to apply consistently to physical events or logical statements about them. I put this by saying that probability requires the events which it subsumes to have a distribution, but a theory and all its possible alternatives do not have a unique distribution. It is true that a theory can contain a *parameter* whose possible values have a distribution, so that we can assign a probablility to the hypothesis that the parameter has one range of values rather than another. But this is not the same thing as calculating a probability for the theory as a whole.

Since this is a fine distinction, yet is fundamental, I shall spell it out in an example. Johannes Kepler[23] in 1609 put forward the theory that the orbit of a planet is an ellipse, with the sun at one focus. This theory contains a free parameter, namely the eccentricity of the ellipse, which may have any numerical value between 0 and 1. We can therefore ask what is the eccentricity of the ellipse traced by a particular planet, and we can gather evidence to this end by observing the planet. The evidence can be expressed in summary form as a probability that the eccentricity lies within such and such a range of numbers, and outside the remaining range. When we make more observations, the growing weight of evidence will then be expressed as an increasing probability. In this way, we can show with overwhelming probability (which we may choose to accept as decisive) that the eccentricity falls well above 0, and therefore that the orbit is not that kind of ellipse which is a circle. When we have done this for each planet, we shall have given what (historically) engaged Kepler's mind most, namely decisive grounds for saying that the planets do not run in circles, and good grounds for saying that they run in ellipses.

So, in general, when a theory contains a free parameter, the possible values of the parameter have a distribution, and we can therefore use the experimental evidence to assign a probability to estimated values of the parameter. This looks like assigning a probability to the theory, and it has been so represented in the writings of logical empiricists. The work of Carnap[24] and his students on inductive logic and the confirmation of hypotheses is dogged by this error, which ascribes to a hypothesis a probability that in fact applies only to a numerical parameter embedded in the hypothesis. The parameter may itself be a probability (as when I was tossing pennies earlier in this essay) and this adds to the confusion. But my example from Kepler shows plainly where the confusion lies. We can assign a probability to a parameter, and thus decide whether a curve is a circle or some other ellipse. But we cannot assign a probability to the theory that the curve is an ellipse, when it might be any kind of curve. There is an endless crocodile of curves and their parameters waiting to be fitted to the orbits of the planets, and there is no valid assignment of probabilities that can help to single out the ellipse from the more sophisticated curves; for curves almost the same in shape may express quite different theories.

This point was well made by Popper from the outset, though he argued it differently; and I have chosen to illustrate it with Kepler's ellipses in part because he used that example in *The Logic of Scientific Discovery*. What I have said about theories or hypotheses and the parameters in them will, I hope, help to clear up the recurring puzzle in arguments about confirmation: why the weight of evidence for some hypotheses can be expressed as a probability, when in principle a theory should not be called probable or improbable at all. Popper raises these matters again in his recent proposal to define a measure that he calls verisimilitude, and I shall return to that towards the end of this essay.

X

Those who think that we can calculate the probability of a theory naturally recommend that we explain the known facts or effects by forming the most probable theory that will entail them. Popper aims his fire at this, and points out repeatedly that any scientific theory which is worth having is highly improbable, in any sense of that word. He urges us instead to invent the theory which is most improbable, because it will have the largest number of new consequences, and can therefore be tested most stringently.

I am a little out of patience with this exchange of gestures, but that may be because I am plagued more than Popper by people who send me improbable and silly theories. The point of substance here is that the two advocates are framing their theories to different ends, and therefore have to use different strategies. Nothing follows from this except that there are different strategies in science: it does not even follow that they are incompatible in the long run, or that the words 'probable' and 'improbable' should not be used in either—though, in fact, they should not. The prudent advocate of so-called probable theories is saying that we should stay fairly close to the known effects, because the further we guess beyond them the more likely we are to go wrong. It is extravagant to imply that this is just what we want, because falsification is the only test we accept. It does not help us to be wildly wrong; we do not "learn from our mistakes"[25] if they are gross mistakes; we are only sent back to the effects from which we started, with nothing added. Yes, any theory worth having must take some risks, and go beyond the known effects—because it would not be worth having if it were unable to propose anything new. And it is true that some advocates of so-called probable theories (Carnap among them) are writing of science as a closed system, so that what they have to say has no bearing on the real practice of science, and is fundamentally misconceived. But it is possible to be an advocate of prudence and even of caution and still to talk sense. Caution here is induced not by the fear of straying too far from the known effects, but of getting too far ahead of the pattern or theory that they seem to follow. When we hesitate to speculate too far, it is because we then lack a guide to the shape of the new theory we would like to imagine.

In his essay, "Truth, Rationality, and the Growth of Scientific Knowledge," Popper says that, well, we are not altogether helpless in shaping a new theory, "we *know* what a good scientific theory should be like."[26] Certainly we do, in the sense that we know some of the requirements it should meet, and the pitfalls to avoid. And, in that sense, we know in advance whether a new theory that is proposed to us would be better than the old, if it turned out that it worked. But we do *not* know how to propose a new theory unless it is rather like the old; we have no method to guide us towards a different kind of theory from that; and when Popper says[27] that we know "what kind of theory would be better," that is exactly what we do *not* know. It is the theory different in kind, the new viewpoint from which the effects arrange themselves in another way, the structure that departs from the old model, which we do not know how to project far ahead. Scientists who stick to a cautious strategy which does not venture beyond the known effects (such as the stratagem of induction) do so not from lack of philosophic training but of imagination, for that is the only strategy that will propose a new theory if its structure needs to be radically different from the old. There is a letter from Albert Einstein to Popper which says[28] just this: "dass Theorie nicht aus

Beobachtungsresultaten fabriziert sondern nur erfunden werden kann."

Popper has devised a formula to measure the corroboration of a theory (in a new appendix to *The Logic of Scientific Discovery*) and he has applied it to compare Einstein's theory of gravitation with Newton's. It turns out that Einstein scores higher than Isaac Newton, because he explains more effects. This is fair enough, although it is not exactly a revelation. But the trouble is that a register of the effects would also get Einstein's score, and would equally beat Newton's theory. This cannot really satisfy us—either Popper or me; a theory that interests us must have more content than the sum of effects; and the *more* is evidently the structure of the theory, the way it organizes the effects. What characterizes an original theory (relativity, or quantum mechanics, or Gregor Mendel's distribution of inheritance) is that it is structurally different from the old. The total content of a theory is larger than its empirical content, and includes its structure.

XI

If this is accepted, it forces us to take a new view of the growth of knowledge. Popper himself has done so in a long essay on "Truth, Rationality, and the Growth of Scientific Knowledge" which he published for the first time in *Conjectures and Refutations*. The essay is something of a philosophical testament, and is also remarkable as a human account of the march of Popper's mind in thirty years. At some points, it is as challenging to the prejudices of the 1960s as *The Logic of Scientific Discovery* was to the 1930s. It will be seen that I should have liked it to go even further, but it is an absorbing document as it stands, and I shall end my assessment with it.

The question, what is the content of science, throws its shadow forward from the first page:[29]

> It is not the accumulation of observations which I have in mind when I speak of the growth of scientific knowledge, but the repeated overthrow of scientific theories and their replacement by better or more satisfactory ones.

The central issue here is the meaning that Popper will develop to justify the description of one scientific theory as "better or more satisfactory" than another. But before we reach that, we have to examine his older favorite, "the repeated overthrow of scientific theories."

The overthrow of a scientific theory is accomplished when we show as a matter of experiment or observation that one of its consequences is false. This cannot be the whole story; for any theory can be patched up to save the phenomenon—so that, if this were all, the theory of phlogiston would still be with us. But in principle, this had been Popper's original method: to challenge a theory by testing its empirical consequences, and discarding it if one of them failed the test. The growth of knowledge was to be promoted by clearing away the rubbish of mistaken theories or superstitions.

The trouble with this negative method is that it is preoccupied with the idea of testing. What it asks of a scientific theory, and the criterion by which it judges it, is that it shall stand up to test. Yet, testing in science, as in any human activity, is by nature only a diagnostic procedure: it does not express the function of the activity—it only marks out conditions for it. Scientific theories are not invented for the *purpose* of passing tests, any more than motor cars and courses in philosophy. Whatever it is for which we want theories, it is not to test them; so that this certainly cannot be a criterion to show that a theory does what we want of it. The test by falsification will diagnose when a theory falls sick, but it does not reflect what we ask a healthy theory to be or to do.

Science is a human activity, in which the theories that we make for it play the part both of an account and of a general plan or brief. As in any activity, we make the plan to guide us: we want it to work, in some unwritten but positive sense—to inform and interest us, to show how things are and guess how they will turn out, to organize our outlook. And an inquiry into the nature of science must tackle these functional demands, because they are the issues of substance and the nub of the matter. Science is meant to work, not to be tested; and though it must be tested as a diagnostic or instrumental safeguard, to alert us when there is malfunction, we must not let that tail wag the dog. Even as a mere matter of language, we invite error if we constantly describe every scientific action as a test. The functional requirement is that a scientific theory should work, however we define that; and we shall surely lose this concept if we let the language of diagnosis distort it, and call every occasion when it is put to work a test. If we classify theories by the tests they have passed, we shall have only two categories: *unproved* theories, and *disproved* ones.

XII

Accordingly, the essay on "Truth, Rationality, and the Growth of Scientific Knowledge" does not stop at the overthrow of scientific theories. Fostering the growth of knowledge is now conceived as a more active undertaking than merely clearing away the older growth of mistaken theories. The real task is[30] "their replacement by better or more satisfactory ones." Presumably a better theory is not simply any theory which can pass all the tests that have been tried so far; and Popper therefore squarely faces the question: What makes one scientific theory better than another?

What makes a theory better or worse, what makes it a theory at all (and not a register of effects) must express what we want from a theory. What we want stipulates the purpose or function of a scientific theory in our usage, and this points in turn to what we expect to read in it (or to read into it) as an integral part of its content. That is, a part of the content is the view of the organization of nature that it presents by the manner in which it arranges the effects; and this is expressed in the structure of the theory. Or so at any rate I see the problems, in sequence; and though Popper does not look at them quite in the same way, they are roughly the topics that now occupy him in "Truth, Rationality, and the Growth of Scientific Knowledge."

Popper does not ask explicitly how we see the purpose or function of science as a guide to conduct. But it is evident, and indeed self-evident, that he does not picture it simply as a book of rules for action. In the language that I use in *The Identity of Man*,[31] science and other provisional modes of knowledge do not bluntly *instruct* our actions—they *inform* them. Both as an account and as a plan, therefore, a theory must attempt to guide us to effects which will be confirmed, that is, which will turn out to be as the theory implies. How shall we characterize this demand made of a theory, that it shall imply the effects truly?

Popper proposes in his essay that we do not beat about the bush, but say firmly that we want the theory to be *true*. Of course we do; but does not that postulate that knowledge will thereupon have completed its growth along this branch? There is no danger of that, says Popper; we can never reach *the* truth, or indeed know what it is; we can only push nearer and nearer to the truth.

This is a startling program, coming from a philosopher who took immense pains in the past to avoid using even the word 'truth'. Popper explains that he has been converted by the new clarity that Alfred Tarski has brought[32] to the definition of truth. Thanks to Tarski, it is now possible to know exactly what we mean when we say that a statement is true, and therefore we no longer need use any circumlocution in saying what we all feel, that we would like scientific theories to be true.

XIII

I am an admirer of Tarski's work, and especially[33] of his simple and searching analysis of the concept of objective truth. It has separated what can from what cannot be said about scientific statements in their own language. As a result it has proved once for all that there is an inherent contradiction in the Vienna Program, which aimed to express all true statements about the world in a single scientific language. Much like Kurt Gödel,[34] but more immediately, Tarski has shown that there is no universal language or system in which we can develop a formal way to say everything that is true. This is a deep finding, and Popper has been tireless in making it known and in his tribute to Tarski.

Tarski's achievement rests on his elucidation of a consistent logical basis for the realistic view, that a statement is true when it corresponds to the facts. But, in the nature of things, his analysis applies only to statements of fact: 'snow is white'. We need not read the phrase 'statements of fact' too narrowly; plainly it can be made to include what I call statements of effect, 'snow melts at such and such a temperature', and would be happier if it were confined to those. But there is nothing in Tarski's analysis that sanctions our applying to *theories* the concept of truth as correspondence with the facts. Quite the contrary. Scientific theories are not statements of fact; they are not even descriptions of effects; they are explanations, which means that only their consequences are open to inspection and available to be compared with our experience. The theory as such, the explanation which it offers, is simply not accessible to any scrutiny that we can devise; so that there is nothing that we can put beside it in order to say with a pointing finger, "Yes, the theory as stated is true, because it corresponds to that." Neither is the theory as explanation accessible to Popper's preferred test: there is nothing that we can put beside it which would make us able to say, "No, the theory as stated is false, because it does not correspond to that." We falsify a theory by comparing its *consequences* with something that we can inspect—not by comparing the theory, for there is nothing that we can inspect (even in principle) that is comparable.

Popper is evidently exercised by this problem, for he discusses some versions of it elsewhere in *Conjectures and Refutations,* chiefly in an essay on "Three Views Concerning Human Knowledge." Nevertheless, the argument as I have stated it seems to me conclusive. I think that its conclusion can only be avoided if we suppose that the true theory, the ultimate theory, is different in kind from any theory that we make, and is open to inspection of every part. (We have to *look* at the bad penny to prove that it has two heads.) Such a theory would have to encompass all effects at once, and would no longer be an explanation as we understand that, but a gigantic register or description of them all. No doubt there are philosophers of science who picture nature in this way, as the memory store of a universal computer; but neither Popper nor I (nor Tarski) would accept that this is a necessary projection or model of scientific theory.

XIV

Yet, strangely enough, it does not matter here whether we do or do not believe that nature is a closed mechanism. The argument that I have given against extending to scientific theories the correspondence view of truth is powerful if we do not, but it is not the strongest objection that can be made. For there is in any case a more practical objection, and I think a decisive one. It arises when we want to compare two theories, neither of which claims to be ultimately true. Which has the better claim to our confidence? The one that is nearer to the truth, says Popper: theories form a progression from less true to more true, and the growth of knowledge is an asymptotic approach towards the truth. Popper grants that we cannot know what theory will be true, and we cannot expect to reach it; nevertheless, he holds that we can measure which of two theories contains more truth than the other.

On the contrary, I do not think we know how to measure the partial correspondence to the truth of two theories, as theories. If we do not know what the true theory is, there is no way to assess that we are approaching it, as a theory. Indeed, it does not make sense to say that an explanation is approaching the truth, when we do not know the true explanation, and must therefore foresee that it may have an altogether different and unforeseeable form. How could we have anticipated that a better theory than Newton's would have the form of relativity? So long as we are comparing theories as explanations, the correspondence view of truth cannot give us a yardstick which will measure that one is closer to the unknown truth than the other.

Popper anticipates this objection, and he replies to it in advance that:[35]

> there is no reason whatever why we should not say that one theory corresponds better to the facts than another.

But this is not a legitimate use of the word 'corresponds' in Tarski's scheme. A statement of fact is true if it corresponds to the fact; a theory is true if it corresponds to what it asserts—and what a theory asserts is not an array of facts, but their *explanation*. There is nothing in Tarski's work which justifies measuring the truth of a theory by counting the true and false statements of fact that can be derived from it.

Of course we all agree that it makes sense—more, that it is essential—to say that one theory is better than another, if it accounts for more facts or effects. There is a yardstick here for measuring theories comparatively, one against another. But it does not measure their truth as theories, that is, as explanations, and gives no ground for saying one has moved closer to the truth than another. A criterion of distance from the true *explanation* cannot be derived from any definition of truth as correspondence.

When Popper in the same essay develops a count of true and false assertions of fact or effect, he is therefore returning to an older criterion—a formula for the confirmation of a theory, on familiar lines. He now calls the formula 'verisimilitude' and offers it as a measure of the content of truth in the theory; but, of course, what it measures is the content of facts or effects. (Presumably the true theory would entail an unbounded set of consequential effects.) The criterion of verisimilitude distinguishes a more ample theory from a less ample one, and nothing more; and this is the only ground which it advances for calling one theory better than another. All theories which subsume the same array of effects would rank as equally true and equally good—even if they did not look in the least like explanations.

XV

The practice of science shows that scientists looking for explanations patently prefer some kinds of theory to other kinds. Popper does not miss this point. Having described science as the search for true theories, he goes on to say:[36]

> Yet we also stress that *truth is not the only aim of science.* We want more than mere truth: what we look for is *interesting truth.*

He offers several glosses on the word 'interesting', but I shall go straight to the practical criterion in his mind for thinking one of two theories better than another when they are equally ample. At the end of a list which repeatedly (and rightly) prefers a more ample theory to one that is less ample, he comes to a different kind of preference, namely for a theory which[37] "has unified or connected various hitherto unrelated problems." In the list in which it first appears, the criterion of unity is out of place (it does not increase the verisimilitude), but in the essay as a whole its position is cardinal. It becomes the first and, to my mind, the most searching of the "Three Requirements for the Growth of Knowledge"[38] which Popper puts forward in the essay. The other two are still concerned with the tangible content of effect, and are really beyond dispute (even though I have quoted a funny footnote about them). But the requirement of unity includes a different constituent in the content of a theory.[39]

> The new theory should proceed from some *simple, new, and powerful, unifying idea* about some connection or relation (such as gravitational attraction) between hitherto unconnected things (such as planets and apples) or facts (such as inertial and gravitational mass) or new 'theoretical entities' (such as field and particles).

This is admirably conceived and said. In the most practical way, it leaves no doubt that there is something more in the human search for knowledge than the wish to get the facts right—basic as that is. We want to feel that the world can be understood as a unity, and that the rational mind can find ways of looking at it that are simple, new, and powerful exactly because they unify it.

It is also clear that the demand for unity in a theory goes outside the principle of correspondence, however this is applied. It is an appeal for coherence, and I myself express it by saying that a theory must be *rich*, by which I mean that it must contain a wealth of connections to other theories and to the effects that flow from them. Whatever words we use, they express the same conclusion, namely that a scientific theory has to combine the view which sees truth in correspondence with that which sees it in coherence. We cannot expect a theory to be true, but we cannot rightly assess its content unless we give weight both to correspondence, that is, to fact or effect, and to coherence, that is, to unity or richness.

Since Popper does not develop the concept of unity, let me say something about the concept of richness that I use. It starts from the same recognition that the organization or structure of a theory is a part of its content. However, Popper confines himself to single theories, while I think of the axiomatic system of a science as a whole. Popper has remarked (following Joseph Agassi) that systems of axioms are only provisional, and[40] "should be regarded as stepping stones rather than as ends"; and he has taken issue[41] with Pierre Duhem and Willard V. Quine for involving the whole system whenever a single theory is challenged. Nevertheless, I hold that the state of a science can only be characterized by the set of axioms which govern it at the time, and the content of a theory can only be measured when we see it embedded in them. But a set of axioms in an empirical science is not a linear array of separate statements (even when they are formally independent). A set of axioms is a topological network, in which the knots or joints are the inferred or theoretical entities which the science has had to create so that it will hold together as a unity. The network is given its character by the pattern of linkages that it forms across the joints, and it is the topological invariants of connection that describe it which I call the richness of the system. A new theory changes the system of axioms, and sets up new connections at the joints which change the topology. And when two sciences are linked to form one (electricity with magnetism, for instance, or evolution with genetics), the new network is richer in its articulation than the sum of its two parts.

What I call the richness of a scientific system therefore has dual aspects (as any network does). In the first place, a system to be rich must be compact: that is, a variety of effects must flow as consequences from a small body of axioms. But of course it will not do merely to count the 'number' of axioms, for such an enumeration has no meaning in itself. To be rich, the body of axioms must be internally connected, so that as many as possible take part in explaining many different effects which otherwise would seem to be unrelated. It is the connections between the axioms which give the system its coherence and its specific structure. And the connections are made by having several axioms share the same pivotal concept, namely one of the unobserved entities that we postulate to explain the observed effects. Thus a scientific system is rich not so much because its axioms are few in number, as because they are linked at and radiate from a small number of postulated entities—such as force, curvature, valency, binding energy, quanta, elementary particles, and so on.

But this is only my own sketch of an extended concept of unity which will pinpoint the crucial place of the connections made by the inferred or theoretical entities in a scientific system. I close this essay with it as a reminder that the structure of scientific theories is still unexplored territory; that we know roughly what we mean by unity, but not how we mean it to work; and that "Truth, Rationality, and the Growth of Scientific Knowledge" takes a long look forward towards its exploration.

XVI

It is the pride of the rationalist and empiricist tradition in England that it raises philosophers who combine intellectual power with liberality of spirit. Bertrand Russell has been an example in our lifetime, and Karl Popper was preordained to be a recruit to the tradition. Coming at a time in the 1930s when a generation of young scientists despaired of philosophy, he helped to reestablish its credit and its relevance in the face of authoritarianism. For he insisted in his philosophy as much as in his life that there is no final sanction and authority for knowledge, even in science; that only that is knowledge which is free to change and grow; and that a condition for its growth is the challenge by independent minds. An informal definition from Popper's Preface to *Conjectures and Refutations* makes the point:[42]

> by a liberal I do not mean a sympathizer with any one political party but simply a man who values individual freedom and who is alive to the dangers inherent in all forms of power and authority.

This is the humanist view which reaches from philosophy into conduct, because it derives the social responsibility of each man from his consciousness of human dignity. On this view, the growth of knowledge is indeed an organic growth. Like the evolution of a living species, there is no model in the mind of God towards which knowledge moves, and yet it moves from lower to higher forms by a process of selection which discards the errors, and step by step elevates those mutations that fit the world.

J. BRONOWSKI

THE SALK INSTITUTE FOR BIOLOGICAL STUDIES
SAN DIEGO, CALIFORNIA
OCTOBER, 1968

[1] K. R. Popper, *The Logic of Scientific Discovery* (London: Hutchinson, 1959; New York: Basic Books, 1959). Hereinafter cited as *L.Sc.D.*

[2] Alfred North Whitehead and Bertrand Russell, *Principia Mathematica,* 3 vols. (Cambridge: University Press, 1910-13).

[3] Ludwig Wittgenstein, *Tractatus Logico-Philosophicus* (London: Routledge & Kegan Paul, 1922).

[4] Baruch Spinoza, *Tractatus Theologico-Politicus* (Hamburg: Henricum Künraht, 1670).

[5] Kurt Gödel, "Über formal unentscheidbare Sätze der *Principia Mathematica* und verwandter Systeme, I.," *Monatshefte für Mathematik und Physik,* **38** (1931), 173-98.

[6] A. M. Turing, "On Computable Numbers with an Application to the Entscheidungsproblem," *Proceedings of the London Mathematical Society,* Series 2, **42** (1936), 230-65, and **43** (1937), 544-46.

[7] Frank Ramsey, *The Foundations of Mathematics* (London: Routledge & Kegan Paul, 1931).

[8] Pierre Simon de Laplace, "Essai philosophique sur les probabilités," Introduction to the Second Edition of his *Théorie analytique des probabilités* (Paris, 1814).

[9] Marginal note by William Blake in J. G. Spurzheim, *Observations on the Deranged Manifestations of the Mind, or Insanity* (London, 1817).

[10] Maurice Cornforth, *Science versus Idealism* (London: Lawrence and Wishart, 1946).

[11] B. Hessen, "The Social and Economic Roots of Newton's *Principia*," delivered at the International Congress of the History of Science at London in 1931; reprinted in *Science at the Crossroads* (London: Kniga, 1932).

[12] G. N. Clark, *Science and Social Welfare in the Age of Newton* (London, 1937).

[13] J. D. Bernal, *The Social Function of Science* (London: Routledge & Kegan Paul, 1939).

[14] A. J. Ayer, *Language, Truth, and Logic* (London: Victor Gollancz, 1936).

[15] K. R. Popper, *Conjectures and Refutations: The Growth of Scientific Knowledge* (London: Routledge & Kegan Paul, 1963; New York: Basic Books, 1963). Hereinafter cited as *C.&R.*

[16] *L.Sc.D.*, p. 202.

[17] Jerzy Neyman and Egon S. Pearson, "On the Use and Interpretation of Certain Test Criteria," *Biometrika,* **20**-A (1928).

[18] *L.Sc.D.*, p. 202.

[19] *C.&R.*, p. 241.

[20] *C.&.R.*, p. 248 n.

[21] J. M. Keynes, *A Treatise on Probability* (London: Macmillan and Co., 1921).

[22] Rudolf Carnap, *Logical Foundations of Probability* (Chicago: University of Chicago Press, 1950).

[23] Johannes Kepler, *Astronomia Nova* (Heidelberg, 1609).

[24] Carnap, *Logical Foundations.*

[25] *C.&R.*, p. 222.

[26] *C.&.R.*, p. 217.

[27] *C.&R.*, p. 217.

[28] *L.Sc.D.*, p. 462.

[29] *C.&R.*, p. 215.

[30] *C.&R.*, p. 215.

[31] J. Bronowski, *The Identity of Man* (New York: Natural History Press, 1965).

[32] Alfred Tarski, "Der Wahrheitsbegriff in den formalisierten Sprachen," *Studia philosophica,* **1** (1936), 261-405.

[33] J. Bronowski, "The Logic of the Mind," *American Scientist,* **54**, No. 1 (1966), 1-14.

[34] Gödel, "Unentscheidbare Sätze der *PM*."

[35] *C.&R.*, p. 232.

[36] *C.&R.*, p. 229.

[37] *C.&R.*, p. 232.

[38] *C.&R.*, p. 240.

[39] *C.&R.*, p. 241.

[40] *C.&R.*, p. 221.

[41] *C.&R.*, pp. 238-39.

[42] *C.&R.*, p. viii.

Czesław Lejewski

POPPER'S THEORY OF FORMAL
OR DEDUCTIVE INFERENCE

1. Popper's daring and challenging reappraisal of inductive logic is very well known to logicians and philosophers, and has won him many a staunch supporter. Less known, however, is the fact that, after publishing his *Logik der Forschung* in 1934, he embarked, among other projects, on a slow but thorough and painstaking enquiry into the nature and foundations of deduction. Accounts and discussions of the results obtained by him in this field of study began to appear in print in 1947, headed by "New Foundations for Logic", "Logic without Assumptions", and "Functional Logic without Axioms or Primitive Rules of Inference". To these essays were soon added three others, "On the Theory of Deduction, Part I. Derivation and its Generalizations", "On the Theory of Deduction, Part II. The Definitions of Classical and Intuitionist Negation", and "The Trivialization of Mathematical Logic", all published in 1948. But here the series ends, and since 1948 there have been no further contributions from Popper to the problem of deductive inference.[1]

Unlike his views on induction, Popper's reappraisal of deductive logic was received with marked caution. The far reaching claims put forward by him on behalf of his theory of formal or deductive inference —for the sake of brevity I shall refer to it as **TDI**—were not conceded by the reviewers.[2] Moreover, preoccupied as they were with these claims, the critics paid less attention to the theory itself, which in fact has not yet been assigned its proper place in the ramified hierarchy of disciplines which are of interest to logicians. The prevailing opinion seems to be that **TDI** is akin to Gentzen's logical calculi **LJ** and **LK**, but the nature of the affinity has not been explored, let alone determined.[3] Professor Bernays was alone in pointing out that **TDI** was closely related to Tarski's theory of consequence published in 1930.[4] It is this clue that I propose to follow in the present essay.

2. Since **TDI** and Tarski's theory of consequence—**TC** for short—happen to be formulated in different types of language, any attempt at eluci-

dating the relationship between the two theories will involve, of necessity, either a critical reconstruction of the one in the language of the other, or a critical reconstruction of both in a third type of language. For various reasons which will become clearer as we proceed, I prefer the latter course, and I will try to reconstruct both **TDI** and **TC** in the language which we owe to Leśniewski. A task of this sort would, of course, be impossible, were the two theories purely formal. As it is, both presuppose a very definite interpretation, which can be used as the standard for checking the correctness of our reconstruction. Moreover, by taking into account the intended interpretation we may find it possible to make explicit those presuppositions of either theory which its author has taken for granted or has preferred to suppress for the sake of simplicity.

TDI consists of two parts, which in "Logic without Axioms" Popper calls "Propositional Logic" and "Quantification Theory" respectively.[5] I shall refer to them simply as **PL** and **QT**. And it may be advisable to point out at the outset that by "Propositional Logic" Popper does not understand a Calculus of Propositions nor is his Quantification Theory to be confused with, say, the Lower Predicate Calculus in one of its forms. Since the space at my disposal is not unlimited, I find it necessary to confine my enquiry to **PL**, which is the core of **TDI**, and to leave the examination of **QT** for another occasion.

3. The subject matter of **PL** is a language L, concerning which Popper makes as few assumptions as possible. Naturally, he assumes that statements are available in L. They constitute the range of values of the variables required for the formulation of **PL**. The fundamental undefined concept of **PL**, and of **TDI** as a whole, is that of derivability or, better, deducibility. It occurs in assertions of the following type:

(1) from the premise a the conclusion b is deducible

(2) from the premises a and b the conclusion c is deducible

and generally

(3) from the premises $a_1, a_2, \ldots, a_n$ the conclusion b is deducible

In Popper's symbolic language such assertions are expressed by means of the following formulae:

(1') $a \mid b$

(2') $a, b \mid c$

(3') $a_1, a_2, \ldots, a_n, \mid b$

with the sign "/" embodying the concept of deducibility.

It would be quite legitimate to argue that formulae (1')-(3') do not exhibit a *single* concept of deducibility but rather a *family* of such concepts, and that the constant "/" as used in these formulae is affected by ambiguity, being in one context a two term predicate, and a three term predicate, or a predicate requiring some other number of terms, in another context. Now, is this ambiguity an intrinsic feature of the concept of deducibility or is it forced on us by the symbolism used? As far as I can see, the latter is the case, and the unity of the concept of deducibility can be easily restored if, first of all, we rephrase (1)-(3) to read as follows:

(1″) from the set consisting of the premise a the conclusion b is deducible

(2″) from the set consisting of the premise a and the premise b the conclusion c is deducible

(3″) from the set consisting of n a's each of which is a premise the conclusion b is deducible

(1″)-(3″) can now be subsumed under

(4) from the set of a's each of which is a premise the conclusion b is deducible

Clearly the concept of set is used above in the *distributive* sense whereby "the set of a's" means the same as "a's". Thus, if we allow the qualifications put on a's and b in (1″)-(3″), and (4) to be encapsulated in the concept of deducibility then we are left with a comprehensive formula

(5) $a \mid b$ (to be read: from a's b is deducible)

The stroke "/" in (5) is to be construed as a proposition-forming functor for two arguments each of which is a noun expression. In a true statement of this form the noun expression represented by "b" must designate exactly one statement belonging to L, whereas the noun expression represented by "a" may designate one or more such statements. While in Popper's symbolism the variables "a_1", "a_2", . . ., "a_n", "b", . . ., "c", . . . represent names, that is to say noun expressions each of which designates exactly one object, the variables "a", "b", "c", . . . in the language we are going to use, represent noun expressions which may designate any number of objects, as well as noun expressions which do not designate anything. It is to be noted that (5) is convertible *salva congruitate*: if an expression of the form "$a \mid b$" is meaningful then so is the corresponding expression of the form "$b \mid a$". It is needless to add that this is not a truth transmitting convertibility. Finally, in the Leśniewskian language the concept of deducibility as expressed in (5) abstracts from the order of the premises in an inference, which seems to be in accord with Popper's intentions. In his own symbolism, however, the irrelevance of the order in which the premises occur in an inference has to be asserted axiomatically.

4. Among various other constants available in **PL** we have "∧", ">", and "—". Although, for the most part, we will be concerned with ">"

and "—", I propose to discuss the meaning of "∧" at some length, because in this connection Popper's comments appear to be particularly illuminating. He tells us that the expression "$a \wedge b$" stands for "conjunction of the two statements a and b", which is to be understood in accordance with the following definition:

> (6) the statement c is a conjunction of the two statements a and b if and only if (i) from the premise c the conclusion a is deducible, (ii) from the premise c the conclusion b is deducible, and (iii) from the premises each of which is a or b, the conclusion c is deducible.[6]

No assumption is made by Popper as to how a conjunction of two statements is effected in L. If L is a part of English then a conjunction of two statements in L can be expressed with the aid of the usual "and"; but it can also be expressed with the aid of "if . . . then" and "it is not the case that", or in some other manner. Thus, for instance, the statement

> (7) if Smith retires or Brown retires then there will be a change in the management of the firm

could be regarded as a conjunction of the following two statements:

> (8) if Smith retires then there will be a change in the management of the firm

and

> (9) if Brown retires then there will be a change in the management of the firm.

For from (7), as the premise, (8) is deducible as the conclusion; again, from (7), as the premise, (9) is deducible as the conclusion; and, finally, from (8) and (9), as the premises, (7) is deducible as the conclusion.

Given two statements a and b in L there may be in L several different conjunctions of them. Consequently, as Popper himself points out, a statement which is $a \wedge b$, "is *a* conjunction of a and b, rather than it is *the* conjunction of a and b."[7] *Mutatis mutandis* all this holds of "$a > b$" and "$—a$", of which the former stands for "implication with the antecedent a and the consequent b" while the latter stands for "negation of a". Thus, "$a > b$" designates any statement c of L that is inferentially equivalent to an implication involving a as the antecedent and b as the consequent and effected in L, say, with the aid of "if . . . then". And "$—a$" designates any statement b which is inferentially equivalent to a negation of a effected, for instance, with the aid of "it is not the case that". Accordingly, the statement

(10) Smith retires or Brown retires

can, in accordance with classical logic, be regarded as an implication of

(11) it is not the case that Smith retires

as the antecedent, and

(12) Brown retires

as the consequent. And the statement

(13) if it is not the case that Smith retires then Smith retires

can be viewed as a negation of the statement

(14) it is not the case that Smith retires.

It has been assumed, of course, that (10)-(14) are statements of L.

5. The interpretation of "∧", ">", and "—" just considered is based entirely on Popper's informal discussion of the meaning of "∧" in "Foundations for Logic", and seems to take into account all his intentions. However, it does not tally with the way he uses these constants in the formal sections of his papers. For there we come across expressions such as

(15) $c \,/\, a \wedge b$,   (16) $c \,/\, a > b$,   and   (17) $c \,/\, -a$,

which, in accordance with the intended meaning of "/" imply that, contrary to informal explanations, there can be, in L, only one conjunction of a and b, only one implication with the antecedent a and the consequent b, and only one negation of a. The postulates, as Popper calls them, for "∧", ">", and "—" seem to imply the same. For they can be stated as follows:

(18) whatever a and b may be: if a is a statement of L and b is a statement of L then $a \wedge b$ is a statement of L,

(19) whatever a and b may be: if a is a statement of L and b is a statement of L then $a > b$ is a statement of L,

(20) whatever a may be: if a is a statement of L then $-a$ is a statement of L.[8]

If the formal version were to be in complete harmony with the informal explanations then (15), (16), and (17) would have to be replaced, respectively, by

(15') for some d: both d is an $a \wedge b$ and $c \mid d$,

(16') for some d: both d is an $a > b$ and $c \mid d$,

and

(17') for some d, both d is a $-a$ and $c \mid d$.

Now, (15'), (16'), and (17') are not formulae as simple as (15), (16), or (17), and it is likely that faced with the choice between simplicity and emphasis on concreteness Popper opted for the former at the expense of the latter. By doing so he laid himself open to the charge of committing what Leśniewski would call the fallacy of identifying inferentially equivalent statements. This kind of error is often consciously committed by logicians engaged in metalogical studies. They do not regard it as serious because without having recourse to any formal changes in their language they can escape criticism by reinterpreting the constant terms of the theory so as to make them apply to classes of inferentially equivalent statements rather than to individual statements. Tarski utilised this procedure in connection with his **TC**.[9] Since **PL** and **TC** appear to be at one on this important point, our reconstruction of either will conform.

The postulates mentioned above remind us that **PL** makes use of the notion "statement of L". We will use "s" to symbolize this notion, so that the proposed reconstruction of **PL** will eventually be based on "/", ">", "—", and "s" as the only constants characteristic of the theory. In addition, a very limited vocabulary from logically prior theories will be involved.

6. We now turn to the presuppositions of **PL**. In the present context by "presupposition" I understand any thesis of **PL** which is not derived from other theses already available in **PL**. And while with many logicians presuppositions often take the form of comments or conventions outside the system, I will, in my reconstruction, adhere to the principle of expressing such presuppositions, wherever possible, within the system. The problem of whether or not the presuppositions of **PL** can be reduced to a set of definitions, as Popper argues they can, will occupy us at a later stage.

It was mentioned earlier that in the case of **PL** the universe of discourse is restricted to statements of L. Now this kind of restriction can easily be expressed within the system. In connection with "/" we simply require a presupposition to the effect that

(21) whatever a's and b may be: if from a's b is deducible then every a is a statement of L and b is a statement of L

Translated into Leśniewski's language (21) reads thus:

PA1 $[a\ b]:a\ /\ b.\ \supset.\ [\exists c].c\ \epsilon\ a.a\ \subset\ \text{s}.b\ \epsilon\ \text{s}^{10}$

PA1, which has been made explicit on the basis of informal comments, does not appear in Popper's actual formulation of **PL**. Yet it has
a part to play in many deductions within the framework of the theory.
By including it in our reconstruction of **PL** we do not alter or expand the
original system. We only make it explicit.

Next come what Popper calls the *generalised principle of reflexivity*
and the *generalised principle of transitivity*.[11] The former says that

(22) whatever *a*'s and *b* may be: if all *a*'s are statements of L and
      b is an *a* then from *a*'s *b* is deducible

According to the latter

(23) whatever *a*'s, *b*'s, and *c* may be: if from *b*'s *c* is deducible and
      from *a*'s each of the *b*'s is deducible then from *a*'s *c* is deducible

In our symbolic language the two principles have the following form:

PA2 $[a\ b]:a\ \subset\ \text{s}.b\ \epsilon\ a.\ \supset\ .a\ /\ b$

PA3 $[a\ b\ c]:\ :b\ /\ c:.[d]:d\ \epsilon\ b.\ \supset\ .a\ /\ d:.\ \supset\ .a\ /\ c$

The presuppositions that follow concern the concepts of implication and negation. They are:

PA4 $[a\ b]:a\ \epsilon\ \text{s}.b\ \epsilon\ \text{s}.\ \supset\ .a\!>\!b\ \epsilon\ \text{s}.\ -\!a\ \epsilon\ \text{s}$

PA5 $[a\ b\ c]:c\ \epsilon\ a\!>\!b.\ \supset\ .a\ \epsilon\ \text{s}.b\ \epsilon\ \text{s}$

PA6 $[a\ b]:b\ \epsilon\ -\!a.\ \supset\ .a\ \epsilon\ \text{s}$

It is easy to see that PA4 is just the symbolic version of the postulates (19) and (20) combined into one thesis. PA5 and PA6 mean the
same as:

(24) whatever *a*, *b*, and *c* may be: if *c* is the implication with *a* as
      the antecedent and *b* as the consequent then both *a* is a state-
      ment of L and *b* is a statement of L

and

(25) whatever *a* and *b* may be: if *b* is the negation of *a* then *a* is a
      statement of L.

Neither (24) nor (25) occurs in Popper's actual formulation of **PL**. They
are embedded in his informal comments.

The remaining two presuppositions determine the meaning of
implication and negation respectively. They correspond to Popper's

"inferential definitions" of the two concepts and have the form of the following equivalences:

(26) whatever *a, b,* and *c* may be: *a* and the implication with *b* as the antecedent and *c* as the consequent are inferentially equivalent, i.e., deducible from one another, if and only if (i) *b* is a statement of L, (ii) *c* is a statement of L, and (iii) whatever *d*'s may be: if *d*'s exist then from *d*'s *a* is deducible if and only if from *d*'s or *b c* is deducible.

(27) whatever *a* and *b* may be: *a* and the negation of *b* are inferentially equivalent, i.e., deducible from one another, if and only if (i) *a* is a statement of L, (ii) *b* is a statement of L, and (iii) whatever *c*'s and *d* may be: if *d* is a statement of L and from *a* or *c*'s *b* is deducible then both from *a* or *c*'s *d* is deducible and from *c*'s or *d b* is deducible.

In symbols we have:

PA7 $[a\ b\ c]::.a\ |\ b > c.b > c\ |\ a. \equiv ::b \in \text{s.}c \in \text{s}::[d\ e]:.e \in d.$
$\supset :d\ |\ a. \equiv .d \cup b\ |\ c$

PA8 $[a\ b]::a\ |\ -b.\ -b\ |\ a. \equiv :.a \in \text{s.}b \in \text{s}:.[c\ d]:d \in \text{s.}\ a \cup c\ |$
$b. \supset .a \cup c\ |\ d.\ c \cup d\ |\ b^{12}$

The presuppositions PA1-PA8 characterize that part of **PL**, call it System *P*, which I propose to correlate with Tarski's **TC**. They are expressed in a language which differs from the language used by Popper, but as regards their contents they seem to be in complete harmony with the intended interpretation of his **TDI**. As it has already been pointed out, PA1, PA5, and PA6 do not occur explicitly among the presuppositions of the original version of **PL** but they are most obviously implied by Popper's informal comments and explanations. PA2, PA3, PA4, PA7 and PA8 have explicit analogues among the theses of his theory.

7. Unlike **TDI** Tarski's **TC** is formulated in the language of set theory. Since there is nothing in the formulation which would prevent us from interpreting the concept of set *distributively,* the problem of recasting **TC** into Leśniewskian language presents no difficulty.

The undefined constants of **TC** are "cn", ">", "—", and "s". Different symbolism is used in the case of ">", "—" and "s", but I retain the Popperian signs, since no difference in meaning seems to be involved. The constant "cn" occurs in expressions of the form "$b \in \text{cn}(a)$". Now, "$b \in \text{cn}(a)$" means the same as "*b* is a consequence of *a*'s". Thus "cn" is a noun-forming functor for one argument, which is also a noun. It is clear that "$b \in \text{cn}(a)$" can be regarded as a sort of converse of "$a\ |\ b$", except that, as we shall see presently, in **TC** some statements of the object language can be described as consequences of the null set.

The system of **TC** required for our purpose will be referred to as System *T*. It is based on the following presuppositions:

TA1 $[a\ b]:b\ \epsilon\ \mathrm{cn}(a). \supset .b\ \epsilon\ \mathrm{s}.a \subset \mathrm{s}$

TA2 $[a\ b\ ]:a \subset \mathrm{s}.b\ \epsilon\ a. \supset .b\ \epsilon\ \mathrm{cn}(a)$

TA3 $[a\ b]:.a \subset \mathrm{s}. \supset :b\ \epsilon\ \mathrm{cn}(\mathrm{cn}(a)). \equiv .b\ \epsilon\ \mathrm{cn}(a)$

TA4 $[a\ b\ c]:a \subset \mathrm{s}.c \subset a.b\ \epsilon\ \mathrm{cn}(c). \supset .b\ \epsilon\ \mathrm{cn}(a)$

TA5 $[a\ b]:a\ \epsilon\ \mathrm{s}.b\ \epsilon\ \mathrm{s}. \supset .a > b\ \epsilon\ \mathrm{s}. -a\ \epsilon\ \mathrm{s}$

TA6 $[a\ b\ c]:c\ \epsilon\ a > b. \supset .a\ \epsilon\ \mathrm{s}.b\ \epsilon\ \mathrm{s}$

TA7 $[a\ b]:b\ \epsilon\ -a. \supset .a\ \epsilon\ \mathrm{s}$

TA8 $[a\ b\ c]:b > c\ \epsilon\ \mathrm{cn}(a). \equiv .b\ \epsilon\ \mathrm{s}.c\ \epsilon\ \mathrm{cn}(a \cup b)$

TA9 $[a\ b]:a\ \epsilon\ \mathrm{s}.b\ \epsilon\ \mathrm{s}. \supset .b\ \epsilon\ \mathrm{cn}(a \cup -a)$

TA10 $[a\ b]:.a\ \epsilon\ \mathrm{s}. \supset :b\ \epsilon\ \mathrm{cn}(a).b\ \epsilon\ \mathrm{cn}(-a). \equiv .b\ \epsilon\ \mathrm{cn}(\wedge)$[13]

The system of presuppositions TA1-TA10 differs a little from the original system of presuppositions of **TC** as adopted by Tarski. To be more precise, the following presuppositions have been dropped:

(28) $\bar{\bar{\mathrm{s}}} \leq \aleph_0$

(29) $[a\ b]:a \subset \mathrm{s}.b\ \epsilon\ \mathrm{cn}(a). \supset . [\exists c].c \subset a.\bar{\bar{c}} < \aleph_0 .b\ \epsilon\ \mathrm{cn}(c)$

(30) $[\exists\ a]:.a\ \epsilon\ \mathrm{s}:.[b]:b\ \epsilon\ \mathrm{s}. \supset .b\ \epsilon\ \mathrm{cn}(a)$[14]

TA6, TA7 and the following presupposition:

(31) $[a\ b]:b\ \epsilon\ \mathrm{cn}(a). \supset .a \subset \mathrm{s}$

which is embedded in TA1, have been added.

It is not difficult to see that "/" and "cn" are definable in terms of one another. Thus in *P* we can have

PD1 $[a\ b]::.a\ \epsilon\ \mathrm{cn}(b). \equiv ::a\ \epsilon\ \mathrm{s}::b\ /\ a. \vee :.[c]. \sim (c\ \epsilon\ b):. [c]:c$
$\epsilon\ \mathrm{s}. \supset .c\ /\ a$

On the other hand "/" can, in *T*, be defined as follows:

TD1 $[a\ b]:.a\ /\ b. \equiv :b\ \epsilon\ \mathrm{cn}(a):[\exists c].c\ \epsilon\ a$

Given these definitions *P* and *T* turn out to be inferentially equivalent as is shown in the Appendix. Now, this goes beyond Professor Bernays's result, which amounts to showing that PA1-PA3 imply, and are implied by, TA1-TA4.

8. In *P*, which is our reconstruction of **PL**, the system of presuppositions PA1-PA8 is in fact an axiom system. The constants "/", ">", "—", and "s" are the primitive or undefined terms of *P*; the remaining voca-

bulary belongs to theories which are logically prior to P. Thus "ϵ", "$\subset$", and "$\cup$" belong to Leśniewski's ontology (and so does "$\wedge$" in T) while "$\supset$", "." (or a cluster of dots standing for "and"), "$\equiv$", "$\vee$", and "$\sim$" belong to prototethic. In other words P presupposes a logic of "is", including a few related concepts, and also a logic of propositional connectives such as "if . . . then", "and", "if and only if", etc. A theory of identity, that is to say a logic of "is the same object as" with its derivatives could be used instead of ontology in reconstructing **PL** and **TC**. This would, however, involve using a language different from that of Leśniewski.

New theses are introduced into P, and into T for that matter, in virtue of the following rules of inference: substitution, quantification, and detachment. A rule for propounding *propositional* definitions and an appropriate rule for *nominal* definitions are also assumed to be available. It goes without saying that all these rules have to be adapted to the vocabulary of the respective systems.

In the deductions presented in the Appendix no explicit reference is made to any protothetical or ontological theses. This, of course, does not mean that, insofar as P and T are concerned, protothetic or ontology are logically redundant. Their relevance becomes apparent as soon as we try to make our deductions complete.

Systems P and T are reconstructions of what can be regarded as the nuclei of **TDI** and **TC** respectively. While the nuclei are inferentially equivalent the theories have been expanded by their authors in different directions. Thus in developing his **TC** Tarski is anxious to define and investigate such metalogical concepts as "deductive system", "consistency of a set of statements", "completeness of a set of statements", "the degree of completeness of a set of statements", "axiomatizability of a set of statements", and the like.[15] Now, Popper's principal objective in expanding **TDI** is to make available concepts required for the purpose of describing those logical relations which in the object language under consideration would normally be exhibited in terms of quantifiers. This part of **TDI** is called by him "Quantification Theory". In addition he tries to accommodate modal logic within the framework of **TDI**.[16]

9. The limits of the present essay make it impracticable to follow in detail Popper's method of expanding **TDI**. It appears to be preferable to consider, in the light of our reconstruction of **PL**, some of the claims advanced by Popper on behalf of his **TDI**. An evaluation of the claims seems to be important since their apparent unorthodoxy has tended to obscure the virtues of the theory.

Let us begin with the claim, embodied in the title of the 1947 article in *Mind,* that **TDI** provides new foundations for logic. In this context the operative term is of course "logic". Popper assumes that "the central topic of logic is the theory of formal or deductive inference", and in making such an assumption Popper is not alone.[17] Carnap, for instance, thinks along the same lines when he writes that logical questions do not refer directly to nonlinguistic objects, but to statements, terms, theories, and so on, which themselves refer to the objects in a direct manner.[18] More recently a similar view of logic has been advocated by W. Kneale.[19] Clearly, if by logic we are to understand a theory of formal or deductive inference then Popper's claim is justified. He has worked out new foundations for a theory of deductive inference, and he has done so independently of the earlier work by Tarski. We must remember, however, that there are logicians who hold that the principal logical theory is the one which exhibits the use of such terms as "if . . . then", "and", "or", "if and only if", "it-is-not-the-case-that", and the like. Leśniewski calls it protothetic; it has been called logic of propositions by some, while others refer to it as propositional or sentential calculus. The terminology is, of course, of secondary importance, but it remains a fact that no theory can be developed without protothetical vocabulary, which means that prototetic is in a sense prior to any other theory. It is significant that Popper is rather uneasy and apologetic about the theoretical status of propositional connectives. In his presentation of **TDI** he uses "→", "&", and "↔", but he goes out of his way to assure us that these symbols are "mere abbreviations" of "if . . . then", "and", and "if and only if".[20] As regards the latter he describes them as "the normal means of expression", and argues that there is no question of introducing a logical symbolism in an underhand manner.[21] And indeed no such question arises because the availability of a theory which exhibits their use is presupposed by **TDI**. It is taken for granted in "Foundations for Logic" and in "Logic without Assumptions", and in "Logic without Axioms" it is implied by a reference to the positive part of the Hilbert-Bernays calculus of propositions.[22]

Another theory which in "Foundations for Logic" and in "Logic without Assumptions" is taken for granted and in "Logic without Axioms" is referred to explicitly, is the theory which exhibits the use of "is the same object as" and the use of quantifiers. In System *P* this theory has been replaced by Leśniewski's ontology. Now, both ontology and the theory of identity with quantifiers are regarded by some logicians as logical theories, second in generality to prototetic or calculus of propositions. I do not propose to argue whether or not these theories should be regarded as parts of logic, but I would like to point out that the foundations of **TDI**, if stated explicitly, would be found to consist of the following three layers: (i) the foundations of protothetic or the foundations of a part of protothetic such as the calculus of propositions; subjoined to these are (ii) the foundations of ontology or the foundations of the theory of identity with quantifiers; to these are added (iii) the foundations of **TDI**, in the narrower sense of foundations. And the order of the layers cannot be altered.

10. So much concerning the presuppositions, implicit or explicit, of **TDI**, expressible in the language of **TDI**. We turn now to the problem of definitions. Examples of definitions, which obtain in **TDI**, can conveniently be quoted from "Logic without Assumptions". Having reminded us that "$a \mid \mid b$" can be defined as mutual deducibility, that is to say as "$a \mid b$ and $b \mid a$" Popper continues as follows:

There is an alternative definition of equivalence, viz.:

(7.1) $a \mid \mid b$ if, and only if, for every c: $a \mid c$ if, and only if, $b \mid c$.

Now just as this defines the phrase: "*a has the same force as b, whatever the logical form of a and b may be*", so we can also define the phrase: "*a has the same force as the negation of b, whatever the logical form of a and b may be*" by:

(7.2) $a \mid \mid$ the negation of b if, and only if, for every c: $a, b \mid c$ and, if $a, c \mid b$ then $c \mid b$

Similarly we can define:

(7.3) $a \mid \mid$ the disjunction of b_1 and b_2 if, and only if, for every c_1 and c_2: $a, c_1/c_2$ if, and only if, $b_1, c_1/c_2$ and $b_2, c_1/c_2$.[23]

Two types of definition are exemplified in this passage. In (7.1) we recognize a *propositional* definition. It introduces a term which in concatenation with two arguments "a" and "b" forms a statement or a proposition. Definitions (7.2) and (7.3) introduce terms which in concatenation with their respective arguments form name expressions, viz., "the negation of b" and "the disjunction of b_1 and b_2". Thus, the definitions of this sort are *nominal* definitions. But, prima facie, they appear to be nominal definitions with a difference. The nominal definitions of the most familiar type make use of the functor of singular identity, viz. "$=$", in their definienda. In Leśniewski's systems the definiendum in a nominal definition is written with the aid of "ϵ", which is the functor of singular inclusion. Other functors can be used for the purpose, but as far as I know Popper is the first to have suggested nominal definitions whose definienda involve the use of the functor of mutual deducibility or inferential equivalence, that is to say the use of "/ /". Following Popper, I will refer to this latter sort of nominal definition as *inferential*. They appear to be an innovation, and it is rather surprising that Popper makes no attempt at establishing their legitimacy, which he simply takes for granted, insisting only that a definition should always introduce a new symbol. *"But this, indeed, is the main precaution necessary,"* he writes in "Logic without Assumptions". And he continues as follows:

> We need not make sure, in any other way, that our system of definitions is consistent. For example, we may define (introducing an arbitrarily chosen name "opponent"):
>
> (7.8) $a \mid \mid$ the opponent of b if, and only if, for every c: $b \mid a$ and $a \mid c$
>
> This definition has the consequence that every language which has a sign for "opponent of b" — analogous to the sign for "negation of b" — will be inconsistent (i.e. every one of its statements will be paradoxical). But this need not lead us to abandon (7.8); it only means that no consistent language will have a sign of "opponent of b".[24]

The first sentence in this passage is so strange that one doubts whether it was meant to be understood as it stands. Indeed, the rest of the quotation appears to suggest that, according to Popper we need not be alarmed if our definitions imply that the language under consideration, i.e., the object language L, is uninteresting — if, for instance, it allows us to make false statements only. This much could perhaps be conceded, but surely our theory of such an object language should itself be consistent. If so, then the consistency of the definitions which are part of the theory, should be one of our main concerns. Let us then enquire into their nature a little further.

It would appear that, if (7.8) is a legitimate definition, then so is the following one:

(32) $a \mid \mid$ the opponent* of b if, and only if, for every c: both $b \mid a$ and it is not the case that $b \mid c$

Now from (7.1) it follows that $a \mid \mid a$, which in the presence of (32) implies that the opponent* of $b \mid \mid$ the opponent* of b, and this, in turn, enables us to infer that for every c: both $b \mid$ the opponent* of b and it is not the case that $b \mid c$. Hence we have: both $b \mid$ the opponent* of b and it is not the case that $b \mid$ the opponent* of b, which is a contradiction. Moreover, it is a contradiction not in the object language under consideration, but in our theory of it! What has gone wrong?

As far as I can see we were wrong in propounding (32) as a legitimate definition without first satisfying ourselves that, in accordance with our explicit or tacit presuppositions, for every statement b of L the opponent* of b was also a statement of L. If this condition were secured by our presuppositions then (32) would be a legitimate definition, and our whole theory would, of course, be inconsistent. On the other hand, without the condition being satisfied, we would not be able to have (32) as a definition, and, consequently, the contradiction would not arise. This, however, is not the end of the story; it only brings to our attention the problem of the postulates in Popper's version of **TDI**, and of **PL** in particular.

11. In "Foundations for Logic" Popper acknowledges the role of the postulates in an unequivocal manner. They are on a par with the other presuppositions of his systems. Telling us how "the logic of compound statements" can be constructed, he points out that "We first assume postulates" . . ., "one for each of the compounds we wish to introduce, in order to assure, for every pair of statements, say a and b, the existence of the corresponding compound statement." . . . "These postulates have the function of confining our investigations to languages in which such compounds exist."[25] Less is said about postulates in "Logic without Assumptions", and in "Logic without Axioms" postulates are mentioned only after **PL** has been shown, as Popper claims it, to be derivable from a definition of "/ /" and a set of inferential definitions alone. "If we wish to apply our system to some object language L," he writes, "then certain existential postulates must be added which correspond to the definitions."[26] It seems to me that this is misleading, and that a sounder procedure is described in "Foundations for Logic". We should first lay down the postulates, make sure that they are consistent, and then add definitions, which should correspond to the postulates. For it is the consistency of the postulates that guarantees the consistency of the corresponding definitions.

A critic may say that, if we begin construcing a system of **PL** by first setting out postulates, then our subsequent inferential definitions corresponding to them will violate the principle in accordance with which each definition should introduce a new symbol,. not to be found in the earlier part of the system. This is a valid objection, but it can easily be met by our rephrasing the postulates so that the symbols to be defined are eliminated from them without any loss of content. Thus, for instance, instead of the old postulates for ">" and "—" we can have:

(33) if b and c are both statements of L then for some a: both (i) for every d: d / a if and only if d, b / c and (ii) for every f: if for every d: d / f if and only if d, b / c then $a = f$

and

(34) if b is a statement of L then for some a: both (i) for every c: $a, b \mid c$ and if $a, c \mid b$ then $c \mid b$ and (ii) for every d: if for every $c: d, b \mid c$ and if $d, c \mid b$ then $c \mid b$ then $a = d$

Consider, now, a fragmentary system of **PL** based on postulate (34) as the only axiom. We can subjoin to it a propositional definition such as (7.1), and, what is more important, we can introduce a new symbol, "the negation of", by proposing a nominal definition such as (7.2). With the aid of (34), (7.1) and (7.2) we can prove that

(35) $a \mid \mid$ the negation of b if and only if $a =$ the negation of b

For suppose that (i) $a \mid \mid$ the negation of b; from (7.1) we learn that (ii) the negation of $b \mid \mid$ the negation of b; then we note that (7.2), (i) and (ii) imply both (iii) for every c: both $a, b \mid c$ and if $a, c \mid b$ then $c \mid b$, and (iv) for every c: both the negation of $b, b \mid c$ and if the negation of $b, c \mid b$ then $c \mid b$; considering what has been agreed about the universe of discourse of **PL** we realise that a, b, and the negation of b are all statements of L; hence from (34), (iii), and (iv) we can infer that (v) for some c: both $c = a$ and $c =$ the negation of b; (v), in turn, implies that (vi) $a =$ the negation of b. Conversely, assuming (vi) we can infer (i) in virtue of (7.1).

Proposition (35) is not a surprising result. It only emphasises what was said earlier about the fallacy of identifying inferentially equivalent statements. More important, however, is that we can repeat our argument in the case of any inferential definition whose legitimacy has been secured by an appropriate postulate, which suggests, in turn, that in the definiendum of an inferential definition we may, legitimately, replace "/ /" by "=". In order to satisfy ourselves that such a replacement is indeed justified, we have to derive (7.2) from (34), (7.1) and

(36) $a =$ the negation of b if and only if for every c: both $a, b \mid c$ and, if $a, c \mid b$ then $c \mid b$,

with the help, perhaps, of some other theses of **PL**. What in fact will be needed is simply the generalised principle of reflexivity and the generalised principle of transitivity.

Suppose then that (i) $a =$ the negation of b; from (7.1) and (i) we infer that (ii) $a \mid \mid$ the negation of b. Now, conversely, suppose that (ii) is true; (7.1), (ii), and the generalised principle of reflexivity imply that (iii) $a \mid$ the negation of b; since the negation of $b =$ the negation of b, we infer from (36) that (iv) for every c: both the negation of $b, b \mid c$ and if the negation of $b, c \mid b$ then $c \mid b$; from (iv) and (iii), by applying the

generalised principle of reflexivity and that of transitivity, we obtain
(v) for every c: both $a, b \mid c$ and if $a, c \mid b$ then $c \mid b$; considering that b
is a statement of L we now make use of (34), (iv), and (v) with a view to
deriving (vi), i.e., for some c: both c = the negation of b and $c = a$; (vi)
implies (i). Thus, starting with a different set of presuppositions, we have
proved (35), which in conjunction with (36) yields (7.2).

Now, this result shows that we can replace "/ /" by "=" in our inferential definitions, which means that they are nothing else but the traditional nominal definitions in another guise. As is well known, the
traditional nominal definitions involving the use of the functor of singular
identity in the definiendum are not *unconditional*. They cannot be introduced into the system irrespective of what is, or is not, already in the
system. To be more precise it is the existence and uniqueness of the
object whose name is to be introduced by a nominal definition based on
"=" (or "/ /") that has to be guaranteed, in the last instance, by postulates, i.e., axiomatically. Postulates cannot be regarded as integral parts
of nominal definitions, as is obvious from our example of the would-be
definition of "the opponent* of". They are independent of definitions
and prior to them.

The upshot seems to be that Popper's claim to have constructed a
logic without assumptions or a logic without axioms, i.e., a logic based
on definitions alone, can hardly be upheld.

12. According to Popper the concept of deducibility as used in **PL** enables us to define formative, or logical, signs such as "and", "or", "if
. . . then", "neither . . . nor", "it is not the case that", etc. Indeed in
"Logic without Assumptions" he argues that a *sign s of a language*
L *is a formative sign if and only if s can be defined by an inferential definition*.[27] The claim that formative signs can be defined within **PL** or **TDI**
is likely to create misgivings. It is, therefore, important that we should
first try and understand the language of the claim.

Expressions of the form "definition D defines x" or "definition of
x" are often used by logicians in their informal comments on systems
under construction, or under discussion. But such expressions are
notoriously ambiguous. Thus, for instance, the question "What does
(36) define?" can elicit the following answers:

(37) definition (36) defines the term, or the functor, "the negation of"
(38) definition (36) defines the name-function "the negation of b"
(39) definition (36) defines the negation of a statement b in language L

Adapting the very well-known terminology of Carnap we can say
that in (37) and (38) the verb "defines" is used to mean the same as ·

"*formally* defines" whereas in (39) it is used to mean the same as "*materially* defines". And these are two different meanings. For the expression formally defined by (36) belongs to the language of **TDI** and is not a statement while the expression materially defined by (36) is a statement belonging to the object language L. As far as I can judge Popper's use of "defines" and "definition of" is not meticulously uniform, but in claming that in **PL** he can define formative signs in terms of deducibility, he clearly claims that he can do so materially. Thus, for instance, on the assumption that L is a part of English, the formative sign "it is not the case that" can, following Popper, be defined as follows:

> (40) *a* is a sign of negation in L if and only if it is a sign which placed
>   before a statement *b* of L forms a new statement *c* of L such
>   that *c* is the negation of *b*,

where "the negation of *b*" is to be understood in the light of (36).[28]

The possibility of materially defining formative signs of a language by first formally defining such name-functions as "the negation of *b*", "the conjunction of *b* and *c*", "the implication with *b* as the antecedent and *c* as the consequent", etc., is not surprising. But it would be a sensation, of course, if formative signs could formally be defined in terms of deducibility. One can easily be misled into attributing this sort of claim to Popper if one fails to distinguish the two senses of "defines".

13. Now that the problem of definitions in **PL** has been clarified a little, it will be easier for us to evaluate Popper's comments on the relationship between **TDI** and systems such as *Principia Mathematica*. In the first section of his "Logic without Axioms" Popper claims that the procedure adopted by him in constructing his **TDI** is considerably simpler than the procedure adhered to in constructing the customary systems, which by and large are modelled on *Principia*. I will illustrate Popper's argument insofar as it applies to propositional logic.

The setting up of a customary system involves, according to Popper, the following stages: (a) undefined primitive *formative* signs are laid down; (b) unproved primitive propositions or axioms are laid down; (c) primitive rules of inference are laid down; (d) principles stating that the inference relation is transitive and reflexive are assumed, either explicitly, or, more often, tacitly. Now, Popper points out, the traditional procedure must make use of a language of communication in which it discusses and describes the linguistic systems under consideration. In particular, use must be made of concepts such as that of deducibility. But once the characterization of the concept of deducibility by means of (d), i.e., by means of the principles stating that the inference relation is transitive and reflexive, is given, then, urges Popper, (a') no formative signs need be laid down as primitive since names for them can be defined in terms of deducibility; (b') no unproved axioms need be assumed since they can be shown to be demonstrable, demonstrability being defined in terms of deducibility; and (c') no primitive rules of kind (c) need be laid down. Since the principles of transitivity and reflexivity for the concept of deducibility can be incorporated into one of the inferential definitions, we can obtain, so Popper concludes, the whole structure of logic from inferential definitions alone.[29]

I must confess that I am puzzled by the second half of this argument. As far as I understand the system of *Principia* or any other system of the so-called calculus of propositions, I agree that their authors make use of a language of communication, usually ordinary language, but they do so in order to discuss, informally, the system they are set out to construct. And while the system is being developed they keep up a running commentary, usually in ordinary language, on its growth. The system under construction, however, neither discusses nor describes nor refers to any linguistic system conceived as an object language. It simply exhibits the use of formative signs, "∨", "⊃", ".", "~", ..., i.e., "or", "if ... then", "and", "it is not the case that", etc. Systems of **PL** or **TC**, on the other hand, discuss and describe an object language by establishing various logical relations that may hold between its expressions. They, too, make use of formative signs, but in addition they exhibit the use of such signs as "from.. .. ...is deducible", "consequence of", "the negation of", etc., and this is their characteristic feature. Like the formative signs of a customary system these latter signs or concepts are also discussed, in terms of ordinary language, at a presystematic level or in the comments outside the actual system of **PL**.

The system of *Principia* and Popper's system of **PL** are, undoubtedly, two different sorts of systems; their content is different, and neither can be regarded as a simplification of the other, but the system of *Principia* is logically prior to the system of **PL**. Both, however, are deductive systems and, as such, they have a number of features in common. For example, the setting up of a system of **PL**, such as Popper's, involves, I would say, stages exactly analogous to those indicated by Popper in connection with customary systems. First, (a″) undefined primitive signs, e.g., "/", that is to say, "from.. .. ...is deducible", are laid down; formative signs are regarded as "the normal means of expression", which to my mind amounts to assuming them as available from logically prior theories. Secondly, (b″) unproved presuppositions, i.e., primitive propositions or axioms (Popper prefers calling them principles or rules, which appears to be a matter of terminology) are laid down, viz., the

generalised principle of reflexivity and the generalised principle of
transitivity for the concept of deducibility; the stating of postulates belongs to this stage too. Finally, (c″) primitive rules of inference and
definition for the system under construction, not for the object language
L, are tacitly assumed as is evidenced by the presence of definitions in
the system and the fact that we are expected to expand the system by
making inferences from the definitions and from the presuppositions
mentioned by (b″); the rules of inference and definition are not stated
explicitly, to be sure, but this is only because the presentation of the
system of **PL** is not formalised to the extent to which the presentation
of the customary systems usually is. The various rules of inference prov-
able in Popper's system of **PL** are applicable to the object language L,
while the rules of inference applicable to the system itself are not statable
in the language of **PL**. If we were to formulate them, we would have to
do so outside the system, just as the rules of inference applicable to a
system of propositional calculus have to be stated outside the framework of that system.

As regards **PL**, Popper's stage (d) coincides with stage (b″) in our
account. I do not quite understand how it affects the setting up of a
customary system such as that of *Principia*.[30]

In connection with (a′) one can point out that, as we saw earlier,
a material definition of a formative sign does not amount to its formal
definition. If, in a system, we wanted to use a new formative sign, say,
"neither . . . nor . . .", we could not introduce it with the aid of an inferential definition. For such a definition could only introduce into the
system "the joint denial of . . . and . . .", which is not the same thing as
"neither . . . nor . . .". The former forms name expressions; the latter
forms statements.

Concerning (b′) it would appear that by showing a statement *s* to
be demonstrable in an object language L we do not, by the same token,
avail ourselves of a licence to use it in our system of **PL**. Admittedly,
within the framework of **PL**, or **TC**, we can derive a sort of model of a
customary system of the propositional calculus. This, however, does not
mean that without assuming a system of the propositional calculus as a
theory logically prior to **PL** we can derive it as part of **PL**.

The claim under (c′) has already been discussed under (c″).

To sum up, it seems to me that Popper's claims put forward under
(a′), (b′), and (c′) in the description of his procedure are in need of
revision. And so is his claim that by his method one can obtain the whole
structure of logic from inferential definitions alone. It is true that in
Popper's language the principles of reflexivity and transitivity for the
concept of deducibility can be incorporated into an inferential definition,

although this makes the definition inorganic.[31] More important, however, is the fact that at least one of his postulates cannot be so incorporated, namely the one which makes the definition legitimate.

14. I have examined Popper's claims in connection with his **PL** at some length but I have hardly any criticism to offer as regards the theory itself. It seems to be based on intuitively sound ideas and provides an important conceptual framework for general metalogical investigations. The concepts of deducibility, implication, negation, conjunction, etc., are constantly used in informal comments on deductive systems under construction, and the merit of theories such as **PL** or **TC** is that they determine the meaning of these and many other concepts on a firm axiomatic basis. Moreover, both **PL** and **TC** can be expanded in various directions as has been shown by Popper and, in the case of **TC**, by Tarski. In "Logic without Axioms" Popper shows that by means of appropriate definitions one can introduce into **PL** the traditional modal concepts, i.e., the concepts of necessity, possibility, impossibility, and contingency.[32] Usually logicians try to accommodate such concepts by expanding ordinary calculi of propositions, which presuppose no object language. Popper appears to be right in urging that modalities belong to metalogic and should be treated within the framework of such a theory as **PL**. Another sort of expansion of **PL** explored by Popper aims at providing conceptual apparatus for the purpose of articulating those logical relations which in a sufficiently rich object language would normally be exhibited in terms of quantification. This new line of enquiry seems to be both interesting and promising, and Popper's **QT** deserves a careful and thorough study, but as I said earlier an adequate examination of this part of Popper's **TDI** would exceed the limits of the present essay.

In "Foundation for Logic" Popper urges that logic, by which he means the theory of deducibility, should be simple. He accordingly tries to reduce the number of undefined terms of **TDI** by an extensive use of definitions, a method which has led him to believe that he could dispense with axioms. Now, this requirement of formal simplicity can hardly be said to be satisfied by the axiomatic foundations of *P*, which embodies our reconstruction of **PL**. It turns out, however, that on closer examination the axiom system PA1-PA8 lends itself to a formal simplification of no negligible extent. Thus, for instance, axioms PA1-PA3, which characterize the concept of deducibility, can be replaced by a single axiom and a definition of "s", to wit, by

(41) $[a\ b]:::a\ /\ b. \equiv ::.b\ \epsilon\ b.b\ /\ b::.[\ \exists\ c]::c\ \epsilon\ a:.[d]:d\ \epsilon\ a.$
$\supset .d\ /\ d:: \sim (a\ /\ c). \lor :.[\ \exists\ d]:.d\ /\ b:.[e]:e\ \epsilon\ d.\supset .a\ /\ e$

and

(42) $[a]:a \in s. \equiv .a \in a.a / a$

In fact the whole axiom system PA1-PA8 can be replaced by a single axiom with "/" as the primitive term, the remaining constant terms, i.e., "s", ">", and "—" being introduced by definitions. For details the reader is invited to consult the Appendix, which shows **PL** "at work".

CZESŁAW LEJEWSKI

DEPARTMENT OF PHILOSOPHY
UNIVERSITY OF MANCHESTER, ENGLAND
JANUARY 28, 1967

APPENDIX

The proof that System **P** and System **T** are inferentially equivalent is by no means obvious. It is given below in outline. A complete version of the proof offers no theoretical difficulties. The outline consists of two parts. In the first part it is shown that any thesis of **T** is obtainable within the framework of **P**. In the second part evidence is given to the effect that, conversely, any thesis of **P** is also a thesis of **T**. For the convenience of the reader I state the axioms of the two systems again:

The axioms of P.

PA1 $[a \, b]:a / b. \supset .[\exists c].c \in a.a \subset s.b \in s$

PA2 $[a \, b]:a \subset s.b \in a. \supset .a / b$

PA3 $[a \, b \, c]::b / c:.[d]:d \in b. \supset .a / d:. \supset .a / c$

PA4 $[a \, b]:a \in s.b \in s. \supset .a > b \in s.-a \in s$

PA5 $[a \, b \, c]:c \in a > b. \supset .a \in s.b \in s$

PA6 $[a \, b]:b \in -a. \supset .a \in s$

PA7 $[a \, b \, c]::.a / b > c.b > c / a. \equiv ::b \in s.c \in s::[d \, e]:.e \in d. \supset :d / a. \equiv .d \cup b / c$

PA8 $[a \, b]::a / -b.-b / a. \equiv :.a \in s.b \in s:.[c \, d]:d \in s.a \cup c / b. \supset .a \cup c / d.c \cup d / b$

The axioms of T.

TA1 $[a \, b]:b \in cn(a). \supset .b \in s.a \subset s$

TA2 $[a\ b]: a \subset$ s.b ϵ a. $\supset$ .b ϵ cn(a)

TA3 $[a\ b]:.a \subset$ s. $\supset$:b ϵ cn(cn(a)). $\equiv$ .b ϵ cn(a)

TA4 $[a\ b\ c]: a \subset$ s.c $\subset$ a.b ϵ cn(c). $\supset$ .b ϵ cn(a)

TA5 $[a\ b]: a \epsilon$ s.b ϵ s. $\supset$ .a $> b \epsilon$ s.$-a \epsilon$ s

TA6 $[a\ b\ c]: c \epsilon a > b.$ $\supset$ .a ϵ s.b ϵ s

TA7 $[a\ b]: b \epsilon -a.$ $\supset$ .a ϵ s

TA8 $[a\ b\ c]: b > c \epsilon$ cn(a). $\equiv$ .b ϵ s.c ϵ cn(a $\cup$ b)

TA9 $[a\ b]: a \epsilon$ s.b ϵ s. $\supset$ .b ϵ cn(a $\cup$ $-a$)

TA10 $[a\ b]:.a \epsilon$ s. $\supset$:b ϵ cn(a).b ϵ cn($-a$). $\equiv$ .b ϵ cn($\wedge$)

Our proof involves the following deductions within the framework of System **P**:

PD1 $[a\ b]:::.a \epsilon$ cn(b). $\equiv$ ::a ϵ s::b / a. $\vee$:.[c]. $\sim$ (c ϵ b):.[c]:c ϵ s. $\supset$ .c / a   (definition)

PT1   (=TA1) $[a\ b]: b \epsilon$ cn(a). $\supset$ .b ϵ s.a $\subset$ s   (follows from PD1, PA1)

PT2   (=TA2) $[a\ b]: a \subset$ s.b ϵ a. $\supset$ .b ϵ cn(a)   (from PA2, PD1)

PT3 $[a\ b\ c]: c \epsilon a.$cn(a) / b. $\supset$ .b ϵ cn(a)
        $[a\ b\ c]::$
        (1) $c \epsilon a.$
        (2)   cn(a) / b. $\supset$:.
        (3) $[d]: d \epsilon$ cn(a). $\supset$ .a / d:.   (PD1, 1)
        (4) a / b.   (PA3, 2, 3)
              $b \epsilon$ cn(a)   (PD1, PA1, 4)

PT4 $[a\ b\ c]: a$ / b.b / c. $\supset$ .a / c
        $[a\ b\ c]::$
        (1) a / b.
        (2) b / c. $\supset$:.
        (3) $b \epsilon$ s:.   (PA1, 1)
        (4) $[d]: d \epsilon b.$ $\supset$ .a / d:.   (1, 3)
              a / c   (PA3, 2, 4)

PT5 $[a\ b\ c]::a \subset \text{s}.c \in a:.[d]:d \in \text{s}. \supset .d \mid b:. \supset .b \in \text{cn}(a)$

       $[a\ b\ c]::$
- (1) $a \subset \text{s}.$
- (2) $c \in a:.$
- (3) $[d]:d \in \text{s}. \supset .d \mid b:. \supset .$
- (4) $c \mid b.$ (3, 1, 2)
- (5) $a \mid c.$ (PA2, 1, 2)
- (6) $a \mid b.$ (PT4, 5, 4)

       $b \in \text{cn}(a)$ (PD1, PA1, 6)

PT6 $[a\ b\ c]:.c \in \text{s}:[d]. \sim (d \in a):b \in \text{cn}(a): \supset .c \mid b$

       $[a\ b\ c]:.$
- (1) $c \in \text{s}:$
- (2) $[d]. \sim (d \in a):$
- (3) $b \in \text{cn}(a): \supset .$
- (4) $\sim (a \mid b).$ (PA1, 2)

       $c \mid b$ (PD1, 3, 4, 1)

PT7 $[a\ b\ c]:.[d]. \sim (d \in a):\text{cn}(a) \mid b.c \in \text{s}: \supset .c \mid b$

       $[a\ b\ c]::$
- (1) $[d]. \sim (d \in a):$
- (2) $\text{cn}(a) \mid b.$
- (3) $c \in \text{s}: \supset :.$
- (4) $[d]:d \in \text{cn}(a). \supset .c \mid d:.$ (PT6, 3, 1)

       $c \mid b$ (PA3, 2, 4)

PT8 $[a\ b]:.[d]. \sim (d \in a):\text{cn}(a) \mid b: \supset .b \in \text{cn}(a)$

       $[a\ b]::$
- (1) $[d]. \sim (d \in a):$
- (2) $\text{cn}(a) \mid b. \supset :.$
- (3) $[d]:d \in \text{s}. \supset .d \mid b:.$ (PT7, 1, 2)

       $b \in \text{cn}(a)$ (PD1, PA1, 2, 1, 3)

PT9 $[a\ b]: a \subset \text{s}.b \in \text{cn}(\text{cn}(a)). \supset .b \in \text{cn}(a)$

       $[a\ b]::$
- (1) $a \subset \text{s}.$
- (2) $b \in \text{cn}(\text{cn}(a)). \supset :.$
- (3) $[\exists d].d \in a. \lor .[d]. \sim (d \in a):$
- (4) $b \in \text{s}:.$
- (5) $\text{cn}(a) \mid b. \lor :[d]:d \in \text{s}. \supset .d \mid b:.$ $\Big\}$ (PD1, 2)

       $b \in \text{cn}(a)$ (3, 5, PT3, PT5, 1, PT8, PD1, 4)

PT10 $[a\ b]: b\ \epsilon\ \text{cn}(a).\ \supset\ .b\ \epsilon\ \text{cn}(\text{cn}(a))$
        $[a\ b]:$
    (1) $b\ \epsilon\ \text{cn}(a).\ \supset\ .$
    (2) $\text{cn}(a)\ \subset\ \text{s}.$ (PD1)
        $b\ \epsilon\ \text{cn}(\text{cn}(a))$ (PT2, 2, 1)

PT11   (=TA3) $[a\ b]:.a\ \subset\ \text{s}.\ \supset\ :b\ \epsilon\ \text{cn}(\text{cn}(a)).\ \equiv\ .b\ \epsilon\ \text{cn}(a)$ (PT9, PT10)

PT12 $[a\ b\ c]: a\ \subset\ \text{s}.c\ \subset\ a.c\ |\ b.\ \supset\ .b\ \epsilon\ \text{cn}(a)$
        $[a\ b\ c]::$
    (1) $a\ \subset\ \text{s}.$
    (2) $c\ \subset\ a.$
    (3) $c\ |\ b.\ \supset\ :.$
    (4) $[d]:d\ \epsilon\ c.\ \supset\ .a\ |\ d:.$ (PA2, 1, 2)
    (5) $a\ |\ b.$ (PA3, 3, 4)
        $b\ \epsilon\ \text{cn}(a)$ (PD1, PA1, 5)

PT13 $[a\ b]::a\ \subset\ \text{s}.b\ \epsilon\ \text{s}:.[c]:c\ \epsilon\ \text{s}.\ \supset\ .c\ |\ b:.\ \supset\ .b\ \epsilon\ \text{cn}(a)$
        $[a\ b]::$
    (1) $a\ \subset\ \text{s}.$
    (2) $b\ \epsilon\ \text{s}:.$
    (3) $[c]:c\ \epsilon\ \text{s}.\ \supset\ .c\ |\ b:.\ \supset\ :.$
    (4) $[\exists c].c\ \epsilon\ a.\ \vee\ .[c].\sim(c\ \epsilon\ a):$
        $b\ \epsilon\ \text{cn}(a)$ (4, PT5, 1, 3, PD1, 2)

PT14   (=TA4) $[a\ b\ c]: a\ \subset\ \text{s}.c\ \subset\ a.b\ \epsilon\ \text{cn}(c).\ \supset\ .b\ \epsilon\ \text{cn}(a)$
        $[a\ b\ c]::$
    (1) $a\ \subset\ \text{s}.$
    (2) $c\ \subset\ a.$
    (3) $b\ \epsilon\ \text{cn}(c).\ \supset\ :.$
    (4) $b\ \epsilon\ \text{s}:.$ $\Big\}$ (PD1, 3)
    (5) $c\ |\ b.\ \vee\ :[d]:d\ \epsilon\ \text{s}.\ \supset\ .d\ |\ b:.$
        $b\ \epsilon\ \text{cn}(a)$ (5, PT12, 1, 2, PT13, 4)

PT15 $[a\ b\ c\ d]::.a\ \subset\ \text{s}.b\ \epsilon\ \text{s}::[e\ f]:.f\ \epsilon\ e.\ \supset\ :e\ |\ d.\ \equiv\ .e\ \cup\ b\ |\ c::$
        $[e]:e\ \epsilon\ \text{s}.\ \supset\ .e\ |\ d::\ \supset\ .a\ \cup\ b\ |\ c$
        $[a\ b\ c\ d]::.$
    (1) $a\ \subset\ \text{s}.$
    (2) $b\ \epsilon\ \text{s}::$
    (3) $[e\ f]:.f\ \epsilon\ e.\ \supset\ :e\ |\ d.\ \equiv\ .e\ \cup\ b\ |\ c::$
    (4) $[e]:e\ \epsilon\ \text{s}.\ \supset\ .e\ |\ d::\ \supset\ .$
    (5) $b\ |\ d.$ (4, 2)

    (6) $b \mid c$.   (3, 2, 5)

    (7) $a \cup b \mid b$.   (PA2, 1, 2)

         $a \cup b \mid c$ (PT4, 7, 6)

PT16 $[a\ b\ c]: .b > c \ \epsilon \ \mathrm{cn}(a): [\ \exists d].d\ \epsilon\ a: \supset .b\ \epsilon\ \mathrm{s}.c\ \epsilon\ \mathrm{cn}(a \cup b)$

         $[a\ b\ c]:.$

    (1) $b > c\ \epsilon\ \mathrm{cn}(a):$

    (2) $[\ \exists d].d\ \epsilon\ a: \supset$.

    (3) $a \mid b > c$.   (PD1, 1, 2)

    (4) $b > c \mid b > c$.   (PA2, PA1, 3)

    (5) $a \cup b \mid c$.   (PA7, 4, 2, 3)

         $b\ \epsilon\ \mathrm{s}.c\ \epsilon\ \mathrm{cn}(a \cup b)$ (PD1, PA1, 4, PA5, 5)

PT17 $[a\ b\ c]:.b > c\ \epsilon\ \mathrm{cn}(a): [d]. \sim (d\ \epsilon\ a): \supset .b\ \epsilon\ \mathrm{s}.c\ \epsilon\ \mathrm{cn}(a \cup b)$

         $[a\ b\ c]:.$

    (1) $b > c\ \epsilon\ \mathrm{cn}(a):$

    (2) $[d]. \sim (d\ \epsilon\ a): \supset$.

    (3) $\sim (a \mid b > c)$.   (PA1, 2)

    (4) $b > c \mid b > c$.   (PA2, PD1, 1)

    (5) $b\ \epsilon\ \mathrm{s}$.   (PA7, 4)

    (6) $b \mid b > c$.   (PD1, 1, 3, 5)

    (7) $b \mid c$.   (PA7, 4, 5, 6)

    (8) $a \cup b \mid c$.   (2, 7)

         $b\ \epsilon\ \mathrm{s}.c\ \epsilon\ \mathrm{cn}(a \cup b)$ (5, PD1, PA1, 8)

PT18 $[a\ b\ c]: b > c\ \epsilon\ \mathrm{cn}(a). \supset .b\ \epsilon\ \mathrm{s}.c\ \epsilon\ \mathrm{cn}(a \cup b)$ (PT16, PT17)

PT19 $[a\ b\ c]:.b\ \epsilon\ \mathrm{s}.c\ \epsilon\ \mathrm{cn}(a \cup b): [\exists d].d\ \epsilon\ a: \supset .b > c\ \epsilon\ \mathrm{cn}(a)$

         $[a\ b\ c]:.$

    (1) $b\ \epsilon\ \mathrm{s}$.

    (2) $c\ \epsilon\ \mathrm{cn}(a \cup b):$

    (3) $[\exists d].d\ \epsilon\ a: \supset$.

    (4) $a \cup b \mid c$.   (PD1, 2, 3)

    (5) $b > c\ \epsilon\ \mathrm{s}$.   (PA4, 1, PA1, 4)

    (6) $b > c \mid b > c$.   (PA2, 5)

    (7) $a \mid b > c$.   (PA7, 6, 3, 4)

         $b > c\ \epsilon\ \mathrm{cn}(a)$ (PD1, 5, 7)

PT20 $[a\ b\ c]:.b\ \epsilon\ \mathrm{s}.c\ \epsilon\ \mathrm{cn}(a \cup b): [d]. \sim (d\ \epsilon\ a): \supset .b > c\ \epsilon\ \mathrm{cn}(a)$

         $[a\ b\ c]::$

    (1) $b\ \epsilon\ \mathrm{s}$.

    (2) $c\ \epsilon\ \mathrm{cn}(a \cup b):$

    (3) $[d]. \sim (d\ \epsilon\ a): \supset :.$

(4) $b \mid c.$ (PD1, 2, 3, 1)
(5) $b > c \, \epsilon \, \text{s}.$ (PA4, 1, PA1, 4)
(6) $b > c \mid b > c :.$ (PA2, 5)
(7) $[d] : d \, \epsilon \, \text{s}. \supset .d \cup b \mid b :.$ (PA2, 1)
(8) $[d] : d \, \epsilon \, \text{s}. \supset .d \cup b \mid c :.$ (PT4, 7, 4)
(9) $[d] : d \, \epsilon \, \text{s}. \supset .d \mid b > c :.$ (PA7, 6, 8)
     $b > c \, \epsilon \, \text{cn}(a)$ (PD1, 5, 3, 9)

PT21 $[a \, b \, c] : b \, \epsilon \, \text{s}.c \, \epsilon \, \text{cn}(a \cup b). \supset .b > c \, \epsilon \, \text{cn}(a)$ (PT19, PT20)

PT22 $(=\text{TA8})$ $[a \, b \, c] : b > c \, \epsilon \, \text{cn}(a). \equiv .b \, \epsilon \, \text{s}.c \, \epsilon \, \text{cn}(a \cup b)$
                                                                     (PT18, PT21)

PT23 $(=\text{TA9})$ $[a \, b] : a \, \epsilon \, \text{s}.b \, \epsilon \, \text{s}. \supset .b \, \epsilon \, \text{cn}(a \cup -a)$
      $[a \, b] :$
      (1) $a \, \epsilon \, \text{s}.$
      (2) $b \, \epsilon \, \text{s}. \supset .$
      (3) $-a \, \epsilon \, \text{s}.$ (PA4, 1)
      (4) $-a \mid -a.$ (PA2, 3)
      (5) $-a \cup a \mid a.$ (PA2, 3, 1)
      (6) $-a \cup a \mid b.$ (PA8, 4, 2, 5)
      $b \, \epsilon \, \text{cn}(a \cup -a)$ (PD1, 2, 6)

PT24 $[a \, b] : -a \mid a.b \, \epsilon \, \text{s}. \supset .b \mid a$
      $[a \, b] :$
      (1) $-a \mid a.$
      (2) $b \, \epsilon \, \text{s}. \supset .$
      (3) $-a \, \epsilon \, \text{s}.$ (PA4, PA1, 1)
      (4) $-a \mid -a.$ (PA2, 3)
      (5) $-a \cup b \mid -a.$ (PA2, 3, 2)
      (6) $-a \cup b \mid a.$ (PT4, 5, 1)
      $b \mid a$ (PA8, 4, 2, 6)

PT25 $[a \, b \, c \, d] : -c \mid b.d \, \epsilon \, a.a \cup b \mid c. \supset .a \mid c$
      $[a \, b \, c \, d] :: $
      (1) $-c \mid b.$
      (2) $d \, \epsilon \, a.$
      (3) $a \cup b \mid c. \supset :.$
      (4) $a \subset \text{s}.$ (PA1, 3)
      (5) $b \, \epsilon \, \text{s}.$ (PA1, 1)
      (6) $c \, \epsilon \, \text{s}.$ (PA1, 3)
      (7) $-c \, \epsilon \, \text{s}.$ (PA4, 6)
      (8) $-c \mid -c :.$ (PA2, 7)

(9) $[e]: e \in a. \supset .-c \cup a / e:.$ (PA2, 7, 4)
(10) $[e]: e \in -c. \supset .-c \cup a / e:.$ (PA2, 7, 4)
(11) $[e]: e \in b. \supset .-c \cup a / e:.$ (PA3, 1, 10, 5)
(12) $-c \cup a / c.$ (PA3, 3, 9, 11)
(13) $a \cup d / c.$ (PA8, 8, 2, 4, 12)
    a / c (13, 2)

PT26 $[a\ b]: -a / b. \supset .-b / a$
      $[a\ b]:.$
    (1) $-a / b. \supset :$
    (2) $[\exists c].c \in -a:$ (PA1, 1)
    (3) $a \in s.$ (PA6, 2)
    (4) $b \in s.$ (PA1, 1)
    (5) $-b \in s.$ (PA4, 4)
    (6) $-b / -b.$ (PA2, 5)
    (7) $-b \cup b / b.$ (PA2, 5, 4)
    (8) $-b \cup b / a.$ (PA8, 6, 3, 7)
      $-b / a$ (PT25, 1, 5, 8)

PT27 $[a\ b\ c]: a \in s.b \in cn(a).b \in cn(-a).c \in s. \supset .c / b$
      $[a\ b\ c]:$
    (1) $a \in s.$
    (2) $b \in cn(a).$
    (3) $b \in cn(-a).$
    (4) $c \in s. \supset .$
    (5) $a / b.$ (PD1, 2, 1)
    (6) $-a \in s.$ (PA4, 1)
    (7) $-a / b.$ (PD1, 3, 6)
    (8) $-b / a.$ (PT26, 7)
    (9) $-b / b.$ (PT4, 8, 5)
      c / b (PT24, 9, 4)

PT28 $[a\ b]: a \in s.b \in cn(a).b \in cn(-a). \supset .b \in cn(\wedge)$
      $[a\ b]::$
    (1) $a \in s.$
    (2) $b \in cn(a).$
    (3) $b \in cn(-a). \supset :.$
    (4) $b \in s:.$ (PD1, 2)
    (5) $[c]: c \in s. \supset .c / b:.$ (PT27, 1, 2, 3)
      $b \in cn(\wedge)$ (PD1, 4, 5)

PT29 $[a\ b]: a \in s.b \in cn(\wedge). \supset .b \in cn(a).b \in cn(-a)$

$[a \; b]::$

    (1) $a \; \epsilon$ s.

    (2) $b \; \epsilon \; \text{cn}(\wedge). \supset :.$

    (3) $— a \; \epsilon$ s.   (PA4, 1)

    (4) $\sim(\wedge \; / \; b).$ (PA1)

    (5) $b \; \epsilon$ s:.

    (6) $[c]: c \; \epsilon$ s. $\supset .c \; / \; b:.$ $\left.\right\}$ (PD1, 2, 4)

        $b \; \epsilon \; \text{cn}(a).b \; \epsilon \; \text{cn}(—a)$ (PD1, 5, 6, 1, 3)

PT30 (=TA10) $[a \; b]:.a \; \epsilon$ s. $\supset :b \; \epsilon \; \text{cn}(a).b \; \epsilon \; \text{cn}(—a). \equiv .b \; \epsilon \; \text{cn}(\wedge)$

                                                                (PT28, PT29)

PT31 (=TD1) $[a \; b]:.a \; / \; b. \equiv :b \; \epsilon \; \text{cn}(a):[\exists c].c \; \epsilon \; a$ (PD1, PA1)

    It is evident from PT1, PT2, PT11, PT14, PA4, PA5, PA6, PT22, PT23, PT30 and PT31 that any thesis of T can be derived within the framework of P, which concludes the first part of our outline of the proof that the two systems are inferentially equivalent. We now turn to the second part of the outline, which is effected within the framework of System T:

TD1 $[a \; b]:.a \; / \; b. \equiv :b \; \epsilon \; \text{cn}(a). [\exists c].c \; \epsilon \; a$ (definition)

TT1   (=PA1) $[a \; b]:.a \; / \; b. \supset :[\exists c].c \; \epsilon \; a:a \subset$ s.$b \; \epsilon$ s (TD1, TA1)

TT2   (=PA2) $[a \; b]:a \subset$ s.$b \; \epsilon \; a. \supset .a \; / \; b$ (TA2, TD1)

TT3 $[a]:a \; \epsilon$ s. $\supset .a \; / \; a$ (TT2)

TT4   (=PA3) $[a \; b \; c]::b \; / \; c:.[d]:d \; \epsilon \; b. \supset .a \; / \; d:. \supset .a \; / \; c$

    $[a \; b \; c]::$

      (1) $b \; / \; c:.$

      (2) $[d]:d \; \epsilon \; b. \supset .a \; / \; d:. \supset :.$

      (3) $c \; \epsilon \; \text{cn}(b).$ (TD1, 1)

      (4) $b \subset \text{cn}(a).$ (2, TD1)

      (5) $\text{cn}(a) \subset$ s.   (TA1)

      (6) $c \; \epsilon \; \text{cn}(\text{cn}(a)):.$ (TA4, 5, 4, 3)

         $[\exists d]:$

      (7) $d \; \epsilon \; b:$ $\left.\right\}$ (TT1, 1)

      (8) $[\exists e].e \; \epsilon \; a:$ (2, 7, TT1)

      (9) $d \; \epsilon \; \text{cn}(a):.$ (4, 7)

    (10) $a \subset$ s.   (TA1, 9)

    (11) $c \; \epsilon \; \text{cn}(a).$ (TA3, 10, 6)

        $a \; / \; c$ (TD1, 11, 8)

TT5 $[a\ b\ c]:a\ /\ b.b\ /\ c.\ \supset\ .a\ /\ c$
        $[a\ b\ c]::$

(1)	$a\ /\ b.$	
(2)	$b\ /\ c.\ \supset :$	
(3)	$b\ \epsilon\ s:.$	(TT1, 1)
(4)	$[d]:d\ \epsilon\ b.\ \supset\ .a\ /\ d:.$	(3,1)
	$a\ /\ c$	(TT4, 2, 4)

TT6 $[a\ b\ c\ d]:a\ /\ b > c.d\ /\ a.\ \supset\ .d\ \cup\ b\ /\ c$
        $[a\ b\ c\ d]:.$

(1)	$a\ /\ b > c.$	
(2)	$d\ /\ a.\ \supset :$	
(3)	$d\ /\ b > c.$	(TT5, 2, 1)
(4)	$b > c\ \epsilon\ \mathrm{cn}(d).$	(TD1, 3)
(5)	$c\ \epsilon\ \mathrm{cn}(d\ \cup\ b):$	(TA8, 4)
(6)	$[\exists e].e\ \epsilon\ d:$	(TT1, 2)
	$d\ \cup\ b\ /\ c$	(TD1, 5, 6)

TT7 $[a\ b\ c\ d\ e]:b > c\ /\ a.e\ \epsilon\ d.d\ \cup\ b\ /\ c.\ \supset\ .d\ /\ a$
        $[a\ b\ c\ d\ e]:.$

(1)	$b > c\ /\ a.$	
(2)	$e\ \epsilon\ d.$	
(3)	$d\ \cup\ b\ /\ c.\ \supset :$	
(4)	$[\exists f].f\ \epsilon\ b > c:$	(TT1, 1)
(5)	$b\ \epsilon\ s.$	(TA6, 4)
(6)	$c\ \epsilon\ \mathrm{cn}(d\ \cup\ b).$	(TD1, 3)
(7)	$b > c\ \epsilon\ \mathrm{cn}(d).$	(TA8, 5, 6)
(8)	$d\ /\ b > c$	(TD1, 7, 2)
	$d\ /\ a$	(TT5, 8, 1)

TT8 $[a\ b\ c]::.a\ /\ b > c.b > c\ /\ a.\ \supset ::b\ \epsilon\ s.c\ \epsilon\ s::[d\ e]:.e\ \epsilon\ d.\ \supset :d$
        $/\ a.\ \equiv .d\ \cup\ b\ /\ c$ (TT1, TA6, TT6, TT7)

TT9 $[a\ b\ c]::.b\ \epsilon\ s.c\ \epsilon\ s::[d\ e]:.e\ \epsilon\ d.\ \supset :d\ /\ a.\ \equiv .d\ \cup\ b\ /\ c::\ \supset$
        $.a\ /\ b > c.b > c\ /\ a$
        $[a\ b\ c]::.$

(1)	$b\ \epsilon\ s.$	
(2)	$c\ \epsilon\ s::$	
(3)	$[d\ e]:.e\ \epsilon\ d.\ \supset :d\ /\ a.\ \equiv .d\ \cup\ b\ /\ c::\ \supset .$	
(4)	$b > c\ \epsilon\ s.$	(TA5, 1, 2)
(5)	$b > c\ \epsilon\ \mathrm{cn}(b > c).$	(TA2, 4)
(6)	$c\ \epsilon\ \mathrm{cn}((b > c)\ \cup\ b).$	(TA8, 5)
(7)	$(b > c)\ \cup\ b\ /\ c.$	(TD1, 6, 1)

(8) $b > c \mid a.$ (3, 4, 7)
(9) $a \in s.$ (TT1, 8)
(10) $a \mid a.$ (TT3, 9)
(11) $a \cup b \mid c.$ (3, 9, 10)
(12) $c \in cn(a \cup b).$ (TD1, 11)
(13) $b > c \in cn(a).$ (TA8, 1, 12)
      $a \mid b > c. b > c \mid a$ (TD1, 13, 9, 8)

TT10 (=PA7) $[a \; b \; c]::.a \mid b > c.b > c \mid a. \equiv :: b \in s.c \in s::[d \; e]:.$
      $e \in d. \supset :d \mid a. \equiv .d \cup b \mid c$ (TT8, TT9)

TT11 $[a \; b \; c]:a \in cn(b). \sim (b \mid a).c \in s. \supset .c \mid a$
      $[a \; b \; c]:.$
      (1) $a \in cn(b).$
      (2) $\sim(b \mid a).$
      (3) $c \in s. \supset :$
      (4) $[d]. \sim (d \in b):$ (TD1, 1, 2)
      (5) $a \in cn(c).$ (TA4, 3, 4, 1)
            $c \mid a$ (TD1, 5, 3)

TT12 $[a \; b]::a \in s:[c]. \sim (c \in b):.[c]:c \in s. \supset .c \mid a:. \supset .a \in cn(b)$
      $[a \; b]::$
      (1) $a \in s:$
      (2) $[c]. \sim (c \in b):.$
      (3) $[c]:c \in s. \supset .c \mid a:. \supset .$
      (4) $a \in cn(a).$ (3, 1, TD1)
      (5) $-a \in s.$ (TA5, 1)
      (6) $a \in cn(-a).$ (3, 5, TD1)
      (7) $a \in cn(\wedge).$ (TA10, 1, 4, 6)
            $a \in cn(b)$ (7, 2)

TT13 $[a \; b]:a \in s.b \in s. \supset .a \mid (b > -b) > -b$
      $[a \; b]:$
      (1) $a \in s.$
      (2) $b \in s. \supset .$
      (3) $-b \in s$ (TA5, 2)
      (4) $b > -b \in s.$ (TA5, 2, 3)
      (5) $b > -b \in cn(b > -b).$ (TA2, 4)
      (6) $-b \in cn((b > -b) \cup b).$ (TA8, 5)
      (7) $(b > -b) > -b \in cn(b).$ (TA8, 4, 6)
      (8) $-b \in cn(-b \cup (b > -b)).$ (TA2, 3, 4)
6   (9) $(b > -b) > -b \in cn(-b).$ (TA8, 4, 8)
      (10) $(b > -b) > -b \in cn(\wedge).$ (TA10, 2, 7, 9)

(11) $\sim (\wedge \mid (b > -b) > -b)$.   (TD1)

        $a \mid (b > -b) > -b$ (TT11, 10, 11, 1)

TT14 $[a\ b] :: a \in \text{s}.b \in \text{s} :. [c\ d] : d \in \text{s}.a \cup c \mid b. \supset .a \cup c \mid d.c \cup d \mid$
      $b :. \supset .a \mid -b$

      $[a\ b] ::$

      (1) $a \in \text{s}.$

      (2) $b \in \text{s} :.$

      (3) $[c\ d] : d \in \text{s}.a \cup c \mid b. \supset .a \cup c \mid d.c \cup d \mid b :. \supset .$

      (4) $a \cup b \mid b.$ (TT2, 1, 2)

      (5) $-b \in \text{s}.$ (TA5, 2)

      (6) $a \cup b \mid -b.$ (3, 5, 4)

      (7) $b > -b \in \text{s}.$ (TA5, 2, 5)

      (8) $b > -b \mid b > -b.$.   (TT3, 7)

      (9) $a \mid b > -b.$ (TT7, 8, 1, 6)

    (10) $a \mid (b > -b) > -b.$ (TT13, 1, 2)

    (11) $a \mid a.$ (TT3, 1)

    (12) $a \cup (b > -b) \mid -b.$ (TT6, 10, 11)

        $a \mid -b$ (TT4, 12, 1, 7, 11, 9)

TT15 $[a] : a \in \text{s}. \supset .-a > a \mid a$

      $[a] :$

      (1) $a \in \text{s}. \supset .$

      (2) $-a \in \text{s}.$ (TA5, 1)

      (3) $-a > a \in \text{s}.$ (TA5, 2, 1)

      (4) $a \mid a.$ (TT3, 1)

      (5) $-a > a \mid -a > a.$ (TT3, 3)

      (6) $a \cup (-a > a) \mid a.$ (TT2, 1, 3)

      (7) $(-a > a) > a \in \text{cn}(a)$ (TD1, 6, TA8, 3)

      (8) $-a \cup (-a > a) \mid a.$ (TD1, 5, TA8, 2)

      (9) $(-a > a) > a \in \text{cn}(-a).$ (TD1, 8, TA8, 3)

    (10) $(-a > a) > a \in \text{cn}(\wedge).$ (TA10, 1, 7, 9)

    (11) $-a > a \mid (-a > a) > a.$ (TT11, 10, TD1, 3)

        $-a > a \mid a$ (TD1, 11, TA8)

TT16 $[a\ b] : -a \mid b. \supset .-b \mid a$

      $[a\ b] :.$

      (1) $-a \mid b. \supset :$

      (2) $[\exists c].c \in -a :$ (TT1, 1)

      (3) $a \in \text{s}.$ (TA7, 2)

      (4) $-a \in \text{s}.$ (TA5, 3)

      (5) $b \in \text{s}.$ (TT1, 1)

      (6) $-b \in \text{s}.$ (TA5, 5)

(7) $b > a \in$ s.   (TA5, 5, 3)

(8) $b > a / b > a.$ (TT3, 7)

(9) $b \cup (b > a) / a.$ (TT6, 8)

(10) $-a \cup (b > a) / a.$ (TT3, 9, 1, 5, TT2, 4, 7, TT5)

(11) $-a > a \in$ s.   (TA5, 4, 3)

(12) $-a > a / -a > a.$ (TT3, 11)

(13) $b > a / -a > a.$ (TT7, 12, 7, 10)

(14) $-a > a / a.$ (TT15, 3)

(15) $b > a / a.$ (TT5, 13, 14)

(16) $-b \cup b / a.$ (TA9, 5, 3, TD1)

(17) $-b / b > a.$ (TT7, 8, 6, 16)

    $-b / a$ (TT5, 17, 15)

TT17 $[a\,b]::a \in$ s.$b \in$ s:.$[c\,d]:d \in$ s.$a \cup c / b. \supset .a \cup c / d. c \cup d /$
$b:. \supset .-b / a$
$[a\,b]::$

   (1) $a \in$ s.

   (2) $b \in$ s:.

   (3) $[c\,d]:d \in$ s.$a \cup c / b. \supset .a \cup c / d.c \cup d / b:. \supset .$

   (4) $-a \in$ s.   (TA5, 1)

   (5) $a \cup -a / b.$ (TA9, 1, 2, TD1)

   (6) $-\grave{a} / b.$ (3, 4, 5)

      $-b / a$ (TT16, 6)

TT18 $[a\,b\,c\,d]:a / -b.-b / a.d \in$ s.$a \cup c / b. \supset .a \cup c / d$
$[a\,b\,c\,d]::$

   (1) $a / -b.$

   (2) $-b / a.$

   (3) $d \in$ s.

   (4) $a \cup c / b. \supset :.$

   (5) $a \in$ s.   (TT1, 2)

   (6) $a \cup c \subset$ s.   (TT1, 4)

   (7) $-b \in$ s.   (TT1, 1)

   (8) $b \in$ s.   (TA7, 7)

   (9) $b \cup -b / d.$ (TA9, 8, 3, TD1)

  (10) $a \cup c / a.$ (TT2, 5, 6)

  (11) $a \cup c / -b:.$ (TT5, 10, 1)

  (12) $[e]:e \in b \cup -b. \supset .a \cup c / e:.$ (8, 4, 7, 11)

      $a \cup c / d$ (TT4, 9, 12)

TT19 $[a\,b\,c\,d\,e]:-b / a.d \in$ s.$a \cup c / b.e \in c. \supset .c \cup d / b$
$[a\,b\,c\,d\,e]::$

   (1) $-b \mid a.$

   (2) $d \in s.$

   (3) $a \cup c \mid b.$

   (4) $e \in c. \supset :.$

   (5) $a \in s.$ (TT1, 1)

   (6) $b \in s.$ (TT1, 3)

   (7) $-b \in s.$ (TA5, 6)

   (8) $c \cup -b \subset s:.$ (TT1, 3, 7)

   (9) $[e]:e \in a \cup c. \supset .c \cup -b \mid e:.$ (5, 1, TT2, 8, TT5)

 (10) $c \cup -b \mid b.$ (TT4, 3, 9)

 (11) $-b > b \in s.$ (TA5, 7, 6)

 (12) $-b > b \mid -b > b.$ (TT3, 11)

 (13) $c \mid -b > b.$ (TT10, 12, 4, 10)

 (14) $-b > b \mid b.$ (TT15, 6)

 (15) $c \mid b.$ (TT5, 13, 14)

 (16) $c \cup d \subset s:.$ (8, 2)

 (17) $[e]:e \in c. \supset .c \cup d \mid e:.$ (TT2, 16)

       $c \cup d \mid b$ (TT4, 15, 17)

TT20 $[a\ b\ d]:-b \mid a.d \in s.a \mid b. \supset .d \mid b$

      $[a\ b\ d]:$

   (1) $-b \mid a.$

   (2) $d \in s.$

   (3) $a \mid b. \supset .$

   (4) $-b \mid b.$ (TT5, 1, 3)

   (5) $b \in s.$ (TT1, 3)

   (6) $b \mid b.$ (TT3, 5)

   (7) $b \in \mathrm{cn}(b).$ (TD1, 6)

   (8) $b \in \mathrm{cn}(-b).$ (TD1, 4)

   (9) $b \in \mathrm{cn}(\wedge).$ (TA10, 5, 7, 8)

 (10) $\sim(\wedge \mid b).$ (TD1)

       $d \mid b$ (TT11, 9, 10, 2)

TT21 $[a\ b\ c\ d]:.-b \mid a.d \in s.a \cup c \mid b:[e]. \sim (e \in c): \supset .c \cup d \mid b$

      $[a\ b\ c\ d]:.$

   (1) $-b \mid a.$

   (2) $d \in s.$

   (3) $a \cup c \mid b:$

   (4) $[e]. \sim (e \in c): \supset .$

   (5) $a \mid b.$ (3, 4)

   (6) $d \mid b.$ (TT20, 1, 2, 5)

       $c \cup d \mid b$ (4, 6)

TT22 $[a\ b\ c\ d]:-b\ /\ a.d\ \epsilon\ \text{s}.a\ \cup\ c\ /\ b.\ \supset\ .c\ \cup\ d\ /\ b$
       $[a\ b\ c\ d]:.$
          (1) $-b\ /\ a.$
          (2) $d\ \epsilon\ \text{s}.$
          (3) $a\ \cup\ c\ /\ b.\ \supset\ :$
          (4) $[\exists e].e\ \epsilon\ c.\ \vee\ .[e].\ \sim (e\ \epsilon\ c):$
               $c\ \cup\ d\ /\ b$ (TT19, TT21)

TT23   (=PA8) $[a\ b]::a\ /\ -b.-b\ /\ a.\ \equiv\ :.a\ \epsilon\ \text{s}.b\ \epsilon\ \text{s}:.[c\ d]:d\ \epsilon\ \text{s}.a$
       $\cup\ c\ /\ b.\ \supset\ .a\ \cup\ c\ /\ d.c\ \cup\ d\ /\ b$
                                    (TT1, TA7, TT18, TT22, TT14, TT17)

TT24 $[a\ b]::.a\ \epsilon\ \text{cn}(b).\ \supset\ ::a\ \epsilon\ \text{s}::b\ /\ a.\ \vee\ :.[c].\ \sim (c\ \epsilon\ b):.[c]:c$
       $\epsilon\ \text{s}.\ \supset\ .c\ /\ a$ (TA1, TD1, TT11)

TT25 $[a\ b]::a\ \epsilon\ \text{s}:[c].\ \sim (c\ \epsilon\ b):.[c]:c\ \epsilon\ \text{s}.\ \supset\ .c\ /\ a:.\ \supset\ .a\ \epsilon\ \text{cn}(b)$
       $[a\ b]::$
          (1) $a\ \epsilon\ \text{s}:$
          (2) $[c].\ \sim (c\ \epsilon\ b):.$
          (3) $[c]:c\ \epsilon\ \text{s}.\ \supset\ .c\ /\ a:.\ \supset\ .$
          (4) $a\ \epsilon\ \text{cn}(a).$ (TA2, 1)
          (5) $-a\ \epsilon\ \text{s}$ (TA5, 1)
          (6) $a\ \epsilon\ \text{cn}(-a).$ (3, 5, TD1)
          (7) $a\ \epsilon\ \text{cn}(\wedge)$ (TA10, 1, 4, 6)
              $a\ \epsilon\ \text{cn}(b)$ (7, 2)

TT26   (=PD1) $[a\ b]::.a\ \epsilon\ \text{cn}(b).\ \equiv\ ::a\ \epsilon\ \text{s}::b\ /\ a.\ \vee\ :.[c].\ \sim (c\ \epsilon$
       $b):.[c]:c\ \epsilon\ \text{s}.\ \supset\ .c\ /\ a$ (TT24, TD1, TT25)

It is evident from TT1, TT2, TT4, TA5, TA6, TA7, TT10, TT23, and TT26 that any thesis of *P* can be derived within the framework of *T*. This completes the outline of the proof that *P* and *T* are inferentially equivalent.

The axiom system consisting of PA1, PA2, and PA3 corresponds to what Popper calls the basis I. It conveniently collapses into the following simple proposition:

PA1* $[a\ b]:::a\ /\ b.\ \equiv\ :::.[\exists c]:::.c\ \epsilon\ a.a\ \subset\ \text{s}::.\ \sim (a\ /\ c).\ \vee\ ::b\ \epsilon$
       $\text{s}::[\exists d]:.d\ /\ b:.[e]:e\ \epsilon\ d.\ \supset\ .a\ /\ e$

The proof that the system consisting of PA1, PA2, and PA3 is inferentially equivalent to PA1* involves the following deductions within System **P**.

PT32 $[a\ b]::a\ /\ b.\ \supset\ :.\ [\exists d]:.d\ /\ b:.[e]:e\ \epsilon\ d.\ \supset\ .a\ /\ e$
$[a\ b]::.$
   (1) $a\ /\ b.\ \supset\ ::$
   (2) $a\ \subset\ s:.$ (PA1, 1)
   (3) $[e]:e\ \epsilon\ a.\ \supset\ .a\ /\ e::$ (PA2, 2)
       $[\exists d]:.d\ /\ b:.[e]:e\ \epsilon\ d.\ \supset\ .a\ /\ e$ (1, 3)

PT33 $[a\ b]:::a\ /\ b.\ \supset\ ::.[\exists c]::.c\ \epsilon\ a.a\ \subset\ s::.\ \sim\ (a\ /\ c).\ \vee\ ::b\ \epsilon$
$s::[\exists d]:.d\ /\ b:.[e]:e\ \epsilon\ d.\ \supset\ .a\ /\ e$ (PA1, PT32)

PT34 (=PA1*)   (PT33, PA2, PA3)

The deductions that follow show that PA1* implies PA1, PA2, and PA3.

PT34.1 (=PA1) $[a\ b]:a\ /\ b.\ \supset\ .[\exists c].c\ \epsilon\ a.a\ \subset\ s.b\ \epsilon\ s$
$[a\ b]:.$
   (1) $a\ /\ b.\ \supset\ :$
       $[\exists c]:$
   (2) $c\ \epsilon\ a.$
   (3) $a\ \subset\ s:$ $\left.\begin{array}{c} \\ \\ \\ \end{array}\right\}$ (PA1*, 1)
   (4) $\sim(a\ /\ c).\ \vee\ .b\ \epsilon\ s:$
   (5) $a\ /\ c:$ (PA1*, 2, 3)
       $[\exists c].c\ \epsilon\ a.a\ \subset\ s.b\ \epsilon\ s$ (2, 3, 4, 5)

PT34.2 (=PA2) $[a\ b]:a\ \subset\ s.b\ \epsilon\ a.\ \supset\ .a\ /\ b$ (PA1*)

PT34.3 (=PA3) $[a\ b\ c]::b\ /\ c:.[d]:d\ \epsilon\ b.\ \supset\ .a\ /\ d:.\ \supset\ .a\ /\ c$
$[a\ b\ c]:::$
   (1) $b\ /\ c:.$
   (2) $[d]:d\ \epsilon\ b.\ \supset\ .a\ /\ d:.\ \supset\ :::.$
       $[\exists d]:.$
   (3) $d\ \epsilon\ b.$ (PT34.1, 1)
   (4) $a\ /\ d:$ (2, 3)
       $[\exists e].$
   (5) $e\ \epsilon\ a.$ $\left.\begin{array}{c} \\ \\ \end{array}\right\}$ (PT34.1, 4)
   (6) $a\ \subset\ s::.$
   (7) $c\ \epsilon\ s::[\exists d]:.d\ /\ c:.[e]:e\ \epsilon\ d.\ \supset\ .a\ /\ e::.$
                               (PT34.1, 1, 2)

$a \mid c$ (PA1*, 5, 6, 7)

Thus our outline of the proof that PA1* is inferentially equivalent to the system consisting of PA1, PA2, and PA3 is completed.

In the main part of my paper I have shown that Popper's inferential definitions are in fact definitions involving the use of the functor of singular identity. This being so, we can define ">" and "—" by means of nominal definitions which make use of "ϵ". The constant term "s" can also be so defined as is clear from PA1 and PA2. The three definitions have the form of the following three statements:

PD1* $[a]:a \epsilon \text{ s.} \equiv .a \epsilon a.a \mid a$

PD2* $[a\ b\ c]::.a \epsilon b > c. \equiv ::a \epsilon \text{ s.}b \epsilon \text{ s.}c \epsilon \text{ s::}[d\ e]:.e \epsilon d. \supset :d \mid$
$a. \equiv .d \cup b \mid c$

PD3* $[a\ b]::a \epsilon -b. \equiv :.a \epsilon \text{ s.}b \epsilon \text{ s:.}[c\ d]:d \epsilon \text{ s.}a \cup c \mid b. \supset .a \cup$
$c \mid d.c \cup d \mid b$

In view of PD1* we can now eliminate "s" from PA1*, which becomes:

PA1** $[a\ b]:::a \mid b. \equiv ::.b \epsilon b.b \mid b::.[\exists c]::c \epsilon a:.[d]:d \epsilon a. \supset$
$.d \mid d:: \sim (a \mid c). \vee :.[\exists d]:.d \mid b:.[e]:e \epsilon d. \supset .a \mid e$

It is easy to see that PA1* implies, and is implied by PA1** and PD1*.

Now, PD2* and PD3* imply, respectively, PA5 and PA6, which thus become redundant as axioms. On the other hand, PA4 has to be rephrased as it contains constant terms which we want to be introduced into the system by means of definitions. We, accordingly, replace it by the following two statements:

PA2** $[a\ b]:::.a \mid a.b \mid b. \supset :::[\exists c]:::c \mid c::[d\ e]:.e \epsilon d. \supset :d \mid$
$c. \equiv .d \cup a \mid b:::[f]::.f \mid f::[d\ e]:.e \epsilon d. \supset :d \mid f. \equiv .d \cup$
$a \mid b:: \supset .c \epsilon f$

PA3** $[a]:::a \mid a. \supset ::.[\exists b]::.b \mid b:.[c\ d]:d \mid d.b \cup c \mid a. \supset .b$
$\cup c \mid d.c \cup d \mid a::.[e]::e \mid e:.[c\ d]:d \mid d.e \cup c \mid a. \supset .e \cup$
$c \mid d.c \cup d \mid a:. \supset .b \epsilon e$

It may, perhaps, be pointed out that the axiomatic foundations of P can be reduced to a single though rather lengthy axiom. It is inferentially equivalent to the axiom system consisting of PA1**, PA2**, and

PA3**, and has the following form:

PA1*** $[a\ b]:::::.a\ /\ b. \equiv :::::b \in b.b\ /\ b:::::[\exists c]:::::.c \in a:.[d]:d$
$\in a. \supset .d\ /\ d:::::. \sim (a\ /\ c). \lor ::::[\exists d]:.d\ /\ b:.[e]:e \in d. \supset$
$.a\ /\ e::::[d]:::.d\ /\ d. \supset :::[\exists e]:::e\ /\ e::[fg]:.g \in f. \supset :f$
$/e.\equiv.f \cup b\ /\ d:::[h]::.h\ /\ h::[fg]:.g \in f. \supset :f\ /\ h. \equiv .f \cup$
$b\ /\ d:: \supset .e \in h::::[\exists d]::.d\ /\ d:.[ef]:f\ /\ f.d \cup e\ /\ b. \supset .d$
$\cup e\ /\ f.e \cup f\ /\ b::.[g]::g\ /\ g:.[ef]:f\ /\ f.g \cup e\ /\ b. \supset .g \cup$
$e\ /\ f.e \cup f\ /\ b:. \supset .d \in g$

PA1*** satisfies all the conditions set up by Leśniewski for well-constructed axiom systems.[33]

In conclusion I should like to mention that System *P*, as well as System *T*, has an interpretation in prototethic, which means that it is consistent if prototethic is consistent. Under this interpretation nominal variables of the two systems become propositional variables and the ontological constants change their meanings as follows:

"ϵ" becomes "and", i.e., the functor of conjunction,
"$\subset$" becomes "if . . . then", i.e., the functor of implication,
"$\cup$" becomes "or", i.e., the functor of alternation,

and, for the purpose of System *T*,

"$\land$" becomes "0", i.e., the standard false statement.

The vocabulary characteristic of *P* is then interpreted thus:

"/" becomes "and", i.e., the functor of conjunction,
"s" becomes "1", i.e., the standard true statement,
">" becomes "and", i.e., the functor of conjunction,
"—" becomes "it is the case that", i.e., the functor of assertion,

and, for the purpose of System *T*,

"cn" becomes "it is or it is not the case that", i.e., the functor of verum.

The reader can easily see for himself that under the suggested interpretation the axiom of ontology and the axioms of *P*, and those of *T*, turn out to be theses of prototethic while the rules of inference, quantification and definition obtaining in *P* and *T* become valid prototethetical rules.[34]

NOTES

[1] K. R. Popper, "New Foundations for Logic", *Mind*, 56 (1947), 193-235. Hereinafter cited as "Foundations for Logic".

K. R. Popper, "Corrections and Additions to 'New Foundations for Logic' ", *ibid.*, 57 (1948), 69, 70.

K. R. Popper, "Logic without Assumptions", *Proceedings of the Aristotelian Society*, 47 (1947), 251-92. Hereinafter cited as "Logic without Assump.".

K. R. Popper, "Functional Logic without Axioms or Primitive Rules of Inference", *Proceedings of the Koninklijke Nederlandsche Akademie van Wetenschappen*, 50 (1947), 1214-24. Hereinafter cited as "Logic without Axioms".

K. R. Popper, "On the Theory of Deduction, Part I. Derivation and its Generalizations", *ibid.*, 51 (1948), 173-83. Hereinafter cited as "Deduction I".

K. R. Popper, "On the Theory of Deduction, Part II. The Definitions of Classical and Intuitionist Negation", *ibid.*, 322-31. Hereinafter cited as "Deduction II".

K. R. Popper, "The Trivialization of Mathematical Logic", *Proceedings of the Xth International Congress of Philosophy*, 1 (Amsterdam, 1948), 722-27. Hereinafter cited as "Trivializ. of Logic".

[2] Cf.,e.g., the review of "Foundations for Logic" and "Logic without Assump." by J. C. C. McKinsey in *The Journal of Symbolic Logic*, 13, p. 114 [hereinafter cited as *JSL*]; the review of "Logic without Axioms" by S. C. Kleene in *JSL*, 13, p. 173; and by H. B. Curry in *Mathematical Reviews*, 9 (1948), 321, and the review of "Deduction I", "Deduction II", and "Trivializ. of Logic" by S. C. Kleene in *JSL*, 14, p. 62.

[3] Cf. S. C. Kleene in *JSL*, 14, p. 62.

[4] Cf. "Foundations for Logic", p. 204[1]. Tarski's theory of logical consequence is developed in his "Über einige fundamentale Bergriffe der Metamathematik", *Comptes rendus des séances de la Societé des Sciences et des Lettres de Varsovie*, 23 (1930), class III, pp. 22-29; "Fundamentale Begriffe der Methodologie der deduktiven Wissenschaften. I", *Monatshefte für Mathematik und Physik*, 37 (1930), 361-404; and "Grundzüge des Systemenkalkül", *Fundamenta Mathematicae*, 25 (1935), 503-26, and 26 (1936), 283-301. These papers are available in an English translation by J. H. Woodger in A. Tarski, *Logic, Semantics, Metamathematics* (Oxford, 1956). Hereinafter cited as *LSM*.

[5] "Logic without Axioms", p. 1218.

[6] "Foundations for Logic", p. 206.

[7] *Ibid.*, p. 208.

[8] *Ibid.*, pp. 211, 212, and "Logic without Axioms", p. 1222.

[9] A. Tarski, *LSM*, p. 31[3].

[10] Throughout the present paper I will be using Leśniewski's version of the symbolism of *Principia Mathematica*. In this symbolism " $\supset$ " stands for "if . . . then", " $\vee$ " – for "or" in its inclusive sense, " $\equiv$ " – for "if and only if", " $\sim$ " – for "it is not the case that"; "and" is represented by a dot or a cluster of dots, which also serve the purpose of indicating the scope of logical constants and the scope of the quantifiers " $[a\ b\ . . .]$ " and " $[\exists\ a\ b\ . . .]$ ", to be read "for all a, for all b . . ." and "for some a, for some b, . . ." respectively.

In accordance with Leśniewski's use of " ϵ " a statement of the form " $a\ \epsilon\ b$ " is true if and only if the noun expression in the place of " a " designates exactly one object, which is also designated by the noun expression in the place of " b ". In his "ontology" the meaning of " ϵ " can be determined by means of the following axiom: $[a\ b] :: a\ \epsilon\ b. \equiv :. [\exists c]\ .c\ \epsilon\ a.c\ \epsilon\ b :. [c\ d] : c\ \epsilon\ a.d\ \epsilon\ a. \supset .c\ \epsilon\ d$. A statement of the form " $a\ \subset\ b$ " is true if and only if whatever is designated by the noun expression in the place of " a " is also designated by the noun expression in the place of "b", that is to say, the following definition holds: $[a\ b] : .a \subset b. \equiv : [c] : c\ \epsilon\ a. \supset .c\ \epsilon\ b$. An elementary presentation of ontology can be found in my paper "on Leśniewski's Ontology", *Ratio*, 1 (1957-58), 150-76.

[11] "Foundations for Logic", pp. 197, 198.

[12] *Ibid.*, p. 218; alternative "inferential definitions" of negation are given in "Logic without Assump.", p. 282, in "Logic without Axioms", p. 1218, and in "Deduction II", p. 323. The sign "$\cup$" belongs to Leśniewski's ontology. The following equivalence determines its meaning: $[a\ b\ c]:.a \in b \cup c. \equiv :a \in b. \vee .a \in c$. An expression of the form "$b \cup c$" is a noun expression; it can be read "b or c", where "or" is a noun-forming functor for two nominal arguments.

[13] In Leśniewski's ontology "$\wedge$" is defined as follows: $[a]:a \in \wedge. \equiv .a \in a. \sim (a \in a)$. It can be read "object which does not exist" or, metaphorically, "the null set".

[14] (28) means the same as "the number of statements in L is less than or equal to $\aleph_0$". In (29) the expression "$\bar{c} < \aleph_0$" means the same as the "the number of c's is less than $\aleph_0$".

[15] Cf. the papers quoted in footnote 4 above.

[16] "Logic without Axioms", p. 1223.

[17] "Foundations for Logic", p. 193.

[18] Rudolf Carnap, *Logical Syntax of Language* (London and New York, 1937), p. 277.

[19] W. Kneale and M. Kneale, *The Development of Logic* (Oxford, 1962), p. 1.

[20] Cf., e.g., "Foundations for Logic", pp. 197, 203.

[21] "Logic without Axioms", p. 1216.

[22] See n. 21 above.

[23] "Logic without Assump.", p. 282 et seq.

[24] *Ibid.*, p. 284.

[25] "Foundations for Logic", p. 212 et seq.

[26] "Logic without Axioms", p. 1222.

[27] "Logic without Assump.", p. 286.

[28] See n. 27 above.

[29] "Logic without Axioms", p. 1214 et seq.

[30] In a customary system of the calculus of propositions with, say, the rules of substitution, distribution of the universal quantifier, and detachment, a complete proof can be given of every thesis other than an axiom, that is to say, every thesis can be derived from the axioms by simple steps each of which involves a single application of one of the rules. No such proof makes any use of rules of inference which state that the relation of inference is transitive or reflexive.

[31] A definition is said to be inorganic if a proper part of its definiens, preceded, if necessary, by a universal quantifier, can be proved as a thesis of the system.

[32] "Logic without Axioms", p. 1223.

[33] Cf. B. Sobociński, "On Well Constructed Axiom Systems", *VI Rocznik Polskiego Towarzystwa Naukowego na Obczyźnie* (London, 1956), pp. 54 et seq.

[34] For details related to the interpretation of Lesniewski's ontology within the framework of his protothetic see my article "The Consistency of Leśniewski's Mereology" forthcoming in *JSL*. [Added in proof: now published in Vol. **34**, No. 3 (1969), 321-28. —EDITOR]